INDIA DEVELOPMENT REPORT
2008

INDIA DEVELOPMENT REPORT 2008

edited by
R. RADHAKRISHNA

OXFORD
UNIVERSITY PRESS

YMCA Library Building, Jai Singh Road, New Delhi 110 001

Oxford University Press is a department of the University of Oxford. It furthers the
University's objective of excellence in research, scholarship, and education
by publishing worldwide in

Oxford   New York

Auckland Cape Town Dar es Salaam Hong Kong Karachi Kuala Lumpur
Madrid Melbourne Mexico City Nairobi New Delhi Shanghai Taipei Toronto

With offices in

Argentina Austria Brazil Chile Czech Republic France Greece Guatemala
Hungary Italy Japan Poland Portugal Singapore South Korea Switzerland
Thailand Turkey Ukraine Vietnam

Oxford is a registered trademark of Oxford University Press
in the UK and in certain other countries

Published in India
By Oxford University Press, New Delhi

© Oxford University Press and Indira Gandhi Institute of Development Research 2008

The moral rights of the author have been asserted
Database right Oxford University Press (maker)

First published 2008

All rights reserved. No part of this publication may be reproduced
or transmitted, in any form or by any means, electronic or mechanical,
including photocopying, recording or by any information storage and
retrieval system, without permission in writing from Oxford University Press.
Enquiries concerning reproduction outside the scope of the above should be
sent to the Rights Department, Oxford University Press, at the address above

You must not circulate this book in any other binding or cover
and you must impose this same condition on any acquirer

ISBN-13: 978-0-19-569351-5
ISBN-10: 0-19-569351-5

Typeset in Minion in 10.5/12.5
by Excellent Laser Typesetters, Pitampura, Delhi 110 034
Printed by Roopak Printers, Delhi 110 032
published by Oxford University Press
YMCA Library Building, Jai Singh Road, New Delhi 110 001

Preface

The Indian economy has been one of the fastest growing economies of the world since 2003–4 and there are signs that it is on its way to emerging as a major economic power. At the same time it has experienced severe agrarian crises which have manifested in farmer suicides. There has been a growing recognition among policy makers that achieving high growth is one issue, but making it pro-poor is another. In recent years, there has been a decisive shift in policy in favour of inclusive growth. However, it is to be seen how far policy pronouncements translate into concrete action.

The IDR series provides a comprehensive view of the contemporary problems faced by the Indian economy. The IDR 2008 (the fifth in the series), prepared mostly by the faculty and researchers of the Indira Gandhi Institute of Development Research (IGIDR), focuses on inclusive growth and carries forward the debate initiated in IDR 2004–5. It analyses issues associated with sustaining high growth, achieving macroeconomic stability, quality, and adequacy of higher education, employment, agrarian crisis, implications of globalization, and so on. The statistical appendices contributed by S.L. Shetty of Economic and Political Weekly Research Foundation (EPWRF), constitute a comprehensive database on the Indian economy. The report is lucid and written keeping the general reader in mind. The views expressed here are those of the individual authors.

I would like to thank Sheila Bhalla, Nirmal Chandra, S.R. Hashim, Amitabh Kundu, D. Narasimha Reddy, Mihir Rakshit, V.M. Rao, C. Ravi, J.C. Sandesara, and K.K. Subramanian for acting as peer reviewers and S. Chandrasekar, Rohit Mutatkar, and Shovan Ray for their editorial support. Patrick Lewis has ably co-ordinated the production and Lavina D'Souza has provided considerable secretarial assistance. I am also grateful for the editorial support and help provided by Oxford University Press, New Delhi.

R. RADHAKRISHNA

Contents

List of Tables x

List of Figures xiii

List of Boxes xv

List of Statistical Profile xvi

List of Abbreviations xix

List of Contributors xxii

1. **Overview: Growth: Achievements and Distress** 1
   R. Radhakrishna • S. Chandrasekhar

   Performance of the Indian Economy   1
   Emerging Indian Economy   2
   Growth and Well-being   5
   Employment   9
   Agrarian Crisis   12
   Higher Education   13
   Emerging Issues in the Financial System   14
   India in a Globalizing World   17
   Concluding observations   18

2. **Macroeconomic Overview** 20
   Manoj Panda

   Introduction   20
   National Income Growth   20
   Other Macroeconomic Developments   27
   Asian Economic Integration   32
   Poverty and Distribution   34
   Conclusion   38

3. **Crisis in Agriculture and Rural Distress in Post-Reform India** 40
   D. Narasimha Reddy • Srijit Mishra

   Introduction   40
   Agrarian Structure on the Eve of Economic Reforms   41
   Reforms and Impact on the Farming Community in Agriculture   41
   Rural Distress and Farmers' Suicides   47
   Reform-led Growth, Small Peasant Adjustment Cost, and The Need for State Support   50

4. Employment and Unemployment Since the Early 1970s 54
   T.N. Srinivasan

   Introduction 54
   Trends in Employment and Unemployment Rates 56
   Conclusions 63

5. State of Higher Education in India 71
   S.R. Hashim

   Changing Perception about Value of Higher Education 72
   Education and Earning 74
   Household Expenditure on Education 75
   Growth of Higher Education 76
   Investment in Higher Education 79
   Using the Existing Research Infrastructure for Teaching at Higher Levels 81
   The Rural–Urban Gap in Education 83
   Summary and Conclusion 84

6. Exploring Intra Urban Differences in Economic Well-Being in India 87
   S. Chandrasekhar • Tesfayi Gebreselassie

   Introduction 87
   Data 88
   Extent, Distribution, and Characteristics of Slum Population 89
   Heterogeneity in Slum Population 91
   Intra Urban Differences in Economic Condition of Households 92
   Conclusion 95

7. Macroeconomic Policy and the Exchange Rate: Working Together 96
   Ashima Goyal

   Introduction 96
   India's Changing Exchange Rate Regime 97
   Stability of Forex Markets 98
   Internal and External Balance 101
   Inflation and the Labour Market 106
   Structure, Monetary, and Fiscal Policy 109
   Conclusion 110

8. Emerging Policy Regime for Bank Credit Delivery and Tasks Ahead: A Critical Review 112
   S.L. Shetty

   Introduction: Importance Assigned to Finance for Development 112
   Post-nationalization and Post-reform Banking Developments 113
   Micro-credit Movement in India 124
   Disappointing Ground Reality After the 1990s 126
   More decisive evidence from AIDIS and Other Field Studies 128
   New Initiatives for Expanding Credit Flow to Agriculture and Other Priority Sectors 129
   New Policy Regime for Better Credit Delivery: Tasks Ahead 131

9. Non-Perfoming Assets in Indian Banking: Magnitude, Determinants, and
   Impact of Recent Policy Initiative 134
   Kausik Chaudhuri • Rudra Sensarma

   Introduction 134

Literature Review　　135
　　　Indian Banking System and its NPA Problem　　135
　　　Prudential Norms and Regulatory Response to NPAs　　138
　　　Empirical Methodology and Data　　140
　　　Empirical Results　　140
　　　Impact of Policy Response　　142
　　　Policy Implications and Concluding Remarks　　143

10. **India and China: Changing Patterns of Comparative Advantage?**　　145
    C. Veeramani

    Trade Policy Reforms　　146
    Growth of Exports　　147
    Structure of Exports and Changing Comparative Advantages　　148
    Conclusion and Implications　　155

11. **Indian Textile and Apparel Sector: Performance, Employment, and Demand**　　157
    G. Badri Narayanan

    Introduction　　157
    Indian Textile Sector in the International Market　　158
    India's Organized Textile Sector: Performance and Employment　　161
    Performance of India's Unorganized Textile Sector　　166
    Domestic Consumption of Textiles in India　　172
    Conclusions　　175

12. **Globalization, Employment, and Labour Market Flexibility: The Case of India**　　178
    K.V. Ramaswamy

    The Issues　　178
    Globalization and Employment　　179
    Aggregate Employment　　179
    Job Security Regulations: Impact on Labour Markets　　180
    Empirical Studies　　182
    Manufacturing Employment in India: Past Trends and the Debate　　183
    Trade and Manufacturing Employment in India in the 1990s　　183

    A Statistical Profile of India's Development　　189

Tables

2.1	Average Annual Growth Rates in Real GDP	21
2.2	Index Number of Agricultural Production, Area, and Yield	23
2.3	Growth in Index Number of Industrial Production by Use-based Sectors	25
2.4	Savings and Capital Formation	28
2.5	Fiscal Parameters of Central Government	30
2.6	Fiscal Parameters of State Governments	30
2.7	Fiscal Parameters of Central and State Governments Combined	31
2.8	Major Foreign Trade Parameters	31
2.9	Direction of India's Exports	32
2.10	HCR of Poverty for Major Indian States	35
2.11	Urban–Rural Differences in MPCE	37
3.1	Important Measures of Economic Liberalization in Indian Agriculture	43
3.2	Capital Formation and Plan Expenditure in Agriculture	44
3.3	Per Worker Income in Agriculture and Non-agriculture Sectors in india	45
3.4	Number of Poor and Undernourished Persons in Various Farm Categories in Rural India	46
3.5	Trends in CDR and SMR in India, 1981–2003	47
3.6	Age-adjusted Male SMRs in India and Selected Indian States	48
3.7	Age-adjusted SMRs for Male Population and Male Farmers	49
A3.1	Returns Per Hectare and Expenses as Per Cent of Value of Output, 2002–3	53
4.1	Employment Rates	58
4.2	Unemployment Rates	59
4.3	Employment Status	60
4.4	Labour Force Participation Rates	61
4.5	Within Reference Week Distribution of Labour Force, 1999–2000	62
4.6	Change in Employment Rate	64
4.7	Per 1000 Distribution of Usually Employed by Broad Groups of Industry for Various Rounds, All India	65
A4.1	Employment Rates: Number of Persons (person-days) Worked Per 1000 Persons (person-days) According to US, CWS, and CDS Approaches for Different Rounds	69
A4.2	Unemployment Rates: Number of Persons (person-days) Unemployed Per 1000 Persons (person-days) in the Labour Force for Different Rounds	69
A4.3	Employment Status: Per 1000 Distribution of Usually Employed by Status of Employment for Different Rounds	70
A4.4	Labour Force Participation Rates: Number of Persons (person-days) Employed and Unemployed Per 1000 Persons (person-days) for Different Rounds	70
5.1	Incidence of Poverty by Landholding Groups, 1993–4	72
5.2	Percentage Share of Number and Area under Marginal Holdings	73

5.3	Sectoral Share in GDP	74
5.4	Percentage Distribution of Households and Income by Education Level of the Head of the Household	74
5.5	Household Income by Head's Education and Age	75
5.6	Income Elasticity of Household Expenditure on Education	75
5.7	Per Capita Consumption Expenditure on Education by Income Group	75
5.8	Educated Youth in the Labour Force, Middle Level of Schooling, and Above	76
5.9	All India Growth of Student Enrolment (Higher Education), 1982–3 to 2001–2	77
5.10	Expenditure on Education in Five Year Plans	79
5.11	Growth in Public Expenditure on Education in India	79
6.1	Differences Across Slum and Non-slum Households	90
6.2	Variation in the Characteristics of Slum Population Residing in Different Wards of the Same Municipal Corporation	91
6.3	Mean of Assets by Resident Type	93
6.4	Scoring Factors based on the First Principal Component and Summary Statistics	94
7.1	Depreciation or Appreciation, End December	98
7.2	Yearly Volatility of the Exchange Rate	98
7.3	Taking Account of the Trade Basket and Inflation	106
8.1	Spread of Bank Branch Network in India	114
8.2	Population Group-wise C–D Ratio as per Sanction and Utilization	115
8.3	Regional Scenario of C–D Ratios	115
8.4	C–D Ratios for Selected States	115
8.5	State-wise Classification of Districts by Size of C–D Ratios, March 2005	116
8.6	District-wise Aggregate Deposits and Bank Credit for Maharashtra and Andhra Pradesh	117
8.7	Number of States and UTs in Different Ranges of C–D Ratio, March 2003	118
8.8	Region-wise CDR and C+I/D Ratio of Scheduled Commercial Banks	118
8.9	Region-wise Credit Plus Investment Plus RIDF to Deposit Ratio	118
8.10	Outstanding Credit of SCBs Against Agriculture and SSIs	119
8.11	Direct and Indirect Finance for Agriculture and Allied Activities by SCBs	120
8.12	Flow of Total Institutional Credit for Agriculture by Institution	120
8.13	Agency-wise Break-up of Term Credit flow	121
8.14	Flow of Institutional Credit for Agriculture by Category	122
8.15	Data Reported on Agricultural Advances of Public Sector Banks	122
8.16	Trends in the Number of Small Borrowal vis-à-vis Other Bank Loan Accounts	123
8.17	NABARD: Bank-SHG Credit Linkage Programme Cumulative Progress upto 2004–5	125
8.18	Progress under SIDBI Foundation for Micro Credit (SFMC)	125
8.19	Cumulative Growth in SHG-Linkage in Priority Status	125
8.20	Relative Share of Borrowing of Cultivator Households from Different Sources	129
8.21	Indebtedness of Farm Households Classified According to Land Possessed	129
9.1	Asset Structure of Indian Commercial Banking System	135
9.2	Incidence of Gross and net NPAs of SCBs	137
9.3	Cross-country Comparisons of Gross Non-performing Loans to Total Loans	138
9.4	Nature and Strength of Impact of Various Factors on NPAs	141
9.5	Nature and Strength of Impact of Policy Responses on NPAs	142
10.1	Average Import Tariff Rate	146
10.2	Average Annual Growth Rate of Exports	147
10.3	Structure of Exports by Commodity Group	149

10.4	Composition of Exports by Factor Intensity	150
10.5	Patterns of Comparative Advantage According to Factor Intensity	151
10.6	Patterns of Comparative Advantage According to Commodity Group	152
10.7	Shares of India and China in World Exports by Commodity Group	153
10.8	Expansion of Trade by Products, 1980–4 to 2000–3	153
10.9	Structural Change of Exports and Comparative Advantage Across Products	154
11.1	Annual Growth Rates of Textile and Apparel Exports	161
11.2	Average Annual Growth Rates in the Organized Indian Textile Sector	162
11.3	Trends in Some Ratios of Capital (K), Output (Y), and Employment (N)	162
11.4	Trends in Effective Rates of Protection for Different Sub-sectors in the Indian Textile Sector	163
11.5	Salient Features of the Organized Textile and Apparel Sector in India: Recent Trends	165
11.6	Shares of Various Sub-sectors in Different Sectors, 2000–1	166
11.7	Annual Average Growth Rates in Unorganized Textile Sector	168
11.8	Trends in Partial Productivity Measures in Unorganized Textile Sector in India	169
11.9	Growth Trends of Partial Productivity Measures in Unorganized Textile Sector in India	170
11.10	Trends in Per capita Consumption Expenditures and Shares on Clothing in Rural India	172
11.11	Trends in Per Capita Consumption Expenditures and Share of Clothing in Urban India	173
11.12	Indian Textile and Apparel Sector—Trends in Growth of Supply and Demand	173
11.13	Trends in Excise Structure of Various Textile Staple Fibres in India, 1992–2005	173
11.14	Trends in Excise Structure of Various Textile Yarns Based on Filaments and Staple Fibres in India, 1992–2005	174
11.15	Trends in Excise Structure of Various Textile Fabrics in India, 1992–2005	174
11.16	Elasticities of Various Textile Commodity Groups to their Prices and Textile Expenditure	175
11.17	Credit Applications that were Received and Disbursed under TUFS	176
12.1	Distribution and Growth of Non-agricultural Employment, 1994–2000	179
12.2	Key Industries in Six Industry Groups	184
12.3	Employment in Six Industry Groups, 2001–2	184
12.4	Employment Growth Rates in Indian Manufacturing, 1989–2001	184
12.5	Employment Elasticity in Indian Manufacturing by Industry	184
12.6	Organized Sector Jobs by Industry, 1994–2000	185
12.7	Growth of Contract Labour in Factories	185
12.8	Distribution of Factories by Employment Size and Trade Orientation, 2000–1	186

Figures

1.1	All-India and Statewise Incidence of Poverty (Rural + Urban)	6
1.2	Percentage Share of States in All India Poor (Rural + Urban)	6
1.3	Index of Average Monthly Per Capita Expenditure in the Rural Sector	7
1.4	Incidence of Malnutrition among Children in All India and Selected States (Rural + Urban)	9
1.5	Trends in Unemployment, 1987–8 to 2004–5	11
2.1	Real GDP Growth on Annual Basis and 3-year Moving Average Basis	21
2.2	Composition of GDP by Major Sectors (per cent)	22
2.3	Average Annual Growth Rates in Index Number of Agricultural Production	23
2.4	Gross Capital Formation in Agriculture (at 1993–4 prices)	23
2.5	Annual Growth in Index Number of Industrial Production	24
2.6	Average annual growth rate of service sectors, 2000–5	26
2.7	Growth in Monetary Variables (per cent)	28
2.8	Inflation Rate for WPI and CPI	29
2.9	Average Annual Growth Rate in Per Capita GSDP Across States	36
2.10	Coefficient of Variation in Per Capita GSDP among Major States	36
3.1	Indices of FBI and CPIAL	45
3.2	SMR for Male Farmers and Non-farmers in India, 1995–2004	48
5.1	Percentage Distribution of Households and Income	74
5.2	Per Household Income by Head's Education and Age	75
5.3	All India Growth of Student Enrolment (Higher Education), 1982–3 to 2001–2	78
5.4	Expenditure on Education in Five Year Plans	79
5.5	Growth in Public Expenditure on Education in India	80
6.1	Share of India's Slum Population	89
6.2	Distribution of Households Based on Asset Index Quantiles by Location	94
7.1	Post-reform Exchange Rates	97
7.2	Recent Daily Fluctuations in Spot Exchange Rates	99
7.3	Shrinking the Impossible Trinity	104
8.1	Trends in Agriculture Credit: Number of Borrowal Accounts	126
8.2	Trends in Credit for SSI Sector: Number of Borrowal Accounts (For SCBs)	127
8.3	Percentage Shares of Agriculture and SSI Credit in Total Bank Credit (By SCBs)	127
8.4	Number of Small Borrowal Accounts (For SCBs)	127
8.5	Prcentage Share of Credit of Small Borrowal Accounts to Total Credit (By SCBs)	128

9.1	Gross NPAs to Gross Advances, 2001–5 Public Sector and Private Sector Banks	136
9.2	Gross Non-performing Loans to Total Loans, 2001–5	138
10.1	Trends in India's Exports, Imports, and Trade Balance	147
10.2	Comparative Export Performance, 1950–2004	148
11.1	Exports of Silk and Silk Products at Constant Prices	159
11.2	Exports of Wool and Wool Products at Constant Prices	159
11.3	Exports of Cotton and Cotton Products at Constant Prices	159
11.4	Exports of Products from Manmade Filaments at Constant Prices	159
11.5	Trends in Percentage Shares of Exports of some Non-cotton Textile Products in Total Exports from India.	160
11.6	Trends in Percentage Shares of Exports of some Cotton Textile and all Apparel Products in Total Exports from India	160
11.7	Employment Trends in Non-mill Textile Sector	164
11.8	Employment Trends in Different Sub-sectors of Textile Wet Processing Sector	164
11.9	Employment Trends in Textile Wet Processing Sector	165
11.10	Employment Trends in Sub-Sector in Textile Sector	165

Boxes

2.1	Long-term Scenarios for Asian Growth: Need for Asian Economic Integration	33
2.2	National Rural Employment Guarantee Act, 2005	37
5.1	Pressure of Competition for Available Seats in the Institutions of Higher Learning	72
5.2	Farming has Become a Risky Vocation	73
5.3	The Goal of Spending Six Per cent of GDP on Education	78
5.4	Need for Regulating Quality of Curricula and Institutions	80
5.5	Research Support Structures	81
5.6	Success Rate by Medium—UPSC Civil Services Main Examination	83
7.1	Speculation versus Hedging	99
7.2	Forex Markets and Central Bank Intervention	100
7.3	Monetary Policy Shocks	101
7.4	The Road to Full Capital Convertibility	102
7.5	The impact of Monetary Policy in an EME: The Mundell–Fleming Model	103
7.6	The Difference Between Indian GDP and GNP	105
7.7	Strategies to Absorb Foreign Inflows	107
10.1	Major Reforms in China	146
10.2	Major Reforms in India	146
10.3	Contribution of FDI to Export Growth in China and India	148
10.4	Market Seeking vs Export Promoting FDI	148
12.1	Introducing Flexibility: The Case of Spain	182
12.2	Fixed-term Contract in Indian Industry	185
12.3	Job Security Regulations in India	186

A Statistical Profile

REAL SECTOR

A1 National Income
- A1.1 Key National Accounts Aggregates (at Constant Prices) — 191
- A1.2 Gross and Net Domestic Savings by Type of Institutions (at Current Prices) — 195
- A1.3 Gross Capital Formation by Type of Institutions at Current Prices — 197
- A1.4 Net Capital Stock By Type of Institutions and Capital-Output Ratios — 201
- A1.5 Rank of States in Descending order of Per Capita State Domestic Products in Real Terms (Three-yearly Annual Averages) — 203

A2 Production
- A2.1 Production Trends in Major Agricultural Crops — 205
- A2.2 Trends in Yields of Major Crops — 207
- A2.3 Horticulture and Live Stock Production — 208
- A2.4 Value of Output from Agriculture, Horticulture, and Livestock — 209
- A2.5 Structural Changes in Indian Industry and Decadal Growth — 211
- A2.6 Index of Industrial Production with Major Groups and Sub-groups — 212

A3 Budgetary Transactions
- A3.1 Budgetary Position of Government of India — 216
- A3.2 Consolidated Budgetary Position of State Governments at a Glance — 218

A4 Money and Banking
- A4.1 Money Stock Measures — 219
- A4.2 Selected Indicators of Scheduled Commercial Banks Operations (Year-End) (Outstandings) — 220
- A4.3 Trends in Statewise Bank Deposits and Credit and Credit-Deposit Ratios (For Scheduled Commercial Banks) — 221
- A4.4 Trends in Districtwise Deposits and Credit (as per Utilisation) and Credit-Deposit Ratios — 223
- A4.5 Distribution of Outstanding Credit of Scheduled Commercial Banks According to Occupation — 224
- A4.6 Resources Mobilisation from the Primary Market — 226

A5 Capital Market
- A5.1 Trends in Resource Mobilisation by Mutual Funds — 228
- A5.2 Trends in Resource Mobilisation by Mutual Funds — 230
- A5.3 Trends in FII Investments — 231
- A5.4 Business Growth of Capital Market Segment of NSE — 232
- A5.5 Settlement Statistics of Capital Market Segment of National Stock Exchange of India (NSE's) — 233
- A5.6 Business Growth Of The Futures and Options Market Segment, NSE — 234
- A5.7 Settlement Statistics In Futures and Options Segment, NSE — 235
- A5.8 Business Growth On The WDM Segment, NSE — 235

A STATISTICAL PROFILE xvii

A5.9	Business Growth and Settlement of Capital Market Segmen, BSE	236
A 5.10	Secondary Market Turnover in Financial and Commodities Market	237

A6 Investment

A6.1	Trends in Total Investment and Investment Under Implementation by Industry	238
A6.2	Trends in Total Investment and Investments Under Implementation by States & Union Territories	240

A7 Prices

A7.1	Wholesale Price Index: Point-to-Point and Average Annual Variations	241
A7.2	Cost of Living Indices	243

EXTERNAL SECTOR

A8 Balance of Payments

A8.1	Foreign Exchange Reserves (End Period)	246
A8.2	Balance of Payments 1990–1 to 2005–6	247
A8.3	Invisibles Account on Balance of Payments	251

A9 Exchange Rate

A9.1	Exchange Rate for the Indian Rupee vis-à-vis Some Select Currencies (Indian Rupee per Currency)	253
A9.2	Indices of Real Effective Exchange Rate (REER) and Nominal Effective Exchange Rate (NEER) of the Indian Rupee	255
A9.3	Weighing Diagrams for RBI's NEERs and REERs.	256

A10 Foreign Trade

A10.1	Changing Scenerio in Foreign Trade	257
A10.2	Foreign Trade with Major Trading Partners	259

A11 Foreign Investment and NRI Deposits

A11.1	Foreign Investment Inflows	260
A11.2	NRI Deposits - Outstandings as at the End Period	261
A11.3	FDI Inflows: Year-wise, Route-wise, Sector-wise Break-up and Country-wise Break-up	262

DEMOGRAPHY AND SOCIAL SECTOR

A12 Population

A12.1	Statewise Population 1951–2001	264
A12.2	Statewise: Rural and Urban Population of India: 1951–2001	265
A12.3	Statewise: Sex Ratio	266
A12.4	Statewise—Literacy Rate: 1951 to 2001	267
A12.5	Statewise Infant Mortality Rate: 1961, 1981, 1991, 2001, 2002, and 2003	268

A13 Human Development Indices

A13.1	Human Development Index for India by State 1981, 1991, and 2001	269
A13.2	State-wise Poverty Estimation HCR	270

A14 Employment

A14.1	Total Population, Workers and Non-Workers as Per Population Censuses	271
A14.2	Number of Persons Employed per 1000 Persons according to Usual Status and Current Weekly Status Approaches	272

A14.3	Per 1000 distribution of the Usually Employed by Status of Employment for All (Principal and Subsidiary Status Workers)	273
A14.4	Unemployment Rate	274
A14.5	State-wise Labour Force and Work Force Participation Rates by Place of Residence and Sex: 1983 to 1999–2000	275
A14.6	State-wise Sectoral Distribution of Usual (Principal + Subsidiary) Status Workers: 1983 to 1999–2000	276
A14.7	State-wise Composition of Rural and Urban Usual (Principal + Subsidiary) Status Workers: 1983 to 1999–2000	277
A14.8	Trends in Number and Employment of Agricultural (excluding crop production and plantation) and Non-Agricultural Enterprises,1980–2005 and growth	278
A14.9	Percentage Distribution of Gainfully Employed Persons (ie by usual status for all workers ie PS+SS), by Industry	282

A15 Household Indebtedness

A15.1	Household Indebtness A Profile	288

A16 International Comparison

A16.1	Development Characteristics of Some Selected Countries	290

Abbreviations

ADB	Asian Development Bank
AFTA	ASEAN Free Trade Agreement
AoA	Agreement on Agriculture
ASEAN	Association of South East Asian Nations
ASI	Annual Survey of Industries
BSE	Bombay Stock Exchange
BSR	Basic Statistical Returns
CAD	Current Account Deficit
CAR	Capital Adequacy Ratio
CB	Central Bank
C–D	Credit–Deposit
CDR	Crude Death Rate
CDR	Corporate Debt Restructuring
CDS	Current Daily Status
CPI	Consumer Price Index
CPIAL	CPI for Agricultural Labour
CRAR	Capital to Risk-Weighted Assets Ratio
CRR	Cash Reserve Ratio
CSO	Central Statistical Organization
CV	Coefficient of Variation
CWS	Current Weekly Status
DFI	Development Finance Institution
DGET	Directorate General of Employment and Training
DHS	Demographic Health Survey
DME	Directory Manufacturing Establishment
DRT	Debt Recovery Tribunal
EME	Emerging Market Economy
EMI	Employment Market Information
EO	Export Oriented
ES	Enterprise Survey
EU	European Union
EUS	Employment and Unemployment Surveys
FBI	Farm Business Income
FDI	Foreign Direct Investment
ffr	Federal Fund Rate
FI	Financial Institution
FRBM	Fiscal Responsibility and Budget Management
FSU	First Stage Unit
GCC	General Credit Card

GCF	Gross Capital Formation
GDCF	Gross Domestic Capital Formation
GSP	Generalized System of Preferences
HCR	Head Count Ratio
HYV	High Yielding Variety
IC	Import Competing
ICT	Information and Communication Technology
IGIDR	Indira Gandhi Institute of Development Research
IIT	Indian Institute of Technology
IMF	International Monetary Fund
IT	Information Technology
JSR	Job Security Regulations
KCC	Kissan Credit Card
LR	Labour Reserve
MCPS	Monopoly Cotton Procurement Scheme
M–F	Mundell-Fleming
MFA	Multi-fibre Agreement
MFI	Microfinance Institutions
MOF	Ministry of Finance
MPCE	Monthly Per Capita Consumption Expenditure
MSP	Minimum Support Price
MTFR	Medium Term Fiscal Reform
NABARD	National Bank for Agriculture and Rural Development
NAFTA	North American Free Trade Agreement
NAS	National Account Statistics
NCAER	National Council for Applied Economic Research
NCL	National Commission for Labour
NCRB	National Crime Records Bureau
NDME	Non-directory Manufacturing Establishment
NEER	Nominal Effective Exchange Rate
NFA	Net Foreign Assets
NGO	Non-governmental Organization
NIC	Newly Industrialized Countries
NPA	Non-performing Asset
NREG	National Rural Employment Guarantee
NSSO	National Sample Survey Organization
NTC	National Textile Corporation
OAME	Own Account Manufacturing Enterprise
OCR	Operating Cost Ratio
ODL	Open and Distance Learning
OECD	Organization for Economic Co-operation and Development
OEM	Open Economy Macroeconomics
OGL	Open General Licensing
OTS	One Time Settlement
PC	Population Census
PPP	Purchasing Power Parity
PSU	Public Sector Unit
QR	Quantitative Restrictions
RBI	Reserve Bank of India
RCA	Revealed Comparative Advantage
REC	Regional Engineering College
REER	Real Effective Exchange Rate

RFAS	Rural Finance Access Survey
RIA	Regional Integration Agreements
ROA	Return on Assets
ROW	Rest of the World
RRB	Regional Rural Bank
RTA	Regional Free Trade Agreement
SAFTA	South Asia Free Trade Agreement
SAP	Structural Adjustment Programme
SCB	Scheduled Commercial Bank
SEZ	Special Economic Zone
SFMC	SIDBI Foundation for Micro Credit
SHG	Self-Help Group
SIDBI	Small Industries Development Bank of India
SLR	Statutory Liquidity Ratio
SME	Small and Medium Enterprise
SMR	Suicide Mortality Rate
SSI	Small Scale Industry
TFP	Total Factor Productivity
TFR	Total Fertility Rate
UGC	University Grants Commission
US	Usual Status
VRS	Voluntary Retirement Scheme
WPI	Wholesale Price Index
WPR	Work Force Participation Rate
WTO	World Trade Organization
WUA	Water Users Association

List of Contributors

S. Chandrasekhar	Assistant Professor, Indira Gandhi Institute of Development Research, Mumbai
Kausik Chaudhuri	Associate Professor, Indira Gandhi Institute of Development Research, Mumbai
Tesfayi Gebreselassie	MEASURE DHS, Macro International Inc., Calverton, MD, USA
Ashima Goyal	Professor, Indira Gandhi Institute of Development Research, Mumbai
S.R. Hashim	Director, Institute for Studies in Industrial Development, Delhi
Srijit Mishra	Associate Professor, Indira Gandhi Institute of Development Research, Mumbai
G. Badri Narayanan	Research Economist, Center for Global Trade Analysis, Purdue University, USA
Manoj Panda	Professor, Indira Gandhi Institute of Development Research, Mumbai
K.V. Ramaswamy	Associate Professor, Indira Gandhi Institute of Development Research, Mumbai. At present Visiting Senior Research Fellow, Institute of South Asian Studies, National University of Singapore, Singapore
D. Narasimha Reddy	Professor of Economics (Rtd), University of Hyderabad. At present Visiting Professor, Institute for Human Development, Delhi
Rudra Sensarma	Maxwell Fry Research Fellow in Finance Birmingham Business School, UK
S.L. Shetty	Director, Economic and Political Weekly Research Foundation, Mumbai
T.N. Srinivasan	Samuel J. Park, Jr Professor of Economics, Economic Growth Center, Yale University, CT, USA
C. Veeramani	Assistant Professor, Indira Gandhi Institute of Development Research, Mumbai

1

Overview
Growth: Achievements and Distress

R. Radhakrishna • S. Chandrasekhar

PERFORMANCE OF THE INDIAN ECONOMY

GDP Growth

The Indian economy has emerged in recent years as one of the fastest growing economies of the world. The Indian market along with that of China is considered as one of the major engines of growth for the global economy. Domestic factors have led to the recent robust economic growth. The key factors that underpin the transition from moderate to high growth are the favourable supply side factors as well as continuous strong domestic demand. These include the savings surge resulting from improvement in corporate and household savings; and more importantly, high investment rates aided by easy liquidity. The major contributors of growth other than savings and investment are a spurt in exports, resurgence of the manufacturing sector, and substantial flow of foreign direct investment (FDI) that has complemented the domestic investment. Many observers of the Indian economy argue that India can achieve a still higher growth rate and sustain it over a longer period. However, future growth would depend on sustaining the growth of investible resources, achieving widespread productivity improvement on the supply side, and maintaining macroeconomic stability on the demand side. In the medium term, infrastructure bottlenecks, shortage of skilled manpower, and poor performance of agriculture will be the major constraints to rapid growth. Sluggish agricultural growth will also be a major constraint in achieving inclusive growth. There is a fear that excessive dependence on crude oil imports—that account for about 70 per cent of domestic consumption—may become a limiting factor.

There has been a significant improvement in macroeconomic stability. This is reflected in the lower year-to-year variations in the gross domestic product (GDP) growth rate; the standard deviation of growth rate of GDP is observed to be declining steadily over time. The improvement in macroeconomic stability could be due to macroeconomic policies. While the prospects for achieving high growth are good, the prospect of maintaining macroeconomic stability must be rated low. The Indian economy is likely to be susceptible to periodic shocks originating from the global economy such as those related to global financial crises and volatility in crude oil prices. As India moves towards full convertibility of the rupee, it is likely to be vulnerable to the contagion effect flowing from any major global financial crisis. Business expectations are governed not only by the macro fundamentals of the economy, but also by the outcomes of the global markets.

A distinct acceleration in GDP growth has occurred between the Ninth and Tenth Plan periods that reversed the deceleration observed between the Eighth and Ninth Plans. The annual growth rate averaged 6.5 per cent during the Eighth Plan period (1992–7), slipped to 5.5 per cent during the Ninth Plan (1997–2002), but accelerated to 7.6 per cent during the Tenth Plan period (2002–7). The growth performance in recent years is even more impressive. The growth rate rose to 9 per cent in 2005–6, 9.4 per cent in 2006–7, and is projected to grow at close to 9 per cent in 2007–8. A recent assessment of the economy attributes the better performance to better capital utilization and a turnaround in the total factor productivity (TFP) in manufacturing since 2002–3, and a steady improvement in productivity growth in services (RBI 2007a). The long-term growth has, however, been intercepted by periodic cycles (Figure 2.1). Arguably, the recent high growth witnessed since 2003–4 might be a cyclical phase—the GDP growth rate may peak soon and then fall as was seen in the past between the two periods 1993–7 and 1997–2003. Concerns have been raised about overheating in certain sectors as manifested in the full utilization of their capacities, rapid expansion of credit, surge in asset and commodity prices, and rising inflation rates. For instance, during the past three years, capacity utilization in all industries exceeded 80 per cent. And what is more, it exceeded 90 per cent in electricity. The tight monetary policy being adopted reflects the need for caution. However, recent high investments may augment the capacities with a lag, and to some extent relieve the pressure and restore macroeconomic stability.

Sectoral Performance

The industrial sector GDP grew by 8 per cent in 2005–6 and 11 per cent in 2006–7. The revival of industrial growth that began in 2002–3 has entered the fifth consecutive year of high growth. The industrial sector, in which the manufacturing sector played a critical role, has become very competitive at home and abroad. The growth of the manufacturing sector which was for long stuck at modest annual rates of 7 to 8 per cent, accelerated to 9.1 per cent in 2005–6, and further to 12.3 per cent in 2006–7. This has been achieved despite infrastructural bottlenecks and competitive pressures. The acceleration in manufacturing growth has been triggered by investment and consumption demand. Within the manufacturing sector, capital goods production registered an impressive increase of 15.8 per cent in 2005–6 and 18.2 per cent in 2006–7. The growing investment demand was met partly through imports of capital goods which increased by more than 40 per cent in 2005–6 and 2006–7. The high growth of capital goods production as well as the spurt in capital goods imports was due to fresh investment in automobiles, power equipment, metals, oil and gas, and petrochemicals (Naik 2006). Restructuring, better capacity utilization, and better inventory management seem to be the factors that contributed to the recovery of the capital goods sector that faced stiff competition from imports in the 1990s due to a reduction in customs duties (Panda, Chapter 2). Infrastructure bottlenecks and shortage of skilled manpower are likely to constrain the manufacturing growth. If the falling demand for consumer durables (recorded in the recent period), persists, it may affect future overall industrial growth (IEG 2007). Despite favourable growth of the global economy at about 5 per cent per annum, growth of exports started slowing down much before the recent appreciation of the Indian rupee. These factors may have an adverse effect on the future prospects of industrial growth.

The services sector has sustained its high growth and contributed substantially to overall growth. In 2006–7, this sector grew by 11 per cent, slightly up from 10.3 per cent in 2005–6, and contributed to 71.5 per cent of the increase in overall GDP (RBI 2007b). Communications has been the fastest growing sub-sector of services sector. Removal of monopoly and adoption of cost-reducing technologies contributed to its growth (Panda Chapter 2). Sub-sectors such as trade, hotels, restaurants, transport, storage, and communication contributed to more than one third of the overall growth rate of GDP (RBI 2007b). There has been a spurt in the growth of travel and tourism as a result of expansion in business and trading activities. Foreign tourist arrivals increased from 2.65 million in 2000 to 4.43 million in 2006 and foreign exchange earnings from $ 3.2 billion to $ 6.6 billion over the period (EPWRF 2007).

Agriculture has been experiencing deceleration since the mid-nineties, with no recovery in sight (GOI 2007b). The annual agricultural GDP increased at 2.7 per cent in 2006–7, 6 per cent in 2005–6, and was stagnant in 2004–5. In the post-reform period, high GDP growth accompanied by low agricultural growth has brought about a distinct shift in the sectoral distribution of GDP, which is skewed against agriculture. The share of agriculture in GDP declined by 10 percentage points between 1993–4 and 2004–5 whereas its share in employment declined by 7 percentage points. These trends have further worsened income disparities. In 2004–5, the share of agriculture in total workforce was 56.5 per cent but it accounted for only 20.2 per cent of total GDP. In contrast, services constituted less than one-fourth of the total workforce, but accounted for more than half of GDP. What is even more disquieting is the fact that the ratio of worker productivity in agriculture to that in non-agriculture declined from 28 per cent in 1993–4 to 20 per cent in 2004–5. Clearly, this growing disparity may bring to naught the efforts at achieving inclusive growth (Reddy and Mishra Chapter 3). Year-to-year fluctuations in agricultural production may not affect the aggregate growth to the same extent as in the past, but such fluctuations would put at risk the livelihood of about 60 per cent of the population.

EMERGING INDIAN ECONOMY

Growth Projections

India's potential GDP growth rate has been estimated to be about 7 per cent per annum over two decades (Rodrik and

Subramanian 2004). Growth accounting exercises reveal that TFP contributed 21 per cent of GDP growth during 1961–81, 38 per cent during 1981–91, and 40 per cent in 1991–2000 (Acharya et al. 2003). Moreover, TFP accounted for more than half of per worker GDP growth during 1981–2000 (Rodrik and Subramanian 2004). Endogenous growth theory and evidence suggest that a number of factors—research and development, human capital, FDI with technological spillovers, trade openness, competition, economic policies, and institutions—play a major role in increasing TFP. Their relative contribution, however, varies across countries and also between different growth phases in a country. India has put in place most of the drivers of productivity growth. It is not clear why the contribution of TFP to GDP growth remained the same for the 1980s and 1990s despite the introduction of economic reforms in the 1990s. However, annual growth rate of TFP increased marginally from 2 to 2.6 per cent between 1980s and 1990s (Acharya et al. 2003). Little is known about the underlying factors of TFP growth between pre- and post-reform periods. In all probability, India can better its growth, provided the recent higher investment rate and TFP improvement are sustained.

The Planning Commission has set a growth target of 9 per cent per annum for the duration of the 11th Five Year Plan starting from April 2007. The Planning Commission estimates that the investment rate would need to be stepped up to 32 and 35.1 per cent corresponding to 8 and 9 per cent growth targets, respectively. Higher growth rates and reduction in population growth rate will imply a significant improvement in per capita GDP growth over time. In order to achieve higher growth rates, there is a need to increase not only the savings and investment rates but also to improve efficiency. The real challenge, however, will remain in achieving a target growth rate of 4 per cent per annum set for agriculture.

Growth Drivers

India has the advantage of a relatively large size of population in the working age group. However, this advantage has not been exploited fully so far. Some of the East Asian countries including Japan, South Korea, and China have already started facing the problem of lesser number of persons of working age to retired persons—a phenomenon being experienced by the developed countries. India has yet to face this problem and hence, has the advantage of increasing relative proportion of working age population. If employment opportunities can be created and persons of working age are equipped with knowledge and skills, India is ideally poised to reap the benefits of demographic dividend given the bulge in the working age population. Moreover, a side effect is likely to be an increase in savings rate and this would finance higher levels of investment (GOI 2007a). These factors are favourable for achieving high GDP growth. There are, however, some major obstacles to be addressed if India is to benefit from demographic advantages. These include widespread malnutrition and illiteracy. For example, in 2004–5, about 40 per cent of adults suffered from chronic energy deficiency, 35 per cent of workers were illiterate, and 20 per cent of workers were in the households below the poverty line. These factors underlie the low productivity of labour.

The gross domestic savings (investment) as a percentage of GDP has increased from 23.4 per cent (24 per cent) in 2000–1 to 34.3 per cent (35.1 per cent) in 2006–7. Higher levels of investment aided by higher efficiency could reinforce the confidence in sustaining high growth. New growth sectors, beyond information technology (IT) and IT-enabled service industries, could bolster the belief of sustainability of the high growth phase. An example of a sunrise sector industry would be tourism that has shown a double digit growth rate in the last three years. The emerging middle class which is expected to increase from an estimated 220 million people in 2000 to about 370 million by 2010 (NCAER 2002) would expand the demand for consumer goods as also the supply of skilled labour.

The prevailing environment is conductive for the growth of the manufacturing sector. The investment boom—supported by increased savings as well as increased flow of credit, and improvement in TFP—underlies the growth of the manufacturing sector. It is widely believed that India will emerge as a base for global production in sectors such as auto-components, electronic hardware, and pharmaceuticals (Naik 2006). In line with the optimistic predictions, the *National Strategy for Manufacturing* released by the National Competition Council suggests a growth rate target of at least 12 to 14 per cent per annum for manufacturing sector and an increase of its share in GDP from the present 17 per cent to 23 per cent by 2015.

Outward FDI from India is expected to grow rapidly as restrictions on India's foreign investments are relaxed by the government. In recent years, India's outward FDI has been in the manufacturing and service sectors. Outward FDI increased from $701 million in 2000–1 to $1.6 billion in 2004–5, $4.5 billion in 2005–6, and further to $11 billion in 2006–7. The numbers for the current year are expected to be much higher. In 2005–6, 57 per cent of outward FDI was on account of manufacturing, 6 per cent for financial services, 20 per cent for non-financial services, and 8 per cent for trading. Indian companies are acquiring companies abroad, some examples being Tata Motors Limited's takeover of Daewoo Commercial Vehicles Company (Republic of Korea), Tata Tea's takeover of Tetley Tea (United Kingdom), and Tata Steel's takeover of Corus. Outward FDI can be utilized to reduce pressure on some scarce domestic resources if they are complemented by the products of outward FDI. For instance, it is argued that India can benefit from outward FDI in the oil fields of sub-Saharan Africa and Central Asia. The outward FDI can also contribute to the promotion of exports.

FDI into India started increasing after the opening up of the economy, including relaxing of the restrictive policy towards FDI. It has risen substantially in recent years, from $4.3 billion in 2003–4 to $5.7 billion in 2005–6 and further to $19.5 billion in 2006–7. FDI inflows into India originated mainly from Mauritius, the United States, and United Kingdom and had flowed into manufacturing, financial services, banking services, IT services, and construction (RBI, *Macroeconomic and Monetary Development in 2006–7*, 24 April 2007). Studies suggest that, overall macroeconomic growth, growth of domestic investment, revival of industrial growth, availability of skilled manpower, and FDI global flows contributed to the growth of FDI flows into India. It is pertinent to note that the overall impact of FDI on investment and growth depends crucially on whether it crowds out or crowds in domestic investment, its positive externalities particularly in technology, management practices etc., and linkages with domestic industry. The East Asian experience suggests FDI inflows would have a positive impact on economic growth under a specific policy regime—which is situation specific. Given its strong private sector and entrepreneurial base, India can gain from FDI if it flows into capital and knowledge intensive sectors and foreign enterprises get vertically integrated with domestic labour intensive enterprises.

Risk Factors and Constraints

Certain risk factors, however, cannot be overlooked. There are apprehensions about the lopsided growth patterns and the underlying regional imbalances. During the 1990s and beyond, inter-state inequalities in per capita state domestic product (SDP) worsened and the laggard states, Bihar, Orissa, and Uttar Pradesh, recorded low growth rates (Figure 2.9). If these states continue to grow slow, the overall GDP growth rate will be pushed down. It is critical that adequate investments and credit are made available towards meeting the growth requirements of these backward states. Some of the backward states are also faced with severe governance problems. Concerns have also been raised over the state of higher education and the employability of the graduates who are joining the workforce. While the situation on the infrastructure front appears to be improving, there is substantial scope for further improvements. Energy sufficiency remains an area of concern and the adverse impact of rising crude oil prices on industry cannot be underplayed.

The declining share of consumption in aggregate demand caused by the slowdown in the growth of domestic household consumption would make effective demand susceptible to greater volatility since investment is prone to greater risks than consumption. This could push the economy towards a path of instability. Moreover, household consumer demand—driven by growth of income, urbanization and more importantly, tastes and changing lifestyles of the rich—has been experiencing substantial diversification, calling for continuous adjustment by the producers. Such adjustments involve huge costs. Besides, the liberalization of trade is also likely to increase producers' risks. It is clear then that the domestic economy will face problems of effective demand associated with both demand deficiency as well as diversification of consumer demand. To some extent, demand deficiency can be overcome by adjusting investment and export components of the effective demand. It is imperative that India put in place proper instruments to fine-tune the effective demand. Increasing capital flows as well as better integration of India's financial markets with the global financial markets would make the choice of instruments extremely difficult over time. It is important to recognize that growth biased in favour of lower income groups would ensure stability since their consumption patterns are likely to be more stable. Such a growth process would also revive the stagnating per capita food consumption that co-exists with widespread undernutrition witnessed in recent years.

While India can sustain high GDP growth and improve its position in the world GDP ranking, the moot question is whether this growth would be inclusive. Inclusive growth is not only desirable from the equity point of view, but is also important for ensuring stable growth. For inclusive growth, it is not enough to achieve high growth; nor should it mean simply income transfers through a plethora of government schemes. The experience, by and large, is that countries which achieved rapid reduction in poverty are those which combined rapid growth with equity-promoting growth. In such a strategy, public policies influence both the distribution of income and the process of income generation. Neither a strategy which focuses primarily on growth nor one that concentrates on reducing inequality through redistribution of assets is likely to succeed in reducing poverty. Excessive focus on redistribution while ignoring growth may undermine the incentive system and also impose constraints on finding resources required for financing the targeted antipoverty programmes in the absence of growth. Therefore, growth needs to be rapid enough to significantly improve the condition of the poor. Also, for maximum impact, there should be an improvement in the relative position of the poor, and the share of poor in the incremental income should be greater than their share in the average.

It is widely held that acceleration of both growth and poverty reduction cannot be achieved without increasing growth rates in the laggard states such as Bihar, Madhya Pradesh, Orissa, and Uttar Pradesh. These states are also worse-off in terms of the non-income dimensions of poverty. What is even worse, the deprived social groups are concentrated in these states. Of particular importance for poverty reduction are policies that would increase both agricultural productivity and rural non-farm employment. Faster growth of the rural non-farm sector can provide jobs to the labour force released from agriculture. Public intervention should be holistic and tailored to the specific and heterogeneous needs of the poor.

GROWTH AND WELL-BEING

Poverty Trends

The process of poverty reduction has been modest over the past two decades. The incidence of poverty as measured by the head count ratio (HCR) declined at 0.85 percentage point per annum during 1983–94 and at 0.7 percentage point per annum during 1994–2005. The decline in terms of annual compound growth rate works out to 2.3 per cent and 2.4 per cent, respectively. The decline in poverty has not been smooth. Poverty increased during the early years of the 1990s, before it started declining in the latter years. The absolute number of poor declined by 5.4 million between 1983 and 1993–4 and by 17.8 million between 1993–4 and 2004–5. The growth process could uplift a mere 23.2 million persons out of poverty over a span of two decades and has left an unacceptably high level of 303 million poor in 2004–5. The reduction in the absolute number of poor was slightly faster in the latter period because of lower population growth. A slow process of urbanization of poverty is also taking place. The number of rural poor declined by 31.4 million between 1983 and 2005 and, in contrast, the number of urban poor increased by 8.3 million. The worsening situation in urban areas was due to their high population growth attributed to natural growth as well as rural–urban migration.

Growth and Poverty Nexus

The strength of the relationship between growth and poverty is usually measured by the poverty elasticity with respect to per capita GDP. Our estimate of poverty elasticity is in the range of –0.86 to –0.77. The trickle-down effect of growth is rather weak. Moreover, preliminary analysis suggests further weakening of the relationship in the post-reform period. This is supported by the fact that there has been no significant acceleration in the process of poverty reduction during 1980–2005 despite an acceleration in the growth of per capita GDP. Empirical studies reveal that lack of assets such as land, human capital, and skills constrain the poor from participating in, and benefiting from, growth. There is now a growing consensus that the poverty reduction strategy must also rely on direct measures since the present high growth, given its sectoral composition and degree of inclusiveness, may not eradicate poverty completely even by 2015. The National Rural Employment Guarantee (NREG) Scheme which came into force in 2006, and is being implemented in 330 districts across the country can make a difference to the lives of those who have thus far been excluded from the growth process (Panda, Chapter 2). Also relevant for poverty reduction are the programmes such as the self-employment programmes (*Swarnajayanti Gram Swarozgar Yojana*), rural housing for the houseless, and social assistance to the aged and disadvantaged.

What do Recent Poverty Studies Reveal?

A reading of the poverty situation in India reveals some disturbing facts. Issues relating to equity and growth and the rate of poverty reduction in rural and urban areas have been under the microscope. It is disquieting that there has been no acceleration in the pace of poverty reduction in the states where it matters the most. The poorer states of Bihar, Madhya Pradesh, Orissa, and Uttar Pradesh have not exhibited any significant increase in the rate of reduction of poverty over the two periods 1983–93 and 1993–2005 (Figure 1.1). Poverty has increasingly become concentrated in these states (Figure 1.2). While 46 per cent of India's poor lived in the states of Bihar, Madhya Pradesh, Orissa, and Uttar Pradesh in 1983, over 54 per cent lived in these states in 2004–5. Moreover, rural poverty has also become concentrated in these four states which accounted for 56 per cent of all-India rural poor in 1983 and 61 per cent in 2004–5. These trends indicate tendencies towards economic apartheid. It is politically risky to ignore this problem as it could potentially become a source of social conflict. North-western states (Punjab, Haryana, Himachal Pradesh, and Jammu and Kashmir) had made substantial progress in poverty reduction even by the early 1980s and their combined share in all-India poor was 2.7 per cent in 1983; this further declined to 2.2 per cent in 2004–5. These states have comparatively low rural–urban disparity in per capita expenditure (Panda, Chapter 2). Further, they had higher wage rate for workers engaged in agricultural operations and lower gender disparity in wage rates. Contrary to expectations, the highest per capita income state of Maharashtra had a disproportionately larger share in poverty which increased from 9 per cent in 1983 to 9.7 per cent in 1993–4 and further to 10.4 per cent in 2004–5. It had higher rural–urban disparity, low wage rate for workers engaged in agricultural operations, and high gender disparity in wage rates.

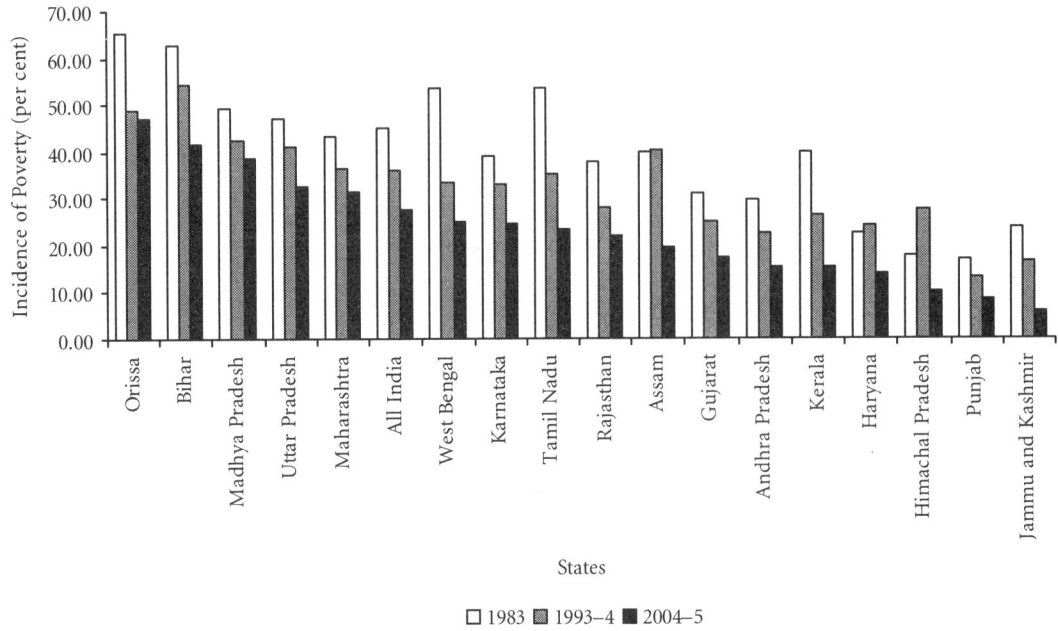

Note: Bihar, Madhya Pradesh, and Uttar Pradesh refer to the undivided states.
Source: C. Ravi, Centre for Economic and Social Studies (CESS), personal communication.

Figure 1.1: All-India and Statewise Incidence of Poverty (Rural + Urban)

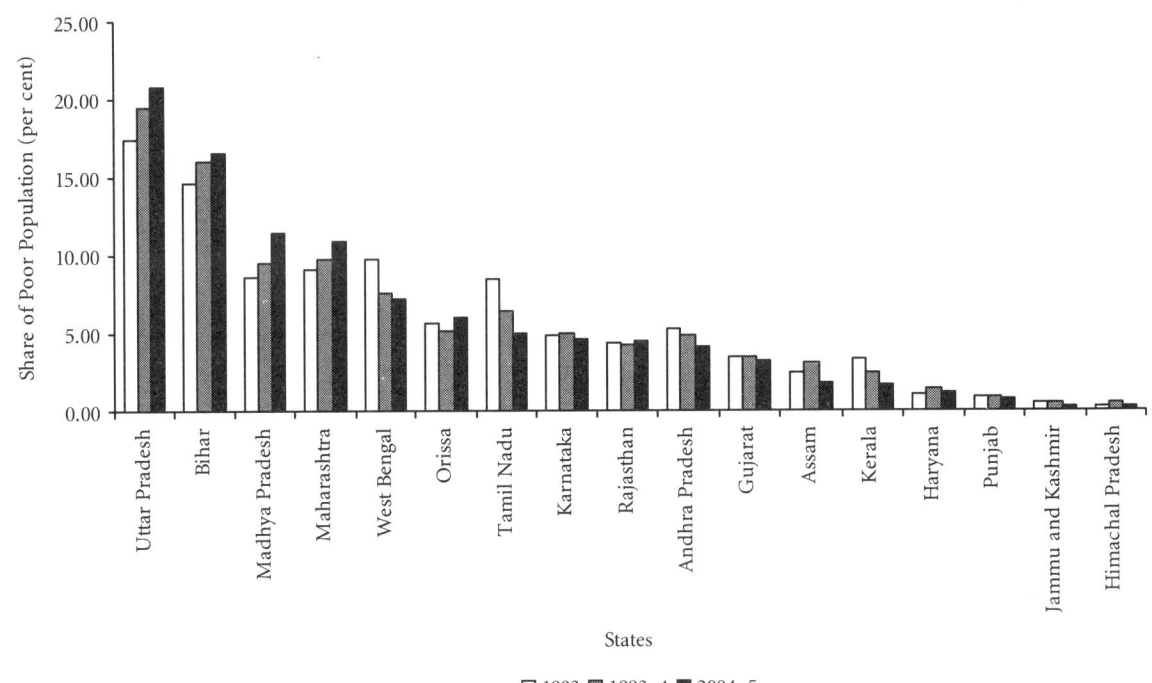

Note: Bihar, Madhya Pradesh, and Uttar Pradesh refer to the undivided states.
Source: C. Ravi, Centre for Economic and Social Studies (CESS), personal communication.

Figure 1.2: Percentage Share of States in All India Poor (Rural + Urban)

More than half of India's urban poor lived in the states of Maharashtra, Madhya Pradesh, Uttar Pradesh, and Tamil Nadu. The first three states also had larger shares of rural poverty. Larger population size accompanied by higher urbanization rates as well as higher incidence of urban poverty explains the large share of Maharashtra in all-India urban poor; and higher urbanization explains the large share of Tamil Nadu. Though urbanization rate was low, the large size of the urban population as well as high incidence of urban poverty explains the larger share of Uttar Pradesh and Madhya Pradesh in all-India urban poor.

There is no evidence for convergence in the incidence of poverty across the states of India. The states of Kerala, Tamil Nadu, and West Bengal achieved reduction in the incidence of poverty faster than for All India (Figure 1.1) and reduced their share of all-India poor (Figure 1.2) in both the periods. The states of Bihar, Madhya Pradesh, Maharashtra, and Uttar Pradesh experienced slower rate of poverty reduction and higher share of all-India poverty in both the periods. As expected, the coefficient of variation (CV) of poverty reveals widening inter-state inequalities in poverty reduction. The CV of estimates of rural poverty by state declined from 41 in 1983 to 36 in 1993–4. However, it increased to 54 in 2004–5. The CV of estimates of urban poverty by state increased from 32 per cent in 1983 to 46 per cent in 1993–4 and further to 57 per cent in 2004–5. The reduction in inter-state inequality in rural areas between 1983 and 1993 could be due to the better reach of agricultural growth during the 1980s. The widening inequalities in the later period could be attributed to the worsening inter-state income inequalities, growing rural–urban disparities in per capita expenditure (Figure 1.3), and worsening inequalities within rural as well as urban areas.

Chronic Poverty

Chronic poor (poor persons/households who have been poor for a long duration) were 14 per cent of all-India rural households and 11 per cent of all-India urban households; and comprised about half of the poor in both rural and urban areas (Radhakrishna et al. 2006, 2007) in the late 1990s. The incidence of rural [urban] chronic poverty was high in Orissa (28 [26] per cent), Uttar Pradesh (12 [18]), Madhya Pradesh (19 [25]), West Bengal (19 [6]), and Bihar (19 [19]) but low in Jammu and Kashmir (2.7 [5.6]) and Punjab (4.8 [3.2]).

The incidence of chronic poverty varied significantly across social and occupational groups, and is among social groups, the highest for scheduled castes (SCs) (21[19] per cent) in rural [urban] areas. In some of the states, chronic poverty was more of a social problem than an economic one. For example, in rural areas, the share of SCs in chronically poor households was as high as 84 per cent in Punjab and 66 per cent in Haryana and the corresponding percentages in urban areas were 61 and 58, respectively. This suggests that economic instruments may not be sufficient for eradicating poverty and their efficacy tends to reduce with poverty reduction in states with high incidence of poverty among social groups.

The incidence of chronic poverty was higher among rural casual labour households (19 per cent), urban casual labour households (24 per cent), and urban self-employed households (12 per cent). It is noteworthy that in rural

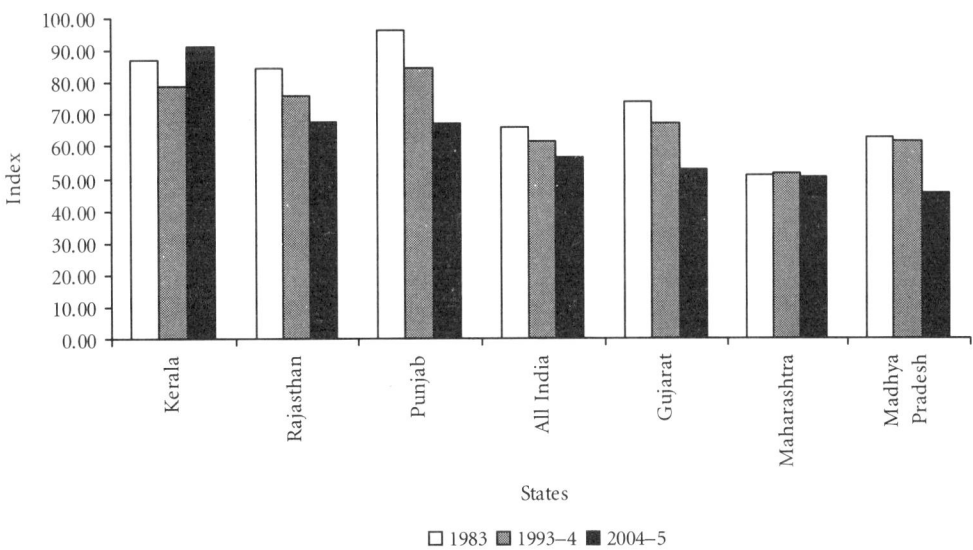

Note: Madhya Pradesh refers to the undivided state.
Source: C. Ravi, Centre for Economic and Social Studies (CESS), personal communication.

Figure 1.3: Index of Average Monthly Per Capita Expenditure (1993–4 prices) in the Rural Sector (Urban = 100)

areas, agricultural labour households accounted for 45 per cent of the chronic poor households; and in urban areas, chronic poverty was spread among self-employed and casual labour households with self-employed households accounting for 36 per cent urban chronic poor and casual labour accounting for 29 per cent.

It is essential to recognize that the poor are heterogeneous and the strategies for elimination of poverty should be specifically designed to address the chronic poor and other poor. Safety nets have to be designed to remove chronic poverty and to free this population from the multiple deprivations so as to enable them to become more responsive to development opportunities. These programmes must strengthen the livelihood base and gradually make them productive. In the case of chronic poor, external support should play a major part in the beginning.

Comparison of India and China in terms of Poverty Reduction

India's record in poverty reduction pales before the achievements of China, which has been far more effective in reducing poverty. The incidence of poverty in China declined by a staggering 45 percentage points in two decades: from 53 per cent in 1981 to 8 per cent in 2001 (Ravallion and Chen 2004). In contrast, India could reduce poverty by a mere 17 percentage points in two decades. India fares badly even on non-income dimensions of poverty. For instance in the recent period, the incidence of malnutrition in India was four times more than that in China, the infant as well as under-five mortality rate in 2002 was double that in China and maternal mortality rate was ten-fold higher in India (UNDP 2003). Though China managed to reduce poverty rapidly, the progress has been uneven across its regions (Ravallion and Chen 2004). In China too, there are concerns about whether all sections of society have benefited equally from the growth process. Whether the poor benefit from economic growth or not, depends on the country's geographic spread and the sectoral composition of growth. In India a similar concern emerges with apprehensions over its lopsided growth marked by its lagging agricultural sector, worsening rural urban disparity, and growing regional imbalances. However, it is noteworthy that India fared better than China in achieving lower inequality. This is reflected in the higher income shares of the bottom groups. For instance, the share of the poorest 20 per cent in income (expenditure) was 8.1 per cent in India whereas it was only 5.9 per cent in China (UNDP 2003).

Non-income Poverty Dimensions

Data from the National Family Health Survey (NFHS-3) carried out in 2005–6 and District Level Household Survey on Reproductive Health (RCH) carried out during 2002–4 show the worst forms of deprivation in India. As high as 46 per cent of children under 3 years of age (NFHS-3) and 49 per cent children under 6 years (RCH) suffered from malnutrition; and 79 per cent of children from anaemia (NFHS-3). These unfavourable child health outcomes could be, inter alia, attributable to failures in health care. For instance, 56 per cent of children were not fully immunized and 79 per cent did not receive Vitamin-A dose in the last 6 months prior to the survey (NFHS-3). The position was equally dismal for adolescent girls (10–19 years) and women—33 per cent of ever-married women suffered from chronic energy deficiency, 58 per cent suffered from anaemia, 59 per cent deliveries did not take place in institutional agencies (NFHS-3), and 76 per cent of adolescent girls suffered from severe and moderate anaemia (RCH). The access of households to basic amenities was equally poor. According to NFHS-3, 32 per cent of households did not have electricity, 58 per cent did not have piped drinking water, 55 per cent did not have toilet facility, and 59 per cent did not live in pucca houses. These data suggest that the incidence of non-income poverty is much more alarming than the incidence of income poverty. Studies suggest that even if income poverty is eliminated in India, other forms of poverty may persist. NFHS-3 data also reveal rural–urban and intra-household inequalities in nutritional outcomes. For example, the incidence of chronic energy deficiency in rural (urban) women was 38.8 (19.8) per cent among ever-married women and 33.1 (17.5) per cent among men. The performance of India in terms of nutritional outcomes is worse than that of less developed African countries in recent years (UNDP 2003).

The national averages mask the huge variations in the incidence of child malnutrition across the states of India (Figure 1.4). In 2005–6, the incidence of child malnutrition varied among the major states from 27 per cent in Punjab and 29 per cent in Kerala and Jammu and Kashmir to 60 per cent in Madhya Pradesh (NFHS-3). It is to be noted that the nutritional status of children and adults in some of the middle-income states such as Kerala and Tamil Nadu was better than that in higher income states such as Maharashtra and Gujarat. This could be attributed to public interventions in the nutrition and health sectors. Factors such as public provision of safe drinking water and health care are also important determinants of nutritional well-being. Analysis of inter-household variations in child nutrition shows that the risk of malnutrition decreases with an improvement in household income, mother's nutritional status, her education, and access to health care during child delivery. The mother's present nutritional status, in turn, depends on her childhood nutritional status.

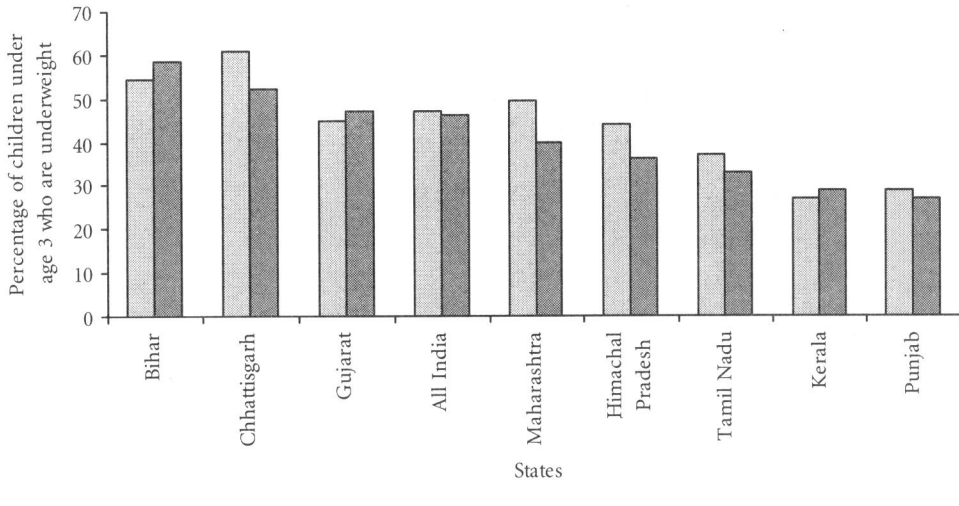

Note: Bihar excludes Jharkand.
Source: NFHS-2 and NFHS-3.

Figure 1.4: Incidence of Malnutrition among Children in All India and Selected States (Rural + Urban)

Malnutrition is seriously retarding human development and is hampering further reduction in child mortality. Adults who survived malnutrition in their childhood are less healthy, physically less productive, and have poor intellectual abilities. The economic costs of the current scale of malnutrition are enormous. Improvements in incomes of the poor and supply of environmental and health services are the long-term solutions for the eradication of malnutrition. However, in the short run, direct nutrition intervention should be the priority.

Despite legislative orders passed in 2001, the coverage and progress of the Integrated Child Development Scheme (ICDS) has been tardy. In response to a petition on the 'non-implementation of the directions' given by Supreme Court relating to ICDS, the Supreme Court in its order in December 2006 issued the following directive: 'Government of India shall sanction and operationalize a minimum of 14 lakh AWCs in a phased and even manner starting forthwith and ending December 2008. In doing so, the Central Government shall identify SC and ST hamlets/habitations for AWCs on a priority basis'. The universalisation of the ICDS involves extending all ICDS services (supplementary nutrition, growth monitoring, nutrition and health education, immunization, referral and pre-school education) to every child under the age of 6, all pregnant women and lactating mothers and all adolescent girls'. The Central Government has recently sanctioned 173 ICDS projects, 107, 274 Anganwadi centres, and 25,961 mini-Anganwadi centres. The budgetary allocation for ICDS has been raised from Rs 4087 crore in 2006–7 to Rs 4761 crore in 2007–8. The impact of these initiatives depends largely on reforming the delivery system. Hopefully, lessons can be drawn from the success of Kerala and Tamil Nadu in reducing the incidence of malnutrition.

Urban Slums

Projections show that over 534 million people, constituting 38 per cent of India's population are likely to be living in urban areas by 2026. Concomitant with higher levels of urbanization would be a growth in the slum population. Intra-urban differences (slums versus non-slums) in economic outcomes are expected to get even more stark in the coming years and may become a source of urban conflicts. If there is a pick up in the rate of migration it would swell the slum population further. It has been well documented that individuals living in the slums are worse-off in terms of non-income poverty dimensions and do not have access to many public services. There is growing empirical evidence lately, that suggests huge disparities in health outcomes even within urban areas. It also shows substantial heterogeneity within both slums and non-slum urban areas. It is evident from the discussion in Chapter 6 that India has a long way to go before it meets the Millennium Development Goal of achieving 'a significant improvement' in the lives of slum dwellers.

EMPLOYMENT

Employment Growth

The provision of gainful employment for all in the labour force is essential for reducing poverty and achieving inclusive growth. Accelerating productive employment is important because wage income is the main source of income for the poor. It is well-recognized that employment generation by itself is not enough to lift people out of poverty as poverty is widespread even among the employed. What is required is the growth of productive employment. Expansion of productive employment, employment security, and favourable working conditions are imperative for poverty reduction. According to the regional profile document of the South Asian Association for Regional Cooperation (SAARC), employment growth rate should be equal to labour force growth rate in the first instance and surpass it later (Bhalla 2007). The most favourable situation for India is one in which labour demand outpaces its supply and food supply outpaces its demand.

During the last two decades, employment expansion, more or less, kept pace with labour supply growth; both grew at 2 per cent per annum. Between 1983 and 1993–4, employment (by usual principal status) increased at 2.09 per cent per annum and labour force at 2.02 per cent per annum, and between 1993–4 and 2004–5, employment increased at 1.98 per cent per annum and labour force at 2.02 per cent per annum (GOI 2007a). However, because of cyclical behaviour, short-term growth rates deviated from the long-term growth rates. For example, employment (labour force) growth rate fell to 1.57 (1.60) per cent per annum from 1983 to 1999–2000, and then rose to 2.48 (2.54) per cent per annum from 1999–2000 to 2004–5. This raises a question about the validity of inferring long-term trends from short-period growth rates. However, many economists inferred the slowdown of employment growth by comparing the growth rates of the two periods, viz. 1987–8 to 1993–4 and 1993–4 to 1999–2000. On the basis of a rigorous econometric analysis, Srinivasan (Chapter 4) shows that there was no such slowdown in employment growth and observes 'that the pronouncements on slowdown in employment growth since 1993–4 are based on inappropriate measurement and invalid employment elasticity analysis and that the long-term trends in usual status and current weekly status employment rates do not support the same'. However, it is a fact that employment growth did not accelerate in consonance with GDP growth. Srinivasan sees barriers to accelerating employment growth in labour laws and regulations and suggests a reform of labour laws. It is important to recognize that the real issue in the Indian context is whether the accelerated growth generated decent work. There is a need to differentiate between effort-intensive work, associated with drudgery and long hours, and decent work.

Quality Dimension of Employment

Out of the 60.7 million workers absorbed between 1999–2000 and 2004–5, 52.3 million (86 per cent) were absorbed in the informal economy and the rest in the organized sector (NCEUS 2007). In fact, the entire additional employment in the formal sector was of informal type and did not have employment security or social security. In this context, two questions arise: What proportion of informal employment was decent? And has it been increasing? The available data show that in 1999–2000, about 65 per cent of the informal workers were in agriculture; 45 per cent of the non-agricultural employment was in rural areas and most of the informal workers did not have either employment and income security let alone health insurance (NCEUS 2006).

There has been increasing casualization of the labour market without a safety net, increasing feminization of agricultural labour with low wages, persistence of child labour (about 12.6 million in 2001), and increasing flow of interstate distress rural migrant workers (for example, every year 200,000 workers migrate from Bihar for livelihood). It is pertinent to note that despite the ban on child labour, its incidence was high in hazardous activities. The conditions of the long distance distress migrants also was bad. They were engaged in work associated with drudgery and long hours. They were also subject to social hostilities. For example, it is reported that in the North-eastern Assam, militants recently killed nearly 90 Hindi-speaking migrants, mostly from Bihar, some of whom migrated decades earlier. However, migrants faced less hostility in prosperous Punjab during the green revolution period or in northern Ladakh where tourism had fuelled a construction boom. Clearly, social conflict would be lower in situations where migrant labourers do not compete with local labourers or in situations with severe local labour shortage.

Employment Structure and Status

Over the years, there has been a slow change in the composition of the workforce in rural India, with an increasing tendency to move out of the agriculture sector. The dependency of rural male (female) workers on agriculture declined from 81 (88) per cent in 1977–8 to 71 (86) in 1993–4, and further to 67 (83) per cent in 2004–5. Despite the decline, India continues to have a relatively large rural population dependent on agriculture and allied activities. In urban areas, there has been a slight increase in the share of industrial sector in the total urban workforce from 31.6 (28.5) per cent in 1993–4 to 33.5 (32.2) per cent in 2004–5. The share of the tertiary sector remained almost unchanged during the above-mentioned periods.

The employment status (self employment, regular salaried employment, and casual employment) has also been changing. In rural areas, while self-employment is on the decline, casual employment is on the rise for both males and females. In urban areas, for males, the relative sizes of self-employment and casual employment have been on the rise and that of regular salaried has been on the decline;

and in contrast, for females, regular and salaried employment has been on the rise and self-employment has been on the decline. In 2004–5, in rural areas, 58 (64) per cent male (female) usual status workers (principal plus subsidiary) were self-employed, 33 (33) were causal labour; and in urban areas, 45 (47) per cent were self-employed and 15 (17) per cent were casual labour (NSSO 2006). It is important to recognize that self-employed and casual workers who constitute more than 90 per cent of the rural work force and more than 60 per cent of the urban workforce are not covered by effective social security and are, therefore, likely to be exposed to the risks originating from various shocks.

What is worse, employment insecurity, particularly in rural areas, is on the rise. The National Employment Guarantee Scheme has the potential to reduce the risks associated with the labour market and thereby contribute to the protection of rural casual wage labour from transient poverty.

Unemployment

The unemployment situation has not improved, but among the four measures of unemployment, only current daily status (CDS) unemployment rate shows a worsening of the unemployment situation between 1993–4 and 2004–5 (Figure 1.5).

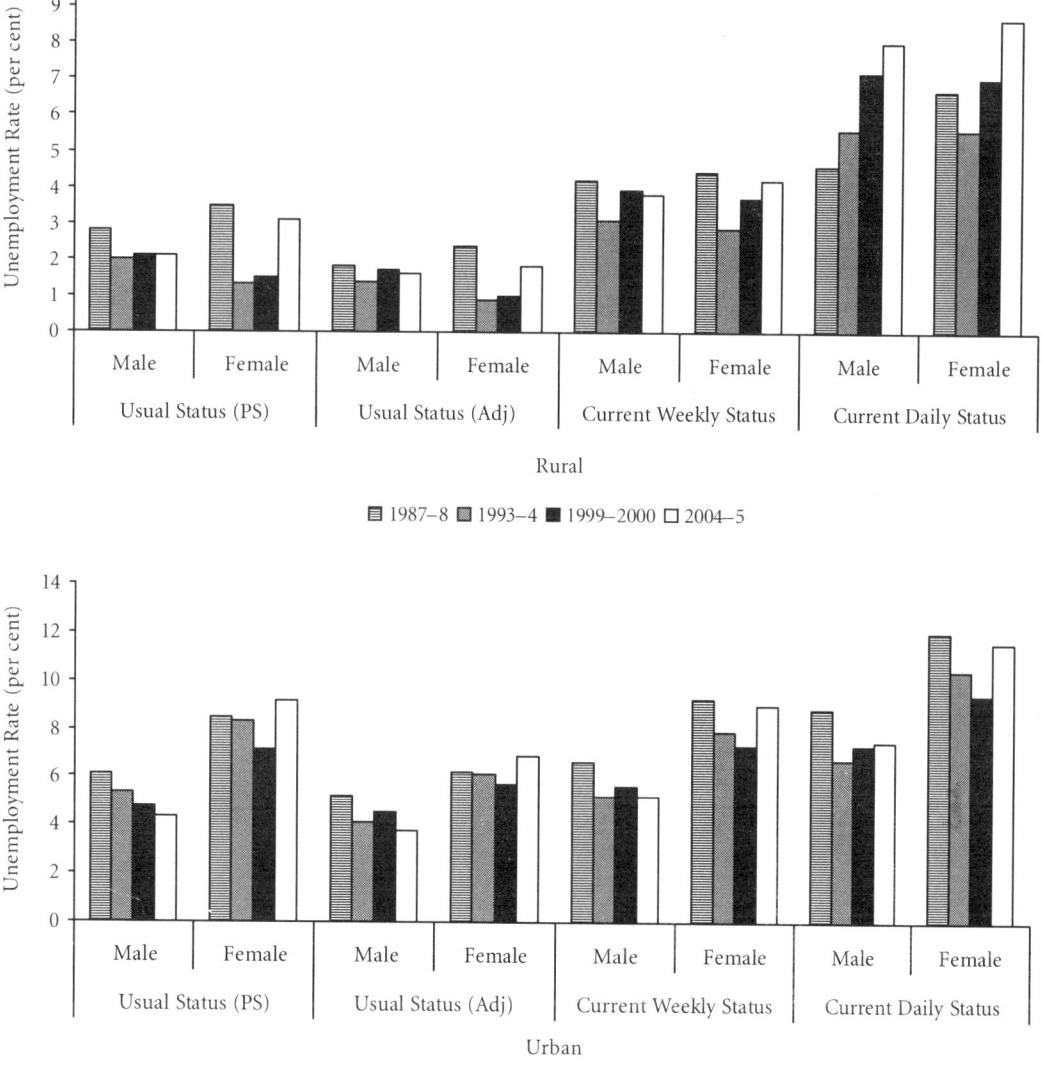

Notes: PS—primary status; adj—adjusted; for concepts of employment, see Srinivasan (Chapter 4).
Source: NSS 2006.

Figure 1.5: Trends in Unemployment, 1987–8 to 2004–5

The CDS unemployment rate for rural males (females) increased from 5.6 (5.6) per cent in 1993–4 to 8 (8.7) per cent in 2004–5 and for urban males (females) from 6.7 (7.9) per cent in 1993–4 to 7.5 (11.6) per cent in 2004–5. Although the CDS unemployment rate indicates some worsening of unemployment in the post-reform period, its long-term trend does not reveal any worsening situation (Srinivasan, Chapter 4). It is important to note that when the employment rates follow a cyclical pattern, inferences about long-term trends based on two period comparisons would be misleading (Srinivasan, Chapter 4). Much of the debate on India's progress on the employment front is based on such two-period comparisons.

A high level of unemployment was evident in West Bengal, Kerala, and Tamil Nadu (NSSO reports). In urban areas, levels of unemployment were, in general, lower than those observed in rural areas. Kerala and Tamil Nadu reported relatively higher levels of urban unemployment. A better measure of underemployment (invisible) would be the percentage of currently employed persons seeking additional or alternative work. The percentage of usually employed persons seeking alternative/additional work was very significant in 1999–2000 (19.6 per cent for males and 14.3 per cent for females). The incidence of underemployment was widespread in both developed and backward states.

Wages

Recent studies on rural agricultural wage rates show that these continued to increase in the 1990s but at a reduced rate than in the 1980s (Himanshu 2005). However, non-agricultural wage rates increased at a faster rate in the 1990s (Himanshu 2005). There is a growing body of empirical evidence which suggests that an improvement in agricultural wages would reduce not only rural poverty but also urban poverty. Normally, the wage rate of the unskilled agricultural labour usually acts as a reservation wage for the rural non-agricultural worker and as well as for the urban unskilled informal worker. However, improvement in agricultural productivity is a prerequisite for wage improvement; otherwise wage increases cannot be sustained over time.

There are substantial inter-state variations in the wage rates (in rural labour households in agricultural operations), even within a state. In 1999–2000, the male worker wage rate varied from Rs 94.52 (Kerala) to Rs 26.31 (Chhattisgarh) among major states (Rural Labour Enquiry Report 1999–2000). For female workers, the range was Rs 73.98 (Punjab) to Rs 22.31 (Orissa). In general, wage rates as well as their growth rates were lower in the laggard states of Bihar, Madhya Pradesh, Orissa, and Uttar Pradesh. At the all-India level, the average wage rate for female casual workers was 60 per cent of the wage rate of male workers. Inter-state differences were higher than gender differences.

Challenges for Employment Generation

The problem of low wage rates, particularly in laggard states, lack of employment opportunities in agriculture, increasing casualization of employment, gender disparities in wage rates, and high levels of underemployment among those employed, continue to remain formidable issues that need to be addressed. The declining employment opportunities in agriculture and slow employment growth in the organized sector suggest that the policy focus for the promotion of employment should be on the development of the unorganized sector including allied activities of agriculture. It is important to recognize the need for massive rural and peri-urban industrialization. Further, small enterprise clusters could emerge as hubs of economic activities. With necessary policy and infrastructure support, such clusters could emerge as engines of industrial growth in the peripheral economies. Simultaneously, efforts should be made to develop demand based skills. NCEUS recommended that 25 growth poles (cluster of clusters) be supported during the Eleventh Plan period. If implemented, this would facilitate labour-intensive industrialization, with strong forward–backward linkages. However, the key tasks would remain to be capacity building and creation of effective support systems. It is useful to learn about the role of state and local institutions from some of the successful clusters in India such as the Tirupur Knitwear cluster. It would also be a challenge to provide social security cover to all the unorganized workers, many of whom are covered neither by any formal system of social security nor regulation of conditions of work (see NCEUS 2006).

AGRARIAN CRISIS

The disquieting trends in Indian agriculture that have persisted since the mid-1990s include: declining profitability of agriculture, increasing risks, degradation of natural resources, steep fall in technological innovations in agriculture, and collapsing agricultural extension. Agricultural growth has hardly been 2.2 per cent per annum, falling short of the targeted 4 per cent growth in the Tenth Five Year Plan. The crop sector has witnessed a marked decline in its growth rate. Livestock and horticultural crops which provided the lead during the first half of the 1990s have been experiencing deceleration in their growth since 1995–6. The slowdown in agricultural growth has been accompanied by a slowdown in agricultural credit and in agricultural investment (especially public investment)—the most powerful drivers of agricultural growth. Private investment in agriculture has been increasing but could not compensate for the fall in public investment. Growing evidence shows declining TFP in the 1990s. The large number of farmers' suicides reported in states such as Andhra Pradesh,

Karnataka, Kerala, Maharashtra, and Punjab in recent years is symptomatic of the deep-rooted crisis in agriculture.

The Report of the Expert Group on Agricultural Indebtedness (GOI 2007b) has highlighted the twin dimensions of the current widespread agricultural crisis—an agricultural development crisis and an agrarian crisis. The root cause of the agricultural development crisis is the neglect of agriculture in designing development programmes and in effective implementation of agricultural programmes at the micro level. On the other hand, the agrarian crisis is characterized by the high dependence of rural population on farm incomes which are too meagre to withstand weather and price shocks and are also vulnerable to technological risks. In addition to low growth and declining productivity, the failure of growth in creating adequate productive employment outside agriculture underlines the agrarian crisis.

There is a consensus that growth of irrigation, a major driver of growth, has slowed down owing to a decline in public investment in irrigation infrastructure. Despite the fact that 40 per cent of the irrigation potential (140 million hectares) remains untapped, only 0.8 million hectares per annum was added during the 1980s and 1990s. This is in contrast to 2.5 million hectares annual additions to irrigated area during the Green Revolution. Over 400 major and medium projects were in the pipeline at various stages during the Ninth Plan Period and the situation might not have changed since then. Poorer states such as Bihar, Madhya Pradesh, Orissa and Uttar Pradesh account for more than half of the unfinished major and medium irrigation projects. Poor maintenance of the existing system of surface irrigation has contributed to low efficiency in water use (water use efficiency was less than 40 per cent, much below the attainable 65 per cent). The situation with respect to minor irrigation has been relatively better but there is overexploitation of ground water by rich farmers.

Public expenditure on agricultural research and extension was low at 0.49 per cent of GDP (on average developing countries spend 0.7 per cent and developed countries 2 to 3 per cent). It is important to recognize that the research requirements are high in view of substantial variations in agro-climatic conditions that warrant region-specific and crop-specific technologies, compatible with the endowments of the farm community. Needless to say, efforts in this direction are grossly inadequate. It is worrying that no technological innovations are in the offing which could make decisive impact on agricultural productivity, particularly in dry land agriculture. What is worse, in many states the agricultural extension system has virtually collapsed.

A major area of concern is the sluggish growth of institutional credit (Shetty, Chapter 8). Agriculture's share of about 10–11 per cent in the institutional credit was way below the stipulated target of 18 per cent. Half of the farmers had no access to institutional finance in 2003; institutional agencies accounted for 57.7 per cent of the outstanding loan amount of farmers, followed by money lenders (25.7 per cent) and traders (5.2 per cent). These data suggest heavy dependence of farmers on informal sources of finance. The picture is even worse for small and marginal farmers. Interest rates charged by informal sources are not affordable given the low productivity levels in agriculture. For instance, about 40 per cent of the cash debt from informal sources outstanding in 2003 was at interest rates of 30 per cent or more. In contrast, the interest rate was less than 20 per cent for 99 per cent of the debt from institutional sources. A field survey conducted in Punjab showed that farmers incurred 3 to 8 per cent of the loan amount over and above the interest to obtain institutional credit (GOI 2007b). Inadequacy of formal credit, enormous delays in obtaining credit from scheduled commercial banks (SCBs), and cumbersome documentation have compelled farmers to avail of high-cost credit from informal sources. Recent decisions to reduce the interest rate to 7 per cent and double the amount of rural credit are welcome steps. However, given the weaknesses of the formal credit institutions, these measures may not yield the expected outcomes.

The agricultural deceleration has had differential impact on small holders with limited resources and the relatively better-off large farmers, as also between rain-fed and irrigated regions. Reddy and Mishra (Chapter 3) pose a pointed question, viz. whether small-marginal farming is sustainable without substantial public infrastructure support and comprehensive social security including health, education, employment, and old age support? The Indian farmer is under severe stress. Water is becoming a scarce resource and the absence of adequate irrigation facilities has meant that farmers in dry regions incur large debts by investing in unstable groundwater resources. There has been a steep increase in the costs of farming across the country. Faced with multiple risks, a number of farmers have committed suicide under duress. Reddy and Mishra point out that this is probably due to the sequencing of the reform process. The twin issues of cost of cultivation and depletion of water resources need to be tackled on a war footing.

HIGHER EDUCATION

India's achievements in higher education in the post-independence period have been significant in view of the slender base from which it started (Hashim, Chapter 5). From 1950–1 to 2004–5, the number of universities increased from 28 to 348, and colleges from 578 to 17,625. Enrolment in higher education increased from 0.17 million to 10.48 million. By March 2006, India had 20 central universities, 217 state universities, 102 deemed universities,

10 private universities, 13 institutions of national importance, and 5 universities established under the State Legislature Act. The quantum jump in numbers, however, hides the great disparities that exist between institutions, between states and regions, and among central and state universities.

India has one of the largest stock of trained and educated manpower, equipped with considerable scientific and technical capabilities. And yet the country's capacity and capabilities are inadequate to meet the growing demand that is being made on our educated youths and managers in various disciplines of higher education. The pace of expansion of higher education has been very slow and the quality by and large uneven across the spectrum. For instance, hardly a third of universities and 10 per cent of colleges meet the minimum standards of quality of educational services. To a great degree, this has been the consequence of the state having a considerably diminished role in higher education (Hashim, Chapter 5). One important result is the lack of reach and equity in higher education even as the demand on the system is huge; excellence cannot be evenly distributed when the base is slender (Hashim, Chapter 5).

Severe capacity constraints have emerged, particularly in those segments of higher education where demand has increased sharply with the changing competitive edge of the Indian economy. This has resulted in huge premium on specific skills and, consequently, there has been a great competitive rush to cash in on the opportunities offered. In the face of niggardly allocation of public resources in the last two decades, the spread of education in these spheres has been inadequate and iniquitous. The entry of the private sector has met a part of this supply constraint but with undesirable consequences on several fronts in terms of both excellence and equity. It is not surprising that private players are cashing in on this market with products that are not altogether high class. India's main competitors are investing heavily in higher education as we seem to pedal the excuse of resource crunch in meeting the required budget. This being the state of affairs, the quality of students' training has been disappointing. The quality of training can be gauged from the following example. Out of six lakh engineering graduates produced by the engineering colleges, a mere one lakh get hired through on-campus interviews, another 2.5 lakh graduates manage to get jobs after some waiting period, and the rest are considered unemployable and end up in odd jobs. Most of the IT companies are compelled to recruit diploma holders and graduates and subject them to rigourous training by incurring huge costs. There is also an associated problem of quality teachers as the market is driving out some of the best talent into industry and to greener pastures abroad. This will accentuate the problem for the next generation of students.

India is committed to allocating 6 per cent of GNP to education since the mid-1960s when the Education Commission went into the issue and the target has been accepted by all subsequent policy pronouncements. This target is far from achieved throughout the period. Expectedly, the largest share goes to elementary (primary and secondary) segment and an inadequate part is left for higher and technical education. The combined share of higher and technical education is not only inadequate but has also declined since the 1990s—as a share of both GNP and public expenditure. In 1990–1, they together accounted for 0.61 per cent of the GNP but declined to about 0.46 per cent in 2004–5. As share of the budget, it declined in the same period from 2.09 per cent to 1.60 per cent. It fluctuated around the declining trends in the intervening period.

In the age group of 18–24 years for higher education, the gross enrolment ratio in 2003–4 was 9.2 per cent, up from 1.0 per cent in 1950–1. The enrolment rate, however, needs to be raised to at least 15 per cent to meet the target of a competitive economy in the global context. This requires a substantial step up of resources, for which serious concerns have been expressed, and ways and means need to be explored to garner the requisite resources. At the same time, meeting the challenge of equity, access, and competitive efficiency is also an issue of importance.

Chapter 5 argues that it is imperative to bridge the supply–demand gap in high quality manpower if India is to retain its competitive edge in the world market. The chapter suggests some measures to enhance quality of education and also addresses equity concerns. Expansion of higher education not only has intrinsic value of its own, it also plays a significant role in facilitating economic development and bringing about social change. It is important to note that the neglect of this sector acts as a drag on India's development in the context of its opening up to globalizing forces.

EMERGING ISSUES IN THE FINANCIAL SYSTEM

Monetary and Fiscal Situation

The avowed objective of the monetary policy is to maintain price stability and promote economic growth. However, the serious task of exchange rate management in the wake of large, two-way capital flows continues to complicate the conduct of monetary policy. The Reserve Bank of India has been saddled with the problems of rising real estate prices, increasing inflationary expectations, and appreciating rupee. There are apprehensions in certain quarters over the current level of asset prices. The quantum of funds garnered by companies via primary issues has increased, buoyed by the sentiments in the stock markets. A sum of Rs 17,721 crore was raised by primary issues during the three years 2000–1 to 2002–3. In the next three years, a whopping sum of Rs 78,910 crore was raised and the figure for April–January 2006–7 was Rs 28,143 crore. While stock prices have remained buoyant, real estate prices have moved northward. With inflation rearing its head and concerned by the rising asset prices, RBI took indirect measures following which interest rates hardened. To moderate the effect of the large capital inflows on the exchange rate, the RBI has been accumulating foreign exchange reserves, which crossed the level of $ 230 billion. This has resulted in rapid growth of money supply. The measures taken by the RBI to moderate the growth of money supply tended to increase the interest rates. Contrary to expectations, the rising interest rate has so far had no effect on industrial activities (IEG 2007).

The government has been making concerted efforts to reduce the fiscal and revenue deficits by increasing revenues as well as improving the allocative and technical efficiencies of public expenditure. However, the burden of fiscal adjustment during the 1990s mostly fell on capital outlays. This distorted the structure of government expenditure and there was a shift away from public investment. The wide fiscal deficit and skewed government expenditure towards salaries, pensions, and interest payments provided limited scope for the government to allocate resources towards investment expenditure for physical and social infrastructure. Against this backdrop, the government enacted the Fiscal Responsibility and Budget Management Act in July 2004. This act requires that the Central Government's fiscal deficit be not more than 3 per cent of GDP by 2008–9 and that the Central Government should have a zero revenue deficit by 2008–9. Responding to the debt relief package offered in return for fiscal correction, 24 of the 29 states enacted fiscal responsibility acts which require reducing fiscal deficit to 3 per cent of GSDP and revenue deficit to zero by 2008–9.

There has been a reduction in the combined revenue and fiscal deficits of the Central and state governments in recent years, consistent with legislative commitments on fiscal reforms over the medium run. The fall in revenue deficit from 6.6 per cent of GDP in 2000–1 to 3.1 per cent in 2005–6 is thus a significant change. It further declined to 2.1 per cent of GDP in 2006–7 (budgetary estimate). In the same period, the gross fiscal deficit declined from 9.4 per cent in 2000–1 to 7.4 per cent in 2005–6. It is estimated to be 6.3 per cent of GDP in 2006–7. Tax receipts of the Central and state governments (combined) increased from 13.8 per cent of GDP in 2001–2 to 16.6 per cent of GDP in 2005–6. In 2006–7, the tax receipts are estimated at 16.8 per cent. The reduction in the gross deficit has been attributed to the harmonized fiscal policies followed by the Central as well as the state governments. According to Economic Advisory Council to the Prime Minister (EAC), while fiscal deficit is on the course to achieve the target set for 2008–9,

it would be difficult to phase out the revenue deficit. Improving the tax revenues by widening tax base and improving tax compliance and pruning wasteful expenditure would be needed not only for maintaining macroeconomic stability but also for providing resources for pro-poor public programmes. Concerns have been expressed about the growing off-budget liabilities of the Centre and states (EAC 2007). Quite a few state-level public sector undertakings (PSUs) have raised finances in the domestic market with an 'unconditional and irrevocable guarantee' from state governments. These borrowings are kept outside the purview of the budget and do not need the approval of the legislature. Consequently, the actual revenue and fiscal deficits are much higher than the official figures. Also, an increasing proportion of the growing budget deficit is being financed by funds from various public accounts, some of which are reserve funds in poverty reduction schemes. State governments have created special purpose vehicles (SPVs) in recent years. Debt charges—interest and principal—of these SPVs are not from the state government budgets, but they are actually part of government borrowings.

Trade and Balance of Payment (BOP)

The Indian financial system has come a long way since the onset of the reform process. The reforms have had a far-reaching impact on the domestic financial system and BOP management. The globalization of capital markets has been faster than that of commodity markets. This is manifested in substantial increase in FDI and non-FDI capital inflows. Capital flows have emerged as a major determinant of money supply and domestic inflation is being influenced more by global supply–demand imbalances than domestic ones. There is a belief that India has benefited more from globalization of capital markets than the globalization of commodity markets.

The critical question is whether India has become resilient to domestic and external shocks. On the external front, in 2005–6, the current account deficit was at a manageable level of 1.1 per cent of GDP. India's exports stood at $44.56 billion in 2000–1 and had increased to $102.72 billion by 2005–6. In 2006–7, exports grew at 36.3 per cent, up from 23.4 per cent in the previous year. The days of the foreign exchange crisis seem to be a distant memory as foreign exchange reserves have crossed $230 billion.

Exchange Rate

Goyal (Chapter 7) reviews the behaviour of the Indian exchange rate and its interactions with the macroeconomic cycle over the past few years. The chapter examines the extent to which exchange rate policy has been able to contribute to lowering the probability of currency and banking crises, ensuring sustainable internal and external balance, and containing inflation. The chapter makes the case for limited volatility in exchange rates that improves the structure of incentives, thus contributing to four objectives. First, external balance: a real exchange rate that follows its trend competitive value can stimulate the real sector, so that eventual current account surpluses follow initial deficits. Steady progress on the road to full convertibility can also contribute to absorbing excess foreign exchange reserves. It requires reduction of instability of markets along with releasing their strengths. As controls disappear, incentive structures have to be in place to induce responsible behaviour to ensure that both policy and individual responses do not amplify shocks. Second, smoother and more counter-cyclical interest rates can stimulate activity. Higher activity allows more inflows to be absorbed. Third, an appreciation is an antidote to price shocks coming from food, oil, and other intermediate inputs—typical temporary supply shocks faced by an economy. These affect aggregate inflation through the wage–price process. For example, whatever the underlying trend, a steeper short-term appreciation can counter the supply shock, contributing to control of inflation, thus allowing interest rates to be tuned to the macroeconomic output cycle. Fourth, limited two-way movement of the exchange rate creates incentives to hedge, reduces noise trader entry, and contributes to the deepening of forex markets.

The impossible trinity implies a loss of autonomy in monetary policy-making in a more open economy. But there are a number of deviations from the simple case, some of which are valid for the Indian economy. In the context of the political economy, the structural wage–price processes, and the degree of backward and forward looking behaviour, monetary policy can have considerable impact. Using structure, combined with openness, can increase the degree of freedom and impact of monetary policy. India's labour market structure implies an elastic aggregate supply curve, but one which is subject to frequent shocks. One such shock is a rise in food prices, which triggers off a rise in wages. Goyal feels that more openness can contribute to stabilizing food prices; so can changes in the nominal exchange rate, thus giving the Central Bank more weapons to fight inflation, as well as maintain demand. Policy transparency as in an inflation targeting regime gives sufficient discretion to allow flexible response to market signals; but the transparent constraints on the discretion may be sufficient to prevent inflation expectations from setting in, even without monetary tightening.

Banking Sector—Non-performing Assets

Growing competition from foreign banks and private sector banks has meant that the market share of public sector banks as measured by their share of total assets declined from 84.4 per cent in 1995–6 to 72.3 per cent by 2005–6. The effect of competition is also captured in the decline in interest spread from 3.13 to 2.78 per cent during this period. The next phase of banking reforms will see Indian banks with foreign operations complying with the Basel II norms (by March 2008).

An important development in the last the decade relates to the decline of non performing assets (NPAs) of all SCBs from 15.7 per cent of gross advances in 1995–6 to 3.3 per cent in 2005–6. A similar decline was evident in NPAs as a percentage of total assets. Even though Indian banking has done reasonably well in controlling NPAs, there is little room for complacency. Low incidence of NPAs is a crucial precondition for ensuring financial stability in any economy.

Chaudhuri and Sensarma (Chapter 9) provide a comprehensive review of the problem of NPAs in Indian banking. The authors assess the magnitude of the problem in India by presenting the prudential norms with respect to classifying assets and NPAs. They also review the policy responses that have been implemented to address the problem. The authors identify the financial, microeconomic, and macroeconomic determinants of the level of NPAs of banks. They find that the impact of priority sector lending on NPA levels is ambiguous. They also show that setting up of debt recovery tribunals, implementing the Corporate Debt Restructuring and passing of the Securitization and Reconstruction of Financial Assets and Enforcement of Security Interest (SARFAESI) Act have resulted in lowering NPAs in Indian banking.

Bank Credit Delivery

The SCBs' credit flow to agriculture, small-scale industries, and other small borrowers was sluggish in the 1990s and thereafter till 2003. This is reflected in the declining shares of bank credit for agriculture, small-scale industries, and small borrowal accounts in total bank credit. More significantly, drastic reduction has taken place in the number of borrowal accounts for all these informal sector categories. Also, there has been no expansion of SCB branches in rural areas.

Shetty (Chapter 8) shows the worsening of inter-regional disparities and disparities within states in the credit from SCBs including regional rural banks, which were getting corrected in the post-nationalization period but deteriorated in the 1990s. For instance, in the 1990s there were just about 20–8 out of 401–78 districts which had credit–deposit ratios of less than 20 per cent but in March 2000, the number of such districts had risen to 105 out of 565 districts. Lately, the role of co-operatives in farm credit has been on the decline. Their share of total farm credit has steadily declined from about 40 per cent in 1999–2000 to

24 per cent in 2005–6. As a result, the traditional role of co-operatives in providing term credit suffered considerably.

Concerned at the glaring agrarian crisis and crisis in the status of non-farm informal sectors, the authorities have taken a series of measures to mitigate the situation. Arrangements for the revitalization of the co-operative credit system were put into place. RRBs are being consolidated. To supplement the branch banking infrastructure, the concept of 'agency banking' has been introduced, with two models, namely, 'business facilitator' model and 'business correspondent' model, being commended to banks for adoption. With greater focus on the micro-finance system, the self-help group (SHG)–bank linkage programme is proposed to be expanded. Apart from thus strengthening the institutional structure, the government has adopted the policy of doubling of bank credit to agriculture in three years and for small and medium enterprises in five years. As a measure of 'financial inclusion', the issuance of a general credit card (GCC) has been adopted for bank customers in rural and semi-urban areas. A 7 per cent rate of interest has been prescribed for crop loans as a short-term measure.

Recent data show substantial increase in the flow of credit to agriculture (since 2002). However, the growing proportion of the credit was in favour of large-size loans. Shetty argues that the system of 'agency banking' can only supplement the branch network. Further spread of bank branches is necessary along with adequate qualified personnel. While micro-finance is extremely useful for meeting the credit needs of poor households, it cannot fully meet the credit needs of the extremely large number of small enterprises.

INDIA IN A GLOBALIZING WORLD

Asian Economic Integration

There is a growing feeling that India should expand its trade with other Asian countries. It is possible that outward FDI could lead trade patterns in the future. An Asian Development Bank study concluded that Asian economic integration could be the main stimulus for future growth in the region (see Chapter 2). The study notes that Asian Free Trade Agreement (AFTA), with steady improvements in trade facilitation, would help regional income growth to a larger extent than global free trade.

India—China

There is considerable interest in the engagement of India and China with the rest of the world, apart from India–China trade. Veeramani (Chapter 10) analyses the emerging patterns of comparative advantage in India and China in a comparative perspective. He finds that the comparative advantage of both the countries lies primarily in unskilled labour-intensive goods. At the same time, a gradual improvement of comparative advantage in human capital and technology-intensive goods is being seen in both the countries. India's share in world exports is much lower than that of China even in those products where we have a comparative advantage. China's exports and comparative advantage had undergone a greater degree of structural change over the years than India's. The findings indicate that China's gain of market share (or comparative advantage) in a given product does not necessarily mean India's loss of market share (or comparative advantage) in the same product and vice versa. The two countries have been expanding their exports by specializing in different product lines within each of the product categories. Overall, Veeramani's findings indicate the growing significance of intra-industry specialization in both the countries. The resource reallocation process under trade liberalization is not causing a polarization wherein certain industries are forced to vanish while certain other industries gain prominence. In a liberalized environment, domestic industries and firms are able to survive and compete through specialization in narrow product lines. The apprehension that import liberalization would lead to a large-scale demise of domestic industries (the fear of de-industrialization) is unwarranted. The chapter shows that certain bottlenecks (such as poor physical infrastructure) and policy-induced rigidities in the factor markets (such as those in the organized labour market) stand in the way of the resource reallocation process as well as rapid export growth in India.

Textile Industry in the International Market

India and China would be competing in the textile market following the phasing out of the Multi Fibre Arrangement (MFA). Narayanan (Chapter 11) gives an overview of the current state of, and recent developments in, the Indian textile sector, with an emphasis on international trade, employment, performance of the supply and demand sides, with a developmental perspective. Though Indian textile and apparel exports rose during the last stage of the gradual phasing out of MFA quotas, the increase has not been sustained after 2004–5. In fact, the export shares of all textile products in total exports have been falling since 2000–1 and those of apparel exports are on the decline after 1999–2000. Given that the development of emerging economies in the past such as newly industrialized countries in South East Asia and Japan was heavily dependent on exports from labour-intensive sectors such as textiles and apparel, this is a worrisome trend. The organized apparel sector has performed quite well in terms of employment in recent years, showing a recovery from the decline in the past. The same is not true in the case of the textile sector, barring some signs of recovery. Promotion of huge investment requires not only good credit disbursement schemes, but also ensuring awareness about these among the entrepreneurs. In the unorganized textile sector, urban and larger enterprises have been performing better than rural and smaller ones. Policies are required to facilitate equity in the performance of unorganized textile firms. There is also a domestic demand constraint in Indian textile sector. Since the own-price demand elasticities of synthetic fibres are higher than those of cotton, and cross-price demand elasticities are negligible, a tariff cut in synthetics may help in removing this demand constraint.

Globalization and the Labour Market

There is increasing interest in the impact of globalization on domestic labour markets. Ramaswamy (Chapter 12) discusses the issue of globalization and employment in India with a focus on labour regulations. Three major reasons for anxiety are: the loss of good jobs in industries that are losing competitiveness, technological change biased against unskilled workers, and the informalization of workforce. In the Indian context, formal sector jobs in the non-agricultural sector have grown by just 0.6 per cent per annum in the 1990s. The IT sector is an exception. The Indian economy needs to create a large number of jobs for the unskilled workers. The high rate of job creation in the IT sector will be for college educated (skilled) workers with specific skills. In this situation, the pressure is on the manufacturing sector to absorb unskilled labour. Here the role of job security regulations (JSR) is emphasized as a constraint as it increases the expected cost of workforce adjustment. This reduces the incentive for firms to hire regular workers. Labour regulations have restricted the size expansion of factories to take advantage of economies of scale. Ramaswami provides evidence that there is a greater concentration of factories in the size group less than 100 employees across industry groups. According to the author, policy initiatives are required to create incentives for firms to absorb workers by simplifying procedural requirements for worker retrenchment in the future due to changes in market conditions. This calls for a constructive social dialogue between the three stakeholders, namely, the state, the corporate sector, and the workers.

CONCLUDING OBSERVATIONS

Growth in the near future, given the business expectations, and the macroeconomic management, is likely to be driven by investment. Even if it is sustained through appropriate policy measures, the social consequences of higher growth assume much greater importance. In this context, the following questions are relevant. Will the higher growth result in an increase in the demand for labour and eventually tighten the labour market? Will the growth, per se, improve the level of living of the poorer groups and integrate them with the development process? Answers to these questions would depend not merely on the quantum of growth but also on the structure of growth. While the performance of the Indian economy in achieving and sustaining higher growth is laudable, much is left to be desired in achieving equitable growth.

The stability of growth in the short run would depend on the efficacy of macroeconomic management in maintaining macroeconomic balances and in the long run on both the maintenance of macroeconomic balances and location of effective demand. Macroeconomic management has largely been successful in reversing the progressive worsening trends in macroeconomic balances during the pre-reform period. Moreover, it has been overcoming fresh problems that arise from opening up of the economy, particularly the integration of the domestic financial markets with the global financial markets. However, India has, so far, not been successful in locating the effective demand in a desirable manner. It is important to recognize that if effective demand is located away from wage income and into the non-wage income of the upper strata, it would be susceptible to greater risks of uncertainty since the consumption patterns of the upper strata change fast. The other components of effective demand viz., investment and exports are prone to a greater degree of volatility. Clearly, growth will be more stable if it is skewed in favour of the poor.

The trickle-down process of growth has been weak, since growth is not located in sectors where labour is concentrated (for example, agriculture) and in states where poverty is concentrated (for example, Bihar, Orissa, Madhya Pradesh, and Uttar Pradesh). There is now a greater appreciation of the fact that if inequality increases beyond a limit, social disarticulation would set in that may become a major barrier to higher growth. The present pattern of growth has the potential for widening inequality. The recent policy emphasis on inclusive growth is a step in the right direction. To achieve inclusive growth, it is imperative that agriculture is revived, the rural non-farm sector is accelerated, and the poor are integrated with the dynamic sectors of growth. These are challenging tasks but by no means formidable. The solutions are also well-known, however, problems lie in their implementation.

References

Acharya, Shankar, Isher Ahluwalia, K.L. Krishna, and Ila Patnaik (2003), *Indian Economic Growth 1950–2000*, Indian Council for Research on International Economic Relations, New Delhi.
Bhalla, Sheila (2007), 'Inclusive Growth? Focus on Employment' (mimeo), Institute of Human Development, New Delhi.
EAC (2007), *Economic Outlook for 2007–08*, Economic Advisory Council to the Prime Minister, July.

EPWRF (Economic and Political Weekly Research Foundation) (2007), *Monthly Economic Review*, EPWRF, July.

GOI (2007a), *Economic Survey, 2006–07*, Ministry of Finance, Government of India, New Delhi.

——— (2007b), *Report of the Expert Group on Agricultural Indebtedness*, Ministry of Finance, Government of India, New Delhi, July.

Himanshu (2005), 'Wages in Rural India: Sources, Trends and Comparability', *The Indian Journal of Labour Economics*, Vol. 48, No. 2, April–June.

IEG (2007), *Monthly Monitor*, Institute of Economic Growth, New Delhi, July.

International Institute for Population Sciences (2000), *National Family Health Survey (NFHS) 2, 1998–9*, Mumbai.

——— (2006), *District Level Household Survey on Reproductive Health Survey, 2002–4*, Mumbai.

——— (2007), *National Family Health Survey (NFHS) 3, 2004–5, Fact Sheets*, Mumbai.

Naik, S.D. (2006), 'Manufacturing Needs a Policy Crack Up', *Business Line*, Mumbai, 20 September.

NCAER (2002), *The Consuming Class*, National Council for Applied Economic Research, New Delhi.

NCEUS (2006), *Report on Social Security for Unorganised Workers*, National Commission for Enterprises in the Unorganized Sector, Government of India, May.

——— (2007), *Report on Conditions of Work and Promotion of Livelihood in the Unorganised Sector*, NCEUS, July.

National Manufacturing Competitive Council (2007), *National Strategy for Manufacturing*, New Delhi.

NSSO (2006), *Employment and Unemployment Situation in India, 2004–5, Report Nos 515 (61/10/1), Parts I and II*, National Sample Survey Organization.

Radhakrishna, R., K. Hanumantha Rao, C. Ravi, and B. Sambi Reddy (2006), 'Estimation and Determinants of Chronic Poverty in India, An Alternative Approach', Working Paper No. WP-2006–7, Indira Gandhi Institute of Development Research, Mumbai.

——— (2007), 'Estimation and Determination of Chronic Poverty in India, An Alternative Approach', Working Paper No. 90, Chronic Poverty Research Centre, Manchester, United Kingdom.

Ravallion, Martin and Shaohua Chen (2004), 'Learning from Success: Understanding China's (uneven) Progress against Poverty', *Finance and Development*, December.

RBI (2007a), *Annual Report, 2006–7*, Reserve Bank of India, Mumbai.

——— (2007b), *Macroeconomic and Monetary Development*, Reserve Bank of India, Mumbai, July.

Rodrik, Dani and Arvind Subramanian (2004), 'Why India Can Grow at 7 per cent a Year or More: Projections and Reflections', IMF Working Paper, WP/04/118, International Monetary Fund, Washington D.C.

UNDP (2003), *Human Development Report 2003*, United Nations Development Programme, New York.

2

Macroeconomic Overview

Manoj Panda

INTRODUCTION

There have been several interesting developments in the Indian economy in recent years. Substantial market friendly reforms initiated in 1991 created a favourable economic environment for high rates of growth in the economy. Real gross domestic product (GDP) has grown between 7.4 and 9.4 per cent for four successive years in a row since 2003–4 and its growth in 2007–8 is likely to be along the same trajectory. This fascinating aggregate growth makes India currently the second highest growing economy in the world, next only to China. The pessimism that prevailed during the period 1997–2002 about the economy's growth rate being stuck at a moderate level of 5–6 per cent has been replaced by a new optimism for a higher growth. Exports have surpassed the target and foreign demand has contributed substantially to the GDP acceleration—reflecting greater integration of the Indian economy with the world economy. Despite the strong upward pressure in international oil prices, inflation has been moderate but for certain short periods and the balance of payment position has remained comfortable. New policy initiatives have been undertaken to introduce fiscal discipline, specially at the state level. Another major step has been the enactment of the Rural Employment Guarantee Act which, if implemented properly, could substantially benefit the poor. Yet, there is a disquieting feeling that the growth process has not benefited all sections of the people. In line with the tradition of viewing growth and social justice as the twin major objectives of economic policy formulation, the Approach Paper to the Eleventh Plan advocates for a 'more inclusive' growth process to bridge the current 'divides' even as it targets for a faster growth rate of 9 per cent. It is against this backdrop that the chapter reviews the macroeconomic developments in India from a medium term perspective.

We start with a discussion of the GDP growth by broad sectors in the section 'National Income Growth' followed by other macroeconomic developments such as fiscal and trade scenes in the next section 'Other Macroeconomic Development'. The section 'Asian Economic Integration' discusses a specific policy agenda on Asian economic integration to promote trade and growth further. 'Poverty and Distribution' relates to recent developments in the poverty and distribution fronts. Finally, the last section makes concluding remarks.

NATIONAL INCOME GROWTH

Table 2.1 gives the average annual growth rates in national income for three broad sectors—agriculture, industry, and services—for various periods spanning over 1951–2006. The Indian economy grew at an average rate of 3.5 per cent per annum for about three decades till 1980. It witnessed a breakthrough around 1980 and moved onto a higher growth trajectory of above 5.5 per cent during 1980–2000. In per capita terms, this meant a jump from about 1.5 per cent to 3.5 per cent per annum. National income has accelerated further, resulting in per capita income growth of 5–6 per cent per annum since 2000. A sustained increase in the average level of living of about 4 per cent per annum for

TABLE 2.1
Average Annual Growth Rates in Real GDP

	1951–2 to 1980–1	1981–2 to 1990–1	1991–2 to 1999–2000	2000–1 to 2006–7	2002–3 to 2006–7 (Tenth Plan Period)
Agriculture	2.6	3.8	3.0	2.5	2.2
Industry	5.3	7.0	5.7	7.8	9.1
Service	4.6	6.7	7.9	8.5	9.4
GDP (total)	3.6	5.6	5.8	6.9	7.6
Per capita GDP	1.4	3.4	3.6	5.2	6.0

Note: The last two columns relate to data with new 1999–2000 base. The sector 'agriculture' includes other primary sectors such as livestock, forestry, fishing, and mining and quarrying.

Source: National Account Statistics (various issues), Central Statistical Organization.

a quarter of a century marks a break from the previous historical trends of several centuries.

The acceleration of the economy during the decade of the 1980s was essentially triggered by an expansionary fiscal policy with limited reforms in the mid-1980s. Substantial control on trade and industrial activities continued; fiscal deficit was high and trade performance was weak. A balance of payment crisis occurred in 1991 in the wake of the Gulf war and rise in international oil price. The crisis led to the realization by policy makers of the need for wide ranging economic reforms which were initiated in 1991 and have continued at varied pace till now.[1] One major component of the reform process related to trade liberalization through a gradual abolition of import quotas, reduction of tariff rates to moderate levels, and market determined exchange rate. Another component related to the promotion of private enterprises through abolition of the system of industrial licensing, encouragement of foreign investment including majority share holding in several industries, interest rate deregulation, and disinvestment of government equity in several public sector enterprises.

During the post-reform period, the Indian economy has, in fact, witnessed two phases of strong average growth of 7.5 per cent during the triennium 1995–6 to 1997–8 and of 8.5 per cent more recently during 2003–4 to 2006–7 (as seen from Figure 2.1). The high and moderate growth phases are clearly evident from the 3-year moving average line in Figure 2.1. Note that both the downward and upward phases were of longer duration during the last decade. The average growth in the economy during the Tenth Five Year Plan (2002–3 to 2006–7) was 7.6 per cent, the highest growth recorded during any plan period, although it falls short of the target of 8 per cent. Per capita GDP has expanded by 6 per cent per annum during the Tenth Plan. Available evidence indicates that the high growth phase is likely to continue in 2007–8 as well.

More importantly, however, the average growth rate achieved during the post-reform era appears to be sustainable in the long term. The economy has developed sufficient resilience to short term fluctuations such as drought and international oil price rise. The post-reform period has witnessed macroeconomic stability—evident from low to moderate inflation, reasonably stable exchange rate, adequate foreign exchange reserves, and sufficient food grains

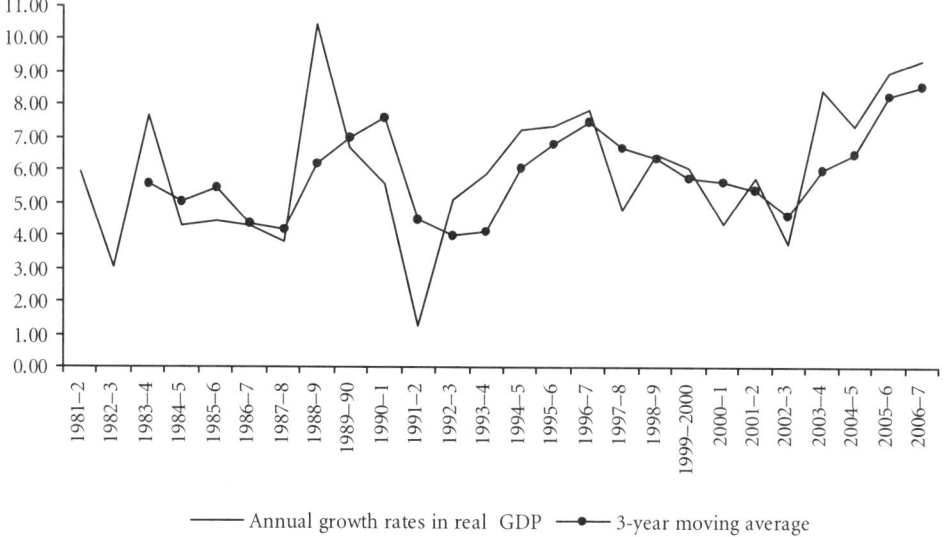

Figure 2.1: Real GDP Growth on Annual Basis and 3-year Moving Average Basis

[1] While the balance of payment crisis was the immediate cause, the reform measures were influenced by several other factors including the success of the outward oriented East Asian economies, end of the cold war, and collapse of the Soviet Union.

stocks on a medium-term basis. Using a growth accounting framework, Rodrik and Subramanian (2004) estimate India's growth potential to be about 7 per cent over the next two decades. There is optimism about an even higher growth potential in the medium run as reflected in the growth target of 9 per cent per annum fixed by the Planning Commission for the 11th Five year Plan which began in April 2007.

It is being recognized in international circles that India is steadily progressing on the path to become a major economy in the world in aggregate income terms. The annual income generation in the country was valued at US$ 793 billion in 2005. In per capita terms, its income is low at $720 (in 2005) compared to the world average of $6280 based on the market exchange rate. When adjusted for purchasing power parity (PPP) to reflect command over commodities, per capita income works out to $PPP 3450. The level of living as reflected in purchasing power of an average Indian is roughly one-third of the world average and one-tenth of the developed high-income countries.

Composition of GDP

The structure of the Indian economy has undergone substantial changes with a steady fall in the share of agriculture and rise in share of services sector. Agriculture accounted for about 55 per cent of GDP in 1950–1. Its share in GDP has fallen to about 20 per cent of GDP in 2006–7. The share of industry (including construction), which was only about 14 per cent in the early 1950s, rose to 27 per cent in 1990–1. Industry's share has virtually stagnated since then. The composition of GDP has been continuously moving in favour of services, which now accounts for about 55 per cent of GDP. The structural change away from agriculture is broadly consistent with the international experience. The economy is no longer as much driven by agriculture and has been able to absorb shocks in rainfall more smoothly in recent decades. Indeed, annual growth rate in real GDP has exceeded 3.5 per cent in all the years since 1992–3. This new lower limit on annual growth rates reflects the dynamism and strength of the economy.

Agriculture

The index number of agricultural production has increased by about 120 per cent since 1970–1 (Table 2.2). This increase in output can be attributed mostly to rise in yield per hectare rather than to expansion of area. Table 2.2 reveals that total area under principal crops has changed very little in recent decades, though area allocation within agriculture has changed from foodgrain crops in favour of non-foodgrain crops. Foodgrain output growth in recent decades is almost entirely due to increase in yield per hectare. Area under non-foodgrain crops increased by about 50 per cent in 2005–6 over 1970–1 while the yield per hectare of these crops increased by 70 per cent over the same period.

The deceleration in agricultural production for both foodgrains and non-foodgrains crops since 1990 is shown in Figure 2.3. The deceleration is more evident for foodgrains. The relative shift in cropping pattern is largely driven by the changing demand pattern. Huge buffer stocks of cereals built up by the government—reaching above 60 million tonnes for several months in 2002[2]—points to the limited future consumption growth potential for cereals and the need for further agricultural diversification. Gross production of foodgrains has increased from 130 million tonnes in 1980–1 to 209 million tonnes in 2006–7. The implied

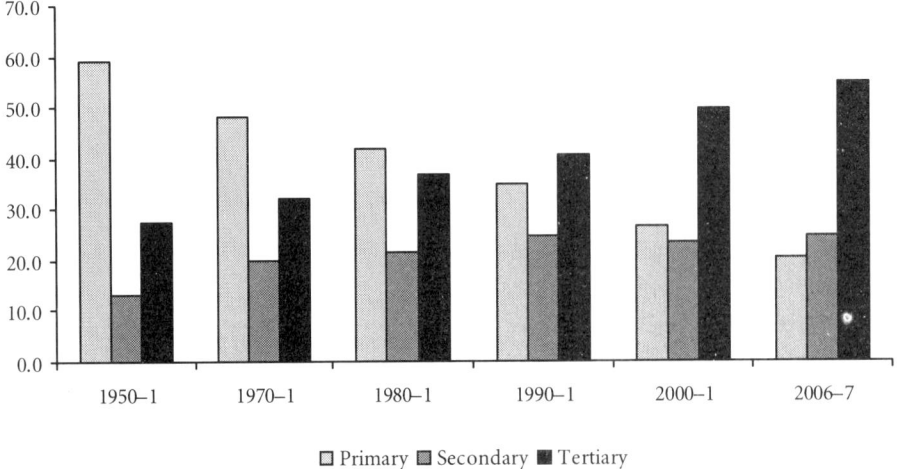

Figure 2.2: Composition of GDP by Major Sectors (per cent)

---

[2] The agricultural year 2002–3 turned out to be a drought year and the peak level of foodgrains stock of 64.7 MT in June 2002 came down sharply to 32.8 MT in April 2003 due to lower procurement, higher offtake for relief operations, and some exports. Further depletion in stocks, particularly of wheat below the buffer stock norm, prompted the government to import 5.5 MT of wheat in 2006–7.

TABLE 2.2
Index Number of Agricultural Production, Area, and Yield

(1981–2 =100)

	1970–1	1980–1	1990–1	2000–1	2002–3	2003–4	2004–5	2005–6
			Agricultural Production					
Foodgrains	87.9	104.9	143.7	158.4	140.4	172.0	159.9	168.6
Non-foodgrains	82.6	97.1	156.3	178.2	167.2	201.0	205.7	224.4
All Commodities	85.9	102.1	148.4	165.7	150.4	182.8	176.9	189.3
			Area Under Principal Crops					
Foodgrains	97.9	99.8	100.7	95.4	89.7	97.3	94.6	96.1
Non-foodgrains	91.1	99.4	120	127	115.6	125.4	137.5	139.9
All Commodities	96.3	99.7	105.2	102.7	95.7	103.8	104.8	106.2
			Yield Of Principal Crops					
Foodgrains	93.2	105.1	137.8	152.8	143.2	165.3	156.5	161.4
Non-foodgrains	91.4	99.2	128	133.2	126.3	151.3	147.6	157.5
All Commodities	92.6	102.9	133.8	144.4	135.7	159.2	152.5	159.7

Source: Economic Survey, 2006–7, Ministry of Finance, Government of India.

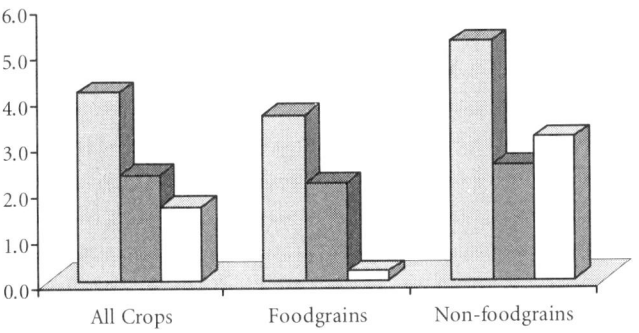

Figure 2.3: Average Annual Growth Rates in Index Number of Agricultural Production

long-term growth rate of about the same as 1.8 per cent per year is just about the same as the population growth rate. Per capita net availability of foodgrains has been fluctuating around 450 grams per day. Given the very low income elasticity, domestic demand for foodgrains is likely to grow slowly in the future, mostly in response to population pressure. Growth potential in non-foodgrains sectors, on the other hand, is large and its realization would require stronger linkages with agro-processing sectors.

The fall in public investment in agriculture during the 1980s and subsequent near stagnation in the post-reform period has been a matter of concern (Figure 2.4). Chadha (2003) points out that the public sector accounted for 54 per cent of agricultural total gross capital formation in

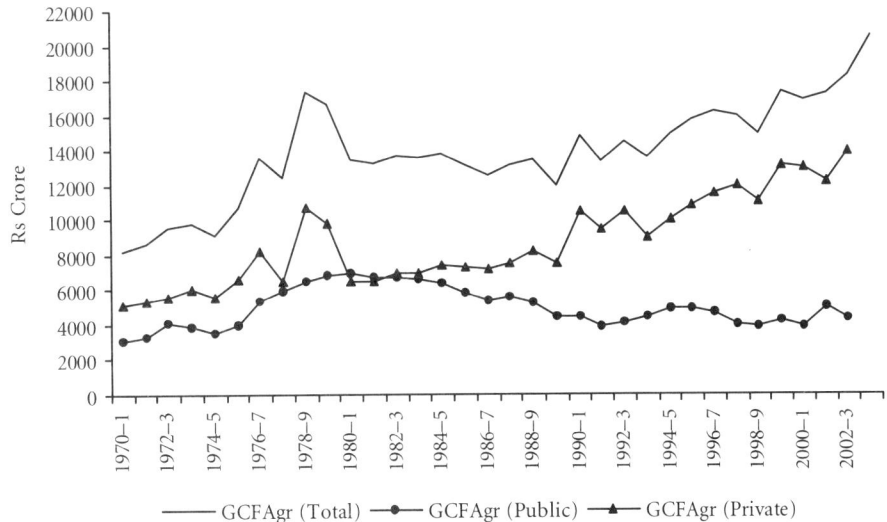

Source: Based on NAS, Back Series 1950–1 to 1992–3 and NAS (2005).

Figure 2.4: Gross Capital Formation in Agriculture (at 1993–4 prices)

1980–1, but this share fell to about 30 per cent in 1990–1 and further to a quarter by the end of 1990s. He points out that this has led to the net irrigated area remaining stagnant at around 53–5 million hectares since mid-1990s. Agricultural public investment in the National Account Statistics (NAS) mostly covers expenditure on medium and major irrigation systems. Chand (2002) constructs a broad series of rural investment by extending it to include investment in rural roads, markets, storage, and rural electrification which are important for agricultural development. He finds that this broad series also indicates a declining trend. Figure 2.4 shows that total capital formation in agriculture has picked up in recent years primarily due to the private investment component. Despite this investment increase, agricultural growth has stagnated; this reflects rising capital intensity of agricultural production due to factors such as rising cost of land development and depletion of water table in areas dependent on ground water.

The Government provides a large fertilizer subsidy by way of meeting the difference between administered selling price and the cost of production. The same stood at about Rs 16000 crore in 2004–5—that is, about 3 per cent of agricultural GDP. Public irrigation is also highly subsidized and irrigation charges are not able to recover even the operating costs. There is a growing realization that the fall in agricultural public investment is partly due to a diversion of a growing volume of resources to input subsidies. Overall, the agricultural sector would benefit by a reallocation of public expenditure from input subsidies to public investment. In recent years, the Government has initiated measures to streamline and control subsidies.

Indian farmers have traditionally tried to supplement their crop income with earnings from livestock produce, which also safeguards them against large year-to-year fluctuations in crop income. India has become the largest producer of milk in the world in recent years and per capita availability of milk has increased from 128 grams per day in 1980–1 to 241 grams in 2005–6. Accounting for about a quarter of GDP in agriculture and allied sectors, livestock has recently emerged as the most important sub-sector within this broad category. The income generated in this sector gets more equitably distributed since livestock ownership is skewed in favour of small farmers in India. Further, women account for a majority of the workforce in livestock.

Given the large variability in climate and soil conditions in the country, India is well-suited for producing a wide range of high value and employment-intensive horticulture crops including floriculture. Commercial horticulture, targeting the exports markets with good profit opportunities, could attract educated entrepreneurs to agriculture and change the nature of agricultural operations. It is necessary to develop modern infrastructure such as cold storage for preservation, refrigerated transportation, grading, and quality control for these emerging sectors.

Industry

Industrial deregulation and trade reforms introduced considerable changes in the overall environment and organizational structure in Indian industry. Competition has forced Indian firms to accord priority attention to improvements in product quality, reliability, and durability. Induction of foreign technology has expanded significantly through the equity-linked technology collaboration route.

Growth in the industrial sector remained sluggish for several years after 1997–8 to reach the bottom in 2001–2 with less than 3 per cent growth in the index number of industrial production. An upturn occurred in 2002–3 and the overall industrial growth has been fairly good in the range of 8–11 per cent since 2004–5 (Figure 2.5). The manufacturing sector has been the prime driver in this revival

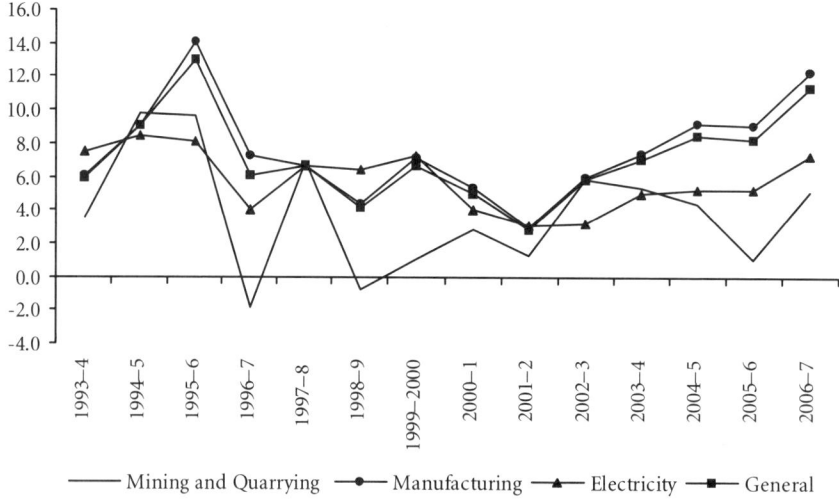

Figure 2.5: Annual Growth in Index Number of Industrial Production

process. Production in the mining and quarrying sector has decelerated since 2003–4. Growth of the electricity sector of about 5 per cent is a matter of concern since it is in the nature of a universal intermediate good. Its supply is not keeping pace with the growing demand, forcing power cuts in several parts of the country.

Industrial growth in recent years has spread over all use-based sectors (Table 2.3). The capital goods sector was a major contributor to the growth process during the 1980s. It saw the largest tariff reduction during the reforms and its growth reduced during the 1990s to about half of pre-reform growth, partly due to expansion of imports. Its recovery in recent years, to meet the strong investment demand, indicates its inherent strength to compete in an open environment. The fast growth of consumer durables is explained by several factors such as disposable income growth, access to a range of imported goods, and easy availability of credit. Although the average manufacturing growth during the post-reform period has remained somewhat lower than that during 1980s, the manufacturing sector has slowly but surely revealed, during the last decade, its strong ability to compete in both domestic and external markets in several spheres.

The construction sector has grown at 8.2 per cent per year during 2000–5, reflecting increased investment activity and priority assigned to road connectivity in public investment in recent years. Accounting for 6.5 per cent of GDP, higher than average growth of this labour intensive sector, helps in better income distribution as well.

Services

Figure 2.6 depicts the average growth rates for various components of the services sector during 2000–5. Most segments of the services sector have been growing at 6 per cent or more, led by communications and non-railway transport. Communication continues to be the fastest growing component within the services sector with an average growth rate of about 24 per cent per annum. Its contribution to GDP (at constant 1999–2000 prices) has more than doubled over six years (1999–2000 to 2004–5) from 1.6 to 3.5 per cent. As a result of falling prices, however, its share in GDP in nominal terms has increased very little from 1.6 to 1.8 per cent during the same period. Consumers have obviously benefited not only from high growth, but also from the steep price fall due to the removal of state monopoly and fast technological changes.

Trade, which is the largest segment in the services sector and accounts for one-seventh of GDP, has been showing strong performance with an average growth of 8 per cent. Similarly non-railway transport, real estate, and personal services have been growing above the overall growth rate of the economy and thus helping the services sector to increase

TABLE 2.3
Growth in Index Number of Industrial Production by Use-based Sectors

(*per cent per annum*)

Year	Basic Goods	Capital Goods	Intermediate Goods	Consumer Goods	Consumer Durables	Consumer Non-durables	General Manufacturing
1990–1	6.9	16.0	4.7	6.8	10.7	5.8	8.9
1991–2	6.5	−8.5	−2.1	1.0	−10.9	4.0	−0.8
1992–3	2.6	−0.1	5.4	1.8	−0.7	2.4	2.2
1993–4	9.4	−4.1	11.7	4.0	16.1	1.3	6.1
1994–5	5.5	24.8	3.7	8.7	10.2	8.4	9.1
1995–6	10.7	5.4	19.3	12.8	25.8	9.8	14.1
1996–7	3.0	11.4	8.1	6.2	4.6	6.6	7.3
1997–8	6.8	5.8	8.0	5.5	7.8	4.9	6.6
1998–9	1.7	12.6	6.1	2.2	5.6	1.1	4.4
1999–2000	5.5	6.9	8.8	5.7	14.1	3.2	7.1
2000–1	3.6	1.7	4.7	8.0	14.6	5.8	5.3
2001–2	2.7	−3.4	1.6	6.0	11.5	4.1	2.9
2002–3	4.8	10.5	3.9	7.1	−6.3	12.0	6.0
2003–4	5.5	13.6	6.4	7.2	11.6	5.8	7.4
2004–5	5.5	13.9	6.1	11.7	14.3	10.8	9.2
2005–6	6.7	15.7	2.5	12.0	15.2	11.0	9.1
2006–7	10.2	17.7	11.7	10.0	na	na	12.3
Averages							
1982–90	7.5	12.0	6.2	5.9	14.2	4.5	7.6
1991–9	5.7	6.0	7.7	5.3	8.1	4.6	6.2
2000–6	5.6	10.0	5.3	9.0	10.2	8.3	7.5

Source: RBI, *Annual Report* (various issues).

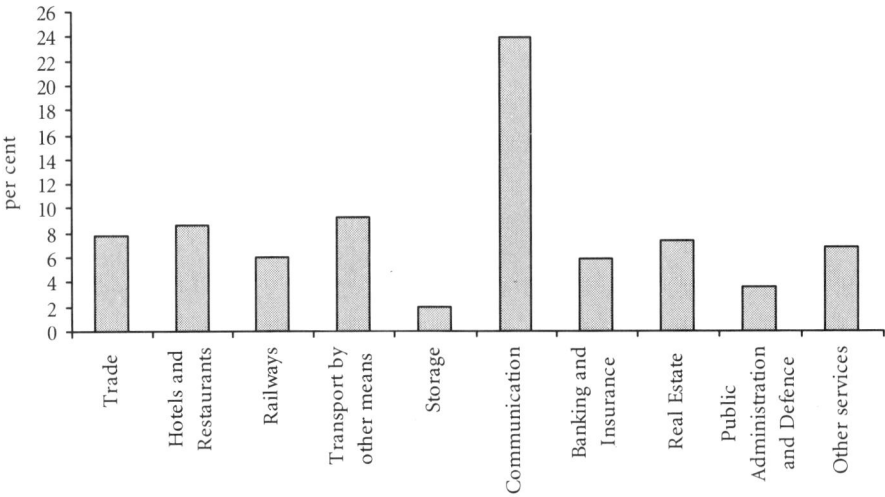

Figure 2.6: Average Annual Growth Rate of Service Sectors, 2000–5

its share in GDP. Railways and banking have maintained their share in GDP, posting a growth of about 6 per cent. Storage and public administration are two segments in the service sector where growth is relatively low. Downsizing of public administration reflects restructuring of government expenditure through reduction of excess staff and containing non-developmental expenditure. More attention, however, needs to be given to the storage sector in the future. A countrywide network of storage facilities would complement road connectivity in integrating the rural areas to the mainstream of economic activities.

Questions have been raised about the sustainability of service-led growth in India. The shift in composition of GDP away from agriculture has been a natural feature of the growth process. Historical experience of Europe and USA reveals that the falling share of agriculture was accompanied by a near-compensating shift in favour of industry and the service sector growth followed at a later stage of development. More recently, China and East Asia too had a similar experience with fast expansion of labour-intensive manufacturing activities. The Indian experience differs from this classical pattern since the share of industry has remained nearly unchanged for more than two decades (as noted earlier).

Virmani (2004) examines whether the share of services in Indian GDP is excessively high compared to other countries at similar stages of development. He undertakes a cross-country regression of the average share of services during 1992 to 2000 on the average per capita GDP (at constant PPP) and derives a normative value of the service share corresponding to different income levels. His finding is that India's actual share of service sector in GDP is almost normal in relation to the predicted value; it was just one percentage more during this period. Though historically atypical, India's experience thus seems to be in line with the current international experience. If the current pattern is influenced by, inter alia, emerging international comparative advantage, India should take advantage of its complementary role.

Sources of Growth

Expansion in the volume of production can take place either by increasing the quantum of inputs used in the production process or by increasing the productivity of the inputs used. Productivity growth is recognized as a major source of economic growth in various economies. Total output growth can be decomposed into contributions of changes in inputs and changes in total factor productivity (TFP). When the contribution of changes in various inputs to change in output is accounted for, the residual is attributed to change in TFP.

Dholakia (1992) and Rosengrant and Evenson (1995) show that TFP growth contributed to as much as 40–50 per cent of total growth in the agricultural sector in India during the Green Revolution era. For the organized manufacturing sector, on the other hand, Ahluwalia (1991) found that there was hardly any growth in TFP during 1959–86. Her sub-period analysis of TFP growth revealed a turnaround in the positive direction in the early 1980s. In a recent study, Sivasubramonian (2004) estimated the sources of economic growth in India using NAS data during 1950–1 to 1999–2000 for agriculture and non-agriculture (excluding dwelling). He found an increase in TFP for both agriculture and non-agriculture during the 1980s, but virtually no change between 1980s and 1990s, the pre- and post-reform decades. There has been a big fall in the utilization of labour input in both agriculture and non-agriculture during the 1990s.

The conventional growth accounting framework does not distinguish between technological progress (shift in production frontier) and technical efficiency (efficiency with which factors are used given the technical frontier). Recognizing importance of this distinction, Kalirajan et al. (2000) decomposed output growth into technical efficiency change, technological progress, and input growth. They found that input utilization was the dominant source of agricultural output growth during 1985–95 in all major states in India. While the contribution of technical efficiency to output growth continued to be in the range between 20–35 per cent during 1985–90 to 1991–5, contribution of technical progress was low at about 12–15 per cent during 1985–90 and fell further to 5–9 per cent for most states during 1991–5. The dynamism generated during the Green Revolution era has been lost.

OTHER MACROECONOMIC DEVELOPMENTS[3]

Savings and Investment

Gross domestic savings rate rose from 22.1 per cent of GDP in 1991–2 to 25.1 per cent in 1995–6. This trend got reversed during the second half of 1990s and the savings rate of the economy fell to 21.5 per cent in 1998–9, driven by the fall in savings from the public sector from 2 per cent of GDP in 1995–6 to -1 per cent in 1998–9. Aggregate savings rate has improved since then, despite the negative contribution of the public sector during 1998–9 to 2002–3. Improved contributions from both private and public sectors helped gross domestic savings rate to reach a record level of 32.4 per cent of GDP in 2005–6. Savings by the household sector, which accounts for the bulk of the total savings in India, had declined to 17 per cent of GDP in 1996–7.[4] It showed a rising trend since then to reach a peak of 23.5 per cent in 2003–4 but fell to 22.3 per cent in 2005–6.[5] Savings by the private corporate sector increased from less than 3 per cent of GDP prior to 1990–1 to 4.9 per cent in 1995–6. It exhibited a downward trend till 2001–2 but has improved since then and stood at 8.1 per cent in 2005–6. Fiscal discipline undertaken by Central and state governments as well as the tax buoyancy have led to a turnaround in public sector savings from –2.0 per cent in 2001–2 to 2.0 per cent in 2005–6. Public sector savings behaviour would be crucial for financing the higher investment that is needed for the acceleration of the economy.

Along with the savings rate, gross domestic capital formation (GDCF), adjusted for errors and omissions, has also witnessed a substantial jump from 22.9 per cent in 2001–2 to 33.8 per cent in 2005–6. While both private and public sectors have contributed to the improvement in investment rate, it is the private sector that has played a major role in the revival process. The net capital outflows during 2001–2 to 2003–4 kept the investment rate lower than the savings rate. However, there was a turnaround in 2004–5 and investment has again exceeded savings, the gap being bridged by net capital inflows. Net capital inflows or outflows have ranged between 0.5 to 1.5 per cent of GDP.

India's savings and investment rates are still lower than those of East Asian economies. Achievement of a higher growth target of 8–9 per cent on a medium-term basis would depend upon the economy's ability to raise the savings and investment rates even further. Starting from a baseline scenario of 29.1 per cent investment rate for 7 per cent GDP growth, the Planning Commission estimates the required investment rate to be 32.0 and 35.1 per cent of GDP corresponding to 8 and 9 per cent growth targets, respectively.[6]

Money and Credit

Both reserve money and broad money grew by about 17 per cent during 2005–6 compared to about 12 per cent in the previous year (Figure 2.7). This was mainly due to the Reserve Bank's liquidity injection operations in the face of redemption of India Millennium Deposits of about $8 billion. The reserve money growth in 2005–6 was driven largely by net domestic assets while it was mostly driven by foreign exchange reserves in the previous year. Demand for bank credit remained relatively strong during 2005–6 due to expanding economic activities. This led to liquidation by commercial banks of some of their excess holdings of government securities, which reduced to 31 per cent of net demand and time liabilities by the end of 2005–6 from a

---

[3] Behaviour of several macroeconomic variables has been discussed below by normalizing their size with respect to nominal GDP. The Central Statistical Organization has brought out the new national income series with 1999–2000 base for 1999–2000 onwards. GDP data prior to 1999–2000 are with 1993–4 base. Thus, the figures for post-1999–2000 period are not strictly comparable with those for the earlier period. Current price GDP for 1999–2000 in the new series is 1.1 per cent higher than that in the old series. As far as possible, we have relied on recent issues of *Economic Survey* and RBI *Annual Reports* for updating the data.

[4] Savings and investment estimates for 'household' sector are obtained as residual and include those of private non-corporate enterprises and non-profit institutions (see, EPWRF 2004, p. 51).

[5] Preliminary estimates of household financial savings for 2005–6, given in RBI *Annual Report* 2005–6, indicate a rise to 11.5 per cent of GDP from 10.1 per cent in the previous year.

[6] Planning Commission (2006). Note that China's growth rate of 9.5 per cent during 1990–2003 has been accompanied by an investment rate of 40–2 per cent.

TABLE 2.4
Savings and Capital Formation

Year	Gross Domestic Savings				Gross Capital Formation		
	Household Sector	Private Corporate Sector	Public Sector	Total Savings	Private Sector	Public Sector	GDCF
1990–1	19.3	2.7	1.1	23.1	14.7	9.4	26.3
1991–2	17.0	3.1	2.0	22.1	13.1	8.8	22.6
1992–3	17.5	2.7	1.6	21.8	15.2	8.6	23.6
1993–4	18.4	3.5	0.6	22.5	13.0	8.2	23.1
1994–5	19.7	3.5	1.7	24.9	14.7	8.7	26.0
1995–6	18.2	4.9	2.0	25.1	18.9	7.7	26.9
1996–7	17.0	4.5	1.7	23.2	14.7	7.0	24.5
1997–8	17.6	4.2	1.3	23.1	16.0	6.6	24.6
1998–9	18.8	3.7	–1.0	21.5	14.8	6.6	22.6
1999–2000	20.9	4.4	–1.0	24.2	16.7	6.9	25.3
				New Series with 1999–2000 base			
1999–2000	21.1	4.5	–0.8	24.8	17.9	7.4	25.9
2000–1	21.0	4.3	–1.9	23.4	16.5	6.9	24.0
2001–2	21.8	3.7	–2.0	23.5	16.3	6.9	22.9
2002–3	22.7	4.2	–0.6	26.4	18.4	6.1	25.2
2003–4	23.8	4.7	1.2	29.7	19.4	6.3	28.0
2004–5	21.6	7.1	2.4	31.1	21.3	7.1	31.5
2005–6	22.3	8.1	2.0	32.4	23.6	7.4	33.8

Notes: GDCF total includes (i) errors and omissions and (ii) valuables (introduced in the new series); 'valuables' covers expenditure made on acquisition of items such as precious metals and stones but excludes works of arts and antiques.
Source: RBI, *Annual Report* (various issues).

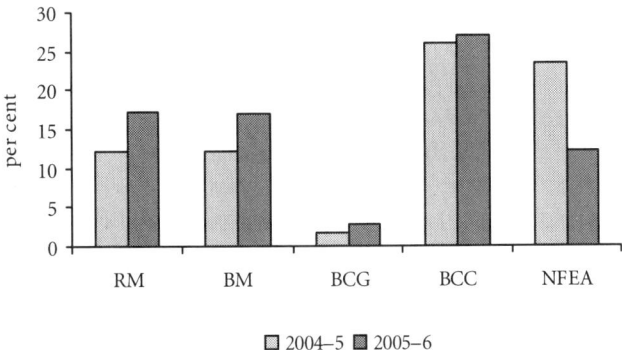

Notes: RM–reserve money; BM–broad money (M3); BCG–net bank credit to government; BCC–bank credit to commercial sector; NFEA–net foreign exchange assets of banking sector

Figure 2.7: Growth in Monetary Variables (per cent)

level of 38 per cent in the previous year. The reduced level is still in excess of the statutory minimum limit of 25 per cent. Credit to the government by the banking sector as a whole, however, rose due to the liquidity injection operation.

Inflation

International crude oil prices have more than doubled during the last two years, generating inflationary pressures at the global level. The Central government permitted partial pass through of price hike in imported oil to the domestic economy. Simultaneously, the Reserve Bank of India (RBI) adopted a pre-emptive monetary tightening policy to contain inflationary expectations. The current phase of inflation started in the second half of 2005 (Figure 2.8). On an annual basis, the rate of inflation, measured by wholesale or consumer price, has been moderate in the range of 4–5 per cent during 2005–6. On a monthly basis, the consumer price indices (CPI) have indicated a higher inflation rate of more than 7 per cent for several months in the half of 2006. Expectedly, fuel prices have been the major source of inflation with mineral oils contributing to more than 40 per cent of aggregate price rise, though their weight in wholesale price index (WPI) is only 7 per cent.

Public Finance

The combined total expenditure of the government was 28.6 per cent of GDP in 2005–6. The government collected tax revenue of 16.8 of GDP (5.7 per cent direct tax and 11.1 per cent indirect tax) and non-tax revenue of 4 per cent. The balance between expenditure and revenue is met by capital receipts most of which are borrowings constituting the fiscal deficit. The combined gross fiscal deficit of the Central and state governments stood at 7.5 per cent of GDP in 2004–5 and revised estimates for 2005–6 indicate no change from the previous year. Imbalance of this magnitude is not a sign of a healthy fiscal position, although it is

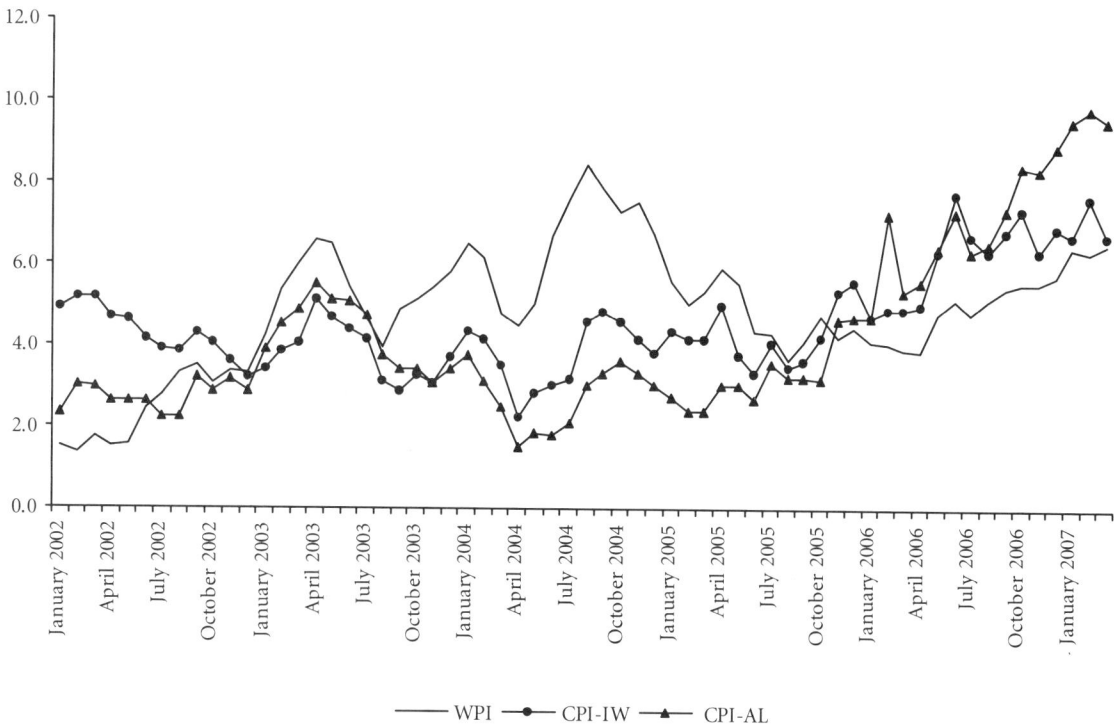

Figure 2.8: Inflation Rate for WPI and CPI

an improvement over the deteriorating situation noticed for five years till 2002–3 when it reached a peak of 10 per cent of GDP. This level of fiscal deficit was similar to the level that prevailed during the 1991 crisis, yet it did not get precipitated in an external crisis. Ahluwalia (2002) explained that this was due to a neutralizing shrinkage in demand effect from the private sector, which witnessed only a marginal rise in investment–GDP ratio while savings of the private sector rose substantially by 4–5 percentage points of GDP during the 1990s.

Other deficit indicators such as revenue deficit and primary deficit too have improved. The most significant change has been in the revenue deficit—defined as the excess of revenue expenditure over revenue receipt. It indicates a situation where the government borrows to meet those expenditures which do not directly support the income generation process. A revenue balance, on the other hand, provides resources for capital expenditure. The fall in revenue deficit from 6.6 per cent of GDP in 2000–1 to 3.1 per cent in 2005–6 is thus a welcome sign. The governments have undertaken time-bound legislative commitments to eliminate the fiscal deficit. Larger volume of tax and non-tax revenue receipts due to higher growth, widening of the tax base to the service sector, and steps to contain revenue expenditure have all contributed to this improvement. Tax collection rise by 1 per cent of GDP in 2005–6 is particularly noteworthy. The burden of fiscal adjustment during the 1990s fell mostly on capital outlays and distorted the structure of government expenditure away from investment. The rise in salary and pension payments consequent upon the Fifth Pay Commission recommendations further distorted the structure in favour of current expenditure for several years.

Non-tax revenue receipts of both Central and state governments increased in the first half of the 1990s, but have stagnated after that at around 4 per cent of GDP. Price rationalization in utilities such as power, transport, and irrigation and other public sector units (PSUs) needs to occur on a continuous basis through independent and credible regulatory authorities to ensure that users do not pay for increasing inefficiency of the utilities.

While social sectors such as health and education with large expenditures mostly fall under state jurisdiction under the Indian constitution, the tax base of the state governments has remained narrow, resulting in a heavy dependence of the states on the Centre for grants and shareable taxes. The Eleventh Finance Commission had recommended the creation of a Fiscal Reform Facility by the Central government during 2000–1 to 2004–5 to provide incentives to state governments for undertaking medium term fiscal reform (MTFR). The Twelfth Finance Commission, covering the period 2005–6 to 2009–10, also laid emphasis on a time-bound fiscal restructuring path to eliminate revenue deficit by 2008–9 and fiscal deficit to 3 per cent of GDP by 2009–10, even as it recognized the need for restructuring of expenditures by state governments in favour of capital outlay and social sector. In order to reduce the debt burden and interest payments by the states, it recommended an incentive linked debt relief scheme provided the states enact fiscal responsibility legislation with specific targets. Adoption of such legislation by most state governments has helped to reduce fiscal distortions at the state level.

Public debt of the Centre and the states rose sharply from 61.3 per cent of GDP in 1995–6 to 82.5 per cent in 2004–5, though revised estimates for 2005–6 show a fall by 3 percentage points. The average interest rate on outstanding loans of the Centre has fallen from 13 per cent in 2000–1 to 8.8 per cent in 2005–6 reflecting a fall in market rate over the years. Total interest payment is still large at about 6 per cent of GDP; it has fallen slowly and continues to pre-empt about a fourth of total revenue. A primary surplus on a sustained basis would be needed to reduce the debt–GDP ratio in the liberalized context. The outstanding government guarantees to loans raised by other agencies such as PSUs continue to be large at about 10 per cent of GDP. Two-thirds of these contingent liabilities are by state governments.

The wide fiscal deficit and skewed government expenditure towards salaries, pensions, and interest payments provides limited scope for the government to allocate resources for developmental and productive activities. Notwithstanding this constraint, the government did play an important role in arresting adverse welfare effects of the drought in 2002–3 by provision of adequate relief measures. To a lesser

TABLE 2.5
Fiscal Parameters of Central Government

(as percentage of GDP)

	1980–91	1990–1	1996–7	2001–2	2002–3	2003–4	2004–5	2005–6 (RE)	2006–7 (BE)
Total Expenditure	17.70	17.2	14.69	15.88	16.87	17.07	15.94	14.40	14.27
Revenue Expenditure	11.70	12.9	11.62	13.21	13.83	13.12	12.31	12.47	12.35
Interest Payments	2.80	3.8	4.35	4.71	4.81	4.50	4.07	3.68	3.54
Subsidies	1.70	1.7	1.13	1.37	1.78	1.61	1.40	1.33	1.17
Capital Disbursements	6.00	4.4	3.08	2.67	3.04	3.95	3.63	1.94	1.92
Capital Outlay	2.51	2.1	1.04	1.16	1.19	1.24	1.66	1.61	1.69
Total Tax	10.00	10.1	9.40	8.2	8.8	9.2	9.8	10.5	11.2
Direct Tax	2.00	1.9	2.80	3.0	3.4	3.8	4.3	4.8	5.3
Indirect Tax	7.90	7.9	6.60	5.2	5.4	5.4	5.5	5.7	5.9
Non-Tax Revenue	2.40	2.11	2.38	2.97	2.95	2.78	2.60	2.10	1.93
Gross Fiscal Deficit	6.80	6.6	4.11	6.18	5.92	4.47	4.01	4.14	3.76
Gross Primary Deficit	3.90	2.8	−0.24	1.47	1.11	−0.03	−0.06	0.46	0.22
Revenue Deficit	1.90	3.3	2.39	4.39	4.40	3.56	2.51	2.60	2.14

Source: RBI, *Annual Report* (various issues).

TABLE 2.6
Fiscal Parameters of State Governments

(as percentage of GDP)

YEAR	1990–1	2002–3	2003–4	2004–5	2005–6 (RE)	2006–7 (BE)
Total Expenditure	16.0	17.2	18.7	21.7	19.5	16.7
Developmental Expenditure	11.1	9.2	9.9	9.4	10.3	9.7
Social Sector Expenditure		6.0	6.0	5.4	6.0	5.8
Non-developmental Expenditure	4.0	6.1	6.0	6.0	5.8	5.8
Revenue Expenditure	12.6	13.5	13.4	13.1	13.3	13.0
Interest payments	1.5	2.8	2.9	2.8	2.5	2.5
Capital outlay	1.16	1.5	1.8	2.0	2.4	2.4
Total revenue Receipt	11.7	11.4	11.2	11.9	12.9	13.0
Tax Revenue (own)	5.3	5.8	5.7	6.1	6.4	6.4
Non-Tax Revenue (own)	1.6	1.4	1.3	1.5	1.3	1.3
Central Transfers	4.7	4.1	4.1	4.3	5.2	5.3
Grants	2.2	1.8	1.8	1.8	2.6	2.5
Shareable Taxes	2.5	2.3	2.4	2.5	2.6	2.7
Gross Fiscal Deficit	3.3	4.2	4.4	3.5	3.2	2.7
Gross Primary Deficit	1.8	1.3	1.5	0.7	0.7	0.2
Revenue Deficit	0.9	2.2	2.2	1.17	0.49	0.05

Source: RBI, *Annual Report* (various issues).

TABLE 2.7
Fiscal Parameters of Central and State Governments Combined

(as percentage of GDP)

	1990–1	1995–6	2001–2	2002–3	2003–4	2004–5	2005–6 (RE)	2006–7 (BE)
Revenue Receipts	18.6	18.3	17.5	18.5	18.8	19.7	20.8	21.1
Tax Revenue	15.4	14.7	13.8	14.6	15.0	15.8	16.8	17.4
Direct Tax Revenue	2.5	3.5	3.6	4.1	4.6	5.0	5.7	6.1
Indirect Tax Revenue	12.9	11.2	10.2	10.5	10.5	10.8	11.1	11.4
Non-tax Revenue	3.2	3.6	3.8	3.9	3.7	3.9	4.0	3.7
Total Disbursements	28.7	25.4	28.3	28.8	28.9	27.9	28.6	27.9
Developmental Expenditure	17.1	13.9	14.6	14.6	14.9	14.3	15.5	n.a.
Social Sector Expenditure	6.8	6.4	7.7	7.8	7.5	7.4	8.1	7.8
Non-developmental Expenditure	11.6	11.5	13.5	13.9	13.6	13.6	12.8	n.a.
Interest payments	4.4	5.0	6.2	6.5	6.4	6.2	5.8	5.7
Gross Fiscal Deficit	9.4	6.5	9.9	9.6	8.5	7.5	7.5	6.5
Gross Primary Deficit	5.0	1.6	3.7	3.1	2.1	1.4	1.6	0.8
Revenue Deficit	4.2	3.2	7.0	6.7	5.8	3.7	3.1	2.2

Source: RBI.

extent, government policies also helped in the revival of industrial activities through extensive road construction activities.

International Trade

The world economy has witnessed significant growth of about 5 per cent per annum since 2003 led by more than 7 per cent growth in the emerging market economies. The world trade volume too expanded considerably at 10.4 and 7.3 per cent in 2004 and 2005, respectively. Taking advantage of world trade growth, India's merchandise exports have nearly doubled from US$ 54 billion in 2002–3 to $105 billion in 2005–6. The average annual growth in exports has been as high as 24 per cent during 2003–4 to 2005–6. Imports grew even more sharply from $64.5 billion in 2002–3 to $156 billion in 2005–6 due to rise in international oil prices and in non-oil imports attributable to domestic growth. Trade deficit rose to $51.6 billion in 2005–6 or 6.5 per cent of GDP. Current estimates for 2006–7 show that trade flows have expanded by 20–5 per cent with export and import levels reaching about $125 and $180 billion. Merchandise exports and imports respectively accounted for 13.1 and 19.6 per cent of GDP in 2005–6 (Table 2.8). With the current shares, the additional 10–12 per cent export growth over and above the trend has thus roughly contributed to more than 1 percentage point of GDP growth. In this sense, one might say the acceleration noticed in GDP since 2003–4 is largely export driven.

Invisible earnings too have been rising steadily to reach 11.5 per cent of GDP in 2005–6 thanks to substantial expansion in two components: (i) transfers (remittances) from abroad and (ii) service exports in information technology and business process outsourcing. In absolute terms, remittances were of the order of about US$ 25 billion while

TABLE 2.8
Major Foreign Trade Parameters

(as percentage of GDP)

	1990–1	1995–6	2000–1	2001–2	2002–3	2003–4	2004–5	2005–6
Export	5.8	9.1	9.9	9.4	10.6	11.0	11.8	13.1
Import	8.8	12.3	12.6	11.8	12.7	13.3	17.1	19.6
Trade balance	–3.0	–3.2	–2.7	–2.4	–2.1	–2.3	–5.3	–6.5
Invisible receipts	2.4	5.0	7.0	7.7	8.3	8.9	10.3	11.5
Invisible payments	2.4	3.5	4.9	4.5	4.9	4.3	5.8	6.4
Net invisibles	–0.1	1.6	2.1	3.1	3.4	4.6	4.5	5.1
Current receipts	8.0	14.9	16.8	16.9	18.8	19.8	22.0	24.5
Current account balance	–3.1	–1.7	–0.6	0.7	1.3	2.3	–0.8	–1.3
Foreign investment	0.03	1.4	1.5	1.7	1.2	2.6	2.1	2.5
Debt–GDP ratio	28.7	27.0	22.4	21.1	20.4	17.8	17.3	15.8
Debt–Service ratio	35.3	24.3	16.6	13.4	16.4	16.3	6.1	10.2
Import cover of reserves (in months)	2.5	6.0	8.8	11.7	14.2	16.9	14.3	11.6

Source: RBI, *Annual Report* (various issues).

software exports were close to US$ 18 billion. India ranks first as a remittance recipient and second as a software related exporter in the world.

Invisible payments too have risen to 6.4 per cent of GDP in 2005–6 due to liberalization of travel, transport, dividends, and other service related payments. The net surplus on the invisibles account has been about 5 per cent of GDP which helped the overall balance of payments to remain comfortable with a deficit of 1.3 per cent of GDP. The economy had witnessed a surplus in current account balance for three years during 2001–2 to 2003–4, but is back to the deficit phase because of the rise in oil prices. While the ratio of merchandise trade (imports and exports together) to GDP has increased to 32.7 per cent, current account transactions (including invisibles) to GDP ratio has jumped above 50 per cent.[7] These ratios are clear indicators of India's steady movement towards integration with the global economy.

Foreign direct investment (FDI) and portfolio investment flows have increased to $7.7 and $12.4 billion in 2005–6 reflecting liberalized policy changes as well as an improved investment climate. FDI could play a critical role in manufacturing export promotions, market diversification, technology transfer, and productivity increase. India needs to increase the share of high technology manufactured products in its export basket.

Following phased liberalization in the capital account, a significant recent development has been overseas investment by Indian companies which has picked up recently from $ 0.7 billion in 2000–1 to 2.7 billion in 2005–6. Such investments have flown to sectors such as iron and steel, information technology (IT), pharmaceuticals, and petroleum. Indian companies have acquired controlling shares in some of the global giants in recent months. This would open up global business opportunities for Indian entrepreneurs and provide new means of economic co-operation for India with other countries.

India's outstanding external debt stood at $125 billion or 15.8 per cent of GDP at the end of fiscal 2005–6. Of this, about $9 billion was in the nature of short-term debt. Debt services of about $20 billion as a ratio of total current receipt was 10.2 per cent.

The overall surge in capital flows exceeded the current account deficit and led to a further build up of RBI's net foreign assets (NFA) of $10.1 billion in 2005–6. Foreign exchange reserves reached US$ 151 billion by March 2006 and have recently crossed the $200 billion mark. The reserves were adequate to pay for import bill of 11.6 months in 2005–6 as against the import cover of 16.9 months in 2003–4. This fall in reserves relative to imports in the face of increase in world oil prices serves as a caution against world market price volatility.

India continues to have among the highest tariff rates across developing countries. The import weighted average basic tariff rates turn out to be 18 per cent for all commodities in the year 2004–5.[8] India has recently announced its intention to align its tariff structure with those of Association of South East Asian Nations (ASEAN) countries.

The direction of India's exports has undergone considerable change in recent years. Share of Eastern Europe and Organization for Economic Co-operation and Development (OECD) countries has been going down and getting replaced by that of Asian countries (Table 2.9). In fact, Asia and ASEAN together accounted for as much as 48 per cent of India's exports in 2005–6.[9] The movement towards a stronger intra-Asian trade linkage in recent years is evident for other Asian countries too. China is the largest market for Asian exports with a share of 10 per cent. Though India's trade linkage with China has historically not been strong, it has been expanding fast in recent years. China has become the second biggest trading partner of India with a share of 7 per cent in total Indian trade in 2005–6 next to USA (10.6 per cent). Some influential think tanks in Asia have been advocating the need for a stronger integration of the Asian economies and we turn to this issue in the next section.

TABLE 2.9
Direction of India's Exports

(*percentage share*)

	1990–1	1995–6	2001–2
OECD	53.5	55.7	49.3
OPEC	5.6	9.7	12.0
Eastern Europe	17.9	3.8	2.3
Asia (excluding Japan and OPEC)	14.3	21.3	22.4
Rest of world	8.7	9.5	14.0
Total	100.0	100.0	100.0

Source: Economic Survey 2004–5, Government of India.

ASIAN ECONOMIC INTEGRATION

There has been a strong move towards regional economic integration in recent decades following the successful experimentation of the European Union (EU) and the North American Free Trade Agreement (NAFTA). The EU has gradually expanded to become a 25-member large unified market with free flow of trade, capital, and labour among

---

[7] Note that these are accounting ratios that indicate openness in relation to size of the economy and do not by any means imply relative position of trade in the domestic production structure.

[8] See Mathur and Sachadeva (2005) who report the weighted average basic import duty rates of 29 per cent, 5 per cent, 50 per cent, 19 per cent, and 18 per cent for agriculture, mining, consumer goods, intermediates, and capital goods, respectively in 2004–5.

[9] Data for recent years are not reported by *Economic Survey* in the same format as shown in Table 2.9.

the members and a common currency for a large part of the Union. It currently accounts for about a quarter of world income and a third of world exports. Similarly, NAFTA contributes to about 35 per cent of world income and 20 per cent of world exports. Co-operative arrangements in Asia, however, have been weak till now and are limited to sub-regional levels as evident from the ASEAN Free Trade Agreement (AFTA) and the South Asia Free Trade Agreement (SAFTA).

Developing Asia accounted for 52 per cent of world population and 25 per cent of world income in PPP terms in the year 2004 (IMF 2005). Developed Japan and the newly developed Asian economies (Hong Kong–China, Korea, Singapore, and Taiwan) contribute another 3 per cent of world population and 10 per cent of world income. The developing and developed Asian economies together generate income of $8 trillion in nominal terms and $18 trillion in PPP terms which are 23 and 35 per cent of the respective world totals (in 2003). On a comparative perspective, the size of Asian economy is comparable to that of the EU and NAFTA.

Several Asian countries such as China, Indonesia, Hong Kong–China, Korea, Singapore, and Thailand have been among the fastest growing countries in the world for more than two decades. They opened up their economies to foreign trade and investment in the 1970s and early 1980s and reaped the benefits of the globalization process.[10] Exports and imports expanded faster than overall income growth. Foreign trade flows as a proportion of GDP rose from 47 per cent in 1990 to 61 per cent in 2001 in East Asia and from 32 per cent to 44 per cent in China during the same period. FDI accounting for 3–5 per cent of GDP, also played a major role in the growth process of the East Asian economies.

India has been a latecomer in Asia to the globalization process, but is moving fast. It accounts for 18 per cent of Asia's income in PPP terms and 6 per cent of trade (2004). In recent years, India has joined several bilateral or sub-regional trade agreements with other Asian countries and adopted the Look East policy in the early 1990s. Its economic relation with other Asian countries has progressed considerably. Recent initiatives have resulted in a free trade area (FTA) agreement with the SAARC countries, dialogue partnership with ASEAN, a protocol with Thailand to implement the Early Harvest Scheme under the FTA framework. It is engaged in negotiations for Regional Trade and Investment Agreement (TRIA) with ASEAN and a comprehensive economic co-operation agreement with Singapore. Sen et al. (2004) note that the mindset of Indian policy makers has changed considerably in favour of East Asia and adequate reciprocation would help progress in overall cooperation.

A recent study by the Asian Development Bank (ADB) concludes that Asian economic integration could be the main stimulus for future growth in the region (see Box 2.1).

Box 2.1

Long-term Scenarios for Asian Growth: Need for Asian Economic Integration

A recent research project undertaken by the ADB highlights the critical role of Asian economic integration for stimulating future growth in the region (Ronald-Holst et al. 2005). Improvements in intra-Asian trade efficiency would help to expand as Asian income to a greater extent as compared to global trade liberalization.

The study develops a baseline scenario for growth and trade movements for major countries in Asia till 2025 and then examines the potential for raising this baseline growth using international trade enhancing instruments. The baseline forecast is obtained by means of calibration of a dynamic computable general equilibrium model to average consensus growth rates from several macroeconomic projections. Such a 'business as usual' scenario is optimistic about the continuation of the good growth performance of the Asian regions seen in the past decade or so. In order to examine the prospects for trade-induced higher growth rate for Asia, the papers have developed scenarios related to: (i) trade liberalization at the global and continental levels and (ii) trade facilitation measures that reduce transportation, distribution, and transit costs captured by 2 per cent annual increase in intra-Asian trade efficiency.

The first set of results indicates that income growth from Asian trade liberalization per se is rather small for various Asian countries and ranges between 0.6 to 17.3 per cent over a period of two decades. China seems to be deriving the maximum gains from Asian trade liberalization. India's equivalent income gain is about 9 per cent from both Asian trade liberalization and global trade liberalization over the baseline projection in the year 2025—implying an average income rise of about 0.5 per cent per annum.

The second set of results relating to trade facilitation, on the other hand, indicates relatively large gains ranging between 22 and 62 per cent for various Asian countries. India's income gain from trade facilitation is about 25 per cent in 2025. This would mean India's GDP growth could accelerate further by 1 per cent per year. Thus, the most interesting result from this analysis is that an AFTA with slow but steady improvements in trade efficiency could help regional income growth to a larger extent rather than global free trade alone.

The study argues that the benefits need not be seen as those due to classical trade diversification as the detailed regional trade pattern indicates that the volume of trade flows of each region expands not only with other Asian regions but also with the rest of the world (ROW) except for a minor fall in South Asia's trade with ROW. Thus, diversion would take place in incremental trade volumes rather than in existing trade volumes. Realization of these potential gains from intra-Asian trade requires a fresh look by Asian countries on the evolution of their policies and institutions.

---

[10] Admittedly, the nature and speed of opening up varied from country to country and the governments did play an active role in several cases.

The study notes that Asian Free Trade Agreement (AFTA)—with steady improvements in trade facilitation—helps regional income growth to a larger extent than global free trade. There has been substantial progress on the removal of formal trade restrictions by means of tariffs and quotas all over the world in recent decades and as such liberalization of remaining tariffs or tariff equivalent of quotas would provide only limited gains in the future. Current attention is getting shifted to trade facilitation and institutional issues. It has been recognized that trade facilitation could substantially enhance world income and issues related to this have been on the WTO negotiation agenda since the Singapore Ministerial Meeting in 1996.

Trade facilitation measures refer to expedition of the movement and clearance of goods, greater transparency, and procedural uniformity of cross-border transportation of goods. Transport and communication is a major element of costs associated with trade, and efficiency in their provision could reduce trade margins considerably. Border formalities for clearance of inter-country movement of goods have improved but still continue to be tedious and wasteful. Adoption of standardized customs compliance forms would avoid duplication and international norms could be followed to complete the formalities. An agreement on product standard is another major area to facilitate trade within an RTA.

Formation of regional integration agreements (RIAs) has caused significant changes in the pattern of world trade due to faster rise of trade and investment flows within the RIAs. There is general agreement that a multilateral trade arrangement across the globe is the first best option from the global welfare point of view. Yet, the trend towards RIAs seems to continue unabated[11] as a second best option and to improve bargaining strength in international negotiations.[12] In such an environment, Asia would lose its relative strength in the world economy unless it moves as a strong block through a fast track economic integration process. Asian economies can reduce cost, enhance competitiveness, and accelerate overall regional growth by making use of the opportunity of a continent-wide expanded market.

Regional economic co-operation in Asia need not involve a classic South–South type trade. The level of development among the Asian countries varies a lot; for example, one could look at the contrast between Japan and Korea on the one hand, and India and Pakistan on the other. There is sufficient diversity in relative factor endowments, capital, labour, technology, and skills among Asian countries. Several papers in Kumar (2004) discuss prospects of Asian economic integration from various angles and find that there is sufficient scope for viable integration among the Asian countries. They provide examples of potential areas of co-operation and it may be appropriate to state some of them here, involving India as a partner. Korea and Singapore have underutilized capacity in construction which could be fruitfully used to develop infrastructure in India. East Asia can make use of India's well developed R&D infrastructure in biotechnology, pharmaceuticals, and space research. India is seen as having relative advantage in the services sector, while it is manufacturing in China and East Asia. In the newly developed ITC sector, India specializes in software development while East Asia's focus has been on hardware manufacturing.

The current trend for formation of RTAs seems to be strong and all but a few countries in the world have signed one or more RTAs. In such an environment, there is a strong feeling that Asia would lose its long-term bargaining power and face adverse terms of trade effects unless it moves as a strong block by adopting a fast track economic integration process. A pan-Asian market would be large enough to derive sufficient economies of scale and enhance regional growth. The large size of the market would hopefully avoid a situation where a single enterprise drives away others in the same product line due to economies of scale. It is necessary to guard against creation of monopoly that could effectively kill competition. As World Bank (2000) states, the success of RTAs would lie in increasing scale as well as competition in the integrated market compared to the pre-RTA scenario.

Asian integration calls for a fresh look by the Asian countries on the evolution of their policies and institutions. The ADB study advocates a 'policy coherence' approach to Asian integration similar to the OECD type arrangement, which is less binding in nature than the 'policy harmonization' approach in the EU type arrangement. An Asian co-operative arrangement could have adequate bargaining power with EU or NAFTA and could bring about a tripartite balance on global negotiation tables. By representing views of a wide cross-section of nations at different stages of development, such a forum could play a significant role in further advancement of the globalization process.

POVERTY AND DISTRIBUTION

We now turn to current concerns on the poverty and distribution side. Given the widespread and intense poverty among a large section of the population, poverty reduction has been a major goal of economic policy in India along with aggregate income growth. Low per capita growth

---

[11] Nearly 200 RIAs/FTAs have been notified to the GATT/WTO.

[12] A country can join an RIA without necessarily compromising on its commitment to the multilateral trading regime. But, whether formation of RIA would complement or conflict with the multilateral liberalization process has been a matter of debate.

coupled with near invariance of the distribution parameter led to little improvement in the level of living of the poor for about three decades after independence. The incidence of poverty did not show any declining trend in India till the mid-1970s and started to fall only when the economy moved up to a phase of higher economic growth of 5 per cent or more. Hence, policy makers and analysts have advocated the need for higher GDP growth to facilitate poverty reduction. Trade liberalization can reduce poverty through sustained economic growth. International evidence indicates that poverty effects of growth, including trade led growth, are very much circumstance specific.[13]

Poverty estimates by the Planning Commission show that the percentage of population below the poverty line, also known as head count ratio (HCR), has fallen from 55 per cent in 1973–4 to 36 per cent in 1993–4 and further to 27 per cent in 2004–5 for rural and urban areas taken together.[14] The absolute number of total poor stood at 302 million in 2004–5—accounting for about a quarter of the poor in the world. India thus would pose a major challenge for meeting the first Millennium Development Goal which aims at reducing poverty to half the 1990 level by 2015.

Accelerated economic growth has not led to as fast a fall in poverty as expected earlier. Between 1993–4 and 2004–5, HCR fell by only 22 per cent while per capita real income grew considerably by 62 per cent. The implied elasticity of poverty with respect to per capita income (NNP) is less than 0.40 which is not very encouraging, to say the least. Accentuation of inequality might have partly neutralized the potential poverty reducing effects of growth.

Poverty ratios in Table 2.10 reveal substantial variation across the states in India. Among the major states, Orissa, Bihar, and Madhya Pradesh (including the new states of Jharkhand and Chhattisgarh) have substantially higher HCR than all-India, while Punjab has single digit HCR. Note that the high poverty states are contiguous, lying in the central and eastern parts of India. This leads us to the question of regional disparity.

Figure 2.9 arranges the major states by descending order of their per capita GSDP in 1993–4 and shows the growth rates in per capita GSDP during 1993–4 to 2004–5. Punjab, Maharashtra, Haryana, and Gujarat were among the richest states in India in 1993, while Bihar, Orissa, Uttar Pradesh, and Assam were the poorest. Average level of living in Punjab was about four times that of Bihar in 1993–4. During the post-reform period, states on the low rung of the income ladder had the lowest growth rates too. Thus their divergence from all-India average has widened. States in the middle rung such as West Bengal, Gujarat, Karnataka, and Kerala witnessed above 5 per cent growth in per capita income as

TABLE 2.10
HCR of Poverty for Major Indian States

States	Rural		Urban		Total	
	1993–4	2004–5	1993–4	2004–5	1993–4	2004–5
Andhra Pradesh	15.9	11.2	38.3	28.0	22.2	15.8
Assam	45.0	22.3	7.7	3.3	40.9	19.7
Bihar	58.2	43.0	34.5	28.7	55.0	41.1
Gujarat	22.2	19.1	27.9	13.0	24.2	16.8
Haryana	28.0	13.6	16.4	15.1	25.1	14.0
Karnataka	29.9	20.8	40.1	32.6	33.2	25.0
Kerala	25.8	13.2	24.6	20.2	25.4	15.0
Madhya Pradesh	40.6	37.9	48.4	41.9	42.5	39.0
Maharashtra	37.9	29.6	35.2	32.2	36.9	30.7
Orissa	49.7	46.8	41.6	44.3	48.6	46.4
Punjab	12.0	9.1	11.4	7.1	11.8	8.4
Rajasthan	26.5	18.7	30.5	32.9	27.4	22.1
Tamil Nadu	32.5	22.8	39.8	22.2	35.0	22.5
Uttar Pradesh	42.3	33.7	35.4	31.0	40.9	33.1
West Bengal	40.8	28.6	22.4	14.8	35.7	24.7
India	37.3	28.3	32.4	25.7	36.0	27.5

Notes: Based on Uniform Recall Period (URP) consumption in which the consumer expenditure data for all the items are collected from 30-day recall period; Bihar, Madhya Pradesh, and Uttar Pradesh include the new states of Jharkhand, Chhattisgarh, and Uttarakhand, respectively.

Source: Government of India.

---

[13] See, for example, a recent review article by Winters et al. (2004).

[14] These estimates are based on comparable uniform recall period of 30 days. Estimates based on the 1999–2000 survey data are not used here due to the controversy over the mix-up of the recall period.

36 INDIA DEVELOPMENT REPORT

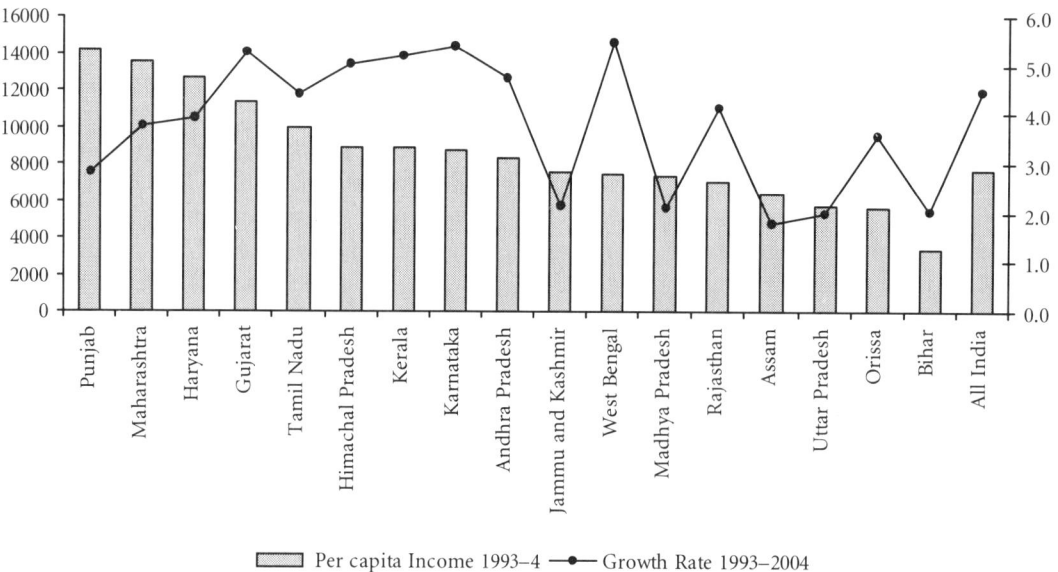

Figure 2.9: Average Annual Growth Rate in Per Capita GSDP Across States
(Arranged by 1993–4 Per Capita GSDP)

against all-India growth of 4.4 per cent. The three richest states had lower than average growth, though not as low as some of the poorest states.

Figure 2.10 presents the coefficient of variation (CV) in per capita GSDP among the major states. Disparity in average level of living among states has clearly increased after the reforms, though it remained somewhat stable during the late 1990s. Curiously, it seems that the high growth phases in national income have been accompanied by increase in inter-state inequality.

Along with an accentuation of regional disparity, urban–rural disparity too has widened after the reforms (Table 2.11). All-India urban per capita consumption expenditure was 63 per cent higher than that in rural areas in 1993–4. It has jumped to 88 per cent in 2004–5. The rise in urban–rural disparity has taken place across all the major states in India. Relatively low agricultural growth is one of the factors contributing to the rising urban–rural inequality.

Several other factors too might have led to an increase in inequality during the post-reform period. Pay packages in multinational companies are substantially higher than those for comparable jobs in domestic companies, leading to a widening differential in wage rates. The technical progress in information and communication sectors and consequent large expansion in demand for skilled and semi-skilled labour during the 1990s has contributed to a rise in the relative gap in wages between skilled and unskilled labour. The most intensively used factor of production in these newly emerging sectors strongly linked to the world market is not likely to be provided by the poor households who typically

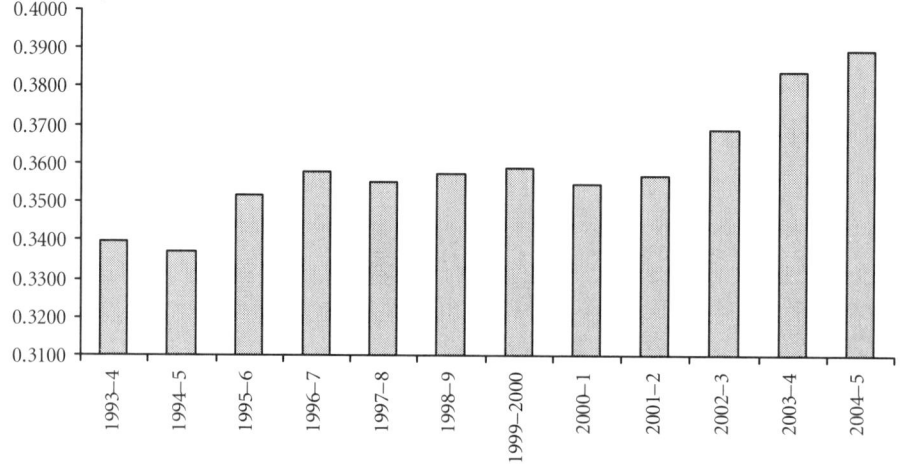

Figure 2.10: Coefficient of Variation in Per Capita GSDP among Major States

TABLE 2.11
Urban–Rural Differences in MPCE

States	Urban MPCE as per cent of Rural MPCE	
	1993–4	2004–5
Andhra Pradesh	141.5	173.9
Assam	177.9	194.8
Bihar	161.9	186.2
Gujarat	149.8	187.1
Haryana	123.1	132.3
Karnataka	157.2	203.3
Kerala	126.7	127.4
Madhya Pradesh	161.9	212.0
Maharashtra	194.1	202.1
Orissa	183.2	189.7
Punjab	118.0	156.6
Rajasthan	132.0	163.1
Tamil Nadu	149.0	179.4
Uttar Pradesh	142.0	151.5
West Bengal	169.9	200.0
All India	163.0	188.2

Source: Based on NSSO data.

possess 'unskilled' labour. Of course, as demand for consumer goods by skilled labour households expands, indirect benefits for the poor are generated through the multiplier process.

Since the poor did not gain considerably from the market-driven growth process, the government is expanding the scope of complementary policies to make economic development more broad based. Most of the poor households are endowed with labour power and wage is their most important source of income. Hence, employment has been recognized as an important monitoring variable for public policy, though it has not occupied a central place in the development plans. In the initial decades of development planning, it was thought that economic growth as such would help in substantial reduction of unemployment. But, actual experience turned out to be different. While the structure of income moved rapidly in favour of non-agriculture, the structure of employment changed very slowly. Industries and services did not generate adequate employment to absorb the growing labour force. About 55 per cent of the workforce continues to depend on agriculture, though they produce only 20 per cent of GDP. Thus, the per capita income of a typical worker in agriculture is one-fifth of his counterpart in non-agriculture. Bulk of the rural poor are landless labourers or marginal farmers dependent on wage income for a good part of the year.

It is against this structural background that several public employment programmes, aimed at providing the poor with manual work, were introduced under different names—*Swarnajayanti Grameen Rozagar Yojana* being the most recent one. The volume of such direct intervention programmes has expanded over time with rising unemployment, but there was no guarantee till recently that employment would be provided to all those who need it. The recent National Rural Employment Guarantee (NREG) Act is a welcome move from this point of view (see Box 2.2). This is an important policy initiative taken by the government that

---

BOX 2.2

National Rural Employment Guarantee Act, 2005

The Indian Parliament enacted a law in 2005 making it mandatory for the government to provide at least 100 days of wage employment in a financial year to every household whose adult members are willing to undertake unskilled manual work at the minimum wage rates enacted for agricultural labourers. This act is a recognition by the state of employment entitlement by poor manual workers and constitutes a form of social security measure for them. The new scheme to be implemented in phases throughout the country would subsume other current public employment programmes.

The programme involves both the central and the state administration. The Central government assumes responsibility to provide the required fund to run the programme, while the state governments would be in charge of implementing it. An applicant is entitled to an unemployment allowance of about a third of the wage rate if he is not provided work within 15 days by the state government. This sum would be met by the state government.

There was a heated debate on the merits and demerits of the Employment Guarantee act. Opponents were quick to point out the likely huge additional cost of the programme involving 1–2 per cent of GDP and large leakages noticed in other poverty reduction programmes. Advocates, on the other hand, emphasised the 'self-selection' character of public employment programme in so far as only those willing to do manual work at the minimum wage would demand it. Such people normally belong to the lowest income brackets. Evaluation studies have also shown that employment programmes are more cost effective in transferring resources to the poor compared to other poverty alleviation programmes. Besides, public employment programmes have a positive effect on rural wage rate which is an important determinant of poverty.

One lesson from the debate is that a socially acceptable norm may be worked out to devote a certain percentage of national income to programmes directly aimed at benefiting the low income classes. Since the natural growth process may not ensure full employment in a market economy, minimum income or employment entitlement to the people requires government intervention. Minsky (1986) says creation of an 'infinitely elastic demand' for labour could be possible only by government at a floor wage—operating at 'a base level during good times and expanding during recession'.

reconciles the poverty reduction objective with the growth objective. Distributional conflict management by the state could play a crucial role in the success of reforms. The state should design innovative instruments that have least conflict with the growth process.

CONCLUSION

Economic policies in India have been formulated with the twin objectives of growth and social justice. The economic reform process has placed the economy on a strong growth path. An average GDP growth of about 8 per cent since 2003–4 is particularly noteworthy. Revival of industry after a transition phase has generated new optimism about its inherent strength to compete in the global market. Growth of the services sector continues to be strong with a near revolution in telecommunication and IT. Growth of exports has played a key role in the current high growth phase.

The agricultural sector, however, has been stagnant and needs a big push to make the development process broad-based. The divergence of income and employment pattern does pose a main problem for India. With the majority of population still depending on agriculture, higher growth of agriculture and agro-based industries is essential for poverty reduction. Another emerging divide is the slow expansion of employment in the organized sector. According to NAS data, as much as 40 per cent of GDP originates in the organized sector which accounts for only about 15 per cent of employment. The need for removal of rigidities in the land and labour markets, consistent with growth and distribution objectives, cannot be overemphasized.

Inflation has been an area of concern in recent months with the CPI rising at above 7 per cent triggered by the rise in world prices of crude oil. There has been a partial pass-through of this price hike to the domestic economy. The RBI has adopted a pre-emptive monetary tightening policy to contain inflationary expectations.

Combined revenue and fiscal deficits of the Central and state governments have reduced in recent years, consistent with legislative commitments on fiscal reforms over the medium term. Reduction in revenue deficit, particularly, has generated positive savings from the public sector contributing to overall savings growth. Composition of government expenditure has improved with a reorientation towards the social sector and capital outlay. Overall fiscal deficit continues to be high at 7.5 per cent of GDP and fiscal distortions need to be further contracted through measures on the revenue and expenditure fronts.

The acceleration noticed recently in the Indian economy is largely driven by strong export growth which has averaged 24 per cent during the last three years. Imports too have grown considerably due to the economic buoyancy effect and international crude price rise. Strong growth in invisible earnings has helped to keep the current account deficit at a moderate level.

While the upturn in world economy did contribute to the high growth phase, the rising savings and investment ratio is indicative of domestic supply-side response to take advantage of global demand. A move towards faster integration with other Asian countries could potentially contribute to a continuation of the export-led growth process in the medium run.

Given the low growth in employment, the poor do not seem to be benefiting equally from the growth process. Effective implementation of direct intervention measures such as the NREG programme could be important steps towards an inclusive growth process. The targeted schedule to cover the whole country under NREG should not be delayed. Economic acceleration should help us to divert a part of the incremental income to poverty reduction programmes so that those not getting absorbed in productive employment created by the growth process are not left behind. Distributional conflict management by the state could play a crucial role in the success of reforms.

References

Ahluwalia, Isher J. (1991), *Productivity and Growth in Indian Manufacturing*, Oxford University Press, New Delhi.

Ahluwalia, Montek S. (2002), 'India's Vulnerability to External Crisis: An assessment', in M.S. Ahluwalia, Y.V. Reddy, and S.S. Tarapore (eds), *Macroeconomics and Monetary Policy—Issues for a Reforming Economy*, Oxford University Press, New Delhi.

Brooks, Douglas, David Roland-Holst, and Fan Zhai (2005), 'Growth, Trade and Integration: Long-Term Scenarios of Developing Asia', Asian Development Bank, Manila.

Chadha, G.K. (2003), 'Indian Agriculture in the New Mellennum', *Indian Journal of Agricultural Economics*, Vol. 58, No. 1.

Chand (2002), 'Indian Agriculture', *Indian Journal of Agricultural Economics*, Vol. 56, No. 2.

Dholakia, Bakul H. (2002), 'Sources of India's Accelerated Growth and the Vision of Indian Economy in 2020', *Indian Economic Journal*, Vol. 49, No. 4.

EPWRF (EPW Research Foundation) (2004), *National Account Statistics of India 1950-51 to 2002-03*, Fifth Edition, EPW Research Foundation, Mumbai.

International Monetary Fund (2005), *World Economic Outlook*, Washington, D.C

Kalirajan, K.P, R.T. Shand, and S. Bhide (2000), 'Economic Reforms and Convergence of Income across Indian States: Benefits for the Poor', in Shubhashis Gangopadhyay and Willima Wadhwa (eds), *Economic Reforms for the Poor*, Konark Publishers Pvt. Ltd., Delhi.

Kumar, Nagesh (ed.) (2004), *Towards an Asian Economic Community: Vision of a New Asia*, Research and Information System for Developing Countries, New Delhi and Institute for Southeast Asian studies, Singapore.

Mathur, Archana S. and Arvinder S. Sachdeva (2005), 'Customs Tariff Structures in India', *Economic and Political Weekly*, Vol. 39, No. 6.

Minsky, Hyman P. (1986), 'Stabilizing an Unstable economy', A Twentieth Century Fund Report, Yale University Press, New Haven and London.

Planning Commission (2006), 'Towards Faster and More Inclusive Growth: An approach Paper to the 11th Five Year Plan', (Draft), Government of India, New Delhi.

Rodrik, Dani and Arvind Subramanian (2004), 'Why India can Grow at 7 per cent a Year or More: Projections and Reflections', *Economic and Political Weekly*, Vol. 39, 17 April.

Ronald-Holst, David, Jean-Pierre Verbiest, and Fan Zhai (2005), 'Growth and Trade Horizons for Asia: Long Term Forecasts for Regional Change', Asian Development Bank, Manila.

Rosengrant, Mark W. and Robert E. Evenson (1995), 'Total Factor Productivity and Sources of Long-Term Growth in Indian Agriculture', EPTD Discussion Paper No. 7, International food Policy Research Institute, Washington, D.C.

Sen, Rahul, Mukul G. Asher, and Ramkishen S. Rajan (2004), 'ASEAN-India Economic Relations: Current Status and Future Prospects', *Economic and Political Weekly*, Vol. 39, No. 29.

Sen, Abhijit and Himanshu (2004), 'Poverty and Inequality in India', *Economic and Political Weekly*, Vol. 39, 18 and 25 September.

Sivasubramonian, S. (2004), *The Sources of Economic Growth in India 1950–1 to 1999–2000*, Oxford University Press, New Delhi.

Virmani, Arvind (2004), 'India's Economic Growth: From Socialist Rate of Growth to Bharatiya Rate of Growth', Working Paper No. 122, Indian Council for Research on International Economic Relations, New Delhi.

Winters, L. Alan, Neil McCulloch, and Andrew McKay (2004), 'Trade Liberalization and Poverty: The Evidence So Far', *Journal of Economic Literature*, Vol. XLII.

World Bank (2000), *Trade Blocks*, Oxford University Press, New York.

3

Crisis in Agriculture and Rural Distress in Post-Reform India

D. Narasimha Reddy • Srijit Mishra

INTRODUCTION

After more than half a century of planned economic development and high levels of aggregate growth over the last two decades, the Indian economy still remains predominantly rural. In 1999–2000, 72 per cent of population and 76 per cent of workforce in India were rural. In terms of overall growth, the last two decades have witnessed unprecedented high rates. What is puzzling is that high rates of growth, contrary to expectations, have been accompanied by a marked deceleration in the growth of urban share, from 1.1 per cent during 1981–91 to less than 0.8 per cent during 1991–2001. This is reflected in the slowing down of the growth of urban population from 3.2 per cent in the 1980s to 2.8 per cent in the 1990s (Sen 2003, pp. 479–80).

Rural India, however, was never closed or isolated but had its own dynamism and was on a steady path of articulation with the rest of the Indian economy and the world at large. Much of this transformation, during the post-independence period, was due to a series of development programmes where the state had a dominant protective as well as promotional role. However, during the last two decades, especially since the early 1990s, as a part of the neo-liberal wave of globalization aided by the revolution in information and communication technology (ICT), which has compressed time and space drastically, rural India too, somewhat rudely, has been exposed to the surge towards integration into the global market economy. This exposure, instead of lifting the rural economy, has been a cause of growing concern. In terms of the share in the national income and in the levels of living there have been growing rural–urban disparities during the 1980s and 1990s (Bhalla 2005). Within rural India, agriculture continues to still be the dominant occupation. There was hardly any substantial increase in the share of rural non-farm sector employment. This paper addresses the nature and causes of the unfolding agrarian crisis and rural distress.

This paper is divided into five sections. The first section brings out the fact that the Indian economy is still predominantly rural, with slow urbanization but growing rural–urban disparities in income and levels of living. Agriculture continues to be the most important economic activity in the countryside with a disproportionate retention of high share in the total workforce, but with a fast declining share in the national product. The second section deals with the structural changes in employment as well as land holdings. The agricultural sector evolves as the one with a preponderance of self-employed small farms in terms of land holdings and growing proportion of hired-casual labour, awaiting the spread of appropriate technology for a breakthrough towards improved productivity. The third section analyses the nature of economic reforms in the Indian agriculture and their impact on the farming community. The fourth section brings out the broad contours of agrarian crisis that manifests in the form of a series of suicides. The fifth section discusses reforms, rural stress and suicides and closes with a few reflections on a possible way out of this existing situation.

AGRARIAN STRUCTURE ON THE EVE OF ECONOMIC REFORMS

To understand the severity of impact of economic reforms on rural India we begin with an analysis of the changes in the basic agrarian structure and the nature of peasantry who are sucked into the vortex of market forces. An analysis of changes in the landholding structure (Reddy 2006a) reveals that: (i) there has been a general tendency of increase in the share of households and the area cultivated by small–marginal farmers, (ii) there has been a reduction in the share of holdings as well as the area cultivated by the large farmers, and (iii) the average size of holdings in all size-classes is on the decline. There has been a marginal increase, nonetheless, in the concentration ratios. The asset concentration would be much higher if non-land assets such as farm machinery and buildings are included. But, unlike the East-Asian small-farm agrarian structure where there is hardly any landlessness, the Indian situation shows a phenomenal increase in the 'near landless households'. Although rural landless households increased only marginally from about 10 per cent in 1970–1 to 11 per cent in 1991–2, if we include those households with less than about half an acre of land, which are referred to as 'near landless', along with the landless, their proportion has increased from about 30 per cent in 1970–1 to about 48 per cent—nearly half of the rural households by 1990–1 (Sharma 2000). These are the households, which constitute the vast and growing rural underclass.

If we consider all the households with about 10 acres (about 4 hectares) or more (medium and large holdings) as constituting the rich (!) peasantry, it is this class, which has emerged as the 'masters of the countryside'. Until 1970–1, there had been no substantive change either in the share of households or in the share of land operated. They still constituted 15 to 20 per cent of the households and held 60 to 65 per cent of the operational holdings. But in 1970–1, this group of rich peasantry had already emerged as a class which wielded power, not only in the countryside, but also acquired the capability to influence public policy, apparently to appease the masses; and at the same time, to manipulate the implementation of these policies to their own advantage. It is well-known that land reform legislation, particularly relating to land ceilings, had hardly any effect on the landholdings of the rich peasantry till the end of the 1960s. By the 1970s, when considerable political pressure called for effective legislation and implementation, the rich peasant class was well entrenched. Wherever land was emerging as an increasingly productive asset, both because of public investment and new technology, the land reforms were subverted with impunity. The ceiling surpluses were kept to the minimum, and the surplus land surrendered was often of very poor quality. Even with surrenders of sub-standard surplus land, the total ceiling surplus land redistributed to the poorer peasantry hardly constitutes about 2 per cent of the total cultivated land in India, in comparison to about 25 to 40 per cent in the case of East Asian countries. What is retained by the rich peasantry is not only better quality land but also the land, which became a better productive asset because of benefits of state investments in providing infrastructure such as irrigation and power facilities. This was also the land of the rich peasantry that was ready to receive the improved technology along with heavy doses of state subsidies.

Thus, when we refer to the top 15 per cent of the rural households operating about 50 per cent of the land, at the end of the 1960s a substantial proportion of this land was more productive land, while the small–marginal farmers constitute about 80 per cent of the households operating only about 40 per cent of the land, a substantial part of which was relatively low quality land. The gini ratios, or worsening nature of land concentration, in some of the states need to be read along with the qualitative differences in the land operated by the rich and the poor farmers. To return to land reforms, it was not until the 1970s, when the revised land ceiling legislative measures acquired a certain cutting edge, that there appeared a tendency towards a decline in the proportion of households as well as area held under the large peasant category. The tenancy legislation, which apparently had the objective of transferring land to the cultivator (with the exception of tenants under the *zamindars* and other intermediaries who became owners in 1950s), has never been near reaching this objective. The class character of the entire gamut of agrarian reforms in all its variations is best summed up as a classic instance of how the capitalist farmers were the net beneficiaries of both the ill-implemented and the well-implemented agrarian reform programmes (Rao 1992) till the 1980s. But by late the 1980s, the 'rich peasantry' as a class appears to have developed stakes elsewhere than agriculture. Agriculture for them served only as a political base but no longer as a source of their economic strength which came from contracts, commissions, commerce and speculative activities including real estate. The reform-induced withdrawal of the state in agriculture doesn't hurt this class that matters politically as much as it does those who are powerless. Part of this process is discussed in the next section.

REFORMS AND IMPACT ON THE FARMING COMMUNITY IN AGRICULTURE

Besides the economic reforms which overwhelmed the peasant stability, the roots of the present all pervading crisis in Indian agriculture can be traced back to the complacency and benign neglect of agriculture since the mid-1980s. Agriculture had fallen from policy priority under the euphoria that the country had left behind the days of shortages and achieved sustainable self-sufficiency in food grain production; that agriculture had reached a level of development where it could respond to the domestic market as well as global prices, if only the market restrictions were reversed; and that preferential and institutional interventions were anachronisms. But the worse deal had to wait till the 1990s when the reforms influenced every measure of public policy including agriculture at the behest of the Central Government, and were carried on with different degrees of zeal at the state level. The unfinished distributive land reforms were seen as obstacles to incentives, and liberal markets were expected to bring about technological breakthroughs. The result is a rapid decline of institutional support to agriculture based on well-deliberated principles of growth with equity. The evidence compiled here, both from the macro and micro levels, suggests that rapid retrogression in the public agricultural support systems is manifesting in unprecedented stress that has been causing the widespread health hazard of farmers' suicides.

Crisis in agriculture was well underway by the late 1980s and the economic reforms beginning in the 1990s have only deepened it. The crisis in agriculture in the post-reform period has become all pervasive. The manifestation of the crisis is felt in different forms in different agro-climatic and institutional contexts. For instance, the absence of irrigation facilities has forced farmers in dry regions to incur serious debts by investing in unstable groundwater resources, the growing pressure on land in command areas has resulted in rapid increase in the highly exploitative tenancy system. The volatile prices of commercial crops, including certain plantation crops, have suffered ruination because of the agricultural trade liberalization. The exposure to externally engineered crops with a hope of very high yields and with very scant regard of their suitability to domestic conditions has resulted in inappropriate technological practices that has meant severe loss of not only livelihoods but also resource degradation.

In 1991, when India officially went along the structural adjustment path and introduced a series of neo-liberal economic reforms, there was apparently not much explicitly by way of reforms in agriculture. But very soon, at least by mid-1990s when the World Trade Organization (WTO) was in place, there did unfold many policy reforms directly addressed to agriculture. Table 3.1 lists some of the important policy changes and measures of reform relating to Indian agriculture. International trade in agriculture has been liberalized. Beginning in 1997, all Indian product lines have been placed under the Generalized System of Preferences (GSP). By 2000, all agricultural products were removed from quantitative restrictions (QRs) and brought under the tariff system. Canalization of trade in agricultural commodities through state trading agencies was almost removed and most of the products brought under Open General Licensing (OGL). The average tariffs on agricultural products, which stood at over 100 per cent in 1990, were brought down to 30 per cent by 1997 and targeted to come down further.

Internally, the structural adjustment process initiated in 1991 at the behest of the International Monetary Fund (IMF), and pursued with the aid of the World Bank had far reaching implications for Indian agriculture. The single-minded pursuit of fiscal reforms had much greater effect on the agricultural input support system and institutions than even the provisions of the Agreement on Agriculture (AOA) of WTO. Much of the Green Revolution initiated in 1960s in India was built with a system of state-supported incentives or subsidies and public investment in agricultural infrastructure such as irrigation. The National Seed Corporation established in 1963, and later, a network of State Seed Corporations established since 1975 had virtual monopoly and responsibility of developing and distributing better and high yielding variety (HYV) seeds in collaboration with the agricultural universities. Though trade in seeds was opened to private trade in the 1980s, in 1991, 100 per cent foreign equity was allowed in the seed industry in India and restrictions on import of seeds were relaxed.

Fertilizer subsidy, which continues to be the major explicit agricultural incentive system directly funded by the Union Government of India, has been considerably reduced. Fertilizer subsidy, which amounted to 3.2 per cent of GDP and 6 per cent of the Union revenue expenditure in 1990–1, was reduced to 2.5 per cent and 5 per cent, respectively by 1997–8 (Acharya 2004, p. 67). It was further reduced to 0.69 per cent of GDP by 2003–4 (Sen and Bhatia 2004, p. 275). Low electricity charges for agriculture are an incentive system provided through state budgets. Since 1997, several state governments introduced power sector reforms at the behest of the World Bank loans, and increased power tariffs with the ultimate objective of cost recovery. As part of the reforms, the power sector was thrown open to private sector investment. Low water rates for irrigation have been yet another implicit incentive to farmers provided through the state budgets. Many states revised the water rates upwards with the objective of recovering operation and maintenance costs. Some states like Andhra Pradesh had announced a ban on investment in new major irrigation projects, unless the 'stakeholders' also contributed to part of the investment. The irrigation reforms included introduction of participatory water management through water users' associations (WUAs), which did not have much impact on the efficiency of utilization of irrigation water resources. A comprehensive study of the working of the

TABLE 3.1
Important Measures of Economic Liberalization in Indian Agriculture

Area of Liberalization	Policy Changes and Measures of Implementation
1. External Trade Sector	a. In tune with the WTO regime, since 1997 all Indian product lines placed in GSP. b. In 1998, QRs for 470 agricultural products dismantled. In 1999, further 1400 agricultural products brought under OGL and canalization of external trade in agriculture almost reversed. c. Average tariffs on agricultural imports reduced from 100 per cent in 1990 to 30 per cent in 1997. d. Though India is in principle against Minimum Common Access, but actually already importing 2 per cent of its food requirements.
2. Internal Market Liberalization	
(i) Seeds	a. Since 1991, 100 per cent foreign equity allowed in seed industry. b. More liberalized imports of seeds.
(ii) Fertilizers	a. Gradual reduction of fertilizer subsidies since 1991.
(iii) Power	a. Since 1997, power sector reforms were introduced at the behest of the World Bank in states such as Andhra Pradesh and power charges increased. b. Power sector opened to the private sector.
(iv) Irrigation	a. Water rates increased in some states. b. Participatory water management was sought to be introduced through water users' associations (WUAs). c. States such as Andhra Pradesh made new large irrigation projects conditional on 'stakeholder' contribution to part of investment.
(v) Institutional Credit	a. Khursro Committee and Narasimham Committee (1992) undermining the importance of targeted priority sector landing by commercial banks. b. The objectives of regional rural banks' (RRBs) priority to lending to weaker sections in rural areas diluted since 1997.
(vi) Agricultural Marketing	a. Changes in the provisions of the Essential Commodities Act. b. Relaxation of restrictions on the inter-state movement of farm produce. c. Model Agricultural Market Act. d. Encouragement of contract farming. e. Agricultural commodity forward markets.
3. Fiscal Reforms	a. Fiscal reforms with an emphasis on tax reduction and public expenditure turned to reducing fiscal deficit as priority (grave implications for public investment in agriculture and rural infrastructure).

Sources: Acharya (2004, p. 677); Chand (2006); Dorin and Jullian (2004, p. 206); and Vakulabharanam (2005, p. 975).

WUAs in Andhra Pradesh concludes that though a substantial amount of money was spent on the reform process, money was used mainly for improving the ailing irrigation systems rather than strengthening formal institutional structures. Contrary to the expectations, political involvement dominates their functioning. There is little devolution of powers to WUAs, as most important functions like assessments, collection of water charges, and sanctioning of works remain with the irrigation departments (Reddy and Reddy 2005).

Even at the risk of repetition, it must be emphasized that a substantial proportion of the Indian agriculture is a 'small farm' based economic activity,[1] which is increasingly moving from a system of farmers' own-resource-based subsistence farming to purchased-input-based intensive commercial farming. Further, since small farmers' own resources are much too meager, timely and assured credit at reasonable interest rates has become a critical input in Indian agriculture. In the face of inadequacy or non-functioning of agricultural co-operatives, part of the radical banking reforms of the 1960s in the form of 'social control', and later by way of bank nationalization, were aimed at increasing the flow of institutional credit to agriculture by prioritizing lending to this sector. But beginning with 1991, at the behest of pressures from the reform agenda, 'targeted priority lending' or 'directed credit' to agriculture

---

[1] As per the situation assessment survey of farmers, NSS 59th Round (2003), distribution of farmer households by size of land possessed suggests that a little more than one per cent are near-landless (less than 0.01 hectare), 64 per cent are marginal (0.01–1.00 hectare), 18 per cent are small (1.01–2.00 hectares), 11 per cent are semi-medium (2.01–4.00 hectares), 5 per cent are medium (4.01–10 hectares) and the remaining one per cent are large (more than 10.00 hectares).

was put on the back burner. The Narasimham Committee on Financial Reforms (1992) recommended the dilution of priority sector lending, including lending to the agricultural sector by the commercial banks. Though for political reasons, there was no explicit policy of removing priority lending to agriculture, the insistence on adherence to commercial performance placed a severe constraint on bank credit to agriculture, with disastrous consequences. Instead of an expansion in rural bank branches, there was actually closure of such branches, which declined from 34,867 in 1990 to 32,386 in 2003 (Rao 2004b). The regional rural banks (RRBs), which were meant for lending specifically to 'weaker sections', were opened to all on commercial principles, with upward revision of interest rates (Rao 2004a).

The economic reforms in Indian agriculture intensified the process of public as well as private resource crisis brewing from the mid-1980s. Gross capital formation (GCF) in Indian agriculture declined drastically. The public sector GCF in agriculture declined to one-third in 1999–2000, of the level in 1980–1 (Reddy 2006b). Contrary to expectations, the reform measures did not stimulate much increase in private investment. On the contrary there was deceleration of growth of private investment in agriculture (Sen 2003) and as a result, the overall GCF in agriculture as a share of total capital formation in the country, declined by almost half, during the period, from 13.1 per cent to 7.4 per cent. The proportion of Plan expenditure on agriculture and allied activities declined from 6.1 per cent to 4.5 per cent (Table 3.2). Further, there was a drastic reduction in the share of developmental expenditure on rural development from 11.7 per cent of the GDP in 1991–2 to 5.9 per cent in 2000–1 (Gupta 2005, p. 5). One of the severe consequences of the reforms, as mentioned earlier, was felt in the provision of institutional credit to agriculture.

TABLE 3.2
Capital Formation and Plan Expenditure in Agriculture

Year	GFCF in agr. as percentage of GDP	GFCF in agr. as percentage of total GFCF	Exp. on agr. and allied as percentage of total plan exp.
1980–5, Sixth Plan (actuals)	3.1	13.1	6.1
1985–92, Seventh Plan (actuals)	2.3	9.6	5.9
1992–7, Eighth Plan (actuals)	1.9	7.4	5.1
1997–2002, Ninth Plan (actuals)	1.6	7.4	4.5

Note: GFCF indicates gross fixed capital formation, GDP indicates gross domestic product at factor cost, Exp. indicates expenditure, Agr. indicates Agriculture.
Source: Mishra (2006a).

Scheduled commercial banks' share of credit to agriculture declined from 18 per cent in December 1987 to 11 per cent by March 2004 (Shetty 2006). A study of credit from formal institutional sources shows that between 1980–1 and 1999–2000, agricultural sector's share of short–term credit declined from 13.3 per cent to 6.1 per cent. During the same period, agriculture's share in terms of lending declined from 16.9 per cent to 8.3 per cent (Rao 2002). The acceleration in the decline in share of much needed long–term credit for investment was witnessed since the early 1990s. The number of agricultural loan accounts in scheduled commercial banks that had reached a peak of 27.7 million by March 1992 declined to 20.3 million by March 2002 and was at 21.3 million by March 2004 (Shetty 2006). The worst sufferers of the formal institutional resource crunch have been the small borrowers, mostly small farmers. Beginning with the early 1990s, especially since 1993, the small borrowers' share in bank credit declined steeply from 21.9 per cent in 1992 to 7 per cent in 2001 (Rao 2002). This doesn't mean that small farmers' needs have gone down or that small farmers were restrained from borrowing. It only means that small farmers were forced to borrow from non-institutional sources such as moneylenders, fertilizer and pesticide dealers and friends and relatives. The interest charges of these informal sources are disproportionately high compared to institutional credit.

A recent nation wide survey (NSS 59th Round, Report 498, 2005) also brings out the grave agrarian situation in terms of farmer indebtedness. Almost 50 per cent of the farming households are indebted, but the proportion is much higher in states like Andhra Pradesh (82.0 per cent), Tamil Nadu (74.5 per cent), Punjab (65.4 per cent), and Kerala (64.4 per cent), which are also states with relatively higher investment. More than 50 per cent of the borrowing is for investment in agriculture, but it is much higher in Andhra Pradesh (77 per cent), Karnataka (73 per cent), and Maharashtra (83 per cent). Institutional sources account for about 50 per cent on an average, but it is much lower at 30 per cent in states like Andhra Pradesh, where the remaining 70 per cent comes from informal sources.

There has been a steep increase in the costs of farming across the country, which is substantially due to the reforms. The fertilizer price index increased from 99 in 1990–1 to 228 in 1998–9 at a compound annual growth rate of 11 per cent (Acharya 2004, p. 73). And one estimate, across the crops and country, suggests that fertilizers presently account for 29 per cent of farmers' input costs (Acharya 2004, p. 78). There have also been increases in the water charges in many states. One of the often cited reasons for agricultural trade liberalization is that it provides access to higher prices in the global markets. However, there has actually been a decline in global prices of some of the agricultural commodities such as rice and cotton for which India enjoyed comparative advantage. Before 1998–9, the Indian domestic lint prices were lower than world prices and India was an exporter of cotton. With the removal of QRs and with the recent fall in the global cotton prices, India has turned into an importer of cotton, which has depressed domestic prices of cotton and has been the cause of serious losses to cotton farmers (Vakulabharanam 2005). According to one estimate, most of the global agricultural commodity prices in 2002 were lower than those in 1994, and particularly cotton prices were 30 per cent lower (Vakulabharanam 2005). Farm business income (FBI), the difference between the value of output produced and the costs actually paid out, which was on the rise in the 1980s, started declining in the 1990s. The growth of FBI per hectare decelerated from 3.21 per cent in 1980s to 1.02 per cent in the 1990s. The growth of real FBI per cultivator declined from 1.78 per cent in 1980s to 0.03 in 1990s and in actual terms also it seems to have declined in the states of Andhra Pradesh, Bihar, Gujarat, Karnataka, Maharashtra, Orissa, and Rajasthan (Sen and Bhatia 2004).

Figure 3.1 shows the steep rise in cost of living in rural areas as indicated by the CPI for agricultural labour (CPIAL) while the farmers' income languishes. This is a familiar scissors crisis in agriculture often resulting in pauperization of the peasantry. This has also resulted in widening of disparities between agricultural and non-agricultural incomes (see Table 3.3). The disparities have doubled over the last two and a half decades, leaving agriculture way behind.

In 2002–3, the average returns from cultivation per hectare in India were Rs 6756 in *kharif* and Rs 9290 in *rabi* (Appendix 3.1). From the total farmer households, 86 per cent with an average land size of 1.2 hectares and 62 per cent with an average land size of 0.9 hectare cultivated during kharif and rabi, respectively. For all farm households in India, cultivation accounts for 74 per cent of their returns (value of output minus paid out expenses), farm animals contribute 7 per cent, and the remaining 19 per cent is from non-farm business. Overall, there is not much diversification and the income of an average farmer household would hardly suffice to meet basic day-to-day requirements. Paid out expenses as a percentage of value of output are about 44 per cent in kharif and 42 per cent in rabi. This is likely to be higher if one includes imputed family labour or excludes output used for domestic consumption. There is wide inter-state variation. Compared to the national average,

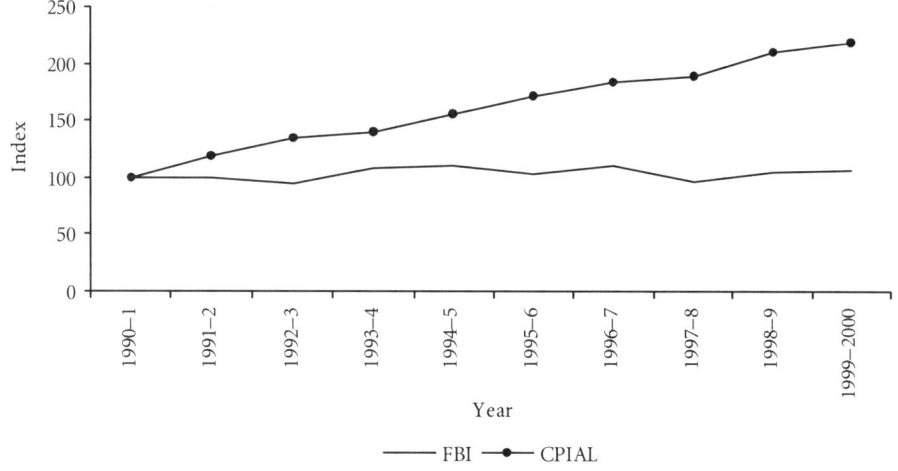

Sources: Government of India (2005) and Sen and Bhatia (2004, p. 241).

Figure 3.1: Indices of FBI and CPIAL

TABLE 3.3
Per Worker Income in Agriculture and Non-agriculture Sectors in India

(1993–4 prices)

Period	Income Per Worker (rupees)		Ratio of Non-agriculture to Agriculture	Growth Rates in the Last Decade (per cent)	
	Agriculture	Non-agriculture		Agriculture	Non-agriculture
1978–9 to 1983–4	9961	28,430	2.85	–	–
1988–9 to 1993–4	11,179	39,355	3.52	1.16	3.31
1998–9 to 2003–04	11,496	59,961	5.22	0.28	4.30

Source: Chand (2006).

one observes relatively lower returns per hectare and greater share of expenses in the states of Andhra Pradesh, Gujarat, Haryana, Karnataka, Maharashtra, Madhya Pradesh, Orissa, Rajasthan, and Tamil Nadu during kharif. This could be indicative of high costs or crop failure. Share of expenses to the value of output is less than 30 per cent in most of the hilly states: Himachal Pradesh, Jammu and Kashmir, Jharkhand, the North-eastern states, and Uttaranchal, indicating that dependence on market based inputs could be much lower here. Besides, some pattern could be hidden because the calculations are aggregated across all crops.

A case study of a farmer owning eight acres of unirrigated land in Yavatmal suggests the following. In 2004, he cultivated cotton on five acres, he had to go in for a second sowing due to delay in rain. This led to an increase in seed expenses, but the expenses incurred in the second instance were reduced by half by using for a different variety and using some leftover seeds.[2] The total expenditure on seed was Rs 7500. After including expenditure on fertilizer (Rs 5000), pesticides (Rs 3000), and labour (Rs 2000) his total costs were Rs 17,500. He got a produce of 15 quintals, which he sold to the Maharashtra State Co-operative Cotton Growers Marketing Federation (MSCCGMF) through the Monopoly Cotton Procurement Scheme (MCPS). At the time of the survey, he had received Rs 1500 per quintal and was expecting another Rs 500 per quintal. After receiving this balance amount his net income will be Rs 12,500. The remaining three acres, used for cultivating crops for consumption purposes, under a deficient rain did not give much return (Mishra 2006a). A good crop (say, 4 quintals of cotton per acre) would have taken this farmer above the poverty line, but now he is below the poverty line.[3] This depicts the transient state of poverty of even a semi-medium farmer household. The situation would be worse for marginal/small farmers who are likely to have lower access to credit from formal sources. A tenant farmer will also have additional costs in the form of rent. Further, because of lower volumes of produce or immediate cash requirement or non-legal status of tenancy, they may end up selling their produce to traders at a price lower than that prevailing in market centres. A slight dip in the price of produce will also have an adverse affect on their income.

Opening up of the economy has led to certain cash crops like cotton and pepper among others being exposed to greater price volatility. Excess international supply of cotton at a lower price is also because of direct and indirect subsidies, leading to dumping by the USA. Domestic policies in India have led to the removal of QRs and the subsequent reduction of import tariff from 35 per cent in 2001–2 to 5 per cent in 2002–3 has increased our vulnerability to the volatility of international prices. It is at this critical juncture when there is a greater need of price stabilization that the MCPS of Maharashtra has become non-functional. Disbanding of this scheme in 2005–6 has in fact led to a reduction of Rs 500 per quintal advance additional price that had in recent years acted as a cushion against the higher costs in the state. The Commission for Agricultural Costs and Prices estimates the cost of production for cotton in Maharashtra at Rs 2303 per quintal, but the all-India minimum support price for the long staple variety of fair average quality is only Rs 1980.

If one goes by the consumption expenditure based headcount estimates of poverty, one may not be in a position to perceive the stress on agricultural communities. However, if one looks at the undernourishment, the stress becomes apparent. Table 3.4 gives data separately on the number of

TABLE 3.4
Number of Poor and Undernourished Persons in Various Farm Categories in Rural India

(in million)

Year	Agricultural		Farm Classe									
			Marginal (<1 ha)		Small (1–2 ha)		Semi-medium (2–4 ha)		Medium (4–10 ha)		Large (>10 ha)	
	Poor	Under-nourished	Poor	Under-nourished	Poor	Under-nourished	Poor	Under-nourished	Poor	Under-nourished	Poor	Under-nourished
1983–4	44.6	33.7	131.2	98.0	41.1	25.8	29.5	18.0	15.0	9.2	2.8	1.9
1987	40.0	30.2	115.1	84.0	29.6	18.8	16.6	12.3	7.2	5.3	1.2	0.7
1993–4	39.5	39.2	123.5	105.5	26.7	24.7	15.0	12.4	8.4	7.4	0.8	1.0
1999–2000	36.5	42.8	95.2	122.0	16.4	28.7	8.5	18.7	3.2	10.3	0.0	0.7

Source: Kumar (2005, pp. 223–4).

[2] It is generally the case that for an acre of land, one packet of seeds (910 grams) costing around Rs 450 to Rs 500 for non-Bt varieties and Rs 1600 for legal Bt varieties would suffice (in 2006–7 agricultural season, due to a court judgement, price of legal Bt varieties has come down to about Rs 1250 per packet). However, due to a guaranteed germination rate of 65 per cent only, farmers end up sowing two instead of one seed and thereby increasing the seed requirement. Under assured water, such practices might reduce.

[3] Updating the Planning Commission poverty line for rural Maharashtra to 2004 one gets an income of Rs 4037 per person per annum (that is, Rs 336.45 per capita per month).

poor and undernourished persons in various farm categories in rural India. What is of significance is that even as the head-count of persons who are poor is coming down, there has been a spurt in the number of undernourished across all farming classes, especially in the 1990s. This clearly brings out the adverse impact of reforms on the health conditions of the farming community. Unfortunately, we do not have sufficient data that would capture undernourishment in terms of the health status of the farming community.

RURAL DISTRESS AND FARMERS' SUICIDES

In addition to the factors that manifest a situation of crisis in agriculture, there has been increasing pressure on the farmers in terms of meeting basic social services such as education and health, which are increasingly being privatized and which are becoming a considerable part of domestic expenditure needs. A combination of these stress factors has been at the root of the unusual phenomenon of farmers' suicides in rural India, especially since 1997. Though there are limitations of data on suicides, an attempt is made here to look into the nature of sources, the nature of data and, to the extent possible, use the same in understanding the crisis.

The main official source of data on suicide deaths is police records made available by the National Crime Records Bureau (NCRB), Ministry of Home Affairs, Government of India. The limitation of the annual data provided by the Bureau is the routine reporting of suicides, which may not reflect the current crisis in agriculture. Further, it is likely to be under-reported because the act is identified with shame and stigma and also because of a legal sanction against it.[4] Notwithstanding these limitations, attempts have been made to analyse the trends in mortality, suicide mortality and farmers' suicides at the district, state, inter-state, and national levels (Mishra 2006a, b, c, d, and Mohan Rao 2004).

The NCRB data are available from 1975 but profession-wise distribution is available only from 1995 onwards. Table 3.5 shows that even as the overall crude death rate (CDR) is coming down, suicide mortality rate (SMR) is on the rise for the country as a whole. Since most of the suicides are among male farmers, it would be interesting to focus on male SMR in India as well as on states reporting high incidence of farmers' suicides. Table 3.6 presents age-adjusted SMRs for India and selected states for the period 1975–2001. The male SMR is much higher than the overall SMR observed in Table 3.5. The rate of growth of male SMR is much higher in the 1990s than earlier. The male SMRs of Andhra

TABLE 3.5
Trends in CDR and SMR in India, 1981–2003

Year	CDR	SMR
1981	12.5	6.0
1982	11.9	6.5
1983	11.9	6.6
1984	12.6	7.0
1985	11.8	7.2
1986	11.1	7.2
1987	10.9	7.6
1988	11.0	8.1
1989	10.3	8.5
1990	9.7	8.9
1991	9.8	9.3
1992	10.1	9.3
1993	9.3	9.6
1994	9.2	9.9
1995	9.0	9.7
1996	9.0	9.5
1997	8.9	10.1
1998	9.0	10.8
1999	8.7	11.2
2000	8.5	10.8
2001	8.4	10.5
2002	8.1	10.5
2003	8.0	10.4
Growth rate	−2.1	2.6

Note: CDR is crude death rate: deaths per 1000 population; CDR estimates exclude Jammu & Kashmir from 1991 to 1995 and in 1997, Mizoram from 1991 to 1996 and Nagaland (rural) from 1995 to 2002; SMR is suicide mortality rate: suicide deaths per 1,00,000 population; Growth rates are linear trend estimates, b in $lnYt=a+bt$ (where t is time), calculated using CDR/SMR rounded off to the first decimal. Both the growth rates are statistically significant at 95% CI.

Source: CDR is from *www.indiastat.com* (accessed 12 June 2006) and SMR is from Mishra (2006d).

Pradesh and Maharashtra which were close to national average till late 1980s, started rising at much faster rates in 1990s. These are two of the four states which have reported the highest incidence of farmers' suicides since early 1990s. The other two states, Karnataka and Kerala which had much higher SMRs than the national average up to 1980s, show further rise in 1990s.

As observed earlier, profession-wise SMRs are available only from 1995. Figure 3.2 shows that SMR for male farmers has been rising steeply since 1995, while SMR for male non-farmers has been more or less stable especially since 1999. Table 3.7 shows the age-adjusted SMRs for all male population as well as SMRs for male farmers for India and the four states under discussion. For India as well as the three states other than Kerala, the gap between male SMRs

---

[4] Attempt to suicide is considered a criminal act as per the Indian Penal Code (IPC) 309. There have been court rulings calling for a humane perspective, but without legislative backing the statute remains.

TABLE 3.6
Age-adjusted Male SMR in India and Selected Indian States

Year	India	AP	Karnataka	Kerala	Maharashtra
1975	9.7	9.3	19.5	30.2	8.6
1976	8.7	11.3	16.4	23.9	9.0
1977	8.3	8.1	16.4	24.7	7.6
1978	8.4	7.5	18.6	24.0	7.1
1979	7.8	8.5	18.1	22.6	6.8
1980	8.0	4.5	20.9	23.0	6.1
1981	7.7	6.6	13.8	24.5	6.6
1982	8.4	6.9	18.9	28.2	7.6
1983	8.4	7.5	16.6	31.1	6.9
1984	8.9	7.9	16.7	33.3	7.7
1985	9.0	9.0	15.5	36.5	8.2
1986	9.0	8.4	14.8	36.2	8.8
1987	9.7	9.6	18.5	38.7	8.1
1988	10.4	9.8	21.2	41.4	9.8
1989	10.9	11.1	23.1	39.6	11.1
1990	11.5	11.3	24.5	43.2	12.7
1991	12.0	12.5	23.2	44.2	14.2
1992	12.0	12.5	23.2	44.2	14.2
1993	12.4	14.4	23.8	43.5	15.6
1994	12.8	12.8	26.0	46.3	15.2
1995	12.5	11.4	31.8	42.0	17.4
1996	11.9	13.3	24.8	40.2	16.0
1997	12.9	14.8	28.1	45.7	17.7
1998	13.8	16.6	30.0	47.4	18.9
1999	14.4	18.1	33.4	49.6	18.5
2000	14.2	17.4	32.2	47.4	19.6
2001	14.0	18.2	32.3	48.3	20.6
Growth rate	2.4*	3.6*	2.8*	3.1*	4.7*

Note: Age-adjusted SMR is suicides per 1,00,000 population of 5 years and above, as suicide is medically not defined for the 0–4 population.
Source: Mishra (2006c).

in general and male farmer SMRs has been on the rise. There was a decline in this gap in Karnataka in 2004. In Kerala, the gap was very high and it started further widening since 1997, though there was a decline in 2001 and again in 2004.

Regression and correlation results based on cross-sectional data of 1995 for 19 states in the country show that the rate of suicides of farmers is more in areas with favourable ratio of area to holdings among small farmers, higher rate of suicide in the general public, high per centage of deaths due to economic bankruptcy, and higher proportion of area under non-food crops. The results also show that farmer suicides are higher in areas with predominance of small holdings, minor irrigation, low share of bank credit to rural areas, and low share of priority sector advances to agriculture. In this connection, the negative association between area under cotton and share of rural credit in total credit also deserves attention (Mohan Rao 2004).

The second, and more widely used source of data, is press reports, particularly from 1997, which are based on suicides specific to farming related causes. The data based on press reports may have an element of over-emphasizing the failure of institutional facilities because of linking it to all suicide deaths by farmers Nonetheless studies such as the one by Mohan Rao (2004) do provide some insights into this issue. Mohan Rao made a content analysis of 337 media reports and brought out economic causes as the dominant factor for the suicides of farmers in Andhra Pradesh. Among the economic factors, indebtedness, crop failure, and lower prices are prominent though higher rates of interest and liberalization also figured. Among the non-economic causes, harassment from creditors particularly input dealers and

Note: SMR for farmers is based on interpolated/extrapolated population for cultivators using 1991 and 2001 census. For details, see Mishra (2006c).
Source: NCRB, Various Years.

Figure 3.2: SMR for Male Farmers and Non-farmers in India, 1995–2004

TABLE 3.7
Age-adjusted SMR for Male Population and for Male Farmers

Year	India		Andhra Pradesh		Karnataka		Kerala		Maharashtra	
	All	Farmers	All	Farmers	All	Farmers	All	Farmers	All	Farmers
1995	12.5	9.7	11.4	13.6	31.8	33.7	42.0	127.6	17.4	14.7
1996	11.9	12.3	13.3	24.4	24.8	30.9	40.2	109.4	16.0	23.5
1997	12.9	12.7	14.8	17.5	28.1	31.3	45.7	138.9	17.7	23.9
1998	13.8	14.8	16.6	28.8	30.0	30.1	47.4	172.9	18.9	29.0
1999	14.4	15.3	18.1	30.1	33.4	41.4	49.6	182.5	18.5	30.6
2000	14.2	15.7	17.4	22.8	33.2	43.5	47.4	184.7	19.6	37.3
2001	14.0	16.2	18.2	25.6	32.3	44.5	48.3	161.8	20.6	44.1
2002	14.3	18.1	21.2	31.7	32.6	41.6	50.5	258.3	20.3	47.3
2003	14.2	17.5	20.7	28.5	33.2	48.2	48.5	297.6	20.6	50.8
2004	14.4	19.2	24.7	44.5	31.2	35.4	45.8	183.0	20.3	57.2

Note: As in Table 3.6.
Source: NCRB, Various Years, as in Mishra (2006c).

moneylenders emerged as a major factor, though spurious inputs, overuse of pesticides, and erratic power supply also figured. Next in order are institutional factors namely the lack of institutional credit, limited purchases by Andhra Pradesh State Co-operative Marketing Federation Limited (MARKFED) and Cotton Corporation of India (CCI). Among the natural factors, inadequate rainfall during sowing season and heavy rainfall at the time of harvest figured prominently.

The third source is the official data released by the state governments, but this suffers from underestimation because it is strictly linked to compensation paid by the government departments. Official scrutiny is often known to treat even genuine instances of suicide as arising out of disease or old age or some other reason, with a view to restricting the payment of compensation. On 10 April 2006, the Union Ministry of Agriculture convened a meeting of Chief Ministers and Agriculture Ministers from the four states that have been reporting high incidence of suicides. Statistics relating to farmers' suicides during five years 2001–2 to 2005–6 were released. Officially the total number of suicides during the period are reported as 5910 in Karnataka (Karnataka disputed it as an overestimate), 1835 in Andhra Pradesh (AP disputed it as underestimate and corrected it to 2035), 981 in Maharashtra, and 201 in Kerala (*The Hindu*, 11 April 2006), but these are much lower than the NCRB data which indicates that between 2001 and 2004 there were more than 35,000 suicide deaths by farmers in these four states and nearly 70,000 for the country as a whole.

Notwithstanding these limitations, the available data on suicides do indicate their links to the impact of reforms on small-farmer Indian agriculture, and the resulting rural stress. Although, it is not an exemplar methodology for social science researchers to visit the households of the suicide victims with an investigative zeal, particularly when the households realize that these investigators are not empowered to recommend compensation, still many small sample-based studies of the households of suicide victims do exist, to which we shall return in the next section. Though suicides are reported from many parts of the country, the magnitude varies.

The available evidence thus tends to show that the farming community is passing through a particularly high stress situation during this high growth reform period. Though the specific and immediate triggers may vary from region to region, the overall macroeconomic context is the one of structural adjustment and trade liberalization. The evidence available from the states emphasizes the reform induced stress. In Andhra Pradesh, declining public investment in irrigation and unavailability of credit from institutional sources meant heavy investment in digging of bore-wells by borrowing from informal sources at a higher interest burden (AWARE 1998; Citizen's Report 1998; RSC 1998; Shiva et al. 2000). This search for water led to a fall in the water table and the expected returns from agriculture did not come about, resulting in debt burden that threatened the individual's self-respect. An enterprising hard working farmer is now identified as someone who is reneging on contracts—he cannot repay his loans. It is the government sponsored mission on oilseeds that led to shifts in cropping pattern shifts in expectation of higher returns (Vidyasagar and Chandra 2004). This not only reduced the farm-based risk mitigation available from multiple cropping cultivation in dry regions but the recent developments in liberalizing imports has also led to a crashing of domestic prices and returns even during normal times. The study further notes that 55 per cent of farmers in the state do not get minimum support prices (MSP). The worst affected are the marginal, small, and even medium farmers who do not get the MSP because of their dependence on traders for credit at high rates of interest, along with a system where they are tied up with sale of output to the trader at prices lower than the MSP. A study by Bhushan and Reddy (2004), based on a survey of suicide households, indicates that the households had taken to mono-cropping of input-intensive, non-food, commercial crops and even leased in land, but the crops failed due to inadequate water. Another study (Rao and Suri 2006) points out that increasing costs and low returns add to the crisis and this has come about because of neo-liberal policies which are, in turn, a consequence of loss of power of the farming community resulting in their removal from the policy making process.

The rain dependent cotton growing farmers of Vidarbha in Maharashtra are faced with declining profitability because of dumping of cotton in the global market by the USA, low import tariffs, failure of MCPS, and withdrawal of supporting state investment and subsidies (Mishra 2006a). Another study of suicides of farmers in the same region of Maharashtra in the Durkheimian framework also observes that lower and middle caste peasant smallholders found themselves trapped between enhanced aspirations generated by land reform and other post-1947 measures, and the reality of neo-liberalism reflected in rising debt and declining income (Mohanty 2005).

The global exposure of the plantation-based farmer in Kerala also led to crisis situations because of depressed world prices (Nair and Menon 2004). A study on farmers' suicides in Kerala concludes that farmers' distress over the past one decade is closely linked to the neo-liberal policy regime in the 1990s. 'The association between the two is more in the regions of the state which are heavily dependent on export-oriented crops, such as coffee and pepper' (Mohanakumar and Sharma 2006). In drought prone Karnataka, it is the liberal imports of edible oil, exposure to fluctuating agricultural commodity markets, and decline in public investment and state support systems to agriculture that triggered suicides (Assadi 1998; Deshpande and Nagesh Prabhu 2005; Vasavi 1999; and Vidyasagar and Chandra 2004).

REFORM-LED GROWTH, SMALL PEASANT ADJUSTMENT COST, AND THE NEED FOR STATE SUPPORT

It would be futile to explain away the manifestation of agrarian distress as psychological aberrations of the farming community. Failure of certain social institutions does serve as a contingent factors to an extent, but does not explain the present distress entirely. There are questions which bring in the social dimensions from the Durkheimian analysis of suicides (Durkheim 2002/1897). The spread of neo-liberal values and highly rationalized individual relations call for attention to the growing alienation and social disintegration in rural areas. The failure of the village as a social community and the growing disintegration of the joint family as a protective and supportive collective also calls for closer analysis.

But the much larger question is whether small–marginal farming is sustainable without substantial public infrastructure support and comprehensive social security including health, education, employment, and old age support? Even at the early stages of the structural adjustment programme (SAP) there was a clear warning that neo-liberal reforms would face adjustment among poor farmers, which without assistance from the state, would intensify their suffering (Cornia et al. 1987). By and large, the incidence of suicides has been higher among small–marginal farmers moving from subsistence agriculture to the high value crops with a strong motivation to improve their social and economic status. They are indeed risk-taking small agricultural entrepreneurs whose success would be the basic premise for the transformation of rural India towards better and equitable incomes and livelihoods. To sum up, 'farmers' distress is not due to lack of agricultural growth but paradoxically due to enterprising qualities of farmers who pursue growth and even achieve it in good measure. But, drought-prone environment and non-caring policy regime turn those who bring growth into victims' (Rao and Gopalappa 2004).

Recognizing growing disparities between the agricultural and non-agricultural sectors and deterioration of the quality of the public services in rural India, Vaidyanathan (2006) calls for a radically different approach to make the farm sector improve its growth performance. It is a cruel paradox that the state is agriculturally self-sufficient, and the policy makers have designs and dreams about high export growth of agricultural commodities including foodgrains, but farmers who are the architects of these surpluses are allowed to die due to distress. What is needed is a caring policy but what exists is exposure to predatory market forces instead. There is increasing evidence that there cannot be rural development, even in relatively prosperous regions like Andhra Pradesh and Punjab, without high agricultural growth. Nor is there any instance in the world of dry land farmers moving to high productivity agriculture in the face of gross exposure to volatile market forces. There is no instance of small–marginal farmers earning adequate livelihood without appropriate social security and economic support or without succour provided by supplementary non-farm employment. Small–marginal farmers in dry regions are the most vulnerable but least cared for in the economic reforms framework. It is policy neglect that has been forcing these farmers to shoulder all the costs and risks of high investment, including land and water resource development (with borrowed capital at usurious interest rates). They have lifted the states' agriculture to relatively better productivity agriculture at a cost that they can ill afford.

These costs are the costs of transition of agriculture in the state from subsistence levels to higher productivity. These costs are necessarily social costs, which should not be compounded on to the shoulders of the distressed peasantry. The state has to own up to the responsibility for these social costs of investment in the development of land and water (including groundwater) resources, provision of adequate economic support by way of institutional credit, extension, supply of quality inputs, and remunerative prices as well as social sector support of ensuring quality education and health facilities in the countryside. There is incontrovertible evidence that agricultural growth driven by improved productivity of small–marginal farmers would result in much more equitable distribution of income, augmentation of effective demand with its spread effects on non-farm sector, and would be more sustainable as well. The essential condition is the need for a policy shift from the mindless neo-liberal market centred reforms to building of economic and social support systems to make small–marginal farming, especially in dry regions, viable, and to ensure that these farmers are protected against exposure to distress due to vagaries of domestic and global market forces.

References

Acharya, S.S. (2004), 'Fertilizer Subsidy in Indian Agriculture: Some Issues' in Bruno Dorin and Thomas Jullien (eds), *Agricultural Incentives in India: Past Trends and Perspective Paths Towards Sustainable Development*, Manohar, New Delhi and Centre de Sciences Humains, pp. 67–82.

Assadi, Muzaffar (1998), 'Karnataka: Farmers' Suicides—Signs of Distress in Rural Economy', *Economic and Political Weekly*, Vol. XXXIII, No. 14, 4 April, pp. 747–8.

AWARE (1998), *Farmers' Suicides in Andhra Pradesh*, AWARE, Hyderabad.

Bhalla, Sheila (2005), 'India's Rural Economy: Issues and Evidence', Working Paper No. 25, Institute for Human Development, New Delhi.

Bhushan, Shashi and T. Prabhakar Reddy (2004), 'A Moving into Poverty Syndrome: Debt and Differentiation in Small Farm Economies: A Casual Study of Farmers' Suicides in AP', Poverty and Social Analysis Monitoring Unit (PSAMU–SERP), Hyderabad, November, Mimeo.

Chand, Ramesh (2006), 'India's Agricultural Challenges and their Implications for Growth and Equity', Paper presented at Silver Jubilee Seminar on Perspectives on Equitable Development: International Experience and What can India Learn? Centre for Economic and Social Studies, Hyderabad.

Citizen's Report (1998), *Gathering Agrarian Crisis—Farmers' Suicides in Warangal District (A.P.) India*, Centre for Environmental Studies, Warangal, *http://www.artsci.wustl.edu/~stone/suicide.html*.

Cornia, G., R. Jolly, and F. Stewart (1987), 'Introduction' in G. Cornia, R. Jolly, and F. Stewart (eds) *Adjustment with A Human Face*, Vol.1, Clarendon Press, Oxford, pp. 1–8.

Deshpande, R.S. and Nagesh Prabhu (2005), 'Farmers' Distress: Proof Beyond Question', *Economic and Political Weekly*, Vol. XL, Nos 44–5, 29 October, pp. 4663–5.

Dorin, Bruno and Thomas Jullien (2004), 'The Product-Specificity of Indian Input Subsidies: Scope and Effects on Equity and Competitiveness' in Bruno Dorin and Thomas Jullien (eds), *Agricultural Incentives in India: Past Trends and Perspective Paths towards Sustainable Development*, Manohar, New Delhi and Centre de Sciences Humans, pp. 151–94.

Durkhiem, E. (2002, French 1897), *Suicides*, Routledge Classics, London.

Gupta, Smita (2005), 'The Crisis of Indian Agriculture under Neo-Liberal Policy', Working Paper No. 24, Institute for Human Development, New Delhi.

Government of India (2005), *Economic Survey 2004–5*, Ministry of Finance, New Delhi.

Kumar, Praduman (2005), 'Empowering the Small Farmers Towards a Food Secure India', in Ramesh Chand (ed.), *India's Agricultural Challenges: Reflections on Policy, Technology and Other Issues*, Centad, New Delhi, pp. 197–225.

Mishra, Srijit (2006a), *Suicide of Farmers in Mahrashtra*, Indira Gandhi Institute of Development Research, Mumbai, *http://www.igidr.ac.in/suicide/suicide.htm*.

——— (2006b), 'Farmers' Suicides in Maharashtra', *Economic and Political Weekly*, Vol. XLI, No. 16, 22 April, pp. 1538–45.

——— (2006c), 'Suicide Mortality Rates Across States of India, 1975–2001: A Statistical Note', *Economic and Political Weekly*, Vol. XLI, No. 16, 22 April, pp. 1566–9.

——— (2006d), 'Suicides in India: Some Observations', in K.S. Bhat and S. Vijaya Kumar (eds), *Undeserved Death: A Study on Suicide of Farmers in Andhra Pradesh (2000–5)*, Allied Publishers, New Delhi, pp. 93–113.

Mohan Rao, R.M. (2004), *Suicides Among Farmers—A Study of Cotton Growers*, Concept Publishing Company, New Delhi.

Mohanakumar, S. and R.K. Sharma (2006), 'Analysis of Farmer Suicides in Kerala', *Economic and Political Weekly*, Vol. XLI, No. 16, 22 April, pp. 1553–8.

Mohanty, B.B. (2005), 'We are Like the Living Dead': Farmer Suicides in Maharashtra, Western India', *The Journal of Peasant Studies*, Vol. 32, No. 2, April, pp. 243–76.

Nair, K.N. and Vineetha Menon (2004), 'Reforming Agriculture in a Globalizing World—The Road Ahead for Kerala', IP6 Working Paper No. 3, NCCR–North South, Swiss National Science Foundation, Berne.

NCRB (Various Years), *Accidental Deaths and Suicides in India*, Ministry of Home Affairs, Government of India, New Delhi.

NSSO (2005), *Situation Assessment Survey of Farmers: Indebtedness of Farmer Households*, NSS 59th Round (January–December 2003), Report No. 498 (59/33/1), Ministry of Statistics and Programme Implementation, Government of India, New Delhi.

Rao, P. Narasimha and K.C. Suri (2006), 'Dimensions of Agrarian Distress in Andhra Pradesh', *Economic and Political Weekly*, Vol. XLI, No. 16, 22 April, pp. 1546–52.

Rao, P.S.M. (2002), *Regional Rural Banks: Equity goals Versus Commercial Viability*, PhD Thesis, CESS and Dr B.R. Ambedkar Open University, Hyderabad.

———— (2004a), 'Weaker Sections' Rural Credit in India: A Post-reform Scenario', Mimeo.

———— (2004b), 'Growing Rural Indebtedness and Increasing Institutional Apathy', Mimeo.

Rao, V.M. (1992), 'Land Reform Experiences: Perspective for Strategy and Programmes', *Economic and Political Weekly*, Vol. XXVII, No. 26, 27 June, pp. A50–A64.

Rao, V.M. and D.V. Gopalappa (2004), 'Agricultural Growth and Farmer Distress: Tentative Perspectives from Karnataka' *Economic and Political Weekly*, Vol. XXXIX, No. 52, 25 December, pp. 5591–8.

Reddy, D. Narasimha (2006a), 'Changes in Agrarian Structure and Agricultural Technology: Is Peasant Farming Sustainable under Institutional Retrogression', in R. Radhakrishna, S.K. Rao, S. Mahendra Dev, and K. Subba Rao (eds), *India in a Globalising World: Some Aspects of Macroeconomy, Agriculture and Poverty, Essays in Honour of C.H. Hanumantha Rao*, Academic Press, New Delhi, 2006.

———— (2006b), 'Economic Reforms, Agrarian Crisis and Rural Distress', 4th Annual Prof. B. Janardhan Rao Memorial Lecture, Prof. B. Janardhan Rao Memorial Foundation, Warangal, Telangana.

Reddy, V. Ratna and P. Prudhvikar Reddy (2005), 'How Participatory is Participatory Irrigation? Water Users' Associations in Andhra Pradesh', *Economic and Political Weekly*, Vol. XL, No. 53, 31 December–6 January.

RSC (1998), *Farmers' Suicides in Andhra Pradesh: Report of the Peoples Tribunal*, Raithu Sahaya Committee, Hyderabad, July.

Sen, Abhijit (2003), 'Globalization, Growth and Inequality in South Asia: The Evidence from Rural India', in Jayati Ghosh and C.P. Chandrasekhar (eds), *Work and Well-being in the Age of Finance*, Tulika Books, New Delhi.

Sen, Abhijit and M.S. Bhatia (2004), *State of the Indian Farmer: A Millennium Study—Cost of Cultivation and Farm Income*, Vol. 14, Academic Foundation, New Delhi.

Sharma, H.R. (2000), 'Agrarian Structure and Agricultural Development in Rural India: Emerging Trends and Patterns', Man and Development, Vol. 22, No. 2, pp. 22–38.

Shetty, S.L. (2006), 'Monetary Policy and Financial Sector Liberalization', in *Macroeconomics of Poverty Reduction: India Case Study*, Report submitted to United Nations Development Programme, Indira Gandhi Institute of Development Research, Mumbai, April.

Shiva, V. A. H. Jafri, A. Emani, and M. Pande (2000), *Seeds of Suicide: The Ecological and Human Costs of Globalisation of Agriculture*, Research Foundation for Science, Technology and Ecology, New Delhi.

Vaidyanathan, A. (2006), 'Farmers' Suicides and the Agrarian Crisis', *Economic and Political Weekly*, Vol. XLI, No. 38, 23 September, pp. 4009–13.

Vakulabharanam, Vamsi (2005), 'Growth and Distress in a South Indian Peasant Economy During the Era of Economic Liberalisation', *Journal of Development Studies*, Vol. 41, No. 6, August, pp. 971–97.

Vasavi, A.R. (1999), 'Agrarian Distress in Bidar: Market, State and Suicides', *Economic and Political Weekly*, Vol. XXXIV, No. 32, 7 August, pp. 2263–8.

Vidyasagar, R and K. Suman Chandra (2004) *Farmers' Suicides in Andhra Pradesh and Karnataka*, National Institute of Rural Development, Hyderabad.

ANNEXURE 3.1

TABLE A 3.1
Returns Per Hectare and Expenses as Per Cent of Value of Output, 2002–3

States	Kharif				Rabi			
	Farmer households cultivating (per cent)	Average cultivated land per cultivating household, hectares	Gross returns per hectare (rupees)	Paid out expenses as per cent of value of output (rupees)	Farmer households cultivating (per cent)	Average cultivated land per cultivating household (hectares)	Gross returns per Hectare (rupees)	Paid out expenses as per cent of value of output (rupees)
Andhra Pradesh	81.7	1.2	5243	62.3	39.1	0.9	7815	52.8
Arunachal	74.8	1.3	13909	13.5	68.4	0.8	8433	22.1
Assam	95.9	0.8	16257	12.7	84.7	0.4	16089	19.0
Bihar	87.0	0.7	8065	39.6	95.2	0.6	10180	37.8
Chattisgarh	98.6	1.3	5355	39.2	26.9	0.8	4296	39.4
Gujarat	85.2	1.6	6005	46.8	39.3	1.2	8621	49.3
Haryana	64.1	1.6	5832	56.9	64.0	1.6	14537	40.7
Himachal Pradesh	97.1	0.5	16432	28.2	94.6	0.4	5377	50.8
Jammu & Kashmir	94.7	0.7	28445	17.7	84.9	0.6	10833	26.8
Jharkand	96.9	0.7	10420	21.1	41.8	0.3	14117	28.1
Karnataka	95.1	1.5	6522	46.0	47.1	1.3	6536	36.6
Kerala	93.6	0.4	17724	38.8	94.5	0.4	18220	34.1
Maharashtra	94.4	1.6	6609	45.0	45.2	1.1	5505	47.9
Manipur	84.3	0.6	16697	28.2	51.3	0.2	6682	41.9
Meghalaya	99.5	1.0	22860	18.1	96.1	1.3	11082	17.9
Mizoram	90.9	1.0	18905	3.8	89.3	1.1	14823	3.5
Madhya Pradesh	77.3	1.6	3882	45.3	67.3	1.7	7305	35.8
Nagaland	91.2	0.5	29592	7.2	96.3	0.3	17578	17.1
Orissa	98.1	0.8	3633	48.1	25.2	0.4	5284	50.9
Punjab	36.9	2.5	19974	38.4	27.6	2.6	20929	37.5
Rajasthan	91.3	1.9	271	89.0	37.0	1.4	10954	40.5
Sikkim	98.9	0.7	11807	22.3	97.6	0.4	7275	33.8
Tamil Nadu	79.1	0.8	6682	57.9	44.1	0.8	8562	45.1
Tripura	91.3	0.5	15333	30.5	62.7	0.3	17500	31.0
Uttar Pradesh	81.8	0.7	7025	44.1	87.8	0.9	8490	46.0
Uttaranchal	93.1	0.5	36646	11.9	93.0	0.4	8914	28.0
West Bengal	89.7	0.5	10942	44.6	71.0	0.4	10976	57.2
Group of UT	77.0	0.7	12528	35.8	47.4	0.6	15322	33.3
All India	86.2	1.2	6756	43.9	62.3	0.9	9290	42.2

Note: Gross returns equal value of output minus paid out expenses; Expenses exclude imputed expenditure on family labour and value of output includes amount used for domestic consumption.

Source: Calculated from unit level data using 33rd Schedule, 59th round, NSS (2003) on 'Situation Assessment Survey of Farmers'.

4

Employment and Unemployment Since the Early 1970s

T.N. Srinivasan

INTRODUCTION

An overwhelming majority of India's population depend on their own labour as the dominant source of livelihood, through its productive use, either in self-employment or in work for others. Labour and issues such as employment, productivity, and wages have been at the centre of attention in pre- and post-independence plans for national development. Sadly, the available employment and unemployment data from various sources in India are inadequate to document the trends in employment since planning for national development began in 1950.

Two of the main sources of data on workers and their distribution across economic activities in the economy as a whole are the decennial population censuses (PC) and the Employment and Unemployment Surveys (EUS) of the National Sample Survey Organization (NSSO). Other sources include the Directorate General of Employment and Training (DGET) which publishes data on the organized part of the economy under its Employment Market Information (EMI) Programme. The Annual Survey of Industries (ASI) conducted by the Central Statistical Organization (CSO) is another source of employment data. With some exceptions and changes over time, its coverage is restricted to the establishments listed as factories under Sections 2m (i) and 2m (ii) of the Factories Act of 1948.

Another important source is the Economic Census, initiated in 1977 as a countrywide census of all economic activities (except crop production and plantation) and followed by detailed sample surveys of unorganized segments of different sectors of the non-agricultural economy in a phased manner during the intervening period of the two successive economic censuses. These 'Economic Census Follow-up Surveys', also called Enterprise Surveys (ESs), produce estimates of production, inputs, employment, factor income, and capital formation, etc.

The definitions used are not the same across all sources and have even varied over time within the same source, as in the PC. Also, some of the sources such as the Economic Census are of recent origin, while the PC goes back to 1881! The EUS was carried out by the NSSO in its 9th round (May–September 1955), also in the 17th–20th rounds for the urban sector, and again for rural and urban sectors in the 27th round (1972–3). Only from the 32nd round (1977–8) has the EUS formally become a part of the national quinquennial household surveys of the NSSO using essentially identical concepts of employment and unemployment. Apart from the large quinquennial surveys, the NSSO also

Samuel C. Park Jr Professor of Economics and Non-resident Senior Fellow, Stanford Center for International Development, Stanford University. I thank Treb Allen for his very able research assistance. Thanks are also due to Sheila Bhalla, S.R. Hashim, Amitabh Kundu, and John Pencavel for their comments on an earlier version. This paper draws extensively from Srinivasan (2006).

collects data annually from a smaller sample of households distributed over the same number of first stage units as its normal socioeconomic survey.

The estimates of employment and unemployment from the rounds other than quinquennial rounds in which EUS is conducted, particularly those meant for ESs, besides being subject to larger sampling errors because of smaller sample size (particularly at the state and regional levels), are suspected to be biased as well. It is suggested that in such rounds:

The selection procedure of first stage units is designed to produce efficient estimates of enterprise-related parameters or other households and individual characteristics. *As a result, the workforce estimates based on the data collected in these rounds are not only subject to higher sampling error but are also suspected to be biased owing to the lesser attention paid to the employment–unemployment component of the survey.* Nevertheless, from the data collected in these rounds, it is possible to generate distribution of workers over the activity-groups that deserve to be considered, albeit critically.

(NAD 2004, p. 10, emphasis added)

Since no concrete evidence has thus far been adduced in support of suspected biases in estimates from smaller-sample rounds, I will assume that there are no biases but only higher sampling errors in these estimates in the trend analysis in the second section. The coverage of sources of data other than PC and EU is limited either in geographical area or sectors or in other ways. The Economic Censuses and ESs exclude crop production and plantation activities in which a large proportion of the rural workforce is employed. Even in the PC and EUS, which are supposedly national in coverage, some states (Jammu and Kashmir and North-eastern states) have been excluded on occasion for various reasons, primarily civil disturbances and insurgencies.

The methods of coverage by PC and EUS differ as well. As noted earlier, the ASI covers only establishments registered under the Factories Act of 1948. DGET

covers all establishments in the public sector (except the defence establishments and armed forces) and those establishments in the private sector that employ 25 or more persons on the last day of the quarter under reference. Apart from this, since 1966, the establishments employing 10 to 24 persons are also covered on a voluntary basis.

(NAS 2004, pp. 11–12)

There are many other sources of partial data on employment, unemployment, wages, and other aspects of labour, which are based on reports required to be submitted by employers under various acts. The report of the National Commission of Labour (NCL) (the Second Labour Commission), has a comprehensive discussion of sources and limitations of labour statistics (NCL 2002). The very first Royal Commission on Labour in 1931 had already identified the need for reliable and representative data on labour.

There has been significant progress in the 75 years since the Royal Commission first reported the need for better labour market data such as the start of regular EUSs by the NSSO. Yet the NCL (2002) laments, 'We regret to say that the Labour Statistics as it stands today is not dependable. The industries do not have an obligation to submit the returns prescribed under the law. The collectors of data do not have any obligation to publish the data on time. In some cases there is a gap of more than 32 months in the publication of the data. Some state governments have a gap of 3 to 4 years before the data is released. As a result of this poor quality and unreliable frequency of data, policy makers do not find it easy to rely on them or make use of them', (NCL 2002, Chapter XII, Part IV, p. 28). I do not wish to underplay the importance of accurate and timely reporting by public agencies and of the need for incentives and penalties for non-compliance for those who are to provide the agencies with the data. However, many of the conceptual, measurement, and data gathering problems relating to labour statistics arise largely from the complexity of the Indian labour market.

From the employee or worker side, complexities arise from the fact that individuals (particularly females) frequently move in and out of the workforce within a year, and even those who participate in the workforce and are employed throughout the year could move from self-employment on their own farms in one season to wage employment in another season within the same year. Self-employment continues to be the single largest source of employment in the economy. Although the proportion of population living in households whose major source of income is self-employment declined from 55.6 per cent in 1987–8 to 50.9 per cent in 1999–2000 in rural areas, it increased slightly from 38.9 per cent to 39.2 per cent during the same period in urban areas (NSS 2001, Table 4.2). Also, an individual could be engaged in more than one economic activity at the same time or at different times in a year.

From the employer side, the situation is just as complex. A farmer employs workers not only from his/her own household but also hires agricultural labourers during peak agricultural season. The same farmer could be employed in casual work (or looking for such work) outside the farm during slack agricultural season. Outside of crop production activities, as the data from the latest economic census show, 98.6 per cent of the number of enterprises in existence in 2005 in the economy employed less than 10 workers.[1] In the earlier census of 1998, this proportion was similar at 98.1 per cent, accounting for 76.5 per cent of the number of

---

[1] GOI (2006). Strictly speaking, the data from the economic censuses refer to the *number of positions and not to workers*. Thus the same position could be held by different persons during a year.

usually working persons. A large majority (61.3 per cent) of the enterprises operated in rural areas. Also, 20 per cent of rural and 15.5 per cent of urban enterprises operated with no premises (GOI 2006). It is very unlikely that enterprises employing less than 10 workers would maintain written records of their activities. There is no way one could gather data on their employment, other than by canvassing such enterprises directly though a well-designed survey or census. This is indeed what an Economic Census and its follow up surveys attempt to do. However, as noted earlier, the census excludes a large share of the workforce employed in crop production activities.

Given the wide differences in their concepts and definitions and the extent of coverage among sources it should cause no surprise that it is virtually impossible to adjust for these differences and arrive at comparable estimates. The dissatisfaction with the then available PC and EUS statistics of unemployment led to the appointment by the Planning Commission of a committee of experts under the chairmanship of M.L. Dantwala (known as the Dantwala Committee) on Unemployment Estimates. The Committee submitted its report in 1970. The EUSs of NSSO have since adopted the committee's recommendations regarding concepts of employment and unemployment.

The focus of this paper is the EUS of the NSSO, since it is the only comprehensive source of data using the same concepts and methods of data collection over more than three decades. Importantly, compared to PC, NSSO data are available for many more years. My purpose is two-fold. First, I fit a simple trend regression to the data, from 27th Round (1972–3) to 61st Round (July 2004–June 2005) on persons (person-days) employed per 1000 persons (person-days), unemployed per 1000 persons (person-days) in the labour force, employment status and labour force participation rate per 1000 persons (person-days), taking into account that sample sizes in terms of the number of households of various rounds were different. Observations from each round are weighted by the square root of the sample size, thus placing greater importance on observations from the large quinquennial surveys (see the second section). The time trend analysis is meant to extract the time patterns in the data efficiently. Also, the estimation allows for possible serial correlation in the disturbance term in the regression equation, taking into account that the observations are not evenly spaced over time. It is important to stress that the friend analysis is not equivalent to a structural economic analysis of the labour market based on a model of labour supply and demand that brings in endogenous and exogenous determinants of both, including importantly variables capturing labour market policies and regulations.[2] Thus the trends are best viewed as trends in labour market equilibria in a loose sense. In the second section, it is pointed out that among the 12 regressions (male–female, rural–urban, and usual current weekly, and current daily statuses) on employment rate (that is, number of employed persons (person days) per 1000 persons (1000 person days)) only two, for rural and urban females using usual status, showed a significant downward trend. Six showed no significant trend and four showed a significant upward trend. Unemployment rate regressions also are consistent with these findings, with five showing a significant downward trend and only one (for rural males using usual status) showing an upward trend. These time patterns do not support the widespread belief that the economy has been experiencing what is often called 'jobless growth' since the reforms. Interestingly, the labour force participation rates showed a significant upward trend for rural males only, with significant downward trend in four cases and no significant trends in the remaining six cases.

Second, besides fitting time trends in the second section, I also analyse the time patterns of employment, unemployment, and being out of the workforce 'within the seven day reference period'. The observed time pattern enables an assessment of the belief that there is considerable churning in the labour market because 'the activity pattern of the population, particularly in the unorganized sector, is such that during a week, and sometimes, even during a day, a person, could pursue more than one activity. Moreover, many people could even undertake both economic and non-economic activities on the same day of a reference week' (NSS 2005, Report 506). If this is the case, we should observe that the distribution of the number of days within a week of a given activity status (employed, unemployed, and not in workforce) should be well dispersed. We shall see that this is not what we observe in general,[3] except for females. I offer some concluding remarks in the last section.

TRENDS IN EMPLOYMENT AND UNEMPLOYMENT RATES

Person and Person-Day Rates

Before describing the trends in employment and unemployment rates, I want to draw attention to the fact that the important distinction between the 'person rate' of usual

---

[2] To the best of my knowledge, no such general equilibrium model is available in the empirical literature. I return to this issue in the last section.
[3] In ongoing research in collaboration with Treb Allen, I fit a Markov transition model to the transition in status of employment (employed, unemployed and not in workforce) from one day to the next within the seven day reference period. We had transition data for the quinquennial rounds and not for other quinquennial rounds. Such data were not collected in the annual rounds yet preliminary findings from this research also broadly confirm this finding.

(US) and current weekly (CWS) status and the 'person-day rate' of current daily status (CDS), seems to have been ignored in the discussion of the employment issue in some of the official publications (Planning Commission 2001, 2002, 2005; MOF 2004).

In the EUS, a person could be in one or a combination of the following three broad activity statuses during the relevant reference period (year, week, or day): (i) 'working' (that is, being engaged in economic activity), (ii) 'unemployed' in the sense of not working, but either making tangible efforts to seek work or being available for work if work is available and (iii) 'not working and not available for work'. Statuses (i) and (ii) correspond to being in the workforce and status (iii) to being out of the workforce. It is possible for a person to be in all three statuses concurrently depending on the reference period. Under such a circumstance, one of the three was uniquely identified in the EUS as that person's status by adopting either the 'major time or priority criterion'. The former was used in identifying the 'usual activity status' and the latter for 'current activity status' (NSS 2005). More precisely, the principal usual activity status of a person among the three was determined as follows: first it was determined whether the person spent a major part of the year in or out of the workforce. Next, those who were in the workforce who spent a major part of their time during the 365 days preceding the date of survey in the workforce working (not working) were deemed as employed (unemployed) (that is, major time criterion). In addition to his or her principal activity in which a person spent a major part of his or her time, he/she could have pursued some economic activity for a relatively shorter time during the preceding year. This minor time activity was that person's subsidiary activity.

The CWS of a person during a period of seven days preceding the date of survey is decided on the basis of a 'certain priority cum major time criterion'. The status of 'working' gets priority over the status of 'not working but seeking or available for work', which in turn gets priority over the status of 'not working and not available for work'. A person is classified as 'working (employed)' while pursuing an economic activity, if he or she had 'worked for at least one hour during the seven day reference period'. A person who either did not work or worked for less than one hour is classified as 'unemployed' if he or she actively sought work or was available for work for any time during the reference week, even if not actively seeking work in the belief that no work was available. Finally, a person is classified as not in the workforce if he or she neither worked nor was available for work any time during the reference period. The CDS of a person was determined on the basis of his/her activity status in each day of the reference week using a priority-cum-major time criterion.[4]

Which of the three rates, namely 'usual status (principal and secondary capacity work combined)', 'weekly status', and 'daily status' should be used estimating the levels and trends in workforce or the number of unemployed? The first two of the three are 'person rates', that is, they refer to persons, for example, the number of persons employed or unemployed per 1000 persons in the population. The third is a person-day rate that is, it refers to the number of person days employed or unemployed per 1000 person-days. Thus, if a person in the sample was deemed to have worked (that is, been employed) for 3.5 days in the reference week, his employed person-days is 3.5 and total person-days is seven so that his employed person-day rate is 0.5, that is, 500 person days of employment in the week per 1000 person days. Averaging this daily rate over all persons and multiplying it by the population figures will yield the total number of person-days of employment per day.

The total number of person-days of employment is not the same as the total number of employed persons. The reason is that a given total number of person-days of employment could be distributed among the same number of persons in many ways so as to lead to different numbers of persons employed. For example, consider a four-person economy in which all four participate in the workforce and together they were employed for ten person-days in the week. This yields a person-day rate of employment of 10 out of 28 or 36 per cent. If the ten person-days are distributed in a way that one person is employed for seven days, another for three days and the remaining two are unemployed, then person-rate of employment is two out of four or 50 per cent. On the other hand, if it is distributed in a way that three persons work for three days each and one person works for just a day, the person rate of employment is four out of four or 100 per cent, given the priority given to the status of employment! Unfortunately, official publications ignore the distinction between persons and person-days, and possible heterogeneity among the population in number of days worked.

For example, MOF (2004, Table 10.7, p. 209) purports to present the number of persons in the workforce, employed and unemployed, using daily status rates that refer to person-days. Interestingly, at the top of the table, the phrase 'person-years' is used, suggesting that the numbers in the table refer not to persons but to person-years. Apparently, MOF wants to have it both ways!

---

[4] See sub-section 'Within reference week Distribution of Employment Status' for details.

Employment, Unemployment, and Employment Status: Time Trend Regressions

The following weighted regression was estimated from the data, taking into account that our data are unequally spaced in time.

$$\sqrt{n_t}\, E_t = \alpha \sqrt{n_t} + \beta t \sqrt{n_t} + \sqrt{n_t}\, u_t \qquad (4.1)$$

with $\dfrac{u_t}{\sqrt{n_t}} = \dfrac{\rho u_{t-1}}{\sqrt{n_{t-1}}} + \varepsilon_t \qquad (4.2)$

Where n_t: number of households canvassed in the round of period t;

E_t: employment rate, unemployment rate, or employment status;

u_t: random disturbance terms with expectation zero and variance

$$\frac{\delta^2}{n_t - (1-\rho^2)}$$

and ε_t: Independent and identically (over time) distributed random terms with mean zero and variance δ^2.

Since the various rounds covered different time spans (year, six months, etc.) and also different year types (calendar year, agricultural year (July 1–June 30) etc.), period t has been defined so that the interval between any two consecutive t is a year. Thus the slope coefficient β represents the annual rate of change in the expected value of E_t. There are only seven observations on person-day rates based on CDS. This fact has to be kept in mind in assessing the CDS regressions.

Employment

Table 4.1 gives the slopes of the regression (4.1) fitted to data on employment rates in Table A4.1. It is evident from the very high R^2 values that the linear time trend regressions fit the data very well, perhaps too well. The serial correlation coefficients are also generally high, suggesting significant persistence in the rates over time. Also, as expected, the trends for males and females are somewhat different. For males, regardless of the reference period (one year for US, a week for CWS, and a day for CDS) and of the concept (person rate for US and CWS and person-day rate for CDS) used, 'there was no statistically significant

TABLE 4.1
Employment Rates

Type of Labour	Reference Period*	Time trend	ρ (autocorrelation coefficient)	R^2
Rural Male	US (PS + SS)	.0225305	.7789102***	0.9999
		(0.32)	(6.67)	
	CWS	–.0899111	.8027889***	
		(–0.94)	(8.46)	0.9999
	CDS	.1134735	–.6083863***	
		(0.51)	(–41.36)	0.9990
Rural Female	US (PS + SS)	–.265162*	.8854497***	
		(–1.79)	(16.81)	0.9991
	CWS	–.1027198	.6119123**	
		(–0.84)	(2.60)	0.9990
	CDS	.0537878	–.8159445)*	
		(0.41)	(0.086)	0.9979
Urban Male	US (PS + SS)	.1046882**	.730777***	
		(2.39)	(5.10)	0.9999
	CWS	.263721**	.1979554	
		(2.71)	(0.28)	0.9998
	CDS	.3261643***	–.852007***	
		(6.51)	(–3.97)	0.9999
Urban Female	US (PS + SS)	–.2151739***	.8715346***	
		(–6.11)	(10.05)	0.9992
	CWS	–.0793651	.7725452***	
		(–0.97)	(4.15)	0.9981
	CDS	.1129917**	–.8494254*	
		(2.80)	(–2.27)	0.9990

Notes: Robust *t*-values reported in parentheses. *** significant at .01, ** significant at .05, * significant at .1
* US (PS + SS)—Usual Status (Principal and Secondary) per 1000 persons; CWS—Current Weekly Status per 1000 persons; CDS—Current Daily Status per 1000 person-days

trend' in rural employment rate and a statistically significant (at 5 per cent or better levels of significance) upward trend in urban employment rate. These finding are particularly noteworthy since the period of analysis covered the reforms of 1991 and thereafter. According to widely shared assessments, the reforms did not encompass rural areas to any extent and were largely urban oriented and as such, could not have had any impact on employment of rural males. The fact that there was a significant upward trend in the employment rate of urban males but not rural males is consistent with the fact that reforms by and large had no rural components. However, the fact that reforms had a positive impact in employment rates of urban males, though encouraging, certainly does not establish a causal relationship between reforms and employment rates. From an overall employment perspective also there are important findings since males, after all, constituted 51 per cent of the total population and accounted for 74 per cent of total employed person-days in 1999–2000 (according to the NSS).

It is well known that the participation rates of females in the workforce and their employment rates are not only much lower than those of males, but they are also more variable, particularly within short periods of time such as a week. The trends for females in Table 4.1 give a mixed picture: in 'rural' areas, there is a significant (at a 10 per cent level) 'downward' trend in the employment rate according to US and no significant trend in the other two measures. In urban areas there is a significant (at a 1 per cent level) downward trend according to US and a significant (at a 5 per cent level) upward trend according to CDS.

Unemployment

Table 4.2 reports the slopes of the trends in unemployment rates documented in Table A4.2. In all regressions, R^2 and serial correlations are again high. The slopes for males are basically consistent with the trends in employment rates: for 'rural' males there is a significant (at a 10 per cent level) upward trend according to US and a significant downward

TABLE 4.2
Unemployment Rates

Type of Labour	Reference Period*	Time trend	ρ (autocorrelation coefficient)	R^2
Rural Male	US (PS + SS)	.0226547*	−.7156501***	
		(2.08)	(−4.62)	0.9917
	CWS	−.0625306	.8128619***	
		(−1.48)	(8.11)	0.9876
	CDS	.0765274	.9335281***	
		(0.44)	(12.43)	0.9594
Rural Female	US (PS + SS)	−.1483735	.6906727***	
		(−1.65)	(3.70)	0.7858
	CWS	−.1702609**	.8737716***	
		(−2.74)	(9.57)	0.9787
	CDS	−.1538805	.9577055***	
		(−0.74)	(26.38)	0.9652
Urban Male	US (PS + SS)	−.1658847***	.7449245***	
		(−4.83)	(4.41)	0.9964
	CWS	−.2587472***	.8231158***	
		(−6.01)	(6.91)	0.9950
	CDS	−.2282298*	.631999***	
		(−2.21)	(42.51)	0.9903
Urban Female	US (PS + SS)	−.9626916*	.6161466	
		(−1.95)	(1.69)	0.8758
	CWS	−.4512313	.6377532**	
		(−1.68)	(2.33)	0.9553
	CDS	−.3066979	.8171305	
		(−1.42)	(1.90)	0.9891

Notes: Robust *t*-values reported in parentheses. *** significant at .01, ** significant at .05, * significant at .1
* US (PS + SS): Usual Status (Principal and Secondary) per 1000 persons in the labour force
CWS: Current Weekly Status per 1000 persons in the labour force
CDS: Current Daily Status per 1000 person-days in the labour force

trend by all measures in urban areas. For females there was a significant downward trend according to CWS in rural areas as well as a significant downward trend according to US in urban areas.

For females, the unemployment picture is very different from that of employment. Both in rural and urban areas, female unemployment rates exhibit either no significant trend or a significant downward trend. It is likely that the divergent picture between trends in unemployment and employment rates arises from the fact that females move in and out of the workforce often.

Employment Status

Table 4.3 details the slopes of the trends in the proportion of self-employed, employed in regular wage/salaried jobs, and employed as casual labour, among those usually employed (principal and secondary status). The relevant data are in Tables A4.3 and A4.4. They show that self-employment is the dominant mode of employment accounting for more than 50 per cent of usually employed males and females in rural areas even in the 61st round (July 2004–June 2005), and is an important (though not the dominant) mode in urban areas, accounting for 45 per cent of usually employed males and 48 per cent of usually employed females. Since the shares of the three categories, self-employment, wage/salary employment and employment as casual labour by definition add to 1, the trend coefficients in the regressions for the three categories have to add to zero. However, if we allow the serial correlation coefficient in the residuals for the three regressions to be different, the estimation procedure that takes into account the serial correlation in residuals will result in estimated trend coefficients for the three categories not adding to zero. But if we restrict the serial correlation coefficient to be the same this problem will not arise. The regressions in Table 4.3 were estimated by imposing this restriction. There is a significant increase in the status of employment as casual labour for rural males and a significant decrease in the staus of employment in regular wage/salaried work for urban males. For rural and urban females there is a downward, but insignificant, trend in employment as casual labour. There is a downward, though insignificant trend in self-employment for rural males and a significant upward trend for rural females Urban females experience a significant

TABLE 4.3
Employment Status

Type of Labour	Reference Period	Time trend	ρ (autocorrelation coefficient)	R^2
Rural Male	Self-employed	−.2170437*** (−1.64)	.5593385 (2.51)	0.9992
	Regular wage/salaried	−.1447657*** (−1.36)		0.9847
	Casual labour	.3618089* (2.05)		0.9976
Rural Female	Self-employed	−1.327904* (−1.94)	.9629305*** (52.49)	0.9848
	Regular wage/salaried	−.0849406 (−0.63)		0.8520
	Casual labour	1.242964 (−1.74)		0.9528
Urban Male	Self-employed	−.3107037* (1.82)	.6788774*** (6.75)	0.9986
	Regular wage/salaried	−.3920492*** (−4.79)		0.9992
	Casual labour	.0813463 (0.42)		0.9883
Urban Female	Self-employed	−.1290026 (−0.37)	.8678653*** (15.52)	0.9903
	Regular wage/salaried	.9234643*** (4.06)		0.9909
	Casual labour	−.7944618 (−1.66)		0.9449

Notes: Robust *t*-values reported in parentheses. *** significant at .01, ** significant at .05, * significant at .1.

increase in employment as wage/salaried workers. Clearly the picture emerging from these trends is complex. It is conceivable, though there is no way of judging this from the trends alone, that casual labour is a transitional status for those who move from self-employment in low productivity activities in rural areas to more productive wage employment in urban areas.

Taken together, Tables 4.1–4.3 paint a more optimistic picture of the Indian labour market than that suggested by official publications.

Labour Force Participation Rates

Table 4.4 depicts the time trends of labour force participation rates. Because the NSSO did not regularly publish these statistics, the data are computed using employment rates (which are reported per 1000 people in the general population) and unemployment rates (which are reported per 1000 people in the labour force). The computed labour force participation rates are given in Table A4.4. As noted in the Introduction, participation rates increased significantly only for rural males. For urban males two measures (US and CDS) showed significant declines while CWS rate showed no trend. For females, either participation rate declined significantly (CWS in rural areas and US in urban areas) or showed no trend at all. In order to interpret these trends, additional analysis of age-specific participation rates is necessary, as one would expect the participation of school-age children in the workforce to decline as the economy grows.

Within Reference Week Distribution of Employment Status

The NSS collects data on the time disposition of each member of the household on each day of the reference week.

This involved the recording of different activities pursued by the members along with the time intensity in quantitative terms for each day of the reference week…each day of the reference week was looked upon as comprising either two 'half days' or a 'full' day for assigning the activity status…

TABLE 4.4
Labour Force Participation Rates

Type of Labour	Reference Period*	Time trend	ρ (autocorrelation coefficient)	R^2
Rural Male	US (PS + SS)	.0226547* (2.08)	−.7156501*** (−4.62)	0.9917
	CWS	−.0625306 (−1.48)	.8128619*** (8.11)	.09876
	CDS	0.765274 (0.44)	.9335281*** (12.43)	0.9594
Rural Female	US (PS + SS)	−.1483735 (−1.65)	.6906727*** (3.70)	0.7858
	CWS	−.1702609** (−2.74)	.8737716*** (9.57)	0.9787
	CDS	−.1538805 (−0.74)	.9577055*** (26.38)	0.9652
Urban Male	US (PS + SS)	−.1658847*** (−4.83)	.7449245*** (4.41)	0.9964
	CWS	−.2587472 (0.9950)	.8231158*** (6.91)	0.9950
	CDS	−.2282298* (−2.21)	.631999*** (42.51)	0.9903
Urban Female	US (PS + SS)	−.9626916* (0.074)	.6161466 (1.69)	0.8758
	CWS	−.4512313 (−1.68)	.6377532** (2.33)	0.9553
	CDS	−.3066979 (−1.42)	.8171305 (1.90)	0.9891

Notes: Robust *t*-values reported in parentheses. *** significant at .01, ** significant at .05, * significant at .1.
* US (PS + SS): Usual Status (Principal and Secondary) per 1000 persons
CWS: Current Weekly Status per 1000 persons in the labour force
CDS: Current Daily Status per 1000 person-days in the labour force

A person was considered 'working' (employed) for the entire day if he/she had worked for 4 hours or more during the day.

If a person was engaged in more than one of the economic activities for 4 hours or more on a day, he/she was assigned two out of the various economic activities on which he/she devoted relatively longer time on the reference day (for each of those two activities, the intensity was 0.5).

If the person had worked for 1 hour or more but less than 4 hours he/she was considered 'working' (employed) for half-day and 'seeking or available for work' (unemployed) or 'neither seeking nor available for work' (not in labour force) for the other half of the day depending on whether he was seeking/available for work or not.

If a person was not engaged in any 'work' even for 1 hour on a day but was seeking/available for work even for 4 hours or more, he was considered 'unemployed' for the entire day. But if he was 'seeking/available for work' for more than 1 hour and less than 4 hours only, he was considered 'unemployed' for half day and 'not in labour force' for the other half of the day.

A person who neither had any 'work' to do nor was available for 'work' even for half a day was considered 'not in labour force' for the entire day and was assigned one or two of the detailed non-economic activity statuses depending upon the activities pursued during the reference day.

(NSS 2001, Chapter 2)

Table 4.5 presents these data as a distribution of the days within the week (in half-days) of those employed, unemployed, and in the workforce. Thus, the entry corresponding to, say, 7 days in Table 4.5 for the employed, is the proportion of those in the respective column who were classified as employed in the CWS who were employed in 'all seven days of the week'. Analogously, the entry corresponding to zero is the proportion of those who were classified as employed in the CWS who were employed for 'no day of the week'. Since by definition the distribution refers to only those who are classified as employed in the CWS, the entry corresponding to zero is zero in the employed column as well as all other columns.

It is remarkable that the proportion who were employed on all seven days of the week among those classified as employed was very high, exceeding 80 per cent for rural and urban males, and 70 per cent for urban females. Only for rural females was this proportion lower at 58 per cent, which is still fairly high. Thus, the perception that there is a lot of 'churning' within the week in the employment of individuals is not borne out in the aggregate. The picture with respect to unemployment is different—only in urban areas the proportion who were unemployed all seven days of the

TABLE 4.5
Within Reference Week Distribution of Labour Force, 1999–2000

(distribution of labour force in per cent)

Number of Days/Week	Rural Males*			Rural Females*			Urban Males*			Urban Females*		
	E	UE	WF	E	UE	WF	E	UE	WF	E	UE	WF
0.0	0.00	0.00	0.00	0.00	0.00	0.00	0.00	0.00	0.00	0.00	0.00	0.00
0.5	0.02	0.00	0.01	0.08	0.00	0.06	0.01	0.06	0.01	0.15	0.09	0.13
1.0	0.47	0.13	0.27	1.09	0.67	0.94	0.32	0.00	0.21	1.01	0.60	0.94
1.5	0.14	0.04	0.10	0.86	0.54	0.81	0.04	0.04	0.03	0.56	0.03	0.51
2.0	1.18	0.19	0.52	3.33	0.96	2.72	0.49	0.08	0.20	2.09	1.00	1.61
2.5	0.13	0.05	0.07	0.98	0.56	0.93	0.05	0.01	0.03	0.82	0.02	0.74
3.0	1.88	0.11	0.72	4.03	0.81	2.97	0.81	0.09	0.29	2.56	1.04	1.88
3.5	0.64	0.15	0.48	12.79	4.83	12.48	0.30	0.17	0.23	8.66	3.45	8.20
4.0	3.72	0.19	1.41	6.83	0.61	4.84	1.73	0.19	0.69	3.28	0.69	2.35
4.5	0.23	0.07	0.13	0.67	0.26	0.64	0.09	0.05	0.05	0.35	0.40	0.37
5.0	4.25	0.15	2.06	6.12	0.55	4.46	2.70	0.14	1.31	3.13	0.26	2.17
5.5	0.26	0.09	0.18	0.64	0.21	0.60	0.10	0.00	0.07	0.30	0.00	0.30
6.0	4.06	0.10	2.74	4.06	0.30	3.15	5.69	0.25	4.16	4.65	0.22	3.52
6.5	0.13	0.00	2.10	0.11	0.00	0.11	0.14	0.00	0.10	0.12	0.00	0.10
7.0	82.90	98.73	91.21	58.40	89.70	65.30	87.53	98.91	92.62	72.31	92.20	77.18

Notes: * E: Distribution of persons classified as employed (according to CWS) by number of half-days employed during the reference week. Note that persons classified as employed according to CWS by definition have worked at least one-half during the reference week, so the zero days/week cell is necessarily 0%.

UE: Distribution of persons classified as employed (according to CWS) by number of half-days employed during the reference week. Note that persons classified as employed according to CWS by definition have not been employed for any half-day have been actively seeking or are available for worked at least one-half day during the reference week, so the zero days/week cell is necessarily 0%.

LF: Distribution of persons in the labour force (unemployed or employed according to CWS) by number of half-days in the labour force (unemployed or employed) during the reference week. Note that persons reporting 0 days in the labour force are not in the labour force, so the zero days/week cell is necessarily 0%.

week is high, 55 per cent for males and 60 per cent for females. The rural proportions for both sexes is about a third. My interpretation of these results is that people move in and out of unemployment more frequently in rural areas, probably because it is easier to find employment in some activity there. On the other hand, both the unemployed and unemployed statuses are persistent in the sense that once one is employed (or unemployed), he or she is more likely to stay employed (or unemployed) for all seven days.

CONCLUSIONS

Before turning to policy questions, a few remarks are in order on the vast literature on employment in India.[5] First, the literature based on NSSO data almost always focuses on the quinquennial rounds, virtually ignoring the annual rounds. Second, the distinction between person-rates of employment and unemployment, US and CWS and the person-day-rates of CWS is very often ignored and all three are treated as if they refer to persons. Third, the literature also usually discusses trends in absolute numbers of employed and less often the trends in employment rates. Fourth, in many of the scholarly articles as well as in some official publications the concept of employment elasticity and estimates of its trends play a crucial role. Related concepts of labour absorption per unit of output or per hectare of land used in the cultivation of various crops are also invoked.

Each of the four aspects of the analyses and findings in the literature can be questioned on analytical and empirical grounds. First, the sample sizes (in numbers of rural and urban households) for India as a whole are large in annual rounds although, in the quinquennial rounds, they are much larger. This being the case, there is no reason to ignore the annual or 'thin' round estimates, at least at the all-India level (and possibly at the level of major states) on grounds of small sample size. The argument that because in these rounds the main subject of inquiry is not necessarily employment and unemployment and for this reason there may be biases (due to investigator neglect) in estimates is not persuasive since no concrete evidence has been offered documenting such bias. Further, given that a large majority of Indian labour is employed in agriculture and activities that process agricultural products, employment in years of quinquennial round may be affected by shocks (particularly monsoon) to agriculture in those years, which could unduly influence the trends between such years. For all those reasons, in this paper I have used all the available data from 'thin' (annual) and 'thick' (quinquennial) rounds.

Second, as I argued in the previous section, since a 'given' number of 'person-days' of employment can be distributed differently among 'persons', it is inappropriate to ignore and treat as irrelevant the distinction between 'person-day rates' and 'person rates'.

Third, in official publications as well as in scholarly writings, a concern has been expressed about the growth of employment having declined in the 1990s. To cite only three among many: 'Concern is often expressed that the process of growth in recent years has not generated employment at the pace required for absorbing the additional entrants to the labour force' (Planning Commission 2006, p. 59); 'rate of growth of employment, on CDS basis, declined from 2.7 per cent per annum during 1983 to 1993–4 to 1.07 per cent per annum during 1994–2000' (MOF 2004, p. 208); 'The rate of growth of employment picked up from the 1960s, but declined in the mid-1970s. There appears to have been a second period of higher growth during the 1980s and early 1990s. But during the most recent period (1993–4 to 1999–2000) there is evidence to suggest a significant deceleration... The growth rate of employment increased from 2.2 per cent in 1983–5 to 3.2 per cent in 1988–93 (2.8 per cent during the decade) and then plummeted to 1.5 per cent during 1993–2000... There has been a virtual collapse of rural employment as per the NSS estimates for the latest period' (Srivastava 2006, pp. 1 and 7).

All these statements are based on growth in estimates of absolute numbers of employed persons, derived by multiplying the relevant census-based population totals by the CDS employment rates from the EUS of the NSSO[6] for the relevant category. Thus, the differing growth rates of absolute numbers employed to which the statements quoted in the previous paragraph refer, combine the effect of trends in CDS person-day employment and that of the census-based growth of persons in the relevant category. Unfortunately, the 'plummeting growth rate of employment' and 'the collapse of rural employment' cited by Srivastava (2006) and echoed by MOF (2004) and Planning Commission (2006) also only use data from quinquennial rounds and, in the case of MOF (2004), mistakenly use the CDS person-day rate as if it were a person rate.

The CDS rates are available only for quinquennial rounds. On the other hand, the US (PS + SS) and CWS rates are person rates and are available for thin as well as thick rounds. In the second section, we noted that for males there was no significant trend in employment rates (either US or CWS)

---

[5] The paper of Srivastava (2006) to which S.R. Hashim drew my attention, cites many of the important contributions to the literature. I found Srivastava's paper extremely helpful both from the perspective of the comprehensiveness of its coverage and of its references to the literature.

[6] The procedure of using census-based population figures as multiplicand for NSS employment rates is not innocuous. As I argue in Srinivasan (2006), NSS underestimates the total population relative to the censuses and the extent of underestimation is increasing over time. One cannot rule out the possibility that whatever is causing the increasing underestimation could affect the NSS employment rates as well.

in rural areas and a significant upward trend in urban areas. Only in the cases of rural and urban females are there significant downward trends, and that too only if we use US data. This being the case, the use of longer term trends in person-rates of US or CWS, rather than the inappropriate person-day rates of CDS based only on quinquennial rounds, would reverse the pessimistic conclusion about the collapse of employment for males.[7] As is to be expected, the employment picture is mixed for females.

Even if one ignored thin rounds and used only the quinquennial rounds, one would find that the changes in employment rates according to US, CWS, and CDS are different (see Table 4.6). For example, if we focus on males who constitute the overwhelming majority (in excess of 75 per cent) of those employed, we find, that although the signs of the change of the three (US, CWS, and CDS) employment rates are the same except in one instance, the magnitudes of the change are very different. If instead of using the inappropriate CDS rates, one had used CWS rates, aggregate employment growth between 1983 and 1999–2000 would have been faster in rural areas, slower in urban areas and faster overall. But between 1983 and 1987–8 on the other hand, the use of CWS would lower the growth of employment in both rural and urban areas. The point is that it matters which of the three employment rates is used for projecting aggregate employment.

Not only have official publications and academic writers wrongly concluded that employment growth has slowed, but in attempting to explain the slowdown, they have also identified a fall in 'employment elasticity' as the culprit. For example, MOF (2004, p. 207) suggests that 'In view of the declining employment elasticity of growth, observed during 1994–2000, the Special Group (constituted by the Planning Commission on targeting ten million employment opportunities per year over the Tenth Plan period)

TABLE 4.6
Change in Employment Rate
(*per cent*)

	Rural Areas			Urban Areas		
	US (PS+SS)	CWS	CDS	US (PS+SS)	CWS	CDS
1983 to 1987–8	–0.46	–0.37	3.9	–1.17	0.00	0.35
1983 to 1993–4	1.10	3.91	4.6	1.76	3.80	4.86
1983 to 1999–2000	–3.10	–0.19	–0.82	1.18	3.45	3.59
1987–8 to 1993–4	2.60	5.35	0.60	2.16	3.36	3.78
1987–8 to 1999–2000	–1.48	1.19	–4.59	2.37	3.45	2.72

Source: Table A4.1.

has recommended (Planning Commission 2002) that over and above employment generated in process of present structure of growth, there is a need to promote certain identified labour intensive activities'. The Planning Commission (2005, Table 8.1) generates its estimates of employment generated during the Tenth Plan using observed employment elasticities and actual GDP growth. Srivastava (2006, Table 18) also computes trends in employment elasticities and comments on their decline.

Unfortunately, such projections and policy pronouncements based on the same have no analytical foundation. Elementary economics would suggest that the observed employment in any period represents equilibrium between labour supply and labour demand. In principle, both supply and demand functions could shift over time. For example, GDP growth, ceteris paribus, would shift the labour demand function outward. Similarly, growth of the number of individuals in the prime working ages due to population growth, ceteris paribus, would shift the supply curve outward. Depending on the relative strengths of these shifts, almost any trend (up, down, or no change) in equilibrium employment is possible. In other words, the so-called 'employment elasticity' is not a deep behavioural parameter and can take on any value.

I conclude that the pronouncements on the slowdown in employment growth since 1993–4 are based on inappropriate measurement and invalid employment elasticity analysis and that the long term trends in US and CWS employment rates do not support such pessimistic pronouncements. However, there is no denying the fact that during the six decades since independence, with the state playing a dominant role in the economy, and a conscious attempt at industrialization, the industrial structure of employment in the economy has changed extremely slowly (see Table 4.7), although the structure of value added (GDP) has changed much more. The shares of agriculture and services in GDP, which respectively were 50 per cent and 30 per cent in 1960 (World Bank 1978, Table 3) changed significantly to 21 per cent and 52 per cent in 2004 (World Bank 2006, Table 4.2). The share of industry increased only modestly from 20 per cent in 1960 to 27 per cent in 2004. Primary activity (mostly agriculture) is still the dominant source of employment (around 66 per cent in the first half of 2004 as compared to 78 per cent in 1977–8) for rural males, the largest single group among the usually employed persons. Additionally, the industrialization strategy that emphasized investment in capital intensive, heavy industry on the one hand and promoted small-scale industry (SSI)

---

[7] Sheila Bhalla comments that my findings are 'unremarkable' and is surprised that I find that the trends that I document paint a more optimistic picture of employment. I am puzzled by her comments, since my quotes from official publications and from Srivastava (2006) amply show that my findings are not shared by them and that the long term trends in US and CWS employment rates do not support such pessimistic pronouncements.

TABLE 4.7
Per 1000 Distribution of Usually Employed by Broad Groups of Industry for Various Rounds, All India

Round	Male						Female					
	Primary		Secondary		Tertiary		Primary		Secondary		Tertiary	
	ps	all	ps	all	ps	all	ps	all	ps	all	ps	all
(1)	(2)	(3)	(4)	(5)	(6)	(7)	(8)	(9)	(10)	(11)	(12)	(13)
Rural												
60	654	659	163	160	183	180	820	841	102	94	78	65
59	704	708	143	141	153	151	841	852	99	95	60	53
58	685	688	140	138	175	174	834	849	91	87	75	65
57	672	678	148	145	180	177	819	840	124	109	57	51
56	688	690	137	136	175	174	812	818	139	133	49	49
55*	712	714	127	126	161	160	841	854	93	89	66	57
54	755	757	103	102	142	141	876	885	70	66	54	49
53	757	758	106	106	137	136	875	885	77	72	47	42
52	746	748	115	114	139	137	854	868	87	80	59	52
51	752	756	104	103	144	141	862	871	88	83	50	46
50*	739	741	113	112	148	147	847	862	91	83	62	55
49	749	750	110	109	141	141	862	872	77	74	61	54
48	753	757	106	104	141	139	858	862	78	78	64	60
47	748	749	112	112	140	139	859	863	79	79	62	58
46	705	710	123	121	172	169	842	849	83	81	75	70
45	716	717	120	121	164	162	800	814	130	124	70	61
43*	739	745	123	121	138	134	825	847	112	100	63	53
38*	772	775	102	100	123	122	862	875	78	74	57	48
Urban												
60	61	63	348	347	591	590	126	161	289	309	584	530
59	60	63	338	336	602	601	145	190	299	312	556	497
58	69	70	338	337	594	593	156	171	298	315	546	513
57	78	78	322	321	601	600	173	211	309	332	519	457
56	63	66	359	356	579	578	136	183	342	342	522	475
55*	65	66	329	328	606	606	146	177	293	293	561	529
54	90	92	324	322	586	586	187	221	292	280	520	499
53	76	78	343	340	582	581	165	200	328	324	507	476
52	81	82	335	335	584	583	179	209	310	309	512	482
51	86	88	330	329	584	583	154	205	354	343	492	452
50*	87	90	331	329	582	581	193	247	299	291	508	462
49	101	102	345	344	554	554	232	258	306	306	462	436
48	104	107	345	343	551	550	195	224	304	308	501	468
47	95	95	306	307	599	598	217	237	278	282	505	481
46	91	92	336	336	573	572	223	249	318	316	459	435
45	95	100	323	319	582	582	214	241	297	303	489	456
43*	85	91	343	340	572	569	218	294	324	317	458	389
38*	97	103	344	342	551	550	255	310	307	306	430	376

Notes: The board group of industries viz., primary, secondary, and tertiary refers to the group of NIC-98 industry divisions 01–05, 10–45, and 50–99, respectively. Industry group 01–05 actually refers to the agricultural sector; * indicate quinquennial rounds.

Source: NSS (2005), Report No. 506: Employment and Unemployment Situation in India: January–June 2004, Statement II.

through reservation of many products for production by SSI only on the other, has failed to substantially increase employment. This failure is seen from the stagnation in the share of the secondary sector as a source of employment for rural males since 1977–8 and an alarming fall in the share of manufacturing in both rural and urban areas. The only redeeming feature is a slow rising trend in the small share for both males and females in rural areas. As is well known, historically the transformation of less developed economies into developed ones consisted in shifting workforce from employment in lower productivity primary activities to higher productivity secondary and tertiary sectors. Viewed from this perspective, the Indian development strategy has thus far been disappointing. Despite the fact that recent huge growth has been led by huge growth of the services sector rather than manufacturing, any expectation that India can leap-frog the stage of manufacturing growth and shift less educated and unskilled workers employed in agriculture and other primary activities with lower productivity to employment in high productive service activities is extremely unrealistic.

One of the contributors to the dismal performance is the set of labour laws enacted after independence. These laws made it costly for large enterprises to hire workers for long-term employment. Once hired, workers could not, in effect, be dismissed for economic reasons because of the costly and time consuming procedure for dismissal. The potential deleterious effects of these laws on economic growth and income inequalities was noted long ago by no less a person than P.C. Mahalanobis (1969, p. 442 and 1961, p. 157):

...certain welfare measures tend to be implemented in India ahead of economic growth, for example, in labour laws which are probably the most highly protective of labour interest in the narrowest sense, in the whole world. There is practically no link between output and remuneration; hiring and firing are highly restricted. It is extremely difficult to maintain an economic level of productivity or improve productivity ... the present form of protection of organized labour, which constitutes, including their families, about five or six per cent of the whole population, would operate as an obstacle to growth and would also increase inequalities ... it would seem better to try to attain the highest possible efficiency of labour and increasing productivity, and use the additional value obtained in this way to create more employment rather than lower the industrial efficiency by slack or restrictive practices through overstaffing.

Mahalanobis not only made a prescient diagnosis of the detrimental effects of labour laws, but also prescribed an alternative way of assuring the legitimate interests of workers and their families while at the same time preserving the right incentives for efficient employment and increasing productivity. It consisted of creating a labour reserve (LR),

...to absorb such industrial workers as may be considered surplus and be 'laid off' by existing industrial enterprises at their dis-cretion, and also to serve as a pool for other enterprises to draw upon, again, at their own discretion. The Labour Reserve Service (LR) would then act as a buffer against unemployment and would serve as a (perhaps socially more useful and psychologically more preferable) form of or substitute for unemployment insurance.... The LR would provide training of various kinds and would continually try to use the men for productive purposes. Workers in the LR would have an incentive to find better jobs at the earliest opportunity.

(Mahalanobis 1961, pp. 157–8).

Considerations of efficiency, rightly emphasized by Mahalanobis, appeared to have played no role in the small-scale sector reservation policy. This policy not only failed to deliver its employment objectives but also crippled India's competitiveness in world markets, since many of the reserved products were major export items. Nearly a decade ago, a committee headed by Abid Hussain concluded that '...the case for reservations is fundamentally flawed and self-contradictory...the policy crippled the growth of several industrial sectors, restricted exports and has done little for the promotion of small scale industries' (p. 130, as quoted in World Bank 1998, p. 27). Although some products (including, most importantly garments, which are one of India's major exports) have been recently de-reserved, many still remain in the reserved category.

The fact that Indian labour laws are highly protective of labour, noted long ago by Mahalanobis, has at last received official recognition by the Ministry of Finance (MOF). The latest economic survey (MOF 2006, p. 209) notes, 'these laws apply only to the organized sector. Consequently, these laws have restricted labour mobility, have led to capital-intensive methods in the organized sector and adversely affected the sector's long run demand for labour'. Interestingly, the survey notes that 'perhaps there are lessons to be learnt from China in the area of labour reforms. China, with a history of extreme employment security, has drastically reformed its labour relations and created a new labour market, in which workers are highly mobile. Although there have been many lay-offs and open unemployment, high rates of industrial growth especially in the coastal regions helped their redeployment'. However, the survey fails to point out that in the special economic zones (SEZs) in the coastal areas of China, employers were free to hire and fire workers and 100 per cent foreign ownership was allowed,[8] whereas in India's recently legislated SEZs, the power to exempt them from

---

[8] There are some studies (Roy 2004; Nagaraj 2004; Deshpande, Standing, and Deshpande 1998) which claim that India's labour laws have not adversely affected growth. These are not entirely persuasive for the reason that they either ignore completely or do not carefully account for the fact that the regulations critically affect the entry and exit dynamics of firms. As such, any analysis based on establishments or firms in existence has to allow for selection effects to be valid. The firms in existence represent those who chose to enter at various points of time earlier and have not exited as yet. After all firms that anticipate their being able to either comply with or evade labour laws at a cost would enter if it is profitable for them to do so, taking into the cost of compliance. Having entered they would stay unless unanticipated events, such as, for example, an increase in costs of corruption for evading labour laws or changes in product prices and non-labour costs make staying unprofitable.

labour laws is in the hands of the governments of the states in which they happen to be located.[9]

Given the slow change in the employment structure in the context of faster output growth, and its implications for the poor as noted earlier, it is understandable that an expanded Employment Guarantee Programme is being implemented. N.S.S. Narayana, Kirit Parikh and I (1988) long ago analysed the growth-enhancing and poverty reducing potential of a well-designed (that is, creating productive assets) and well-executed (that is, involving no leakage to the non-poor) rural work programme. I very much hope that the current programme would indeed be well-designed and well-executed. However, it is important to note that even if it is, it can only be a palliative and not one that will eradicate poverty once and for all within a recognizable time horizon (Srinivasan 2005). The latter goal has been the vision of our founding fathers and mothers. Realizing that vision requires, in my mind, not only a deepening, widening, and acceleration of economic reforms, but also a rethinking of our agricultural policies ranging from price supports, input subsidies, and credit to foreign trade.

Developing a foundation for policy that is based upon sound analysis of variations across states and over time is obviously essential for effective policy formulation; crude aggregate projections void of any economic foundation are no substitutes. Projections based on 'employment' elasticities are crude. I am not dismissing valuable and informative studies by scholars cited by Srivastava (2006). However, they do have some limitations. For the reason that a large majority of Indian workers are employed in agriculture and allied activities, a large number of studies are addressed to analysing the determinants of employment in agriculture. Srivastava (2006) also presents a model of such determinants and estimates it econometrically, carefully allowing for the endogeneity of some of the determinants. Yet it must be said that few, if any, of the studies look at the observed employment levels and returns to labour as being determined in an equilibrium between supply and demand, with both supply and demand being shifted by exogenous variables including policy and technology. The analysis of the informal and formal employment outside of agriculture is less extensive. I should say that the scholars in the past were limited by the data available to them that was largely of an aggregate nature. Now that the NSSO has made available the rich household level data from the quinquennial and annual rounds of EUS, it should be possible to analyse the determinants of household labour supply, including occupational choice decisions and of labour demand decisions of producers such as farmers and owners of household enterprises. I very much hope that many such studies will be undertaken in the future.

References

Deshpande, Sudha, Guy Standing, and Lalit Deshpande (1998), *Labour Market Flexibility in a Third World Metropolis*, Vedams eBooks, New Delhi.

GOI (2006), 'Provisional Results of Economic Census 2005: All India Report', Government of India, Ministry of Statistics and Programme Implementation, Central Statistical Organization, New Delhi, *http://www.mospi.gov.in*

Mahalanobis, P.C. (1961), *Talks on Planning*, Indian Statistical Series No. 14, Statistical Publishing Society, Calcutta.

——— (1969), 'The Asian Drama: An Indian View', *Sankhya: The Indian Journal of Statistics*, Series B (31), Parts 3&4.

MOF (2004), *Economic Survey 2003–04*, Ministry of Finance, New Delhi.

——— (2006) *Economic Survey, 2005–06*, Ministry of Finance, New Delhi.

NAD (2004), Report of the Working Group on Workforce Estimates for Compilation of National Accounts Statistics with Base Year 1978–2000, National Accounts Division, Central Statistical Organization, New Delhi.

Nagaraj, R. (2004), 'Fall in Organised Manufacturing Employment: A Brief Note', *Economic and Political Weekly*, Vol. 39, No. 30, 24 July.

Narayana, N.S.S., Kirit S. Parikh, and T.N. Srinivasan (1988), 'Rural Works Programs in India: Costs and Benefits', *Journal of Development Economics*, Vol. 29, No. 2, pp. 131–56.

NAS (2004), 'Report of the Working Group on Workforce Estimates for Compilation of National Accounts Statistics with Base Year 1978–2000', National Accounts Division, Central Statistical Organization, New Delhi.

NCL (2002), 'Report of the National Commission on Labour', Ministry of Labour, New Delhi.

NSS (1997), 'Employment and Unemployment Situation in India, 1993–4, Report No. 409, NSSO, New Delhi.

——— (2001), 'Employment and Unemployment in India, Parts I and II', Report No. 458 (55/10/2), NSSO, New Delhi.

——— (2005), 'Employment and Unemployment Situation in India', January–June 2004, Report No. 506 (60/10/1), NSSO, New Delhi.

——— (2006), 'Employment and Unemployment Situation in India, Parts I and II, Report No. 515(61/10/1 and 2), NSSO, New Delhi.

Planning Commission (2001), 'Report of the Task Force on Employment Opportunities', Planning Commission, New Delhi.

---

[9] The controversy over the use of farm lands for SEZs seems to confound the legitimate issue of ensuring that landowners get the fair market value of their land in selling to the operators of SEZs, with the issue of whether the use of farm land for SEZs is inappropriate. Demands for a ban on farm lands being used for SEZ make no economic sense. In a well-functioning land market, land will be put to its best economic use, be it for farming or for use in an SEZ. If land markets are not functioning well, the failure should be addressed. The proposed ban is no solution to land market failure.

——— (2002) 'Report of the Special Group on Targeting Ten Million Employment Opportunities Per Year', Planning Commission, New Delhi.

——— (2005), 'Mid-term Appraisal of the 10th Five Year Plan (2002–7)', Planning Commission, New Delhi.

——— (2006), 'Towards Faster and More Inclusive Growth: An Approach to the 11th Five Year Plan', Planning Commision, New Delhi.

Roy, Sudipta Dutta (2004), 'Employment Dynamics in Indian Industry: Adjustment lags and the impact of job security regulations', *Journal of Development Economics*, Vol. 73, pp. 233–56

Srinivasan, T.N. (2005), 'Guaranteeing Employment: a Palliative?', *The Hindu*, Chennai.

——— (2006), 'Trends in Employment, Unemployment and Wages in India Since the Early Seventies', Mahendra Dev (ed.), to be published by Academic Foundation, New Delhi (forthcoming).

Srivastava, R.S. (2006), 'Trends in Rural Employment in India with Special Reference to Agricultural Employment', forthcoming in the World Bank's *India Employment Report*.

World Bank (1978), *World Development Report*, World Bank, Washington, DC.

——— (1998), *India: 1998 Macro-Economic Update*, World Bank, Washington, DC.

——— (2006), *World Development Indicators*, World Bank, Washington, DC.

ANNEXURE 4.1

TABLE A4.1
Employment Rates: Number of Persons (person-days) worked per 1000 Persons (person-days)
According to US, CWS, and CDS Approaches for Different Rounds

Round (survey period)	Rural						Urban					
	Male			Female			Male			Female		
	Usual adjusted	CWS	CDS	Usual adjusted	CWS	CDS	Usual adjusted	CWS	CDS	Usual adjusted	CWS	CDS
61 (7/04 to 6/05)	546	524	488	327	275	216	549	537	519	166	152	133
60 (1/04 to 6/04)	542	511	471	315	245	190	540	525	504	150	136	118
59 (1/03 to 12/03)	547	525		311	236		541	528		146	121	
58 (7/02 to 12/02)	546	529		281	219		534	523		140	118	
57 (7/01 to 6/02)	546	523		314	241		553	542		139	111	
56 (7/00 to 6/01)	544	525		287	217		531	519		140	117	
55 (7/99 to 6/00)	531	510	478	299	253	204	518	509	490	139	128	111
54 (1/98 to 6/98)	539	524		263	202		509	504		114	99	
53 (1/97 to 12/97)	550	535		291	222		521	513		131	114	
52 (7/95 to 6/96)	551	538		295	233		525	520		124	109	
51 (7/94 to 6/95)	560	541		317	241		519	511		136	117	
50 (7/93 to 6/94)	553	531	504	328	267	219	521	511	496	155	139	120
49 (1/93 to 6/93)	545	527		311	232		509	504		130	109	
48 (1/92 to 12/92)	556	536		313	244		507	501		146	122	
47 (7/91 to 12/91)	546	534		294	238		516	509		132	117	
46 (7/90 to 6/91)	553	535		292	230		513	506		143	124	
45 (7/89 to 6/90)	548	528		319	230		512	503		146	121	
43 (7/87 to 6/88)	539	504	501	323	220	207	506	492	477	152	119	110
38 (1/83 to 12/83)	547	511	482	340	227	198	512	492	473	151	118	106
32 (1977 to 1978)	542	519	458	331	232	194	508	490	472	156	125	109
27 (1972 to 1973)	545	530	503	318	217	231	501	491	477	134	123	108

Source: NSS (1997, 2001, 2005, 2006).

TABLE A4.2
Unemployment Rates: Number of Persons (person-days) Unemployed per 1000 Persons (person-days)
in the Labour Force for Different Rounds

Round (survey period)	Rural						Urban					
	Male			Female			Male			Female		
	Usual adjusted	CWS	CDS	Usual adjusted	CWS	CDS	Usual adjusted	CWS	CDS	Usual adjusted	CWS	CDS
61 (7/04 to 6/05)	16	38	80	38	52	75	18	42	87	69	70	116
60 (1/04 to 6/04)	18	47	90	40	57	81	13	45	93	67	90	117
59 (1/03 to 12/03)	15	28		40	51		6	16		35	49	
58 (7/02 to 12/02)	15	28		45	55		6	16		47	57	
57 (7/01 to 6/02)	11	26		39	46		14	26		38	48	
56 (7/00 to 6/01)	14	23		39	48		4	18		29	39	
55 (7/99 to 6/00)	17	39	72	45	56	73	10	37	70	57	73	94
54 (1/98 to 6/98)	21	29		51	54		15	27		68	78	
53 (1/97 to 12/97)	12	20		39	43		7	8		44	58	
52 (7/95 to 6/96)	13	18		38	41		7	9		61	35	
51 (7/94 to 6/95)	10	18		34	39		4	12		34	40	
50 (7/93 to 6/94)	14	30	56	40	52	67	8	30	56	62	84	105
45 (7/89 to 6/90)	13	26		39	45		6	21		27	40	
43 (7/87 to 6/88)	18	42	46	52	66	88	24	44	67	62	92	120
38 (1/83 to 12/83)	14	37	75	51	67	92	7	43	90	49	75	110
32 (1977 to 1978)	13	36	71	54	71	94	20	41	92	124	109	145
27 (1972 to 1973)	12	30	68	48	60	80	5	55	112	60	92	137

Source: NSS (1997, 2001, 2005, 2006).

TABLE A4.3
Employment Status: Per 1000 Distribution of Usually Employed by Status of Employment for Different Rounds

Round (survey period)	Rural						Urban					
	Male			Female			Male			Female		
	Self-employed	Regular wage/ salaried	Casual labour	Self-employed	Regular wage/ salaried	Casual labour	Self-employed	Regular wage/ salaried	Casual labour	Self-employed	Regular wage/ salaried	Casual labour
61 (7/04 to 6/05)	581	90	329	537	37	326	448	406	146	477	356	167
60 (1/04 to 6/04)	572	93	335	615	38	347	441	406	153	446	362	192
59 (1/03 to 12/03)	578	87	335	616	33	351	429	415	156	454	339	207
58 (7/02 to 12/02)	569	88	344	558	36	406	443	407	150	459	308	233
57 (7/01 to 6/02)	580	81	339	589	29	382	430	415	154	441	298	261
56 (7/00 to 6/01)	589	95	316	593	32	375	414	411	175	444	315	241
55 (7/99 to 6/00)	550	88	362	573	31	396	415	417	168	453	333	214
54 (1/98 to 6/98)	553	70	377	534	25	442	425	395	181	384	327	288
53 (1/97 to 12/97)	594	73	333	570	21	409	400	415	185	397	313	290
52 (7/95 to 6/96)	590	77	333	564	24	412	410	425	165	400	332	268
51 (7/94 to 6/95)	604	68	328	570	22	408	414	431	165	426	301	273
50 (7/93 to 6/94)	577	85	338	586	27	387	417	420	163	458	284	258
49 (1/93 to 6/93)	591	79	330	585	23	392	389	395	216	407	262	331
48 (1/92 to 12/92)	608	83	309	591	32	377	412	394	193	425	288	287
47 (7/91 to 12/91)	595	92	313	568	31	401	489	399	172	470	280	250
46 (7/90 to 6/91)	557	128	315	586	38	376	407	442	151	490	259	251
45 (7/89 to 6/90)	597	98	305	609	28	363	423	413	164	486	292	222
43 (7/87 to 6/88)	586	100	314	608	37	355	417	437	146	471	275	254
38 (1/83 to 12/83)	605	103	292	619	28	353	409	437	154	458	258	284

Source: NSS (1997, 2001, 2005, 2006).

TABLE A4.4
Labour Force Participation Rates: Number of Persons (person-days) Employed and Unemployed Per 1000 Persons (person-days) for Different Rounds

Round (survey period)	Rural						Urban					
	Male			Female			Male			Female		
	Usual adjusted	CWS	CDS	Usual adjusted	CWS	CDS	Usual adjusted	CWS	CDS	Usual adjusted	CWS	CDS
61 (7/04 to 6/05)	555	545	530	571	566	561	333	287	237	178	163	150
60 (1/04 to 6/04)	552	536	518	563	557	548	319	257	209	161	149	134
59 (1/03 to 12/03)	555	540		564	556		313	240		151	127	
58 (7/02 to 12/02)	554	544		559	553		283	223		147	125	
57 (7/01 to 6/02)	552	537		575	568		318	247		144	117	
56 (7/00 to 6/01)	552	537		553	545		288	221		144	122	
55 (7/99 to 6/00)	540	531	515	542	539	529	302	263	219	147	138	123
54 (1/98 to 6/98)	551	540		536	533		267	208		122	107	
53 (1/97 to 12/97)	557	546		542	536		293	224		137	121	
52 (7/95 to 6/96)	558	548		546	542		297	235		132	113	
51 (7/94 to 6/95)	566	551		537	532		318	244		141	122	
50 (7/93 to 6/94)	561	547	534	543	539	532	331	275	232	165	152	134
45 (7/89 to 6/90)	555	542		533	527		321	235		150	126	
43 (7/87 to 6/88)	549	526	525	534	527	523	331	230	222	162	131	125
38 (1/83 to 12/83)	555	531	521	540	527	521	342	237	218	159	128	119
32 (1977 to 1978)	549	538	493	537	527	521	338	242	214	178	140	127
27 (1972 to 1973)	552	546	540	526	522	518	320	230	260	143	135	125

Source: NSS (1997, 2001, 2005, 2006).

5

State of Higher Education in India

S.R. Hashim*

India's achievements in higher education in the post-independence period appear to be quite remarkable, given the initial conditions from which we started. We have been able to create a large base of educational institutions and some of them are known to be excellent. We are a country with one of the largest trained and educated manpower with considerable scientific and technical capabilities. Our research in agricultural sciences has contributed significantly to our food security. Our engineers have constructed huge dams, seaports, aerodromes, and power houses. Big industrial plants have been erected and are being run by personnel trained within the country. We have made significant strides in nuclear and space research. We have produced excellent scientists in a number of other fields. We have produced fine practioners of medicine and surgery. Good advances are being made in biotechnology, genetics, and material sciences. We have developed comparative advantages in knowledge-based industries such as pharmaceuticals and IT. We have been able to develop entrepreneurial and managerial skills. And yet, we find today that our capacity and capabilities in higher education are woefully inadequate to meet the needs of a fast growing, knowledge-based economy of 21st century, on the one hand, and the demand from the youth aspiring to enter and be part of this dynamic world of growth and progress, on the other. The pace of expansion of facilities for higher education has been very slow and the quality has been uneven.

Severe capacity constraints have emerged, particularly in those segments of higher education which are most in demand. This has been mainly due to niggardly allocation of public resources to higher education. This resource crisis has assumed alarming dimensions in the past two decades (Azad 2005). India's main competitors—especially China but also Singapore, Taiwan, and South Korea—are investing much more in large differentiated higher education systems. They are providing access to large numbers of students at the bottom of the academic system while at the same time building some research-based universities that are able to compete with world's best institutions (Altbach 2005).

The demand for higher education has surged forward and is growing rapidly as: (i) larger and larger number of students are completing school education, (ii) Indian middle class is expanding, (iii) land-based economic system is declining, (iv) higher education is being looked upon as the means of entry into the dynamic world of growth and progress and as a basis of enduring economic security, and (v) the economy has recorded high growth and is shifting to a still higher growth path with such continuing changes in economic structure as are supported and sustained by higher education inputs. Higher education is no longer the

* The author would like to acknowledge with thanks the assistance received from various sources in preparing this paper. ISID made available its online data-base-clipping-service for reference and rendered the necessary secretarial assistance. The Institute for Human Development (IHD) helped in procuring reference literature and extracting some data from websites. IGDRI invited me to work and stay with them for 10 days and provided secretarial assistance. R. Radhakrishna read an earlier draft of this paper and made valuable suggestions.

> **Box 5.1**
> **Pressure of Competition for Available Seats in the Institutions of Higher Learning**
>
> The pressure of competition for available seats in the institutions of higher learning is enormous. This can be gauged just from the following example. The top nine institutes of technology which include seven IITs, that is, Bombay, Delhi, Guwahati, Kanpur, Kharagpur, Madras, and Roorkee and IT BHU at Varanasi and ISM at Dhanbad hold a combined entrance test for selecting candidates for admission to various degree courses. For the year 2006, they held a combined entrance test for a total of 5444 seats that they offered altogether in 108 specializations. The number of seats offered in any one institute in any one discipline is not very large. For example, the highest number of seats offered in the overall matrix of institution and speciality is 77 in civil engineering in IIT Roorkee. The smallest number of seats offered is just 7 in the speciality of naval architecture and ocean engineering in IIT Madras. The only other institute which offers this speciality is IIT Kharagpur, and this institute has only 9 seats. IITs are regarded as the best of the educational institutions for higher studies in technology. It may not be out of place to mention here that last year London Times Higher Education Supplement ranked the world's top 200 universities which included three from China, three from Kong Kong, three from South Korea, one from Taiwan, and one from India, an Indian Institute of Technology. It is well-known in academic circles and particularly among the aspirants that competition for admission to IIT is one of the toughest. A lot of hard work is required even for appearing in the admission test. And hence it would not be wide off the mark to surmise that those aspirants who take the test would be good enough for aspiring for a seat in IIT. For these 5444 seats, 2,99,456 students took the entrance examination. The ratio of aspirants to available seats works out to 55:1. Is it difficult not to believe that if the available seats were 5 to 10 times more, even then one could have got enough students worthy of these institutions? Further, it was recently reported that even a score of 90 per cent does not ensure a student a course in a college of choice in Delhi University this year.

preserve of the elite in the society, but has become a commodity in high demand from the middle and lower middle classes and is aspired to even by the poor.

This chapter attempts to address some of the demand as well as supply side issues pertaining to higher education. On the demand side, the factors responsible for changes in the perception about the value of higher education are examined, particularly with reference to the decline in the land-based economy and shift in the economic structure in favour of services and knowledge-based industries. The relationship between education and earnings is also explored. On the supply side, the expansion and growth of higher education in India is traced over time, particularly with reference to allocation of public funds. Ways of enhancing the capacity of higher education are explored and, in this context, the existing and potential role of private providers and foreign providers of higher education is examined. The possibility of using the excellent faculty and infrastructure that has been built over the years in various research institutes (mostly supported by public funds) for teaching purposes (towards post-graduate degrees) is also explored. Open and distance learning systems and the institution of deemed to be universities are also mentioned in this context. Certain other issues like the rural–urban divide in the quality of education and the question of relevant education are also discussed. Some of these issues were raised by the author on an earlier occasion (Hashim 2005).

CHANGING PERCEPTION ABOUT VALUE OF HIGHER EDUCATION

Land has been traditionally perceived by people as the most enduring basis of economic security and social status. In a largely agrarian society, everything revolved around land. Owning a piece of land gave a social identity to the owner, and also made a significant difference in the economic status of the household. Hunger and poverty were extremely high among the landless. Ownership of 5–6 acres of land (to be categorized as 'small' or 'medium' farmer, depending on irrigation status of the land) could keep the farming household mostly above poverty line and could even make some of them relatively prosperous in the rural setting. It may be seen from Table 5.1 that 68 per cent of the landless wage earners and 45 per cent of the marginal farmers were below the poverty line in 1993–4, but only 16 per cent of the small farmers were poor.

TABLE 5.1
Incidence of Poverty by Landholding Groups, 1993–4

Landholding Group	HCR (Percentage)
Landless wage earner	68
Marginal farmer	45
Small farmer	16
Large farmer	11
Other landless	37
All landowners	31
All landless	52

Source: Shariff (1999).

Given that the rate of average earning was not very high in other sectors, including the services sector (except for a minutely small proportion of high class earners), one could not build up enough savings in alternative occupations for the type of economic security that the land could provide. No wonder that people clung to land, sometimes putting their lives at stake even for a small holding. Migrants seeking work elsewhere in the country or abroad did not, for generations, give up their village connection if they had a piece of land back home.

Increasing pressure of population on land due to much slower absorption of workforce in non-agricultural occupations resulted in continuing marginalization of farmers. Percentage share of number of marginal holdings in all holdings increased from 50.6 in 1970–1 to 61.6 in 1995–6. The area under marginal holdings increased from 9.0 per cent to 17.2 per cent over the same period (Table 5.2). The green revolution regenerated hopes of a better livelihood even among the small and the marginal farmers as the new technology was acclaimed to be size-neutral. However, the benefits of the green revolution accrued more to those farmers with command over larger resources, since the input intensity of new agriculture was much higher. During the last decade and a half the agricultural growth has declined and the green revolution has lost much of its shine. The burden of structural adjustment and economic reforms fell on agriculture somewhat more severely than on other sectors. Public investment in agriculture had slowed down even earlier, beginning in the early 1980s (Reddy 2006). Input prices started rising since the early 1990s. Withdrawal of subsidies raised the prices of fertilizers and pesticides and seed costs have gone up enormously. There has been a steep fall in the allocation of credit to agriculture. Since agricultural imports and exports have been liberalized, demand for agricultural products has become highly unpredictable. Agriculture has become a highly risky business. 'On account of the resulting decline in output and income, a large number of small and marginal farmers were pushed below the poverty line in the immediate post-reform period' (Rao 2005). Unemployment rates in rural areas (measured on the basis of principal and secondary status as well as weekly status) were significantly higher in the NSS 54th round (1998) and 55th round (1999–2000) than in the past (Kundu et al. 2005). A state like Punjab which gave the lead in green revolution and had achieved the highest rate of growth and was the highest per capita income state, all on the basis of high value and high intensity agriculture, has lost its rank both in terms of growth rate and in terms of per capita income. The phenomenon of farmers' suicides has spread over the states of Andhra, Karnataka, Maharashtra, and now even Punjab. People seem to have lost confidence in land as the enduring basis of economic security.

TABLE 5.2
Percentage Share of Number and Area under Marginal Holdings
(*less than one hectare*)

Year	No. of Holdings	Area
1970–1	50.6	9.0
1980–1	56.4	12.1
1990–1	59.0	14.9
1995–6	61.6	17.2

Source: Reddy (2006).

The economy as a whole, on the other hand, has experienced a much higher growth rate during the post-reform period—nearly 6 per cent per annum over the long period of a decade and a half. Agriculture has not contributed much to this growth, as already noted. Even the industrial sector, particularly manufacturing, has made only a modest contribution to the growth, ultimately losing its share in total GDP (Table 5.3). The overall growth rate of the economy is boosted mainly by very high growth rates in the services sector and a few segments of manufacturing such as motor-vehicles etc. This growth is manifested in fast modernizing metro-towns, growth in a variety of 'service' activities, pervading growth and influence of IT, bullish trends in stock exchanges, globalization of retail trade, boom in the construction industry, and unprecedentedly

---

BOX 5.2

Farming has Become a Risky Vocation

A. Farmers' Suicides in Vidarbha

According to a recent report, in the current kharif season, more than 550 farmers—mostly cotton growers—have chosen the easy way out from the vicious cycle of debt and crop failure in the Vidarbha region of Maharashtra alone; on an average at least three farmers have committed suicide in the region every day. The factors are multiple: crippling debts, pressure from private and unscrupulous money lenders, high interest rates, soaring input costs, low output prices, and corporate seeds supplied by MNCs which perish faster than the homegrown variety (*Hindustan Times*, New Delhi, 20 May 2006).

B. Farming—An Unprofitable Vocation

Recently, the Minister of State for Agriculture stated in the Rajya Sabha—citing figures from NSS—that 27 per cent of farmer households found the vocation unprofitable, eight per cent felt it was risky and five per cent disliked it because of lack of social status and other reasons. Thus 40 per cent of the farmers would like to try out something new for a living (*Hindustan Times*, New Delhi, 20 May 2006).

TABLE 5.3
Sectoral Share in GDP
(percentages)

Year	Agriculture	Manufacturing	Secondary sector	Tertiary sector
1997–8	26.5	17.7	27.7	45.8
2001–2	24.1	16.9	26.6	49.3
2002–3	21.5	17.3	27.3	51.2
2003–4	21.7	17.0	26.9	51.4

Source: Mid-term Appraisal of the Tenth Plan, Planning commission, Government of India, 2005.

TABLE 5.4
Percentage Distribution of Households and Income by Education Level of the Head of the Household

Educational Level of Head	Rural		Urban	
	HHS	Income	HHS	Income
No formal Education	50.81	42.34	15.69	9.72
Below primary	11.41	11.08	4.93	4.45
Below middle	14.39	15.64	12.15	8.34
Below secondary	8.50	9.99	10.40	7.53
Below higher secondary	10.14	13.41	21.88	22.31
Undergraduate	2.43	3.61	9.22	9.13
Graduate and above	2.43	3.93	25.74	38.52

Source: MIMAP (2003).

high incomes in certain segments of the fast growing economy. This growth is largely urban oriented and is contributing to a fast expansion of urban middle class.

EDUCATION AND EARNING

The relationship between the levels of education and long earning has been a subject of interest. A more systematic recent study based on household surveys is available from MIMAP India Survey Report, (NCAER 2003). It is based on a survey of 5000 households for the reference period July 1994 to June 1995. A positive correlation is found between average household income and the education level of the head of the household for both rural and urban households. Lack of education is disadvantageous to earnings in rural and urban settings, but more so in the latter. While some education below undergraduate level can help in improving earning levels in rural areas, in urban areas it is education at graduate and higher levels only which makes a real difference in earning levels (Table 5.4). With the thrust and the focus of the economy shifting in favour of more urban-oriented economic activities (mainly in the services sector) it is no wonder that demand for higher education has suddenly gone up and will continue to move upwards. Perhaps people's response to the changing trends is much quicker and sharper than our understanding of these trends.

The data also reveal another interesting feature of the relationship between levels of earning and education. It is generally known that earnings rise with age/experience. The data show that the experience, as reflected in age, matters for earnings only if the educational level is high enough (Table 5.5). Earnings of illiterates and those with lower than secondary level of education initially decline with age, picking up only at later stages though at slow rate. Earnings of the better educated rise sharply with age/experience.

Thus, it is higher education that matters for substantial improvement in earning levels, particularly in the urban

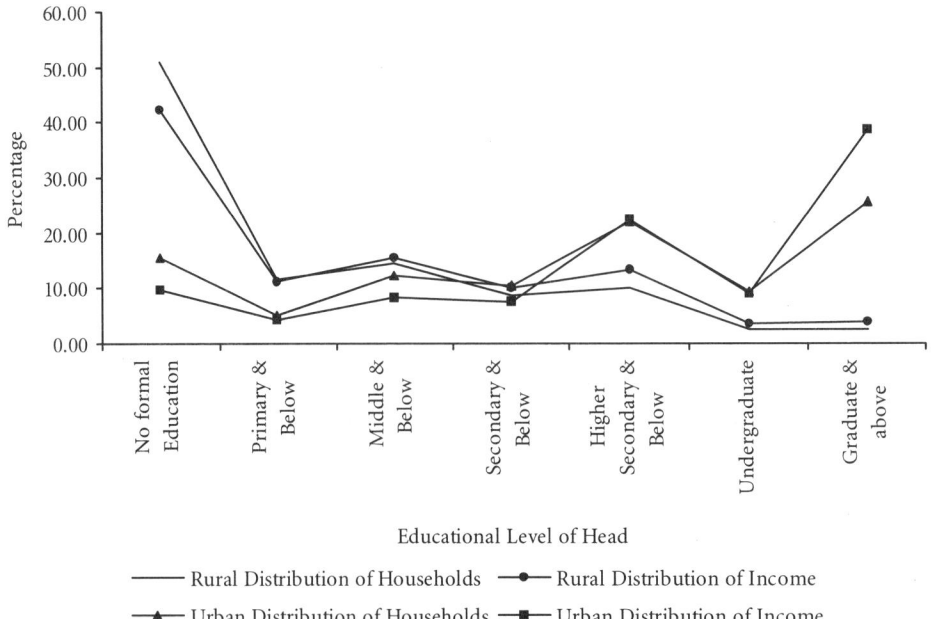

Figure 5.1: Percentage Distribution of Households and Income

TABLE 5.5
Per Household Income (Rs per annum) by
Head's Education and Age

(All India)

Age Group in years	Education Level of Head		
	Illiterate	Below secondary	Above secondary
Below 30	20,134	28,422	32,871
30–9	18,323	23,755	46,729
40–9	21,749	29,898	54,065
50–9	26,710	37,972	76,085
60 & above	29,950	42,202	80,974

Source: MIMAP (2003).

Data from the MIMAP Survey on per capita consumption expenditure on education by income groups are presented in Table 5.7. Average per capita expenditure on education in urban areas is 5–6 times higher than that in rural areas. Ninety per cent of the households in urban areas spend Rs 289 and above per capita per annum on education, while only about 10 per cent of households in rural areas spend Rs 173 per capita per annum or more on education. This table reflects strong tendencies. The data presented in Table 5.7 are over ten years old, as they pertain to the year 1994–5. Over these ten years, as the urban-oriented, knowledge-based

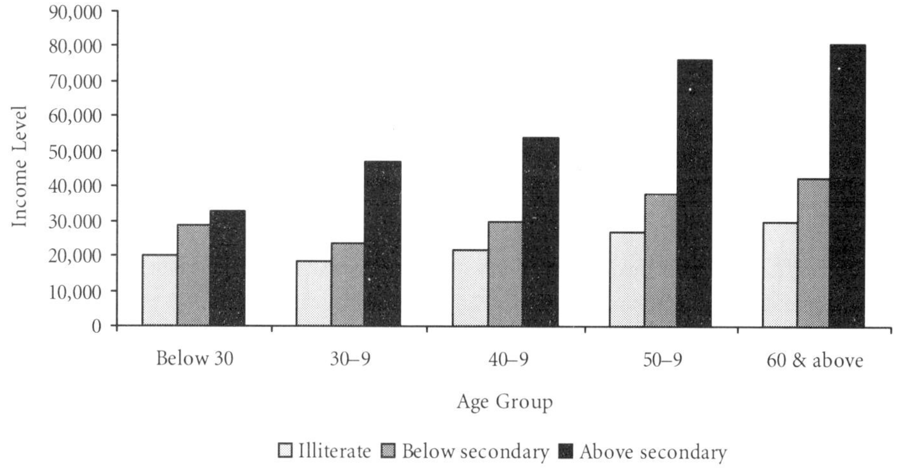

Figure 5.2: Per Household Income by Head's Education and Age

setting which represents the more modern and futuristic economic activity pattern. Higher education is, therefore, is seen as the more enduring basis of economic security and social status.

HOUSEHOLD EXPENDITURE ON EDUCATION

The change in perceptions about the value of education, to an extent, is captured in the pattern of household consumption expenditure. Household expenditure on education as per NSS has been generally low since large segments of population have been traditionally dependent on education provided by the government. However, household expenditure on education goes up sharply as income rises.

The income elasticity of expenditure on education (worked out across 12 expenditure classes) is very high for both urban and rural areas (see Table 5.6).

TABLE 5.6
Income Elasticity of Household Expenditure on Education

Year	Rural	Urban
1993–4	1.685	1.834
1999–2000	1.821	1.617

Source: Calculated from Household Consumption Expenditure data from NSS 50th and 55th Rounds.

segments of the economy have expanded at a much faster rate and there has been a decline in the land-based segments of the economy, urban attitudes about education have spread fast even to the rural areas.

In this context there is another bit of interesting data. Table 5.8 presents data on educated youth (age group 15–29) in the labour force. 'Educated', here, is defined as those having

TABLE 5.7
Per capita Consumption Expenditure on Education by
Income Group

Income Group (Rs)	Rs Per capita per annum		Percentage of households	
	Rural	Urban	Rural	Urban
Up to 12,000	42	40	16.2	2.3
12,001–18,000	62	58	25.7	7.7
18,001–24,000	79	289	17.9	9.5
24,001–48,000	135	276	29.9	35.8
48,001–72,000	173	496	5.9	19.8
72,001–96,000	142	662	2.1	11.4
> 96,001	182	951	2.2	13.5
All	81	455	100.0	100.0

Note: The last two columns of the table have been calculated from the number of households given in the source table.
Source: MIMAP (2003).

TABLE 5.8
Educated Youth in Labour Force, Middle Level of Schooling, and Above

(as percentage of labour force in relevant age group)

Sex	Age Groups	Rural		Urban		All	
		1993–4	1999–2000	1993–4	1999–2000	1993–4	1999–2000
Male	15–29	44.2	50.9	66.7	72.1	49.8	56.4
	15–19	49.5	55.1	67.4	71.9	52.1	58.7
	20–4	47.4	53.8	69.7	73.8	53.1	59.2
	25–9	36.6	45.2	63.5	70.7	44.0	52.3
Female	15–29	21.7	29.0	54.5	62.5	26.5	33.5
	15–19	30.6	40.6	63.6	69.7	34.7	44.3
	20–4	21.1	28.9	56.0	64.6	26.2	33.9
	25–9	14.2	21.3	47.0	55.9	19.6	25.9
Persons	15–29	36.6	43.4	64.1	70.3	42.5	49.3
	15–19	43.1	50.2	66.5	71.4	47.2	54.2
	20–4	38.0	45.3	66.7	72.1	44.3	51.5
	25–9	29.4	36.7	60.2	68.0	36.9	44.1

Notes: Data pertain to the 50th and 55th Rounds of NSS. The original table has been re-cast here.
Source: Planning Commission (2003).

completed middle level of schooling and more. Urban areas, as expected, have a significantly higher proportion of educated youth in the labour force than the rural areas—the percentage of all educated persons in labour force in urban areas is 70.3 while the corresponding percentage for rural areas is 43.4. What is interesting is that the proportion of educated youth in labour force has increased over the five year period 1993–4 and 1999–2000 in all the sub-groups of age and sex in rural as well as in urban areas. What is even more interesting is that those groups which had a smaller proportion of educated youth in the labour force, that is, all groups in rural areas and females in both rural and urban areas, have shown a faster rate of growth of 'educated' in the labour force.

It needs to be noted that higher education in India has been the single most potent means of social mobility, that is, for moving from the poor, the rural, and the downtrodden sections of population to respectable status in society. It was the access to higher education with the help of financial support by way of scholarships, etc., which brought about the social mobility which we have seen so far and which has further raised the aspiration for such transitions. The growth in facilities for higher education has, however, not kept pace with the need and demand for higher education in recent years, making the competition for admissions very tough and thus, almost closing the avenues for higher education for the less privileged, who need it the most.

GROWTH OF HIGHER EDUCATION

India has a long tradition in learning and higher education was imparted mostly through family lines or gurukul traditions. Formal institutions of learning such as *Pathshalas*, *Vihars*, and *Madrasas* came into existence and flourished at various points in history, particularly during the Pre-British period. However, 'barring a few exceptions higher education has been the monopoly of the few. If Manu in his Smriti showed his preferences in this regard, the Great Akbar in his Aine did not show much enthusiasm for providing education to all classes. Indeed he even thought education if made generally available would make the maintenance of law and order difficult' (Singh 1998). British education policy got a clear direction following the minutes of Lord Macaulay in 1835. Lord Macaulay favoured educating the 'elite' and made a vigorous plea for spreading western learning through the English language (Kaur 2003). The British also, at times, appeared to show concern for the education of the masses. But the fact is that education, particularly higher education, remained, by and large, the preserve of the elite.

The involvement of the British in the Indian Education system, particularly from the middle of the nineteenth century led to a rapid growth of schools, colleges, and Universities established by the government as well as by Missionaries and other private agencies for spreading the western system of education. Universities of Bombay, Madras and Calcutta were established in 1857 and Universities of Allahabad and Punjab (at Lahore) in 1887. During 1880–1900, three different agencies came forward to spread education: (i) mission schools and colleges, (ii) educational institutions established by the government, and (iii) private institutions. Thus a westernized education system (through English language) came to be established. The nationalist movement raised the question of education for the masses. Demand for education in the native language and development of Indian languages was raised in the early part of the 20th century. The nationalist view was that education should develop a nationalist character. The need for technical and vocational education was also emphasized (Kaur 2003). However, the overall provision of educational facilities remained extremely inadequate. There was just a little over one person per thousand of population enrolled in higher educational institutions in 1951.

The main thrust of the education policy after independence has been education for the masses, which is quite natural given the woeful state of literacy and elementary education among the people. Recognizing that economic development made growing demands on human resources, and in a democratic set-up it called for values and attitudes for which the quality of education was an important element, the Second Five Year Plan—which was the first elaborate articulation of the philosophy of India's development and its translation into schemes and programmes—provided for a larger emphasis on basic education, expansion of elementary education, diversification of secondary education, improvement of standards of college and university education, extension of facilities for technical and vocational education, and the implementation of social education and cultural development programmes. The Second Plan document expressed concern that the rapid increase in the number of students in universities and colleges had affected the standards of education. The Plan stipulated a number of measures for improving the quality of university and college education and for reducing wastage and stagnation of students who were unable to qualify. These included the institution of three-year degree courses and improvement in the overall environment and infrastructure, etc. The Plan also considered the diversification of courses at the secondary level mainly with a view to checking the rush of students to Arts Colleges. The main concern was that university education should acquire greater purpose and direction. However, the plan had a much more enthusiastic approach toward higher technical education. The IIT at Kharagpur was established during the first Five Year Plan and the establishment of other technological institutions, in a phased manner, was envisaged for different regions of the country. That is how the other IITs and Regional Engineering Colleges (RECs) came into existence. Over the years after independence, a large number of teaching and research institutions/universities have been established, covering almost all the major disciplines in technology, sciences, social sciences, management, and arts. However in terms of priority, as reflected in resources spent on higher education, higher education really had a back seat.

The changes in the post-independence period in terms of absolute numbers, however, have been impressive. By the year 1991, we had 5.8 persons per thousand population enrolled in institutions of higher education and by the year 1998–9 this number had reached 7.5 persons per thousand,

marking an almost 11-fold increase over the base of 1951. The number of colleges increased from 750 in 1950–1 to 11,089 in 1998–9, a 15-fold increase. The number of universities increased from 30 to 238 over the same period. The number of students increased from 263,000 to 7,417,000 over the same period, an increase of 28 times. The number of teachers went up from 24,000 to 342,000, that is, 14 times. Thus, over this period the student–teacher ratio has doubled. In 2004, there were 300 universities/deemed universities including 18 medical universities and 40 agricultural universities and more than 15,000 colleges, of which over 5000 were in rural areas (approximate numbers). Enrolment in higher education rose from less than half a million in 1950–1 to over 9 million in 2003. Table 5.9 gives the growth rate of enrolment from 1982–3 to 2001–02. It can be seen that the growth of enrolment has slowed down since 1991–2.

Even with great strides in the expansion of education, the enrolment in higher education today would be less than nine persons per thousand population. Vast numbers of aspiring youth do not have access to higher education. In fact, the constraints on the access to education start right from the primary level and become more acute at the secondary level and even more so at higher levels of education. In the early years after independence, since the literacy rate as well as the rate of schooling was very low, the demand for college education was much less. The demand for college education was mostly from a very small section of urban population. Aspiring students could easily get admission in

TABLE 5.9
All India Growth of Student Enrolment (Higher Education) 1982–3 to 2001–02

Year	Total Enrolment (in thousand)	Percentage increase
1982–3	3133	6.1
1983–4	3308	5.6
1984–5	3404	2.9
1985–6	3605	5.9
1986–7	3757	4.2
1987–8	4020	7.0
1988–9	4285	6.6
1989–90	4603	7.4
1990–1	4925	7.0
1991–2	5266	6.9
1992–3	5535	5.1
1993–4	5817	5.1
1994–5	6114	5.1
1995–6	6574	7.5
1996–7	6843	4.1
1997–8	7260	6.1
1998–9	7706	6.1
1999–2000	8051	4.5
2000–1	8399	4.3
2001–2	8821	5.0

Source: Kaur (2003).

universities/colleges in any subject they liked if they had the necessary minimum schooling. Starting from such a low base, the expansion appears to have been vast. However, the facilities for higher education have not grown in proportion to the demand and in proportion to the growing aspirations among the people for a higher degree or for real higher education. In countries where job opportunities are good and rates of earnings are not so widely different between jobs requiring higher education and other jobs requiring somewhat lower education but particular skills, many young people voluntarily branch off towards skilled jobs requiring school education and vocational skills. However, even in international comparison, the current enrolment ratio in higher education in India is less than the average for lower middle-income countries in the world. The gross enrolment ratio is less than 9 per cent in India, while it is 15 per cent in China, more than 20 per cent in many developing countries such as Mexico, Malaysia, Thailand, Chile and Brazil, and 40 to 50 per cent in most of the developed countries (PROPHE, <http://www.albany.edu/dept/prophe/data/data.html>).

As the literacy base of population and the base of schooling is expanding at faster rate now, the demand for higher education will also grow at a faster pace. Literacy rate of the population has increased from 18.33 per cent in 1951 to 65.4 per cent in 2001. Enrolment in high schools and higher secondary schools increased from 15 lakh in 1950–1 to 282 lakh in 1999–2000, nearly 19-fold increase, or an increase from 4.2 persons per thousand of population to 28.5 persons per thousand, that is, a 7-fold increase. The result of slow expansion of capacity and fast increasing demand is, an acute scarcity of access to higher education. In such an environment of scarcity, the poor are more deprived of access while the unscrupulous private providers flourish extorting huge rentals from the scarcity. Quality of supply too suffers under scarcity.

It is clear from the discussion here that capacity for higher education in India, today, is very inadequate. It has been built up in the past at a very slow rate and needs to be stepped up at a much higher rate in the coming years. Looking at the perception and mood of the people, it appears that if capacity is not enhanced adequately in the next few years, it might even become the cause of a major social unrest. As a target, let us say, we need to double the capacity in the next five years. Towards this goal, we need to explore all the possible ways of adding to capacity through private and public investments and also use more innovatively and more intensively some of the existing research capacities that have already been created.

Box 5.3

The Goal of Spending Six Per Cent of GDP on Education

The National Policy on Education, 1986 had recommended: 'from the Eighth Plan (1992–7) onwards, it (the expenditure on education) will uniformly exceed 6% of the national income.' How far away we are from this magic figure! The US with its astronomical national income, was spending 5.6 per cent of its GDP on education in 2002. The percentage for France was 5.8 and for Germany 4.6. Even Thailand and Kenya were spending 5 per cent and 6.2 per cent, respectively of their GDP on education in 2002 (J.L. Azad, *Higher education: rethink required*, Financial Express, 15 January 2005).

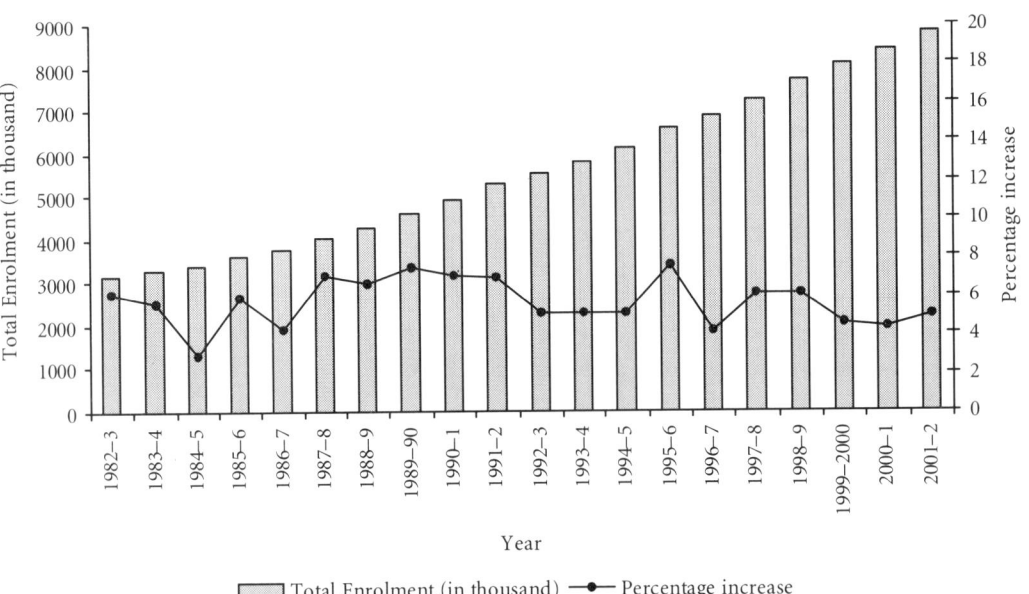

Figure 5.3: All India Growth of Student Enrolment (Higher Education), 1982–3 to 2001–2

INVESTMENT IN HIGHER EDUCATION

The main constraint to the expansion of higher educational facilities has been the meager public resources allocated to education. Priority within the available resources naturally goes to primary and secondary education (Table 5.10). The Education Commission (1964–6) had recommended that at least 6 per cent of GDP should be spent on education. Many countries, developed as well as developing, spend more than 6 per cent of their GDP on education. Stated as one of the goals of the National Policy on Education, the need to step up expenditure on education towards the goal of 6 per cent of GDP often finds an important place in political statements on education, and has been a persistent demand from those concerned with education. However, we find that in recent years public expenditure on education as a percentage of GDP has declined, and it was only 3.49 per cent in 2004–05 (Table 5.11).

TABLE 5.10
Expenditure on Education in the Five Year Plans
(*as percentage of total expenditure in the FY plans*)

Five Year Plan	Total Education	Elementary	Secondary	Higher
Fifth Plan	3.27	0.8	0.4	0.5
Sixth Plan	2.70	0.8	0.7	0.5
Seventh Plan	3.55	1.3	0.8	0.5
Eighth Plan	4.50	2.1	0.8	0.3
Ninth Plan	6.23	3.2	1.1	0.5

Note: Other levels and types of education are included in Total.
Source: Tilak (2006).

Public expenditure on higher education per student was Rs 7676 (at 1993–4 prices) in 1990–1. It came down to Rs 6954 (at constant prices) in 1999–2000 and further to Rs 5522 in the year 2002–3 (Tilak 2004). Also, the ratio of proposed outlay on secondary education in the Tenth Plan to the actual expenditure on secondary education in the Ninth Plan (at current prices) was 1.8. The same ratio for higher education was lower at 1.6. Thus, while the economy is booming and a 6 per cent (per annum) growth rate has been sustained over a decently long period of a decade and a half, and it is well recognized that it is our knowledge base which has largely contributed to this high growth achieved with poor infrastructure and acute shortages of energy, our per capita public expenditure on higher education, in real terms, has not increased. We also need to note, in this context, that whatever knowledge base we have been able to create in the country, public expenditure has almost entirely been the source of it, in spite of its frugality. Even in terms of quality, the best has come from the public supported institutions of higher learning. If we want to press on the advantages that our knowledge base has given us, there is a case for massive additional public investment in higher education.

TABLE 5.11
Growth in Public Expenditure on Education in India

Year	Percentage of GDP	Percentage of Budget	Per capita (Rs) (1993–4 prices)
1990–1	4.07	13.97	329
2000–1	4.26	12.23	509
2001–2	3.82	10.80	470
2002–3	3.97	12.60	495
2003–4	3.74	12.31	498
2004–5	3.49	12.27	–

Source: Tilak (2006).

The recently released Planning Commission's paper on approach to the 11th Plan has shown a promising awareness of the issue. The approach paper states 'It (The 11th Plan)

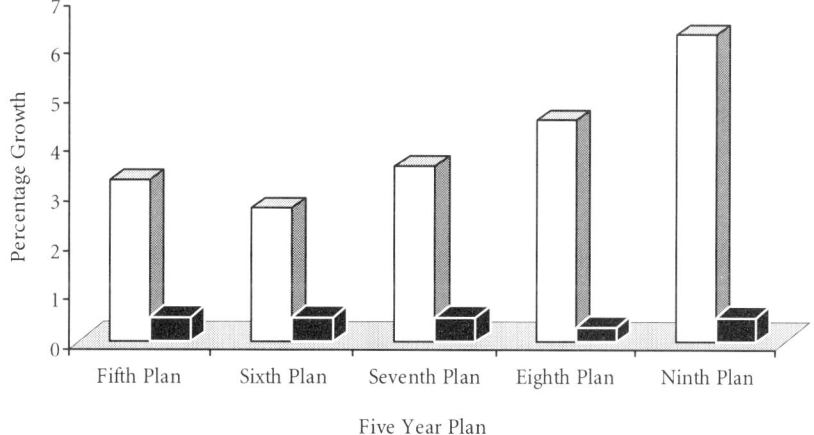

Figure 5.4: Expenditure on Education in the Five Year Plans

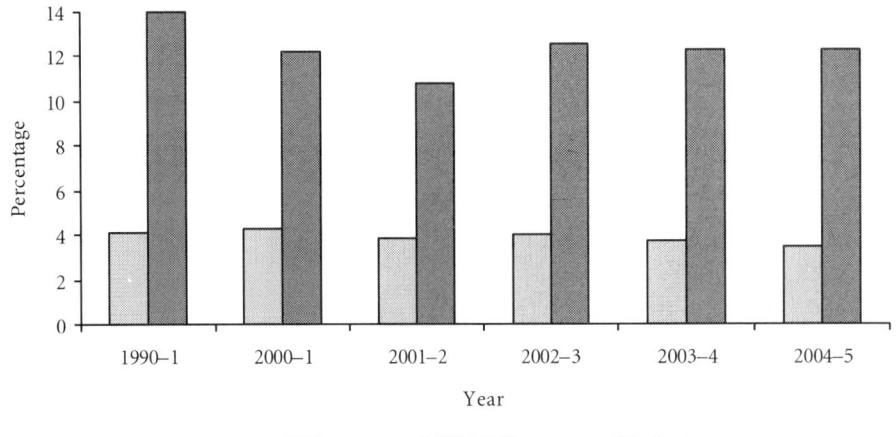

Figure 5.5: Growth in Public Expenditure on Education in India

must address simultaneously the issues of increasing enrolment in universities and colleges especially the high-end institutions like the IITs and IIMs, the problems of varying standards, outdated syllabi, inadequate facilities, and most of all the need to create an environment that will attract top class faculty'. The 'approach' further says, 'Achievement of these objectives will require a substantial increase in resources devoted to this sector and successive annual plans will have to provide rising levels of budgetary support. However, this must be accompanied by internal resource generation by duly and realistically raising fees. Simultaneously, efforts will be made to develop wider merit-cum-means based loan and scholarship programmes through the banking system and other agencies' (Planning Commission 2006).

Private Providers

In as much as it adds to the much needed capacity, the participation of private providers in higher education is welcome in the given situation of resource crunch. In earlier days, private initiative in education came mainly from religious and charitable endowments, which established 'non-profit' institutions. Today a new crop of institutions of higher learning has come up to fill in the gap in capacity creation, and most of them are 'for-profit' types. According to some estimates these account for nearly one-third of all the institutions of higher learning. The private providers are still welcome as they do create the much needed and sought after capacity for higher education. But 'for profit' considerations naturally raise the costs to a very high level and put the facilities out of reach for the less privileged. In much sought after branches of education such as medicine, management, or certain branches of engineering, where capacity constraints in publicly provided facilities are very acute, private providers even manage to obtain a very high

> **BOX 5.4**
> **Need for Regulating Quality of Curricula and Institutions**
>
> 'India's higher education needs policy. The Government has to play the role of facilitator and regulator of quality in curricula and institutions' wrote S. Neogi (*Hindustan Times*, 28 November 2005). Neogi further pointed out, 'The mushrooming of medical and engineering colleges in Karnataka, Andhra Pradesh and Maharashtra is another example of how an overwhelming demand got around an indifferent government. In fact, private sector engineering colleges, which accounted for 15 per cent of the seats in 1960, now account for 84.4 per cent of seats. The proportion of private medical colleges is also rising. From 6.8 per cent seats in 1960 it is 40 per cent now. The irony is that despite UGC affiliations, many of these universities and colleges are no more than education shops'.

rental on each of the seats offered, most of the time in an unaccounted manner. Even the quality of education offered in some of these institutions leaves much to be desired. Among the higher educational institutions in India, one must admit, the best ones in terms of quality of education provided are still those in the public domain, or some of those among the private 'non-profit' providers. The experience so far has been that the profit motive in education dilutes quality. It is no wonder that the most sought-after institutions of higher learning happen to be in the public domain, including the autonomous institutions largely supported by public funds and the level of competition for admission in these publicly provided institutions has become enormously tough.

It is these concerns about privatization which are reflected in the views of some of the eminent educationists. They believe that even while encouraging private investment in education, it must be made clear that such initiative in education cannot be for profit-making purposes in however disguised a form. Further, the entry of the private sector cannot be seen as a solution to all the various problems of quantity and quality. However, in the face of acute capacity constraints in higher education, private providers may be allowed but they should be subjected to a regulatory framework which ensures careful accreditation and monitoring of working of the institutions and quality of education that they provide.

Foreign Providers

In order to add to the scarce capacity for higher learning, we need also to encourage the entry of foreign education providers particularly the well-known ones to India. A foreign university/institute may open its branch in India either as its sole subsidiary or in partnership with an Indian university/institute. Investment in infrastructure, design of curricula, faculty recruitment and development will be the responsibility of the providing institution, and the degree is awarded by the providing foreign institutions (Bhushan 2005). A regulatory framework will, of course, be required for the entry and working of the foreign education provider. Apart from creating the much needed capacity, entry of a reputed foreign education provider will bring in quality and may have an indirect impact on the quality of indigenous providers as well. The cost of education in this arrangement will be higher, but certainly not as high as in the indigenous rent-seeking institutions. Moreover, it will also cater to the demand of those who would in any case like to acquire a foreign degree. The number of students going to the USA alone was 47,411 in 2000–1 which rose to 74,603 in 2002–3 (MHRD 2003–4). The total number of students going abroad for education would be more than 100,000 by now. The demand for foreign education is growing at a fast rate. The entry of reputed foreign education providers will also satisfy demand for foreign education for those who cannot afford to go abroad.

There are also other forms of arrangement with foreign providers, that is, twinning or franchising arrangements with Indian partners. Under the twinning arrangement, the foreign institutions in India attract Indian students for a year or two in their own countries. Under the franchise, the foreign institutions permit Indian partner institutions to execute the programme and conduct the examinations. The foreign institution keeps a control over the quality and curriculum design. As per information collected by the National Institute of Educational Planning and Administration (NIEPA), there were over 100 institutions/universities providing foreign courses/programmes in India. It is reported that there has been a spurt in the demand for courses/programmes offered by Indian institutions working in collaboration with foreign universities. However, in the absence of a simple and transparent approach to recognize, supervise, and monitor foreign education providers in India, students feel uncertain about their career prospects having followed such courses of study (NIEPA 2004). There is a need for a regulatory body to register, approve, and monitor the overall operation of foreign education providers in India.

USING THE EXISTING RESEARCH INFRASTRUCTURE FOR TEACHING AT HIGHER LEVELS

There is immense possibility of using the existing research infrastructure for teaching at higher levels, and thus adding to the capacity for higher education within a short period and with marginal additional investments only.

It was understood from the very beginning of the era of planned development that a strong foundation in research in science and technology as well as in social sciences was necessary for building up a self-reliant, modern, industrial society, even though planners were somewhat sceptical about the usefulness of university degree holders in non-technical subjects, generally desiring that university education should acquire greater purpose and direction and fit more closely into plans of economic and social development (Planning Commission 1956). Towards this end a large number of research support structures were created and nurtured through the Plans. Departments were created within the government for focusing on research in science and technology. A number of councils and organizations were created for supporting research establishments (research centres, institutes, laboratories, etc.) Some of these (such as the Indian Council

---

Box 5.5
Research Support Structures

Some of the most important research support structures created by the Central Government in the fields of social science and science and technology are listed here:

In the field of Social Science
Indian Council of Social Science Research (ICSSR)
Indian Council of Historical Research (ICHR)
Indian Council of Philosophical Research (ICPR)
National Council of Rural Institute (NCRI)

In the field of Science and Technology
Department of Science and Technology (DST)
Department of Biotechnology (DBT)
Department of Oceanography (DO)
Council of Scientific and Industrial Research (CSIR)
Indian Council of Agricultural Research (ICAR)
Indian Council of Medical Research (ICMR)
Defence Research and Development Organization (DRDO)

Note: This is not an exhaustive list.

of Agricultural Research, ICAR) have supported teaching institutions/universities also, but most of them have remained involved with research alone. We take up for discussion two of these research support structures, that is, Indian Council of Social Science Research (ICSSR) and Council of Scientific and Industrial Research (CSIR), but the possibilities which exist with these structures, by and large, exist with all the other support structures also. ICSSR supports—by way of part-financing—a number of research institutes in social sciences, while CSIR fully supports and controls a number of institutes/laboratories and research centres in science and technology.

The ICSSR was established in 1969 to promote research in social sciences. It supports 28 research institutes spread over different parts of the country in partnership with state governments. It provides funds for research and also awards scholarships and fellowships. Most of the research institutes supported by ICSSR, have, after passing through some difficult times in respect of financial resources, established themselves well and have been able to mobilize considerable amount of resources on their own which has given them stability and strength. These institutes have, over time, built up excellent faculty, supportive infrastructure, and academic culture and environment. Many of them have been guiding research scholars for PhD in collaboration with some university. Many of them have also undertaken teaching towards a variety of training programmes. The Institute of Economic Growth (IEG), for example, provides training to Indian Economic Service (IES) probationers. Most, or rather all, of these institutes are in an excellent position to take up teaching at the post-graduate level. Experience shows that a combination of post-graduate teaching and research produces best results. There are a number of other well reputed autonomous institutes which are not under the auspices of ICSSR, and some of these have obtained the status of deemed university and have undertaken teaching the at post-graduate level, for example, Gokhale Institute of Politics and Economics (GIPE) at Pune and Indira Gandhi Institute of Development Research (IGIDR) at Mumbai. Results of this venture have been laudable. It is understood that for ICSSR-supported institutions, there are difficulties in obtaining deemed-to-be university status since ICSSR has narrowly interpreted its mandate so as to not support those institutes which obtain deemed to be university status from the University Grants Commission (UGC), while the UGC, though willing to confer deemed- to-be university status on the institutes which qualify as per the laid down norms, is unwilling to takeover the extra financial burden in compensating them for the loss of ICSSR grants. These are minor turf conflicts between two support structures within the same government and can certainly be settled through mutual understanding.

The CSIR has a countrywide network of 40 laboratories and 80 field centres which undertake fundamental and applied research in diverse areas of science and technology. The so-called laboratories are in fact full-fledged research institutes with outstanding scientists on their faculty and having excellent infrastructure. Areas of particular strength in the CSIR, which have won global recognition for excellence are aerospace engineering, drugs and pharmaceuticals, bio-science and bio-technology, chemicals (catalysts and polymers), petroleum (refining and petrochemicals), materials (composites), leather (processing, chemicals and product design), geophysics, and radio-physics (Kaur 2003). CSIR labs also have live interactive linkages with industries. CSIR institutes/labs guide research scholars for PhD in arrangement with universities and undertake a variety of training programmes. As such, each of the CSIR labs/institutes would be an excellent candidate to become a deemed-to-be university and undertake post-graduate teaching towards MSc, MTech, and PhD degrees. It was recently announced that the government had taken a decision that CSIR would become a deemed-to-be university (*The Economic Times*, 5 June 2006). However, it was said that the move would not result in any major structural changes in CSIR. The senior fellows and scientists working in various CSIR labs would double up as faculty. It was also reported that CSIR as deemed university would provide degrees such as MPhil, PhD, and post-doctorate. It is a step in the right direction, no doubt, but our main concern is the capacity constraints in providing education at graduate and post-graduate levels. These research institutions may not be able to bear the burden of undergraduate teaching, but they could certainly be opened up for teaching at MSc/MTech levels in addition to teaching for MPhil and guiding research for PhD. With the resources and expertise at their command they could produce the best quality of post-graduates, comparable with the best from anywhere in the world. Towards this end, it is advisable that instead of CSIR becoming a deemed university, each of the laboratories/institutes under CSIR should become a deemed university. Each of these institutes has developed its own identity and specializations, and deserves a degree of autonomy to develop further as a first-rate research and teaching institution. CSIR would keep performing the role of a support structure, guiding and regulating the work of these various institutes and rendering the necessary financial assistance—similar to the role played by UGC in respect of universities.

Deemed-to-be universities are playing an important role today. There are 102 deemed-to-be universities today, and 62 of them have come up post-2002. There is need to further evolve the accreditation system as well as a system of continuous monitoring of academic standards and proper regulation.

Open and distance learning (ODL) caters to about 10 to 15 per cent of candidates for higher education at present. The mandate in the current Five Year Plan is to raise this figure to around 30 per cent. The ODL system alone can extend the reach of higher education to remote and rural areas. There is a need for diversification of courses, making them job-oriented, and constantly improving the quality of lessons. Forums for close interaction between the ODL system and conventional universities and research institutions need to be evolved and strengthened.

THE RURAL–URBAN GAP IN EDUCATION

Higher education is still basically an urban phenomenon. Colleges and universities and other institutions of higher learning are mostly located in urban areas and are accessible mostly to the urban population. No doubt there are a number of degree colleges in rural areas. Out of a total of about 15,000 colleges, only about 5000 were located in rural areas with 72 per cent of the country's population resides. The quality of education in rural colleges is recognizably much lower than what it is in the urban areas. Rural colleges are mostly housed in inferior building structures, have poor libraries and labs, have poorer quality of sports and other facilities, and can afford only low paid teachers. The access to literature, books, journals, and other sources of knowledge is exceptionally poor in rural areas as compared to the average colleges in urban areas. Most of the rural colleges run without even moderately adequate sources of funds. In most cases they pay less than the official salaries to the teachers. All these factors together account for a lower quality of education. The concept in older times was that those few who desired to obtain higher education would go to an accessible urban centre, live in a hostel, and get the desired education. The assumption worked in practice because there were very few who desired higher education while living in rural areas and those who did they usually belonged to the top-most income group in that setting. That concept is no longer true. Today, there is a rising demand for higher education in rural areas. Even if the quality is not available, at least a degree is sought after in the hope that it would lead to some improvement in living standards.

It also appears that the urban–rural gap in the quality of education, over the years, has increased. There was a time, maybe the pre-independence period and a decade or two after independence, when schools in the rural areas were very few, but those few schools used to do a good job of educating students. The few who desired college education, had to migrate to cities, but with their background in schooling they did reasonably well in colleges, sometimes even better than students who came from urban schools. The gap in the quality of education between urban and rural schools was not so huge. One reason could be the resource endowments of the schools were more or less equal. If urban schools were run by municipal corporations, rural schools were run by district boards. If the schools were run by charitable trusts, again their resource endowments were similar in rural and urban areas. Today, the resource endowments of the schools vary enormously. Even among government schools, there are vast differences in resource endowments. Proficiency in English language among students from well-endowed urban schools gives them a head start. Rural schools have remained poor. Rural colleges get their students from these poor schools.

Students taught in rural colleges, therefore, do not do well in competition for good jobs. Young people who do well in the civil services examinations or other competitive tests for good jobs are largely from urban backgrounds (meaning urban education, and not necessarily urban place of birth). Candidates from amongst those who have had an opportunity of receiving urban education right from the primary or the secondary stage do well. The parents of a typically successful candidate would belong to 'service class'

Box 5.6

Success Rate by Medium—UPSC Civil Services Main Examination

Competitive advantage of the English Language can be seen in the Civil Services (Main) examinations conducted by the Union Public Service Commission (UPSC) for recruiting young people to the best and the most sought after Civil Services in the country. The candidates are allowed to take the examinations through the medium of English, Hindi, or any other listed language. Majority of candidates for civil services choose to take the exams through the English medium, and the next largest number choose Hindi; though an overwhelming large majority of students in the country obtain their degree through Hindi medium. Those who choose English as their medium have 3 to 4 times higher success rate than those who choose Hindi, as can be seen from the following table.

Success Rates by Medium: UPSC Civil Services Main Examination

Year	Medium	Candidates Appeared (number)	Successful Candidates (number)	Success (per cent)
2002	English	1969	238	12.09
	Hindi	1270	57	4.49
	All Mediums	3301	310	9.39
2003	English	3159	342	10.83
	Hindi	2469	49	1.98
	All Mediums	5750	413	7.18
2004	English	2989	346	11.58
	Hindi	2192	58	2.65
	All Mediums	5328	422	7.02
2005	English	2898	340	12.04
	Hindi	1880	65	3.46
	All Mediums	4923	425	8.63

Source: Union Public Service Commission, New Delhi.

or would be 'professionals such as doctors, lawyers', etc. It does happen but it is rather rare to find a young person coming with a completely rural educational background making it to the list of the successful candidates.

Today, the interactive processes, which contribute to the growth of knowledge, have become universal. Fast communications and virtually unlimited capacities to store and process information have tremendously enhanced our capabilities of learning from global access to knowledge. It is in recognition of these processes and with a desire to take advantage of the global store of knowledge, and with the rejection of the possibilities of being left out of it, that almost all the countries of the world have embarked upon learning of a common language, and that common language today happens to be English. Country after country, such as Russia, China, Japan, which, till only a few decades back, had shunned English altogether, has begun to make vigorous efforts to make learning of English possible for the youth. We, in India, have an inherited advantage in this. Even if only 3 per cent of our population had English education, we have a well-established system of teaching and learning English. It is this advantage that enabled us to a large extent to be able to take early advantage of developments in IT. We should not keep the vast majority of our rural population and also those living in urban areas but not having access to early learning of English, deprived of new opportunities. Mother tongue is no doubt very important—we should be proud of our language and national heritage. But, we should also facilitate early learning of English. The plea is not for making English the medium of instruction necessarily and everywhere, but for facilitating early learning of English in rural as well as in urban areas. The West Bengal Government has just done this. In schools and colleges, proficiency in English gives access to a wide range of books and literature all of which is not available in our own languages. It should not remain the privilege of a few who can afford to send their children to costlier English medium schools. We must participate in the new processes of globalization of knowledge and universalization of education with a new vigour and with full opportunities to all—poor and rich, rural and urban. Approach to rural education has also suffered somewhat from a well-intended but implicitly biased notion that educational needs of the rural population were different from the educational needs of the urban population. The University Education Commission 1948–9 recommended, inter alia, that rural education should evolve its own distinctive pattern and also that it should be administered mainly by persons who have been directly concerned with rural life and with rural education. The commission recommended the establishment of rural universities. Rural institutes were established under the Second Five Year Plan which launched the scheme of rural higher education with a purpose to inculcate among the rural youth 'sprit of service to the community and sympathy for rural way of life'. In fact, Agricultural Universities which got huge support after the launch of the green revolution contributed much more to rural development by developing new agricultural and crop raising technology rather than by sympathizing with the rural ways of life. Educational opportunities and choices available have to be relevant to the available work opportunities and human needs, no doubt. But the argument is sometimes carried to far to imply that if a person is living in a rural household and the occupation of the household is agriculture, the relevant education for that person would be related to rural life and agriculture. The 'relevance' argument is that education should give knowledge which is useful to the immediate surrounding of the pupil. A person from rural areas should be taught about farming, tending animals, or making mud houses. It is difficult to agree with this view. One cannot visualize a situation where a person, born in an agriculture family, has to remain an agriculturist over his lifetime and his children will also remain agriculturists and live in the rural areas. Every person whether he lives in the urban or rural setting has a right to aspire to unlimited boundaries for movement in terms of occupation and place of work. Education is 'universal'. It is only in this sense that the great portals of education are called 'universities'. We do not think education could only be what is relevant to the immediate surrounding of an individual. Education should be relevant to human life and society. Education must contribute to: human development, advancement of science, inventions of techniques, and innovations of new technology. It must aim at making the human mind and human life serene and beautiful. In that sense, it should certainly be relevant to life. Above all, education should facilitate rural–urban, occupational, or social mobility. Today, a rural person would not like to be treated separately. He/she would like to receive the same education and have the same choices that an urban person has.

SUMMARY AND CONCLUSION

The higher education system in India has expanded, but at a slow pace. The result is that our capacity and capabilities in higher education today are severely strained and are totally inadequate to meet the growing needs of the economy and the rising aspirations of the youth. There has been a spurt in the demand for higher education as more youth are passing through schools in larger numbers. Land-based economic systems are declining. The Indian middle class is expanding, urban orientation and attitudes are touching even the rural setting and the economy is shifting to a higher growth path with changes in economic structure and activities that are supported and sustained more by higher education inputs.

Agricultural growth has slowed down for more than a decade now. Declining public investment in agriculture and rising costs of inputs have made agriculture unprofitable. Indifferent quality of seeds and pesticides, non-availability of credit, and uncertain harvest prices have made agriculture a highly risky business. As a result, a large number of small and marginal farmers have been pushed below the poverty line and the phenomenon of farmers' suicides has spread over many states, including a state such as Punjab which was at the forefront of green revolution. Thus, even the rural population is increasingly being pushed to seek security in education, particularly higher education. It is seen from the available evidence that it is education at graduate and higher levels only which makes a real difference in earning levels.

It is seen that household expenditure on education goes up sharply as the income/expenditure of the household increases. Income/expenditure elasticity of expenditure on education is high. The proportion of educated youth in the labour force has been increasing, and this change is faster among rural youth and among females in the labour force—groups which had a lower proportion of educated in labour force.

The main thrust and priority of the education policy after independence has been the education of the masses—spread of literacy, expansion of elementary education, and diversification of secondary education. In the higher education segment, more emphasis was placed on higher technical education. The priority for higher education was rather low in terms of allocation of resources. Even with the apparently impressive growth in the number of colleges and universities and the number of students going in for higher education, enrolment in higher education today is less than 9 per cent of the relevant age-group population. The same ratio in many of the developing countries is around 20 per cent and for developed countries it is around 50 per cent.

The Education Commission (1964–6) had recommended that at least 6 per cent of GDP be spent on education. This target has never been achieved and in recent years expenditure on education as a percentage of GDP has even declined. Expenditure on education as percentage of GDP was 3.49 per cent in 2004–05. Hopefully, the Approach to the 11th Plan stipulates rising levels of budgetary support to education. In spite of its frugality, public expenditure has almost entirely been the basis of the education and knowledge infrastructure in this country. Even in terms of quality, the best has come from public-supported institutions of higher learning.

Participation of private providers in higher education has gone up in recent times—today they account for nearly one-third of all the higher education institutions, majority of them being 'for-profit' type. 'For-profit' considerations raise the costs enormously and do not pay due attention to quality. A well thought out regulatory framework detailing the system of grading, accreditation, and regular monitoring of quality of teaching and academic standards needs to be brought in place for private and foreign providers. Their participation in the system should, however, be welcome in order to ease capacity constraints. Entry of foreign providers of repute (A-grade universities/institutions) may even have a positive impact on the quality of education. Different forms of participation by foreign providers in our educational system need to be facilitated, subject to a well-placed regulatory system.

There is immense possibility of using the existing research infrastructure for teaching at higher levels, and adding to the higher education capacity within a short period and with marginal additional investments only. A large number of research support structures have been created and nurtured through the Five Year Plans in India in the areas of social sciences, sciences, and technology. The ICSSR, for example, supports a number of research institutes in social sciences, while the CSIR fully supports and controls a number of institutes/laboratories and research centres in science and technology. These institutions have over time built up good infrastructure, good faculty, and have a conducive academic and research environment. They are ideal for undertaking post-graduate teaching work in some of the most sought after disciplines. Each one of these institutes/labs could become a deemed university. There is need to further evolve the accreditation system as well as a system of monitoring of academic standards on a regular basis. Th ODL system can also be further expanded to cover the more remote and rural areas.

The urban–rural gap in the quality of education has increased over the years, and this puts those educated in rural areas at a disadvantage while competing for good jobs or higher studies in sought after disciplines. The disadvantage is mainly because of poor infrastructure and poor resources available to rural colleges. Earlier thinking was that those living in rural areas need special education 'relevant' to their surrounding. The 'relevance' question appears to have become irrelevant in today's world—the rural youth would not like to be treated separately.

An acute scarcity of access to higher education is being experienced today. In an environment of scarcity, the poor are more deprived of access. The capacity for higher education needs to be expanded at a much higher rate than in the past and needs to be nearly doubled in the next five years.

Knowledge as the source of growth and development is recognized, however, its full potential still remains to be realized. Our base of higher education is quite narrow and there are limits to the excellence we can achieve on a narrow base. Excellence is like the summit of a pyramid—the larger the base, the higher the summit. We must strive to make education and knowledge the real source of growth and development.

References

Altbach, Philip G. (2005), 'Higher Education in India', *Hindu*, 12 April 2005.

Azad, J.L. (2005), 'Higher Education: Rethink Required', *Financial Express*, 15 January 2005.

Bhushan, Sudhanshu (2005), 'Foreign Education Providers in India—Research Study', National Institute of Educational Planning and Administration, New Delhi.

Hashim, S.R. (2005), 3rd Convocation Address at Indira Gandhi Institute of Development Research, Mumbai, 6 December 2005.

Kaur, Kuldip (2003), 'Higher Education in India (1781–2003)', UGC, New Delhi.

Kundu, Amitabh, Niranjan Sarangi, and Bal Paritosh Das (2005), 'Economic Growth, Poverty and Non-Farm Employment: An Analysis of Rural Urban Inter-Linkages', in Rohini Nayyar and Alakh N. Sharma (ed.), *Rural Transformation in India— The Role of Non-form Sector*, Institute for Human Development, New Delhi.

MHRD (2003–4), *Selected Educational Statistics, 2003–4*, Ministry of Human Resource Development, Government of India.

NCAER, MIMAP (2003), *India Survey Report, The Well-being of Indian Households*, NCAER, Tata-McGraw Hill, New Delhi.

NIEPA (2004), 'Internationalisation of Higher Education, Issues and Concerns', National Conference, 26–7 August 2004, National Institute of Educational Planning and Administration, New Delhi.

Planning Commission (1956), *Second Five Year Plan*, Government of India, 1956.

——— (2003), *Report of the Task Force on Employment Opportunities*, Government of India, 2003.

——— (2005), *Mid-Term Appraisal of the Tenth Plan*, Government of India, 2005.

——— (2006), *An Approach to 11th Five Year Plan*, Government of India, 14 June 2006.

PROPHE (Programme for Research on Private Higher Education), Weblink: <*http://www.albany.edu/dept/prophe/data/data.html*>

Reddy, Narasimha (2006), 'Prof. B. Janardan Rao Memorial Lecture: Economic Reforms, Agrarian Crisis and Rural Distress', Prof. B.J. Rao Memorial Foundation, Warrangal.

Rao, C.H. Hanumantha (2005), 'Economic Reforms, Agriculture and Rural Development' (1997), in *Agricultural Growth, Farm Size and Rural Poverty Alleviation in India*, Academic Foundation, New Delhi.

Shariff, Abusaleh (1999), *Indian Human Development Report: A Profile of Indian States in 1990s*, NCAER and Oxford University Press, New Delhi.

Singh, R.P. (ed.) (1998), *Indian Universities—Towards Nation Building*, University Grants Commission, New Delhi.

Tilak, J.B.G. (2004), 'Absence of Policy and Perspective in Higher Education', *Economic and Political Weekly*, March.

Tilak, J.B.G. (2006), 'Education—A Saga of Spectacular Achievements and Conspicuous Failure', in *Indian Social Development Report*, Council for Social Development, Oxford University Press, New Delhi.

UPSC, Data compiled by Union Public Service Commission (on request).

6

Exploring Intra Urban Differences in Economic Well-being in India

S. Chandrasekhar • Tesfayi Gebreselassie

INTRODUCTION

Recent estimates by UN–Habitat suggest that there are 900 million slum dwellers in the developing world, accounting for 43 per cent of the urban population. It is important to focus on the slum population for the following three reasons. First, among the Millennium Development Goals, the one that explicitly focuses on urban areas is Goal 7 (Ensure Environmental Sustainability), Target 11: 'By 2020, to have achieved a significant improvement in the lives of at least 100 million slum dwellers'. Second, inadequate access to safe water and sanitation in slums can offset the advantage of living in urban areas, thereby making slum dwellers a disadvantaged group. The problem of poor service provision in the urban slums is well recognized. The Panel on Urban Population Dynamics recognized that slums dwellers 'may face additional health penalties that erase the urban health advantage' (Montgomery et al. 2003). Poor reproductive and child health outcomes in slums can be traced to lack of access to clean water, sanitation facilities, and health care services. Recent research shows that there are stark differences within urban areas and there is substantial heterogeneity within the slums as well as in the non-slum urban areas (Rutstein, Johnson, and Montana 2005, Matthews et al. 2005). Using Demographic Health Survey (DHS) data, Rutstein et al. (2005) show that slum dwellers are more disadvantaged in terms of maternal health services compared to households residing in non-slum urban areas. In addition, the unmet need for contraception among currently married women was higher for slum residents than for non-slum urban residents. Third, population growth rate in slums is higher than in other urban locations. In India, the annual growth rate of urban population is 3 per cent, in the large cities it is 4 per cent and in the slums it is between 5–6 per cent (National Population Policy 2000). The total fertility rate (TFR) is higher in the slums than in non-slum urban areas. For urban Maharashtra (not including Mumbai) the TFR was 2.24 while for metropolitan Mumbai it was 2.13. There are differences within Mumbai with the TFR much higher at 2.69 in the slum areas than in the non-slum areas—1.40 (Human Development Report Maharashtra 2002).

Despite the demographic importance of the slum population, research focusing on intra urban differences and in particular on slum populations has been limited because of lack of disaggregated data in urban areas, that is, separately

---

An earlier draft of this paper was presented at the IGIDR–CSH conference on 'Multidimensions of Urban Poverty in India', October 2006. We are grateful to Abhiroop Mukhopadhyay, R. Radhakrishna, and M.H. Suryanarayana for comments on an earlier draft. The usual disclaimer applies.

on slum and non-slum households. However, in India, two nationally representative data sets are available. For the first time, nationwide data were collected as part of 2001 Census of India on slum and non-slum urban households. Also, in 2002, the NSSO conducted a nationwide survey of various aspects of housing conditions. The data cover households from rural, slum, and non-slum urban areas. While household specific information (unit data) is available as part of the data made available by NSSO, unit level data are not available from Census 2001. An examination of these two data sets, albeit separately, sheds light on intra urban differences. Given the large data set and the extent of heterogeneity within India, some generalizations about characteristics of slum households and intra city differences should be possible.

This paper is structured is as follows. In the second section, we briefly describe the two data sets and the definition of slums suggested by UN-Habitat and the definitions used by Census 2001 and NSSO for purposes of collecting data. In third section, the focus is on the extent, distribution, and characteristics of slum population. In the fourth section, we describe the extent of heterogeneity within the slum population. Instead of focusing on wards from all the cities we instead choose to focus on four mega cities; viz. Chennai, Delhi, Kolkata, and Mumbai. Thus our analysis covers inter-state and inter-town differences and differences across slums within the same city. In the fifth section, we draw upon NSSO data on housing conditions and monthly consumption expenditure of households to understand the extent of differences in economic conditions across households living in slum and non-slum urban areas. We estimate the extent of relative poverty in urban areas and compare the distribution of monthly per capita consumption expenditure (MPCE) of households across slums and non slum urban areas. We also construct an asset index similar to those constructed by researchers using the Demographic Health Survey (DHS) data. Filmer and Pritchett (2001) have used principal component analysis to create an asset index as a proxy for long-run household wealth and to predict enrollment status of children.[1] Sahn and Stifel (2003) use factor analysis to construct an asset index and find that their index is a valid predictor of child health and nutrition. We examine the distribution of households based on the asset indices and MPCE and also comment on whether these distributions are similar.[2]

DATA

The UN-Habitat defines slums as areas characterized by inadequate access to safe water, sanitation, poor quality of housing, overcrowding, and insecure residential status.

In India, for the purposes of census operations, slums were identified according to the following criteria.

1. All specified areas in a town or city notified as 'slum' by state/local government and UT administration under any Act including a 'Slum Act'.
2. All areas recognized as 'slum' by state/local government and UT administration, housing and slum boards, which may have not been formally notified as slum under any Act.
3. A compact area of at least 300 population or about 60–70 households of poorly built congested tenements, in unhygienic environment, usually with inadequate infrastructure and lacking in proper sanitary and drinking water facilities.

On the other hand, NSSO defines a slum as a 'compact settlement with a collection of poorly built tenements, mostly of temporary nature, crowded together usually with inadequate sanitary and drinking water facilities in unhygienic conditions' (NSSO 2003, p. 6).

This article provides a description based on three data sets available as part of Census 2001: aggregates on the slum and non-slum urban population in 24 states, information on slum and non-slum urban population in 640 towns and cities from the 24 states, and finally ward-level information on slum households from these 640 town and cities. The estimates of slum population were confined to cities and towns having more than 50,000 population at the 1991 Census since the Directorate of Census Operations decided to identify slum areas in only such towns. In 2001, slum population has been reported from 26 states and union territories. The nine states and union territories not reporting any slum population in their cities or towns are Himachal Pradesh, Nagaland, Mizoram, Sikkim, Arunachal Pradesh, Manipur, Dadra and Nagar Haveli, Daman and Diu, and Lakshadweep. We also use the NSSO 2002 all-India level data set covering a total of 41,916 households from urban areas. Within urban areas, 6138 slum households and squatters, 35,703 households from non-slum urban areas and 75 households without a house were surveyed. Information is

---

[1] In the recent past, there have been disagreements on the appropriate statistical technique for creating an asset index using the dichotomous variables available in DHS data. Montgomery and Hewett (2004) advocate using MIMIC (multiple indicator, multiple cause) models to create a living standards index. Kolenikov and Angeles (2004) have argued that the approach proposed by Filmer and Pritchett (2001) 'is inferior to other methods for analysing discrete data, both simple such as using ordinal variables, and more sophisticated such as using the polychoric correlations'.

[2] Since the NSSO data do not have any information on reproductive or child health or schooling outcomes we are unable to check how well the indices do in terms of predicting health or educational outcomes.

available on various aspects including housing conditions, MPCE, and access to credit.[3]

EXTENT, DISTRIBUTION, AND CHARACTERISTICS OF SLUM POPULATION

India's population stood at 1027 million on 1 March 2001. 72 per cent of India's population lived in rural areas while the remaining 28 per cent lived in the urban areas. In 1991 (1981) less than 26 (24) per cent lived in urban areas. Although the level of urbanization has been rising gradually, and the decadal increase in urban population remains quite high (although slowing), there is still potential for enormous increases in India's urban population. As per the UN projections, if urbanization continues at the present rate, 46 per cent of the total population will be in urban regions of India by 2030 (United Nations 1998).

In the last two decades, growth of slums has become an integral part of urban India. In 1981, nearly 28 million persons lived in the slums, in 1991 there were 45.7 million slum dwellers and as per 2001 Census data, there are 40.6 million persons living in slums.[4] In 2001, the population residing in slums constituted nearly 23 per cent of the total urban population of states or union territories reporting slums. In Maharashtra, 11.2 million people lived in the slums followed by 5.19 million in Andhra Pradesh, 4.4 million in Uttar Pradesh, and 4.12 million in West Bengal. Thus nearly 59 per cent of India's slum population resides in these four states (Figure 6.1). If one includes Tamil Nadu then the top five states account for over 65 per cent of India's slum population (Census of India 2001).

The data have information on the distribution of social groups, viz. scheduled castes (SCs), scheduled tribes (STs), and others. The SCs and STs are minority groups and have been disadvantaged with regard to education and occupation. SCs account for 17.4 per cent of the population in slums all over India. In contrast this group accounts for less than 12 per cent of the non-slum urban population. There is no such variation in the case of ST households. The ST households account for 2.4 per cent of the slum population a nd the non-slum urban population.

The all-India literacy rate in slum areas is 73 per cent. The male literacy rate is 81 per cent and female literacy rate is 64 per cent. In the non-slum urban areas the overall literacy rate is 80 per cent and the male literacy rate and female literacy rates are 86 per cent and 73 per cent, respectively. As will be discussed in the next section, these averages mask the large differences in the literacy across slums in different wards within the same city.

Since literacy data are not available for different social groups, we computed the pair-wise correlation between the share of SCs in the state's slum population and the slum literacy rate. The correlation coefficient works out to –0.33 and is statistically significant at 10 per cent. Similarly, we computed the pair-wise correlation between the share of SCs in the state's non-slum urban population and the non-slum urban literacy rate. This correlation coefficient works out to –0.21 and is not statistically significant. This suggests that slum literacy rates could possibly be explained by the extent of SC population in the slums. If this conjecture is true, then the question that arises is, what would explain

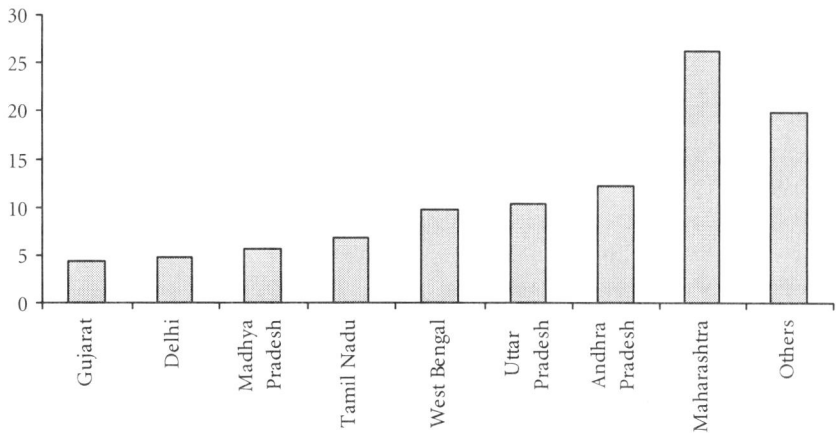

Source: Calculations based on data from 26 states and union territories.

Figure 6.1: Share of India's Slum Population

---

[3] For details on the sampling methodology and framework see NSSO (2003, 2004).

[4] There is reason to suspect that this decline is on account of an underestimation of the number of people living in the urban slums. The latest Census data also reflect the problems inherent in not having an accepted definition of slums and absence of proper listing of slum settlements in the urban offices concerned with slum improvement and civic amenities. The practice of notifying slums under relevant laws is not being followed, especially where the land involved belongs to the government or any of its agencies.

the high levels of illiteracy among the SCs residing in slums. This is an issue that needs to be explored further.

Earlier, we pointed out that the bulk of India's slum population resides in the states of Andhra Pradesh, Maharashtra, Uttar Pradesh, Tamil Nadu, and West Bengal. In 1999–2000, over 55 per cent of India's poor SC households from urban India resided in these five states (Radhakrishna et al. 2004). Also, nearly 56 per cent of India's very poor[5] urban households lived in these five states (Radhakrishna et al. 2004). Based on this, it is possible to conjecture that bulk of the poor households and in particular poor SC households reside in the slums. Though this conjecture cannot be verified since poverty measures are not available for slum and non-slum urban households, the conjecture is not necessarily far-fetched.[6] This has implications for the extent of urban poverty in these states.

There has been a lot of discussion on sex ratios following the release of Census 2001. A total of 6.07 children in the age group 0–6 reside in the slums accounting for 14.3 per cent of the total slum population. Mirroring the distribution of slum population, the bulk of these children (57 per cent) live in the slums of Andhra Pradesh, Maharashtra, Uttar Pradesh, Tamil Nadu, and West Bengal. The sex ratio (0–6 years), that is, girls per 1000 boys, is 919 in the slum population as compared to 906 in the non-slum urban areas. In Punjab and Haryana the sex ratio is 821 and 834, respectively in the slums and 796 and 808 in the non-slum urban areas.

Female literacy rate in slums is 9 percentage points lower than that in the non-slum urban areas. There is evidence in the literature to suggest that maternal education is important for child health and schooling outcomes. Lower levels of female literacy and poor slum infrastructure (water and sanitation) can make slum children particularly vulnerable. It is possible that the positive benefits of growing up in urban areas could bypass them. Godbole and Talwalkar (2000) found that the state of child health in urban slums was in some cases worse than that in rural areas.[7] A survey[8] of 14,500 households from 87 slums in the wards of borough VII revealed that adult female members were the primary decision making authority on issues pertaining to health. What is a of concern is that since a large proportion of females was not educated, it was effectively the uneducated who were taking important decisions on health matters. Maybe it was because of the low levels of literacy and awareness, that the incidence of anaemia in children and adults went unnoticed.

We now turn to the differences in slum population across the 640 cities and towns from the 26 states and union territories reporting slum population. Over 51 per cent of these cities or towns are from the states of Andhra Pradesh, Maharashtra, Tamil Nadu, Uttar Pradesh, and West Bengal.

TABLE 6.1
Differences Across Slum and Non-slum Households

	Mean	Standard deviation	Min.	Max.
Household Size				
Slums	5.35	0.87	3.68	9.52
Non Slum Urban	5.29	0.82	3.77	8.92
Sex Ratio (0–6 years)				
Slums	924	74.28	636	1700
Non Slum Urban	909	57.77	695	1024
Minority Groups: Slums				
Percentage of Scheduled Castes	22.50	14.48	0	100
Percentage of Scheduled Tribes	2.92	5.66	0	50.80
Minority Groups: Non-slum Urban				
Percentage of Scheduled Castes	12.04	6.44	0	49.18
Percentage of Scheduled Tribes	2.03	3.83	0	50.88
Literacy: Slums				
Overall	69.43	10.45	1.99	94.30
Male	78.04	9.72	2.47	96.62
Female	60.01	12.06	1.49	92.03
Literacy: Non-slum Urban				
Overall	79.76	7.57	37.92	96.62
Male	86.36	6.56	44.50	97.90
Female	72.55	9.21	27.87	95.38
WPR: Slums*				
Overall	37.60	6.06	20.26	68.19
Male	58.06	5.76	34.16	78.95
Female	15.19	8.29	0.74	59.33
WPR: Non-slum Urban				
Overall	35.66	4.64	25.05	58.79
Male	56.98	5.07	42.12	75.93
Female	12.33	5.81	2.81	46.53

Note: * The workforce participation rate (WPR) has been arrived at by dividing the total workers by the total population above the age of 6.
Source: Authors' calculations based on census data 2001 on 640 towns from 26 states and union territories.

---

[5] Poor persons are defined as those whose per capita total expenditure is less than 75 per cent of the state specific poverty lines.

[6] Case studies and small sample surveys have shown that a bulk of the slum dwellers are poor. A survey of nine slums in Howrah, West Bengal, undertaken by Sengupta (1999) revealed that one-third of the total population living in the slums spent less than Rs 247 a month and was below the poverty line.

[7] They also found that in the slum areas only 34 per cent women reported a birth interval of more than three years. The corresponding number in non-slum areas was 51 per cent. With regard to women's health, a survey undertaken by Institute of Medical Health, Pune (in 1998) of 27 slums in Pune revealed that 44 per cent of women did not take treatment for reproductive tract infections.

[8] *http://www.cmdaonline.com/plans_gis.html*

The state level aggregates reported in the earlier section mask the variations within the states. In this section we discuss the differences in the variables of interest across the towns of each state and the pattern that emerges is summarized in Table 6.1.

We find that the average household size is bigger in the slums than in non-slum urban areas. The sex ratio too is higher in the slums. The proportion of people from minority groups, in particular those belonging to SC households, is higher in the slums than in the non-slum urban areas.

The average literacy rate in the slums in towns is 69 per cent and this is 10 percentage points lower than that in non-slum urban areas. The difference in the male–female literacy rate in slums is 18 per cent while it is 14 per cent in non-slum urban areas. What is of concern is that while the literacy rate in the non-slum urban areas of these towns varies from 37 per cent to 96 per cent, in the slums of these towns the average literacy rate varies from 2 per cent to 94 per cent.

We do not find substantial difference in the work force participation rate[9] (WPR) across slums and non-slum urban areas. In slums the average WPR is 37.60 per cent while it is 35.66 per cent in non-slum urban areas. However, there are variations across towns in the male and female WPR.

The male WPR varies from 34.16 to 78.95 per cent in slums and from 42.12 to 75.93 per cent in the non-slum urban areas. The female WPR is lower than the male WPR. The female WPR varies from 0.74 to 59.33 per cent in slums and from 2.81 to 46.53 per cent in the non-slum urban areas.

HETEROGENEITY IN SLUM POPULATION

A large proportion of India's slum dwellers live in the slums of Greater Mumbai Municipal Corporation (6.48 million), Delhi Municipal Corporation (1.85 million), Kolkata Municipal Corporation (1.49 million), and Chennai Municipal Corporation (0.82 million).[10] If one considers the urban agglomerations of Mumbai, Delhi, Kolkata, and Chennai then these four agglomerations account for 29 per cent of the population living in the slums. These four urban agglomerations have populations of over six million each. Narrowing the focus from urban agglomeration to the municipal boundaries, we find that a large proportion of households live in the slums. For instance, in the Greater Mumbai Municipal Corporation, 35 per cent of people live in the slums.

There are large variations in the characteristics of the slum population within the wards of these cities (Table 6.2). From

TABLE 6.2
Variation in the Characteristics of the Slum Population Residing in different Wards of the same Municipal Corporation

	Kolkata			Chennai		
	Mean	Min.	Max.	Mean	Min.	Max.
Household Size	5.33	3.89	8.26	4.61	3.94	6.10
Sex Ratio (0–6 years)	927	677	1286	984	621	1393
Percentage of SCs	5.70	0	29.17	33.64	0	84.99
Percentage of STs	0.15	0	2.01	0.21	0	3.79
Overall Literacy Rate	74.43	44.97	92.18	74.73	44.54	93.84
Male Literacy Rate	79.09	47.63	95.09	81.42	52.30	97.69
Female Literacy Rate	68.80	38.98	88.35	67.92	37.54	90.91
Overall WPR Rate	43.56	27.83	70.25	39.40	30.47	51.54
Male WPR Rate	64.77	47.01	87	60.41	50.05	70.23
Female WPR Rate	15.32	3.66	39.57	18.01	7.01	47.62
	Delhi			Greater Mumbai		
Household Size	4.77	3.47	6.96	4.89	4.31	7.18
Sex Ratio (0–6 years)	904	0	1208	923	798	1067
Percentage of SCs	32.40	0	92	6.77	0	60.95
Percentage of STs	0	0	0	1.17	0	6.83
Overall Literacy Rate	60.60	10.80	93.61	82	50.98	93
Male Literacy Rate	69.20	15.03	95.52	88.11	58.11	96.73
Female Literacy Rate	48.65	5.66	92.07	73.96	39.55	88.37
Overall WPR Rate	44.31	33.80	77.78	43.67	34.58	59
Male WPR Rate	64.54	54.71	80	64.21	49.77	75.04
Female WPR Rate	16.30	4.07	75	16.52	3.78	33.66

Source: Authors' calculations based on Census 2001 data.

[9] The WPR has been calculated by dividing the total workers in the slums by the total above the age of 6 in the slums.

[10] Bhagat (2005) provides a discussion on the population growth rate (1981–2001) of these cities and urban agglomerations.

the table it is evident that there are differences in the household size, sex ratio, and share of minorities in the slum population. We also find that there exist substantial differences in the literacy rates in the slums within the same city. We computed the pair-wise correlation between the share of population not from the SC and ST and the overall literacy rate in the slum. The correlation coefficient is 0.36 and is statistically significant at 1 per cent level of significance. This suggests that in slums with a higher share of population from the minority groups, the literacy rate is lower.

We computed the pair-wise correlation between the female literacy rate and female WPR. The correlation coefficient is –0.32 and is statistically significant at 1 per cent level of significance. This suggests that female literacy could be a potential determinant of female work force participation rates.

Mayer (1999) finds causal linkages between sex ratio and female WPR, and sex ratio and female literacy. To examine this matter we computed the corresponding pair-wise correlation coefficients. We find the pair-wise correlation between sex ratio and female WPR to be very low (0.07) but statistically significant at 1 per cent. We find the pair-wise correlation between sex ratio and female literacy to be close to zero and statistically not significant. Interestingly, we find different results when we take the unit of observation as the town and not the ward. Using information at the town level, we find the pair-wise correlation between sex ratio and female WPR to be higher at 0.23 and statistically significant at 1 per cent. We find the pair-wise correlation between sex ratio and female literacy to be 0.14 and statistically significant at 1 per cent. Mayer's (1999) conjecture about a causal linkage between sex ratio and female literacy does not hold true when the unit of observation is the ward instead of the town. This finding is important since it seems to suggest that results could vary depending on the level of aggregation. The findings in this section clearly reflect the extent of heterogeneity in the slum population.

INTRA URBAN DIFFERENCES IN ECONOMIC CONDITION OF HOUSEHOLDS

To begin with, we measure the extent of relative poverty in urban areas. The concept of relative poverty takes into account the general level of income or consumption by considering the median MPCE. Relative poverty is defined as the proportion of people living in households with MPCE lower than 60 per cent of the MPCE[11] of the median household. Since this was not the thick sample of NSSO we are not able to calculate extent of absolute poverty. One limitation of the concept of absolute poverty is that it is defined and measured with respect to an absolute minimum, independent of the general level of income or standard of living. Relative poverty in contrast is measured in reference to the general level of income or consumption by considering the median MPCE. Hence our decision to focus on relative poverty is a fruitful exercise, capable of generating some insights.

We find the median MPCE in urban areas to be Rs 700. For the purpose of calculation of relative poverty we take the relative poverty line at 60 per cent of the median MPCE, that is, Rs 420.

For All India, we find relative poverty in urban areas to be 16.52 per cent, that is, 16.52 per cent of people in urban areas have an MPCE of less than 60 per cent of the median MPCE.[12]

We then focus on the distribution of relatively poor people by location (notified slum, non-notified slum, non-slum urban). In order to do this, we first calculate the total number of relatively poor people by location and also calculate the total number of people who are not relatively poor by location. We then take the ratio of these two numbers for each location and multiply it by 100. We find that for every 100 people residing in non-slum urban areas who are not relatively poor, there are 18 people from non-slum urban areas who are relatively poor. We find that for every 100 people residing in notified (non-notified) slums who are not relatively poor, there are 34 (48) people from notified (non-notified) slums who are relatively poor.

In many data sets such as DHS information on MPCE is not available and authors have constructed a standard of living index. Given that NSSO data have information on assets and MPCE, we construct an asset index in order to find the extent of correspondence between ranking of households as per asset index and MPCE.

Asset indices have been used as a proxy for long-run household wealth. It is often argued that compared to consumption expenditure, asset indices are better indicators of wealth and hence the economic condition of the household. We compute an asset index using the principal components statistical technique, that is, reduce a given number of variables by extracting linear combinations that best describe the variables. The first principal component, the linear combination capturing the greatest variance, can be converted into factor scores that serve as weights to construct a wealth index. The weights are standardized first

---

[11] In developed countries, including, the United Kingdom, the relative poverty line is drawn at 60 per cent of the median MPCE.

[12] We calculated the relative poverty for urban areas using NSS0 data for 1999–2000. These are the data from which official poverty numbers are generated. In 1999–2000, the median MPCE in urban areas was Rs 667 and the relative poverty line works out to Rs 400.2. Relative poverty in urban areas in 1999–2000 was 16.38 per cent. The 1999–2000 data did not have a slum identifier.

principal component of the variance–covariance matrix of the observed household assets. Filmer and Pritchett (2001) use a similar method to construct a wealth index (asset) using DHS data.

The summary statistics of the variables used to construct the asset index[13] are presented in Table 6.3. The definition suggested by UN-Habitat focuses on inadequate access to safe water, sanitation, poor quality of housing, overcrowding and insecure residential status. We focus on water source, availability of electricity, latrines, and drainage system.

TABLE 6.3
Mean of Assets by Resident Type

	Non-slum urban	Notified slum	Non-notified slum
Own Radio	0.51	0.34	0.31
Own Electric Fan	0.82	0.76	0.62
Own Bicycle	0.5	0.35	0.35
Own Sewing Machine	0.27	0.13	0.07
Own Colour TV	0.38	0.18	0.16
Own Black-White TV	0.29	0.37	0.3
Own Telephone	0.28	0.08	0.05
Own Refrigerator	0.3	0.07	0.06
Own Washing Machine	0.12	0.01	0.01
Own Motor Cycle	0.26	0.06	0.03
Own Heater	0.06	0.01	0.01
Own Air Conditioner	0.02	0	0
Own Car	0.05	0	0
Own Computer (PC)	0.03	0	0
Drinking water from Tap	0.73	0.84	0.73
Drinking water from well/tube	0.26	0.13	0.24
Drinking water from Other Source	0.02	0.03	0.03
Main cooking: wood, coal, dung	0.26	0.34	0.41
Main source of lighting electric	0.92	0.89	0.78
Private Pit	0.07	0.02	0.03
Private Flush	0.5	0.19	0.11
Shared Pit	0.05	0.04	0.08
Shared Flush	0.22	0.47	0.36
No Latrine	0.17	0.28	0.43
No Drainage	0.17	0.22	0.41
No Separate Kitchen	0.4	0.74	0.78
Dwelling made with High Quality Material	0.78	0.71	0.58

Source: Authors' calculations based on Census 2001 data.

Among all the sources of water, tap water is probably the most preferred water source. We find that 73 (84) per cent of households in non-notified (notified) slums have access to piped water. In the non slum urban areas 73 per cent of households have access to piped water. Similar differences emerge when one examines availability of latrines and drainage. Nearly 43 (28) per cent of non-notified (notified) slums do not have a latrine; and 41 (22) per cent do not have any drainage facility. In the non-slum urban areas 17 per cent of households do not have a latrine or any drainage facility.

Table 6.4 presents the mean and standard deviation of each item, and unrotated factor scores from principal component analysis. The distribution of non-slum, notified slum, and non-notified slum based on the wealth index quintiles is presented in Figure 6.2. The quintiles distinctively distinguish between the three locations. Based on the wealth index, 17 per cent of non-slum households, 1st 26 per cent of notified slum households, and 41 per cent of the non-notified slum households are in the poorest (1st quintile). On the other hand, 22, 2, and 2 per cent of the richest 20 per cent (5th quintile) reside in non-slum, notified slum, and non-notified slum, respectively.

In order to evaluate whether the rankings based on asset index and MPCE are similar, one can calculate the Spearman rank correlation based on the ranking of households according to the MPCE and the asset index. The overall Spearman's rank correlation between MPCE and the asset index for all households is 0.60. Spearman's test of independence between the reported monthly personal consumption expenditure and the wealth index rejects test of independence of the two distributions.

Alternatively, one can construct a matrix akin to a transition matrix (Sahn and Stifel 2003). Under this, we group households into n quantiles first based on the asset index and then based on MPCE of the households. In order to evaluate whether the rankings based on asset index and MPCE are similar, we compute the following correspondence index

$$\frac{\sum_{i=1}^{n}\sum_{j=1}^{n}(i-j)^2 m_{ij}}{2\sum_{i=1}^{\frac{n}{2}}(i-n)^2} \times \frac{1}{0.322} \qquad (6.1)$$

where 'n' is the number of even number of quantiles, 'i' is the row quantile, 'j' is the column quantile, and m_{ij} is the observation in the (i, j) cell of the matrix. We set n equal to 10. The underlying idea is that it gives weight to the off-diagonal elements of the matrix and the weights increase with distance from the diagonal. If all households are along the diagonal then the correspondence index takes the value 0.

---

[13] The standard of living index using the DHS data is constructed taking into consideration the following variables: type of house, toilet facility, source of lighting, main fuel for cooking, source of drinking water, separate room for cooking, ownership of house, agricultural land, irrigated land, livestock, and durable goods.

TABLE 6.4
Scoring Factors Based on the First Principal Component and Summary Statistics

	Scoring coefficients	Mean	Sandard deviation	Scoring factors
	1	2	3	(1/3)
Own Radio	0.50	0.49	0.50	1.00
Own Electric Fan	0.53	0.81	0.39	1.36
Own Bicycle	0.15	0.48	0.50	0.30
Own Sewing Machine	0.45	0.25	0.43	1.04
Own Colour TV	0.75	0.35	0.48	1.57
Own Black-White TV	−0.19	0.30	0.46	−0.41
Own Telephone	0.73	0.26	0.44	1.67
Own Refrigerator	0.78	0.28	0.45	1.74
Own Washing Machine	0.62	0.11	0.31	2.00
Own Motor Cycle	0.66	0.24	0.42	1.56
Own Heater	0.45	0.06	0.23	1.91
Own Air Conditioner	0.34	0.02	0.14	2.46
Own Car	0.46	0.04	0.20	2.22
Own Computer (PC)	0.35	0.03	0.17	2.02
Drinking water from Tap	0.31	0.74	0.44	0.69
Drinking water from well/tube	−0.31	0.25	0.43	−0.72
Drinking water from other source	−0.01	0.02	0.13	−0.06
Main cooking: wood, coal, dung	−0.56	0.27	0.44	−1.26
Main source of lighting electric	0.43	0.92	0.28	1.54
Private Pit	−0.07	0.07	0.25	−0.27
Shared Pit	−0.16	0.05	0.21	−0.75
Shared Flush	−0.20	0.24	0.43	−0.47
Private Flush	0.66	0.47	0.50	1.33
No Latrine	−0.52	0.19	0.39	−1.34
No Drainage	−0.40	0.18	0.39	−1.03
No Separate Kitchen	−0.60	0.44	0.50	−1.21
Dwelling made with High Quality Material	0.45	0.77	0.42	1.06
Percent covariance explained by 1st factor	22.77			
First eigenvalue	6.15			
Second eigenvalue	2.54			

Scoring coefficients are unrotated factor scores from PCA with mean 0 and standard deviation 1.

Source: Authors.

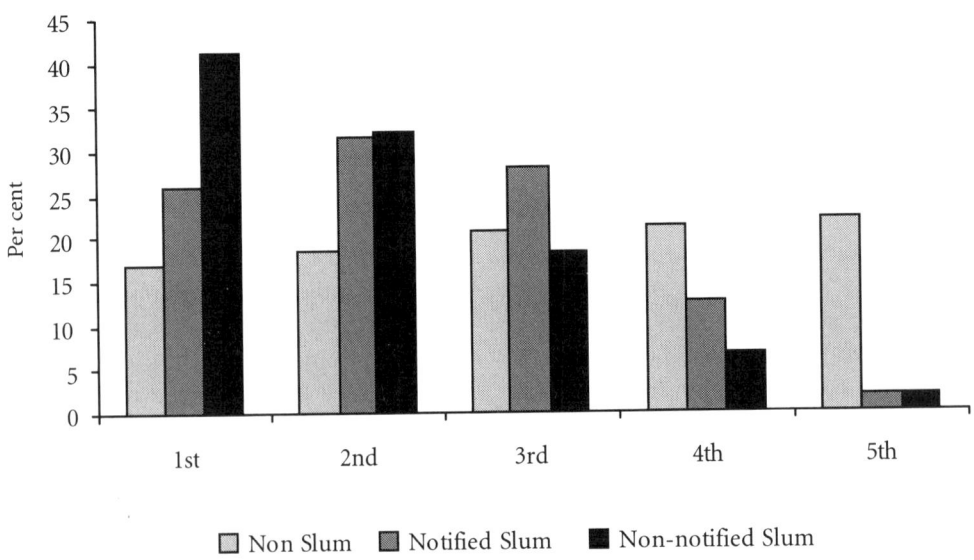

Figure 6.2: Distribution of Households based on Asset Index Quantiles by Location

If the value of the correspondence index is 1 then it implies perfect random association between the distributions based on asset index and MPCE of households. The correspondence indices for non-slum urban, notified slum, and non-notified slum are 0.37, 0.44, and 0.41, respectively. These numbers are comparable with those in the literature (Sahn and Stifel 2003).

CONCLUSION

This article provides a comprehensive picture of India's slum and non-slum urban population using data from the 2001 Census of India and NSSO. The paper establishes that there is substantial heterogeneity in the urban areas. There are large differences in the literacy rates between households living in slums and in non-slum urban areas. It also provides evidence that slums are extremely heterogeneous. There are large variations in the characteristics of slum households not only across the towns and cities of India but also within the wards of a city. We examined variations in the following variables: household size, proportion of minority groups in the urban population, literacy, sex ratio, and WPRs.

In order to highlight the distributional aspects, we estimated the extent of relative poverty in the urban areas. We also constructed an asset index and found a high rank correlation coefficient between ranking of households according to MPCE and asset index. Since asset indices have been used as one of the proximate determinants of reproductive and child health outcomes, our finding of similar rankings based on MPCE and asset index is of significance.

Reference

Bhagat, R.B. (2005), 'Urban Growth by City and Town Size in India', Paper presented at the Annual Meeting of Population Association of America held at Philadelphia, USA, 31 March–2 April 2005.

Census of India (2001), 'Metadata and Brief Highlights on Slum Population', available at *http://www.censusindia.net/results/slum/metadata_highlights.pdf*

Filmer, Deon and Lant H. Pritchett (2001), 'Estimating Wealth Effects without Expenditure Data or Tears: An Application to Educational Enrolments in States of India', *Demography*, Vol. 38, No. 1 (February), pp. 115–32.

Geodbole, V.T. and M.A. Talwalkau (1991a), 'Programme for Children: An Assessment in Urban Areas of Maharashtra 1998', State Family Welfare Bureau, Pune.

Government of Maharashtra (2002), *Human Development Report Maharashtra*.

Kolenikov, Stanislav and Gustavo Angeles (2004), 'The Use of Discrete Data in PCA: Theory, Simulations, and Applications to Socioeconomic Indices', available at *www.cpc.unc.edu/measure/publications/pdf/wp-04-85.pdf*

Matthews, Zoë, M. Brookes, R.William Stones, and Mian Bazle Hossain (2005), 'Village in the City: Autonomy and Maternal Health-Seeking among Slum Populations of Mumbai A Focus on Gender: Collected Papers on Gender Using DHS Data', ORC Macro, Calverton, Maryland, USA, August.

Mayer, Peter (1999), 'India's Falling Sex Ratios', *Population and Development Review*, Vol. 25, No. 2 (June), pp. 323–43.

Montgomery, Mark R. and Paul C. Hewett (2004), 'Urban Poverty and Health in Developing Countries: Household and Neighborhood Effects', Working Paper No. 184, Population Council, USA.

Montgomery, Mark, R. Stren, B. Cohen, and H. Reed (eds) (2003), *Cities Transformed: Demographic Change and Its Implications in the Developing World*, National Academy Press, Washington, DC.

National Commission on Population (undated), 'Role of NGO's', available at *http://populationcommission.nic.in/ngo.htm*

National Sample Survey Organization (2003), 'Condition of Urban Slums—2002' Report no. 488, Ministry of Statistics and Programme Implementation, Government of India.

——— (2004), 'Housing Condition in India', Report no. 486, Ministry of Statistics and Programme Implementation, Government of India.

Radhakrishna, R., K.H. Rao, C. Ravi, and B.S. Reddy (2004), 'Chronic Poverty and Malnutrition in India in the Nineties', Reprint Number 568, Indira Gandhi Institute of Development Research, Mumbai, India.

Rutstein, Shea, Kiersten Johnson, and Livia Montana (2005), 'Targeting Health Services to the Urban Poor: Is Slum Geography Enough?', Paper presented at International Union for the Scientific Study of Population, XXV International Population Conference, Tours, France, July 2005.

Sahn, David and David Stifel (2003), 'Exploring Alternative Measures of Welfare in the Absence of Expenditure Data', *Review of Income and Wealth*, Vol. 49, No. 4, pp. 463–89.

Sengupta, C. (1999), 'Dynamics of Community Environmental Management in Howrah Slums', *Economic and Political Weekly*, 22 May.

7

Macroeconomic Policy and the Exchange Rate
Working Together

Ashima Goyal

INTRODUCTION

Macroeconomic policy has been more intensively studied and is better understood for Latin American economies, but emerging market economies (EMEs) differ from each other in important respects. Greater attention has been focused on Asia after the East Asian crises, and currently on the Chinese exchange rate regime, as reserves grow in Asia and deficits widen in the US. Even so, the unique macroeconomic conditions facing China and India in their rapid catch-up phase of growth are not fully understood. The two countries have more than 2 billion people accounting for a third of the world population. The key transition that both face is one of absorbing labour into more productive modern employment. There are signs that China is reaching the end of this process. Migratory labour is no longer freely available in the SEZs and nominal wages are going up. India lags behind China in this process by about ten years. In this paper we examine the implications of a dualistic labour market structure for macroeconomic policy and, in particular, exchange rate policy for India.

We also examine the implications, for the appropriate exchange rate regime, of other major features that impact policy. Among these are the large inflows of global capital after the reforms, frequent temporary and some permanent supply shocks, the absence of full wage indexation for the majority of the population, prevalence of administered prices, and political factors resulting in an interaction of monetary and fiscal policy that keeps output below potential. The exchange rate regime should be able to contribute to lowering the probability of currency and banking crises, ensuring sustainable internal and external balance, and containing inflation. We examine each in turn in the sections to follow, in the specific structural context.[1]

Ever since the Indian reforms and liberalization, open economy issues have dominated monetary policy making. Dealing with the wall of foreign inflows hitting the economy and managing its impact on money supply has been the major day-to-day issue. Financial markets had to be deepened and an exchange rate appropriate for India's wider interface with the world found. Policy has done a good job, on the whole, and has responded flexibly to rapid changes. Although financial stability has been maintained and export promotion achieved, exchange rate policy has not contributed as much as it could have towards maintaining internal balance and containing inflation. The implications of structure and of more forward-looking behaviour of markets and consumers have been underutilized. Perspectives from

---

I thank an anonymous referee for very useful comments, Ankita Agarwal for prompt research assistance and T.S. Ananthi for help with the processing.

[1] The analysis draws on and updates material contained in Goyal (2002; 2004a; b, 2005a; b; 2006) and Goyal and Pujari (2005). The data and analysis of trends in until 2006 when the paper was written.

modern open economy macroeconomics explored in this paper suggest considerable degrees of freedom for policy even in the context of high capital mobility.

A change in the value of the rupee has widespread affects and, therefore, provokes interest. There have been many such changes after the reforms. Depreciation hurts all those who have to make payments in foreign currency, while those who receive such payments gain. Thus exporters, and beneficiaries of export spillovers, gain at the cost of the importers, the consumers, the holders of foreign liabilities. Nationalists want the rupee to be strong irrespective of the costs of overvaluation, but the current dominant view is that increasing the productive use of unemployed resources, to which exports can contribute, creates wealth.

The structure of the argument is as follows: in the next section, we examine changes in the nominal value of the rupee since the reforms, and then, in the third section, draw out their implications for the stability of forex (foreign exchange) markets. Box 7.1 shows that hedging tends to be incomplete and yet the exchange rate regime can encourage hedging; Box 7.2 explores the role of central bank (CB) intervention in focusing market expectations. Both would make forex markets more stable. The fourth section presents the contribution of Indian exchange rate policy to internal balance and argues that the latter was not achieved. Box 7.3 shows that large negative monetary policy shocks sustained the industrial slowdown. Box 7.4 explores the consequences of capital account convertibility and India's progress in achieving it. Box 7.5 lays out the arguments of the simple Mundell–Fleming (M–F) model for a loss of monetary policy autonomy in a more open economy. But a number of deviations from the simple case, which are valid for the Indian economy, imply that monetary policy has considerable impact. The two aspects of external balance examined in the fifth section are, first, the real exchange rate and its impact on exports; second, the large capital inflows and ballooning reserves. Box 7.7 argues that given the objective of encouraging exports, and the existence of unemployed resources, stimulating demand is a valid way of absorbing foreign resources available. Box 7.6 shows that despite more foreign borrowing, net income from abroad has risen as a ratio of GDP in the period after reforms. The sixth section argues that India's labour market structure implies an elastic aggregate supply curve, but one which is subject to frequent shocks. One such shock is a rise in food prices, which triggers off a rise in wages. More openness can contribute to stabilizing food prices and so can changes in the nominal exchange rate, thus giving the CB more weapons to fight inflation, yet maintain demand. The seventh section draws out the implications of this structure for monetary and fiscal policy and their co-ordination, and the final section concludes.

INDIA'S CHANGING EXCHANGE RATE REGIME

After the dual devaluation in the early 1990s, the rupee was market-determined, in the sense that it was now convertible on the current account and the RBI was no longer fixing buy and sell quotes. But heavy RBI intervention as it bought and sterilized the boom in foreign inflows, kept the rupee rock steady over 1993 and 1994 (see Figure 7.1, Table 7.1 and 7.2).

Periodic bursts of volatility occurred over the years 1995–2000, starting before and continuing past the East Asian currency and banking crisis. The response was to intervene to reduce volatility by raising interest rates and squeezing liquidity. The official policy stance was announced to be market determined exchange rates with intervention to control excess volatility. However, intervention's other aim was to maintain the unannounced real exchange rate target required to stimulate exports. This led to increasing reserves. Trend steady nominal depreciation was continued through the bursts of volatility, since Indian inflation rates

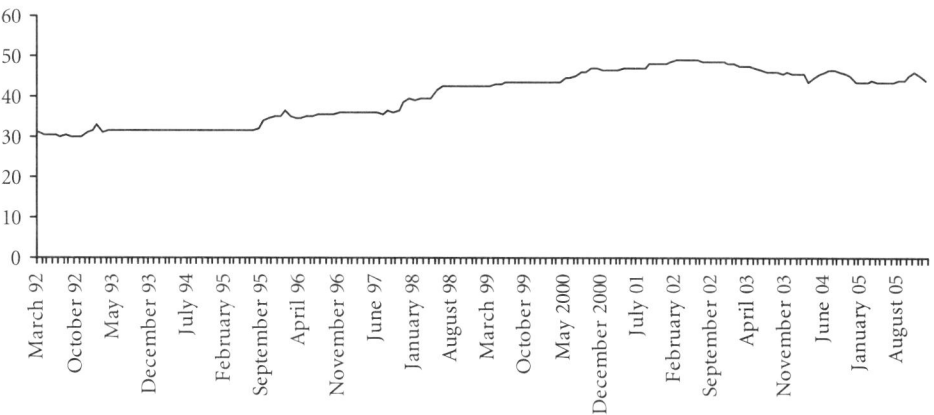

Figure 7.1: Post-reform Exchange Rates

TABLE 7.1
Depreciation (−) Or appreciation (+), End December

Year	Percentage change
1993	−1.6
1994	−0.02
1995	−12.1
1996	−2.2
1997	−9.3
1998	−8.2
1999	−2.4
2000	−7.5
2001	−3.1
2002	0.3
2003	5.0
2004	3.5
2005	−3.0

Source: Calculated using data from *www.rbi.org.in*

were higher than world rates. Table 7.1 shows consistent minus signs (denoting rupee depreciation) all through the 1990s. The trend was reversed for the first time in 2002 when the dollar began to depreciate under large US twin fiscal and balance of payment deficits. The rupee gained against the dollar even while it did not strengthen against other currencies.

Table 7.1 shows yearly changes in nominal rupee dollar exchange rates. In Table 7.2 percentage change between the highest and the lowest daily exchange rate within a year is used to calculate yearly volatility and standard deviation, to get a sense of the changes within a year. The table gives interesting information. Both 1999 and 2002 were periods where the exchange rate reverted to being almost frozen. That was partly why there was so much excitement in the markets, and volatility was high when the trend reversed. Reversals after a period of fixed exchange rates cause overreaction by market players as well as policy makers.

The reversal did establish the possibility of a two-way movement in nominal exchange rates, which can contribute to the stability of forex markets.

STABILITY OF FOREX MARKETS

Policy makers have traditionally regarded traders in Indian markets as prone to destabilizing speculative behaviour,[2] but poor market design and predictable one-way movements in exchange rates contribute to such behaviour.

To make currency markets more stable, policy makers need to avoid two traps: first, attempting to curb speculation through quantitative controls or restrictions on derivatives, which impede the development of financial markets and second, creating moral hazard and incentives to undertake more risk using derivatives. Thus market development has to go side by side with improving the incentives for hedging.

Before the reversal in the trend of Indian depreciation only importers and those who had borrowed from abroad were hedging their forex exposure. After the appreciation, exporters also rushed for cover. There was a 51 per cent rise of activity in rupee derivatives. It continued, however, to be concentrated among a few players, mostly foreign banks. Although there are still some restrictions on hedging indirect currency risk, new technology and regulatory market design are enhancing market activity yet lowering destabilizing speculation (Gopinath 2005).

By 2004, the Indian exchange rate policy evolved further in the required direction, with the RBI maintaining some two-way movement while continuing to prevent excess volatility. The identical percentage change in high–low rates and standard deviation over 2004, 2005, and the first half of 2006 suggests a conscious decision to create volatility. There were still periods when the exchange rate was almost frozen, but they had shrunk. One such period was from February to June 2005 (Table 7.2). In 2006, depreciation and higher volatility began earlier in May, driven partly by the fall-out of a crash in stock market indices. Over one week in May 2006, the Bombay Stock Exchange (BSE) stock index fell from approximately 13,000 to 9000, and then fluctuated.

TABLE 7.2
Yearly Volatility of the Exchange Rate

Years	Monthly high–low (per cent change)	Standard deviation
1993	0.9	0.2
1994	0.2	0.05
1995	12.2	2.7
1996	11.6	2.8
1997	11.3	2.9
1998	11.6	3.2
1999	2.8	0.9
2000	7.8	2.4
2001	4.3	1.4
2002	2.3	0.8
2003	5.3	1.7
2004	6.9	2.1
February 2005–	1.3	0.4
June 2005	6.9	2.1
January 2006–July 2006	6.6	2.1

Source: Calculated with data from *www.rbi.org.in*

---

[2] This has often caused great trauma to traders and to certain communities that specialize in trade. See Hardgrove (2004) for a study of the Indian Marwari community, their self-understanding, and sense of identity. They were said to be gamblers but for example, the traditional gambling on the rains actually served to hedge against income loss. Political rhetoric even equated foodgrain traders to the rats who eat grains and deserve to be shot.

> **Box 7.1**
>
> **Speculation versus Hedging**
>
> Hedging is reducing an existent risk by eliminating exposure to price movements in an asset. Speculation is betting on a one-way price movement. Thus speculators aim to profit by taking a position in the market. If they believe a currency is going to depreciate they sell the currency, or take a position using derivative products. It is not linked to any risk from an existing transaction, but is rather a 'risk-taking attempt to profit from subjective predictions of price movements' (Shiller 1993). It is sometimes argued that since speculators buy when prices are low and sell when prices are high, rational speculative activity stabilizes markets. But this does not always follow since speculators buy when there is a high probability of price appreciation and sell when the probability is low (Hart and Kreps 1986), and can thus cause cumulative movements. Hedging, however, stabilizes markets. First, it removes potential shocks to balance sheets that can destabilize the financial system. Second, if hedging is complete at the aggregate level, long and short positions can be matched with less price volatility.
>
> Hedging through market instruments has a cost* but can be potentially costless, for example, writing an insurance contract with someone who has the opposite currency position. But customized OTC hedging products have to be developed to implement such contracts. Financial innovation and competition should reduce the cost of hedging and this is part of market deepening. Informal hedging is also costless. However, hedging does not necessarily rise with the availability of more market instruments, since the same derivative can be used for hedging or for speculation. Incentives to induce hedging are more important.
>
> Hedging is incomplete even in developed markets. Psychological factors undermine rational decisions. Kahneman and Tversky's (1979) prospect theory showed that while people prefer a sure gain, they prefer an uncertain outcome with a small probability of a gain to a sure loss. Hedging involves a small sure loss or cost, and without it there is a small probability of a gain. Thus they are willing to reduce hedging and undertake more risk than is rational. But subsequent work shows the importance of 'framing' for the outcome. If the same choice is translated in a way sensitive to psychological attitudes, risk-taking behaviour can reduce.
>
> Moreover, an agent will rationally undertake too much risk under limited liability, when the government, debtors, or shareholders absorb bankruptcy costs, while the promoter is able to protect his assets. He will also prefer to speculate rather than hedge if economic structure or policy induces an expected one-way movement in exchange rates. Unhedged, short-term foreign borrowing had played a major role in escalating the East Asian crisis. Burnside et al. (2001) present evidence that markets, instruments, and opportunities existed for hedging in East Asian countries prior to the crisis, although there were some restrictions on the use of currency derivatives, for example in Korea. It was possible for those who took foreign loans to lay off the currency risk. These markets certainly existed in a country like Sweden, which also had a twin crisis in the early 1990s. The failure was more of incentives to hedge. Commitment to a pegged nominal exchange rate and domestic interest rates that exceeded international rates had encouraged firms and banks to over-borrow abroad without covering exchange rate risk. As currencies started depreciating they rushed to buy cover thus increasing the demand for dollars and creating pressure on the domestic currencies.
>
> * The approximate annual cost of hedging an NRI deposit against rupee fluctuations was between 130 to 150 basis points in 2006.

Figure 7.2 graphs daily spot rates over the period July 2005 to February 2006, it shows the concentration of volatility in a few months. An even spread through the year would imply deep markets and active price discovery. But until markets become deep enough, policy has to space its intervention so as to stimulate them. While continuing to limit excess volatility, policy has to consciously create some volatility.

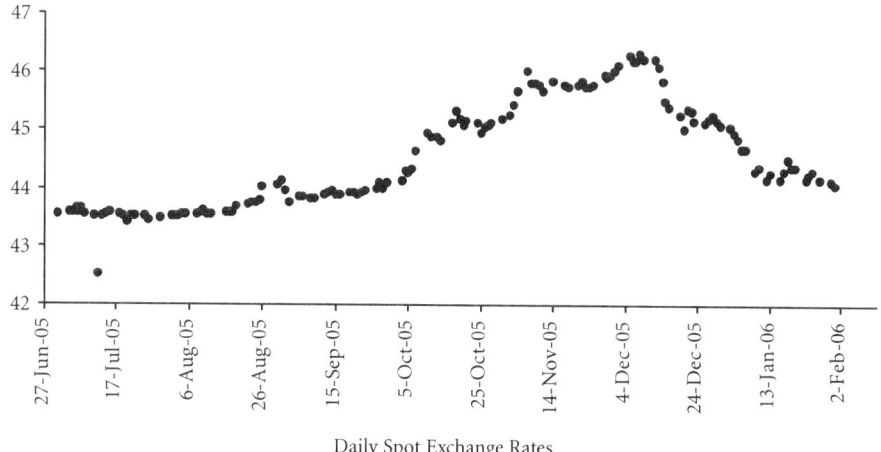

Daily Spot Exchange Rates

Figure 7.2: Recent Daily Fluctuations in Spot Exchange Rates

Box 7.2 presents some of the reasons for the instability of forex markets and discusses the role for, and effectiveness of, non-monetary interventions from the CB. Moreover, the RBI has the added advantage of the absence of full capital account convertibility (see Box 7.4). There are QRs of various kinds on the forex exposures allowed to different kinds of transactors, which give it additional levers of control. The problem is that these raise transaction costs, are impediments in the smooth working of markets, and are difficult to implement in the electronic age. The second advantage that the RBI has is the huge stock of reserves it has built up, so that its market interventions command respect.

Apart from improving one's own markets and policy, other ways to reduce the risk associated with capital inflows are improvements in the international financial architecture, and more regional co-operation (Goyal 2002b). Although the former is stalled, India is making progress in the latter (Reddy 2005). Apart from contributing to the stability of forex markets, exchange rate policy also has to contribute to internal balance—keeping the economy near

---

BOX 7.2

Forex Markets and Central Bank Intervention

There is a basic inequity in forex markets and that is the superior information with the CB and its dominance as a trader. Therefore, the forex market is not like any other market. Even so, the CB has a healthy respect for the market because of the tendency of market participants to follow each other in unstoppable one-way movements, and the sheer volume of forex transactions. CB reserves can be wiped out in minutes if it tries to defend a particular value of the exchange rate against market perceptions. So the CB watches the market and the market watches the CB in a guessing game. Each wants to know what the other is thinking.

Trend following also occurs because people are trying to guess and follow what other people are going to do, rather than base decisions on fundamentals. Herd behaviour is especially prevalent where fundamentals are uncertain, as in forex markets. Such markets are subject to irrational bubbles, especially in EMEs where conditions are less settled. Other psychological traits compound inefficiencies in forex markets. Past trends are expected to persist, leading to overreaction. The tendency towards mean reversion is systematically underrated (Shefrin 2001).

Another frequent psychological factor in financial markets is low error bands; that is, judgements are made with overconfidence. Investors tend to believe in their own evaluations and luck, thus suffer from an 'illusion of control' (Shiller 1993). All this suggests that there may be a role for exchange rate policy in focusing market expectations.

Exchange rate announcements alone can affect exchange rates because of the CB's dominant position in the forex market, and the market's aversion to uncertainty and ambiguity,* provided macroeconomic policy is credible. Ultimately a policy that strengthens fundamentals is credible. Initial intervention with the wind may be required to support an announcement. The intervention would be destabilizing, since the CB would buy the rupee when it signals a further appreciation and sell it when it wants it to depreciate. Since it would lose money if the opposite movement occurred, the intervention would be a credible signal of its intention. Market players would follow the signal since they would make speculative profits, for example as they sold a depreciating currency. They would not overreact since of the CB commitment to limiting the volatility. An announcement can be directional and diffuse, but within a pre-specified band, to minimize 'loss of face' if the market does not follow. This tends to be a concern with CBs.

Noise traders or those bound by contracts or current requirements would lose. They would be providing the net rupee demand on the opposite side of the market. Since rupee supply would far exceed demand, the required depreciation would soon occur. A reversal of the CB's stance, switching from selling the rupee to buying it, for example, may be required if depreciation begins to exceed the required amount. This—against the wind—intervention implies the CB buys when low. Since it would also sell when high, in the opposite case, if it wanted to stop rupee appreciation, it makes money across the two types of transactions. If the time of intervention followed random supply shocks, it would be random, providing incentives to hedge. Since the intervention is sterilized it implies that money supply is not tied to the exchange rate and remains free to respond to the domestic cycle. CB's buying or selling of the rupee, or its announcement of an expected direction of movement can alone initiate the change even without any change in the money supply.

Since in an EME such as India, receiving large capital inflows, the CB is always intervening or buying currency to accumulate foreign exchange reserves and prevent a large appreciation, only some modification of this intervention is required to bring about the required changes. On other occasions, market-driven movements in the exchange rate will continue to occur due to shocks to fundamentals or news from foreign markets; here stabilizing intervention may be required. When the CB influences and limits exchange rate expectations, entry of noise traders is lowered. These are traders without knowledge of fundamentals and who base valuations on actions of others. Such traders tend to gain from higher exchange rate volatility so their entry is lowered when this volatility is limited (Jeanne and Rose 2002), making forex markets more stable. Limited volatility is sufficient to encourage the activity of the well-informed institutional actors that markets in derivative contracts require.

*An example from Indian markets was the 'Manic Monday' on 17 May 2004, due to unexpected election results. Stock markets crashed and had to be shut down. The RBI made a public announcement on its website that it was ready to sell forex and to provide liquidity as required. The availability of the window meant it was not required. Since each player knew that the other knew that liquidity was available there was no need for a panic rush to be the first to draw a limited stock.

full employment—and external balance, that is, maintaining a balance of payments that is sustainable over time.

INTERNAL AND EXTERNAL BALANCE

Internal Balance

The response to bursts of high volatility in exchange rates was normally a sharp rise in interest rates. The first such episode in the mid-1990s triggered an industrial slowdown and subsequent such episodes sustained it over 1997–2001. When the domestic cycle required a macroeconomic stimulus, monetary policy repeatedly tightened in response to external shocks. Box 7.3 explains one way of calculating monetary shocks and the figure shows the large negative monetary shocks estimated over this period.

An analysis of the pattern of macroeconomic volatility across four pre- and post-reform, high and low growth periods (Goyal 2005a), shows that Indian interest rate volatility exceeded exchange rate volatility for much of the 1990s. Limited exchange rate volatility is easier to hedge than interest rate volatility, which has a deeper impact particularly when bank loans are the dominant mode of finance. Since the reliance on bank debt is high in an EME, sharp interest rate volatility delivers a severe shock to the financial system.

Although post-reform foreign financial inflows, measured by the surplus on the capital account rose, their volatility, and that of the major non-controlled components of the capital account fell. The volatility was also much below that of the current account deficit (CAD), which rose in the

---

Box 7.3

Monetary Policy Shocks

The strategy for isolating monetary policy shocks involves making enough identifying assumptions to estimate the parameters of the RBI's feedback rule. These assumptions include functional form assumptions and assumptions about the variables that RBI looks at while setting up its monetary policy instrument and also about the operating instrument.

Monetary policy shocks are identified using a short-run vector autoregression model. Since the variables are simultaneously determined over time, an identification assumption on contemporaneous causality is required to be able to isolate the policy shocks. That is, exogenous shocks (foreign oil price inflation and interest rates), and domestic variables (inflation, IIP growth, and exchange rate changes) affect the policy instrument variable (call money rates, or treasury bill rates) contemporaneously, but the policy variables affects them only with a lag. All these variables go on to affect gross bank credit and the broad monetary aggregate (M3). This is a 'recursiveness assumption'. The foreign variables are block exogenous to the system, since the Indian economy is too small to affect international prices, that is, domestic variables do not enter the lag structure of the foreign variables. The RBI's reaction function or feedback rule to changes in the foreign shocks and non-policy variables determines the setting of the policy instrument variable. The policy shock is the residual after this estimated 'reaction' of the RBI. It is orthogonal to the variables in the RBI's feedback rule. The residuals of the 'monetary policy instrument' equation are our estimate of monetary policy shocks.

The model behaves consistently. Responses to shocks are in directions suggested by theory, and thus it can be considered as a good approximation to reality. Estimated monetary policy shocks are shown in the figure.

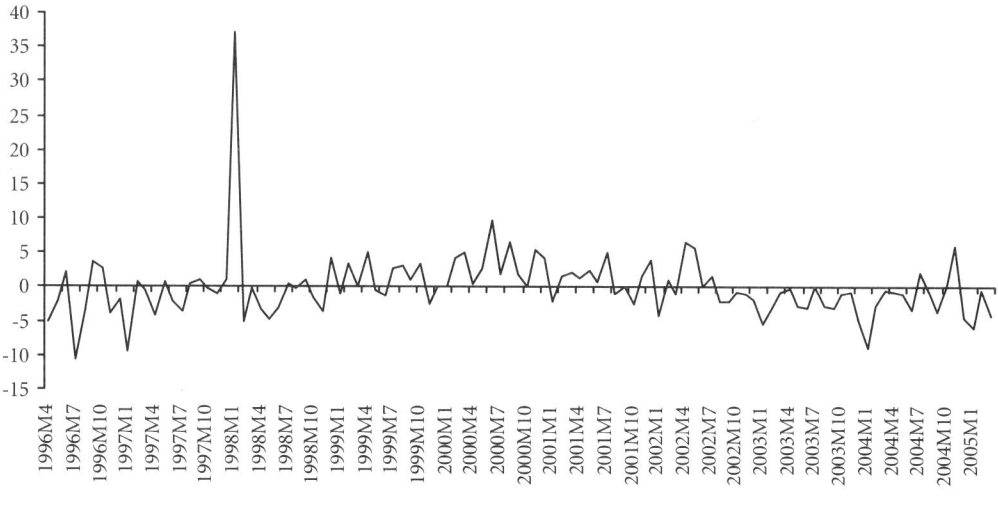

CMR SHOCK

Source of box: Ankita Agarwal.

period of the slowdown.[3] This suggests the latter may have been policy-induced due to the domestic cycle and not due to external volatility. Policy was magnifying the volatility of the inflows, and hindering their absorption. The CAD measures the actual absorption of foreign savings allowing domestic investment to exceed domestic savings.[4] Their trend was stable, but short-term fluctuations of foreign portfolio inflows did contribute to exchange rate volatility. The impact of interest rates rose significantly in the post-reform period. Although in the post-reform period exchange and nominal interest rates were more volatile, volatility in the latter reduced volatility in the real interest rate.

After 2001, two things happened. Falling US interests rates increased capital flows to EMEs. The calming of the so-called EME capital market crises[5] made capital less jittery. There was some reduction in Indian interest rates although not as much as in US rates. Second, the liquidity adjustment facility became operational at this time. It made effective smoothing of liquidity possible and brought all short-term interest rates within a corridor determined by the reverse-repo and the repo rate,[6] short-term policy rates. The steady lowering and smoothing of interest rates stimulated consumer spending and industry. But when the US Fed began raising the federal fund rate (ffr) in mid-2004, the RBI followed with quarter point rises in the reverse-repo rate from mid-2005. The question that arises is, if it is possible for the interest rate to respond to the domestic cycle, with some independence from international rates, in a more open economy? What is the degree of monetary policy autonomy and what is its impact on output?

The RBI also has to control for changes in US monetary policy since that influences capital flows to EMEs. But the US is following a paradigm of monetary policy that smoothes interest rates and gives excess demand time to reveal itself. So the RBI should have no difficulty in keeping Indian rates aligned. Although US rates have been rising since June 2004, the RBI had degrees of freedom since it had never lowered rates as much as the US.[7] Political rigidities that put a floor on the Indian interest rate structure led to large interest differentials, thus inviting short-term inflows seeking arbitrage opportunities. These differentials can be lowered as US interest rates rise. A fall in the risk associated with EMEs also makes it possible to lower interest differentials (BIS 2006). Indian rates can also rule lower than US rates to the extent that the rupee is appreciating against the dollar.

India has had a slow relaxation of controls on the capital account through the 1990s; capital account convertibility is now high for international capital but still low for outflows of domestic capital (see Box 7.4). We are closer to a fixed than a flexible rate.

Box 7.4

The Road to Full Capital Convertibility*

Controls raise transaction costs and create inefficiencies. Moreover, capital controls are difficult to implement in a more open and highly wired economy—the nuisance remains without the benefits. Global movement of capital to EMEs has risen. It is feared that controls may reduce India's share of the pie (although China has had no problem in attracting capital even with controls). India has the human capital to acquire a comparative advantage in the provision of financial services. Their development is handicapped without full rupee convertibility. The latter would also allow productive absorption of excess foreign exchange reserves as individuals optimally diversify their portfolio of assets.

However, short-term capital flows can be excessively volatile, and self-fulfilling panics develop in EMEs when fundamentals are weak and uncertain. Therefore, strong fundamentals and crisis proofing are prerequisites for full rupee convertibility. EMEs that opened their up capital account without the necessary institutional maturity suffered a series of crises in the 1990s. Acquiring external signs of development without the internal strengths is extremely dangerous.

Even so, steady progress is possible on the road to full convertibility. It requires reducing the instability of markets but releasing their strengths through improvements in regulation. As controls disappear, incentive structures have to be in place to induce responsible

(Box 7.4 contd.)

---

[3] The coefficients of variation for the two periods 1992–7 and 1997–2003 were –0.48 and –1.97, respectively, for the CAD and 0.46 and 0.19 for the capital account. The latter period coincided with the industrial slowdown.

[4] Forex reserves rose to 140 billion US dollars in 2005, compared to a paltry 5 billion in 1990–1. 30 billion dollars were accumulated in just 18 months over the period January 2002 to August 2003. Arbitrage occurred at the short end since Indian short real rates were kept higher than US rates.

[5] This was the name given to the East Asian currency crises after contagion spread to Brazil and Russia.

[6] The RBI stands ready to lend collateralized liquidity at the repo rate. The reverse-repo rate is the rate the RBI pays for deposits kept with it. Thus the repo is the rate at which the market can borrow from the RBI, and the reverse-repo the rate at which it lends to the RBI. The first creates injections of liquidity and the second absorbs liquidity.

[7] The lowest value the ffr had reached in mid 2004 was 1 per cent compared to 4.5 per cent for the Indian reverse repo rate (rrr). In August 2006 the two rates were respectively 5.25 (ffr) and 6 (rrr). The US Fed, coming to the end of its rising cycle missed a rise in August, while the RBI raised the rrr in July. Since the ffr is the daily rate at which US banks borrow from each other, it should be compared to the Indian call money rate, which is normally higher than the rrr.

(Box 7.4 contd.)

behaviour, to ensure that both policy and individual responses are such as not to amplify shocks. Market design and incentives have to encourage a shift away from speculative to fundamentals based behaviour.

Crises proofing is required to tackle weaknesses of markets. Part of this is countercyclical macroeconomic policy that supports trend growth—two-way movement of exchange rates, and a transparent exchange rate policy. Foreign capital comes in because of growth expectations and can go if either growth collapses or overheating occurs. Policy has to maintain a fine balance.

Financial markets need to be deepened further. Although reform of legal systems and implementation takes time, regulatory convergence is occurring faster. Debt markets still need to be deepened and international accounting standards adopted. We have made progress on all these fronts. Well-sequenced partial convertibility has already lowered transaction costs and stimulated financial development.

Specific sectoral policy proposals should be assessed in terms of their contribution to the overall objectives outlined above, to encouraging innovation, and inducing more competition in markets. Some examples are as follows:

Banks in SEZs make 75 per cent of loans to firms that are based in SEZs. It is possible to allow more foreign business, giving banks more freedom to compete in providing offshore services in SEZs, in line with the objective to create international financial centres. Since short-term unhedged bank borrowing abroad was a major cause of East Asian crises, limits on open positions should continue longer, but could be relaxed for individual banks depending on the strength of their balance sheets.

Individuals already had the freedom to remit upto $25,000 abroad in 2006. There is an argument that this was not fully utilized so the limit should be raised only for high net worth individuals. But since this is for portfolio diversification and can lead to unstable outflows, limits should be relaxed only for productive purposes, exports business acquisitions, expansions (above the current 200 per cent of a firm's net worth). To develop debt and derivative markets, limits for foreign inflows can be raised for longer-term bonds.

Competition and innovation should be encouraged to reduce the cost of hedging while two-way movement of asset prices encourages hedging. Restrictions on indirect hedging should be relaxed; MIFOR (Mumbai Interbank Forward Offer Rate) swaps for forex exposures, and interest rate futures should be allowed to develop.

Tax distortions should be removed. For example, ECB guidelines should have equal treatment of domestic as well as overseas acquisitions. The withholding tax should be made equal for bank loans and debt issues.

* This box draws on the author's contribution to The Economic Times, Tuesday debate, 28 March 2006, on 'Full rupee convertibility: good, bad or ugly?', and the author's comments made at a brainstorming discussion at the Indian Merchant's Chamber, Mumbai on 'Fuller Capital Account Convertibility', 14 June 2006.

The M–F model tells us that with perfect capital mobility, static expectations, and a fixed exchange rate, monetary autonomy is lost. Policy makers often refer to this impossible trinity, feeling a sense of helplessness before the wave of foreign inflows, and the increasing dominance of the market. But going beyond the simple M–F model (presented in Box 7.5), it turns out that the potential impact of monetary policy has increased with the reforms.

Box 7.5

The Impact of Monetary Policy in an EME: The Mundell–Fleming Model

Analysis* with the simple M–F model (this takes the expected exchange rate to be equal to its current rate) implies that under a float, monetary policy is effective in raising output in the short run but fiscal policy becomes ineffective. The reason is that a rise in money supply depreciates the currency and stimulates exports. But fiscal policy has the reverse effect, which counters the demand stimulus from the fiscal expansion.

Under a fixed exchange rate, a monetary expansion lowers the interest rate and the consequent capital outflow necessitates a sale of reserves, which reduces money supply, in order to maintain the fixed exchange rate. Fiscal policy escapes this neutralizing effect. A fiscal expansion raises interest rates above world rates. Maintaining the fixed exchange rate under the consequent capital inflow requires an expansion of reserves and money supply. The latter supports the fiscal expansion, thus raising demand and output in the short run.

With non-static expectations, the expected exchange rate can differ from the current rate. Now fiscal policy can also be effective under a floating exchange rate. The appreciation that occurs implies an expected depreciation back to equilibrium values. Therefore, higher interest rates do not lead to a further capital inflow and appreciation, crowding out the rise in demand, since uncovered interest parity is satisfied. That is, returns on holding domestic or foreign currency balances are equalized.

Under a fixed exchange rate, a monetary boost is still reversed, but devaluation allows reserves, money supply, and output to increase in the short term. An expected devaluation, however, would raise interest rates and if the latter harmed real fundamentals sufficiently, could lead to a capital outflow or attack on the foreign exchange reserves.

In the long run, of course, macroeconomic policy would not be able to raise output above full employment, and if the economy is at full employment, any monetary impulse would affect only nominal variables.

* Krugman and Obstfeld (2003) offer a textbook treatment that is simple yet in line with modern developments that emphasize asset markets.

The exchange rate regimes in most countries, and especially in EMEs such as India, are somewhere between a perfect fix and a perfect float. Even partial flexibility of exchange rates gives some monetary autonomy, and the absence of complete capital account convertibility (as in India) opens up more degrees of freedom, as Figure 7.3 (Frankel 1999) shows. The bottom two corners represent a fixed and a floating exchange rate and the line between them depicts the whole range of intermediate regimes. The upper point is a closed capital account, so that in approaching the bottom line, convertibility gradually increases until perfect capital mobility is reached on the line. Therefore, the impossible trinity is only point A of the triangle. Everywhere else there are varying degrees of monetary autonomy. The impossible trinity occupies only a point in the policy space even in the simple M–F model.

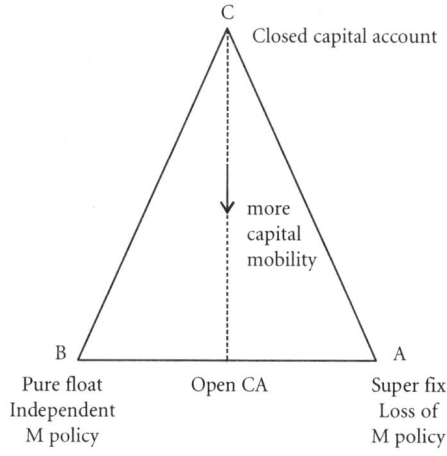

Figure 7.3: Shrinking the Impossible Trinity

If during rapid transition, as is currently occurring in India, productivity rises, and demand for a country's products rises even faster than productivity, the real exchange rate appreciates. From real interest parity this implies that the country's real interest rate has to be lower than world real interest rates, giving monetary policy a further degree of freedom in adjusting interest rates. If output is less than potential, and rising rapidly, as in India, even a rising money supply can be associated with a nominal appreciation, not depreciation, since demand for a currency falls with a rise in its relative money supply but rises with its relative income (Goyal 2005b).

Market efficiency has never been established for forex markets. Markets can sometimes get stuck in the wrong rate. These factors are exacerbated by goods market imperfections. The exchange rate overshoots to compensate for short-term nominal rigidities, and then slowly comes back to equilibrium. Excess volatility raises profits for noise traders and attracts more of them. Reducing excess volatility of the exchange rate can give a free lunch by reducing noise trader entry, and focusing market expectations, thus freeing monetary policy instruments to respond to the domestic cycle (Goyal 2006).

If the exchange rate is managed it cannot overshoot, but the same market imperfections can show up in excess volatility of interest rates in order to satisfy asset market expectations and currency arbitrage. Thus, some exchange rate flexibility can help smooth interest rates, yet give considerable freedom to adjust short-term interest rates to suit the domestic cycle. For example, even if exchange rates vary within a 5 per cent band, six month interest rates can vary 10 per cent while satisfying uncovered interest parity.

EMEs like India also suffer from structural rigidities. But some rigidities actually enhance the power of monetary policy. Interest rates generally exceed international rates. Structural changes allow domestic rates to approach international ones. For example, reform lowers financial repression, deepens financial markets, and improves regulation thus lowering the risk premium and inflation differentials and giving more independence to the CB. While the interest differential can become very narrow for certain types of capital where arbitrage is almost free, capital controls and continuing structural impediments allow large differentials to continue in some segments, and there is a role for policy in aligning them.

There are other factors that increase the impact of monetary policy in an open economy. Thus the new open economy macroeconomics (OEM) (Obstfeld and Rogoff 1996) points out that monetary policy can have persistent effects on output and welfare because of the wealth effects of current account imbalances. A monetary stimulus raises output where industry structure is such that output is below potential. But now the stimulus has long-run effects. This issue is particularly relevant for an EME like India that should be able to invest more than it saves through a CAD, making possible a faster transition to maturity where it reaches its potential output and absorbs all its labour at the technology frontier.

OEM makes it clear that causality runs from macroeconomic policy—affecting savings, investment and consumption smoothing—and, therefore, the current account of the balance of payments. Credible reform and expected future growth can allow a country's consumption and investment to rise, financed by sustainable capital inflows. In both China and India, foreign inflows and reserve accumulation have occurred in the presence of large fiscal deficits and government debt. This is perhaps because in both countries private savings are high enough to cover government dissaving and the foreign savings flowing in are based on sustainable future growth expectations.

OEM emphasizes forward-looking behaviour and expectations not only on the part of consumers and investors, but also workers. EMEs have rigidities that make forward-looking behaviour the exception rather than the rule. In the next sub-section, we see how these rigidities have tempered the absorption of foreign savings, and then go on to argue that even so, labour market rigidities peculiar to a populous democracy can, with suitable policy, actually encourage rapid growth.

External balance

Policy was successful in stimulating exports but less successful in absorbing the foreign savings available. Policy makers were committed to the successful East Asian and Chinese growth strategy of competitive exchange rates. This strategy effectively ruled out a substantial appreciation as a means of absorbing foreign exchange reserves through cheapening and encouraging imports. It is also the correct strategy as long as India, like China, has large reserves of labour that need to be absorbed into higher productivity employment to which exports can contribute.

But what was the specific value of the real and nominal exchange rate policy aimed at? The market value of a currency depends on demand and supply of foreign exchange and how these are expected to change. But these are uncertain, especially in a country without deep markets or full capital account convertibility so that the true demand for the currency cannot be revealed. A short-term market indicator of equilibrium rates is the approximate equality of buyer-initiated and seller-initiated orders. Although in the short term, market perceptions and policy can affect the exchange rate, in the longer-term it cannot depart from equilibrium rates determined by macroeconomic fundamentals such as relative money supply, relative output, productivity, and demand for a country's products. The rate has to allow a sustainable CAD. Investment can initially exceed domestic savings, but the deficit has to turn into a surplus as income levels rise, in order to repay debt. Box 7.6 shows

---

Box 7.6

The Difference Between Indian GDP and GNP

In an open economy, GDP can be very different from gross national product (GNP) because Indian nationals hold assets abroad and foreigners hold assets within India. Net income paid abroad has to be deducted from GDP produced within a nation's boundary to obtain the nation's GNP. If a country has been borrowing from abroad more than it has been lending, the deduction should be high. The figure below shows the adjustment as a ratio to GDP. We pay abroad more than we earn from abroad so the adjustment is negative. But the amount is low, only about minus half a percentage point. The upward trend in the ratio during the period of reforms is surprising since this was a time of more openness and borrowing from abroad. Time series regressions run by teams of students* as a class assignment suggest that rise in GDP, fall in global interest rates, and fall in net interest and service payments (a component of net income from abroad), were the primary reasons for the reduction in the ratio of the payments we made abroad. The last factor was highly significant in the regressions, and had the largest coefficient. As a ratio to GDP it also fell during this period. We had to pay less for what we borrowed and we had also begun to earn from assets held abroad.

* Anindya Sengupta, Anuradha Ghosal, Arjun Singh, Mamta Agrawal, M. Pratima, Rajendra Gupta, Rama Joglekar, Shazeb Kohari, and Sujeet Kumar revised their work and estimated the robust regressions reported here.

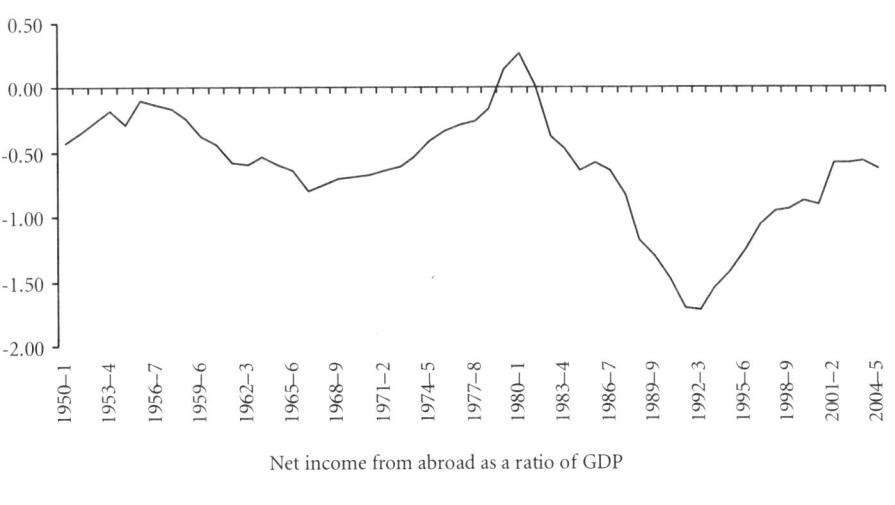

Net income from abroad as a ratio of GDP

Borrowing more but paying less abroad

that payments abroad remained small as a ratio of GDP, and the ratio actually fell during the 1990s.

A number of macroeconomic variables affect the equilibrium real exchange rate, but the latter affects exports. The real effective exchange rate (REER) gives weights according to major trading partners and corrects for relative inflation.[8] The index of the 36-country, export-based REER, with 1993–4 as the base, was at 100.04 in November 2005, and had largely ruled at just below hundred over the past decade. A rise above hundred would have meant an appreciation over the 1993–4 level. The trouble with the REER is that constancy of the aggregate is consistent with large changes against individual countries. It also does not correct for relative changes in productivity and world demand, which affect equilibrium real exchange rates.

A 5-country, trade-weighted REER, with weights based on India's major trading partners, was also calculated. But as the pattern of India's trade changed in this period, a new 6-country, trade-weighted REER was made available from 2005. This included India's trade with China together with the traditional western partners. Table 7.3 shows two-way movements in this REER with sustained appreciation in the past few years. However, lower Indian inflation and higher productivity growth meant the limited appreciation did not hurt exports, which grew at above 20 per cent per annum. Global trade was on the upswing and there was a rise in international demand for Indian products. The nominal effective exchange rate[9] (NEER) largely depreciated since our inflation rates were higher than those of our trading partners.

TABLE 7.3
Taking Account of the Trade Basket and Inflation
(6 country export weights (appreciation +) base 2003–4 = 100)

Year	REER	NEER
1994–5	5.7	–3.1
1995–6	–4.3	–8.7
1996–7	–0.2	–1.9
1997–8	3.2	1.2
1998–9	–7.9	–11.9
1999–2000	1.6	–0.4
2000–1	5.3	0.3
2001–2	–0.2	–1.8
2002–3	–4.9	–6.3
2003–4	1.5	–1.9
2004–5 (P)	2.5	–0.7
2005–6 (December)	6.5	3.4

Source: Calculated using data from www.rbi.org.in.

A fixed nominal exchange rate is supposed to stimulate trade by reducing uncertainties, but hedging can remove the impact of limited currency flexibility on trade. Moreover, there is evidence that while currency crises adversely affect trade, limited fluctuation in exchange rates does not have a large effect on trade (McKenzie 2004). If limited volatility helps prevent crises and lower interest rates, it may even benefit trade. Another constraint on rupee movement is that it cannot appreciate substantially unless the Renminbi does so, since China is a major trade competitor and partner. China's tight band with the dollar had been shifted to a currency basket in July 2005, but the depreciation has been only marginal. China wants to develop its financial markets further and strengthen its weak banks before allowing more exchange rate flexibility.

An economy at full employment requires an appreciation of the exchange rate to absorb foreign inflows since a rise in domestic absorption occurs through a rise in imports. But if there is excess labour, the rise in absorption can occur at an unchanged real exchange rate, through output and capacity expansion (see Box 7.7). But for this, interest rates must be such as to stimulate demand. More capital account convertibility is another way to absorb capital inflows, but this has to be gradual and well-sequenced (see Box 7.4).

Some exchange rate appreciation would help to absorb inflows but it cannot be the major part of the adjustment. Large numbers available to work at low wages prevent the substantial rise in average real wages required for a major currency appreciation. Such a rise in real wages is possible only with a rise in labor productivity in agriculture. Full capital account convertibility, which allows domestic residents to acquire foreign assets, also absorbs reserves, but it raises the risk of capital outflows and crises unless markets and institutions are well-developed. Therefore, it has to be introduced gradually and in a correct sequence.

INFLATION AND THE LABOUR MARKET

Inflation control is another policy objective to which the exchange rate policy can contribute. An appreciation is an antidote to price shocks coming from food, oil, and other intermediate inputs. This also requires a two-way movement of the exchange rate. For example, even if the underlying trend is that of nominal depreciation, a steeper short-term appreciation in response to an adverse supply shock can moderate the relative price shock. Short-term movements in the exchange rate to counter temporary supply shocks can achieve the limited volatility required to stabilize forex

---

[8] The REER is, therefore, the price of Indian output in terms of a basket of foreign currencies.
[9] The NEER is the price of a rupee in terms of a basket of currencies. The RBI estimates the NEER as the summation of the SDR/ rupee rate divided by the weighted average of the other countries SDR/$ rates, so the units of the NEER are $/rupee. Therefore, an appreciation implies a rise in the nominal value.

> **BOX 7.7**
>
> **Strategies to Absorb Foreign Inflows**
>
> The simple Swan diagram here (see Corden 2002) shows how foreign inflows can be absorbed, without a real appreciation, if there is less than full employment.
>
>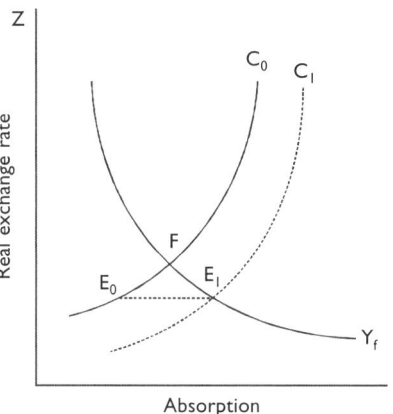
>
> The Swan Balance of Payments
> Model with foreign inflows
>
> The vertical axis gives the real exchange rate, Z, which is the ratio of traded to non-traded goods prices (P_T / P_N), so that a rise is a real depreciation. The horizontal axis gives real absorption, A, or total real expenditure by the country on domestic goods and imports (A = C + I + G). Curve Y_f gives the combinations of Z and A which give output demand equal to full employment output. Values above the curve would generate inflation and those below unemployment. The curve is downward sloping because as domestic absorption rises, Z must appreciate to reduce foreign demand at a given level of output. Curve C_0 gives the combinations of the two variables that yield a given CAD. The C curves are upward sloping because as imports rise with higher domestic expenditure Z must depreciate to encourage exports and keep the current account unchanged. A rise in foreign inflows implies a leftward shift of C_0 to C_1 since foreign inflows now finance the rise in CAD as Z appreciates and imports rise.
>
> It is easy to see that if the initial position of the economy is on the Y_f curve at F, absorbing foreign inflows through a higher CAD will require a real appreciation. But if the economy is at E_0, a demand stimulus can move it along $E_0 E_1$, and absorb the foreign inflows, at the same real exchange rate.

markets and also reduce the effect of supply shocks on the domestic price-wage process, through which they impact inflation. Building in a rule whereby there is an automatic announced response to an expected supply shock would avoid the tendency to do nothing until it becomes necessary to overreact. But better forecasting and estimation of macro models is required for such forward-looking policy. This policy implies using the exchange rate to contribute to supply-side management, and insofar as exchange rate policy can be de-linked from changes in the money supply (the section on internal balance shows why this is sometimes possible), monetary adjustment can be tuned to the domestic output cycle. Even monetary adjustment can change the exchange rate in the right direction. If a negative supply shock occurs under general excess capacity, Goyal (2005b) shows that a monetary expansion can lead to an appreciation of the exchange rate.

Under any kind of wage–price rigidity, a rise in relative prices of key intermediate inputs, or of commodities that have a large share in the consumption basket, can raise the average price level or inflation. The labour market plays a major role in the wage–price process of a specific economy.[10] India has a large informal labour market (accounting for 80 per cent of the work force) without formal cost of living indexation. Therefore, nominal wages respond with a lag to changes in the CPI. But India is also a democracy, and the lack of indexation and large number of poor makes the polity very sensitive to inflation. There are political pressures to keep real wages fixed in terms of food. Therefore, the lag with which wages respond to changes in food prices

---

[10] Thus real wage rigidity constrained the German Central Bank to be strict, while the US Fed could be more accommodative to domestic cycles because customary three-year nominal wage contracts allowed real wages to fall after an unexpected rise in prices (Bruno and Sachs 1985).

is very short. The CPI is a weighted average of home and foreign prices, but with a large weight (about 50 per cent) given to food items. With trade liberalization, food prices become more closely linked to border prices and the weight of the exchange rate in the CPI rises; the exchange rate has a larger effect on the cost of living and, therefore, on wages. Producer prices are marked up on wages, so producer price inflation responds to nominal wage inflation, lagged output (indicating demand pressure), and contemporaneous oil or productivity shocks to supply.

Pressures from well-organized farm lobbies (the rural population exceeds 57 per cent of the Indian population)[11] have in the past led to high and rising farm support prices. The compromise was to subsidize both farmers and consumers; the latter through a low price public distribution system. Since the latter was not very effective, protection was not complete, and nominal wages rose with a lag in response to a rise in food prices. Farmers also did not make long-term gains from this policy combination since the terms of trade advantage were only short term. It was lost as non-agricultural prices rose with inflation. For labour to move from agriculture to urban activities, productivity in agriculture has to rise. The focus on rising support prices came at the expense of development of irrigation and other essential agricultural infrastructure. In general, in a democracy, short-term subsidies gained at the expense of development of infrastructure and human capital. Support polices for farmers should shift from raising prices to stabilizing prices; developing human and physical capital and infrastructure; and giving them greater freedom from marketing monopolies. As populations totally dependent on agriculture for their living shrink, but poverty remains high in the large informal sector, stable food prices will benefit a larger group of voters, while providing insurance to farmers.

This migration of populations implies a labour slack. Therefore, both in the short run and over a horizon exceeding one year, which is long enough for the capital stock to rise, mean output lies below potential output. If food prices are stable, capital is available, specific bottlenecks are alleviated, and institutional reforms undertaken; supply will not be a constraint on output, which is below the potential that absorbs the labour slack.[12] In the absence of full labour absorption, the forward looking marginal cost facing the firms is flat. Large capital inflows and foreign exchange reserves relieve constraints on imports of food stocks, fuel oils, and capital goods.[13] Moreover, new technology makes it possible to bypass some deficiencies in infrastructure while easier availability of finance funds its expansion. Reduction in bureaucratic rationing and continuing reforms shorten lags and delays, making supply more elastic. These factors, together with the large numbers willing to work at a low constant real consumption wage imply constant returns to capital,[14] or an elastic supply curve. But this aggregate supply curve is subject to frequent shocks. Therefore, monetary policy has to find a way to counter these shocks, while maintaining aggregate demand.

Reforms allow faster labour absorption and an upward trend in the mean output. Capital accumulation and organizational change over time will raise labour productivity, and increasing competition through opening up will reduce mark-ups. These factors will tend to reduce inflation further until the economy reaches a mature steady state. As long as monetary policy is able to anchor nominal wages and inflationary expectations, it can stimulate demand. A rise in credit will finance an expansion in output, capital,

---

[11] Kelkar (2005) makes the point that India is urbanizing rapidly. The urban sprawl found outside most towns has a much higher population density compared to rural areas. He quotes the Indian Retirement, Earnings, and Savings database as giving the occupational break-up for India earners as 6.3 per cent in big firms, 9.7 per cent in government, 29 per cent self-employed, 25 per cent in small firms, and only 30 per cent in agriculture.

[12] Indian labour laws that make it difficult to retrench labour in the organized sector can make labour expensive; reform here would also help, but changing power equations have given firms many freedoms, for example, in the use of contract labour. A little bit of investment in training makes a large supply of labour available. For example, the Maharashtra Government and the Retailers Association of India have launched a scheme to train slum-dwelling youth from backward castes to man food and grocery divisions in the ongoing retail boom, ensuring a flat supply curve. These tasks do not require very sophisticated skills. Faster growth has not as yet been successful in absorbing labour. The NSSO 60th round reports that the unemployment rate for rural males increased over the period 1993–4 to 2004 from 5.6 to 9 per cent and for urban males from 6.7 to 8.1 per cent. It increased for women also. Goyal and Pujari (2005) present evidence that the Indian long-run aggregate supply curve is elastic.

[13] It may even relieve India's pressing infrastructure needs. The Indian Government is trying to find innovative ways to use forex reserves to spend more on infrastructure, motivated by the Chinese Government's successful large spending in this area. The inability of the private sector to build infrastructure despite inducements has led to an emphasis on public-private partnerships.

[14] Aghion et al. (1999) derive this in a standard Cobb–Douglas production function $Y = AK^{\beta}L^{1-\beta}$ where Y is the output level, K the capital stock, and L the labour employed. Normalizing the constant consumption wage $W/P_t^c = 1$ (where W is the nominal wage and P the price level) and equating it to the marginal product of labour gives a value for L, which when substituted in the production function gives: $Y = A((1-B)A)^{(1-\beta)/\beta} K = \tau K$ or the standard AK production function with CRS. If the average real consumption wage is around subsistence, firms do not gain from lowering it, since productivity falls commensurately.

and capacity. The ability of the CB to focus exchange rate expectations gives it an additional weapon, independent of monetary policy, to counter relative price shocks that trigger the wage–price process and raise inflation. It can then focus monetary policy on maintaining demand, in a situation of overall excess capacity and unemployment.

To summarize, if food prices are constant, labour cost does not rise; if there is no cost shock, intermediate inputs prices also do not rise; and with labour slack, deviations from mean output are demand-determined, with costs remaining constant. Since keeping inflation low and real wages constant in terms of a basic consumption basket are political imperatives, an exchange rate policy that furthers these objectives is politically feasible. As it reduces the necessity for subsidies and administered prices that distort incentives and result in lower efficiency, it lowers the waste in the system. Two-way movement only pre-empts the effect of temporary supply shocks on the domestic price–wage process. This is different from fixing the exchange rate to bring down high levels of inflation, which often leads to real appreciation and ends in a crisis, as in the Latin American exchange-based stabilization episodes. Svensson (2000) points out that the lag from the exchange rate to consumer prices is the shortest.

STRUCTURE, MONETARY, AND FISCAL POLICY

To sum up, the Indian exchange rate policy has started to contribute to market stability and deepening, and has supported rising exports. Although exchange rates are more flexible, the inflation sensitivity of the electorate ensures that the RBI does not have an inflation bias. Since there was no temptation to raise the exchange rate in order to cause surprise inflation, the exchange rate was not systematically undervalued. As inflation was low there was no need to use the exchange rate as a nominal anchor to stabilize inflationary expectations, thus, there was no overvaluation. However, the exchange rate policy did not support the adjustment of monetary policy to domestic cycles and to the productive absorption of foreign exchange reserves. Although some agricultural liberalization and falling world food prices did reduce the political pressures that had raised food support prices and inflation, the exchange rate policy was not systematically used to moderate the effect of the typical EME supply shocks—oil price shocks and failure of rains. Monetary policy broadly succeeded in preventing an explosive growth in money supply and reined in inflationary expectations, but at a high output cost.

Indian private and corporate savings are high enough to compensate for government dissaving, and a large population employed at low productivity implies that output is below potential. Moreover, political and institutional features result in fiscal–monetary co-ordination such that the economy remains on an elastic stretch of the aggregate supply curve, unable to exhaust excess labour and capacity. Fiscal populism pushes monetary authorities towards conservatism in order to reduce inflationary expectations. But since the populism raises inefficiencies, and therefore, costs, it shifts up the supply curve, while monetary tightening reduces demand, resulting in a large negative effect on output for little gain in reduced inflation. Therefore, optimal co-ordination of monetary and fiscal policy requires the imposition of flexible rules that will constrain discretion and push it in the required direction (Goyal 2002a, 2007). Fiscal surpluses should be built in good times that are available to spend in bad, government expenditure capped at an expected trend growth rate, and its composition changed to make it more effective. The Fiscal Responsibility and Budget Management (FRBM) Act 2003 will put some restraint on the fiscal laxity, but it does not really address the need to change the composition of government expenditure away from consumption and towards investment in infrastructure and human capital, and hence reduce waste. Even so, together with more openness, it may make it possible for monetary policy to be more in tune with the domestic cycle. Higher growth, lower interest rates, and the commitment to reduce the revenue deficit will eventually lower domestic public debt ratios. Public–private partnerships can help leverage public resources available for infrastructure and utilize them more effectively.

In the theory of monetary policy in an open economy (Clarida et al., 2001), optimal policy is derived by minimizing deviations from potential output and from target inflation subject to three constraints. First, forward-looking aggregate demand, second, aggregate supply derived from firms equating wages to expected marginal product, and third, trader arbitrage over currencies linking changes in the exchange rate to real interest differentials over time. With such a framework, a short-run trade-off between inflation and output variability arises only if inflation is positive due to a cost shock, since excess demand can be removed without output cost. This is trivially true for an economy such as India during a catch-up period of rapid productivity growth when potential output exceeds actual output. Moreover, monetary policy based on expectations and forward-looking behaviour has shorter lags; since fiscal policy must go through the political process, fiscal policy lags can be longer.

If the exchange rate is flexible there is automatic adjustment to a demand shock, since depreciation results and increases demand. Under a fixed exchange rate, money supply automatically responds to money demand and financial market shocks in order to maintain the fixed exchange rate, but with a more flexible exchange rate this does not happen. Thus, a monetary policy regime that allows a more automatic response to market conditions is required. Inflation targeting allows a learning from, and response to, the market, while anchoring inflation expectations. Targeting monetary quantities is inadequate as money demand becomes unstable.

As Dash and Goyal (2000) point out, information available in the systematic structural features can be exploited while designing monetary policy. Policy had been accommodating an agricultural shock but tightening as manufacturing prices rose subsequently and this had a large output cost. They argue that a monetary contraction should be completed earlier than in the past, and should coincide with a rise in food prices. But the open economy gives degrees of freedom because it turns out that a monetary relaxation, in response to an anticipated temporary supply shock, can appreciate the exchange rate, and thus reverse the impact of the supply shock (Goyal 2005b). The administered price mechanism implies that there is a lag between a supply shock such as a failure of rains or a rise in international oil prices and its impact on inflation. Forward-looking monetary policy can use its knowledge of this structure to abort the inflationary process. As long as supply shocks are the dominant source of inflation and deviations of output from the potential harm welfare, optimal policy would aim to achieve an inflation target only over the medium-term by which time temporary supply shocks have petered out, or have been countered by exchange rate policy, changes in tax rates, or improvement in efficiencies. Inflation targeting itself will prevent inflationary wage–price expectations from setting in, which can permanently shift up the supply curve in response to a temporary supply shock. Monetary policy has to tighten only if there is excess demand. Thus, exchange rate policy and the management of inflationary expectations can help abort the relative price shocks that contribute to inflation, allowing monetary policy to maintain demand. In a situation of overall excess capacity and unemployment, tightening monetary policy to reduce supply-shock inflation has a high cost in terms of output sacrificed.

Indian financial markets have developed to the point where short-term interest rates are well integrated. Short-term forex market efficiency holds (Mohan 2006). Therefore, exchange rate expectations affect the interest differential. To the extent rapid catch-up implies the exchange rate is expected to appreciate, and the risk premium is low, domestic interest rates can even be lower than international rates, giving greater freedom to adapt monetary policy to domestic needs.

CONCLUSION

Limited volatility in exchange rates improves the structure of incentives, thus contributing to four objectives. First, external balance—a real exchange rate that follows its trend competitive value can stimulate the real sector, so that eventual current account surpluses follow the initial deficits. Second, internal balance—smoother and more countercyclical interest rates can stimulate activity. Higher activity allows more inflows to be absorbed. Third, an appreciation is an antidote to price shocks coming from food, oil, and other intermediate inputs, which are typical temporary supply shocks that the economy faces. These affect aggregate inflation through the wage–price process. For example, whatever the underlying trend, a steeper short-term appreciation can counter the supply-shock, contributing to control of inflation, thus allowing interest rates to be tuned to the macroeconomic output cycle.

A large voting population whose wages are not formally indexed to inflation implies political sensitivity to food price inflation. Administrative restraints are often put on the prices of basic consumption goods. Since political pressure from farmers pushes up farm support prices, consumption subsidies are given. Since these are not complete, nominal wages respond with a lag to a rise in food prices leading to inflation. With more openness, world prices can restrain domestic food prices. An exchange rate policy that lowers domestic food price inflation through its effect on imported food prices also reduces the necessity for other distorting interventions. The resulting improvements in efficiency release a surplus, which can be used, for example, to provide better infrastructure to farmers. Therefore, the policy is compatible with political constraints and the overall macro policy objectives to lower inflation and raise growth.

The fourth benefit is stability in the external sector, and a fall in the likelihood of currency crises. Limited two-way movement of the exchange rate, creates incentives to hedge, reduces noise trader entry, and contributes to deepening of the forex markets.

If monetary policy is loose the currency is expected to depreciate, and a capital outflow occurs; but if it is too tight high interest rates harm activity and a capital outflow can provoke the depreciation it fears. For well-behaved forex markets, credibility of the CB policy is essential. A policy that satisfies the four objectives, with appropriate support from fiscal policy, would be credible. Policy transparency such as through an inflation targeting regime gives sufficient discretion to allow flexible response to markets signals; but the transparent constraints on the discretion may be sufficient to prevent inflation expectations from setting in, even without monetary tightening.

References

Aghion, A., A. Banerjee, and T. Piketty (1999), 'Dualism and Macroeconomic Volatility', *Quarterly Journal of Economics*, Vol. 114, No. 4, November, pp. 1359–97.

BIS (Bank for International Settlements) (2006), 'An Overview', *76th Annual Report, 1 April 2005–31 March 2006*, BIS, Basel.

Bruno, M. and J.D. Sachs (1985), *Economics of Worldwide Stagflation*, Harvard University Press, Cambridge, Massachusetts.

Burnside, C., M. Eichenbaum, and S. Rebelo (2001), 'Hedging and Financial Fragility in Fixed Exchange Rate Regimes', *European Economic Review*, Vol. 45, pp. 1151–93.

Clarida, R., J. Gali, and M. Gertler (2001), 'Optimal monetary policy in closed versus open economies: An integrated approach', *American Economic Review*, Vol. 91, No. 2, May, pp. 248–52.

Corden, W.M. (2002), *Too Sensational: On the Choice of Exchange Rate Regimes*, MIT Press, Cambridge MA.

Dash, S. and A. Goyal (2000), 'The Money Supply Process in India: Identification, Analysis and Estimation', *Indian Economic Journal*, Vol. 48, No. 1, July–September.

Frankel, J.A. (1999), 'No Single Currency Regime is Right for all Countries or at all Times', NBER Working Paper 7338, Cambridge, USA.

Gopinath, S. (2005), 'Recent Developments in Forex, Money and G-sec Markets: Account and Outlook', Address at the 16th National Forex Assembly at Kochi, 13 August 2005, available at *www.rbi.org.in*.

Goyal, A. (2002a), 'Coordinating Monetary and Fiscal Policies: A Role for Rules?', chapter 11 in K.S. Parikh and R. Radhakrishna (eds), *India Development Report 2002*, IGIDR and Oxford University Press, New Delhi.

——— (2002b), 'Reform Proposals from Developing Asia: Finding a Win-win Strategy', in Leslie Elliott Armijo (ed.), *Debating the Global Financial Architecture*, SUNY Press, New York.

——— (2004a), 'Rupee Reversals: More on Real Exchange Rates, Fiscal Deficits and Capital Flows', discussion piece in *Economic and Political Weekly*, Vol. 39, No. 2, 15 May, pp. 2061–3.

——— (2004b), 'Rupee: Changing Trends', commentary piece in *Economic and Political Weekly*, Vol. 39, No. 23, 5 June, pp. 2335–7.

——— (2007), 'Tradeoffs, delegation and fiscal–monetary co-ordination in a developing economy', *Indian Economic Review*, Vol. 42, No. 2, July–December, forthcoming working paper available at *http://ssrn.com/abstract=625861*.

——— (2005a), 'Reducing Endogenous Amplification of Shocks from Capital Flows in Developing Countries', Report for the GDN Coordinated Project on Macroeconomic Policy Challenges of Low Income Countries, available at *http://www.gdnet.org/pdf2/gdn_library/global_research_projects/macro_low_income/Goyal.pdf*.

——— (2005b), 'Incentives from Exchange Rate Regimes in an Institutional Context', IGIDR Working Paper WP-2005-02, available at *http://www.igidr.ac.in/pub/pdf/WP-2005-002.pdf*

——— (2006), 'Exchange Rate Regimes: Middling Through', *Global Economic Review*, Vol. 35, No. 2, June.

Goyal, A. and A.K. Pujari (2005), 'Identifying Long-run Supply Curve in India', *Journal of Quantitative Economics*, Vol. 3, No. 2, July.

Hardgrove, A. (2004), *Community and Public Culture*, Oxford University Press, New Delhi.

Hart, O.D. and D.M. Kreps (1986), 'Price Destabilising Speculation', *Journal of Political Economy*, Vol. 94, No. 5, pp. 927–52.

Jeanne, O. and A.K. Rose (2002), 'Noise Trading and Exchange Rate Regimes', *The Quarterly Journal of Economics*, Vol. CXVII, No. 469, pp. 537–70.

Kahneman, D. and A. Tversky (1979), 'Prospect Theory: An Analysis of Decision under Risk', *Econometrica*, Vol. 47, No. 2, March, pp. 263–92.

Kelkar, V. (2005), 'India's Economic Future: Moving beyond State Capitalism', D.R. Gadgil Memorial Lecture, MEDC, *Monthly Economic Digest*, November.

Krugman, P.R. and M. Obstfeld (2003), *International Economics: Theory and Policy*, 6th edition, Pearson Education, India.

McKenzie, M.D. (2004), 'The Effects of Exchange Rate Volatility on Trade', in G. de Brouwer and M. Kawai (eds), *Exchange Rate Regimes in East Asia*, Routledge Curzon, London and New York.

Mohan, R. (2006), 'Coping with Liquidity Management in India: A Practitioner's View', based on an Address at the 8th Annual Conference on Money and Finance in the Indian Economy, IGIDR, 27 March.

Obstfeld, M. and K. Rogoff (1996), *Foundations of International Macroeconomics*, Cambridge, MIT Press, Massachusetts.

Reddy, Y.V. (2005), 'Monetary Co-operation in Asia', Speech by Governor, RBI at the IMF-MAS High-Level Seminar on Asian Integration held on 3 September, at Singapore.

Shefrin, H. (2002), *Beyond Greed and Fear: Understanding Behavioral Finance and the Psychology of Investing*, Oxford University Press, Oxford.

Shiller, R.J. (1993), *Creating Institutions for Managing Society's Largest Economic Risks*, Clarendon Lectures in Economics, Clarendon Press, Oxford.

Svensson, L.E.O. (2000), 'Open Economy Inflation Targeting', *Journal of International Economics*, Vol. 50, pp. 155–83.

8

Emerging Policy Regime for Bank Credit Delivery and Tasks Ahead
A Critical Review

S.L. Shetty

INTRODUCTION: IMPORTANCE ASSIGNED
TO FINANCE FOR DEVELOPMENT

Public policies in India have always conferred a pivotal role for finance in the process of development. Even in the pre-independence period, when the nation got an independent CB, the importance of institutional credit for the dominant agrarian economy was embedded in the statute. The early part of planning in the post-independence period was devoted to building and nurturing institutions in the financial system so as to facilitate improvements in savings mobilization and in productive deployment of financial resources. This phase of banking consolidation and strengthening of banking regulations (1950–67) was followed by a more decisive thrust in terms of a supply-leading approach to the institutional credit structure (1967–90). The policy of bank nationalization and the associated public policies on banking and financial sector development were predicated on the strong assumption of the need for promoting financial intermediation by building institutions, expanding their geographical spread, mobilizing savings, and promoting better regional, sectoral, and functional as well as small borrower reach of institutional credit in India.

Post-independence banking development, and in particular the post-nationalization banking progress continued for two decades until the end of the 1980s, and received encomia in literature on the positive role played by finance in the process of development in India. Bell and Rousseau (2001) have brought out how financial intermediaries in India played a leading role in influencing the economic performance; their results suggest that the financial sector, amongst other things, was not only instrumental in promoting aggregate investment and output but also in attaining finance-led industrialization. What is more, studies by Burgess and Pande (2003 and 2004) and Burgess, Pande, and Wong (2004) conclusively prove that state-led branch expansion into rural unbanked locations reduced poverty across Indian states; in addition, the directed bank lending requirement was associated with increased bank borrowing among the poor, in particular low caste and tribal groups. Their studies go further and find that while the presence of a nationwide bank branch licencing rule between 1977 and 1990 caused banks to open relatively more branches in Indian states with lower initial financial development during the period, the reverse was true outside this period; they also find

The author wishes to place on record sincere thanks to Bipin Deokar for his unstinted support in preparing the entire banking database; also to V.P. Prasanth for his national accounts/state domestic product data base used in the study and to K. Srinivasan for his repeated typesetting work.

that rural branch expansion in India significantly reduced rural poverty and increased non-agricultural output.

More generally, the financial policies of the 1970s and 1980s have followed Patrick's (1966) supply-leading strategy, or they have resembled an endogenous growth strategy in which finance itself is seen as a crucial factor of production such as knowledge and in which the influence of institutional arrangements with regard to finance on growth rates has been forcefully emphasized (see Eschenbach 2004; see also RBI 2001). We have been repetitively emphasizing that sustained expansions in sectoral credit growth in real terms during the latter half of the 1970s and the whole of the 1980s served inter alia as an important causal factor in the acceleration of growth rates in agriculture and unregistered manufacturing in the 1980s (Shetty 2002). Similarly, the acceleration in employment growth from 1.5 per cent per annum during the period 1977 to 1983 to 2.70 per cent during 1983 to 1993–4, and more significantly, the non-farm employment growth in rural areas that showed an outstanding performance in the 1980s, appear to have been related to better sectoral, regional, and size distributions of bank credit.

Contrari-wise, after the financial sector reforms began in the early part of the 1990s, every banking indicator representing post-nationalization success—spread of branch banking in rural and historically underbanked regions, improved credit–deposit ratios of these regions, better credit delivery for agriculture, small-scale industries (SSIs), small borrowers, and other priority areas—has received a setback. No doubt, the unprecedented growth of the banking system for two decades prior to the 1990s brought in its trail serious infirmities in the working of the whole financial system: reduced bottomlines, large non-performing assets, poor capital base and insufficiency of loan loss provisions, and organizational weaknesses leading to serious deterioration in house-keeping tasks as well as customer service. By the end of the 1980s, even the post-nationalization successes cited above had begun to wear thin. Therefore, the evolution of banking after the 1990s has reflected the enormous challenges that the public sector banks in particular have faced in cleaning up and consolidating their operations in an entirely new competitive and reform-zest environment. Apart from the onerous discipline imposed by regulatory and prudential norms as part of financial sector reforms, there has also occurred a sea change in the role of banks as a result of competitive opportunities thrown up in para-banking activities—merchant banking, housing finance, mutual funds, insurance, and others, and above all, in the notion of universal banking and project finance.

Even as banks have responded to the above challenges, they have very seriously faltered on their traditional developmental role, particularly in their task of credit delivery for varied informal sectors. The resultant distortions in credit distribution, which persisted for over a decade, became very glaring. It is, however, perceived that corrections to these distortions cannot be introduced entirely by resurrecting the traditional control regime. The multiplicity of in-house and independent committees appointed by the RBI and National Bank for Agriculture and Rural Development (NABARD) have recommended a combination of measures involving credit targets, intensive use of microfinance institutions (MFIs), more innovative system of 'agency banking', and even embracing the philosophy of 'financial inclusion' so that banks are obliged to provide banking services to all segments of the population on an equitable basis. The authorities have responded to these recommendations quickly and positively and directed banks to rapidly expand credit delivery to agriculture and small and medium enterprises.

The objective of this paper is to take a close look at the emerging policy regime and its implications for the ultimate goals of widening credit delivery arrangements sectorally, regionally, and by size. To be meaningful, this evaluation has to take cognizance of the ground reality of developments in the post-nationalization and post-reform periods; hence the second section of the study is devoted to a review of these developments as a background. In the post-nationalization period also, the directed credit arrangements had recognized the limited credit absorptive capacities of agricultural and informal sectors as well as the underdeveloped regions and hence, substitute devices were introduced to take cognizance of such infirmities and to mitigate them; their results are also reviewed in this section. The third section presents a review of the micro-credit system in India which has emerged as a major movement to cover the borrowing as well as thrift facility needs of poorer households after the 1990s. The fourth section seeks to bring out the ground reality regarding the growing dependence of farmer/rural households on non-institutional sources for their indebtedness despite varied attempts made to provide institutional credit. In response to the acutely deteriorating ground situation, the official agencies have, of late, introduced a fresh series of innovative measures to fill the institutional gaps in the rural credit structure and to arrest the gaps in credit delivery for the informal sectors. These measures, enumerated in the fifth section, form the basis for a critical evaluation of the emerging policy regime for credit delivery and for offering a set of suggestions to make the delivery mechanism relatively more enduring in the last section.

POST-NATIONALIZATION AND POST-REFORM BANKING DEVELOPMENTS

Changing Rural Credit Structure

An outstanding aspect of banking development after the nationalization of banks in July 1969 was the rapid growth and territorial spread of branch network all over the country, particularly in rural areas and underdeveloped regions. From a base of a little over 8000 bank branches in 1969, the presence of over 68,680 branches today, indeed represents an unprecedented growth of scheduled commercial banking in India. However, the bulk of this expansion took place before the 1990s. In the first two decades (1970–91), 53,537 branches were added, that is, 2550 branches per year. But, thereafter in a 15-year period until March 2006, only 6957 branches were added, that is, 464 branches per year or near one-sixth of what was achieved until the 1990s.

More significantly, by the early 1990s, the number of bank branches operating in rural areas had crossed 35,000 or about 57 per cent of the total number of bank branches operating in the country (as per the centres with 10,000 of population, classified on the basis of the 1981 Population Census). Reclassification of the areas based on the 1991 Census also brought down the number of rural bank branches from 33,017 in March 1995 to 32,981 in March 1996. Since then, on a comparable basis, the number of rural branches has steadily come down to as low as 30,572 by March 2006 (Table 8.1) through mergers and swapping of rural branches. It is significant that the first Narasimham Committee Report on the Financial System (November 1991) had specifically recommended that 'each public sector bank should set up one or more rural banking subsidiaries to take over all its rural branches' and that the operations of regional rural banks (RRBs) should be expanded to embrace all types of banking business.

A major component of the banking policy before reforms had been the spread of branch network into rural areas—a policy which has since been given up in the post-reform period. There was a branch expansion programme monitored by the RBI which was disbanded. On the expiry (on 31 March 1995), of this branch expansion programme 1990–5, no fresh programme was drawn up on the ground that the subject had to be left to the commercial judgements of banks (RBI 1997). Banks were allowed to convert their non-viable rural branches into satellite offices or close bank branches at rural centres served by two commercial banks. RRBs were allowed to relocate their loss-making branches to new places even outside the rural areas. This shows that given the option, banks would not like to open branches in rural areas.

Alongside the opening of rural bank branches between 1970 and 1991, shares of rural deposits and rural credit in aggregate deposits and credit had risen. More significantly, with the prescribed targets of 60 per cent credit–deposit ratio, the credit–deposit (C–D) ratios of rural branches had touched 64–5 per cent by the mid-1980s (Table 8.2).

These positive developments have uniformly suffered a setback since the beginning of the 1990s. No doubt, rural C–D ratios appear much higher based on utilization rather than sanction of bank credit,[1] but even such C–D ratios have experienced sharp reductions between 1990 and 2000; overall only 36 per cent of the incremental deposits in rural areas during the whole of the 1990s have been deployed in the very areas even after taking into account the net in-migration of credit from outside the rural areas. Since 2000, a noticeable improvement has occurred (Table 8.2), but 'the average size of loans mitigating into rural areas, which was around Rs 5 lakh until March 1998, suddenly jumped to Rs 30 lakh or more thereafter, implying that these loans do not have any rural character' (EPWRF 2005).

TABLE 8.1
Spread of Bank Branch Network in India

(Scheduled Commercial Banks including RRBs)

Period-end	Rural		Semi-urban		Total	
	Number of Bank Branches	Per cent to total	Number of Bank Branches	Per cent to total	Number of Bank Branches	Per cent to total
December 1969	1443	17.6	3337	40.8	8187	100.0
March 1991	35,134	56.9	11,566	18.7	61,724	100.0
March 1995	33,017	51.7	13,502	21.2	63,817	100.0
March 1996	32,981	51.2	13,731	21.3	64,456	100.0
March 2002	32,443	47.8	14,910	21.9	67,897	100.0
March 2003	32,283	47.4	15,042	22.1	68,078	100.0
March 2004	32,107	46.8	15,252	22.2	68,645	100.0
March 2005	31,967	45.7	15,619	22.3	69,969	100.0
March 2006*	30,572	44.5	15,274	22.2	68,681	100.0

Notes: Decline in March 1996 is partly due to reclassification of centres based on the 1991 Census.

Source: RBI Basic Statistical Returns, various issues; * RBI's *Quarterly Handout*.

[1] An innovative data set gathered in the RBI's banking statistics relates to the capturing of the phenomenon of migration of bank credit from the place of sanction to the place of utilization. This is the distinction between C–D ratios based on sanction and utilization.

TABLE 8.2
Population Group-wise C–D Ratio as Per Sanction and Utilization

(In percentages)

Year/Population Group	June 1980	March 1990		March 2000		March 2005	
	Sanction	Sanction	Utilization	Sanction	Utilization	Sanction	Utilization
Rural	54.5	61.2	97.1	40.4	49.3	51.6	75.3
Semi-urban	47.2	49.1	48.5	34.7	40.0	44.2	48.3
Urban	60.0	55.6	52.9	41.9	42.1	50.5	56.6
Metropolitan	87.0	69.9	58.0	78.9	73.2	83.7	73.8
All India	67.2	60.7	60.7	56.0	56.0	66.0	66.0

Source: RBI Basic Statistical Returns, various issues; * RBI's Quarterly Handout.

Sanction and Utilization Differences in Bank Credit at the State Level

A significant point to note with regard to interregional disparities in credit flow is that the improvement that took place in narrowing the disparities during the first two decades of bank nationalization, has been reversed and that a sizeable fall in C–D ratios of the less developed regions has occurred in the 1990s in terms of both sanction and utilization (Tables 8.3 and 8.4). However, the only silver-lining in this respect has been that the data show that after March 2000, there has been an improvement in C–D ratios of backward regions, particularly in terms of utilization. It should be recognized that even this has occurred when there has been a sizeable improvement in the overall C–D ratio at the all-India level due to sharp reductions in cash reserve and statutory reserve ratios and due to vast increases in personal loans and other retail sector credit (EPWRF 2006).

TABLE 8.3
Regional Scenario of C–D Ratios

(In percentages)

Region	March 2005		March 2002		March 1996		March 1992		December 1982		December 1972	
	Sanction	Utilization	Sanction	Utilization	Sanction	Utilization	Sanction	Utilization	Sanction	Utilization	Sanction	Utilization
Northern	59.5	62.2	56.2	55.0	51.4	50.4	51.1	49.3	70.0	67.7	47.6	46.6
North-eastern	35.0	44.6	27.2	53.2	35.5	41.1	46.7	66.3	41.2	57.5	36.3	71.4
Eastern	45.5	50.4	37.6	41.4	47.0	46.4	49.5	49.1	56.1	55.2	62.9	62.6
Central	40.8	45.8	33.9	38.4	40.0	42.0	47.6	50.2	47.8	50.6	39.1	44.4
Western	83.5	71.8	79.7	71.3	72.2	71.4	58.2	56.5	73.7	73.0	76.2	71.8
Southern	78.1	83.9	64.6	68.9	74.2	74.8	76.5	77.7	79.2	80.2	91.1	94.7
All India	66.0	66.0	58.4	58.4	59.8	59.8	57.7	57.7	67.1	67.1	66.4	66.4

Source: RBI Basic Statistical Returns, various issues; * RBI's Quarterly Handout.

TABLE 8.4
C–D Ratios for Selected States

(In percentages)

Region	March 2005		March 2002		March 1996		March 1992		December 1982		December 1972	
	Sanction	Utilization	Sanction	Utilization	Sanction	Utilization	Sanction	Utilization	Sanction	Utilization	Sanction	Utilization
Northern	59.5	62.2	56.2	55.0	51.4	50.4	51.1	49.3	70.0	67.7	47.6	46.6
Rajasthan	68.7	76.5	48.4	55.4	45.4	45.3	55.6	59.3	70.1	74.1	48.6	54.5
Bihar	27.7	31.4	21.3	21.9	30.1	31.1	36.9	38.5	42.8	50.7	28.1	53.0
West-Bengal	52.3	56.8	45.8	49.2	55.2	53.3	52.8	51.0	59.3	54.1	76.0	65.5
Madhya Pradesh	54.7	61.2	46.6	50.3	56.2	60.6	61.0	63.2	58.2	61.2	46.6	51.8
Uttar Pradesh	37.9	42.2	29.9	34.3	33.8	35.0	42.5	45.3	44.7	47.3	36.9	42.2
Gujarat	46.5	60.9	44.1	54.7	52.9	56.9	52.4	57.3	52.0	53.9	56.4	64.6
Maharashtra	94.9	75.9	92.3	77.5	79.6	77.3	60.7	57.1	83.7	81.7	83.8	74.8
Tamil Nadu	101.2	105.4	85.4	88.5	94.9	94.4	89.0	89.1	94.6	94.5	109.5	110.0
All India	66.0	66.0	58.4	58.4	59.8	59.8	57.7	57.7	67.1	67.1	66.4	66.4

Source: RBI Basic Statistical Returns, various issues; * RBI's Quarterly Handout.

It may be argued that the credit absorptive capacities of backward states and regions may have been eroded during the decade of the 1990s, but as is shown in a subsequent section, this is only partially true; the supply of credit has been found to have fallen behind the demand for it.

Inter-district disparities in bank credit—
initial improvement and subsequent setback

The improvement in banking development in the post-nationalization period was reflected in a large number of districts showing noticeably higher growth in bank deposits, higher credit growth, and improved C–D ratios. The number of districts with C–D ratios of 60 per cent and above shot up from 136 in March 1980 to 209 in March 1985; thereafter they remained in the range of 177–63 until March 1992. Such improvement took place in rural centres of districts also (EPWRF 2006).

But, as in the case of other banking indicators cited earlier, in the 1990s, a large number of districts began to experience reductions in credit delivery in relation to the deposits that they generated. At one extreme, in March 1990 or even up to March 1992, there were just about 20–8 districts (out of 401–78) which had C–D ratios of less than 20 per cent, but in March 2000, there were as many as 105 districts (out of 565) within this lowest range of C–D ratios.

Classification of districts by their C–D ratios and by states reveals an interesting picture (Table 8.5). As of March 2005,

TABLE 8.5
State-wise Classification of Districts by Size of C–D Ratios, March 2005

Region/State/Union Territory Range	< 20	20–30	30–40	40–50	50–60	60–100	> 100	Total
NORTHERN REGION	10	13	16	13	13	27	4	96
Haryana		1	3	4	3	7	1	19
Himachal Pradesh	1	7		1	2	1		12
Jammu & Kashmir	6	2	5				1	14
Punjab	3	1	2	2	1	7	1	17
Rajasthan		2	6	6	7	10	1	32
Chandigarh						1		1
Delhi						1		1
NORTH-EASTERN REGION	13	9	21	14	8	12	2	79
Arunachal Pradesh	10	3	3					16
Assam		4	11	6	3			24
Manipur	1		1		2	4	1	9
Meghalaya	1		2	3	1			7
Mizoram				3		4	1	8
Nagaland	1	1	1	2	2	4		11
Tripura			1	3				4
EASTERN REGION	12	38	18	11	19	15	1	114
Bihar	5	17	9	4	3			38
Jharkhand	5	10	4	2				21
Orissa			1	2	13	13	1	30
Sikkim		1	1		1	1		4
West Bengal	1	9	3	3	2	1		19
Andaman & Nicobar Islands	1	1						2
CENTRAL REGION	12	27	34	29	18	25	2	147
Chhattisgarh		3	5	5	2		1	16
Madhya Pradesh	1	3	14	8	5	16	1	48
Uttar Pradesh	4	17	14	16	11	8		70
Uttaranchal	7	4	1			1		13
WESTERN REGION	6	8	10	8	14	17	1	64
Goa		2						2
Gujarat	4	6	5	4	5	1		25
Maharashtra			4	4	9	16	1	34
Dadra & Nagar Haveli			1					1
Daman & Diu	2							2

(Table 8.5 contd.)

TABLE 8.5: *Contd.*

Region/State/Union Territory Range	< 20	20–30	30–40	40–50	50–60	60–100	> 100	Total
SOUTHERN REGION	1	2	6	9	15	53	13	99
Andhra Pradesh				2	5	13	3	23
Karnataka			2	1	2	18	4	27
Kerala		1	1	2	3	6	1	14
Tamil Nadu			1	3	5	16	5	30
Lakshadweep	1							1
Pondicherry		1	2	1				4
ALL INDIA	54	97	105	84	87	149	23	599

Note: C–D Ratios are in Percentages.

Source: RBI Basic Statistical Returns, various issues; * RBI's *Quarterly Handout.*

the north-eastern, eastern, and central regions have their districts concentrated in low C–D ratio loops, while the western region districts appear somewhat spread out across various C–D ratio ranges. The southern region enjoys the distinction of its districts being concentrated in high C–D ratio loops.

A glance at the list of districts appearing in the low C–D ratios range suggests that the above mentioned deterioration, since the beginning of the 1990s, may have taken place because of the constricted banking (and economic) activities in Jammu and Kashmir and some states in the north-eastern region due to political tensions. But a large number of districts in the list also belong to bigger states such as West Bengal, Bihar, and UP. Interestingly, some of the deposit-generating districts in many of the relatively advanced states, for example, Gurgaon, Rewari, Rohtak, and Sonipat in Haryana, Bilaspur, Mandi, and Simla in Himachal Pradesh, Amritsar and Gurdaspur in Punjab, Udupi in Karnataka, and Kollam and Thiruvananthapuram in Kerala, appear in the same low C–D ratio list—a phenomenon which, on the face of it, may not appear as unduly disquieting because of the limited number of bankable projects that can absorb higher credit levels.

Nevertheless, while the district banking profiles have to be juxtaposed against the corresponding economic profiles so as to be able to critically evaluate the district-wise performance of banks, the presence of such advanced districts, agriculturally or otherwise, like Ghaziabad, Meerut, and Kheda in the northern/western states and Raigad, Ratnagiri, and Sindhudurg in Maharashtra facing low C–D ratios, typify the observation that overall efforts by banks in promoting borrowers in different parts of the country, particularly in rural and semi-urban areas, leave much to be desired.

Also, as expected, there are acute inter-district disparities within states in banking developments. Interestingly, the district-wise database built by the EPWRF reveals uniform deterioration of these intra-state disparities since the beginning of the 1990s. An example of the data for the two states of Maharasthra and Andhra Pradesh presented in Table 8.6 brings out how such a deterioration occurred between March 1992 and March 2005. The acute concentration of bank credit share amongst the top five districts, further intensified after March 1992 in both the states. Likewise, the credit shares of the bottom five districts slipped between March 1992 and March 2005 in both the states.

Substitute Policy Devices to Promote Larger Credit Absorption in Backward States and Regions

To a significant extent, the credit absorptive potentials of the underdeveloped regions and districts had suffered a setback

TABLE 8.6
District-wise Aggregate Deposits and Bank Credit for Maharashtra and Andhra Pradesh

Districts	End of March 2005		End of March 1992	
	Credit Share (in per cent)	C–D Ratio	Credit–Share (in per cent)	C–D Ratio
Maharashtra				
State total	100.0	77.4	100.0	60.7
Top 5 districts	91.7	75.7	89.9	60.5
Mumbai	77.8	74.8	79.5	61.2
Pune	6.9	86.0	5.4	66.9
Thane	2.9	49.8	1.7	32.4
Nagpur	2.2	85.8	2.1	56.6
Raigad	2.0	229.2	1.2	69.2
Bottom 5 Districts	0.24	46.3	0.67	35.2
Andhra Pradesh				
State total	100.0	83.3	100.0	80.1
Top 5 districts	61.7	85.9	59.3	91.2
Hyderabad	39.0	89.5	36.3	101.3
Visakhapatnam	6.2	48.1	6.7	65.5
East Godavari	6.0	131.3	6.0	80.7
Guntur	5.4	107.4	5.8	71.2
Krishna	5.1	88.0	4.5	132.6
Bottom 5 Districts	5.9	67.8	6.4	55.5

Note: C–D Ratios are in Percentages.

Source: RBI, Basic Statistical Returns, March 1992 and March 2005.

in the 1990s and hence, their C–D ratios were deteriorating. To mitigate this situation, substitute policy devices were considered and put into place. Two such special policy initiatives are: (i) bank investment in securities and bonds of state governments and state-associated bodies; and (ii) resources placed by banks with NABARD in the rural infrastructure development fund (RIDF) which are utilized for funding state governments for rural infrastructure projects including irrigation projects; 216,099 projects for Rs 42,948.51 crore had been sanctioned up to end March 2005.

Though interregional disparity remains, the north-eastern, eastern, and central regions show significant improvements in (credit utilization + investments + RIDF) to deposit ratios. As shown in Table 8.7, the number of states with C–D ratios of 50 per cent and above have steadily increased, from 7 under C^S–D ratio to 15 under C^U–D ratio, to 21 under (C^U+I) to D ratio and to 24 under (C^U+I+RIDF) to D ratio (as of March 2003). But, to add a caveat, C–D ratio based on utilization plus investment improves the position of underdeveloped regions, but it does so even for the advanced southern region (Table 8.8). Further, inclusion of RIDF benefits improves the C–D ratios across all regions—developed as well as underdeveloped (Table 8.9).

TABLE 8.7
Number of States and UTs in Different Ranges of C–D Ratio, March 2003

(In percentages)

Range of CDR	C^S DR	C^U DR	C^U+I/D Ratio	C^U+I+RIDF/D
<30	17	8	2	2
30–50	11	12	14	9
50–60	1	7	4	8
>60	6	8	15	16
Total	35	35	35	35

Note: C^S/DR: Credit as per sanction to deposit Ratio; C^U/D Ratio: credit as per utilization to deposit ratio; C^U+I/D Ratio: credit as per utilization plus Investment to deposit ratio; C^U+I+RIDF/D: credit as per utilization plus investment plus RIDF to deposit ratio
Source: NABARD (2006): Report of the Expert Group on Credit–Deposit Ratio.

TABLE 8.8
Region-wise CDR (as per sanction) and C+I/D Ratio (as per credit utilization) of Scheduled Commercial Banks

(In percentages)

Region/Year	March 1995		March 2000		March 2003	
	C^S/D	C^U+I/D	C^S/D	C^U+I/D	C^S/D	C^U+I/D
Northern	48.6	53.4	51.1	54.8	56.0	60.5
North-eastern	35.6	68.8	28.1	48.9	27.4	67.0
Eastern	47.1	62.7	37.0	48.3	39.6	54.3
Central	39.0	57.3	33.9	48.5	33.3	49.9
Western	63.2	67.2	75.4	78.6	81.0	74.9
Southern	69.4	80.9	66.2	75.5	66.3	79.2
All India	55.6	65.3	56.0	63.6	59.2	66.4

Notes: C^S/D : Credit (as per sanction) + investment to deposit ratio; C^U+I/D: Credit (as per utilization) + investment to deposit ratio.
Source: NABARD (2006): Report of the Expert Group on Credit–Deposit Ratio.

TABLE 8.9
Region-wise Credit Plus Investment Plus RIDF to Deposit Ratio

(In percentages)

Region/Year	March 2000		March 2003	
	C^S/DR	C^U+I+RIDF/D	C^S/DR	C^U+I+RIDF/D
Northern	51.1	55.2	56.0	61.4
North-eastern	28.1	50.2	27.4	69.4
Eastern	37.0	48.9	39.6	55.2
Central	33.9	49.6	33.3	51.3
Western	75.4	79.1	81.0	75.5
Southern	66.2	76.3	66.3	80.5
All India	56.0	64.3	59.2	67.4

Notes: C^S/DR: Credit (as per sanction) + investment to deposit ratio; C^U+I+RIDF/D: Credit (as per utilization) + investment + rural infrastructure development fund (RIDF) to deposit ratio.
Source: NABARD (2006): Report of the Expert Group on Credit–Deposit Ratio.

Bank Credit for Agriculture

Yet another achievement of the banking industry in the 1970s and 1980s was a decisive shift in credit deployment in favour of the agricultural sector, in particular. From a puny level at the time of bank nationalization, the credit share of the sector had moved to near 11 per cent in the mid-1970s and to a peak of about 18 per cent at the end of the 1980s. This was the official target set, at any rate for public sector banks. But, thereafter a steady deterioration, mostly against the declared public policies, has occurred in the sectoral distribution of bank credit. The share of agriculture in total bank credit (both direct and indirect) had dwindled to a low of 10 per cent by March 2005 (Table 8.10).

No doubt, the failure of scheduled commercial banks to expand their credit base for agriculture is to be seen against the relative decline in the share of agriculture in the country's GDP. In a nutshell, the share of agriculture in total GDP has steadily slipped from 38.9 per cent in 1980–1 to 31.3 per cent in 1990–1 and further to 22.0 per cent in 2004–5. An obvious policy question that would be asked is whether the 18 per cent of net bank credit target set for agriculture would still be valid. It appears to be still valid on account of a few important considerations. First, the proportion of paid-out costs in terms of modern inputs has increased considerably in agriculture over the years. Second, vast diversification is taking place in agriculture—away from crop husbandry and in favour of horticultural and livestock products, which require higher amounts of short-term and investment credit. Finally, the proportion of workforce dependent on agriculture remains nearly 60 per cent. Against this background, the stark reality of a sharp reduction in the absolute number of agricultural loan accounts has been indeed disquieting. This number, which had reached a peak of 27.74 million in March 1992, persistently declined thereafter and touched 20.35 million by March 2002, that is, a fall of 25 per cent in a period of ten years; some increase has occurred thereafter to 26.66 million by March 2005 due to socio-political pressures (Table 8.9) but loans for agriculture as a percentage of total loans have remained at about 10 per cent.

Direct vs Indirect Credit for Agriculture

A caveat is to be entered at this stage in the context of the absolute reductions in the number of loan accounts as well as decline in the agriculture sector's share in total bank credit. The annual percentage increases in bank credit rendered by scheduled commercial banks (SCBs) in recent years have been quite sizeable, ranging from 19 per cent to 29 per cent in each of the past four years. There are a few reasons for these apparent accelerated increases in agricultural loans. First, a substantial part of the loans has been in the form of indirect advances, that is, not to individual farmers but to institutions and organizations serving the interest of farmers directly or indirectly. Second, it has occurred in the most recent period after the government introduced the policy of doubling farm credit over a period of three years. Finally, within farm credit, a growing proportion has been in favour of large-size loans, which is evident from the fact that while the number of loan accounts under direct finance has risen by meagre percentages, the loan amounts have risen quite significantly (Table 8.11).

Total Credit Flow for Agriculture (Including that from Co-operatives)

The above picture is based only on credit delivery arrangements by scheduled commercial banks, and that too, in terms of outstandings at year-ends and not in terms of fresh

TABLE 8.10
Outstanding Credit of SCBs against Agriculture and SSIs

(Amount in rupees lakh)

Year	Agriculture				SSIs			
	No. of Accounts	Per cent to All India	Amount	Per cent to All India	No. of Accounts	Per cent to All India	Amount	Per cent to All India
December 72	1,371,975	31.6	50,091	9.0	172,685	4.0	65,926	11.9
December 75	3,042,170	41.3	107,058	10.7	262,301	3.6	117,796	11.8
December 81	11,231,727	50.5	486,330	17.1	765,431	3.4	353,315	12.4
March 1990	24,520,595	45.5	1,662,607	15.9	1,606,146	3.0	1,198,563	11.5
March 1999	19,788,385	37.8	4,088,926	10.7	2,029,920	3.9	3,142,843	8.2
March 2000	20,532,891	37.8	4,563,827	9.9	2,126,150	3.9	3,506,987	7.6
March 2001	19,843,289	37.9	5,173,035	9.6	1,742,544	3.3	3,690,487	6.9
March 2002	20,351,184	36.1	6,400,855	9.8	1,572,798	2.8	3,197,030	4.9
March 2003	20,840,434	35.0	7,593,522	10.0	1,431,421	2.4	3,794,034	5.0
March 2004	21,304,168	32.1	9,624,504	10.9	718,056*	1.1	3,843,255	4.4
March 2005	26,656,308	34.6	12,438,487	10.8	939,186	1.2	4,707,642	4.1

Note: * This does not appear to be correct; the error is in the source. Also, there are significant definitional problems associated with the SSI sector data due to frequent revisions in definitions.
Source: RBI's Basic Statistical Returns, various issues.

TABLE 8.11
Direct and Indirect Finance For Agriculture and Allied Activities by SCBs

(Amount in rupees lakh)

Year	Number of Accounts					
	Agriculture total 1 = (2+3)	Per cent Increase	Direct Finance 2	Per cent Increase	Indirect Finance 3	Per cent Increase
March 97	22,524,364		22,224,763		299,601	
March 98	21,720,055	−3.6	21,407,723	−3.7	312,332	4.2
March 99	19,788,385	−8.9	19,520,405	−8.8	267,980	−14.2
March 00	20,532,891	3.8	20,214,350	3.6	318,541	18.9
March 01	19,843,289	−3.4	19,564,089	−3.2	279,200	−12.4
March 02	20,351,184	2.6	19,740,112	0.9	611,072	118.9
March 03	20,840,434	2.4	20,195,464	2.3	644,970	5.5
March 04	21,304,168	2.2	20,719,954	2.6	584,214	−9.4
March 05	26,656,308	25.1	26,010,380	25.5	645,928	10.6
	Amount Outstanding					
March 97	3,163,415		2,721,736		441,680	
March 98	3,526,252	11.5	3,050,890	12.1	475,362	7.6
March 99	4,088,926	16.0	3,394,114	11.2	694,812	46.2
March 00	4,563,827	11.6	3,856,079	13.6	707,748	1.9
March 01	5,173,035	13.3	4,342,026	12.6	831,008	17.4
March 02	6,400,855	23.7	4,743,042	9.2	1,657,813	99.5
March 03	7,593,522	18.6	5,905,756	24.5	1,687,766	1.8
March 04	9,624,504	26.7	7,009,873	18.7	2,614,631	54.9
March 05	12,438,487	29.2	9,463,537	35.0	2,974,950	13.8

Source: RBI, Banking Statistics: Basic Statistical Returns of Scheduled Commercial Banks in India, March 2005 (Vol. 34) and earlier issues.

annual flows of advances. NABARD provides such data on total credit flow for agriculture separately for co-operatives, RRBs and commercial banks. These data show that with the introduction of special agricultural credit plans, commercial banks and RRBs have come to play an increasing role in the supply of total agricultural credit, while co-operatives have begun to take a back seat. The share of co-operatives in total farm credit has declined steadily from about 40 per cent in 1999–2000 to 24 per cent in 2005–6 (Table 8.12); suggesting that less than one-fourth of institutional credit

TABLE 8.12
Flow of Total Institutional Credit for Agriculture by Institution

(Rs crore)

Years/ Agency	Coopera- tives	Per cent Increase	Scheduled Commercial Bank (4+5)	Per cent Increase	RRBs	Per cent Increase	Commercial Banks	Per cent Increase	Total Institutional Credit (2+3)	Per cent Increase
(1)	(2)		(3)		(4)		(5)		(6)	
1999–00	18,363 (39.7)		27,905 (60.3)		3172		24,733		46,268	
2000–1	20,800 (39.4)	13.3	32,027 (60.6)	14.8	4220	33.0	27,807	12.4	52,827	14.2
2001–2	23,604 (38.0)	13.5	38,441 (62.0)	20.0	4854	15.0	33,587	20.8	62,045	17.5
2002–3	23,716 (34.1)	0.5	45,844 (65.9)	19.3	6070	25.1	39,774	18.4	69,560	12.1
2003–4	26,959 (31.0)	13.7	60,022 (69.0)	30.9	7581	24.9	52,441	31.9	86,981	25.0
2004–5	30,639 (26.6)	13.7	84,604 (73.4)	41.0	11,718	54.6	72,886	39.0	115,243	32.5
2005–6	37,272 (23.7)	21.7	120,228 (76.3)	42.1	14,076	20.1	106,152	45.6	157,500	36.7

Note: Figures in brackets are percentage to total.

Source: NABARD data quoted in GOI (2006), *Economic Survey* 2005–6 up to 2004–5 and from NABARD for 2005–6.

for agriculture comes from co-operatives. 'This is reflected in the increasing concern in recent years over the effectiveness, governance, and financial health of rural co-operative banks and the attention being given to rural lending by commercial banks. Just under a third of rural credit continues to be extended by the co-operative system and hence it is essential that they be revitalised and put on a sound business footing' (Mohan 2006, p. 1017). As explained in a subsequent section, revitalization of the co-operative credit system has been conceived as a major task and the recommendations of the Vaidyanathan Committees (I and II) have been accepted in principle for implementation.

As a result of the sufferance of the co-operative credit system, it is its traditional role rendering term credit that has suffered a serious setback (Table 8.13). Even so, because of sizeable increases in term credit by commercial banks and RRBs ranging from 40 per cent to 70 per cent in the recent period,[2] the share of term credit in total credit has risen from 35 per cent in 2001–2 to 41 per cent in 2004–5 (Table 8.14).

Database Issues on Agricultural Credit

Even though as an aside, it is necessary to take note of the fact that the data published by RBI and NABARD based on their control returns invariably tend to overestimate the size of bank credit outstanding against agriculture and allied activities as compared to that revealed by the *Basic Statistical Returns of Scheduled Commercial Banks* (BSR). The latter is a more scientifically designed annual survey conducted by the RBI, the data for which are collected from the branch offices of scheduled commercial banks individually and hence, their quality is not influenced by the regional offices and head offices of banks. Otherwise, there does not appear to be any valid reason for the persistent overestimation of agricultural credit totals by the control returns as compared with those tabulated by the BSR system. It is also interesting that the overestimation so reported has risen from about Rs 6662 crore in March 2002 to Rs 15,386 crore in March 2005 (Table 8.15). Besides, almost the entire part of

TABLE 8.13
Agency-wise Break-up of Term Credit Flow

(Rs crore)

Year	Cooperatives	Growth rate (per cent)	Commercial Banks	Growth rate (per cent)	RRBs	Growth rate (per cent)	Total term credit	Growth rate (per cent)
(1)	(2)		(3)		(4)		(5)	
1995–6	2148		4827		532		7507	
	(28.6)	21.8	(64.3)	29.1	(7.1)	5.8	(100)	25.4
1996–7	2616		6234		563		9413	
	(27.8)	21.9	(66.2)	20.0	(6.0)	14.4	(100)	20.2
1997–8	3190		7482		644		11316	
	(28.2)	6.1	(66.1)	17.9	(5.7)	16.5	(100)	14.5
1998–9	3386		8821		750		12957	
	(26.1)	3.9	(68.1)	47.8	(5.8)	-0.1	(100)	33.5
1999–2000	3518		13036		749		17303	
	(20.3)	19.9	(75.3)	9.9	(4.3)	30.0	(100)	12.8
2000–1	4218		14321		974		19513	
	(21.6)	13.2	(73.4)	9.5	(5.0)	10.6	(100)	10.4
2001–2	4776		15683		1077		21536	
	(22.2)	-17.2	(72.8)	19.4	(5.0)	20.1	(100)	11.3
2002–3	3956		18724		1294		23974	
	(16.5)	7.7	(78.1)	40.2	(5.4)	15.4	(100)	33.5
2003–4	4262		26249		1493		32004	
	(13.3)	-4.4	(82.0)	70.2	(4.7)	60.3	(100)	59.8
2004–5	4074		44688		2394		51156	
	(8.0)	11.8	(87.4)	*	(4.7)	-3.6	(100)	*
2005–6	4554				2308			
	(*)				(*)			
CAGR (1995–6 to 2004–5)		7.8		24.9		15.8		21.1

Notes: * Not available; Figures in bracket are percentages to total term credit flow.

Source: NABARD (2005), *Expert Group on Investment Credit*, June up to 2002–3 and NABARD sources thereafter.

[2] The growth rates will work out to be more moderate if they are measured over outstandings.

TABLE 8.14
Flow of Institutional Credit for Agriculture by Category

(Rs crore)

Year	Short-term credit	Growth rate (per cent)	Term credit	Growth rate (per cent)	Total Credit	Growth rate (per cent)	Term credit as per cent of pvt. sector GCF in agriculture$
(1)	(2)		(3)		(4)		(5)
1995–6	14,525 (65.9)		7507 (34.1)		22,032 (100)		35.1
1996–7	16,998 (64.4)	17.0	9413 (35.6)	25.4	26,411 (100)	19.9	38.6
1997–8	20,640 (64.6)	21.4	11,316 (35.4)	20.2	31,956 (100)	21.0	43.5
1998–9	23,903 (64.8)	15.8	12,957 (35.2)	14.5	36,860 (100)	15.3	48.5
1999–2000	28,965 (62.6)	21.2	17,303 (37.4)	33.5	46,268 (100)	25.5	53.6
2000–1	33,314 (63.1)	15.0	19,513 (36.9)	12.8	52,827 (100)	14.2	59.5
2001–2	40,509 (65.3)	21.6	21,536 (34.7)	10.4	62,045 (100)	17.4	60.5
2002–3	45,586 (65.5)	12.5	23,974 (34.5)	11.3	69,560 (100)	12.1	61.7
2003–4	54,977 (63.2)	20.6	32,004 (36.8)	33.5	86,981 (100)	25.0	–
2004–5	73,960 (59.0)	34.5	51,349 (41.0)	60.4	125,309 (100)	44.1	–
CAGR (1995–6 to 2004–5)	19.6		23.5		21.1		

Note: Figures in brackets are percentages to total credit; $ This is a rough estimate.
Source: Same as in Table 8.13.

TABLE 8.15
Data Reported on Agricultural Advances of Public Sector Banks: A Comparison of Control Return and BSR Numbers

A. Agricultural Advances Reported as per Priority Sector Data for Public Sector Banks (Control Returns)

(*As on last reporting Friday*)

	No. of Accounts (lakh)				Amount Outstanding (Rs Crore)			
	March 2002	March 2003	March 2004	March 2005	March 2002	March 2003	March 2004	March 2005 @
Agriculture	158	168	190	208	58,142	70,501	84,435	112,475
Direct	153	165	188	191	44,019	51,484	62,170	82,613
Indirect	5	3	2	17	14,123	19,017	22,265	29,862

B. Advances to Agriculture by Public Sector Banks (BSR Data)

(*As on 31st March*)

	No. of Accounts (lakh)				Amount Outstanding (Rs Crore)			
	March 2002	March 2003	March 2004	March 2005	March 2002	March 2003	March 2004	March 2005
Agriculture	137	140	140	177	51,480	59,992	76,445	97,089
Direct	133	136	137	174	36,794	45,000	53,215	71,334
Indirect	4	4	3	3	14,686	14,992	23,230	25,755

Note: @ Data are provisional.

Sources: (i) For A, *Report on Trend and Progress of Banking in India*, 2004–5, p. 236.
(ii) For B, *RBI, Banking Statistics: Basic Statistical Returns of Scheduled Commercial Banks in India, March 2005* (Vol. 34) and earlier issues.

the difference is to be found under direct finance for agriculture as distinguished from indirect finance.

There is yet another reason to believe that the overestimation could be still more because the control returns cover agricultural advances under the 'priority sector' which by definition should normally exclude many big-size advances given against agricultural operations (such as loans beyond Rs 10 lakh against pledge/hypothecation of agricultural produce, and loans for input distribution for allied activities beyond Rs 40 lakh shown as indirect finance), whereas the BSR data include all agricultural advances.

Small-scale Industries

Next to agriculture, the small-scale industrial sector occupies a pivotal position in terms of employment and output share in the economy.[3] Apart from sectoral dispersal and wider promotion of entrepreneurship, the SSIs have a regional dimension in that the SSI units are scattered all over, in the nooks and corners of the country. Immediately after the introduction of social control and subsequent bank nationalization, banks found SSIs to be a lucrative target for lending. Hence, the share of SSI units in total bank credit shot up from 6.9 per cent in June 1968 to 12.0 per cent in June 1973. Thereafter, it was sustained in the range of 11 to 13.5 per cent until the early 1990s. What has happened thereafter is truly disappointing. A steady and drastic fall in the share of bank credit in favour of SSIs has occurred from 13.4 per cent in March 1989 to as low as 4.1 per cent in March 2005 and that of artisans and village industries from 0.9 per cent to 0.7 per cent. The number of bank loan accounts in respect of the SSI sector has dropped from a peak of 21.26 lakh in March 2000 to as low as 9.39 lakh in March 2005—a loss of over 12 lakh or 56 per cent (see Table 8.10). To what extent these are attributable to revisions in the definition of the SSI sector is not known. Besides, while separate data are not available for the SSI sector's GDP, indications are that its share in total GDP may have generally stood firm in recent years. The share of unregistered manufacturing was about 5.7 per cent in 1980–1 and has remained at that level in 2003–4.

Loss of Momentum in the Distribution of Bank Credit in Favour of Small Borrowers and other Vulnerable Groups

Between December 1972 and June 1983, there were 21.2 million additional bank loan accounts in the aggregate, added and nursed by the SCBs, of which 19.8 million or 93.1 per cent were accounts with credit limits of Rs 10,000 or less. This trend of focusing on small borrowal accounts continued for another decade up to March 1992 (despite the loan waiver scheme effective 15 March 1990). Between December 1982 and March 1992, there were 38.1 million additional bank accounts, of which 36.0 million were the redefined small borrowal accounts with credit limits of Rs 25,000 and less.

However, what has happened since the beginning of the 1990s has been most distressing. Between March 1992 and March 2001, there has been an absolute decline of about 13.5 million in the aggregate bank loan accounts and this has happened entirely because of a much larger decline of 25.3 million accounts for the redefined small borrowal accounts with credit limits of Rs 25,000 and less. On the other hand, borrowal accounts with higher credit limits of above Rs 25,000 have shown an unusually large increase of 11.8 million as compared with only 2.1 million increase during the preceding decade (December 1983 to March 1992).

Even in the recent period, March 2001 to March 2005, while an addition of 24.79 million in total loan accounts has occurred, small borrowal accounts have experienced an absolute fall of 0.49 million (until March 2004); during 2004–5, there was a fractional rise of 1.97 million because of the forced expansion in farm loans (Table 8.16).

TABLE 8.16
Trends in the Number of Small Borrowal vis-à-vis other Bank Loan Accounts

Period-End	Total Bank Borrowal Accounts (Lakh)		Small Borrowal Accounts of Rs 25,000 or less (Lakh)		Other Bigger Accounts (Lakh)	
	Number	Increase over the previous period	Number	Increase over the previous period	Number	Increase over the previous period
December 1983	277.48	–	265.21	–	12.27	–
March 1992	658.61	381.12	625.48	360.27	33.12	20.85
March 2001	523.65	(–) 134.95	372.52	(–) 252.96	151.13	118.01
March 2004	663.90	140.25	367.66	(–) 4.86	296.24	145.11
March 2005	771.51	107.61	387.33	19.67	384.18	87.94

Source: Same as for Table 8.11.

---

[3] In the recent period, a paradigm shift from SSI to small and medium enterprises in the official focus on sectoral bank credit flow has taken place (see RBI 2005). Only the SSI credit is treated as part of the priority sector. Data are not as yet available for the medium enterprises sector.

Impact of Credit Contraction on Poor Households[4]

The implications of credit contractions for small borrowers are many. First, RBI data have shown that nearly 80 per cent of small borrowal accounts were in rural and semi-urban areas and hence their contraction is sure to hurt the borrowers in such areas. Second, about 22 per cent of the number of small accounts and 18.1 per cent of the amount outstanding of such accounts have been in respect of women borrowers; over the years this proportion has edged up implying that women borrowers have increased their share of bank borrowings. Such is not the case with the borrowers amongst SCs and STs; their share has remained generally static between 1993 and 1997; the shares of women in these groups are also broadly the same. Third, even within the small borrower category, still smaller loans up to Rs 7500 had accounted for 80.5 per cent of the number of accounts and 50 per cent of the loan amount outstanding in March 1993, which slipped to 64 per cent and 32 per cent, respectively by March 1997. Fourth, the bulk of the small borrowal accounts have been for agricultural and allied activities. Fifth, about 50 per cent of the small borrowal accounts have been granted under special asset-creating employment programmes like the IRDP, SEEUY, SEPUP, DRI, and others. Sixth, RRBs stand out as banks serving the small borrowal accounts; this is more so in rural areas. Many of these phenomena are getting further reinforced in the more recent period. Finally, small borrowal accounts have about two-thirds of credit outstanding as standard assets, which is somewhat lower than that for the public sector banking system as a whole at 88 per cent. Standard assets of small borrowal accounts have risen with the size of loans but have been higher for agricultural activities than for industry, trade, and transport except for personal and professional loans; the latter categories thus have weaker assets.

MICRO-CREDIT MOVEMENT IN INDIA

The rationale behind the micro-credit movement in India is manifold. Despite their phenomenal growth and spread, there is still a vast gap in the availability of banking services in rural areas. Apart from the organizational reluctance on the part of banking institutions to expand their branch network and to cater to the needs of informal sector households, formal credit institutions have a major disability in that they cannot meet the composite borrowing needs of poor households in the form of production as well as consumption credit and in the form of thrift facilities. Apart from large transaction costs involved when they meet such services, the formal institutions face large non-performing loans.

In response to the above problems associated with formal banking institutions, non-governmental organizations (NGOs) and other voluntary agencies have devised the institution of self-help groups (SHGs) and for them, the operation of microfinance arrangements involving both the delivery of credit and thrift-type of saving schemes. Such an arrangement has been co-opted by the official agencies in India as part of the structure of credit institutions in the country. With strong official blessings, the whole arrangement has partaken the character of SHG–bank linkage programme. NABARD has taken a number of steps to intensively promote the microfinance movement in India and the RBI has issued a set of guidelines to banks to be observed by them in rendering micro-credit assistance. Credit disbursals through the scheme are to be covered as part of priority sector advances. Alongside Small Industries Development Bank of India (SIDBI), Foundation for Micro Credit (SFMC) was launched effective January 1999.

There is no doubt that the micro-credit movement has shown significant potential in India, and with intensive official support, the coverage has rapidly expanded in recent years. Almost all SCBs and RRBs have embraced it as an important banking programme. As shown in Tables 8.17 and 8.18, over 22.38 lakh SHGs have obtained bank loans aggregating Rs 11,398 crore for about 330 lakh poor households with the refinance support of Rs 4157 crore from NABARD (at the end of March 2006). Likewise, the cumulative assistance under the SIDBI scheme has aggregated Rs 422 crore for 15 lakh poor households at the end of March 2005.

SHGs comprising only women members have constituted 90 per cent; with of course timely loan repayment (95 per cent). There has been substantial regional concentration of SHGs, with the southern states occupying a pride of place—accounting for 54 per cent of the total SHGs credit linked and much more at 75 per cent in terms of the total amount of bank loans disbursed as at the end of March 2006. Andhra Pradesh alone accounted for 26 per cent of the SHGs credit linked and 38 per cent of cumulative bank loans as at the end of March 2006. This situation was much more acutely concentrated until the recent period and it is claimed to be undergoing a change as may be seen in the latest data provided by NABARD (Table 8.19). However, it is important to note that for the BIMARU (Bihar, Madhya Pradesh, Rajasthan, Uttar Pradesh) states, the proportion of SHGs in the all-India total has remained at about 15–16

---

[4] The summary assessment in this sub-section is based on a series of occasional articles in the RBI's monthly bulletin; See, for example, 'Survey of Small Borrowal Accounts, 2001' in May 2004 issue of the Bulletin; some parts of the data on small borrowal accounts are available in the *RBI's BSR of Scheduled Commercial Banks*, which has been the basic source of information for this note.

TABLE 8.17
NABARD: Bank–SHG Credit Linkage Programme Cumulative Progress up to 2004–5

Year-End (April–March)	No. of SHGs linked	SHGs Refinanced (Number)	Bank Loans (Rs Crore)	Refinance by NABARD (Rs Crore)
2000–1*	263,825	213,213	481	400
2001–2	461,478	340,131	1026	796
2002–3	717,360	493,634	2049	1419
2003–4	1,079,091	611,043	3904	2124
2004–5	1,618,476	824,888	6898	3086
2005–6	2,238,565	900,000	11,398	4157

Note: * In the 2000–1 report, SHGs are excluding those not covered under refinance.

Source: NABARD's Annual Report 2004–5 and various issues.

TABLE 8.18
Progress Under SIDBI Foundation for Micro Credit (SFMC)

(Amount in Rs crore)

Year	Amount Sanctioned	Amount Disbursed	Number of SHGs Involved	Outstanding Loan Portfolio of SIDBI (amount)	Cumulative sanctions of assistance (amount)	Cumulative total number of poor persons benefited (lakh)
1999–2000	21.90	14.03	–	–	52.61	3.14
2000–1	28.28	19.45	20530	33.24 (1.50)	81.05	4.42
2001–2	41.70	21.79	28436	43.45 (1.51)	122.75	7.28
2002–3	38.51	31.04	–	–	161.26	8.62
2003–4	70.84	66.31	–	91.21	232.08	10.41
2004–5	189.73	145.06	–	199.21	421.81	15.10

Note: Figures in brackets represent NPAs of the total portfolio.

Source: SIDBI Annual Reports, various issues.

TABLE 8.19
Cumulative Growth in SHG-Linkage in Priority States (As on 31 March)

(Number of SHGs)

State	2002	2003	2004	2005	2006
Assam	1024	3477	10,706	31,234	56,449
Bihar	3957	8161	16,246	28,015	46,221
Chhattisgarh	3763	6763	9796	18,569	31,291
Gujarat	9496	13,875	15,974	24,712	34,160
Himachal Pradesh	5069	8875	13,228	17,798	22,920
Jharkhand	4198	7765	12,647	21,531	30,819
Maharashtra	19,619	28,065	38,535	71,146	1,31,470
Madhya Pradesh	7981	15,271	27,095	45,105	57,125
Orissa	20,553	42,272	77,588	1,23,256	1,80,896
Rajasthan	12,564	22,742	33,846	60,006	98,171
Uttar Pradesh	33,114	53,696	79,210	1,19,648	1,61,911
Uttaranchal	3323	5853	10,908	14,043	17,588
West Bengal	17,143	32,647	51,685	92,698	1,36,251
Total for 13 priority states	141,804 (30.7)	249,462 (34.7)	397,464 (36.8)	667,761 (41.2)	10,05,272 (44.9)
Southern States	317,276 (68.8)	463,712 (64.7)	674,356 (62.5)	938,941 (58.0)	12,14,431 (54.3)
BIMARU States	57,616 (12.5)	99,870 (13.9)	156,397 (14.5)	252,774 (15.6)	3,63,428 (16.2)
All-India Total	461,478	717,360	1,079,091	1,618,456	22,38,565

Note: Figures in brackets represent percentages to all-India totals.

Source: Progress of SHG–Bank Linkage in India, Various Issues, NABARD.

per cent (at the end of March 2006). As far as data on the sources of support for the SHG sector are concerned, SHGs directly formed and financed by banks still constitute only 20 per cent of the total (as at the end of March 2006); an overwhelming 74 per cent are formed by NGO organizations but directly financed by banks and another 6 per cent are financed by banks using financial intermediaries.

The microfinance movement in India has shown significant potential, and with intensive official support, the coverage has expanded significantly which, as the institutional visions portray, is likely to be further intensified. The RBI has also expanded the scope by giving freedom to institutions to charge interest rates at their own discretion and more importantly, to cover not only consumption and production loans but also credit needs of housing and shelter improvements. SHGs involve thrift as well as credit arrangements. NABARD and SIDBI have provided for SHGs and SHG members scope for capacity building through training and other inputs by NGOs. Peer monitoring helps in better credit recovery. Finally, the SHG movement so far has shown that the outcomes have gone beyond thrift, credit, and economic well-being; they serve as an instrument of social change, especially the empowerment of women. Improvement in literary levels and children's education particularly in awareness of girls' education, housing facilities, abolition of child labour, decline in family violence, and banning of illicit distilleries in the villages have all been reported in different studies. Women have acquired better communication skills and self-confidence; they have also acquired better status within families. However, there are a number of misgivings regarding the working of the microfinance system in India and the possibilities of it emerging as an effective instrument of credit delivery for the vast masses of productive households and enterprises in rural areas—small and medium farmers, tenant farmers, and agriculture labourers desiring to graduate to non-farm activities and artisans and other small-scale, own-account enterprises; these issues are raised in the final section.

DISAPPOINTING GROUND REALITY AFTER THE 1990s

The official statistics on the distribution of bank credit amongst the informal sectors reveal a steady deterioration since the early 1990s. To bring home the seriousness of the deterioration in credit rendered by SCBs, the tabular data presented in earlier sections are depicted in Figures 8.1 to 8.5. The shares of bank credit for agriculture, SSIs, and small borrowal accounts in total bank credit were at their peak levels of 17.7 per cent, 13.4 per cent, and 25.4 per cent around the end of the 1980s or early 1990s; they have fallen steadily since then and reached their lowest levels of 10.0 per cent, 4.1 per cent, and 3.7 per cent of total bank credit around 2000 or 2001 (Figures 8.3 and 8.5). The subject of the possible erosion in the absorptive capacities of these informal sectors, due to significant structural changes taking place in the Indian economy such as reductions in their GDP share, has been addressed earlier. An incisive study calls for more detailed work on the measurement of demand for credit from these sectors and the nature of gap that may have grown over the years (Singh and Sagar 2004). One incontrovertible evidence of the growing gap in the supply of bank credit for all the three categories of informal sectors—agriculture, SSIs, and small borrowals—lies in the drastic

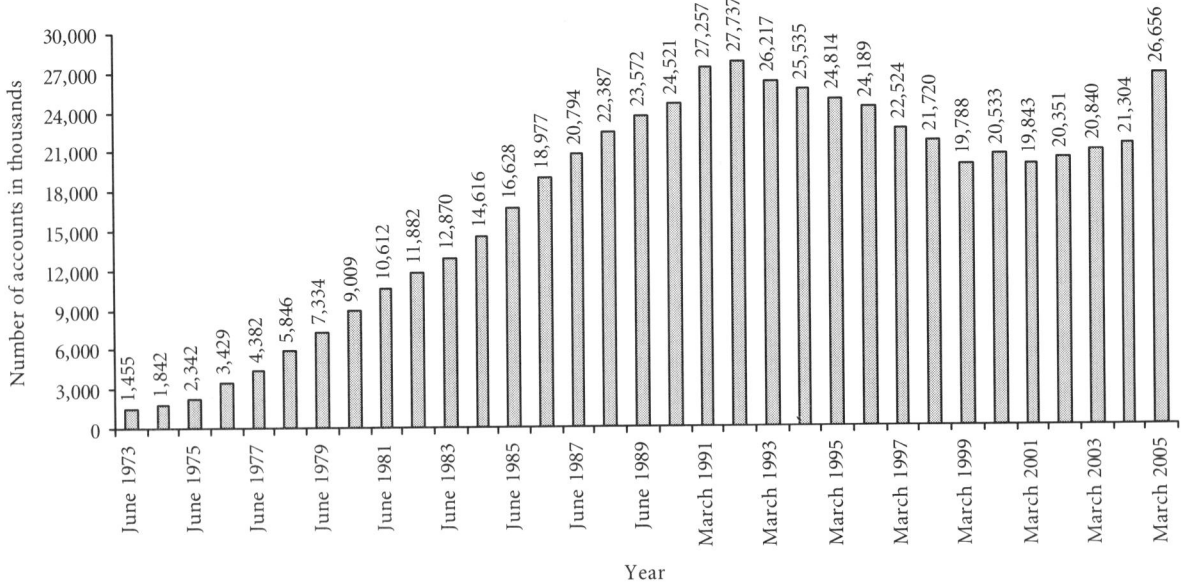

Figure 8.1: Trends in Agricultural Credit: Number of Borrowal Accounts (For SCBs)

EMERGING POLICY REGIME FOR BANK CREDIT DELIVERY AND TASKS AHEAD 127

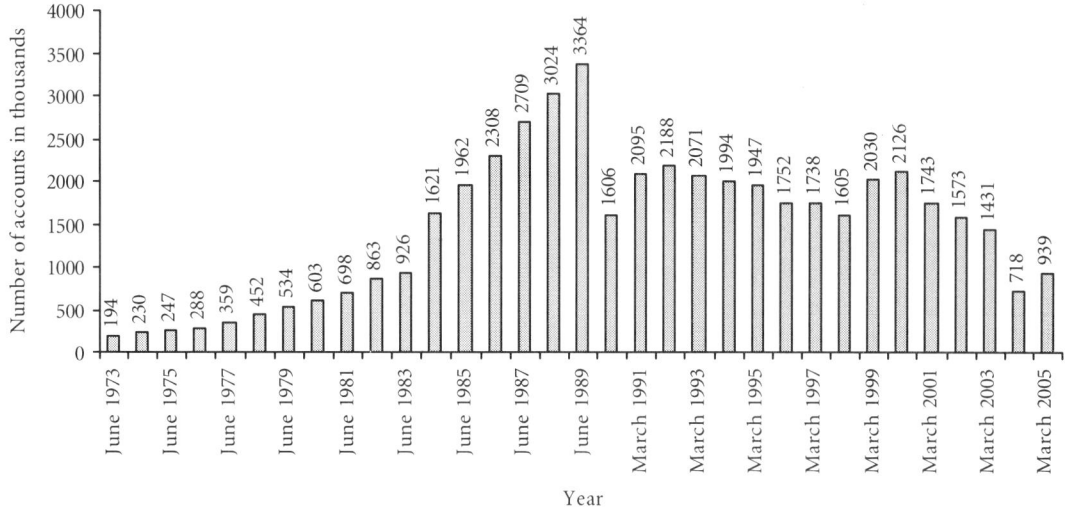

Figure 8.2: Trends in Credit for SSI Sector: Number of Borrowal Accounts (For SCBs)

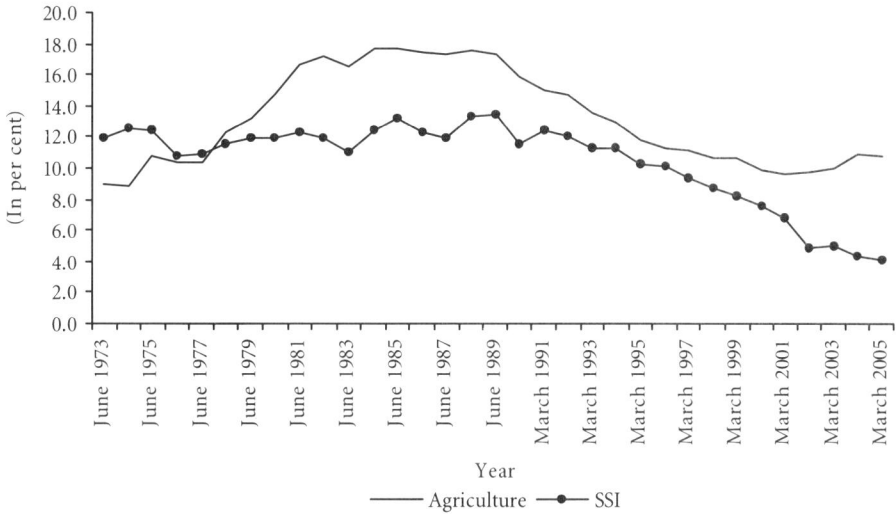

Figure 8.3: Percentage Shares of Agriculture and SSI Credit in Total Bank Credit (By SCBs)

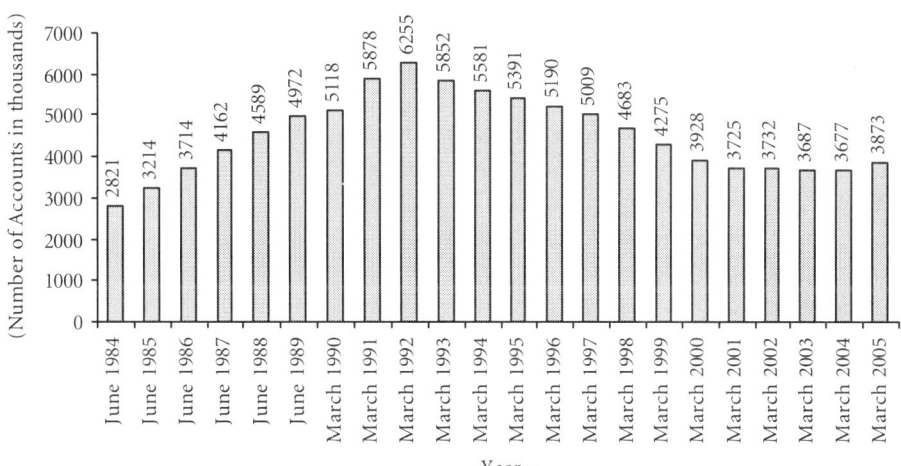

Note: * With credit limits of Rs 25,000 or below

Figure 8.4: Number of Small Borrowal Accounts* (For SCBs)

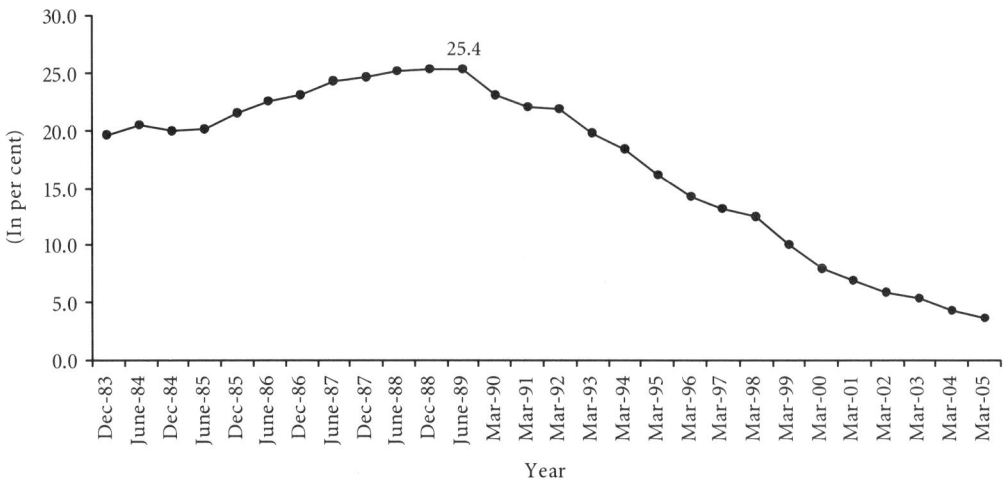

Note: * With credit limits of Rs 25,000 or below

Figure 8.5: Percentage Share of Credit of Small Borrowal Accounts* to Total Credit (By SCBs)

decline in the number of borrowal accounts from their peak levels as shown in Figures 8.1, 8.2, and 8.4. For agriculture, the number of borrowal accounts had touched the peak of 27.74 million at the end of March 1992 and this steadily declined to the lowest level of 19.84 million at the end of March 2001—a loss of about 29 per cent. While the proportion of workforce employed in agriculture and allied activities has declined fractionally from 60.4 per cent in 1993–4 to 56.7 per cent in 1999–2000, the actual number has remained static at around 191 million; between 1983 and 1993–4, there was a rise of 26 per cent from 151.35 million to 190.72 million (NSSO data) (Figure 8.1). Similar declines in the number of borrowal accounts have taken place for SSIs (partly due to definitional changes) and small borrowal categories with credit limits of Rs 25,000 or less.

MORE DECISIVE EVIDENCE FROM AIDIS AND OTHER FIELD STUDIES

The valuable insights provided by the all-India rural credit or debt and investment surveys historically on estimates of household indebtedness divided between institutional and non-institutional sources on a decennial basis are well-known. These show that institutional agencies have accounted for an increasing share of total cash dues outstanding of rural households from about 29 per cent in 1971 to 64 per cent in 1991 (Subba Rao 2005). Considering only the cultivator households, the share of institutional debt had expanded from 31.7 per cent to 66 per cent during the period (Rakesh Mohan 2006). What is evident now is the reversal of this rising trend since the beginning of the 1990s.

In the above respect, there are two survey results on indebtedness of farmer households for the recent period. First, instead of the usual decennial rural–urban debt and investment survey for 2001, the NSSO has covered the subject of indebtedness under a special 'Situation Assessment Survey of Farmers' (SAS) conducted during 2003 and published a separate report on 'Indebtedness of Farmer Households' (NSSO 2005). Second, there is the 'Rural Finance Access Survey' (RFAS), also for 2003, undertaken by the World Bank and the National Council of Applied Economic Research (NCAER) (see Basu 2005). The NSSO survey is a nationwide survey with a major central sample supplemented by a few state/union territory samples, while the RFAS 2003 covered only two Indian states, namely, Andhra Pradesh and Uttar Pradesh.

As the SAS 2003 of NSSO covered only the farmer households, its results are roughly comparable with the data on cultivator households provided by the NSSO's AIDIS in the past (Subba Rao 2005). Such a comparison is shown in Table 8.20—it reveals a decline in the share of institutional debt of cultivator households from 66.3 per cent in 1991 to 61.1 per cent in 2002 and a corresponding increase in the dependence of cultivators on money lenders. What is more revealing in the SAS 2003 survey results is the progressive decline in the proportion of indebted households as well as the share of institutional debt to total debt with the decline in the size of land possessed (Table 8.21). Obviously, this is what has brought to official focus 'the increasing concern in recent years over the effectiveness, governance and financial health of rural co-operative banks and the attention being to rural lending by commercial banks' (Rakesh Mohan 2006).

The results of RFAS 2003 are not comparable as the survey covered only two states. However, the results provide a telling commentary on the state of access to institutional finance for the vast rural masses. The results are best quoted

TABLE 8.20
Relative Share of Outstanding Debts of Cultivator Households from Different Sources

(per cent)

Sources of Credit	1951	1961	1971	1981	1991	2002
Institutional of which:	7.3	18.7	31.7	63.2	66.3	61.1
Co-op Soc/Banks, etc	3.3	2.6	22.0	29.8	30.0	30.2
Commercial Banks	0.9	0.6	2.4	28.8	35.2	26.3
Non-Institutional of which:	92.7	81.3	66.3	36.8	30.6	38.9
Moneylenders	69.7	49.2	36.1	16.1	17.5	26.8
Unspecified	–	–	–	–	3.1	–
Total	100.0	100.0	100.0	100.0	100.0	100.0

Source: All-India Debt and Investment Surveys.

TABLE 8.21
Indebtedness of Farm Households Classified According to Land Possessed

Size of Land Possessed (hectares)	Distribution of Farm Households	Percentage of Indebted Households	Share of Institutional Debt in Total (per cent)
< 0.01	1.4	45.3	22.6
0.01–0.40	32.8	44.4	43.3
0.41–1.00	31.7	45.6	52.8
1.01–2.00	18.0	51.0	57.6
2.01–4.00	10.5	58.2	65.1
4.01–10.00	4.8	65.1	68.8
10.00 +	0.8	66.4	67.6
All Classes	100.0	48.6	57.7

Source: Report No. 498 (NSSO), Quoted from Subba Rao (2005).

in the words of Basu (2005, p. 4009) who is the author of the World Bank–NCAER study.

Notwithstanding the progress made over the decades, the majority of the rural population still does not appear to have access to finance from a formal source. According to the RFAS 2003, some 59 per cent of rural households do not have a deposit account and 79 per cent of rural households have no access to credit from a formal source. The problem of access is even more severe for poorer households in rural areas. Indeed, bank branches in rural areas appear to serve primarily the needs of richer borrowers: some 66 per cent of large farmers have a deposit account; 44 per cent have access to credit. Meanwhile, 70 per cent of marginal farmers do not have a bank account and 87 per cent have no access to credit from a formal source. Another segment that faces serious problems in accessing formal finance is the commercial household (that is, micro-enterprise) segment.

NEW INITIATIVES FOR EXPANDING CREDIT FLOW TO AGRICULTURE AND OTHER PRIORITY SECTORS

Concerned at the glaring agrarian crisis including the widespread incidence of farmer suicides and the growing structural constraints faced by the non-farm informal sectors which alone have the potential for expanding employment opportunities, and concurrently recognizing the acute shortfall in credit flow to these sectors for over a decade since the beginning of the 1990s, the Government of India, the RBI, and NABARD, have initiated a number of measures to mitigate the situation. With renewed emphasis on institutional and structural features in credit policy formulation, the RBI initially appointed three committees for sectoral attention to reduce procedural delays in credit delivery: (i) R.V. Gupta committee for studying credit delivery for agriculture; (ii) S.L. Kapur committee for credit needs of SSIs; and (iii) S.H. Khan committee on harmonizing the regulatory environment for banks and development finance institutions (DFIs).

As discussed earlier, the trends in credit delivery hardly improved for some years up to 2003–4 or thereabout. Consequently, the socio-political pressures became so intense that as many 10 committees were constituted to address the questions of bank lending for agriculture and small and medium-enterprises (SMEs) as well as the institutional issues related to the working of RRBs and the need for revitalizing the short-term as well as long-term co-operative credit structure. The system of priority sector credit has been looked at afresh; likewise, the norms for regional C–D ratios and investment credit for agriculture have been probed at the instance of NABARD. The RBI's internal working groups have examined issues relating to rural credit and microfinance, lending against warehouse receipts and the question of adopting 'financial inclusion' as a policy goal. Broadly, these committees and working groups have departed from the traditional methods of targeted lending and instead proposed more intensive use of microfinance institutions along with an innovative system of 'agency banking' as a substitute for branch banking in rural areas; yet another innovative idea commended by the authorities is that of 'financial inclusion'.[5]

As the recommendations of the various committees and working groups have been by and large inspired by the in-house thinking on various issues (except the Vaidyanathan committees on co-operatives), they have all been accepted including those by both Vaidyanathan committees; and appropriate measures for their implementation have been put into place in official communications. As a result of the acute social pressures to mitigate the travails of the farm community, the Government of India has gone beyond the committee recommendations. To begin with, it announced a credit package envisaging 30 per cent growth in credit flow to agriculture during 2004–5 and sought to double the total flow over a period of three years from Rs 86,981 crore in 2003–4 to Rs 175,000 crore in 2006–7. As shown in Figure 8.1, the number of loan accounts in agriculture rose by 25 per cent from 21.30 million at the end of March 2004 to 26.66 million at the end of March 2005. The Government has also decided to provide a certain level of subvention to NABARD so that farmers receive short-term credit at 7 per cent rate of interest (up to an upper limit of Rs 3 lakh as the principal amount). This measure accepts the principle that interest rate relief to farmers has to be provided through fiscal measures rather than through cross-subsidisation within the banking sector (RBI 2006). The RBI has said that it has commenced implementation of the budget measures, while ensuring the commercial viability of banks and the overall soundness of the credit system (RBI 2006). The issuance of Kisan Credit Cards (KCCs) (introduced in August 1998), has been yet another step in the direction of expanding farm credit. An average of about 90 lakh KCCs have been issued during the past five years 2000–1 to 2004–5, taking the aggregate to 511 lakh; coverage of 100 lakh new farmers was expected during 2005–6. Hitherto, KCCs were only for crop loans but in 2004–5, their scope was expanded to cover term loans. Hence, commercial banks have replaced co-operatives as the maximum issuers of KCCs.

The flow of credit to agriculture had also suffered a setback partly because credit flow from co-operatives had been sluggish. The implementation of the recommendations of the Vaidyanathan Committees (I and II), designed to revitalize the short-term and long-term co-operative credit structures, and to minimize the cost of multi-layering is expected to improve credit delivery, appears to be in a limbo; the process of implementing the recommendations is yet to begin.

With an appropriate definition of medium enterprises (that is, plant and machinery investment in excess of the SSI limits and up to Rs 10 crore), banks have been asked to make concerted efforts to provide credit cover to at least five new SMEs per year on an average at each of their semi-urban and urban branches.

The most innovative measures relate to the more intensive use of MFIs and the introduction of the system of 'agency banking'. The absence of any expansion of branch banking in rural areas for over a decade and a half now, has created a serious institutional vacuum in such areas. Therefore, as a substitute arrangement, the system of agency banking has been introduced whereby two models, namely, 'business facilitator' model and 'business correspondent' model, have been commended to the banks for adoption. The agency system would facilitate the banks to take recourse to local-level institutions—MFIs, other varied civil society organizations, post-offices, and others—as intermediaries in providing financial and banking services through the above two types of models. Through the business facilitator model, the banks would use the services of intermediary agencies as agents for providing various facilitation services such as identification of borrowers, collection of loan applications, and post-sanction monitoring; this model does not involve any conduct of banking business by the concerned intermediaries; they will render services only as agents. On the other hand, the business correspondent model would embrace activities falling within the normal course of a bank's banking business, to be conducted through correspondent intermediaries; such activities would include: (i) disbursal of small value credit, (ii) recovery of principal/collection of interest, (iii) collection of small value deposits, (iv) sale of micro insurance/mutual fund products/pension products/other third party products, and (v) receipt and delivery of small value remittances/other

---

[5] 'The findings of the NSS 59th Round (2003) reveal that out of the total number of cultivator households, only 27 per cent receive credit from formal sources and 22 per cent from informal sources. The remaining households, mainly small and marginal farmers, have virtually no access to credit. With a view to bringing more cultivator households within the banking fold, I propose to appoint a Committee on Financial Inclusion. The Committee will be asked to identify the reasons for exclusion, and suggest a plan for designing and delivering credit to every household that seeks credit from lending institutions', *Union Finance Minister's Budget Speech, 2006–7*, pp. 10–11.

payment instruments. These business facilitator and business correspondent models go beyond the SHG–bank linkage programme described earlier.

Finally, with a view to ensuring greater financial inclusion and aimed at taking banking services to everyone, the RBI has introduced a series of measures, such as the issuance of a general credit card (GCC) to bank customers in rural and semi-urban areas with no prescription of purposes or end-use of funds or security. 50 per cent of the outstanding amount under GCC will be treated as indirect finance to agriculture.

NEW POLICY REGIME FOR BETTER CREDIT DELIVERY: TASKS AHEAD

The fresh thrust conferred on expansion of the bank credit base for agriculture and other informal sectors is greatly welcome. However, a closer examination of different elements of the new policy regime raises a few misgivings; these are required to be addressed if an enduring impact has to be made on the system of credit delivery for the targeted sectors.

First, the target of doubling credit flow to agriculture and allied activities in three years appears a knee-jerk reaction to the serious socio-political pressures that have come to bear on the system due to vast credit supply gaps created over a prolonged period. During this period, it is not only that the credit flow had dried up; even the rural institutional structure in terms of branch-banking had been weakened. Superimposing such a large target on the weak institutional structure will have its repercussions on first, the quality and purposes of lending, and second, the process of loan recovery. Therefore, attempts should be made to resurrect the entire institutional structure in terms of its geographical spread as well as organizational strength. Only such a structure will be able to achieve a steady and healthy delivery of credit for agriculture and rural enterprises.

First and foremost is the need for further spreading of branch network by SCBs and RRBs. The system of 'agency banking' can only supplement the operations of bank branches in rural and semi-urban areas. A palpable cause for the decline in bank lending to agriculture, SSIs, and small borrowers, has been the banks' professional reluctance towards expanding their branch network in rural areas. As shown earlier, the number of bank branches operating in rural areas (classified uniformly on the basis of the 1991 Census) has experienced an absolute reduction from 33,017 (or 51.7 per cent of the total) in March 1995 to 30,572 (44.5 per cent of the total) in March 2006. Any yardstick we apply—30,600 rural branches serving 5.5 lakh villages, the decline in population per bank office, the period in which bank branches reached break-even points in the past, and the positive externalities they provide—justifies the promotion of rural bank branches. Given the option, SCBs would not like to operate in rural areas. This has been proved clearly since March 1995 after the disbanding of branch licencing policy and the granting of freedom to bank boards to decide on their branch expansion programme. Since then, there has been a reduction of roughly 2445 rural branches instead of an addition of at least 10,000 bank branches in rural areas under the erstwhile policy thrust. This approach has thus created a serious institutional vacuum in the rural credit structure. It happened also because no attempt was made by the authorities to substitute it by strengthening RRBs or by building an alternative rural institutional structure for credit delivery. Second, with vast modern input requirements and diversification into horticultural products and other allied areas, agriculture will require a more sophisticated system of credit delivery, for which induction of a sizeable number of qualified agricultural science graduates and graduates with other relevant technical qualifications will be necessary. Considering this felt need, the renewed policy thrust becomes an excellent opportunity for the government to generate an additional employment of about one lakh posts essentially for rural and semi-urban branches of banks; there are about 3.80 lakh employees in these branches (out of a countrywide bank total of about 8.82 lakh, at the end of March 2004). Of the 3.80 lakh employees, about 1.16 lakh are of officers cadre, and considering the past neglect and the enormous business potential, it would not be too ambitious a goal to induct another lakh of technically qualified officers with moderate salaries befitting rural and semi-urban postings in the next five years or so. A rough calculation suggests that the additional burden of wages and perquisites on this count would work out to about Rs 1200–1500 crore per year after five years; it would constitute less than 0.8 per cent of total income or less than 4 per cent of operating profits of SCBs.

Third, it is necessary to reinforce close co-ordination between district planning authorities and banking institutions operating in a district. The system of lead bank scheme and associated district-level co-ordination committees of bankers has apparently become inactive; it needs to be reinvigorated with clear guidelines on respecting the bankers' commercial judgments even as they fulfill their sectoral targets (Shete/NIBM 2004).

Finally, it is necessary to modify the nature of expectations of profitability for rural branches. It is wrong to consider, even as a business proposition, that every rural branch should reach a break-even point and attain positive profits in three years or so. Rather, the expectation should be to achieve positive profits in a cluster of bank branches, say, within a taluka or even a district; the profit so derived should be sufficiently attractive in relation to the totality of business in the whole taluka or district.[6]

Before closing this section, a word of caution is required on the expectations of a pivotal role to be played by the microfinance movement in the rural credit system of the country. First, success stories of MFIs are invariably based on intensely dedicated, selfless, and celebrity services of individuals as NGOs. It is in this context that questions are asked whether the institution of NGOs is a free good, liberally available and whether it can be a substitute for public administration and associated public programmes and policies. Second, NABARD's own experience has shown that over 54 per cent of NGO-supported SHGs are concentrated in the four southern states—over 48 per cent of them in Andhra Pradesh alone. SHG formation in other regions is hampered by the absence of a dedicated NGO movement. Third, upliftment of women is an important goal, but the goal of poverty-alleviation needs to have a wider coverage. The latest report on progress of SHG–bank linkage for 2004–5 states that 90 per cent of the SHGs linked to banks continue to comprise women members only, but this has been commended on the ground that as a result, repayment of loans by SHGs to banks has consistently been over 95 per cent. When the microfinance system is brought into the mainstream, concentration on women SHGs only will not work and formation of SHGs amongst men entrepreneurs is a much arduous task. Fourth, the whole microfinancing programme is at an early stage 'and that the results are an initial outcome of a small-scale and nascent programme. Even studies on Bangladesh's Grameen Bank have revealed that low default rates were confined to loans of small size, that the default rates tended to rise with the loan size and with time and repetitive borrowers' (Hossain 1988). Fifth, the same thing can be said of the impact of high interest rates in micro-credit lendings mediated through NGOs and SHGs. Again, studies on Grameen Bank and other microfinancing schemes have emphasized how high rates of interest, while they are accepted by the poor initially because of their state of helplessness, nevertheless become a burden on their incomes and their future stream of savings (Rahman 1999 and Mosley and Hulme 1998). Sixth, the studies express similar misgivings regarding the apparent prompt and regular loan repayments by the micro borrowers, but in reality they are known to repay not out of the income stream flowing from assets gained, but through further borrowing, even from money lenders (Rahman 1999). In a significant study in northern Bangladesh, Sinha and Martin (1998) reveal that 'most of the informal loans repaid with Grameen loans were taken to repay earlier Grameen loans'. Among the target group households, 45 per cent of the amount of informal sector loans was utilized for repaying loans taken from micro-credit institutions, including Grameen Bank; for the non-target groups this was 15 per cent (Rahman 1999). Hence, Rahman (1999) has characterized the micro credit situation as the creation of 'debt cycles' for the borrowers. Such are the implications of creating a system of MFIs, which are made commercially viable on the strength of higher interest rates charged to the poor than those charged by traditional banking from their normal customers. The caution on the uneconomic levels of rates of interest should also be applicable to the new system of agency banking. The RBI has exempted the whole system from interest rate ceilings and it could have significant adverse repercussions on the finances of micro enterprises.

Seventh, can the micro-credit system substitute for the vast credit needs of the poor in general? Today, only women's needs are being catered to and that also to a limited extent through micro-credit. Small borrowal accounts with credit limits of Rs 25,000 or less account for Rs 42,992 crore of loans, whereas, out of these small borrowal accounts, the SCBs at best may have provided Rs 6900 crore as part of micro-credit arrangement, and that too, with about 80 per cent refinance from NABARD at 6.5 per cent concessional rate of interest. How long such an arrangement can be sustained when the banking system in general shows no commitment to the needs of the small borrowers spread across the country? What is being sought to be hypothesized here is that there is a degree of continuum in the economic relationships, say within a village, and the objective of the socio-economic empowerment of the poor households in the village will be better served only if all sections of a village—myriad small and marginal farmers, farm households in general, village artisans, unincorporated enterprises, and other household enterprises—partake the benefits of increased institutional credit. However, such a requirement is unlikely to be served without co-opting the borrowing needs of all small borrowing households as a responsibility of the banking system and not just the NGO-supported and SHG-based micro enterprises.

References

Basu, Priya (2005), 'A Financial System for India's Poor', H.T. Parekh Finance Forum, *Economic and Political Weekly*, No. 37, 10 September.

Bell, Clive and Peter L. Rousseau (2001), 'Post-independence India: a case of finance-led industrialization?', *Journal of Development Economics*, Vol. 65, pp. 153–75.

Burgess, Robin and Rohini Pande (2003), 'Do Rural Banks Matter? Evidence from the Indian Social Banking Experiment', CMPO Working Paper Series No. 04/104.

---

[6] The suggestions contained in these two paragraphs have also been advanced in another context. See Shetty (2004).

——— (2004), *Can Rural Banks Reduce Poverty? Evidence from the Indian Social Banking Experiment*, Department of Economics, London School of Economics and Yale University, 9 June.

Burgess, Robin, Rohini Pande, and Grace Wong (2004), *Banking for the Poor: Evidence from India*, 2004 EEA Meetings, 22 September. Published in *Journal of European Economic Association*, Vol. 3, Nos 2, 3 (2005).

EPWRF (2005), 'Metamorphic Changes in the Financial System', *Economic and Political Weekly*, No. 12, Special statistics–38, 19 March.

——— (2006), 'Increasing Concentration of Banking Operations: Top Centres and Retail Loans', *Economic and Political Weekly*, No. 11, 18 March.

Eschenbach, Felix (2004), 'Finance and Growth: A Survey of the Theoretical and Empirical Literature', Tinbergen Institute Discussion Paper, TI 2004-039/2, *http://www.tinbergen.nl*

Hossain, M. (1988), *Credit for Alleviation of Rural Poverty: The Grameen Bank in Bangladesh*, Research Paper No. 4, International Food Policy Research Institute, Washington.

Mohan, Rakesh (2006), 'Agricultural Credit in India: Status, Issues and Future Agenda', *Economic and Political Weekly*, No. 11, 18 March.

Mosley, Paul and David Hulme (1998), 'Microenterprice Finance: Is there a Conflict Between Growth and Poverty Alleviation?', *World Development*, Vol. 26, No. 5, May.

NSSO (2005), *Situation Assessment Survey of Farmers, Indebtedness of Farmer Households*, NSS 59th Round (January–December 2003), Report No. 498(59/33/1), May.

Patrick, Hugh T. (1966), 'Financial Development and Economic Growth in Underdeveloped Countries', *Economic Development and Cultural Change*, January.

Rahman, Aminur (1999), 'Micro-credit Initiations for Equitable and Sustainable Development: Who Pays?', *World Development*, Vol. 27, No. 1, January.

Ramachandran, V.K. and Madhura Swaminathan (eds) (2005), *Financial Liberalization and Rural Credit in India*, Agrarian Studies 2, Tulika Books, New Delhi.

RBI (1997), *Report on Trend and Progress of Banking in India, 1996–97*.

——— (2001), 'Financial Development and Economic Growth in India', *Report on Currency and Finance (1999–2000)*, January.

——— (2005), *Report of the Internal Group to Review Guidelines on Credit Flow to SME Sector*, April.

——— (2006), *Basic Statistical Returns of Scheduled Commercial Banks in India—March 2005*, Vol. 34, February.

Shete, N.B./NIBM (2004), *Role of Lead Bank Officers in the Changed Context of Financial Sector Reforms (A Research Report)*, National Institute of Bank Management (NIBM), Pune, 24 December.

Shetty, S.L. (2002), 'Regional, Sectoral and Functional Distribution of Bank Credit', Paper submitted at a Workshop on *Financial Liberalization and Rural Credit in India*, organized by Artis Dasgupta and the editors for the Sociological Research Unit of the Indian Statistical Institute, and held in Kolkata in March 2002, in V.K. Ramachandran and Madhura Swaminathan (eds) (2005).

——— (2004), 'Distributional Issues in Bank Credit: Multi-pronged Strategy for Correcting Past Neglect', *Economic and Political Weekly*, No. 29, 17 July.

Singh, Surjit and Vidya Sagar (2004), *State of the Indian Farmer: A Millennium Study*, Agricultural Credit in India, Department of Agriculture and Co-operation, Ministry of Agriculture and Academic Foundation, New Delhi.

Sinha, Saurabh and Imran Martin (1998), 'Informal Credit Transactions of Micro-Credit Borrowers in Rural Bangladesh', *IDS Bulletin*, Vol. 29, No. 4, April.

Subba Rao, K.G.K. (2005), 'A Financial System for India's Poor', *Economic and Political Weekly*, No. 43, 22 October.

9

Non-Perfoming Assets in Indian Banking:

Magnitude, Determinants, and Impact of Recent Policy Initiative*

Kausik Chaudhuri • Rudra Sensarma

INTRODUCTION

Banking is inherently a risky activity. It entails several risks such as credit risk, market risk, liquidity risk, operational risk etc. Prudent banking practice involves managing the risks and not eliminating them. The same is the case for credit risk which, if not managed effectively, eventually leads to bad loans or non-performing assets (NPAs). While it is neither feasible nor desirable for banks to have zero NPAs, a proper understanding of NPAs is required to manage them, with a view to keeping them under control. In this connection it becomes imperative to understand the determinants of NPAs. This is important both from the regulatory as well as managerial angles. For the regulator, NPAs are crucial since they constitute the first trigger of banking crises. Hence, it is important to ascertain the determinants of NPAs that will help in monitoring the level of bad loans so as to pre-empt any possibilities of a banking crisis. For the bank manager, NPAs eat into the bank's profitability, as banks are not allowed to book income on NPAs and, at the same time, are required to make provision for such accounts as per the regulator's guidelines. Moreover, managerial and financial resources of the bank are diverted towards resolution of NPA problems causing lost opportunities for more productive use of resources. A bank saddled with NPAs might tend to become risk averse in making new loans, particularly to SMEs. According to Merton (1995), the efficiency of the central business activities of financial intermediaries depends critically on their customer liabilities being default-free. Hence an awareness of the determinants of NPAs becomes crucial for efficient decision making at the managerial level. It is with this motivation that we study the problem of NPAs in Indian banking. More specifically, we examine the extent of the problem; and discuss the prudential norms and regulatory responses. Finally, we attempt to identify the determinants of NPAs and examine the impact of policy measures on NPAs in Indian banking.

The rest of the paper proceeds as follows: The second section outlines the relevant literature in modelling problem loans. The third section presents an overview of the Indian banking system and introduces the problem of NPAs in the context of Indian banking. The fourth section discusses the prudential norms and regulatory response to the problem of NPAs in India. The fifth section introduces the empirical methodology and the data for our analysis and the sixth section presents and discusses the empirical

* The authors gratefully acknowledge useful comments received from M. Jayadev, K.L. Krishna, and R. Radhakrishna, on earlier drafts of the paper. The authors are responsible for remaining errors, if any.

results on the determinants of NPAs. The next section explores the impact of policy measures on the level of NPAs. Finally, the eighth section concludes by collating the findings and providing some policy implications.

LITERATURE REVIEW

The academic literature has mostly dealt with determinants of banking crisis, which is the most severe consequence of bad loans in a banking system. Gonzalez-Hermosillo (1999) analysed the role of microeconomic and macroeconomic factors in five episodes of banking system problems in the US. The paper found that low capital equity and reserve coverage of problem loans ratio are the leading indicators of banking distress and failure. Demirguc-Kunt and Detragiache (2000) employed a multivariate logit framework to develop an early warning system for banking crisis and a ratings system for bank fragility. Beck, Demirguc-Kunt, and Levine (2005) examined the interlinkage between bank concentration and banking system fragility. The paper concluded that higher bank concentration is associated with lower probability of banking crisis. Moreover, institutions and regulations that facilitate bank competition are associated with less banking system fragility. Some papers have also specifically looked at the aspect of banking system fragility which we are focusing on, viz. NPAs. Fernandez de Lis, Martinez-Pages, and Saurina (2000) found that GDP growth, bank size, and capital had negative effect on NPAs while loan growth, collateral, net interest margin, debt-equity, market power, and regulation regime had a positive impact on NPAs. According to, Bloem and Gorter (2001), NPAs may be caused by wrong economic decisions or by plain bad luck.

In the Indian context too, a few papers have looked at the determinants of NPAs. Rajaraman, Bhaumik, and Bhatia (1999) and Rajaraman and Vasishtha (2002) explained variations in NPAs across Indian banks through differences in operating efficiency, solvency, and regional concentration. Das and Ghosh (2005) studied the association between risk-taking and productivity using data from public sector Indian banks over the period 1995–6 to 2000–1. They documented that capital to risk-asset ratio and loan growth have a significant negative effect on NPAs. However, the advances to priority sector do not increase NPAs. In another exercise, Das and Ghosh (2003) studied the determinants of NPAs in Indian public sector banks and identified macroeconomic factors such as GDP growth and micro-economic factors such as real loan growth, operating expenses, and size as the main factors associated with NPAs. In addition to these findings, Ranjan and Dhal (2003) found that terms of credit and different measures of bank size also affect the level of NPAs. In this paper, we explicitly try to examine the impact of recent policy initiatives on NPAs after controlling for both bank-specific and macroeconomic variables.

INDIAN BANKING SYSTEM AND ITS NPA PROBLEM

The Indian banking system is characterized by different groups of banks categorized into state-owned or public sector banks, domestic private banks, and foreign banks, which compete amongst each other in almost all areas of banking business. Table 9.1 provides the present structure of the Indian banking industry. The numbers in the table indicate that the state-owned public sector banks dominate the banking industry in terms of presence and asset size. However,

TABLE 9.1
Asset Structure of Indian Commercial Banking System

(as at end-March 2005)

Institutional Category	No. of Institutions	Outstanding Assets (Rs crores)	Assets (per cent to total)
SCBs	286	2,045,748	100.0
(a) Public sector banks	28	1,773,939	72.9
(i) State Bank group	8	627,075	25.8
(ii) Nationalized banks	19	1,065,504	43.8
(iii) Other Public Sector Bank*	1	81,360	3.3
(b) Private sector banks	29	133,494	17.6
(i) Old private banks	20	294,422	5.5
(ii) New private banks	9	154,128	12.1
(c) Foreign banks	31	77,866	6.3
(d) RRBs	196	2,045,748	3.2

Note: * IDBI Ltd, which became an SCB with effect from 11 October 2004.

Source: Compiled based on various tables in *Report on Trend and Progress in Banking in India*, 2004–5.

the new domestic private banks, which were set-up in 1995 subsequent to deregulation, have quickly occupied a significant position as compared to the old private banks.

Prior to the 1990s, the banking regulator, viz. the RBI, strictly controlled the banking system. Policies such as administered interest rates, directed lending, and restricted entry were in place in order to help the government achieve its social objectives. However, towards the early 1990s it was realized that such severe controls were adversely impacting the profitability of banks and the efficiency of the banking system as a whole. In response to this, the RBI initiated the banking sector reforms of 1992 on the recommendations of the first Narasimham Committee on financial sector reforms (1991). Some of the areas where reforms were undertaken are deregulation of entry norms, branch de-licencing, deregulation of interest rate structure, allowing greater autonomy to public sector banks, reduction of the cash reserve ratio (CRR) and the statutory liquidity ration (SLR), setting capital adequacy norms of a minimum 8 per cent capital to risk-weighted assets ratio (CRAR), and the imposition of strict income recognition and provisioning norms. Towards the late 1990s, in the aftermath of the South East Asian Crisis and following the Basel Committee recommendations, the Report of the second Narasimham Committee (April 1998) suggested further reforms in the banking sector. The committee recommended higher CRAR (now at the minimum 9 per cent stipulated by RBI), admitting market risk on government securities, stricter NPA norms, introduction of assets–liabilities management and risk management guidelines. Around the same time (May 1998), the working group for harmonizing the role and operations of DFIs and banks (the Khan Committee) recommended consolidation of the banking system through a move towards universal banking, mergers between banks and DFIs, and harmonizing the operations and regulatory frameworks of these two types of financial intermediaries.

While it is often argued that the banking sector reforms in India were successful in enhancing efficiency and productivity of banks (Sensarma 2006), one of the problems that still remains is the overhang of bad loans or NPAs. As on 31 March 2004, the gross NPAs to gross advances ratio of SCBs in India was 5.2 per cent while the net NPAs (net of provisioning) to net advances ratio was 2.2 per cent. Table 9.2 presents a summary of the state of the NPA problem in the Indian banking system. As can be seen from the table, NPA ratios have been declining over the years for all bank groups. Net NPA ratio was the highest for old private sector banks at end-March 2005 (2.7 per cent), followed by public sector banks, new private banks, and foreign banks. In further analysis we ignore the RRBs since they function with different objectives and business models than the rest of the groups and hence are not comparable with them. They own only 3.2 per cent of the assets of the industry and as is customary in Indian banking studies, we do not include them in our analysis. Furthermore, the numbers in Table 9.2 indicate that the problem of NPAs was more severe for domestic banks as compared to that for foreign banks. Figure 9.1 displays the situation in terms of gross NPAs to gross advances ratio of scheduled domestic banks. Two interesting observations emerge: (i) Over the years the ratio has been decreasing for the public sector banks, the same is true with the private banks except for the year 2002; (ii) In 2005, this ratio for the public sector banks was lower than that of old-private banks for the first time for the years under study. For domestic banks, the problem can be serious since they own more than 90 per cent of the assets of the

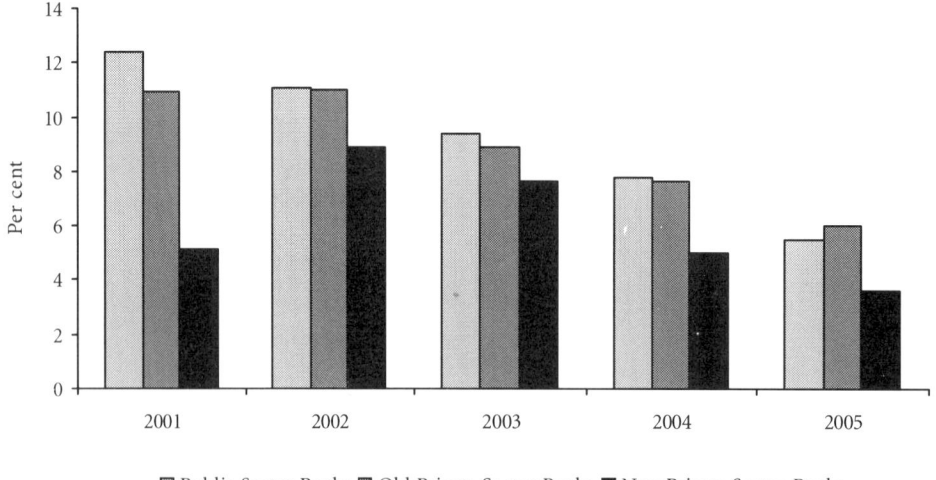

Source: Report on Trend and Progress in Banking in India, Reserve Bank of India, 2003–4 and 2004–5.

Figure 9.1: Gross NPAs to Gross Advances, 2001–5 Public Sector and Private Sector Banks

TABLE 9.2
Incidence of Gross and Net NPAs of SCBs (at end-March)

(amount in Rs crore)

Bank Group/Year	Gross Advances	Gross NPAs	Percentage of Gross NPAs to Gross Advances	Percentage of Gross NPAs to Total Assets	Net Advances	Net NPAs	Percentage of Net NPAs to Net Advances	Percentage of Net NPAs to Total Assets
SCBs								
2001	558,766	63,741	11.4	4.9	526,328	32,461	6.2	2.5
2002	680,958	70,861	10.4	4.6	645,859	35,554	5.5	2.3
2003	778,043	68,717	8.8	4.0	740,473	32,671	4.4	1.9
2004	902,026	64,786	7.2	3.3	862,643	24,617	2.9	1.2
2005	1,152,682	64,439	5.2	2.7	1,115,663	22,289	2.0	0.9
Public Sector Banks								
2001	442,134	54,672	12.4	5.3	415,207	27,977	6.7	2.7
2002	509,368	56,473	11.1	4.9	480,681	27,958	5.8	2.4
2003	577,813	54,090	9.4	4.2	549,351	24,867	4.5	1.9
2004	661,975	51,538	7.8	3.5	631,383	18,860	3.0	1.3
2005	877,825	48,541	5.5	2.7	848,912	17,490	2.1	1.0
Old Private Sector Banks								
2001	39,738	4346	10.9	5.1	37,973	2771	7.3	3.3
2002	44,057	4851	11.0	5.2	42,286	3013	7.1	3.2
2003	51,329	4550	8.9	4.3	49,436	2740	5.5	2.6
2004	57,908	4392	7.6	3.6	55,648	2140	3.8	1.8
2005	70,412	4206	6.0	3.2	67,742	1859	2.7	1.4
New Private Sector Banks								
2001	31,499	1617	5.1	2.1	30,086	929	3.1	1.2
2002	76,901	6811	8.9	3.9	74,187	3663	4.9	2.1
2003	94,718	7232	7.6	3.8	89,515	4142	4.6	2.2
2004	119,511	5963	5.0	2.4	115,106	2717	2.4	1.1
2005	127,420	4576	3.6	1.6	123,655	2292	1.9	0.8
Foreign Banks								
2001	45,395	3106	6.8	3	43,063	785	1.8	0.8
2002	50,631	2726	5.4	2.4	48,705	920	1.9	0.8
2003	54,184	2845	5.3	2.4	52,171	921	1.8	0.8
2004	62,632	2894	4.6	2.1	60,506	900	1.5	0.7
2005	77,026	2192	2.8	1.4	75,354	648	0.9	0.4

Source: Compiled based on various tables in *Report on Trend and Progress in Banking in India*, 2003–4 and 2004–5.

banking industry and thus because of their sheer size are extremely crucial for the financial stability of the economy. Moreover, because of their significant contribution to domestic industrial credit and mobilizing deposits, the issue of prudent lending and effective credit risk management is paramount for these banks. As such, our study concentrates on the NPA management of the domestic banks in India.

To get an idea of the scale of India's bad loans problem in comparison with the rest of the world, we take a look at some cross-country experience with NPAs. Table 9.3 provides a comparison of incidence of NPAs in India with that in some selected countries across geographical regions. In Figure 9.2, we only concentrate on some selected Asian countries. Note that the ratio is lower in India compared to other countries except for Japan and Korea. However, if we look at the average rate of reduction per year, India's performance ranks after Japan, China, and Korea.

We observe that the incidence of NPAs has come down over the past few years for almost all countries reported in the table. Moreover, incidence of NPAs in India appears to be quite low in comparison to some other Asian economies such as China, Indonesia, and Malaysia. However, some emerging economies such as Brazil and Korea have lower incidence of NPAs than India. Developed countries such as USA, Australia, and Canada, expectedly, have the lowest levels of NPAs. Clearly, while India's bad loans problem is not as severe as in several other comparable economies, there is a need to manage NPAs and reduce them further. As we

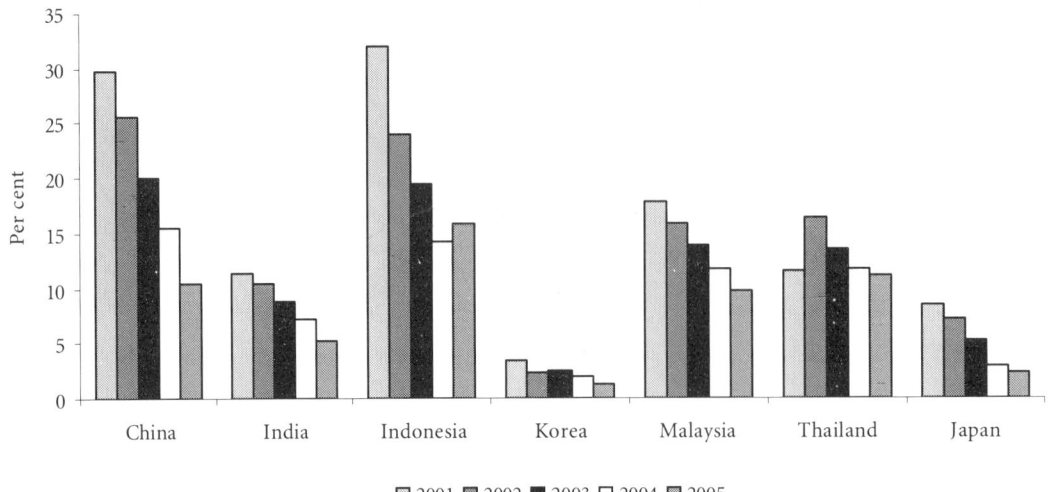

Source: *Global Financial Stability Report*, IMF, April 2006.

Figure 9.2: Gross Non-performing Loans to Total Loans (per cent), 2001–5

TABLE 9.3
Cross-country Comparison of Gross
Non-performing Loans to Total Loans

(per cent, 2001–5)

Country	2001	2002	2003	2004	2005
Brazil	5.6	4.8	4.8	3.8	4.1
Russia	6.2	5.6	5	3.8	3.4
China	29.8	25.6	20.1	15.6	10.5
India	11.4	10.4	8.8	7.2	5.2
Indonesia	31.9	24	19.4	14.2	15.8
Korea	3.4	2.4	2.6	1.9	1.2
Malaysia	17.8	15.9	13.9	11.7	9.8
Thailand	11.5	16.5	13.5	11.8	11.1
Egypt	16.9	20.2	24.2	26.9	26
South Africa	3.1	2.8	2.4	1.8	1.6
Australia	0.7	0.6	0.4	0.3	0.2
Canada	1.5	1.6	1.2	0.7	0.5
Japan	8.4	7.2	5.2	2.9	2.4
United States	1.3	1.4	1.1	0.8	0.7

Source: *Global Financial Stability Report*, IMF, April 2006.

have stated before, the problem of NPAs when ignored has the potential of causing economic and financial deterioration of an economy. To tackle the problem, the regulators have initiated several policy responses, which are discussed in the next section.

PRUDENTIAL NORMS AND REGULATORY RESPONSE TO NPAs

Classification of Assets as Non-performing

An NPA refers to an asset that stops generating income for a bank. As per RBI guidelines (RBI 2005a), an NPA is a loan or an advance where:

1. interest and/or instalment of principal remain overdue for a period of more than 90 days in respect of a term loan;
2. the account remains 'out of order' (that is, if the outstanding balance remains continuously in excess of the sanctioned limit/drawing power), in respect of an overdraft/cash credit;
3. the bill remains overdue for a period of more than 90 days in the case of bills purchased and discounted;
4. a loan granted for short duration crops will be treated as NPA, if the instalment of principal or interest thereon remains overdue for two crop seasons; and
5. a loan granted for long duration crops will be treated as NPA, if the instalment of principal or interest thereon remains overdue for one crop season.

Assets that generate income for the bank, that is, non-NPAs, are known as standard assets. Once an asset becomes an NPA, banks have to make provision for the uncollected income from these assets. The provisioning is made on the basis of the classification of assets into the following categories: sub-standard, doubtful, and loss assets. A Sub-standard asset is one which has remained NPA for a period less than or equal to 12 months. A doubtful asset is one, which has remained in the sub-standard category for a period of 12 months and a loss asset is one where the bank or internal or external auditors have identified loss or the RBI inspection but the amount has not been written off wholly. In other words, such an asset is considered uncollectible and of such little value that its continuance as a bankable asset is not warranted although there may be some salvage or recovery value.

After classifying assets into the above categories, banks are required to make provisions against these assets for the interest not collected by them. The provisioning norms are as follows. Loss assets should be either written off or 100 per cent of the outstanding should be provided for. In case of doubtful assets, provisioning requirement is 100 per cent of the 'unsecured portion' and for the 'secured portion' the requirement ranges from 20 per cent to 100 per cent depending on the age of the NPA.[1] In the case of sub-standard assets, provision of 10 per cent on total outstanding is to be made. Those sub-standard assets that are also 'unsecured exposures' require additional provisioning of 10 per cent, that is, a total of 20 per cent on the outstanding balance. In the case of standard assets, banks are required to make a general provision of a minimum of 0.25 per cent on global loan portfolio basis.

The Response

Several measures have been implemented by the RBI and the Government of India to contain the level of NPAs (RBI 2005b). These include debt recovery tribunals (DRTs), Corporate Debt Restructuring (CDR) scheme, Securitization and Reconstruction of Financial Assets and Enforcement of Security Interest (SARFAESI) Act, and Asset Reconstruction Companies (ARCs). Settlement Advisory Committees have also been formed at regional and head office levels of commercial banks. In order to provide an additional option to banks and to develop a healthy secondary market for NPAs, guidelines on sale/purchase of NPAs were issued in July 2005 where securitization companies and reconstruction companies are not involved.

Some other steps that have been taken to reduce NPAs are: improvement in supervisory mechanism through prompt corrective action (PCA), sharing of borrower information among banks by setting up of Credit Information Bureau of India Limited (CIBIL) and rewarding low NPA banks with freedom in dividend payments to the shareholders. With regard to the first measure mentioned, RBI initiates some structured and discretionary actions against those banks which have hit certain 'trigger points' on three parameters, viz. CRAR, net NPAs, and return on assets (ROA). The two trigger points for net NPAs are 10 per cent and 15 per cent beyond which the concerned bank has to implement measures such as a special drive to reduce NPAs, review its loan and credit-risk management policies, not enter new lines of business etc. With regard to the second measure mentioned above, CIBIL is a repository of information containing credit history of commercial and consumer borrowers that banks can make use of in evaluating their risks and taking their credit decisions. With regard to the last measure mentioned, RBI has granted general permission to those banks to declare dividends (subject to a cap of 40 per cent on dividend payout ratio) for the accounting year ended 31 March 2005 onwards, which comply with: (i) CRAR of at least 9 per cent for preceding two years and the accounting year for which it proposes to declare dividend; and (ii) net NPA ratio of less than 7 per cent. In case any bank does not meet the above CRAR norm, but has a CRAR of at least 9 per cent for the accounting year for which it proposes to declare dividend, it is allowed to declare dividend, provided its net NPA ratio is less than 5 per cent.

Thus, banks have a variety of options and legislations to take recourse to in order to resolve their bad loans problem. There are also supportive supervisory mechanisms available with the RBI and incentives provided to banks for reducing the level of NPAs.

The DRT Act

Coincident with the first phase of banking sector reforms, one of the first legislations to address the problem of NPAs in India was the Recovery of Debts Due to Banks and Financial Institutions Act, 1993, which came into force on 24 June 1993. The Act recommended the setting up of DRTs for speedy adjudication and recovery of debts (where the claim is more than Rs 10 lakh) due to banks and financial institutions (FIs). The Act also recommended setting up Debt Recovery Appellate Tribunals (DRATs) to entertain appeals against any order made by a DRT. Alongside this, the RBI actively promoted the compromise settlements or one time settlements (OTS) to encourage out-of-court settlements of bad debts. *Lok Adalats* (or people's courts), organized by DRTs, help banks to settle disputes involving small loans, but the ceiling has now been raised from Rs 5 lakh to Rs 20 lakh.

As on 31 December 2005, there were 29 DRTs and one DRAT in India. From 1 January 1996 to 31 December 2005, 86,922 cases involving an amount of Rs 184,538.01 crore were filed in DRTs, out of which 59,115 cases involving an amount of Rs 91,866.59 crore were disposed of and recovery of Rs 24,915.28 crore was made (Government of India 2005). In addition to the actual recovery, DRTs are one of the main factors behind the defaulters coming forward for OTS with the Banks and FIs. Recoveries under OTS amounted to Rs 1095 crore and those under *Lok Adalats* amounted to Rs 328 crore as at end-June 2004 (RBI 2004a, b).

---

[1] According to RBI guidelines, 'Unsecured exposure is defined as an exposure where the realisable value of the security, as assessed by the bank/approved valuers/Reserve Bank's inspecting officers, is not more than 10 per cent, ab-initio, of the outstanding exposure. "Exposure" shall include all funded and non-funded exposures (including underwriting and similar commitments). "Security" will mean tangible security properly discharged to the bank and will not include intangible securities like guarantees, comfort letters etc' (RBI 2005a).

The CDR Scheme

On 23 August 2001, the RBI issued guidelines to banks and financial institutions to implement CDR System. CDR is a voluntary and non-statutory arrangement between lenders and borrowers for timely and orderly restructuring of debts of corporate entities affected by certain internal and external factors. As on 31 October 2005, out of 175 cases with total debt of Rs 81,716 crore that were referred for CDR, 138 cases with total debt of Rs 75,756 crore were restructured, 30 cases were rejected, and 7 were under process.[2]

The SARFAESI Act and ARC

The SARFAESI Act was passed on 21 June 2002 to enable banks and FIs to attach the assets of defaulting borrowers without having to approach the courts for recovery. The Act provides for the sale of financial assets by banks and FIs to securitization companies (SCs) and ARCs. SCs and ARCs are institutions that acquire NPAs from FIs and banks with the objective of recovery thereby taking up their burden of NPAs. The first ARC, viz. Asset Reconstruction Company (India) Limited (ARCIL) was also set up under the Act and commenced business on 29 August 2003. This Act was later amended through the Enforcement of Security Interest and Recovery of Debts Laws (Amendment) Act, 2004, which was passed on 29 December 2004. The new Act made it mandatory for borrowers who appeal to a DRAT to deposit upfront 50 per cent of the amount involved in the dispute. This is expected to check borrowers from delaying repayment under the cover of trivial cases. Recoveries under the SARFAESI Act, 2002 amounted to Rs 1748 crore as at end-June 2004 and recoveries under asset sales to ARCIL amounted to Rs 9631 crore (RBI 2004a, b).

EMPIRICAL METHODOLOGY AND DATA

In this section, we introduce the methodology used in our empirical analysis. Our objective is to identify the determinants of NPAs in Indian banking. As such we need to estimate a relationship of the following form, using bank-level data across several years.

$$NPA_{it} = \alpha + \beta X_{it} + \varepsilon_{it} \qquad (9.1)$$

Here, X represents factors, which are supposed to determine NPAs, i and t represent bank and year, respectively, and ε is the unexplained residual. Using panel data across banks and over years, we estimate the above relationship using a random effects regression specification. We could not use the fixed-effects models due to the fact that some of the explanatory variables, for example, growth in GDP remain bank-invariant. For the time being, we refer to X as a variety of bank level financial variables as well as macroeconomic indicators that we employ to explain NPAs.

The financial data are taken from various issues of *Financial Analysis of Banks* and *Performance Highlights of Banks* published by the Indian Banks' Association. Data on macroeconomic variables have been obtained from the RBI's website. We use data on three broadly defined groups of Indian banks, which are homogenous in the nature of their functioning and governance structures. As such, our data set consists of 27 public sector banks (public banks, henceforth), 26 domestic private sector banks (private banks, henceforth) and 9 new domestic private sector banks (new private banks, henceforth) that started operating after deregulation. The time period of analysis is from 1998 to 2003.[3]

EMPIRICAL RESULTS

Our analysis consists of estimating different versions of the NPA equation (9.1). In all our estimations, the dependent variable is taken as the ratio of net NPAs to net advances.[4] As determinants of NPAs, we include the following variables. Proportion of loans to priority sector (PRADV) is included as a determinant in order to account for the argument that the priority sector loans are responsible for the most number of defaults. While it is also argued that it is the non-priority sector that contributes to the biggest defaults in terms of size, controlling for this variable appears sufficient to take care of the nature of the sector to which most of the loans are given as a determinant of NPAs. Size (SIZE) taken as logarithm of assets acts as a control for whether bigger banks are more vulnerable to the NPA problem than smaller banks. Proportion of rural and semi-urban banks (RSUBR) is included as a determinant to study whether the location of banks, that is, in rural or urban areas, matters in causing NPAs. ROA is considered as a determinant since profitability of banks would have a close relation with its NPAs. It is expected that the more profitable banks would have less NPAs. Operating cost ratio (OCR) is included as a determinant to proxy for the importance of operating efficiency. It is expected that inefficient banks with higher operating costs would also

---

[2] Data provided on the website of the Corporate Debt Restructuring Cell (*www.cdrcell.com*).

[3] By 1998, we imply the financial year 1997–8, and similarly for all other years.

[4] It may be noted that even though the dependent variable is truncated between 0 and 1, which may call for a censored regression technique to avoid biased estimates, Greene (2004) pointed out that the bias is very small in case of panel data with T larger than 5, which which is the case in our sample.

have higher NPAs. Both ROA and OCR are accounting indicators of bank performance.[5] Capital adequacy ratio (CAR) is considered to account for the importance of capitalization in causing NPAs. It is expected that adequately capitalized banks would exhibit lower NPAs. GDP growth is included to control for macroeconomic conditions, which, owing to business cycles, have an important role to play in causing defaults. It may be expected that when the macroeconomic conditions are sound and GDP growth is higher, the level of NPAs would be lower. Finally, growth in advances (ADVGR) is included as a determinant to represent the aggressiveness of a bank in its lending behaviour. More aggressive banks may push riskier loans and hence end up with more NPAs (Clair 1992). On the other hand, banks that concentrate on more lending may have developed expertise in effectively managing credit risk and hence may exhibit lower NPAs. Therefore, the role of lending aggressiveness in NPAs is ambiguous.

We begin the discussion of our analysis with the estimation results of the following version of equation (9.1), which we refer to as Model I (sub-scripts are not explicitly shown henceforth):

$$NPA = f(PRADV, SIZE, RSUBR, ROA, OCR, CAR, GDPGR, ADVGR) + \varepsilon \quad (9.2)$$

Column 2 of Table 9.4 summarizes the results.[6] The coefficient of size turns out to be negative indicating that large banks may have better risk management procedures and technology, which allows them to enjoy lower NPAs. The presence of rural and semi-urban branches appears to have a positive association with NPAs. In other words, non-urban branches contribute to the most NPAs. This is not surprising since the maximum amount of priority sector credit disbursed by banks is in the non-urban areas, that are generally perceived to have higher default rates. ROA is found to be negatively associated with NPAs.[7] In other words, profitable banks exhibit lower NPAs. CAR is negatively associated with NPAs implying that well capitalized banks have fewer problem loans. Coming to macroeconomic conditions, we find that GDP growth is negatively associated with NPAs, which would signify that the bad loans problem is less when the economy at large is doing well and the macroeconomic environment is conducive for business growth. We also tried an interest rate variable to proxy for macroeconomic environment in place of GDP growth. Employing the State Bank of India's lending rate in our estimation, we found that its coefficient is positive and significant, indicating that NPAs are higher in periods of high interest rates. This is expected since higher interest rates create pressure on firms' repayment capabilities. However, we do not retain both indicators of macroeconomic conditions in the same estimation and report the results only with GDP growth henceforth. The rest of the variables exhibit theoretically expected relationships with NPAs, but the strengths of the relationships may be weak since the coefficients of these variables are found to be statistically insignificant.

TABLE 9.4
Nature and Strength of the Impact of Various Factors on NPAs
(*Dependent Variable: Ratio of Net NPAs to Net Advances*)

Explanatory Variable (1)	Model I (2)	Model II (3)
PRADV	Positive and insignificant	Negative and insignificant
SIZE	Negative and significant	Negative and significant
RSUBR	Positive and significant	Positive and insignificant
ROA	Negative and significant	Negative and significant
OCR	Positive and insignificant	Positive and insignificant
CAR	Negative and significant	Negative and significant
GDP Growth	Negative and significant	Negative and significant
ADV Growth	Negative and insignificant	Positive and insignificant
PVTDUM	–	Negative and insignificant
NEWPVTDUM	–	Negative and significant (larger (in absolute value) than coefficient of PVTDUM)

Source: Authors.

[5] Net interest margin (NIM) in this regard can also be used as another indicator of bank performance. NIM would indicate the importance of spread in causing NPAs. Once again, it is expected that higher spreads would be associated with lower NPAs.

[6] Throughout the analysis, we do not present the actual coefficients and the associated t-statistics. However, interested readers are encouraged to contact the authors for detailed results.

[7] One may argue that ROA is endogenous. We have also used the first lag of ROA as an independent variable in the regression. Our results as reported remain invariant. We also use the second and third lag of ROA as instruments for ROA and conduct the Davidson–MacKinnon test of exogeneity. The result confirms that ROA can be treated as an exogenous variable in our model.

We are also interested in looking at the impact of ownership on NPAs. In other words, does the nature of ownership have any bearing on the level of NPAs? This issue can easily be investigated by including ownership dummies (PVTDUM for old private banks and NEWPVTDUM for new private banks) in the above specification and estimating the NPA equation (Model II). The results summarized in the last column of Table 9.4 indicate that new private banks may be holding the lowest levels of NPAs in their books, followed by old private banks, and public sector banks in this order. In other words, after controlling for other factors, new private banks appear to be managing their NPAs most effectively followed by the old private banks. Public sector banks appear to be lagging behind their private counterparts in NPA management.

IMPACT OF POLICY RESPONSE

In the fourth section, we referred to several policy responses to the problem of NPAs. In this section we attempt to gauge the impact of some of these policies on the level of NPAs in India. We restrict our focus to only those policies, which our data set allows us to analyse, specifically, these are the DRT Act, the CDR scheme, ARC, and the SARFAESI Act.

Impact of DRT Act

In order to ascertain the impact of DRTs on NPAs in India, we investigate whether the setting up of DRTs in each year had any impact on NPAs. For this we compute the proportion of states that had set up DRTs in each year (PDRT). We then include PDRT in our NPA equation given in (9.2) (Model III). With this reduced structure, we re-estimate the NPA equation and the results are summarized in column 2 of Table 9.5.[8] We can clearly observe that the coefficient of PDRT is negative and statistically significant, thereby indicating that as more and more states have set up DRTs, it may have indeed led to lower NPAs in Indian banking, after controlling for other factors that may affect NPAs. We also note that the signs and significance of most of the other explanatory variables remain the same.

Impact of the CDR Scheme

To find out whether the CDR Scheme had any ameliorating effect on NPAs, we compute a dummy variable (CDRDUM) that takes the value one for the year 2002 when the CDR scheme was implemented and zero for other years. We then include CDRDUM in our NPA equation (9.2) and estimate the equation (Model IV). If the CDR scheme has had a positive impact on the bad loans problem, then the coefficient of this variable should turn out to be negative. The results of this exercise are summarized in column 3 of Table 9.5; they indicate that the coefficient of CDRDUM is negative and statistically insignificant using a two-tailed t-test, however, significant using a one-tailed t-test. This result indicates that, after controlling for other factors that may affect NPAs, it appears that the CDR Scheme may have led to lower NPAs.

Impact of the SARFAESI Act

To analyse whether the SARFAESI Act had any beneficial effects on the problem of bad loans in Indian banking, we create a dummy variable (SARFAESIDUM), this time for the year 2003 when the SARFAESI Act was passed. We then

TABLE 9.5
Nature and Strength of the Impact of Policy Responses on NPAs
(*Dependent Variable: Ratio of Net NPAs to Net Advances*)

Explanatory Variable (1)	Model III (2)	Model IV (3)	Model V (4)
PRADV	Positive and insignificant	Positive and insignificant	Positive and insignificant
SIZE	Negative and insignificant	Negative and significant	Negative and significant
RSUBR	Positive and insignificant	Positive and significant	Positive and significant
OCR	Positive and insignificant	Positive and insignificant	Positive and insignificant
CAR	Negative and significant	Negative and significant	Negative and significant
GDP Growth	Negative and significant	Negative and significant	Negative and insignificant
ADV Growth	Negative and insignificant	Negative and insignificant	Negative and insignificant
PVTDUM	Negative and insignificant	Negative and insignificant	Negative and insignificant
NEWPVTDUM	Negative and significant	Negative and significant	Negative and significant
PDRT	Negative and significant	–	–
CDR Scheme Dummy	–	Negative and insignificant	–
SARFEASI Act Dummy	–	–	Negative and insignificant

Source: Authors.

[8] In this set of estimations, we retain only one accounting indicator of bank performance, viz. OCR. Including ROA or NIM does not change our results qualitatively.

include the SARFAESIDUM in our NPA equation given in (9.2) (Model V). If the passing of the SARFAESI Act has indeed aided recovery of bad loans, then the coefficient of this variable should turn out to be negative. The results of this exercise are summarized in the last column of Table 9.5. We observe that the coefficient of SARFAESIDUM is negative but insignificant. However, note that we just have one year's observation since the passing of this Act. Our evidence in this regard can, therefore, be taken as suggestive.

POLICY IMPLICATIONS AND CONCLUDING REMARKS

This paper reviews the problem of NPAs in Indian banking. We discuss the magnitude of the problem, the associated prudential norms, and present the different policy responses undertaken to address it. Next we undertake an empirical analysis to identify the determinants of NPAs in India banking. Finally, we investigate the impact of various policy responses on NPAs. For the purpose of the empirical analysis we consider data for 62 Indian banks for six years 1998 to 2003. We employ the technique of random effects regression to identify the determinants of bank-wise NPAs and ascertain the impact of policy responses initiated to reduce NPAs.

Our findings may be summarized as follows. The impact of priority sector lending on NPA levels is ambiguous while rural branching is associated with higher NPAs. Larger banks exhibit better credit risk management demonstrated by lower NPAs and more profitable banks also have lower NPAs. Banks with higher operating efficiency have lower NPAs and adequately capitalized banks also appear to have lower NPAs. Favourable macroeconomic conditions help to lower NPA levels while the effect of aggressive lending practices on NPA levels is ambiguous. Nature of ownership has a significant impact on NPA levels. Specifically, new private banks have the lowest NPA levels, followed by old private banks, and public sector banks in this order. Finally, policy measures implemented to tackle the NPA problem have been largely successful in achieving their objective. Setting up of DRTs, implementing the CDR Scheme, and passing of the SARFAESI Act have been successful in lowering NPAs in Indian banking.

The above findings indicate that better credit risk management practices need to be undertaken for bank lending in the non-urban sectors. The RBI should focus on smaller banks and less profitable banks that seem to exhibit higher NPAs. Adequate attention should also be paid to banks with low operating efficiency and low capitalization as also to macroeconomic cycles that appear to be important in determining NPA levels. Finally, after accounting for all the above explanations for NPAs, it appears that the public sector, and to some extent the old private sector, accounts for the bulk of the NPA problem. Thus, we conclude that while the policies that have been implemented to address the NPA problem may have been largely successful, there are further steps that can be taken by the RBI as well as by the banks themselves to tackle the problem of NPAs. These relate to rural branches, smaller banks, unprofitable banks, and inefficient banks, especially during adverse macroeconomic conditions, and more so for the public and old private sector banks. These findings are of crucial importance to banks in order to improve their credit risk management and for the regulatory–supervisory authority in devising its policies, especially in view of the importance that is now being attached to the concept of risk-based supervision in order to prioritize the allocation of supervisory resources.

References

Beck, T., A. Demirguc-Kunt, and R. Levine (2005), 'Bank Concentration and Fragility: Impact and Mechanics', NBER Working Papers 11500, National Bureau of Economic Research, Inc.

Bloem, Adriaan and Cornelis N. Gorter (2001), 'The Treatment of Nonperforming Loans in Macroeconomic Statistics', Working Paper No. 01/209, International Monetary Fund.

Clair, R.T. (1992), 'Loan Growth and Loan Quality: Some Preliminary Evidence from Texas Banks', *Economic Review*, Federal Reserve Bank of Dallas, Third Quarter, pp. 9–21.

Das, A. and S. Ghosh (2003), 'Determinants of Credit Risk in Indian State-owned Banks: An Empirical Investigation', Paper presented at the Conference on Money, Risk and Investment, Nottingham Trent University, UK.

——— (2005), 'Size, Non-Performing Loan, Capital and Productivity Change: Evidence from Indian State-owned Banks', Journal of Quantitative Economics, New Series, Vol. 3, No. 2, pp. 48–66.

Demirguc-Kunt, A. and E. Detragiache (2000), 'Monitoring Banking Sector Fragility: A Multivariate Logit Approach', *World Bank Economic Review*, Vol. 14, No. 2, pp. 287–307.

Fernandez de Lis, S., J. Martinez-Pages, and J. Saurina (2000), 'Credit Growth, Problem Loans and Credit Risk Provisioning in Spain,' Working Paper No. 0018, Banco de Espana.

Gonzalez-Hermosillo, B. (1999), 'Determinants of Ex-Ante Banking System Distress: A Macro-Micro Empirical Exploration of Some Recent Episodes', IMF Working Paper No. 99/33.

Government of India (2005) 'Performance Budget 2005–6'.

Greene, W. (2004), 'Fixed Effects and Bias Due to the Incidental Parameters Problem in the Tobit Model', *Econometric Reviews*, Vol. 23, No. 2, pp. 125–47.

Indian Banks' Association, 'Performance Highlights of Banks', Mumbai, India. Various Issues.

Indian Banks' Association, 'Financial Analysis of Banks', Mumbai, India, Various Issues.

International Monetary Fund (2006), 'Global Financial Stability Report: Market Developments and Issues', Washington, DC, USA, April.

Merton, R.C. (1995), 'A Functional Perspective of Financial Intermediation', *Financial Management*, Vol. 24, No. 2, pp. 23–41.

Rajaraman, I., S. Bhaumik, and N. Bhatia (1999), 'NPA Variations Across Indian Commercial Banks: Some Findings', *Economic and Political Weekly*, Vol. 37, Nos 3 and 4, pp. 16–23.

Rajaraman, I. and G. Vasishtha (2002), 'Non-Performing Assets of Public Sector Banks: Some Panel Results', *Economic and Political Weekly*, Vol. 37, No. 5, pp. 429–35.

Ranjan, R. and S.C. Dhal (2003), 'Non-Performing Loans and Terms of Credit of Public Sector Banks in India: An Empirical Assessment', *RBI Occasional Papers*, Vol. 24, No. 3, pp. 81–122.

RBI (Reserve Bank of India) (1991), 'Report of the Committee on Financial Sector Reforms'.

——— (1998), 'Report of the Committee on Banking Sector Reforms'.

——— (1998), 'Report of the Working Group for Harmonising the Role and Operations of DFIs and Banks.'

——— (2004a), 'Report on Currency and Finance'.

——— (2004b), 'Report on Trend and Progress of Banking in India, 2003–4'.

——— (2005a), 'Master Circular—Prudential norms on Income Recognition, Asset Classification and Provisioning pertaining to Advances'.

——— (2005b), 'Report on Trend and Progress of Banking in India, 2004–5'.

Sensarma, R. (2006), 'Are Foreign Banks Always the Best? Comparison of State-Owned, Private and Foreign Banks in India', *Economic Modelling*, Vol. 23, No. 4, pp. 717–35.

10

India and China
Changing Patterns of Comparative Advantage?

C. Veeramani

During the 1950s, India and China, like many other developing countries, chose the import substitution strategy for industrial development, which involved insulation from the world economy and industrialization under the aegis of state enterprises. Subsequently, there has been a paradigm shift—from import substitution to outward orientation—in many of the developing countries, including in India and China. China started the trade liberalization process in a major way in 1978. India's liberalization initiatives during the 1980s focussed primarily on internal deregulation rather than on trade liberalization. The most pronounced overhaul of India's trade policy regime occurred during the early 1990s in response to a severe balance of payment crisis.

The rationale behind trade liberalization suggests that greater competition would induce the production units to improve productivity, which is instrumental for accelerating overall economic growth. Since firms respond to world market signals, the commodity structure of the country's trade would undergo changes in accordance with the changing patterns of specialization. The conventional wisdom, based on the Heckscher-Ohlin-Samuelson (H-O-S) model, is that trade liberalization would induce reallocation of productive resources from the import competing industries to those industries where the country has comparative advantages. Therefore, while both exports and imports are expected to grow faster, trade liberalization invariably involves some adjustment costs as some of the domestic industries may go out of business.

Does the evidence from India and China support this conventional wisdom? It is well-known that the export performance of China since the 1980s has been spectacular and that India's performance, in comparison, leaves much to be desired. Between 1980 and 2004, China's share in the world exports steadily increased from less than 1 per cent to more than 6 per cent, while India's share increased from 0.4 per cent to only 0.8 per cent. Export expansion under trade liberalization is an offshoot of resource reallocation on the basis of comparative advantage. In other words, rapid export expansion may not materialize if certain rigidities and bottlenecks stand in the way of resource reallocation, whatever the extent of trade liberalization. A question that arises in this context is: Has the process of resource reallocation been smoother in China compared to India, which enabled the former to specialize according to comparative advantage and to achieve export success? The nature and extent of resource reallocation would be reflected in the changing structure of a country's trade flows.

Patterns of specialization can change not only due to the one-time static allocation effects but also due to the long-term dynamic effects of trade liberalization (Baldwin 1992). Accumulation of productive factors, such as human and physical capital, that characterizes economic development,

I thank Nirmal Kumar Chandra for comments. Usual disclaimer applies.

can bring about a dynamic process of changing comparative advantage. For example, the road to export success for the newly industrialized countries (NICs) of Asia started with labour-intensive and low technology manufactures. However, as investments in physical and human capital rose and as labour costs increased with the accumulation of skills, relatively more sophisticated manufacturing activity expanded in these countries at the expense of labour-intensive manufactures.

This paper attempts a comparative analysis of the changing patterns of exports and specialization in India and China since 1980. Drawing upon the Chinese experience, the study throws some light on what needs to be done to accelerate India's exports. The analysis shows that the fear of 'Chinese invasion' of India's export markets is only a popular myth. On a more general level, the analysis provides some insights into the patterns of resource reallocation under trade liberalization and its implications for the cost of adjustments. The analysis excludes the service sector exports and uses data on merchandise exports at the 3-digit level of SITC for the period 1980–2003. The data are taken from the various issues of the *Handbook of Statistics* brought out by the UNCTAD.

The rest of the paper is structured as follows. A brief overview of trade policy changes in India and China is provided in the next section. The impact of the policy changes on aggregate exports in both the countries is briefly discussed in the third section. The changing patterns of exports and comparative advantages in the two countries are analysed in the fourth section. Some concluding remarks and implications of the findings for policy are provided in the fifth section.

TRADE POLICY REFORMS

Prior to the reforms, both India and China followed a relatively autarkic trade policy accompanied by a battery of trade and exchange controls, cutting the link between domestic and world relative prices (Lal 1995). China had a non-market command economy while India always had a large private sector and functioning markets (though subjected to state controls). The exchange rate was overvalued in both the countries, creating a bias against exports. In China, foreign trade activities were monopolized by a handful of centrally controlled foreign trade corporations. In India, an elaborate system of exchange controls and allocation was instituted to ensure that the foreign exchange earned by exporters was used to import only those commodities that conformed to the priorities set in the Five Year Plans (Srinivasan 1990).

Subsequently, there has been a paradigm shift—from import substitution to outward orientation—in both the countries. See Boxes 10.1 and 10.2 for a brief summary of the reforms in China and India, respectively.[1]

BOX 10.1
Major Reforms in China

- Permission for a large number of firms to participate in foreign trade activities.
- Creation of SEZs and promotion of FDI in joint ventures.
- Liberalization of the imports of intermediate inputs (for use in the production of exports) and capital goods (for use in joint ventures).
- Liberalization of the labour market, particularly in the non-state sector (see Meng 2000; Brooks and Tao 2003).
- Progressive reduction of the tariff rates, from about 50 per cent in 1982 (higher than the developing country average) to about 12 per cent by 2002 (lower than the developing country average) (see Table 10.1).
- Major tariff exemptions for processing trade and foreign investments.
- WTO accession in 2001.

BOX 10.2
Major Reforms in India

- Some domestic industrial liberalization during the 1980s (Joshi and Little 1994).
- More comprehensive and systemic liberalization since 1991.
- Complete removal of QRs on the import of capital goods and intermediates in 1992. Removal of QRs in consumer goods in early 2000s.
- Lowering of customs duties from 100 per cent in 1986 to 33 per cent by 2002 (Table 10.1).
- Complete removal of the industrial licencing system (except for a small list of industries on strategic and environmental considerations).
- Elimination of controls on investment and expansion by large industrial houses.
- Opening up of manufacturing industries for FDI.
- Significant disinvestments of government holdings in the equity share capital of public sector enterprises (PSEs).

TABLE 10.1
Average Import Tariff Rate

(unweighted)

Year	India	China	Developing country average
1981	74.3	NA	28.7
1982	NA	49.5	32.6
1986	100	38.1	28.4
1990	81.8	40.3	25.9
1994	47.8	36.3	20.2
1998	30	17.5	16.2
2002	33	12.3	13.6

Source: Downloaded from the World Bank website (*http://siteresources.worldbank.org/INTRANETTRADE/Resources/tar2002.xls*).

---

[1] See Lardy (1992, 2002) for a comprehensive description of China's reform process.

GROWTH OF EXPORTS

The broad trends in the values of India's exports and imports for the period 1950–2004 can be seen from Figure 10.1. It is clear that both exports and imports were almost stagnant in India during the first two decades or so. During this period, India failed to take advantage of opportunities offered by the growing world trade. This is evident from the fact that when the world exports grew at a rate of 7.5 per cent per annum during 1950–70, exports from India grew at a much lower rate of 2.5 per cent (Table 10.2). During the 1970s, India's exports grew at the rate of 17 per cent per annum, which was quite impressive compared to the past performance. However, it must be noted that world exports during this period grew even faster at a rate of 20 per cent per annum. It is striking that India's exports have been growing faster than world exports since the 1980s. The pattern of China's export growth vis-à-vis world export growth is more or less similar, but it must be noted that the rate of growth of China's exports has always been higher than that of India's and that the gap started widening since the 1980s. Import growth generally kept pace with export growth in both the countries, though China often runs a small amount of trade surplus.

India's share of world exports declined steadily from 1.9 per cent in 1950 to as low as 0.4 per cent by 1980 (Figure 10.2). The situation in China is not different either: between 1950 and 1959, China's share in world exports registered an increase from about 0.9 per cent to 2.7 per cent, but then declined steadily, reaching as low as 0.7 per cent by 1977. China's share of world exports, however, has been increasing dramatically since the late 1970s and crossed 6 per cent by 2004 while India's share increased marginally from 0.4 per cent in 1980 to 0.5 per cent in 1990 and to 0.8 per cent by 2004. The share of exports in China's GDP was 35 per cent in 2004 while it was 11 per cent for India.

Several factors might have contributed to the export success of China, such as a favourable exchange rate, low wages, availability of labour, large domestic market, huge volume FDI inflows etc. However, India does not lag much behind China with respect to these factors, except for FDI inflows.[2]

TABLE 10.2
Average Annual Growth Rates of Exports
(Million US dollars)

Period	India	China	World
1950–70	2.49	6.29	7.48
1970–80	17.25	20.04	20.42
1980–90	7.29	12.78	5.99
1992–2004	9.74	15.38	6.33

Source: Author's estimation using data from *Handbook of Statistics*, UNCTAD.

Source: Plotted using data from the *Handbook of Statistics*, UNCTAD.

Figure 10.1: Trends in India's Exports, Imports, and Trade Balance (Million US$)

---

[2] Apart from the domestic economic policies, geo-political elements may also be crucial in understanding China's export success: while the Multi Fibre Agreement stunted India's textile exports, liberal quotas were offered to China (after the Soviet occupation of Afghanistan in 1979) and other US allies in East Asia.

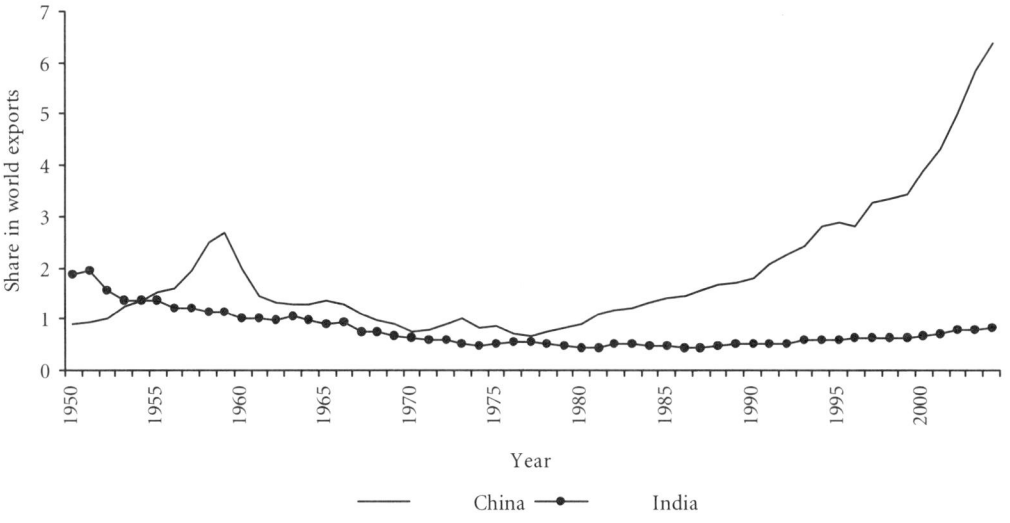

Source: Same as for Figure 10.1.

Figure 10.2: Comparative Exports Performance, 1950–2004

A brief discussion on the contribution of FDI to the export growth of China and India can be seen in Box 10.3.[3] While the multinationals mostly engage in export activities in China, they target the domestic markets in India (Wei 2005). Some explanation for this differential behaviour of multinationals in the two countries is provided in Box 10.4.

STRUCTURE OF EXPORTS AND CHANGING COMPARATIVE ADVANTAGES

Composition of Exports

Table 10.3 shows the composition of exports by commodity groups for both India and China since the 1980s. It is evident that the share of manufactured goods has been increasing steadily, at the cost of other commodity groups, in both the countries. Manufactured goods accounted for about 90 per cent of China's and 75 per cent of India's exports during 2000–3. In the case of China, much of this can be attributed to machinery and transport equipments, the share of which in total exports increased from 7 per cent to 38 per cent between 1980–4 and 2000–3. Manufactured products constitute the major part not only of the export baskets but also of the import baskets in both the countries. Overall, the structure of imports appears to be relatively persistent compared to the structure of exports.

Shifts in the commodity composition of exports according to factor intensity are shown in Table 10.4.[4] Overall, a noticeable shift can be seen in both the countries away

---

Box 10.3

Contribution of FDI to Export Growth in China and India

A significant volume of China's FDI inflows represent 'round tripping' of capital. Wei (2005) reported that even after adjusting for this and other definitional problems, the gap in the volume of FDI into China and India remained very high. According to the *World Investment Report 2003* (UNCTAD 2003), FDI has contributed to the rapid growth of China's merchandise exports at an annual rate of 15 per cent between 1989 and 2001. In 1989, foreign affiliates accounted for less than 9 per cent of total Chinese exports, but by 2002 they provided 50 per cent.

In contrast, FDI has been much less important in driving India's export growth except in IT. FDI accounted for only 3 per cent of India's exports in the early 1990s and even today, it is estimated to account for less than 10 per cent of India's manufacturing exports. The contribution of FDI to India's exports was insignificant before the 1990s as well (Chandra 1994). Most of the FDI flows to India have been domestic market seeking in nature, and go to services, electronics and computer industries.

---

[3] As a large part of reported FDI inflows to China consists of the return flow of capital placed abroad by the state owned enterprises, the contribution of foreign-owned firms to China's exports could be overestimated. The extent of overestimation may not be much, if such 'reverse investments' are more domestic market oriented compared to the true FDI.

[4] We follow Horne (1996), who adopts a scheme devised by Krause to categorize the 3-digit SITC items according to factor intensity. Products at the 3-digit level are divided into five groups according to their intensities in five factors: agricultural resources, mineral resources, unskilled labour, technology, and human capital. There are 239 items at the 3-digit level of SITC. These were classified according to their factor intensity, except for 5 items, which could not be grouped into any of the categories.

> **BOX 10.4**
> **Market Seeking vs Export Promoting FDI**
>
> *Market Seeking FDI:* Also known as 'horizontal FDI' it refers to the situation where the multinational performs essentially the same range of production activities in its plants located in the home and host countries. Much of the FDI flows among the developed countries are horizontal in nature. Theory suggests that, in the presence of positive trade costs (tariffs plus transport costs), multinational enterprises tend to undertake FDI of the 'horizontal type' when their home and host country are very similar with respect to incomes and factor prices (Markusen 1995). A firm has incentive to undertake horizontal FDI in the foreign country, if the saving on trade costs exceeds the fixed costs involved in setting up the new plant.
>
> *Export Promoting FDI:* Also known as 'vertical FDI' represents the international fragmentation of production process by multinationals, locating each stage of production in the country where it can be done at the least cost. The bulk of the FDI that flows to the East Asian developing countries is vertical in nature. According to the theory, multinational enterprises tend to conduct FDI of the 'vertical type' when there exists a sufficient gap in factor prices between their home and host country, and when the trade costs among them are not large. Vertical FDI was initially concentrated in South Korea, Taiwan, Hong Kong, and Singapore. After the mid 1980s, as wage levels in these countries (in relation to labour productivity) began to rise, FDI shifted to China and other Asian countries.
>
> India, however, has been sailing against the wind. Much of the FDI flows into India have been horizontal in nature rather than vertical. It is not difficult to see the reasons why India obtains more horizontal than vertical FDI while the opposite is true for China. For one thing, there has been a powerful incentive for multinationals to undertake tariff jumping horizontal investment in India. This is because the tariff levels have been quite high in India, compared to other countries in Asia, despite their reduction since the early 1990s. At the same time, high trade costs due to tariffs make India an unattractive destination for vertical investments. Trade costs are relatively high in India not only due to high tariffs but also due to the inadequate physical infrastructure in the country compared to China. Further, the well-known rigidities in the organized labour market hobble India's labour-intensive manufacturing activities and discourage vertical FDI into the country.

TABLE 10.3
Structure of Exports by Commodity Group

(per cent of total, averages for the periods)

Commodity Group	India				
	1980–4	1985–9	1990–4	1995–9	2000–3
All food items	26.4 (9.0)	20.5 (7.1)	16.4 (3.8)	17.3 (5.8)	12.4 (5.2)
Agricultural raw materials	3.7 (2.9)	2.6 (3.9)	2.2 (3.7)	1.8 (3.3)	1.2 (3.2)
Fuels	9.5 (30.8)	3.6 (19.5)	2.5 (27.6)	1.0 (25.1)	5.1 (31.7)
Ores and metals	5.9 (6.0)	6.4 (7.5)	4.8 (6.7)	3.1 (6.0)	3.7 (4.5)
Manufactured goods	54.2 (51.1)	65.6 (58.1)	72.8 (50.7)	74.9 (48.9)	75.5 (46.5)
Chemicals	4.0 (9.8)	4.6 (10.0)	6.71 (11.1)	7.64 (10.4)	8.63 (7.4)
Metal Products	2.4 (1.4)	1.6 (0.8)	2.1 (0.7)	2.1 (0.8)	2.7 (0.8)
Iron and Steel	0.8 (7.1)	0.9 (6.7)	2.5 (3.8)	3.1 (3.0)	3.9 (1.6)
Machinery & Transport Equipments	7.0 (19.5)	6.9 (22.2)	7.2 (16.8)	7.5 (17.5)	8.7 (17.7)
Textile & Textile products	20.2 (1.1)	22.9 (0.9)	26.0 (0.9)	26.3 (1.0)	23.1 (1.4)
Other Manufactures	19.9 (12.2)	28.7 (17.4)	28.4 (17.5)	28.2 (16.3)	28.5 (17.6)
Others	0.27 (0.3)	1.24 (3.9)	1.72 (7.6)	2.0 (11.0)	2.14 (9.0)
	China				
All food items	18.2 (8.0)	14.8 (6.8)	11.4 (5.4)	7.2 (5.4)	5.0 (3.7)
Agricultural raw materials	6.2 (9.1)	5.8 (6.4)	2.6 (4.7)	1.5 (4.7)	0.9 (4.1)
Fuels	6.9 (0.9)	13.5 (1.4)	5.7 (3.9)	3.3 (5.3)	2.9 (7.6)
Ores and metals	3.8 (5.0)	2.9 (3.1)	1.8 (3.6)	2.0 (4.8)	1.7 (5.7)
Manufactured goods	64.3 (76.2)	60.2 (81.6)	77.7 (81.8)	85.8 (79.2)	89.3 (78.4)
Chemicals	9.7 (11.1)	5.0 (6.9)	4.6 (7.1)	4.7 (6.2)	3.8 (6.1)
Metal Products	4.8 (2.3)	2.0 (1.3)	2.6 (1.1)	3.2 (1.3)	3.4 (1.0)
Iron and Steel	2.3 (9.0)	1.1 (11.9)	1.8 (6.8)	2.5 (4.7)	1.4 (4.6)
Machinery & Transport Equipments	6.9 (30.1)	9.1 (39.3)	17.4 (41.5)	25.2 (39.9)	37.6 (44.6)
Textile & Textile products	20.7 (6.2)	27.8 (7.9)	27.2 (9.6)	22.5 (8.9)	18.1 (5.2)
Other Manufactures	19.9 (17.5)	15.2 (14.2)	24.1 (15.7)	27.8 (18.3)	25.0 (16.9)
Others	0.7 (0.8)	2.9 (0.7)	0.8 (0.6)	0.2 (0.7)	0.2 (0.6)

Note: Values in parentheses are import shares.

Source: Same as for Table 10.2.

from agricultural and mineral resource-intensive goods towards other goods. Between 1980–4 and 2000–3, the combined share of agricultural and mineral resource-intensive goods declined from 58 per cent to 35 per cent in India and from 35 per cent to 12 per cent in China. In both the countries, the share of unskilled labour-intensive goods showed a steady increase till the mid-1990s and then showed some decline, particularly during 2000–3. Human capital and technology-intensive goods have increased their shares since the 1990s in both the countries. Between 1985–9 and 2000–3, the combined share of human capital and technology-intensive goods in India increased from 20 per cent to 36 per cent. These goods together constituted the largest share of China's exports (52 per cent) by 2000–3.

The share of technology-intensive goods in total exports need not necessarily reveal comparative technological capability (Chandra 1999). A significant part of these exports, especially for China, may represent re-exports after making some domestic value addition and may also be an outcome of the relocation of production into China by firms from industrial countries. At the same time, it is also true that a number of domestic firms have emerged in China in technology-intensive sectors such as consumer electronics, home appliances, computers, and telecom with a significant presence in the global markets. By contrast, most technology-intensive exports from India come from domestic firms.[5]

Changing Patterns of Comparative Advantage and Competitiveness

The commodity pattern of comparative advantage is a central concept in international trade theory. However, the empirical measurement of comparative advantage is difficult because the concept is defined in terms of relative autarkic prices, which are not observable in post-trade equilibria. Thus, if the concept of comparative advantage is to be used empirically, it must be measured indirectly using post-trade events. The index of 'revealed comparative advantage' (RCA) formulated by Balassa (1965) has been widely used to assess the patterns of comparative advantage. The RCA index can be defined as:

$$RCA_{ij} = \frac{X_{ij} / \sum_i X_{ij}}{\sum_j X_{ij} / \sum_i \sum_j X_{ij}}$$

The numerator represents the percentage share of a given sector (or product) in national exports—X_{ij} is exports of sector (or product) i from country j. The denominator represents the percentage share of a given sector (or product) in total world exports. The RCA index, thus, contains a comparison of the national export structure (the numerator) with the world export structure (the denominator). When RCA equals 1 for a given sector (or product) in a given country, the percentage share of that sector (or product) is identical with the world average. Where RCA is above

TABLE 10.4
Composition of Exports by Factor Intensity

(per cent of total, averages)

Classification of commodities	1980–4	1985–9	1990–4	1995–9	2000–3
			India		
Agricultural resource-intensive	35.26	28.80	21.68	21.07	15.75
Mineral resource-intensive	23.09	23.98	21.35	19.26	19.13
Unskilled labour-intensive	22.00	25.64	31.06	30.98	27.25
Human capital-intensive	10.53	8.22	12.08	13.23	15.47
Technology-intensive	8.86	12.13	12.12	13.46	20.72
			China		
Agricultural resource-intensive	25.80	21.05	14.99	9.86	7.14
Mineral resource-intensive	9.64	14.50	7.84	6.14	4.62
Unskilled labour-intensive	31.95	38.46	44.36	42.62	35.87
Human capital-intensive	13.33	10.02	14.81	16.85	20.02
Technology-intensive	18.59	13.08	17.18	24.38	32.13

Source: Same as for Table 10.2.

---

[5] Therefore, more detailed data are required to understand the comparative domestic technological capabilities of the two countries. An analysis of this issue is beyond the scope of the present paper.

1, the country is said to have a comparative advantage (and specialized) in that sector (or product) and vice versa where RCA is below 1.

The H-O-S model explains the patterns of comparative advantage in terms of relative factor endowments and factor intensities. Therefore, it is appropriate to compute the RCA index after classifying the products (SITC 3-digit items), according to their factor intensity. The RCA values at the aggregate level (values in parentheses, Table 10.5) mask important heterogeneities at the product level. Therefore, we look at the number of products within each group where the value of the RCA is greater than 1 and this is shown as percentage shares in Table 10.5. It is clear that every group contains a certain number of products where the RCA value is greater than 1, which is true for both India and China.[6] Nevertheless, the comparative advantage of both India and China lies primarily in unskilled labour-intensive goods, which is truly in accordance with their relative factor endowments. As expected, the comparative advantage of both the countries is the least in technology-intensive goods. However, a gradual gain of comparative advantage in human capital and technology-intensive goods can be seen for both the countries. Compared to India, China holds a comparative advantage in a larger number of unskilled labour and technology-intensive products. In the case of other groups, the pattern has become more or less similar for India and China by 2000–3.

The dynamic process of climbing up the ladder of comparative advantage—from unskilled labour-intensive to human capital and technology-intensive goods—seems to be occurring at a slower pace in both the countries compared to that in the NICs. A much longer period of sustained high economic growth would be necessary for significantly altering the factor endowment conditions of countries such as India and China that have plenty of surplus labour.

TABLE 10.5
Patterns of Comparative Advantage According to Factor Intensity

Factor intensity classification	Total No. of Products	Shares of the total no. with RCA greater than 1				
		India				
		1980–4	1985–9	1990–4	1995–9	2000–3
Agricultural resource-intensive	70	28.6	24.3	25.7	34.3	35.7
		(2.0)	(1.9)	(1.6)	(1.8)	(1.6)
Mineral resource-intensive	29	13.8	24.1	27.6	24.1	27.6
		(1.3)	(1.9)	(1.9)	(1.9)	(1.7)
Unskilled labour-intensive	29	37.9	41.4	55.2	58.6	58.6
		(2.1)	(2.2)	(2.4)	(2.5)	(2.3)
Human capital-intensive	42	28.6	26.2	33.3	33.3	42.9
		(0.5)	(0.4)	(0.5)	(0.6)	(0.7)
Technology-intensive	64	7.8	7.8	7.8	10.9	18.8
		(0.3)	(0.4)	(0.3)	(0.4)	(0.5)
		China				
		1980–4	1985–9	1990–4	1995–9	2000–3
Agricultural resource-intensive	70	57.1	42.9	45.7	35.7	31.4
		(1.5)	(1.4)	(1.1)	(0.8)	(0.7)
Mineral resource-intensive	29	34.5	34.5	37.9	34.5	34.5
		(0.6)	(1.0)	(0.7)	(0.6)	(0.4)
Unskilled labour-intensive	29	82.8	72.4	82.8	86.2	86.2
		(3.1)	(3.2)	(3.5)	(3.4)	(3.0)
Human capital-intensive	42	45.2	23.8	38.1	40.5	40.5
		(0.6)	(0.5)	(0.6)	(0.7)	(0.9)
Technology-intensive	64	25.0	12.5	20.3	25.0	31.3
		(0.6)	(0.4)	(0.50)	(0.6)	(0.8)

Note: Values in parentheses are the RCA index computed by aggregating the export values at the 3-digit level for each group. Averages of the exports values for the given periods are used.

Source: Same as for Table 10.2.

---

[6] We are not giving a detailed list naming the particular products where RCA is greater than 1. Interested readers are referred to Batra and Khan (2005) who provide a list of the particular items where the RCA values are greater than 1 for both India and China. While they use more disaggregated data, their period of the analysis is limited to 2000–3.

Patterns of comparative advantage by commodity groups are shown in Table 10.6. Again, it is clear that every group contains a certain number of products where the RCA value is greater than 1. Since the 1990s, India has been gaining comparative advantage in a number of products within the groups of food items, chemicals, iron and steel, textiles, and other manufactures. China continues to hold high comparative advantage in textiles while improving its position in machinery and transport equipments and other manufactures. China, however, has lost its comparative advantage in certain products within the groups of food items and chemicals.

By definition, each country has a comparative advantage in some products, depending upon the opportunity cost of producing various products in different countries. However, comparative advantage is not the same as international competitiveness or competitive advantage (see Krugman 1996). The notion of comparative advantage has little significance from a macroeconomic perspective; it is not meaningful to say that China has a comparative advantage over India in the aggregate. However, it is meaningful to talk about international competitiveness on both—the macro and micro levels.[7]

The share of a country in world exports (in aggregate or product level) is one of the widely used indicators of international competitiveness. Table 10.7 shows the changes in the shares of India and China in world exports by commodity groups. China has been improving its share remarkably since the 1980s in a number of commodity groups, while India's share has been increasing consistently since the 1990s. Throughout the period, India has been lagging much behind China in almost all the commodity groups including those commodities where India has a higher RCA than China. During 2000–3, there were as many as 118 products (out of 234) where India had a higher RCA value than China, but the former had a higher market share in just 28 products.[8]

TABLE 10.6
Patterns of Comparative Advantage According to Commodity Group

Commodity Group	Total No. of Products	Shares of the total no. with RCA greater than 1									
		India					China				
		1980–4	1985–9	1990–4	1995–9	2000–3	1980–4	1985–9	1990–4	1995–9	2000–3
All food items	44	29.5	25.0	27.3	38.6	40.9	63.6	43.2	47.7	34.1	29.5
		(2.2)	(1.9)	(1.7)	(2.0)	(1.8)	(1.5)	(1.4)	(1.2)	(0.8)	(0.7)
Agricultural raw materials	20	25.0	20.0	20.0	25.0	25.0	40.0	45.0	40.0	35.0	25.0
		(0.9)	(0.7)	(0.8)	(0.8)	(0.7)	(1.5)	(1.5)	(0.9)	(0.7)	(0.5)
Fuels	7	0.0	14.3	0.0	0.0	28.6	14.3	57.1	42.9	57.1	42.9
		(0.6)	(0.4)	(0.3)	(0.1)	(0.5)	(0.5)	(1.2)	(0.6)	(0.4)	(0.3)
Ores and metals	20	15.0	25.0	25.0	20.0	25.0	30.0	30.0	35.0	30.0	30.0
		(1.2)	(1.6)	(1.4)	(1.0)	(1.4)	(0.8)	(0.8)	(0.6)	(0.7)	(0.6)
Manufactured goods	142	21.8	21.8	28.2	30.3	35.2		28.9	40.1	43.0	47.2
of which:		(0.9)	(1.0)	(1.0)	(1.0)	(1.0)		(0.9)	(1.1)	(1.1)	(1.2)
Chemicals	18	27.8	27.8	44.4	44.4	55.6	83.3	33.3	33.3	27.8	22.2
		(0.7)	(0.8)	(1.2)	(1.3)	(1.3)	(1.6)	(0.8)	(0.8)	(0.8)	(0.6)
Metal Products	8	37.5	25.0	37.5	50.0	50.0	75.0	50.0	75.0	87.5	87.5
		(1.1)	(0.8)	(1.0)	(1.0)	(1.3)	(2.1)	(1.0)	(1.3)	(1.5)	(1.6)
Iron and Steel	9	0.0	22.2	44.4	55.6	77.8	22.2	22.2	44.4	33.3	22.2
		(0.2)	(0.3)	(0.9)	(1.2)	(1.7)	(0.6)	(0.3)	(0.6)	(0.9)	(0.6)
Machinery & Transport Equipments	45	8.9	4.4	2.2	2.2	4.4	6.7	6.7	17.8	26.7	33.3
		(0.3)	(0.2)	(0.2)	(0.2)	(0.2)	(0.3)	(0.3)	(0.5)	(0.6)	(0.9)
Textile & Textile products	15	66.7	66.7	86.7	86.7	86.7	93.3	93.3	93.3	93.3	93.3
		(3.9)	(3.8)	(4.0)	(4.2)	(4.2)	(4.1)	(4.6)	(4.2)	(3.6)	(3.2)
Other Manufactures	47	19.1	21.3	23.4	25.5	29.8	55.3	25.5	40.4	42.6	53.2
		(1.3)	(1.7)	(1.6)	(1.5)	(1.6)	(1.3)	(0.9)	(1.4)	(1.5)	(1.4)

Note: Values in parentheses are the RCA index computed by aggregating the export values at the 3-digit level for each group. Averages of the exports values for the given periods are used.
Source: Same as for Table 10.2.

---

[7] See Krugman (1994, 1996) who argues that competitiveness is 'a dangerous obsession' since it may lead to policy choices that are not clearly in the national interest, for example, protectionism when foreign goods 'threaten' local producers.

[8] It is illogical to hold that the huge gap in the market share simply reflects the bigger size of China's economy compared to India's. The logic of international specialization is that individual countries are no longer constrained by the size of their domestic markets. It is indeed possible to identify many products where the relatively smaller countries hold a higher market share compared to the big countries.

TABLE 10.7
Shares of India and China in World Exports by Commodity Group

(per cent, averages for the periods)

Commodity Group	India				
	1980–4	1985–9	1990–4	1995–9	2000–3
All food items	0.98	0.97	0.97	1.29	1.36
Agricultural raw materials	0.40	0.35	0.44	0.52	0.52
Fuels	0.32	0.17	0.15	0.08	0.41
Ores and metals	0.55	0.80	0.82	0.65	1.08
Manufactured goods	0.40	0.48	0.56	0.63	0.79
Chemicals	0.29	0.39	0.66	0.81	1.01
Metal Products	0.48	0.38	0.55	0.62	1.02
Iron and Steel	0.09	0.13	0.48	0.74	1.33
Machinery & Transport Equipments	0.11	0.10	0.11	0.12	0.17
Textile & Textile products	1.76	1.89	2.23	2.69	3.22
Other Manufactures	0.60	0.84	0.87	0.98	1.26
Total	0.45	0.50	0.56	0.63	0.78
	China				
All food items	1.73	2.28	2.75	2.71	3.39
Agricultural raw materials	1.70	2.48	2.17	2.13	2.32
Fuels	0.63	1.95	1.38	1.41	1.38
Ores and metals	0.90	1.19	1.30	2.14	3.00
Manufactured goods	1.23	1.40	2.46	3.66	5.78
Chemicals	1.82	1.32	1.82	2.50	2.72
Metal Products	2.44	1.59	2.87	4.73	7.93
Iron and Steel	0.64	0.50	1.34	2.94	2.95
Machinery & Transport Equipments	0.29	0.44	1.08	2.02	4.57
Textile & Textile products	4.72	7.35	9.53	11.61	15.58
Other Manufactures	1.53	1.41	3.07	4.87	6.77
Total	1.16	1.60	2.29	3.21	4.86

Source: Same as for Table 10.2.

The bottomline is that a mere existence of comparative advantage does not automatically translate into high market shares if there are certain impediments in the country in fully exploiting its comparative advantage.

Notwithstanding the differential performance of India and China, the trade statistics at the 3-digit level suggest that exports (and imports) of the large majority of products have expanded from both the countries, not just of those where the RCA values are greater than 1 (Table 10.8). How is it possible for a country to continuously expand its exports of a product even as the RCA value suggests that the country does not have a comparative advantage in that product? The explanation is very simple: even at a highly disaggregated level, the RCA index masks important heterogeneities within the product. In other words, countries tend to specialize in different types of a given product, indicating the significance of intra-industry reallocation of resources under trade liberalization. Clearly, trade liberalization is not causing a polarization wherein certain industries are forced to vanish while certain other industries

TABLE 10.8
Expansion of Trade by Products, 1980–4 to 2000–3

(Total no. of Products = 239; US $; averages)

Indicator	India	China
No. of products where value of exports increased	223 (93.3)	210 (87.9)
No. of products where value of exports fell to zero	1 (0.4)	3 (1.3)
No. of products where market share of exports increased	196 (82.0)	193 (80.8)
No. of products where value of imports increased	187 (78.2)	214 (89.5)

Note: Values in parentheses are the shares of the total no. of products (=239).

Source: Same as far Table 10.2.

gain prominence.[9] This, however, does not mean that inter-industry movement of resources is not occurring at all, just not to the extent of industries going out of business. A large majority of domestic industries and firms in both India and China are able to survive and compete through specialization in narrow product lines.

In what follows, the extent of structural changes in India and China are examined on the basis of Spearman rank correlation coefficients, computed using the 3-digit level data on exports (Table 10.9). Though some changes (between 1980–4 and 2000–3) can be observed in the structure of exports and comparative advantage in both the countries, the values of the correlations by no means indicates that the changes are substantial. Nevertheless, it is clear that China's exports and comparative advantage have undergone a greater degree of structural change as compared to India's.

The correlations suggest that India and China have become more dissimilar to each other during 2000–3 when compared to 1980–4 with respect to the patterns of comparative advantage and relative market shares of various industries. This implies a greater division of labour in both the countries in recent years compared to the past, which is to be expected in a more competitive and liberalized environment. The statistically insignificant correlation coefficients in the table indicate that China's gain of market share (or comparative advantage) in a given product does not necessarily mean India's lose of market share (or comparative advantage) in the same product and vice versa. The fear of a 'Chinese invasion' of India's export markets is only a popular myth: the two countries have been expanding their exports by specializing in different product lines within each of the product categories. This is also evident from an increasing intra-industry trade in both the countries.[10]

CONCLUSION AND IMPLICATIONS

India and China have been enjoying historically unprecedented average growth rate of GDP since the 1980s.[11] The sectoral composition of growth, however, is an important matter of concern: if the poor people do not own skills sought by the expanding and better paying sectors, the beneficial effect of growth on poverty reduction will be

TABLE 10.9
Structural Changes of Exports and Comparative Advantage Across Products, Rank Correlation Coefficients[#]

Description of the Correlated Variables[a]	Manufactured Goods	Other Goods
Composition of Exports (share of the national exports)		
Export composition of India during 1980–4 and 2000–3	0.60*	0.73*
Export composition of China during 1980–4 and 2000–3	0.53*	0.65*
Values of RCA index		
India's RCA during 1980–4 and 2000–3	0.59*	0.69*
China's RCA during 1980–4 and 2000–3	0.55*	0.47*
RCA during 1980–4 of India and China	0.47*	0.48*
RCA during 2000–3 of India and China	0.25*	0.30*
Point changes of RCA (between 1980–4 and 2000–3) of India and China	–0.09	0.13
Shares in the World Exports		
India's shares during 1980–4 and 2000–3	0.58*	0.70*
China's shares during 1980–4 and 2000–3	0.54*	0.48*
Shares during 1980–4 of India and China	0.47*	0.48*
Shares during 2000–3 of India and China	0.24*	0.31*
Point changes of the shares (between 1980–4 and 2000–3) of India and China	0.13	0.12

Note: [#] lower value of the correlation signifies greater extent of structural change; [a] the variables are the average values for the two periods; * significant at 1 per cent level.
Source: Same as for Table 10.2.

[9] In the case of India, there is only one product for which the export value declined to zero during 2000–3 from a positive value. Interestingly, this is SITC 911 (mail not classified by kind), which is not related at all to trade liberalization. In the case of China, the number of such products is three; one among them is again SITC 911. The others are SITC 286 (uranium, thorium ores) and SITC 675 (iron, steel hoop, and strip).

[10] Intra-industry trade refers to the simultaneous occurrence of exports and imports within the same industry. We estimated the standard Grubel–Lloyd index to measure the extent of intra-industry trade in the total trade of both India and China since the 1980s. In order to save space, we do not discuss this issue in the present paper. See Veeramani (2002, 2004) for more details pertaining to India's intra-industry trade. Hu and Ma (1999) reported significant levels of intra-industry trade for China.

[11] The average annual growth rates during 1980–2000 were around 6 per cent and 10 per cent, respectively for India and China.

limited. This issue is far more serious for India than for China considering that the GDP growth in India has been largely driven by the services sector rather than the industrial sector. However, China has followed the conventional path in transiting from an agricultural economy to an industrial economy—a pattern observed in many developed countries.[12] While the industrial output now accounts for more than a half of the Chinese GDP, it accounts for only one-fourth of India's GDP. The onus to absorb the surplus labour engaged in India's agriculture rests primarily on the industrial sector as the knowledge-based services sector generally has weaker linkage effects and employs mainly the educated urban youth.[13] It is well-known that exports of manufactured goods played an important role in China's industrialization process. In this context, the present study analysed the emerging trends and patterns of merchandise exports in a comparative perspective.

India's share in world exports has been increasing since the 1990s, yet it contributes only 0.8 per cent of total world exports in 2004. The export performance of China, in comparison, has been spectacular, accounting for more than 6 per cent of world exports in 2004. The analysis of export structure by commodity groups indicates a noticeable shift in the export baskets of both the countries away from agricultural and mineral resource-intensive goods towards manufactured goods. Within manufacturing, both the countries continue to hold a comparative advantage in unskilled labour-intensive goods. At the same time, a gradual improvement of comparative advantage in human capital and technology-intensive goods was noticed in both the countries.

In a number of products, India does hold a higher RCA value than China, but its share in the world exports of these products is much lower than that of China. This is not surprising, as comparative advantage does not automatically translate into a high market shares if there are impediments in the country in fully exploiting its comparative advantage. We also found that China's exports and comparative advantage have undergone a greater degree of structural change over the years when compared to India's. These findings indicate that certain bottlenecks (such as poor physical infrastructure) and policy induced rigidities in the factor markets (such as those in the organized labour market) stand in the way of the resource reallocation process and export activities in India.

These constraints notwithstanding, we found that the exports (and imports) of the large majority of the products from India have expanded since the 1990s. A similar pattern was observed for China since the 1980s. We also noticed that China's gain of market share (or comparative advantage) in a given product does not necessarily mean India's loss of market share (or comparative advantage) in the same product and vice versa. The two countries have been expanding their exports by specializing in different product lines within each of the product categories. Overall, our findings indicate the growing significance of intra-industry specialization under trade liberalization in both the countries. The resource reallocation process under trade liberalization is not causing a polarization wherein certain industries are forced to vanish while certain other industries gain prominence. In a liberalized environment, a large majority of the domestic industries and firms are able to survive and compete through specialization in narrow product lines. The apprehension that import liberalization would lead to a large-scale demise of domestic industries (the fear of de-industrialization) is unwarranted.[14] Further, greater intra-industry specialization would imply that trade liberalization entails lower adjustment costs than is generally considered.

China has been quite successful in exploiting the opportunities that arise from the growing international fragmentation of the production process in manufacturing industries. India, so far, has failed to take full advantage of such opportunities due to the bottlenecks and rigidities (indicated already), that stand in the way of resource reallocation both between and within the industries. Policy reforms are required to make the process of resource reallocation smoother—labour market reforms, facilitation of investment in infrastructure, and further reduction of trade barriers are particularly crucial. These policy changes are also necessary to induce the multinationals to conduct FDI of the 'vertical type' and hence to augment the process of integrating Indian industry with the fragmented structure of global production activities. Needless to say, the policy environment should be neutral for the domestic and foreign enterprises unlike in China where domestic private entrepreneurs have been discriminated against for various reasons (as elaborated in Huang 2002). It is important not to borrow the wrong aspects of policies from China as much as it is important to borrow the right aspects.

---

[12] Various available estimates suggest that the proportion of people living below the poverty line has been declining in both India and China since the 1980s. These estimates further suggest that the extent of poverty reduction has been higher in China than in India (Srinivasan 2004). While there exist certain concerns on the comparability of the poverty statistics, the differences in the sectoral composition of growth in the two countries reinforce the statistical finding that poverty reduction has been higher in China than in India.

[13] While the share of agriculture in India's GDP is 22 per cent, roughly two-thirds of the labour force is employed in agriculture.

[14] Such apprehensions about the Indian industry can be seen in Nambiar et al. (1999) and Chaudhuri (2002).

References

Baldwin, R.E. (1992), 'Measurable dynamic gains from trade', *Journal of Political Economy*, Vol. 100, No. 1, pp. 162–74.

Balassa, B. (1965), 'Trade liberalization and revealed comparative advantage', *Manchester School of Economics and Social Studies*, Vol. 33, pp. 99–123.

Batra, A. and Z. Khan (2005), 'Revealed comparative advantage: an analysis for India and China', Working Paper No. 168, Indian Council for Research on International Economic Relations, New Delhi.

Brooks, R. and R. Tao (2003), 'China's labour market performance and challenges', IMF Working Paper 03/210, Asia and Pacific Department, *http://www.imf.org/external/pubs/ft/wp/2003/wpo3210.pdf*.

Chandra, N.K. (1994), 'Planning and foreign investment in Indian manufacturing', in T.J. Byres (ed.), *State and Development Planning in India*, Oxford University Press, Delhi; reprinted in T.J. Byres (ed.), *State, Development Planning and Liberalisation in India*, Oxford University Press, Delhi.

——— (1999), 'FDI and domestic economy: neoliberalism in China', *Economic and Political Weekly*, Vol. 11, 6 November.

Chaudhuri, S. (2002), 'Economic reforms and industrial structure in India', *Economic and Political Weekly*, Vol. 37, 12 January.

Horne, J. (1996), 'East Asia and Eastern Europe: trade linkages and issues', *Pacific Economic Papers No. 261*, Australian National University.

Hu, X. and Y. Ma (1999), 'International intra-industry trade of China', *Weltwirtschaftliches Archiv*, Vol. 135, pp. 82–101.

Huang, Y. (2002), *Selling China: Foreign Direct Investment during the Reform Era*, Cambridge University Press, New York.

Joshi and Little (1994), *India: Macroeconomics and Political Economy, 1964–1991*, World Bank, Washington.

Krugman, P. (1994), 'Competitiveness: a dangerous obsession', *Foreign Affairs* (April/March), Vol. 23, No. 2, pp. 28–44.

——— (1996), 'Making sense of the competitiveness debate', *Oxford Review of Economic Policy*, Vol. 12, No. 3, pp. 17–25.

Lal, D. (1995), 'India and China: contrasts in economic liberalization?' *World Development*, Vol. 23, No. 9, pp. 1475–94.

Lardy, N. (1992), *Foreign Trade and Economic Reform in China, 1978–90*, Cambridge University Press, Cambridge.

——— (2002), *Integrating China into the Global Economy*, Brookings Institution Press, Washington.

Markusen, J.R. (1995), 'The boundaries of multinational enterprises and the theory of international trade', *Journal of Economic Perspectives*, Vol. 9, No. 2, pp. 169–89.

Meng, X. (2000), *Labour Market Reform in China*, Cambridge University Press, New York.

Nambiar, R.G., B.L. Mumgekar, and G.A. Tadas (1999), 'Is Import liberalization hurting domestic industry and employment?', *Economic and Political Weekly*, Vol. 34, 13 February.

Srinivasan, T.N. (1990), 'External sector in development: China and India, 1950–89', *American Economic Review*, Vol. 80, No. 2, Papers and Proceedings of the Hundred and Second Annual Meeting of the American Economic Association, May 1990, pp. 113–17.

——— (2004), 'China and India: economic performance, competition, and cooperation: an Update' *Journal of Asian Economics*, Vol. 15, No. 4, pp. 613–36.

UNCTAD (2003), World Investment Report 2003: FDI Policies for Development—National and International Perspectives, United Nations Publications, UN, New York and Geneva.

Veeramani, C. (2002), 'Intra-industry trade of India: trends and country-specific factors', *Review of World Economics (Weltwirtschaftliches Archiv)*, Vol. 138, No. 3, pp. 509–33.

——— (2004), 'Growing intra-industry trade in manufacturing: implications for policy', *Economic and Political Weekly*, Vol. 39, No. 41, 9 October.

Wei, W. (2005), 'China and India: any difference in their FDI performances?', *Journal of Asian Economics*, Vol. 16, pp. 719–36.

11

Indian Textile and Apparel Sector
Performance, Employment, and Demand

G. Badri Narayanan

INTRODUCTION

The Indian textile[1] and apparel sector[2] is the second largest employer after agriculture, with more than 35 million persons engaged in it. It contributes 5 per cent to the GDP, 30 per cent to the total exports, and 20 per cent to the industrial production of India. By virtue of being among the earliest established industries in the country as well as a major sector responsible for rapid growth of the NICs, in addition to the facts and figures listed above, the textile industry is very significant for the Indian economy. This industry has a rich history in India, in addition to its dimensions in culture and heritage, so much so that any study on Indian history would industry be incomplete without a detailed treatment of textile in India. Textile production has been an integral part of the lives of millions of poor people, including farmers in India, for centuries.[3] In addition, textile production has backward linkages with agriculture and allied activities, as far as natural fibres are concerned. Given these features, the link between the textile sector and development of India is quite obvious.

Strong and diverse raw material base, cheap labour, ever-growing domestic market, and relatively better technologies than the other developing countries are the key strengths of the Indian textile sector that have resulted in such a pronounced prominence of this industry. Development of modern textile industry in India had gained momentum after it did so in Britain owing to the availability indigenous cotton, cheap labour, access to British machinery, and a well-developed mercantile tradition in India.

The co-existence of a broad spectrum of production techniques, a distinct trend towards decentralized manufacturing in the informal sector, sustained, albeit considerably declined, predominance of cotton as the raw material, a very huge sick public sector, a recent trend of the manufacturers of adopting modern techniques; and the existence of quite a few regulations and preferential tariff structure (favouring natural fibres and conventional means of production) are some fundamental features of the Indian textile and clothing industry.[4]

Despite being among the leaders in textile production in 1950 and the fact that India has a self-reliant value chain of textiles, India has been steadily receding from the world textile market, with a loss of importance in industrialization at home also. The decline of the Indian textile industry

---

[1] The textile sector includes spinning that involves producing yarn from fibres, weaving that involves manufacturing fabric from the yarns, and processing that involves chemical treatment and colouration of yarns and fabrics for durability as well as aesthetics.
[2] The apparel sector includes the processes that result in the manufacture of readymade garments from fabrics.
[3] Roy(1996) is a comprehensive study of Indian textile history.
[4] Misra (1993) and Sastry (1984) elaborate on these issues.

is very conspicuous, relative to other industries as well as relative to the textile industries of the other countries in the developing world, as evident from a steep fall in the share of Indian textiles in the international market and that in the total Indian exports.

In the 1990s, the Indian textile industry had been facing a severe recession in terms of employment as well as the number of operational mills/factories, which continued despite fundamental changes in tariff structure (among other policy aspects) in the mid-1980s and in 1991. However, there are symptoms of recovery of late, owing to the market expansion resulting from the phasing out of Multi-Fibre Agreement (MFA) quotas. Thus, the textile sector is not only a significant sector in the Indian economy, but also a sector that is at a crucial stage now.

There are some major issues that arise when we look at the textile sector, with a respect to its role in the development of the country, as well as its performance in the global market as a whole: employment, welfare of the people involved in weaker sections of the economy, typically those involved in the unorganized sector, and provision of sufficient clothing to all Indians. While employment is an issue to be considered in more detail in the organized sector, owing to data availability issues, welfare of the people involved in the unorganized sector would be reflected in the performance of textile enterprises in the unorganized sector. The major objective of this chapter is to document how the Indian textile sector has been performing in recent years, with an inclusion of certain issues of concern to development, namely, employment in the organized sector, performance of the unorganized sector, and the consumption of textiles by Indian households.

The perspective considered in this chapter is one of development. India's performance in international textile trade is linked with development in the sense that enhanced textile trade is critically important for better employment prospects in the economy, as is evident from the contribution of Indian textile sector to India's employment, while employment is primarily a development-related issue. Unorganized sector is emphasized in this chapter, to be inline with its focus on implications for development. By nature, the unorganized sector is a part of relatively less-endowed segment of the economy, employing a major part of the Indian workforce. Hence, examining its performance under increased competition is essential for studying the textile sector with a developmental perspective. Analysis of consumption of textiles is an obviously development-related issue, as much as the food consumption would be, by virtue of clothing being a basic need.

This chapter is divided into six sections. The second section gives a brief description of India's recent performance in international textile trade. Looking at the trends in real and nominal value terms of India's annual exports of various textile products, their shares in total exports and their monthly averages, it is observed that they have not risen much even after the phasing out of quotas. The third section gives an account of performance of the organized textile sector in India, with an emphasis on employment, as this plays a major role in India's development. Region-wise and sub-sector-wise analysis is done over the years. The fourth section analyses the performance of the unorganized textile sector, in terms of various partial productivity measures, as this sector involves manufacturers who are most susceptible to open competition, thereby raising a major developmental issue.

As the external sector and domestic supply sector have been covered in the previous sections, it is imperative to look at another major developmental issue linked with textile sector: consumption of textiles by Indians and the factors affecting it, which is the subject matter of the fifth section. Looking at a few trends in domestic consumption and domestic tariff structure, some policy suggestions are provided to improve domestic consumption of textiles, which is a critical step to ensure the development of both consumers as well as manufacturers involved. The sixth section elucidates the policy aspects of the government with respect to the textile sector. Having set a clear picture about demand and supply in the previous sections, this section briefly evaluates policies from an integrated viewpoint. It also comes up with some policy recommendations to strike a balance between globalizing the sector and preserving the developmental objectives, considering the observations from the perspectives of performance and policies on the supply and demand sides.

INDIAN TEXTILE SECTOR IN THE INTERNATIONAL MARKET

To understand the role played by India in the international textile market, it is essential to summarize the recent history of the international textile trade.[5]

After World War II, there were many bilateral trade agreements among countries, till 1961, when a regulatory framework named Short-Term Agreement, was signed by GATT member countries. This was replaced by Long-Term Agreement since 1962, which imposed controls on the exports of cotton textiles and exports to the developed countries from the developing ones. MFA came into force in 1974 to exercise controls and restrictions over imports of non-cotton textiles as well.

The first stage of MFA, which was in place till 1977, promised an increase in export earnings for developing countries, with due considerations of market disruption that

---

[5] Most of this is discussion based on Gokhale and Katti (1995).

might occur owing to excessive imports to the developed countries. In such cases, the developed countries were empowered to restrain the levels of exports, based on past exports, allowing for some positive growth rates as well. These could be done by bilateral consultations and they did apply for handlooms.

The second stage of MFA was from 1978 to 1981, and was more restrictive than the first one, as it allowed reasonable but temporary departures from the general terms of MFA. As the departures were mostly restrictions and were of a continuing nature, this was detrimental to the export performance of the developing countries.

The third stage of MFA, from 1982 to 1986, was supposed to be less restrictive as it gave more provisions to the developing countries to be compensated for the safeguard measures. Textiles and apparel sectors were treated as two distinct sectors and quotas were worked put accordingly. However, this worsened the situation as regards Indian textile and apparel exports, as most bilateral agreements signed consisted of rigid features on category ceilings, growth rates, carry over, carry forward, and swing provisions.

During its last stage, there was increasing resentment across the world against the MFA, since it had allowed the developed countries to export among themselves without restrictions and to safeguard against all low-price exports. Even the consumers of developed countries were at loss, as they had to pay unnecessarily high prices due to these quotas. Thus, phasing out of MFA quotas was scheduled from 1995 till 2005, based on the Agreement on Textiles and Clothing. The increase in growth rates of all the categories, as agreed, was 16 per cent from 1995 to 1998, 25 per cent from 1999 to 2002, and 27 per cent from 2003 to 2005. The importing countries could postpone the phasing out of certain sensitive categories, selected by them at random. Phasing out of MFA quotas is expected to increase the exports of textiles and apparel from developing countries such as India. Low domestic demand, high cotton prices, fiscal policies skewed against synthetics, quality issues, and infrastructure bottlenecks are the major problems faced by the industry today.

In order to analyse the role of India in the international textile market, it is imperative to look at the trends of exports of various textile product-groups over the years, during the era of phasing out of textile quotas. Once this is known, the trends in relative shares of different textile product groups in India's total exports over years can be noted, so as to pinpoint the relative export performance of sub-sectors within textiles. Since the data available from the export import data bank of Directorate General of Commercial Intelligence and Statistics are annual, from 1996–7 till 2004–5, the data available for 2005–6 (from April to September 2005) could not be used in this analysis.

Figures 11.1–11.4 illustrate the fact that the value in constant (1993–4) prices of Indian textile exports rose sharply

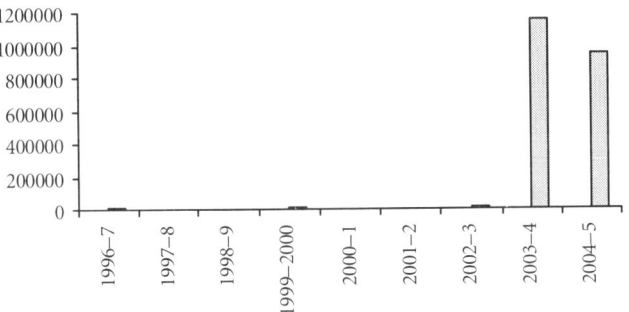

Figure 11.1: Exports of Silk and Silk Products at Constant (1993–4) Prices (in Rs Lakhs)

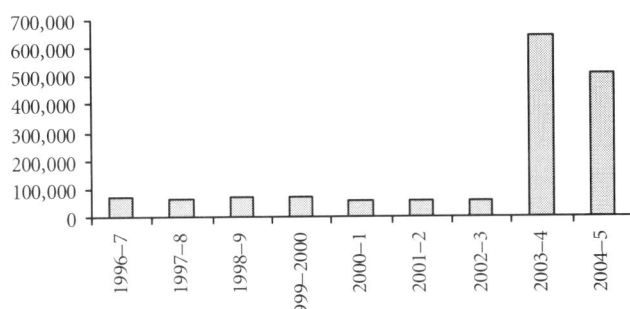

Figure 11.3: Exports of Cotton and Cotton Products at Constant (1993–4) Prices (in Rs Lakhs)

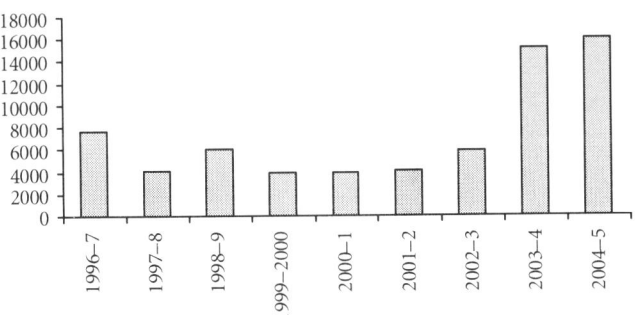

Figure 11.2: Exports of Wool and Wool Products at Constant (1993–4) Prices (in Rs Lakhs)

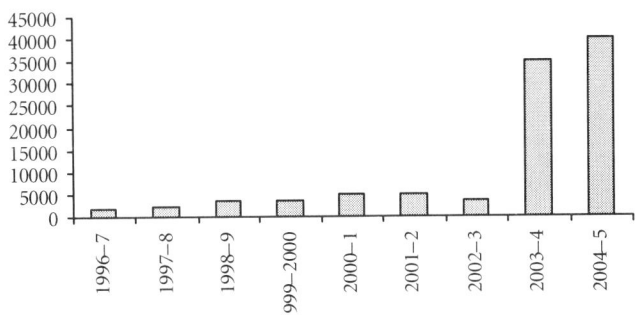

Figure 11.4: Exports of Products from Manmade Filaments at Constant (1993–4) Prices (in Rs Lakhs)

160 INDIA DEVELOPMENT REPORT

in 2003–4 and this break in the stagnant trend, which existed before 2003–4, was just for one year. In 2004–5, the exports either remained the same or fell in most cases, while they marginally rose in a few product groups such as wool, manmade fibres, and filaments. The worrisome fact is that cotton products have suffered a fall in value terms of exports from 2003–4. These being the major sub-sectors in the Indian textile sector, further prospects of the industry are heavily dependent on their performance.

To examine whether these trends are irrespective of the relative sizes of these exports, we need to look at the shares of exports of these product-groups in the total exports of India. However, inclusion of the data for the year 2005–6 would shed more light on this trend. This may be done in two different ways: studying the trends in shares of the exports of the textile commodities in total exports and trends in the monthly average of exports of different textile commodities, in real terms. Examination of monthly averages strengthens the observations made so far and hence this is not shown here to avoid repetition.

A look at the trends in the shares of different textile product groups in the total exports from India from 1996–7 to 2005–6 (April to September), illustrated in Figures 11.5 and 11.6, gives the impression that the shares have been falling in almost all product groups in textiles since 2000–1. This is quite surprising and contrary to general perception that the textile exports have been increasing since 2000. Further, a fall in the share after 2005 is steeper in many categories,

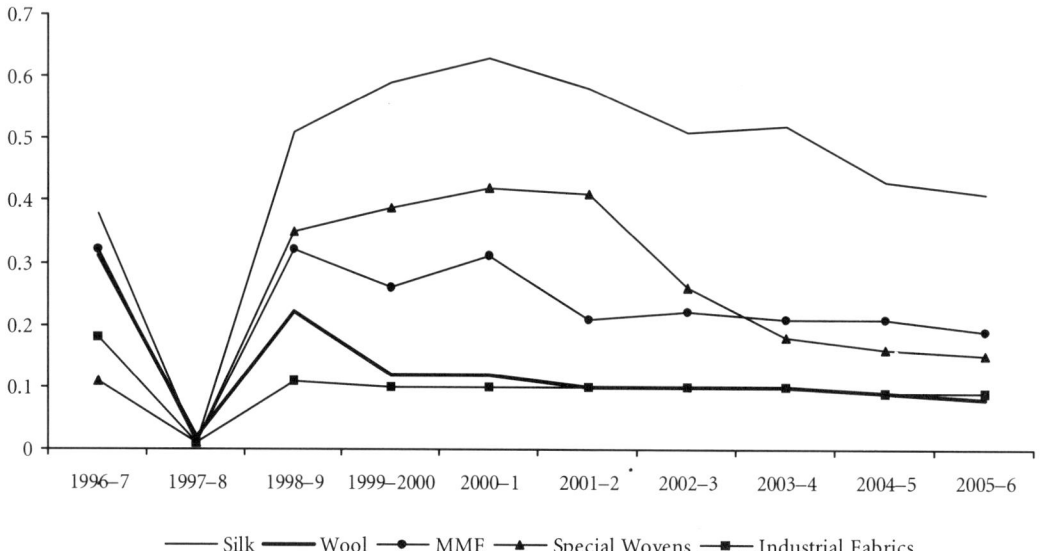

Figure 11.5: Trends in Percentage Shares of Exports of Some Non-cotton Textile Products in Total Exports from India.

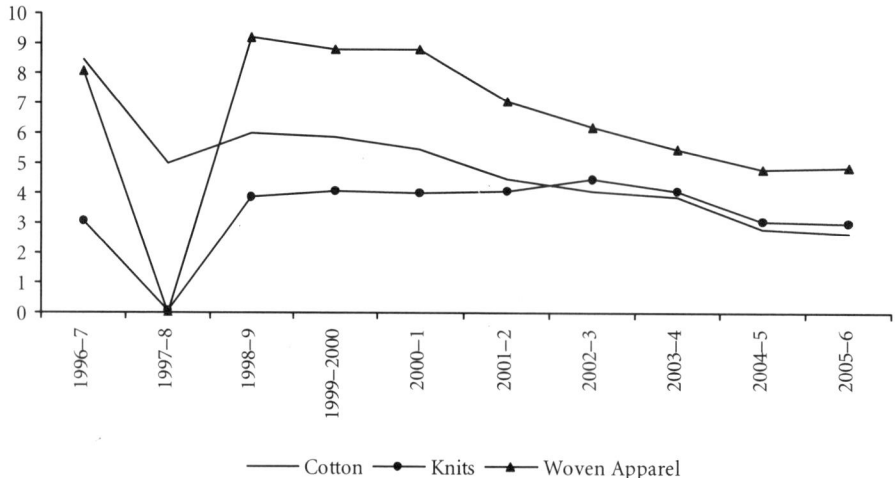

Figure 11.6: Trends in Percentage Shares of Exports of Some Cotton Textile and All Apparel Products in Total Exports from India

which makes the story even more interesting. A marginal increase in the share of woven apparel exports after 2005–6, coupled with the fact that the share of knitted apparel exports in total exports has risen from 4.6 per cent in 2004–5 to 5 per cent in 2005–6, hints at a possibility that the apparel sector is performing better than the textile sector in terms of exports.

Most importantly, these figures lead us to conclude that phasing out of MFA quotas has not affected the relative size of textile exports. This is a very significant observation, given the hype about booming textile exports in an era of free textile trade. To say the least, it can be noted that textile exports have not increased greatly in terms of their value relative to the value of total exports from the country so far and may be expected to pick up in the future, as the data under examination include only eleven months of the post-MFA regime.

Table 11.1 strengthens the observations noted in this section. The annual percentage growth rates from 2002–3 to 2003–4 have been in thousands for most categories, while they have been either negative or small if positive from 2003–4 to 2004–5. Of course, the average annual growth rates from 1996–7 to 2002–3 have been abysmally low if at all positive. Thus, an explosive growth in 2003–4, followed by stagnation in exports in 2004–5, is evident from these figures.

TABLE 11.1
Annual Growth Rates of Textile and Apparel Exports
(*Base Year: 1993–4, Growth rates in per cent*)

Products	1996–7 to 2002–3 (Average Annual)	2002–3 to 2003–4	2003–4 to 2004–5
Silk and its Products	–4.61	2221.61	–3.35
Wool and its Products	–3.58	173.29	9.89
Cotton and its Products	–6.85	1801.34	–20.16
Other Vegetable Fibres	25.78	781.04	16.11
Manmade Filaments	–2.58	980.88	1.57
Manmade Staple Fibres	–4.40	1445.02	–2.93
Felt, non-wovens, cords, etc.	12.32	96.32	–18.77
Carpets and floor coverings	–1.93	1919.05	–1.49
Special Woven Fabrics	3.50	239.64	–7.47
Industrial textiles	5.66	251.88	–6.99
Knitted/crocheted fabrics	–9.01	1033.72	–25.37
Apparel accessories (knits)	–1.50	2779.33	–14.09
Apparel accessories (non-knits)	–5.36	2295.34	–2.63
Made-up textiles including apparel	–16.19	2842.03	5.24

Source: Author's calculations based on data from Office of Directorate General of Foreign Trade.

While it is imperative to note at this point that it is difficult to make strong conclusions on India's performance post-MFA as the data available after 2005 are less, it should also be recognized that the quotas were removed in different phases and hence the export trends after late 1990s should be useful to conclude something, as we have done so far.

Having analysed of the trends in the real values of Indian textile exports, their shares in total exports, and their monthly averages, it seems that India has not really performed as well as it was expected to, in terms of textile exports, at least so far. The reasons should possibly exist on the supply-side, because, thanks to the removal of quotas, the external demand is no more constraining for India. This view is consistent with Beena (2006), who notes that the growth of textile and apparel exports by South Asian countries has been low post-1995, possibly because of various factors including industrial structure.

There are important implications of this analysis from a developmental perspective. Development of emerging economies has, in the past, always been heavily dependent on labour-intensive sectors such as textiles and apparel sectors. Examples are the NICs in South East Asia and Japan to some extent. Most of this development was owing to their performance in international textile trade, despite heavily-constrained trade regimes. Taking this into consideration, the moderate performance of Indian textile exports even after phasing out of the quotas is worrisome from a developmenal viewpoint. Thus, the supply side needs to be looked at, for analysing the state of the Indian textile sector. This motivates us to undertake an overview of the organized textile sector in India. In addition, given the developmental perspective, we also look into the aspects of employment in this sector in the next section.

INDIA'S ORGANIZED TEXTILE SECTOR: PERFORMANCE AND EMPLOYMENT

During the past decades, the organised mill sector in the textile industry has been facing recession. Numerous textile mills have been closed and declared sick, while many of the mills under National Textile Corporation (NTC) are being operated, despite losses, owing to the fact that there are many employees involved. Even in the private sector mills, employment has been a major issue. The recession continued despite fundamental changes in tariff structure among other policy aspects in the mid-1980s and in 1991, though there are symptoms of recovery of late, due to the prospects arising from phasing out of MFA quotas.

In the informal or unorganised sector that is progressing well in the clothing sector, the processes are not planned and systematic. The working conditions are not satisfactory as the labour regulations cannot be enforced and a hire-and-fire principle is in place. This is true even in a part of organised sector, wherein the manufacturers recruit contract labourers in order to minimize the losses that they are facing due to the inflexible labour regulations which stop them from firing their permanent employees even during recessions. In fact, some studies observe a rapid growth of the informal sector in the textile industry, especially after the reforms of 1991.

A wide range of regulations in the textile industry involving bureaucratic difficulties in the expansion of the industry and a highly distortionary tariff structure were partly responsible for this steady recession. For example, hank yarn obligation[6] requires spinners to allocate a fixed part of their production to handloom weavers. This not only restricts the profits of spinners, but also the raw material access and cost for weavers and others up the value chain. The reservation of the garment sector[7] under the SSI had restricted large-scale investment in this sector, which led to huge losses in efficiency that could have otherwise been achieved through economies of scale. Moreover, the Ministry of Environment and Forests (1986) demands proper treatment of certain chemicals used mainly in the processing of textiles, through the Environment (Protection) Act. In addition to domestic regulations, the industry has also been facing import restrictions from the developed countries. For example, the US imports from Asia are being highly constrained by the quotas based on the MFA.

Table 11.2 shows the trends in annual average growth rates of some major variables for the aggregate textile industry. Since this was based on the aggregated textile data, figures could be calculated for four decades with proper concordance of different reports of ASI. It can be seen that output, wages, and fixed capital have been growing at an increasing rate during 1961–2, to 1999–2000, but for a small fall in growth rate during 1991–2 to 1999–2000.

Here, it should be noted that this might partly be due to the omission of cotton ginning sector for the two years after 1997–8, as the NIC-98 has classified this sector under agriculture. The same argument holds for the other variables also and hence the figures for the period between 1980–1 and 1997–8 have been highlighted. The trend in the growth of employment is, however, not uniform. For the period between 1971–2 and 1980–1, it has grown at a much lower rate than the other variables in most periods and, in fact, has declined from 1981–2 to 1990–1.

Though employment has grown on an average after the reforms of 1991, this is nowhere comparable to the growth of the other variables, especially, capital stock, which has grown at about 18 per cent an year.[8] This observation is even more precise if only the period from 1980–1 to 1997–8 is examined, since, in this period, employment has fallen at an approximately annual average rate at which output has grown, despite a remarkable annual growth of capital of over 8 per cent. It would seem from this that, as a whole, textile industry is characterized by substitutability between capital and labour. Given the labour-intensive nature and unionized labour of the organized segment of this industry, entrepreneurs might have had capital to substitute for labour. Even then, the absolute fall of 5 per cent per year in employment when output has increased by 5 per cent per year draws attention.

Even for the latest available data, the rise in employment is very low, though the real total emoluments have grown sharply. The growth in capital has come down to below 3 per cent, which is a reason for worry since huge investment is required to face the competitive market in the free trade regime. Output has, however grown at a higher rate.

Three measures of partial productivity have been analysed in Table 11.3: capital productivity, capital intensity, and labour productivity. Capital productivity is the ratio of gross output to gross fixed assets. This gives the amount of output produced from a unit of capital. Capital

TABLE 11.2
Average Annual Growth Rates in the Organized Indian Textile Sector (*1993–4 prices*)

Period	Output	Employ-ment	Real Wages	Real Fixed Capital
1961–2 to 1970–1	5.034	0.496	2.487	3.645
1971–2 to 1980–1	6.668	3.295	2.882	4.643
1981–2 to 1990–1	8.174	–0.968	5.44	8.802
1991–2 to 1999–2000	6.718	0.997	2.378	17.774
1980–1 to 1997–8	5.34	–5.17	5.35	8.11
2001–2 to 2002–3	9.37	0.98	7.09	2.65

Source: Author's calculations on the basis of data from ASI.

TABLE 11.3
Trends in Some Ratios of Capital (K), Output (Y), and Employment (N)

Year	Y/K	K/N	Y/N
1973–4	2.569	4.523	11.616
1980–1	3.657	4.364	15.958
1985–6	3.092	7.331	22.664
1990–1	3.614	10.332	37.336
1997–8	1.546	34.122	52.76
2001–2	1.403	3.969	6.443
2002–3	1.457	4.195	7.039

Source: Author's calculations from ASI.

---

[6] It came into place in 1974 and was fixed at 50 per cent of the total marketable yarn in 1986, though it was brought down to 40 per cent and then 20 per cent in 2003.

[7] This has been withdrawn with effect from 2 November 2000.

[8] This is quite as expected, since this was the period when the phasing out of MFA quotas was initiated and hence the firms were apparently getting ready for the free trade regime by attempting to invest and enhance their quality and scales as well as the consequent economies and efficiency.

intensity is defined as the ratio of gross fixed assets to total employment. This reflects the relative size of capital and labour in the industries. Labour productivity is the ratio of gross output to total employment. This measures the extent to which labour has been used for production.

Table 11.3—in terms of lakhs of Rupees of gross value of output and gross invested capital per person engaged—makes it more explicit that the textile industry, on an average, has precisely become much less labour-intensive than it was thirty years ago. An unclear trend in labour–capital ratio raises doubt about the existence of substitutability between capital and labour. However, a rise in this ratio despite a fall in capital productivity seems to suggest an existence of mere substitution of labour by capital. After 2001, capital productivity, capital intensity, and labour productivity have fallen sharply. This is another serious problem, given the fact that the international market is becoming more and more competitive, requiring high productivity and capital intensity.

The figures warrant some explanation. Capital productivity (Y/K) has been quite stable from the 1970s till 2003, varying between 1.4 and 3.7. However, there are bulges in capital intensity (K/N) as well as labour productivity (Y/N). Strikingly huge values for these during 1985–6, 1990–1, and 1997–8 could possibly be a result of a rapid fall in employment, which is in the denominator for both these measures, in this period, as can be inferred from Table 11.2. Growth of employment since 2001–2 might have offset the unusually high rises in these ratios before, hence explaining the fall in these ratios to much lower values.

A fall in employment despite an immense rise in labour productivity, possibly because of increased capital intensity, is a cause for concern. Further, a fall in capital productivity suggests that the firms have started investing in expensive automation-oriented machinery, such as autoconers in the case cone-winding and fully automatic shuttleless looms in the case of weaving. Though efficiency-enhancing and skill-oriented-employment-generating, this is not a healthy trend for unskilled labour. Rehabilitation of retrenched/displaced workers, possibly by imparting skills to handle the new machineries, could be a solution to ensure job and income security for the susceptible labour groups.

In recent years, most of the measures of protection have been brought down as a part of the reforms. Table 11.4 shows effective rates of protection for different sub-sectors of textile industry over the past few years. The measure used is based on Das (2003), who defines effective rate of protection as a measure of the extent to which a sector is sheltered from foreign competition. Specifically, this is based on Corden's formula and is the percentage excess of domestic value-added, vis-à-vis world value-added, introduced because of tariff and other trade barriers. This measures the distortion introduced due to tariff on input prices as well as final output prices and, therefore, measures protection to domestic factors of production. We use this measure of protection, because it not only captures the absolute level of effective rate of protection for each sector, but also accounts for intersectoral differences in protection (mentioned above). It is evident from this table that protection has fallen in all sub-sectors, and the reduction has been strikingly sharp in cotton khadi and handlooms. Fall in protection may have implications for employment, to the extent that protected industries that tend to lose because of a fall in protection are employment-intensive.

To explain the factors that could have influenced employment in the organized textile sector in India in the past, we undertake a detailed sector-wise study of trends. Figure 11.7 shows that employment in handlooms and powerlooms has been more or less stagnant from 1973–4 to 1997–8, except for a sharp increase in employment in handlooms in 1986–7 when the Handlooms (Reservation of Articles for Production) Act of 1985 was enforced from 1986. However, employment fell rapidly owing to liberalization which favoured the powerlooms and mill sector in the late 1980s, leading again to the past levels of employment. Figure 11.8 shows that employment has been consistently falling in the cotton mill sector, while it has been almost stagnant in the wool, silk, and other natural fibres and has risen sharply in the synthetics and made-up textiles, more so after the reforms of 1991. This roughly indicates that the highly

TABLE 11.4
Trends in Effective Rates of Protection for Different Sub-sectors in the Indian Textile Sector

NIC-1987 Codes	Description of Sectors	1980–5	1986–90	1991–5	1996–2000
230, 231, 235	Cotton ginning, spinning, and weaving	109.77	125.38	68.38	42.93
262	Embroidery, ornamental trimming, and zari	160.91	151.23	95.79	48.22
232, 233	Cotton khadi and handlooms	109.36	126.85	70.95	0
234, 236	Powerlooms and processing in mills	109.77	125.38	68.38	42.93
260, 265, 267	Hosieries, garments, and other made-ups	138.33	149.89	98.45	54.25
263	Carpets and other furnishings	102.52	91.8	63.3	44.66
268, 269	Water-proof and other speciality textiles	160.91	151.23	95.79	48.2

Source: Based on Das (2003), Working Paper No. 105, ICRIER.

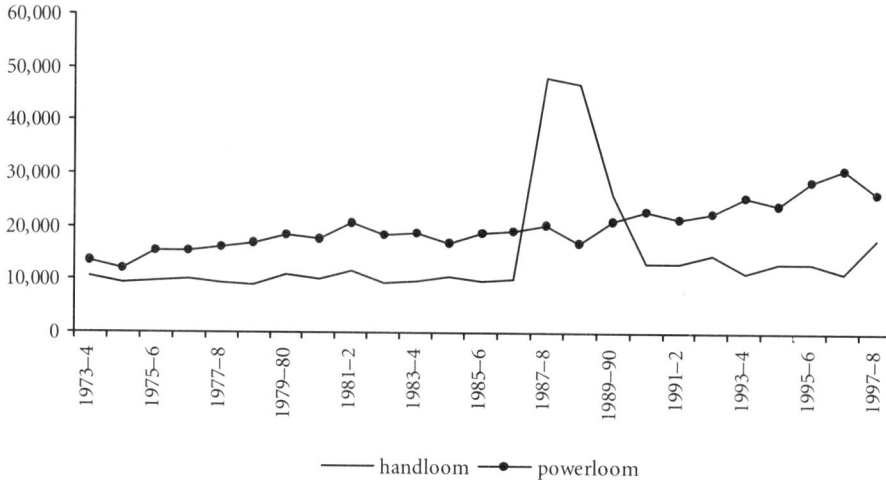

Figure 11.7: Employment Trends in Non-mill Textile Sector

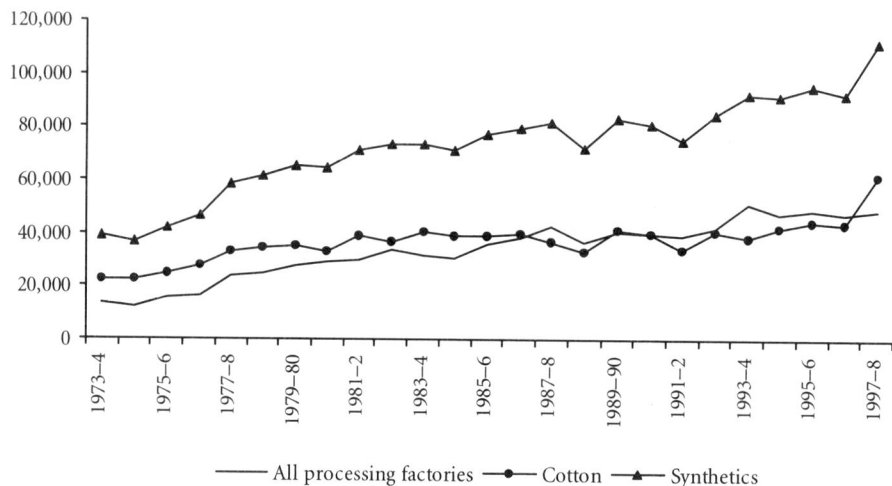

Figure 11.8: Employment Trends in Different Sub-sectors of Textile Wet Processing Sector

regulated conventional cotton mill sector has suffered the most among all the sub-sectors of cotton textiles in terms of employment—implying the existence of a negative relationship between labour regulations and employment. It also suggests a positive effect of liberalization at least in some sub-sectors that come under the made-ups.

Figure 11.9 shows that though employment has been rising as a whole in the textile processing sectors that are prime polluters in the industry, its fall in 1987–8 and 1995–6 in the overall, cotton, and synthetic processing sectors indicates the possible existence of a negative impact, at least in the short term, of the Environmental Pollution Act (1987) and the ban of certain dyes by some members of the EU in 1995. Figure 11.10 strengthens evidence for this statement since the fall in employment is even more conspicuous in the case of wool and silk processing sectors, which are more pollution-intensive in nature. The long-term increasing trend in employment is preserved despite the environmental regulations, suggesting that the rise in employment that might be gained by compliance to these regulations may have played some role in increasing employment. These trends motivate us to test for the existence of an impact of environmental regulations on employment in polluting sectors of the textile industry. Further, figures 11.7 to 11.10 also highlight the fact that the Indian textile sector is extremely heterogeneous in terms of employment trends.

Given the past trends and figures, we examine the salient features of the latest available data for the organized sector (Table 11.5). The number of factories has increased in both textile and apparel sectors, implying a rise in fixed capital, number of workers, total persons engaged, total emoluments, and gross output in the apparel sector. However, employment and wages in the textile sector have fallen, though total emoluments have risen, possibly reflecting the increased requirement of skilled employees other than workers, as seen in the relatively better performance in terms

INDIAN TEXTILE AND APPAREL SECTOR 165

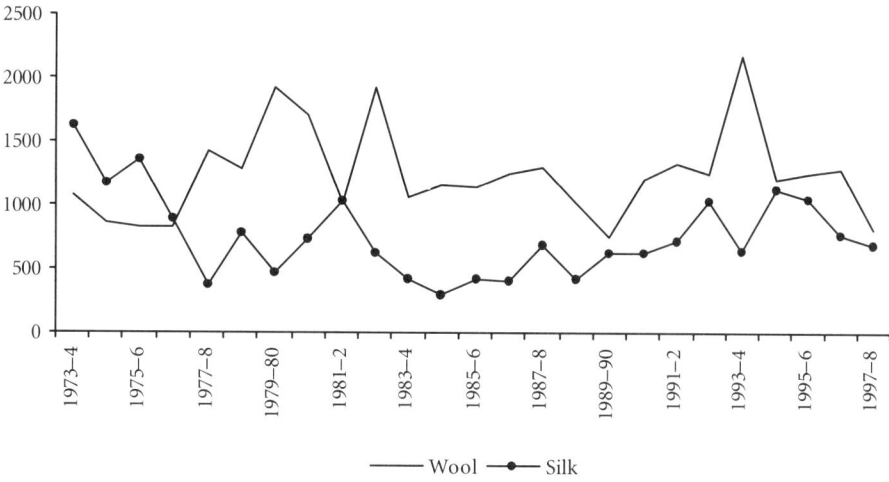

Figure 11.9: Employment Trends in Textile Wet Processing Sector

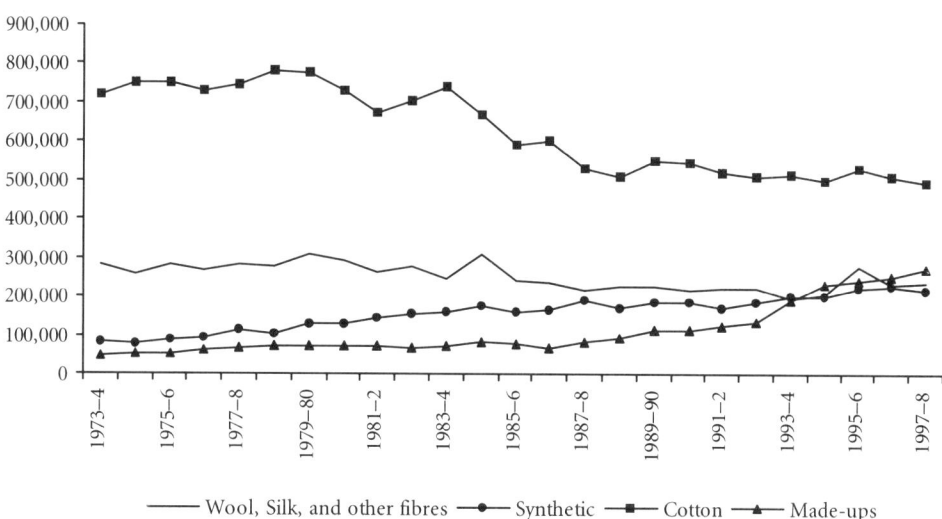

Figure 11.10: Employment Trends in Sub-Sector in Textile Sector

TABLE 11.5
Salient Features of the Organized Textile and Apparel Sector in India: Recent Trends

(values are in Rs lakhs, current prices and others are in number)

Year	Sector	Factories	Fixed Capital	Workers	Total Persons Engaged	Wages to Workers	Total Emoluments	Gross Output
2001–2	Textile	12,557	3,931,489	1,004,848	1,182,124	445,017	602,216	8,202,046
2001–2	Apparel	3283	310,821	272,524	317,089	86,647	127,917	1,456,746
2001–2	Total	15,840	4,242,310	1,277,372	1,499,213	531,664	730,133	9,658,792
2002–3	Textile	12,764	4,011,135	1,001,251	1,178,520	438,814	634,828	8,771,897
2002–3	Apparel	3307	346,560	285,544	335,559	96,242	150,978	1,885,114
2002–3	Total	16,071	4,357,695	1,286,795	1,514,079	535,056	785,806	10,657,011
				Annual Growth Rates				
2001–3	Textile	1.648	2.026	−0.358	−0.305	−1.394	5.415	6.948
2001–3	Apparel	0.731	11.498	4.778	5.825	11.074	18.028	29.406
2001–3	Total	1.458	2.720	0.738	0.992	0.638	7.625	10.335

Source: Author's Calculations from ASI (2001–2 and 2002–3).

of total persons engaged, compared to that in terms of workers. This is another noteworthy issue with respect to development, as both employment and wages are serious issues of concern, more so because textiles is a much bigger sector than apparels in the organized segment.

Looking at the growth rates, it is surprising to note that though growth in the number of factories has been much lower in the apparel sector, capital, employment, wages, and emoluments as well as output have grown at very high rates. This shows that the organized apparel sector is now booming. This could partly be attributed to the fact that the garment sector was dereserved from the SSI Sector in 2000. This is supported by the observation that the number of factories, per se, has not grown much, probably because of the mergers of smaller fragments after dereservation, causing a reduction in number, which could have been outweighed by the number of new factories established.[9] Thus, the organized apparel sector seems to be more prepared for the free-trade regime than the organized textile sector. Therefore, employment from this industry could well become much more dependent on apparel than on textile in the future.

However, a word of caution is necessary while discussing about employment in the organized textile sector. Given the high labour costs and rigidities in the labour markets, coupled with the sickness of factories, the employers go in for sub-contracting employees from the unorganised sector, thereby reducing the employment in the organised sector. This, in addition to showing up as a decline in employment, is not a healthy trend, as far as the welfare of employees is concerned—as they are not protected by any legislation, given their unorganised nature. This issue needs to be taken care of by the policy makers, possibly by ensuring income security for the workers, coupled with some labour flexibility for the employers, so that they are discouraged from sub-contracting.

Having analysed the trends in employment in India's organised textile sector, it is essential to link these observations to the development perspective. The apparel sector has performed quite well in terms of employment in the recent years, showing a recovery from the declines in the past, though the same is not true for the textile sector, though there are some signs of recovery. This seems to be a good indication for the country's development in general, given the immense contribution of textile sector to the economy. However, as shown subsequently, the unorganized sector is a vital part of the Indian textile industry from the viewpoint of development. Therfore, the story on employment and performance of textile industry and its implication for development would not be complete without a comprehensive examination of trends in the unorganized textile sector.

PERFORMANCE OF INDIA'S UNORGANIZED TEXTILE SECTOR

The unorganized manufacturing sector is defined as the collection of those manufacturing units whose activity does not come under any statutory Act or legal provision and/or which do not maintain any regular accounts or which are not registered under Sections 2m(i)[10] and 2m(ii)[11] of the Factories Act, 1948 and which are registered under Section 85[12] of the Factories Act, 1948. As Table 11.6 reveals, the unorganized manufacturing sector contributes 28 per cent of the gross value added and 73 per cent of employment to total manufacturing (including the organized sector), thus playing a vital role in the Indian economy.

Table 11.6 shows that the unorganized textile and apparel sector comprises 31 per cent of gross value added and 79 per cent of employment in the entire textile and apparel sector in India. In fact, the unorganised apparel sector, which

TABLE 11.6
Shares of Various Sub-sectors in Different Sectors, 2000–1

(*current prices*)

Sub-sector	Sector	Share in Gross Value Added (per cent)	Share in Employment (per cent)
Unorganised Manufacturing	Total Manufacturing	28	73
Unorganised Textiles	Total Textiles	18	74
Unorganised Apparel	Total Apparel	59	89
Unorganised Textiles and Apparel	Total Textiles and Apparel	31	79
Unorganised Textiles and Apparel	Unorganised Manufacturing	29	31

Source: Author's calculations from NSSO reports on unorganized Manufacturing and ASI.

[9] It may be noted here that an investment up to Rs 3 crore in plant and machinery and an FDI-cap of 25 per cent is permitted, subject to an export obligation of 50 per cent of total production of garments, even before dereservation.
[10] Factories using power and employing 10 or more workers on any working day.
[11] Factories not using power and employing 20 or more workers on any working day.
[12] Factories, which have less than 10/20 workers with or without power, specially notified by the state government.

contributes about 59 per cent to gross value added and 89 per cent to employment in the apparel sector in India is predominantly unorganized. Thus, any study of Indian textile industry cannot claim to be complete unless it considers unorganised sector in its analysis.

As Misra (1993) notes, the unorganized segment of India's textile sector comprises handlooms, powerlooms, small power-processors, and traditional hand-processors, in addition to the numerous small-scale garment firms in woven as well as hosiery sectors. Powerlooms operate either on an independent basis, or serve a master-weaver system, in which they just process the orders from the master-weaver providing the raw materials and charges based on the quantity of cloth produced. They acquire loans from non-bank sources, while handlooms in rural areas rely on non-institutional sources such as village money lenders.

In the urban areas, where this sector is dominant, the labour is mostly workers migrating from the rural areas, non-unionized, and hence obtained at market-determined wage rates much lower than for the organized sector. All these, in addition to the exemption of grey fabric from excise duty and sales taxes and long working hours, are the sources of competitive advantage for the unorganized powerloom sector, over the organized mill sector. In fact, the rapid growth of the powerloom sector after deregulatory measures introduced in 1985 could be attributed to its unorganized labour market, well-developed input markets, ease of entry and flexible specialization.

Although there are some large production centres of handlooms in urban areas, the major part of this sector is small-scale, and often is an ancillary activity to agriculture in rural areas. Many of the Indian handlooms are non-commercial, such as those in the North East, which produce for local or domestic consumption. There are small-scale, power-processors as well as hand-processors using traditional techniques in India. The fact that the raw material cotton cost is around one-fourth of the total value, and the three stages of spinning, grey weaving, and processing each progressively add one-fourth of final value, illustrates the importance of processing and weaving in the cotton textile value chain.

Further down the value chain, most of the knitted garment manufacturers are in the unorganised sector. For example, many firms in Tiruppur, an industrial town in Tamil Nadu, are either unorganized or depend heavily on sub-contracting to firms in the unorganized sector. Most of these firms are export-oriented and are seasonal/casual in operation, depending on orders from foreign buyers. These firms are usually specialized[13] and small and hence complete their job orders[14] with the help of numerous suppliers. Even some of the woven garment manufacturers, such as a few in Mumbai, Gurgaon, Chennai, and Bangalore are unorganized.

It is worth mentioning that the aforementioned characteristics are almost typical for the cotton sector. However, the features of the other sectors such as wool, silk, and synthetics, which involve similar processes, remain the same. The jute sector, which is concentrated in rural and urban areas of West Bengal, among a few other states, has undergone a major transformation from prosperity in pre-independence times to sickness in recent years. The coir sector is a major cottage industry in many rural areas in Tamil Nadu and Kerala. Other miscellaneous sectors include furnishings, manufacture textiles for industrial purposes such as nylon tyre cords, metallized yarns and rubber thread or cord covered with textile material, speciality textiles such as tapes, cords, and nets, fancy textiles such as embroidery, zari work, and wadded textiles.

As the MFA quotas are being phased out, the Indian textile sector is facing both opportunities and threats. While the organized segment of the sector seems poised for a boom owing to its relatively better economies of scale, the large unorganized sector in this industry is expected to suffer because of its lack of competitiveness and technical efficiency among other related factors such as insufficient scales of operation which limit the levels of efficiency and competitiveness that can be achieved by these firms.

Further, dereservation of the garment sector under the SSI sector (in 2000) is expected to have adverse effects on the unorganized sector, as the enterprises in this sector now have to face stiff competition from big players. Given the huge contribution of the unorganized sector to the textile sector, this is certainly a serious issue for this sector as a whole. On the other hand, small firms are competitive after the recent trade reforms, as decentralized production does have some strengths in terms of costs. In addition, mergers of smaller firms into bigger ones could be one solution to face competition from big players. Combined effluent treatment plants established in clusters of small textile dyeing units, in places such as Tiruppur, are examples of how the small firms can join hands to eliminate their disadvantage of lack of economies of scale.

Given the heterogeneity of the unorganized textile sector, coupled with its potential strengths and drawbacks, it is imperative to examine the trends in productivity in this sector in recent years for which detailed data are available.

This study uses the aggregate summary results of 40th, 45th, 51st, and 56th rounds on unorganized manufacturing

---

[13] Of course, there are a handful of firms that carry out all the activities in the textile value chain.
[14] Most firms are order-based, though there are a few which also market their products.

of the NSSO (NSSO 1989, 1994, 1998, 2002). The different types of enterprises in this study are the following:

- Own account manufacturing enterprises (OAMEs) consisting of no employee other than the working owner.
- Non-directory manufacturing establishments (NDME) employing less than six persons other than the working owner.
- Directory manufacturing establishments (DMEs) employing more than six persons other than the working owner.

The demerits of NSSO data on unorganised manufacturing sector are the possibility of unrepresentative sampling, response errors, inadequate sample size, and absence of sampling error estimates. Owing to the absence of any better source of data for the unorganized textile sector, we use these data for analysis, acknowledging their limitations.

Based on these data, we analyse the average annual growth rates in employment, fixed assets, wages, and output (see Table 11.7). While employment and wages have fallen, on an average, from 1984 to 1990, they have risen in the early 1990s and their growth has been much higher in the late 1990s. This is despite a fall in fixed assets and output throughout this period, though the decline has not been as high in 1990s as it was in 1980s.

TABLE 11.7
Annual Average Growth Rates in Unorganized Textile Sector
(*based on 1993–4 prices*)

Period	Employment	Fixed Assets	Wages	Output
1984–90	−11.803	−24.19	−8.787	−24.512
1989–95	2.724	−8.412	9.174	−3.276
1994–2001	6.781	−9.123	10.946	−7.251

Source: Author's calculations based on NSSO(1989, 1994, 1998, 2002).

Partial productivity measures should be analysed to obtain an overview of the performance of unorganized textile sector. Here, we analyse capital productivity (no units), labour productivity, and capital intensity (in rupees per employee). In large-scale or capital-intensive industries, capital productivity may be expected to be much lower than unity, as output produced would require capital that is much higher than itself, owing to the capital-intensive nature of production. However, as we are considering the unorganized sector, which is not very likely to include such enterprises, this ratio may be even greater than one. This indicates the extent to which capital has been used for production.

As we construct these measures over the years, to facilitate intertemporal comparability, we obtained them in constant prices (base year: 1981–2) by deflating the fixed assets using WPI for textile machineries and gross output using WPI for the respective products, namely, textiles and apparel.

Tables 11.8 and 11.9 show the trends and growth rates, respectively, in capital intensity, capital productivity, and labour productivity across different enterprises and areas in the two sub-sectors of the textile sector, namely, textile manufacture (NIC-98 code: 17) and apparel manufacture (NIC-98 code: 18).

First, we compare the trends in these variables for each year across different enterprise types, areas, and sub-sectors. Second, we look at the average annual growth rates for the variables, for a few years in the past. Third, we derive overall inferences from this analysis.

Capital Productivity

In 1984–5, NDMEs were more capital-productive than OAMEs in almost all categories, except in the rural textile sector, where both were comparable. While the urban textile NDME sector produces output that is more than thrice that of capital, output is as high as capital in most other sectors except apparel OAME. In all cases except rural NDME,[15] the apparel sector is less capital-productive than textile sector. Rural textile NDME is the only exception for the observation that all categories in rural areas are more capital-productive than those in urban areas.

In 1989–90, all categories except rural textile OAME had capital productivity measuring above unity, exhibiting higher levels as compared to those in 1984–5, except urban textile NDME where it had halved. Further, NDMEs are more capital-productive than OAMEs in all categories. All categories in rural areas have been more capital-productive than those in urban areas, except textile NDMEs, just as the case in 1984–5. Further, in all categories except urban NDME, the apparel sector has been more capital-productive than textile sector.

In 1994–5, DMEs were also included in the analysis, owing to the availability of data from the same source (NSSO 1998). In this year, all categories in NDME, except urban apparel sector, were more capital-productive than OAME, while those in DME, except rural apparel sector, were better than those in NDME. Compared to 1989–90, capital productivity has fallen in all categories except rural apparel NDME. While urban textile NDME had been the most capital-productive of all categories till 1989–90, it was just an average category in these terms in 1994–5. Except in urban NDME, capital productivity has been higher in the apparel sector than in textile sector, for all enterprise types and areas. Enterprises in urban areas have higher capital

---

[15] Note that in this case, both textile and apparel sectors are equally capital-productive.

TABLE 11.8
Trends in Partial Productivity Measures in Unorganized Textile Sector in India

Year	NIC-98 Code	Sample	Enterprise Type	Capital Productivity	Capital Intensity	Labour Productivity
1984–5	17	rural	OAME	0.902	2016.479	1819.41
	18	rural	OAME	0.251	8600.825	2154.82
	17	urban	OAME	0.687	3679.076	2527.268
	18	urban	OAME	0.108	39,475.00	4281.939
	17	rural	NDME	0.863	5204.038	4488.943
	18	rural	NDME	0.884	4554.78	4026.569
	17	urban	NDME	3.263	3648.323	11,903.93
	18	urban	NDME	0.695	9940.026	6906.713
1989–90	17	rural	OAME	1.021	1742.425	1778.319
	18	rural	OAME	1.253	1879.168	2354.176
	17	rural	NDME	1.74	2435.485	4238.551
	18	rural	NDME	1.757	3445.447	6054.648
	17	urban	OAME	0.713	4247.893	3030.697
	18	urban	OAME	1.069	4832.785	5165.134
	17	urban	NDME	1.871	10,575.99	19,787.06
	18	urban	NDME	1.303	12,223.04	15,922.37
1994–5	17	rural	OAME	1.143	2033.08	2323.994
	18	rural	OAME	1.166	1596.906	1862.392
	17	urban	OAME	0.836	4524.921	3782.379
	18	urban	OAME	0.889	5100.408	4532.575
	17	rural	NDME	1.279	4335.058	5542.978
	18	rural	NDME	2.31	1965.746	4541.748
	17	urban	NDME	1.251	11,294.63	14,133.05
	18	urban	NDME	0.493	24,059.05	11,871.76
	17	rural	DME	1.578	5905.005	9320.225
	18	rural	DME	2.244	3438.526	7717.756
	17	urban	DME	1.804	9804.714	17,688.04
	18	urban	DME	2.8	6893.022	19,301.48
2000–1	17	rural	OAME	0.906	2577.797	2336.765
	18	rural	OAME	0.612	4986.596	3050.152
	17	rural	NDME	1.16	4680.898	5429.882
	18	rural	NDME	0.794	6554.459	5202.371
	17	rural	DME	1.575	6661.292	10,490.51
	18	rural	DME	1.201	5341.884	6418.246
	17	urban	OAME	0.653	6369.44	4159.148
	18	urban	OAME	0.43	10,000.64	4296.527
	17	urban	NDME	1.49	15,329.54	22,846.26
	18	urban	NDME	0.539	15,875.74	8554.678
	17	urban	DME	1.452	16,719.66	24,275.79
	18	urban	DME	1.049	16,444.34	17,243.16

Source: Author's calculations based on NSSO (1989, 1994, 1998, 2002).

productivity than those in rural areas only for DMEs and the reverse holds true for other enterprise types.

In 2000–1, capital productivity conspicuously declined in all categories. All categories in DME, except urban textiles were more capital-productive than others, while those in OAME were worse than those in others in this aspect. One striking observation is that capital productivity in apparel sector is lower than that in textile sector for all enterprise types and areas. In all cases except textile NDMEs, enterprises in rural areas are more capital productive than those in urban areas.

As seen from Table 11.7, annual average growth rates of capital productivity from 1984–5 to 1989–90 were in two-digits or even higher in all categories barring textile OAME, where they were less than 10 per cent and urban textile NDME, where they had fallen. From 1989–90 to 1994–5, aver-age annual rates of decline in all categories, except textile OAME and apparel NDME in the rural sample,[16]

[16] Note that capital productivity had grown in these categories during this period.

170 INDIA DEVELOPMENT REPORT

TABLE 11.9
Growth Trends of Partial Productivity Measures in Unorganized Textile Sector in India

Year	NIC-98 Code	Sample	Enterprise Type	Capital Productivity	Capital Intensity	Labour Productivity
1984–5	17	rural	OAME	2.623	–2.718	–0.452
	18	rural	OAME	80.007	–15.63	1.85
to	17	rural	NDME	20.351	–10.64	–1.116
	18	rural	NDME	19.756	–4.871	10.073
1989–90	17	urban	OAME	0.772	3.092	3.984
	18	urban	OAME	177.059	–17.551	4.125
	17	urban	NDME	–8.532	37.977	13.245
	18	urban	NDME	17.495	4.594	26.107
1989–90	17	rural	OAME	2.4	3.336	6.137
	18	rural	OAME	–1.381	–3.004	–4.178
to	17	urban	OAME	–4.358	–1.274	–5.354
	18	urban	OAME	–3.37	1.108	–2.449
1994–5	17	rural	NDME	–5.306	15.599	6.155
	18	rural	NDME	6.296	–8.589	–4.997
	17	urban	NDME	–6.624	1.359	–5.715
	18	urban	NDME	–12.424	19.367	–5.088
1994–5	17	rural	OAME	–4.14	5.359	0.11
	18	rural	OAME	–9.51	42.453	12.755
	17	rural	NDME	–1.856	1.596	–0.408
to	18	rural	NDME	–13.129	46.687	2.909
	17	rural	DME	–0.045	2.562	2.511
	18	rural	DME	–9.294	11.071	–3.368
2000–1	17	urban	OAME	–4.376	8.153	1.992
	18	urban	OAME	–10.331	19.215	–1.042
	17	urban	NDME	3.821	7.145	12.33
	18	urban	NDME	1.841	–6.803	–5.588
	17	urban	DME	–3.904	14.105	7.449
	18	urban	DME	–12.511	27.713	–2.133

Source: Author's calculations based on NSSO (1989, 1994, 1998, 2002).

range from 1 per cent to 12 per cent. Between 1994–5 and 2000–1, enterprises were becoming 0.05 per cent to 13 per cent less productive every year, on an average, except in the case of urban NDME, where they had become more productive at an average annual rates of 1.8 per cent to 3.8 per cent. The rates of decline were much higher in the apparel sector than in textile sector. Even in urban NDMEs, apparel sector had become more productive at a rate lower than that for the textile sector. Decline in capital productivity, wherever it occurred, was more rapid in urban enterprises than in rural ones.

Capital Intensity

In 1984–5, capital intensity varied between Rs 2000 and Rs 10,000 per employee, with an outlier of over Rs 39,000 for the urban apparel OAME sector. Capital intensity has been much higher in the apparel sector than in the textile sector, except in rural NDMEs, where it is the other way round. Except in textile NDMEs, the enterprises in urban areas are more capital-intensive than those in rural areas. With the exception of rural textile sector, NDMEs are less capital-intensive than OAMEs.

While these figures vary between Rs 1700 and Rs 12,000 in 1989–90, enterprises in the apparel sector, urban areas, and NDME have been uniformly more capital-intensive than those in textiles sector, rural areas, and OAME, respectively, with no exceptions. Except for the enterprises in urban textile OAME and urban NDME sectors, capital intensity has fallen across all categories, the sharpest fall being more than eight times in the case of urban apparel OAME.

In 1994–5, capital intensity ranged from Rs 2000 to Rs 24,000, and the textile sector was more capital-intensive than the apparel sector in the enterprises in rural areas and those in DME, though urban apparel NDME was most capital-intensive among all categories. Urban enterprises and NDMEs have been more capital-intensive than rural enterprises and OAMEs, respectively. While DMEs in rural areas were more capital intensive than NDMEs in these areas, DMEs in urban areas have been less capital-intensive than NDMEs in these areas. Except for rural apparel NDMEs, capital-intensity has fallen in all categories in 1994–5, compared to that in 1989–90.

Unlike in 1994–5, urban DME has been the most capital-intensive (around Rs 16,000, while the lowest is around

Rs 2600) category in 2000–1, pushing urban NDME to second. The apparel sector has been more capital-intensive than the textile sector in all categories except DMEs. OAME sector is less capital-intensive than NDME, which is less capital-intensive than DME, in all categories except rural apparel sector, where DME is less capital-intensive than NDME. Further, we observe that enterprises in urban areas are much more capital-intensive than those in rural areas. Capital-intensity is much higher during 2000–1 than that during 1994–5 in all categories.

Except for urban NDMEs and textile urban OAMEs, enterprises in all categories had become less capital-intensive, at annual rates of 3–18 per cent during the period 1984–5 to 1989–90. However, annual growth rate has been as high as 38 per cent in textile urban NDMEs. The decline in capital intensity could not be offset by growth in a few categories from 1989–90 to 1994–5, because rapid growth has been seen only in categories which, to begin with, had grown in capital intensity from 1984–5 and growth, if it occurred, in the other categories was not high relative to the rates of decline in the previous period.

Unlike the previous periods, capital-intensity grew quite rapidly, in most categories, from 1994–5 to 2000–1, with the annual average growth rates ranging from 2 per cent to 47 per cent, the only exception being urban apparel DMEs. One more noteworthy observation is that the apparel sector has grown capital-intensive much faster than the textile sector, wherever it has grown, explaining why apparel sector has become more capital-intensive than textile sector in this year, in contrast with 1994–5 figures. While growth rates were much higher in the textile sector in the urban sample than those in the rural sample, the reverse holds true for the apparel sector, with an exception of DMEs. The other observations in growth rates may be made directly from Table 11.7.

Labour Productivity

While the textile sector was less labour-productive than the apparel sector in OAME, the reverse holds true for NDME, during 1984–5. NDMEs were more labour-productive than OAMEs in all sectors and areas. Urban enterprises were more labour-productive than those in rural areas. While rural textile OAME was least labour-productive (Rs 1800), urban textile NDME was most labour-productive (around Rs 12,000).

Except for rural textile enterprises, labour productivity increased in all categories from 1984–5 to 1989–90. Urban enterprises and NDMEs were more labour-productive than rural enterprises and OAMEs, respectively, during 1989–90. The fact that the apparel sector was more labour-productive than the textile sector is violated only by urban NDMEs, which were the most labour-productive (about Rs 19,800). Rural textile OAMEs were least labour-productive (about Rs 1780 per person).

In 1994–5, except in urban OAMEs and DMEs, labour productivity, which varied from around Rs 1800 to Rs 19,000, was lower in the apparel sector than in textile sector. Urban enterprises, DMEs and NDMEs were more labour-productive than rural enterprises, NDMEs and OAMEs, respectively.

During 2000–1, DMEs were more labour-productive than NDMEs which, in turn, were more labour-productive than OAMEs. With an exception of OAMEs, the apparel sector was more labour-productive than the textile sector. Urban enterprises were more labour-productive than rural ones. Labour productivity varied from Rs 2300 to Rs 24,000 during this year.

Between 1984–5 and 1989–90, labour productivity grew in all categories at average annual rates ranging from 1.8 per cent to 26 per cent except for the textile sector in the rural sample, where it declined at relatively lower rates. In contrast, labour productivity declined in all categories except rural textiles, where it had grown at about 6 per cent per year, from 1989–90 to 1994–5. This decline was a bit more pronounced in the apparel sector than in the textile sector.

In the period between 1994–5 and 2000–1, labour productivity has grown in the textile sector in all categories except rural NDMEs, in which it declined at an annual rate of less than 1 per cent. In the rural areas, the apparel sector had grown in this aspect, at 3–13 per cent per year, except in DMEs, which saw a decline of around 3 per cent per year. Urban apparel enterprises became less labour productive in all categories at 1–6 per cent per year.

Overall Inferences on Partial Productivity Measures

With a few exceptions, NDMEs, rural enterprises, and the textile sector were more capital-productive than OAMEs, urban enterprises and the apparel sector, respectively, in 1984–5. While capital productivity grew in most categories during 1984–5 to 1989–90, the other observations are the same as for 1984–5, except that the apparel sector was more capital productive than the textile sector. From 1989–90 to 1994–5, capital productivity declined in almost all categories, with that of DMEs being the highest among all enterprise types. The observation that DMEs in urban areas are more capital-productive than those in rural areas is the only other difference between the figures in 1994–5 vis-à-vis those in 1989–90. In 2000–1, capital productivity conspicuously declined in all categories, more so in urban than in rural areas, explaining the fact that enterprises in rural areas were more capital-productive than those in urban areas. One striking observation is the fall in capital productivity in the apparel sector both in absolute and relative terms and hence the apparel sector was less capital-productive in apparel sector than in textile sector.

In 1984–5, capital intensity was much higher in the apparel sector, urban areas, and NDMEs than, respectively, the textile sector, rural areas, and OAMEs with few exceptions. The same is true for 1989–90 with no exceptions, though capital intensity fell sharply in most categories since 1984–5. Between 1989–90 and 1994–5, there was little, no, or negative growth in the capital intensity.

The textile sector was more capital-intensive than the apparel sector in rural DMEs. While rural DMEs were more capital intensive than rural NDMEs, urban DMEs were less capital-intensive than urban NDMEs in 1994–5 and the other observations were identical to those in 1989–90. In 2000–1, the apparel sector was more capital-intensive than the textile sector in all categories except DMEs. Urban enterprises were much more capital-intensive than rural ones. Capital intensity was much higher during 2000–1 than that during 1994–5 across all categories.

While the textile sector was less labour-productive than the apparel sector in OAME, the reverse holds true for NDME, during 1984–5, when urban enterprises and NDMEs were more labour-productive than, respectively, rural enterprises and OAME. Labour productivity had increased in most categories from 1984–5 to 1989–90. Except for the fact that the apparel sector was more labour-productive than the textile sector in most cases, relative positions remain the same as in 1984–5. In 1994–5, labour productivity was lower in the apparel sector than in the textile sector for all categories except urban OAMEs and DMEs.

Urban enterprises, DMEs and NDMEs were more labour-productive than rural enterprises, NDMEs, and OAMEs, respectively. While labour productivity grew in most of the textile sector during the period 1994–5 to 2000–1, with the exception of OAMEs, the apparel sector was more labour-productive than the textile sector.

To highlight the findings of this section with a developmental perspective, two observations need to be mentioned. First, urban enterprises have been performing better than rural enterprises in most sub-sectors and measures in the unorganized textile sector. This reiterates the dominant problem of the rural–urban divide even in this section of the economy. Second, DMEs have performed better than NDMEs, which have performed better than OAMEs in this sector. This supports the argument that smaller firms may not be in a position to perform better than larger ones. It highlights the need to encourage the relatively susceptible segments of the industry, so as to provide a level-playing field. To sum up, with a viewpoint of development, the unorganized textile sector has been facing an issue of polarization, with certain segments within it being in a better position than the others. This is not a very healthy trend for the development of the economy, given the immense contrubution of the unorganized textile sector to the aggregate textile sector as well as to the manufacturing sector. Policies are required to specifically address this issue in the near future.

DOMESTIC CONSUMPTION OF TEXTILES IN INDIA

Household textile demand holds immense significance in the Indian economy. Given India's population, and more importantly its exploding growth rate, textiles, as a part of the subsistence trio (food, clothing, and shelter), are poised to be among the key factors of demand. Tables 11.10 and 11.11 reveal that the share of clothing in the total expenditure of an average Indian household is around 6–7 per cent in recent years.

The share of textiles and clothing in total expenditure can be considered an indicator of development for the countries, because the more the households in a country spend relatively on clothing, the more developed and comfortable they are with their other basic necessities, especially, food. Thus, there seems to be some scope of increasing the per capita demand for clothing, which could show up as an increase in the share of clothing in the total expenditure. In fact, as a share of non-food expenditure, clothing expenditure has fallen 10 per cent in both urban and rural households, which is clearly a cause for worry.

Sickness of various textile mills in the past has been largely attributed by a number of studies to lack of demand in the country. Though most of these studies were based on the data and scenario till the late 1980s, a demand constraint

TABLE 11.10
Trends in Per capita Consumption Expenditures and Shares on Clothing in Rural India

(*current prices*)

Per-capita Expenditure on	1989–90	1993–4	1999–2000	2000–1	2001–2	2002–3	2003–4	2004–5
Clothing (Rs)	10.52	21.20	33.28	35.94	35.33	37.68	38.58	62.48
Non-food	57.28	108.30	197.36	216.34	221.92	239.21	255.68	619.74
Total (Rs)	158.10	286.10	486.16	494.90	498.27	531.49	555.55	1104.84
Share of Clothing in non-food	0.18	0.20	0.17	0.17	0.16	0.16	0.15	0.10
Share of Clothing in total	0.07	0.07	0.07	0.07	0.07	0.07	0.07	0.06

Source: Author's calculations from the *Report on 60th Round of National Sample Survey on Consumption Expenditure*.

TABLE 11.11
Trends in Per Capita Consumption Expenditures and Share of Clothing in Urban India

(current prices)

Per-capita Expenditure on	1989–90	1993–4	1999–2000	2000–1	2001–2	2002–3	2003–4	2004–5
Clothing (Rs)	15.00	32.70	51.76	58.16	57.81	60.83	60.08	62.48
Non-food	110.18	214.00	444.08	514.01	530.48	582.18	593.56	619.74
Total (Rs)	249.92	464.30	854.92	914.57	932.79	1011.97	1022.68	1104.84
Share of Clothing in non-food	0.14	0.15	0.12	0.11	0.11	0.10	0.10	0.10
Share of Clothing in total	0.06	0.07	0.06	0.06	0.06	0.06	0.06	0.06

Source: Author's calculations from the *Report on 60th Round of National Sample Survey on Consumption Expenditure.*

can be expected to have been persistent in the textile sector, at least till 2005, when the MFA quotas were phased out, leading to a boom in demand from the sector. This demand for clothing seems to have two dimensions relevant for a country's development: its own intrinsic value as an indicator of development; and its implications for the supply-side and hence the employment aspects.

Table 11.12 shows that the aggregate household purchases of textiles have grown over the years, though the per capita purchases have either been stagnant or have fallen, unlike exports, which have been increasing for decades, despite the quota system. The domestic demand trends are not in line with the trends in domestic production. Thus, there is clearly a domestic demand constraint for textiles in India.

TABLE 11.12
Indian Textile and Apparel Sector—
Trends in Growth of Supply and Demand

Period	Aggregate Household Purchases	Per capita Household Purchases	Exports	Supply (Production)
1975–80	3.519	0.991	3.877	6.35
1980–5	4.742	2.225	0.402	4.841
1986–94	0.875	–1.08	14.478	10.518
1995–2000	3.026	1.129	19.045	5.033

Source: Author's calculations from Different yearbooks of ASI, Compendium of Textile Statistics and Consumer's Purchases in Textiles.

The demand constraints are attributed to the excise structure that is highly biased towards cotton and other natural fibres as well as textile commodities that are manufactured by relatively less efficient ways, such as without power and steam. Table 11.13 shows the excise structure over the years in different textile fibres, while Tables 11.14 and 11.15 show this for different yarns and fabrics, respectively.

Before an examination of the figures in these tables, it is imperative to note a few things. First, natural fibres, hank yarn (plain reel and cross reel up to 25s), all fabrics processed without aid of power and steam and products of factories owned by/registered to the National Handloom Development Corporation, State Government Handloom Development Corporations and Khadi and Village Industries Commission have no excise duty to begin with. Second, since 1995–6, a provision was made in the budget to make a part of excise duty in lieu of sales tax for all fabrics and hence the figures from this year are slightly higher than what they effectively are, in comparison with those for the previous years. Third, handloom cotton fabrics and those processed by independent power processors approved by the government have an excise duty that is 40 per cent of that for the mill and powerloom sector.

Woollen fabrics made of shoddy yarn were exempted up to the value of Rs 60/sq. metres till 1992–3 and Rs 100/sq. metres since 1993–4. Hank yarn exemption was withdrawn from 2002–3, but the exemption to hank yarns of coarse counts up to 2s using condenser card machines is maintained. Since 2004–5, duties are applicable with centralized value added taxes for natural fibre yarns and all fabrics.

Considering the fact that the recent figures for excise duties consist of what was sales tax before as well, it can be observed that there is a falling trend in almost all commodity groups.

TABLE 11.13
Trends in Excise Structure of Various
Textile Staple Fibres in India, 1992–2005

Year	Acrylic, Viscose	Polyester	Nylon	Acetate	Polypropylene
1992–3	15.6	13.65	59.15	15.6	17.87
1993–4	14.95	12.65	14.95	14.95	17.25
1994–5	23	23	23	23	23
1995–6	23	23	23	23	23
1996–7	23	23	23	23	23
1997–8	20.7	20.7	20.7	20.7	20.7
1998–9	20.7	20.7	20.7	20.7	20.7
1999–2000	18.4	18.4	18.4	18.4	18.4
2000–1	18.4	18.4	18.4	18.4	18.4
2001–2	18.4	18.4	18.4	18.4	18.4
2002–3	18.4	18.4	18.4	18.4	18.4
2003–4	18.4	18.4	18.4	18.4	18.4
2004–5	16.32	16.32	16.32	16.32	16.32

Source: Compendium of Textile Statistics, Annual Books published by the Office of Textile Commissioner, Ministry of Textiles, Government of India for the years from 1994 to 2005.

TABLE 11.14
Trends in Excise Structure of Various Textile Yarns Based on Filaments and Staple Fibres in India, 1992–2005

(in percentage ad valorem.)

Year	Hank Yarn	Cone Yarn	Polyester Viscose	Polyester Cotton	Polyester Wool	Polyester Filament	Nylon Filament	Viscose Filament	Wool Yarn
1992–3	0.39–2.60	0.35–9.75	15.6	7.8	15.6	80.6	25–71.5	5.2–19.5	0
1993–4	0.23–2.30	0.58–9.78	16.1	8.05	16.1	69	26.5–57.5	5.18–19.55	0
1994–5	3.45	5.75	23	23	23	69	23–34.5	11.5–17.25	11.5
1995–6	3.45	5.75	23	23	23	57.5	23–34.5	11.5–17.25	11.5
1996–7	3.45	5.75	23	23	23	46	23–34.5	11.5–23	11.5
1997–8	3.45	5.75	20.7	20.7	20.7	34.5	20.7–34.5	9.2–20.7	9.2
1998–9	3.45	5.75	20.7	20.7	20.7	34.5	20.7–34.5	9.2–20.7	9.2
1999–2000	0	9.2	18.4	18.4	18.4	34.5	27.6	18.4	9.2
2000–1	0	9.2	18.4	18.4	18.4	36.8	18.4	18.4	9.2
2001–2	0	9.2	18.4	18.4	18.4	36.8	18.4	18.4	18.4
2002–3	0–9.20	9.2	18.4	18.4	18.4	36.8	18.4	18.4	18.4
2003–4	0–9.20	9.2	13.8	13.8	13.8	27.6	13.8	13.8	13.8
2004–5	0–9.2	9.2	8.16	8.16	8.16	24.48	16.32	16.32	8.16

Source: Compendium of Textile Statistics, Annual Books published by the Office of Textile Commissioner, Ministry of Textiles, Government of India for the years from 1994 to 2005.

TABLE 11.15
Trends in Excise Structure of Various Textile Fabrics in India, 1992–2005

Year	Cotton Fabrics	Blended/Synthetic Fabrics	Woollen Fabrics[1]	Woollen Fabrics[2]	Woollen Fabrics[3]
1992–3	0.2–2.5+20% of value > Rs 40/sq. metres	0.5–20%	2.0–9.0	7.1–14.4	10.86–18.00
1993–4	0.2–2.5+20 % of value > Rs 40/sq. metres	0.5–20 %	2.0–9.4	7.95–15.50	10.75–18.80
1994–5	10	10–20%	0–16.50	16.5	16.50–22.25
1995–6	5–10%	10–20%	22.25	22.25	22.25
1996–7	10–20%	20	22.25	22.25	22.25
1997–8	10–20%	20	22.25	22.25	22.25
1998–9	10–20%	20	22.25	22.25	22.25
1999–2000	13–16	16	21	21	21
2000–1	16	16	21	21	21
2001–2	16	16	16	16	16
2002–3	12	12	12	12	12
2003–4	10	10	10	10	10
2004–5	4.08	8.16	8.16	8.16	8.16

Notes: The units are percentage ad valorem for all except woollen fabrics, for which the units are rupees per sq. metre, unless otherwise mentioned; [1] manufactured by independent processors; [2] manufactured by decentralized sector and processed by mills; [3] manufactured and processed by composite mills.

Source: Compendium of Textile Statistics, Annual Books for the years from 1994 to 2005.

Another inference is that the excise structure is now much simpler than it was before. For example, while it was different for each type of staple fibre before, it is the same for all the synthetic stable fibres in the recent years. Filament yarns in general and polyester in particular, are the commodity groups for which the excise duties appear to be the highest.

For simplicity, we have not shown the excise structure of the intermediates involved in the production of synthetics. For most of them, excise has remained static at around 15–18 per cent for the past ten years. Thus, it is very clear that the excise structure is still highly biased towards natural fibres, though this has been reduced to a large extent. Further, less efficient ways of manufacturing such as those that do not use power and steam pay less excise duties, leading to higher relative marginal costs of production for the more efficient manufacturers. This kind of differentiation is removed only in the case of woollen fabrics, as noted in Table 11.15.

A recent exercise on demand estimation, using a dynamic, almost-ideal demand system, performed for a monthly household-level survey data on textile purchases from 1994 to 2003, by the author,[17] shows that the cross-price elasticities among the twelve major commodity groups within textiles are negligible compared to the own-price elasticities, which are very high for synthetic and blended textiles and low for cotton textiles. These findings are in line with the older studies on textile demand, showing that not much has changed in the textile consumption pattern in India over years. This is summarized in Table 11.16, where the own-price elasticities and expenditure elasticities are shown in bold. It is evident that the cross-price elasticities are negligible compared to these. Further, own-price elasticities are strikingly higher in synthetics than in cotton and wool.

All these observations, put together, point towards two major facts. The first is the biased nature of the excise structure that has kept not only synthetic/blended textiles more expensive than they should have been, but has also encouraged the less-efficient means of production, albeit for developmental purposes such as equity. The second is that a reduction of this bias by lowering the excise on synthetics/blended textiles and more efficient means of production, would not cause a fall in demand for conventional textiles, as the cross-price elasticities hardly play a role. Further, such a reduction would enhance the demand for all non-cotton commodity groups, without affecting the demand for cotton and other conventional commodity groups.

Thus, it is quite understandable that a cut in excise duties of synthetic and blended textiles will be beneficial to the Indian textile sector, as a whole. While presenting the Union Budget for the year 2006–7, the Finance Minister probably had these issues in mind while reducing the excise duty of manmade and blended fibres from 16 per cent to 8 per cent. This is, indeed, a welcome step. While we have focussed only on domestic demand, this has implications also for India's competitiveness vis-à-vis the other countries in the textile sector, in international trade.

Thus, it may be said with a reasonable degree of confidence that the Indian textile sector will benefit immensely from this step in the budget. The major point emphasized in this section, which is less obvious, is that a cut in duties will not affect the conventional textiles sector, owing to the low cross-price elasticities between the textile commodity groups. This is essential not only for the well-being and better performance of the sectors, per se, but also for the standards of living of the masses, in terms of textile consumption.

This observation is significant in terms of the developmental perspective as well. It should be highlighted that the consumption of textiles itself is as much a measure of development as is the consumption of food. Hence, enhancing textile consumption should be an inherent feature of developmental policies. In addition, enhanced textile demand would benefit the supply side as well, which is immensely significant for the development of the economy in general.

CONCLUSIONS

This chapter aimed to analyse the integration of the Indian textile sector into the global economy, with the objectives of development being preserved. While doing this, the trends in annual value, shares, and monthly average value of exports from India were studied. It is illustrated that though there was a rapid rise in exports in 2003–4, they

TABLE 11.16
Elasticities of Various Textile Commodity Groups to their Prices and Textile Expenditure

Elasticity of: With Respect to:	Acrylic	Viscose	Cotton	Cotton-Viscose	Nylon	Polyester	Polyester-Cotton	Silk	Polyester-Viscose	Polyester-Wool	Wool
Acrylic	**−0.851**	0.008	0.045	0.013	0.073	−0.070	−0.036	−0.001	−0.109	−0.033	−0.021
Viscose	0.010	**−0.920**	0.035	0.025	0.134	−0.056	0.046	−0.024	−0.031	−0.002	−0.027
Cotton	0.007	−0.020	**−0.667**	−0.024	−0.054	0.042	−0.323	0.002	0.034	0.036	0.021
Cotton-Viscose	0.006	0.010	−0.010	**−0.876**	−0.099	−0.001	−0.017	−0.001	−0.001	0.003	−0.012
Nylon	0.012	0.023	−0.010	−0.037	**−1.334**	0.009	−0.036	0.009	0.046	0.036	−0.0003
Polyester	−0.061	−0.053	0.117	0.001	0.054	**−0.948**	0.188	−0.019	−0.043	−0.032	−0.055
Polyester-Cotton	−0.022	0.055	−0.340	−0.023	−0.157	0.198	**−0.906**	0.015	−0.012	0.036	−0.026
Silk	−0.001	−0.067	0.149	0.005	0.158	−0.054	0.025	**−0.936**	0.011	−0.133	−0.089
Polyester-Viscose	−0.043	−0.014	0.040	0.001	0.107	−0.020	−0.011	0.001	**−0.688**	−0.042	−0.040
Polyester-Wool	−0.021	−0.004	0.044	0.004	0.126	−0.024	0.021	−0.033	−0.066	**−0.730**	−0.045
Wool	−0.035	−0.049	0.110	−0.045	−0.001	−0.109	−0.059	−0.057	−0.179	−0.126	**−0.713**
Textile Expenditure	**1.000**	**1.039**	**0.487**	**0.982**	**0.941**	**1.018**	**1.129**	**1.037**	**1.005**	**0.981**	**1.032**

Source: Author's calculations.

[17] Details of this model, not shown here for simplicity and space constraint, are available on request from the author.

have either been falling subsequently in most sub-sectors, or at best, they are stagnant.

Further, it is seen that the share of textile and apparel exports in the total exports from India has fallen over the years, despite the phasing out of MFA quotas and the subsequent rise in absolute value of textile exports. This is a significant observation, as it contradicts the expectation that textile exports must have exploded, at least in relation to other exports. This is possibly due to bottlenecks on the supply side, as there are no major external demand constraints, given the removal of quotas.

On examining the organized textile and apparel sector, it is seen that employment is stagnant, while capital and output have been increasing in the recent years. In the organized textile sector, employment has been falling for the past few decades, though the effective rate of protection has been falling, indicating elimination of rigidities in the economy. In the apparel sector, it is increasing, along with capital and output, despite a much lower increase in the number of factories. This indicates a structural change, in terms of huge investment and increase in scales of operation, since its dereservation from the SSI sector in 2000. Better prospects of employment seem possible in the apparel sector in the future, though they should be enhanced in the textile sector as well, through promoting investments.

Investment could be encouraged by better credit disbursement policies. In this connection, it should be noted, however, that credit disbursement through the TUFS scheme, as a fraction of credits applied for, has been decent enough (see Table 11.17).[18] A glance at the figures in the table suggest that the disbursement of credit has been fairly good especially in the case of the agencies that are meant for promoting the SSIs (SIDBI and NCDC), with an application-rejection rate of less than 2 per cent and credit disbursement rate of around 70 per cent, though the figures are less impressive for agencies that lend to all industries (ICICI, IDBI, IFCI, IIBI, and EXIM Bank). To the extent that SSIs are more dependent on the sources of credit such as TUFS than the other industries, these figures show that credit disbursement is not a major issue. In fact, the same can be said for other industries too, though not to the extent as that for SSIs. Thus, the reasons for low investment may be a lack of awareness among entrepreneurs about these schemes and the government should take steps to promote them.

As for the unorganized textile sector, employment has been increasing, despite a fall in capital and output, an issue that is in striking contrast with that in the organized textile sector. In the late 1990s and till 2001, capital productivity had declined in this sector, more so in urban than in rural areas. Capital intensity was much higher during 2000–1 than that during 1994–5 in all categories. While labour productivity grew in most of the textile sector between 1994–5 and 2000–1, with the exception of OAME, the apparel sector was more labour-productive than the textile sector. Enterprises in rural areas were more capital-productive, less capital-intensive and less labour-productive than those in urban areas. The apparel sector was less capital-productive, more capital-intensive (except in DMEs) and more labour-productive than in the textile sector. These trends varied across enterprise types as well. A major observation relevant for the developmental perspective is that there has been a divide between various segments within the textile sector, in terms of performance.

The analysis of household demand has shown that per capita textile purchases have been declining in real terms during the past few years. The excise and customs duties on manmade fibre textiles have been a barrier in increasing their purchases due to the fact that they are reflected in their prices

TABLE 11.17
Credit Applications that were Received and Disbursed under TUFS

Nodal Agencies	Credit Applications Received			Credits Disbursed			No. of applications rejected
	No. of applications	Project Cost	Amount of loan required	No. of applications	Project Cost	Amount sanctioned	
Agencies that lend to all industries	1290	23031.07	12237.79	950 (73.64)	14224.00 (61.68)	6682.58 (55.00)	118 (9.15)
Agencies that lend only to SSIs	2379	2498.38	1480.32	1930 (81.13)	1778.29 (71.18)	1006.88 (68.04)	44 (1.85)
Total	3669	25529.45	13718.11	2880 (78.50)	16002.29 (62.26)	7689.46 (56.04)	162 (4.42)

Note: Figures corresponding to costs/amount in the table are in crores of rupees and those in brackets are percentages of the corresponding total.

Source: Author's calculations based on a report on 'Progress of TUFS as on 30.11.2004', issued by the Office of the Textile Commissioner, Mumbai.

[18] See Narayanan (2005) for more details in this regard.

and the demand for these products is highly own-price elastic. Given the fact that the cross-price elasticity between cotton and such fibres is negligible compared to the own-price elasticities, rise in demand for textiles in India without a fall in the demand for the conventional textiles could be ensured by fall in prices of manmade fibre textiles, which is possible only by a cut in excise duties and customs for these products, as has been done in the recent years. This appears to be a significant step in fostering development in the country, from the viewpoints of the supply side as well as the demand side.

References

Beena, P.L. (2006), 'Limits to Universal Trade Liberalisation: The Contemporary Scenario for Textiles & Clothing Sector in South Asia', Centre for Development Studies Working Paper No. 379. Thiruvanthapuram.

Gokhale, C.S. and V. Katti (1995), 'Globalising Indian Textiles: Threats and Opportunities', Tecoya Disseminators, Bombay.

Misra, S. (1993), *India's Textile Sector: A Policy Analysis*, Sage Publishers, New Delhi.

Narayanan, G. Badri (2005), 'Questions on Textile Industry Competitiveness', *Economic and Political Weekly*, 26 February–4 March 2005.

NSSO (1989), *NSS 40th Round (July 1984–June 1985), Tables with Notes on Survey of Unorganized Manufacture: Non-Directory Establishments and Own Account Enterprises, Part I, Part II (Volume 1 and 2)*, Number 363/1, National Sample Survey Organization, Department of Statistics, Government of India, New Delhi.

——— (1994), *NSS 45th Round (July 1989–June 1990), Tables with Notes on Survey of Unorganised Manufacture: Non-Directory Establishments and Own Account Enterprises, Part-I (All-India)*, Number 396/2, National Sample Survey Organization, Department of Statistics, Government of India, New Delhi.

——— (1998), *NSS 51st Round (July 1994–June 1995), Assets and Borrowings of the Unorganised Manufacturing Sector in India*, Number 435, National Sample Survey Organization, Department of Statistics, Government of India, New Delhi.

——— (2002), *NSS 56th round (July 2000 June 2001), Unorganised Manufacturing Sector in India: Characteristics of Enterprises*, Number 477, National Sample Survey Organization, Department of Statistics, Government of India, New Delhi.

Roy, T. (1996), *Cloth and Commerce: Textiles in Colonial India*, Sage Publications, New Delhi.

Sastry, D.U. (1984), *The Cotton Mill Sector in India*, Oxford University Press, New Delhi.

12

Globalization, Employment, and Labour Market Flexibility
The Case of India

K.V. Ramaswamy

THE ISSUES

The impact of global integration of markets on the quantity and quality of jobs has been a contentious issue. This is not surprising as the labour market is one of the main channels through which globalization affects a country's economy and workers. Globalization (a world without barriers to trade and investment) is widely perceived to result in negative labour market outcomes, that is, job losses and reduction in earnings. (are your wage levels set in Beijing?) Three major areas of concern have been the loss of good jobs in industries losing competitiveness, biased technological change against unskilled workers and the informalization of the workforce 'race to the bottom'. All these reasons taken together suggest that globalization could put labour markets under pressure. This outcome could lead to greater social conflicts as a consequence of unemployment and increasing wage inequalities.

In the context of India, accelerating output growth in recent years has not been accompanied by a faster rate of job growth. In particular, the slow growth of regular jobs and the intensification of duality in labour markets (formal versus informal) has become a serious problem. This is evident from the data on non-agricultural employment shown in Table 12.1. Formal sector jobs in the non-agricultural sector have grown by just 0.6 per cent per annum in the 1990s. Recent data suggest that meagre growth rates continue, with the exception of the IT sector (IT and IT enabled services).[1] The Indian economy needs to create a large number of jobs for the unskilled workers who are currently unemployed or employed in the informal sector and those who will be entering the labour force in the next few years. The high rate of job creation in the IT sector will be for the educated (skilled) workers with specific skill sets. In this situation, the pressure is on the manufacturing sector—where currently the growth rate of jobs is only 2 per cent—to absorb unskilled labour. This underlines the need for policies that are conducive to faster growth of regular jobs in the Indian industry.

The employment effects of trade and investment liberalization (prime movers of globalization) may depend, among other factors, on the labour market institutions. Any analysis of globalization needs to recognize the crucial role of labour market institutions on employment outcomes. An inseparable factor complicating the entire issue has been the role of job security regulations (JSR).[2] Countries differ with

---

[1] The IT sector has registered high rates of employment growth of more than 25 per cent in recent years. Total employment of the IT sector is above 1 million (NASSCOM reports).

[2] JSR are one component of labour market institutions. Other components are trade unions and wage bargaining rules, statutory minimum wages, regulations governing working condition, payroll taxes etc.

TABLE 12.1
Distribution and Growth of Non-agricultural Employment, 1994–2000

	1993–4		1999–2000		
	Total (Millions)	Percentage Share	Total (Millions)	Percentage Share	Growth Rate*
Mining and Quarrying	2.7	2.0	2.27	1.4	−2.85
Manufacturing	42.5	32.2	48.01	30.1	2.05
Electricity	1.35	1.0	1.28	0.8	−0.88
Construction	11.68	8.8	17.62	11.1	7.09
Wholesale and Retail Trade	27.78	21.0	37.32	23.4	5.04
Transport, Storage, and Communication	10.33	7.8	14.69	9.2	6.04
Financial Services and Social Services	3.52	2.7	5.05	3.2	6.2
Personal Services	32.13	24.3	33.2	20.8	0.55
Total Non-agriculture	131.99	100	159.44	100	3.2
Organized Sector	25.7	80.5	26.7	83.2	0.6

Note: *Average annual compound growth rate.

Source: Report of the Task Force on Employment Opportunities, Planning Commission, 2001.

respect to the kind of institutions (legislative/administrative rules and procedures) set up to govern worker–employer relations and to regulate working conditions. The JSR may be defined to include all those legal provisions that increase the cost of workforce adjustment by retrenchment of workers. They are supposed to constrain adjustment responses of firms to competitive conditions and inhibit firing decisions (labour market inflexibility). Firms are reported to have responded by hiring more temporary or contract workers and outsourcing production to firms in the informal sector (outside the purview of labour regulations). This is argued to suggest de facto flexibility undermining the need for labour market reforms.[3] Arguably, the existence of de facto flexibility is not a justification for stringent labour laws if the social outcome is greater number of low quality jobs (temporary/contract workers). This raises the question of how to provide social safety nets for workers[4] without harming hiring incentives for firms. This is a major challenge for countries such as India. In this context, it is useful to set out the interlinked factors that determine the employment outcomes of globalization.

GLOBALIZATION AND EMPLOYMENT

Causal Links and Alternative Outcomes

Globalization implies removal of barriers to international trade and investment. The traditional theories of trade predict resource reallocation between sectors. The Ricardian comparative advantage predicts resource movement towards sectors with comparative advantage. Resources move from relatively less productive to relatively more productive industries. This leads to changes in employment in different industries. The alternative approach (Hecksher-Ohlin approach or H-O model) is based on relative factor endowments. The H-O theory, assuming competitive product and factor markets, argues that trade liberalization generates demand for the abundant factor (unskilled labour in developing countries) because of expansion of export sectors, raising both employment and the relative price (wages) of unskilled labour. The demand for skilled workers and their relative wages will fall as the demand for skill intensive goods contracts due to contraction of import competing goods. Consequently, the wage differential between the skilled and unskilled will fall. Therefore, the prediction for developing countries is that the employment opportunity of unskilled workers increases and wage inequality declines. What other market conditions and institutions help or hinder this positive and desirable outcome of trade liberalization?

AGGREGATE EMPLOYMENT

Reinforcing Factors

1. *Slicing up of the value chain.* Globalization implies 'breaking up of the production process into many geographically separated steps'. A good is produced in a number of stages in a variety of locations, adding value at each stage. Producers locate the different stages such that it improves access to resources and facilitates penetration of newly expanding

---

[3] In addition, firms have pursued downsizing by offering 'golden handshakes' or voluntary retirement schemes (VRS) to their employees. VRS are prominent in the public sector enterprises as also in large private sector enterprises such as Tata Steel. This immediately suggests that the use of VRS for workforce adjustment depends on the access to financial resources, which is not available to all firms.

[4] As India does not have unemployment benefits/insurance system, job security law is a form of social security. At the same time, this restricts the job creation capacity of the economic system.

markets. In effect, globalization promotes specialization in terms of the development of market niches. This process of slicing up of the value chain provides greater room for developing countries to specialize in the labour intensive stages of the manufacturing process of a commodity which, as a whole, might be capital intensive. This should create more employment opportunities in low-wage (labour abundant) countries.

2. *Pro-competitive Effect.* Many protected industries are dominated by a few firms and concentrated market structures. Import liberalization, by reducing price mark-ups in imperfectly competitive industries, results in output expansion. This may create more employment. This positive employment effect depends on the employment share of such industries in total industry employment.

3. *Foreign capital and exports.* Openness induces flow of more FDI to the developing economies with large domestic markets. This stimulates output expansion and more employment (for both skilled and unskilled labour) in the aggregate. Employment in both import competing (IC) and export oriented (EO) sectors may experience growth. Export growth relaxes foreign exchange constraints and facilitates access to intermediate goods (machinery and raw materials). This would stimulate growth in output and employment.

Offsetting Factors

1. *Employment in IC Sectors.* The IC sectors (protected industries) may experience large fall in employment. This is not offset by employment creation in industries with competitive advantage in the short to medium run. This could occur because of a variety of reasons, for example, the inadequacy of infrastructure (mainly power and transportation), inadequate financing of industrial investment by the financial sector or simply the short length of adjustment time available for expansion of industries with competitive advantage.

2. *Technology bias and new work organization.* The nature of production technologies that flow in from abroad may be skill-intensive. In other words, the new production methods that are used to improve the competitiveness of developing country exports in the global economy are biased against the use of unskilled labour. Therefore, the new demand for labour will benefit only skilled workers who constitute a small proportion of the workforce.[5]

3. *Organizational Change.* New forms of work organization and management practices introduced either by foreign or domestic firms to attain competitiveness may be biased against the use of unskilled labour.[6]

4. *Dual Labour Markets and Informalization.* Labour markets in developing countries are segmented into formal and informal sectors. In the formal sector of the labour market, government regulations (such as legislation on employment protection and minimum wages) and collective bargaining processes (trade unions) play a significant role in the determination of employment and wages. The informal segment is outside the job security regulations, pays lower wages, is free from union wage agreements, and largely escapes government regulations on health, environment, and safety. Consequently, firm size and quality of employment are positively associated. Globalization can change the composition of employment between formal and informal sectors. Greater competitive pressure forces formal sector firms to outsource labour and production to the informal sector. This will create only low quality jobs and an increasing informalization of workers. Workers laid off from the formal segment of import substituting industries may seek employment in the informal sector. This could cause wages to decline in an already low wage segment, thus increasing wage inequality. The occurrence of a shift from formal to informal sectors has been observed in many countries of Latin America, Asia, and Africa. Recent research on the impact of trade liberalization on labour markets has attempted to take into account the dual structure of labour markets in developing countries as well as the role of labour market regulations.

JOB SECURITY REGULATIONS: IMPACT ON LABOUR MARKETS

JSR play an important role in differentiating formal sectors from non-formal sectors of industry. JSR are mandated by the state to provide protection to workers against unjust termination.[7] The key question is the cost of dismissing a worker for economic reasons, for example, decline in demand or a change in technology used. They are argued to

---

[5] Often called 'skill-enhancing trade'. Note that technological change in the industrialized North also causes a widening of wage inequalities because of increasing demand for skilled workers relative to unskilled workers.

[6] Globalization can affect workers, in a subtle way, by changing the elasticity of labour demand. Globalization makes demand for final products more elastic which, in turn, causes labour demand elasticity to go up (remember that demand for labour is derived demand that depends on the demand for final output that workers help produce). The question of whether globalization has actually led to an increase in labour demand elasticity is an empirical matter.

[7] What constitutes 'unjust' or 'unfair' termination (dismissal) in the eyes of the law (courts) differs across countries. Job loss due to no fault of the worker is considered unjust. This excludes retirement due to superannuation, non-renewal of a pre-determined contract, termination due to misconduct/indiscipline/poor performance, and voluntary retirement.

inhibit the ability of firms to hire and fire workers in response to changing market conditions. JSR result in firing costs as they impose severance pay and procedural conditions on worker terminations. JSR include labour laws that determine the types of contracts offered by firms (permanent/contract (fixed term)/temporary/casual), the lengths of advance period prior to termination, and the compensation for dismissal. Labour laws specify the causes considered justified for dismissal, procedures to be followed for termination of services of a worker, the conditions of work, and the minimum wages.[8]

The Cost of Labour Regulations

This refers to the cost of complying with labour laws. JSR increase the cost of dismissing a worker for economic reasons. JSR require the firm to incur at least four types of costs:[9] (i) administrative procedures for termination, (ii) advance notification, (iii) compensation for dismissal, and (iv) the legal costs of a trial when the firm or the workers contest the decisions of the state authorities. Administrative procedures require the firm to notify and seek the approval of state authorities. This prolongs the period between termination decisions and actual terminations. They may involve negotiations with the trade unions. Advance notification is included because compensation equivalent to wages in lieu of notice is required to be paid. The compensation amount is based on multiples of the most recent wage and the years of service. Firms may be asked to pay the worker a subsistence allowance during the trial period and the foregone wages during trial, depending on the final court decision.

Predictions based on Theory

An important theoretical approach for understanding the impact of firing costs is the model of dynamic labour demand with adjustment costs.[10] The basic principle underlying labour demand when hiring and firing costs exist is that employers (firms) should take into account labour's marginal contribution to expected present discounted profits (shadow value of labour). Employment decisions should not be made on the basis of current profit conditions. The shadow value of labour is defined as the marginal increase in the discounted cash flow of the firm if it hires one additional unit of labour. In this framework, the employer compares the shadow value of labour to hiring (H) and firing (-F) costs. Firing would be optimal when the shadow value of labour (V) is less than the firing costs (-F). That is the marginal cost of severance payments and other costs entailed by dismissals. Concern about future firing costs induces firms to employ fewer units even in periods of strong labour demand (good states of the world). In periods of weak labour demand (bad states of the world), the employer has less incentive to fire, as the annualized cost savings from not firing workers is perceived as lower wage costs. Firing costs, therefore, induce labour hoarding on the part of firms. Firing costs reduce both hiring as well as firing by firms. This microeconomic behaviour implies that employment fluctuations are much narrower than actual fluctuations in marginal productivities experienced by firms. In brief, JSR reduce employment volatility.

However, the impact of firing costs on aggregate average employment rate is ambiguous. The average employment rate increases or decreases depending on whether the decline in hiring rates in expanding firms more than offsets the decline in firings in contracting firms. The net effect of firing costs on aggregate employment is an empirical matter. The JSR may also affect employment through an effect on wages. Firing costs may strengthen the position of insiders (incumbent workers in unionized firms) and increase their wages while reducing employment prospects for outsiders (say, in the informal sector).[11] Actual outcomes depend on many factors, leading to ambiguity in theoretical results. We may note that theoretical models focus on homogenous workers and productivity shocks as reasons for terminations. In reality, the JSR may make worker dismissal difficult even for disciplinary/poor performance reasons, raising expected costs of firing.

Efficiency Wages and Duality

The theory of efficiency wages is based on the idea that firms pay more than the competitive wages in order to prevent workers from shirking. They recognize that lower real wages are associated with lower productivity. Labour cost increases when a firm is expected to downsize by laying off workers. The intuition is that workers have a greater incentive to shirk when they expect the firm to downsize (probability of layoff is higher). To prevent workers from shirking, the firm has to raise future wages. Efficiency wages are, therefore, equivalent to costs of labour adjustment in a firm. In this framework, firms will have an incentive to set up a dual structure within the firm by employing tier-II workers who could be

---

[8] The state also mandates social security contributions like contributions to old age pensions, disability and death, sickness and maternity, unemployment insurance, and other allowances.

[9] This is based on Heckman and Pages (2004). The costs vary from country to country and across regions within a country. The costs are quantified in terms of monthly wages for Latin American and the OECD countries.

[10] See Bertola (1999) for a detailed discussion.

[11] This is the much discussed insider–outsider theory.

fired without cost. Firms will shift the burden of adjustment to tier-II workers and reduce the probability of dismissal of tier-I workers (thus, lowering labour costs).

The dual labour market models can be used to shed light on the response of labour markets in developing countries to trade liberalization and globalization. Consider the following set-up, close to conditions prevalent in India.[12] The firm can hire workers from two pools: a pool of formal workers and a pool of informal workers. The two pools differ in two important respects: first, the employment of workers is regulated by labour market regulations. Formal sector workers receive many benefits. They cannot be dismissed from service unless the firm has accumulated sufficient evidence. They will receive severance payment when dismissed. This implies that adjustment costs associated with the employment of such workers are higher relative to those associated with informal workers. Further, the cost of monitoring formal sector workers is higher. Therefore, the firms need to offer efficiency wages to motivate them. In this set-up, let us introduce tariff cuts (the first step in the move to globalize) that result in price shocks to the firm. Firms need to fire workers to remain in business. Given the efficiency wage, the expected marginal cost of hiring a formal worker increases. Firms will reduce hiring formal workers. Stricter labour market regulation implies probability of detecting and firing shirking workers is lower, which results in higher marginal cost of hiring formal sector workers. The share of the formal sector declines.

EMPIRICAL STUDIES

Many recent studies have consistently shown a negative impact of JSR on average employment rates both in OECD as well as Latin American countries.[13] A recent study (Heckman and Pages 2004) of OECD countries finds a statistically significant negative effect of compensation (indemnities) on employment rates. Another important study (di tella and MacCulloch 2005), examined data for 21 EU countries over a seven-year period (1984–90) using a measure of flexibility given by employers. They found a significant negative relationship between the degree of inflexibility and employment rate (defined as: total civilian employment as a proportion of working age population). According to this study, if France were to make its labour market as flexible as the United States, its employment rate would increase by 1.6 percentage points. This study reports that inflexible labour markets also produce 'jobless recoveries'. In 1997, Spain introduced certain incentives for firms to hire workers using permanent contracts: (i) reduction of severance payments from 45 to 33 days for young workers (below the age of 30 years) and (ii) reduction of payroll taxes paid by the firm for selected categories of workers (young and women workers etc). This reduction of dismissal costs increased the probabilities of employment of young workers on permanent contracts (Kugler et al. 2002). Two studies of labour demand in Peru and Argentina merit mention.[14] Both use firm-level panel data to estimate labour demand equations.

Box 12.1

Introducing Flexibility: The Case of Spain

The EU economies have attempted to introduce flexible provisions in their hiring regulations in recent years. Modification of hiring contract regulations for temporary workers is the chosen method. They are in effect 'marginal' reforms without touching the law on permanent contracts. The objective is 'flexibility at the margin'. In the first half of the 1990s, high unemployment in Spain triggered the adoption of deregulating measures. The key measure allowed the use of temporary workers in regular jobs. (Prior to this, fixed-term contracts could be used only for temporary/seasonal/transitory needs of the firm.) The result of this reform was a dramatic increase in the share of fixed-term contracts from less than 10 per cent prior to 1984 to more than 30 per cent in 1992. This is argued to have been detrimental to workers' welfare as it reduced employment stability (example, increase in the number of workers with jobs of less than 3 months tenure). In 1994, reforms again restricted the use fixed-term contracts to certain age groups and to temporary jobs. In 1997, further reforms led to the introduction of new permanent contracts with reduced 'dismissal costs' (a mandatory redundancy pay of 33 days per year instead of 45 days plus reduced social security contribution for new hires). By 2001, this policy reversal, in combination with the upturn in business cycle, created 1.5 million jobs (76 per cent of these were permanent jobs). In the private sector, a significant decline in the share of fixed contract workers (from 40 per cent to 32 per cent took place between 1995–2002. The lower dismissal costs offered by the new contract have acted as incentives to promote employment on a permanent basis. This case further suggested the possible negative effects of partial reforms that did not touch the nature of permanent contracts.

Sources: Casals (2004) and Dolado et al. (2002).

---

[12] Goldberg and Pavenick (2003).

[13] Empirical studies are large in number. They differ with respect to data (cross-country or cross-firm within a country) and econometric methods. Econometric results of many studies show negative but not necessarily statistically significant impact of JSR on average employment. See Heckman and Pages (2004) for a detailed discussion. We have ignored the studies that focus on unemployment rate in OECD countries, as they are not relevant in the Indian context.

[14] They are Saavedra and Torero (2004, Chapter 2) and Mondino and Montoya (2004, Chapter 6) in Heckman and Pages (2004).

Both introduce an explicit measure of the cost of JSR (expected severance payments/cost equivalence of regulations) on the right hand side of the equation in addition to average wage to explain labour demand. The Peru study includes all firms with more than 10 employees in all sectors and the Argentina study includes only manufacturing firms. They report statistically significant negative association between the cost of JSR and employment. These studies report that a 10 per cent increase in dismissal costs will reduce long-run employment rates by 3 to 6 per cent, keeping wages constant. In brief, the emerging set of labour market studies clearly suggests the negative impact of JSR on employment and hiring decisions of formal sector firms.

MANUFACTURING EMPLOYMENT IN INDIA: PAST TRENDS AND THE DEBATE

A survey of past trends in Indian manufacturing sector output, employment, and investment is available in the *India Development Report 2002* (Chapter 6). I focus here on some selected key arguments in the debate on jobless growth in the Indian manufacturing sector.[15] Slow growth of formal sector jobs in manufacturing has been the focus of debate in India. This is expected as the organized sector, though small in terms of size (formal factory sector's GDP share is around 16 per cent and it employed about 7 million out of a total workforce of 400 million in 2000), is a growing sector providing 'good jobs'. It is also the segment that was expected to absorb the surplus labour in the agricultural sector over time, as India industrialized. The growth rate of these supposedly good jobs has fluctuated during the last four decades. In the 1970s, the average growth rate of jobs in the formal sector was 3.8 per cent per annum while output was growing at 4.5 per cent. In the 1980s (1980–90) employment growth dropped to 0.53 per cent when output growth rate accelerated to 8.7 per cent. A recovery of employment growth rate was observed in the first half of the 1990s (2.1 per cent per annum between 1989–90 to 1994–5). This growth rate could not be sustained and declined in the second half of the 1990s to just 0.7 per cent. An important feature of the 1990s is the decline of employment in the public sector. Employment growth in public sector manufacturing was only 0.39 per cent in contrast to a growth rate of 3.7 per cent in the private sector during the period 1990–7.[16] Since 1999, private sector employment has also declined.

On the basis of the studies that have analysed this jobless growth, several key determinants of formal sector jobs growth may be identified. They are: (i) wages per worker; (ii) labour utilization/working days per worker; (iii) investment/capital formation rate; (iv) relative price of manufacturing goods; (v) growth of small firms; and (vi) labour regulations.[17] Each of these determinants was shown to have had varying importance in impacting employment growth in the 1980s and the 1990s. From today's perspective, the following points may be made. First, the current cost of labour measured by real wages per worker does not show a rising trend.[18] Labour utilization has improved and firms have downsized using VRS etc. Second, the relative prices of manufacturing goods have declined with an improvement in supply and the weakening/reduction of price controls on agriculture and infrastructure goods. This has contributed to greater price competition in the manufacturing sector. Third, investment for modernization and new capacity creation picked up in the first half of the 1990s but slowed down in the second half. Investment for upgrading and modernization continues to be important. Third, evidence on the rapid growth of efficient small–medium scale firms is scarce or unclear at best. Fourth, given our above understanding, accepting the argument that many factors impact employment growth, the question remains why job creation has not picked up even when output growth rates have recovered in recent years? Labour regulations appear to be the crucial factor in influencing the hiring decisions of the firms as they contribute to the expected cost of hiring workers today.

TRADE AND MANUFACTURING EMPLOYMENT IN INDIA IN THE 1990s[19]

A useful way of analysing the impact of trade liberalization on manufacturing employment is to classify industries by their trade orientation and estimate employment growth in two groups of industries; namely, EO and IC industries. An industry is classified as EO if its net exports to output ratio is significantly positive and it figures in the list of leading net

---

[15] I provide only a capsule summary of this debate. A detailed accessible survey of this literature is available in Goldar (2000), Bhalotra (2003), and Rani and Jeeemol (2004) among others.

[16] Goldar (2000).

[17] These are not mutually exclusive but interrelated factors.

[18] See Tendulkar (2006) for an analysis of 2-digit industry groups up to 1998. His analysis supports the idea that slower rate of growth of real product wages in the 1990s facilitated employment growth.

[19] This section draws partly from the study done for the World Bank (see Ramaswamy 2005). It uses the UNIDO database on industrial statistics at a 4-digit level of aggregation. UNIDO presents the data in a convenient format using the ISIC (Revised 2) classification up to the year 1997. For the period 1998 to 2001, the data are presented following the ISIC (Revised 3) classification. We have built the time series using the concordance table available for matching the two series. UNIDO industrial statistics are ASI statistics supplied by the CSO. We have checked the data for consistency using the ASI factory sector results published by the CSO.

export earners in the manufacturing sector in the year 1999. An industry is classified as IC if the net exports to output ratio is significantly negative. Some of the key industries based on this criterion are shown in Table 12.2 and the corresponding number of employees in each group for the year 2001–2 is shown in Table 12.3. The employment growth rates and the employment elasticity of output are estimated for each group of industries (see Tables 12.4 and Table 12.5). Contrary to theoretical predictions, IC industries created more jobs in the first of the 1990s. Import liberalization in the first period presumably improved access to imported inputs and facilitated higher output growth and employment. In the latter half of the 1990s, employment in IC industries declined. A significant fact to note is the impressive employment performance of EO industries. Employment elasticity of output is higher in EO industries. More recently available data also suggest positive employment growth in the automobile and tyre industries. Most of the job losses have occurred in the IC industries that are facing the brunt of structural adjustments. Job creation in other industries is expected to offset this job loss. More worrying factor is the type of structural shift in employment that is taking place within industries. First is the growth of informal sector employment relative to formal sector jobs (see Table 12.6).[20] Second is the growth of contract labour within the factory sector (see Table 12.7). Most of the job gains in the factory sector have taken place in the form of contract

TABLE 12.2
Key Industries in Six Industry Groups

Category	Key Industries
Export-oriented	Textile fabrics, apparel, footwear, drugs, and pharmaceuticals
Import Competing	Paper, iron and steel, electrical and non-electrical machinery, office and computing machinery, TV communication, watches and plastic products
Food, Beverages, and Tobacco	Grain mills, wine, soft drinks, cigarettes
Petroleum Refining and Coal Products	Petroleum refining products (naphtha, gasoline, diesel etc.) and coal and coke products
Auto and Tyre	Four wheelers, two-wheelers, bicycles, tyre and tubes, auto components
Others	Wood containers, cane, paper, rubber products, cement, glass, soap, and cosmetics.

Source: Ramaswamy (2005).

TABLE 12.3
Employment in Six Industry Groups, 2001–2

Industry Group	Employment (Millions)
Export-oriented	2.3
Import-Competing	1.8
Food	1.8
Petroleum	0.1
Auto–Tyres	0.5
Others	1.2
Totals	7.5

Source: Author's estimates based on UNIDO Data.

TABLE 12.4
Employment Growth Rates in Indian Manufacturing, 1989–2001*

	Export oriented	Importcompeting	Food	Petroleum	Auto–Tyres	'Others'
1989 to 1994	2.3	2.6	2.6	5.8	4.5	2.0
1994 to 2001	1.9	–1.4	–1.0	–0.5	–0.2	–2.3

Note: *Average of year over year growth.

Source: Author's estimates based on UNIDO statistics.

TABLE 12.5
Employment Elasticity in Indian Manufacturing by Industry

Years	Industry Groups						
	Export oriented	Import Competing	Food	Auto–Tyre	Petroleum	Others	All Manufacturing
1989–94 Elasticity	0.19	0.19	0.28	0.38	0.38	0.15	0.22
1994–2001 Elasticity	0.45	–0.41	–0.01	–0.03	–0.02	–0.43	–0.11

Source: Author's estimates based on UNIDO statistics.

[20] Rani and Jeemol (2004) present estimates of informal sector employment in different 3-digit industries.

TABLE 12.6
Organized Sector Jobs by Industry, 1994–2000

	1993–4		1999–2000		Share of Organized	
	Total	Organized	Total	Organized	1993–4	1999–2000
	(millions)		(millions)			
Mining and Quarrying	2.7	1.1	2.3	1.0	40.4	44.5
Manufacturing	42.5	6.4	48.0	6.8	15.1	14.1
Electricity	1.4	1.0	1.3	1.0	71.9	78.1
Construction	11.7	1.2	17.6	1.2	10.5	6.7
Wholesale and Retail Trade	27.8	0.5	37.3	0.5	1.6	1.3
Transport, Storage, and Communication	10.3	3.1	14.7	3.2	30.1	21.4
Financial and Social Services	3.5	1.5	5.1	1.7	43.5	32.7
Personal Services	32.1	10.9	33.2	11.5	34.0	34.6
Total Non-agriculture	132.0	25.7	159.4	26.7	19.5	16.8

Source: Report of the Task Force on Employment Opportunities, Planning Commission, 2001.

TABLE 12.7
Growth of Contract Labour in Factories
(*Average Daily Employment in Factory Sector*)

	1999–2000	2000–1	2001–2	2002–3
	Millions			
All Employees	8.2	8.0	7.8	7.9
All Workers	6.3	6.1	6.0	6.2
Contract Workers	1.2	1.3	1.3	1.4
Share in All workers	19.7	20.4	21.8	23.1

Source: http://labourbureau.nic.in/ accessed on 12 May 2006.

worker jobs. Contract jobs have grown at more than 4.5 per cent per annum during the last three years while the regular employment growth rate is negative.[21] This may be directly attributed to the stringent labour regulations and labour laws. The formal sector of the Indian manufacturing industry has responded to the rigidity of labour procedures by using more and more contract labour. Contract workers are not subject to firing regulations applicable to regular workers (see Box 12.2). Therefore, the use of contract labour is an important source of flexibility for Indian firms. The positive relationship between the strictness of JSR and the use of temporary workers is well established in the case of European countries (See Booth et al. 2002).

It is hard to attribute the growth of the informal sector (that is, informalization) entirely to globalization. Industrial firms (both private and public sector) in India have been observed to practice outsourcing of labour, that is, using contract workers, 'on-site only labour', and temporary workers in the 1980s. This process of shifting of labour from the formal to informal segment had started much before the dramatic tariff liberalization and trade liberalization undertaken by India in the 1990s. A substantial shift of jobs from the factory to non-factory sector (informal) was observed between 1981 and 1991.[22] This trend has continued (perhaps accelerated) in recent years. It can be argued that in India, labour regulation is of primary importance in determining the incidence of informal sector employment rather than trade or tariff liberalization.

Labour regulations have restricted the size expansion of factories to take advantage of economies of scale. As is

---

Box 12.2

Fixed-term Contract in Indian Industry

India has introduced a new provision in the Industrial Employment (Standing Orders) Central Rules, 1946, that enables a firm to employ workers on a fixed-term basis. A 'fixed-term employment' workman is a workman who has been engaged on the basis of contract employment for a fixed period. However, his working hours, wages, allowances, and other benefits shall not be less than those of a permanent workman. This provision came into effect in December 2003. It enables an industrial establishment, with more than 100 workers, to access the labour market directly for short-term employment, instead of contractors. Workers under this category can be retrenched without notice or compensation at the end of the contract period. However, most state governments are yet to make the corresponding change in their state rules.

Source: Malik (2006), *Business India* (16–29 February 2004).

---

[21] Contract workers are regulated by a separate labour law called the 'Contract Labour (Regulation and Abolition) Act, 1970'. This empowers the state to prohibit the use of contract workers in core and perennial activities in a firm.

[22] (Ramaswamy 1994 and 1999).

evident from Table 12.8, there is a greater concentration of factories in the size group of less than 100 workers across industry groups.[23] This has adverse effects on the competitiveness of firms, particularly EO firms. It is well-known that India has relatively fewer number of garment making factories with more than 1000 workers.

Need for Flexibility by Consensus[24]

The slow growth of regular jobs in India strongly suggests the need for introducing flexibility in the current set of JSR (for a discussion of JSR in India, see Box 12.3). Firms are utilizing the available avenues of contract labour and product outsourcing to attain some flexibility at the margin.

Some states in India have modified their Contract Labour Act (Andhra Pradesh) to allow the use of contract labour in a wider range of activities of the firm.[25] This will encourage greater use of contract labour in many peripheral activities without inducing the firm to increase regular jobs. The effect of introducing 'fixed-term employment' in the Central government rules will be similar. Policy initiative is required to create incentives for the firms to absorb workers in regular jobs by reducing expected costs of hiring regular workers. This can be achieved by simplifying procedural requirements for retrenchment. International comparisons of severance payments (retrenchment benefits) mandated by the Indian labour laws suggest that they are on the lower

TABLE 12.8
Distribution of Factories by Employment Size and Trade Orientation, 2000–1

Employment Size	Export oriented	Share	Import competing	Share	Auto	Share	Food	Share
0–9	7405	23.1	5182	21.6	751	19.4	7274	27.0
10–49	15360	48.0	13060	54.4	2066	53.2	13167	48.8
50–99	4050	12.7	2566	10.7	434	11.2	3060	11.3
100–199	2300	7.2	1531	6.4	296	7.6	1751	6.5
200–499	1862	5.8	1023	4.3	146	3.8	1074	4.0
500–999	689	2.2	339	1.4	87	2.2	355	1.3
1000–1999	207	0.6	166	0.7	50	1.3	147	0.5
2000–4999	116	0.4	57	0.2	37	1.0	91	0.3
Above 5000	18	0.1	96	0.4	1.4	0.4	49	0.2
Total number of factories	32007	100	24020	100	3881	100	26968	100

Source: Author's estimates based on ASI 2000–1, CSO.

Box 12.3

Job Security Regulations in India

Job security in India is regulated by two key labour laws, namely, the Industrial Disputes Act 1947 (IDA, 1947) and the Industrial Employment (Standing Orders) Act, 1946. The 'Standing Orders' refer to classification of employees, hours of work, procedures for dismissal for disciplinary (misconduct) reasons, and other terms of employment. Section 5B of the IDA lays down rules and procedures for lay-off, retrenchment of workmen, and closure of industrial establishments, namely, factories, mines, and plantations. These provisions are applicable to all establishments having not less than 100 workers since the 1982 amendment (originally applicable to establishments with more than 300 workers; in West Bengal, it is applicable to establishments with not less than 50 workers). Here retrenchment means the termination of the services of a workman for any reasons other than disciplinary action (misconduct). Three conditions are required to be met before a firm can implement a valid retrenchment of any workman with more than 240 days of continuous service: (i) one month's notice indicating reasons for retrenchment or one month's wages in lieu of notice, (ii) payment of compensation (severance pay) equivalent to 15 days of average pay for every year of completed service (45 days in Gujarat), and (iii) obtaining prior permission of the appropriate government (or specified authority either central/state) authority. This requires an

(Box 12.3 contd.)

[23] India continues to suffer from the 'missing middle' syndrome. That is, the smaller employment share of factories in the size class 100 to 500.
[24] In this context, the EU debate on labour market reforms and the concept of flexicurity, that is, flexibility for firing permanent workers and security for temporary workers has many useful lessons. Some scholars have suggested the move should be from 'job security within a job' to 'security of a job', that is security of finding a job easily. What incentives should be put in place such that temporary work becomes a stepping-stone to a permanent job?
[25] The Contract Labour Act of 1970 did not clearly distinguish between core and non-core activities of the firm. An activity carried beyond 120 days is considered as a regular activity, therefore, firms are not permitted to use contract labour for that activity.

(Box 12.3 contd.)

application using the specified form, 'FORM P-A'. This form demands elaborate information on installed capacity, production, and sales for the preceding 3 years, position of the order book (item-wise and value-wise) for the next 18 months, financial conditions supported by balance sheet data, past history of retrenchment, anticipated savings due to retrenchment, proposed savings due to reduction of managerial remuneration, sales promotion, and general administrative expenses, balance sheets for previous six months and the following one year. The firm is required to explain the attempts made to avoid the proposed retrenchment. On receiving the application, the government conveys its decision within a period of sixty days or may chose to refer the matter to a tribunal for adjudication. The tribunal is required to give a decision within a period of thirty days from the date of such reference. However, such permissions to retrench workers are rarely given. (These rules are not applicable to workers employed through contractors or contract worker supplier firms.) The implicit cost of procedural delays on firms seeking to adjust seems to have received less attention. Further, under Section 9-A, firms are required to give notice to workers in case of rationalization, standardization, or improvement of plant/technique that is likely to lead to retrenchment. Firms are prohibited from introducing such changes in the conditions of service within 21 days of such notice (42 days in some states like Andhra Pradesh and West Bengal). In brief, the JSR have increased the expected cost of workforce adjustments (through lay-off or retrenchment) in industrial establishments.

Source: Malik (2006) and Mathur (1992).

side (Asher and Mukhopadhyay 2004). For example, in the case of a worker with four years of service, severance payments add up to six months of pay in Thailand and nine months in Sri Lanka. The same is only two months in India. The report of the Second National Labour Commission has proposed a higher severance payment depending on the size of the establishment, that, is 45–60 days for those working in firms with more than 300 workers and 22.5 to 30 days for those working in firms with less than 100 workers etc. However, as long as we have legal prerequisites of state permissions for retrenchment and lay-offs, firms will have lower incentives to create permanent jobs. The three entities involved in this reform process, namely, the state, the private corporate sector, and the workers need to arrive at a consensus for introducing flexibility. This calls for a constructive social dialogue between the stakeholders.

References

Asher, Mukul and Pundarik Mukhopadhyay (2004), 'Severance Pay in Selected Asian Counries: A Survey', Working Paper, No. 55, School of Public Policy, Singapore University, available at *http:/www.spp.nus.edu.sg* (accessed on 25 May 2006).

Booth, Alison, Juan Dolado, and Jeff Frank (2002), 'Symposium on Temporary work: Introduction', *Economic Journal*, Vol. 112 (June).

Bardhan, Pranab (2001), 'Social Justice in the Globalising Economy', *Economic and Political Weekly*, 3–10 February.

Bertola (1999), 'Microeconomic Perspectives on Aggregate Labour markets' in O. Ashenfelter and D. Card (eds), *Handbook of Labor Economics*, Vol. 3, Chapter 45, Elesvier Science, Holland.

Bhalotra, Sonia (2003), 'The Impact of Economic Liberalization on Employment and Wages in India', Working paper No. 12, ILO, Geneva.

Casals, Joaquim (2004), 'Fixed Term Contracts in Spain: a mixed blessing', *ECFIN Country Focus*, Vol. 1, Issue 1.

Di Tellaa, Rafael and Robert MacCulloch (2005), 'The consequences of labor market Flexibility: Panel evidence based on survey data', *European Economic Review*, Vol. 49, pp. 1225–59.

Dolado, Juan, Garcia-Serrano, Juan Jimeno (2002), 'Drawing Lessons from the Boom of Temporary Jobs in Spain', *Economic Journal*, Vol. 112 (June).

Goldar, Bishwanath (2000), 'Employment Growth in Organised Manufacturing in India', *Economic and Political Weekly*, 1 April, pp. 1191–5.

Goldberg, Pinelopi and Nina Pavenick (2003), 'The response of the informal sector to trade liberalization', *Journal of Development Economics*, Vol. 72, pp. 463–96.

Heckman, James and Carmen Pages (eds) (2004), *Law and Employment: Lessons from Latin American and the Caribbean*, NBER, the University of Chicago Press, Chicago.

Kugler, Adriana, Juan Jimeno, and Virginia Hernan (2002), 'Employment Consequences of Restrictive Permanent Contracts: Evidence from Spanish Labor Market Reforms', Discussion Paper No. 657, Institute for the Study of Labour, Bonn, Available at *http/www.iza.org*.

Malik, P.L. (2006), *Industrial Law*, Vols 1 and 2, Eastern Book Company, Lucknow.

Mondino, G. and Silvia Montoyo, 'The Effect of labor Market Regulations on Employment Decisions by Firms: Empirical Evidence for Argentina', in Heckman and Pages (eds), *Law and Employment*, NBER.

Mathur, Ajeet (1992), 'Employment Security and Industrial Restructuring in India: Separating Facts From Folklore', Paper prepared for Presentation at the national seminar on Restructuring Indian economy, IIM, Calcutta, 17–18 January 1992, Indian Institute of Management, Calcutta.

Ramaswamy, K.V. (1994), 'Small-Scale Manufacturing Industries: Some Aspects of Size, Growth and Structure', *Economic and Political Weekly*, Vol. 29, 29 February, pp. M13–23.

——— (1999),' The Search for flexibility in Indian Manufacturing: New Evidence on Outsourcing activities', *Economic and Political Weekly*, Vol. 34, No. 6, pp. 363–8.

——— (2005), 'Employment in Indian manufacturing and New Services: Impact of Trade and Outsourcing', Unpublished Paper prepared for the World Bank, Washington, DC.

Rani, Uma and Unni Jeemol (2004), 'Unorganized and Organized Manufacturing in India: Potential for Employment Generating Growth', *Economic and Political Weekly*, Vol. 39, No. 4, pp. 4568–80.

Saavedra, James and Maximo Torero (2004), 'Labour Market Reforms and Their Impact over Formal Labour Demand and Job market Turnover: The Case of Peru', in Heckman and Pages (eds), *Law and Employment*.

Tendulkar, Suresh (2006), 'Employment Growth in Factory Manufacturing Sector During Pre- and Post-Reform Periods', in Suresh D. Tendulkar, Arup Mitra, and K. Naryanan (eds) (2006), *India: Industrialisation in a reforming economy; Essays for K.L. Krishna,* Academic Foundation, New Delhi.

Thomas Jayan Jose (2002), 'A Review of Indian Manufacturing', in K. Parikh and R. Radhakrishna (eds), *India Development Report 2002*, Oxford University Press, New Delhi.

Zagha, Roberto (1999), 'Labour and India's Economic Reforms' in J.D. Sachs et al. (eds), *India in the Era of Economic Reforms*, Oxford University Press, New Delhi.

A Statistical Profile
of
India's Development

REAL SECTOR
A1 NATIOANAL INCOME

Table A1.1
Key National Accounts Aggregates (at Constant Prices)

(Rupees, crore)

Year	GDP at factor cost		Net factor income from abroad	GNP at factor cost (2+3)		Consumption of fixed capital	NNP at factor cost (4−5)	NDP at factor cost (2−5)		Indirect taxes less subsidies		GDP at market prices (2+8)		NDP at market prices (7+8)		GNP at market prices (4+8)		NNP at market prices (6+8)	
(1)	(2)		(3)	(4)		(5)	(6)	(7)		(8)		(9)		(10)		(11)		(12)	
1993–4 Series																			
1950–1	140466		−554	139912		7544	132367	132921		8037		148503		140958		147949		140404	
1951–2	143745	2.3	−346	143399	2.5	7848	135551	135897	2.2	9234	14.9	152979	3.0	145131	3.0	152633	3.2	144785	3.1
1952–3	147824	2.8	−281	147544	2.9	8165	139379	139660	2.8	9136	−1.1	156960	2.6	148796	2.5	156680	2.7	148515	2.6
1953–4	156822	6.1	−232	156590	6.1	8431	148159	148391	6.3	9803	7.3	166625	6.2	158194	6.3	166393	6.2	157962	6.4
1954–5	163479	4.2	−354	163126	4.2	8942	154184	154537	4.1	11266	14.9	174745	4.9	165803	4.8	174392	4.8	165450	4.7
1955–6	167667	2.6	−132	167535	2.7	9534	158001	158133	2.3	12863	14.2	180530	3.3	170996	3.1	180398	3.4	170864	3.3
1956–7	177211	5.7	−205	177006	5.7	10213	166793	166998	5.6	13367	3.9	190578	5.6	180365	5.5	190373	5.5	180160	5.4
1957–8	175068	−1.2	−312	174756	−1.3	10854	163902	164214	−1.7	14892	11.4	189960	−0.3	179106	##	189648	−0.4	178794	−0.8
1958–9	188354	7.6	−429	187925	7.5	11442	176483	176913	7.7	15604	4.8	203958	7.4	192517	7.5	203529	7.3	192087	7.4
1959–60	192476	2.2	−759	191717	2.0	12125	179592	180351	1.9	16932	8.5	209408	2.7	197283	2.5	208649	2.5	196524	2.3
1960–1	206103	7.1	−907	205196	7.0	12961	192235	193142	7.1	14457	##	220560	5.3	207599	#	219653	5.3	206692	5.2
1961–2	212499	3.1	−1212	211287	3.0	13773	197514	198726	2.9	16422	13.6	228921	3.8	215148	3.6	227709	3.7	213936	3.5
1962–3	216994	2.1	−1393	215601	2.0	14705	200895	202289	1.8	18840	14.7	235834	3.0	221129	2.8	234441	3.0	219735	2.7
1963–4	227980	5.1	−1403	226577	5.1	15631	210946	212349	5.0	22228	18.0	250208	6.1	234577	6.1	248805	6.1	233174	6.1
1964–5	245270	7.6	−1798	243472	7.5	16832	226640	228438	7.6	23551	6.0	268821	7.4	251989	7.4	267023	7.3	250191	7.3
1965–6	236306	−3.7	−1912	234394	−3.7	18150	216244	218156	−4.5	25723	9.2	262029	−2.5	243879	##	260117	−2.6	241967	−3.3
1966–7	238710	1.0	−1864	236846	1.0	19420	217427	219291	0.5	22876	−11.1	261586	−0.2	242167	##	259722	−0.2	240303	−0.7
1967–8	258137	8.1	−2293	255843	8.0	20425	235418	237712	8.4	23834	4.2	281971	7.8	261546	8.0	279677	7.7	259252	7.9
1968–9	264873	2.6	−2186	262687	2.7	21453	241234	243420	2.4	26886	12.8	291759	3.5	270306	3.3	289573	3.5	268120	3.4
1969–0	282134	6.5	−2342	279791	6.5	22432	257359	259702	6.7	28713	6.8	310847	6.5	288415	6.7	308504	6.5	286072	6.7
1970–1	296278	5.0	−2345	293933	5.1	23336	270597	272942	5.1	30647	6.7	326925	5.2	303589	#	324580	5.2	301244	5.3
1971–2	299269	1.0	−2581	296688	0.9	24436	272252	274833	0.7	33247	8.5	332516	1.7	308080	1.5	329935	1.6	305499	1.4
1972–3	298316	−0.3	−2564	295752	−0.3	25691	270061	272625	−0.8	32278	−2.9	330594	−0.6	304903	−1.0	328030	−0.6	302339	−1.0
1973–4	311894	4.6	−1944	309950	4.8	26888	283061	285005	4.5	29156	−9.7	341050	3.2	314161	3.0	339106	3.4	312217	3.3
1974–5	315514	1.2	−1005	314509	1.5	28092	286417	287422	0.8	29587	1.5	345101	1.2	317009	0.9	344096	1.5	316004	1.2
1975–6	343924	9.0	−751	343173	9.1	29530	313643	314395	9.4	32807	10.9	376731	9.2	347202	9.5	375980	9.3	346450	9.6
1976–7	348223	1.2	−693	347530	1.3	31173	316358	317050	0.8	34940	6.5	383163	1.7	351990	1.4	382470	1.7	351298	1.4

(contd.)

TABLE A1.1 (contd.)

(1)	(2)		(3)	(4)		(5)	(6)	(7)		(8)		(9)		(10)		(11)		(12)	
1977–8	374235	7.5	−771	373464	7.5	32713	340751	341522	7.7	36638	4.9	410873	7.2	378160	7.4	410102	7.2	377389	7.4
1978–9	394828	5.5	−493	394335	5.6	34603	359732	360225	5.5	39609	8.1	434437	5.7	399834	5.7	433944	5.8	399341	5.8
1979–80	374291	−5.2	349	374640	−5.0	36515	338124	337775	−6.2	37372	−5.6	411663	−5.2	375147	##	412012	−5.1	375496	−6.0
1980–1	401128	7.2	842	401970	7.3	38553	363417	362575	7.3	38073	1.9	439201	6.7	400648	#	440043	6.8	401490	6.9
1981–2	425073	6.0	95	425168	5.8	40776	384392	384297	6.0	42066	10.5	467139	6.4	426363	6.4	467234	6.2	426458	6.2
1982–3	438079	3.1	−1503	436577	2.7	43303	393274	394777	2.7	46138	9.7	484217	3.7	440915	3.4	482715	3.3	439412	3.0
1983–4	471742	7.7	−2449	469293	7.5	46028	423265	425714	7.8	46749	1.3	518491	7.1	472463	7.2	516042	6.9	470014	7.0
1984–5	492077	4.3	−2871	489206	4.2	49087	440119	442990	4.1	47797	2.2	539874	4.1	490787	3.9	537003	4.1	487916	3.8
1985–6	513990	4.5	−2930	511058	4.5	51873	459187	462117	4.3	56277	17.7	570267	5.6	518394	5.6	567338	5.6	515464	5.6
1986–7	536257	4.3	−4235	532021	4.1	54863	477158	481393	4.2	61593	9.4	597850	4.8	542986	4.7	593614	4.6	538751	4.5
1987–8	556778	3.8	−5369	551409	3.6	58097	493312	498681	3.6	66593	8.1	623371	4.3	565274	4.1	618002	4.1	559905	3.9
1988–9	615098	10.5	−7891	607207	10.1	61635	545572	553463	11.0	69734	4.7	684832	9.9	623197	##	676941	9.5	615306	9.9
1989–90	656331	6.7	−8223	648108	6.7	65591	582518	590741	6.7	72621	4.1	728952	6.4	663362	6.4	720729	6.5	655139	6.5
1990–1	692871	5.6	−9201	683670	5.5	69465	614206	623407	5.5	78424	8.0	771295	5.8	701831	#	762094	5.7	692630	5.7
1991–2	701863	1.3	−10720	691143	1.1	73771	617372	628092	0.8	76426	−2.5	778289	0.9	704518	0.4	767569	0.7	693798	0.2
1992–3	737792	5.1	−11417	726375	5.1	78193	648182	659599	5.0	81526	6.7	819318	5.3	741125	5.2	807901	5.3	729708	5.2
1993–4	781345	5.9	−12080	769265	5.9	83353	685912	697992	5.8	77875	−4.5	859220	4.9	775867	4.7	847140	4.9	763787	4.7
1994–5	838031	7.3	−13215	824816	7.2	90458	734358	747573	7.1	85318	9.6	923349	7.5	832891	7.3	910134	7.4	819676	7.3
1995–6	899563	7.3	−12602	886961	7.5	99152	787809	800411	7.1	94383	10.6	993946	7.6	894794	7.4	981344	7.8	882192	7.6
1996–7	970082	7.8	−10723	959359	8.2	107275	852084	862807	7.8	97362	3.2	1067444	7.4	960169	7.3	1056721	7.7	949446	7.6
1997–8	1016595	4.8	−10649	1005946	4.9	114860	891086	901735	4.5	98653	1.3	1115248	4.5	1000388	4.2	1104599	4.5	989739	4.2
1998–9	1082747	6.5	−11974	1070773	6.4	122193	948580	960554	6.5	99273	0.6	1182020	6.0	1059827	5.9	1170046	5.9	1047853	5.9
1999–2000	1148367	6.1	−11182	1137185	6.2	129071	1008114	1019296	6.1	117916	18.8	1266283	7.1	1137212	7.3	1255101	7.3	1126030	7.5
2000–1	1198592	4.4	−12154	1186438	4.3	136100	1050338	1062492	4.2	117609	−0.3	1316201	3.9	1180101	#	1304047	3.9	1167947	3.7
2001–2	1267945	5.8	−10309	1257636	6.0	142465	1115171	1125480	5.9	115760	−1.6	1383705	5.1	1241240	5.2	1373396	5.3	1230931	5.4
2002–3	1318362	4.0	−7891	1310471	4.2	148569	1161902	1169793	3.9	122270	5.6	1440632	4.1	1292063	4.1	1432741	4.3	1284172	4.3
2003–4$	1430548	8.5	−8069	1422479	8.5	156474	1266005	1274074	8.9	134072	9.7	1564620	8.6	1408146	9.0	1556551	8.6	1400077	9.0
2004–5$$	1529408	6.9	−9659	1519749	6.8	165150	1354599	1364259	7.1	146092	9.0	1675500	7.1	1510351	7.3	1665841	7.0	1500691	7.2
1999–2000 Series																			
1999–2000	1792292		−15431	1776861		186649	1590212	1605643		166522		1958814		1772165		1943383		1756734	
2000–1	1870387	4.4	−22545	1847842	4.0	194755	1653087	1675632	4.4	166579	0.0	2036966	4.0	1842211	#	2014421	3.7	1819666	3.6
2001–2	1978055	5.8	−20671	1957384	5.9	202104	1755280	1775951	6.0	166428	−0.1	2144483	5.3	1942379	5.4	2123812	5.4	1921708	5.6
2002–3	2052586	3.8	−18805	2033781	3.9	210655	1823126	1841931	3.7	169735	2.0	2222321	3.6	2011666	3.6	2203516	3.8	1992861	3.7
2003–4	2226041	8.5	−17845	2208196	8.6	221338	1986858	2004703	8.8	180283	6.2	2406324	8.3	2184986	8.6	2388479	8.4	2167141	8.7
2004–5$	2393671	7.5	−16942	2376729	7.6	234953	2141776	2158718	7.7	217840	20.8	2611511	8.5	2376558	8.8	2594569	8.6	2359616	8.9
2005–6$$	2595339	8.4	−24029	2571310	8.2	246028	2325282	2349311	8.8	242883	11.5	2838222	8.7	2592194	9.1	2814193	8.5	2568165	8.8

(contd.)

TABLE A1.1 (contd.)

Year	GDP at factor cost				Private final consumption expenditure in domestic market (PFCE)		Government final consumption expenditure (GFCE)		Gross domestic capital formation (adjusted)		Net domestic capital formation (adjusted)		Per capita GNP at factor Cost		Per capita NNP at factor cost		Per capita NDP at factor cost		Population (million)***	
	Public sector	Per cent of GDP	Private sector	Per cent of GDP									(in Rupees)***							
(1)	(13)		(14)		(15)		(16)		(17)		(18)		(19)		(20)		(21)		(22)	
1993–4 Series																				
1950–1	—	—	—	—	128612		9067		20755		13211		3897		3687		3703		359	
1951–2	—	—	—	—	136787	6.4	9161	1.0	26579	28.1	18731	41.8	3929	0.8	3714	0.7	3723	0.6	365	1.7
1952–3	—	—	—	—	142307	4.0	9172	0.1	19554	−26.4	11389	−39.2	3966	1.0	3747	0.9	3754	0.8	372	1.9
1953–4	—	—	—	—	150862	6.0	9287	1.3	20993	7.4	12562	10.3	4132	4.2	3909	4.3	3915	4.3	379	1.9
1954–5	—	—	—	—	155811	3.3	9341	0.6	22661	7.9	13719	9.2	4226	2.3	3994	2.2	4004	2.3	386	1.8
1955–6	—	—	—	—	157301	1.0	9600	2.8	30552	34.8	21018	53.2	4263	0.9	4020	0.7	4024	0.5	393	1.8
1956–7	—	—	—	—	164259	4.4	10268	7.0	39364	28.8	29150	38.7	4414	3.5	4159	3.5	4165	3.5	401	2.0
1957–8	—	—	—	—	161014	−2.0	11563	12.6	37667	−4.3	26813	−8.0	4273	−3.2	4007	−3.7	4015	−3.6	409	2.0
1958–9	—	—	—	—	175796	9.2	11973	3.5	32760	−13.0	21319	−20.5	4496	5.2	4222	5.4	4232	5.4	418	2.2
1959–60	—	—	—	—	177795	1.1	12188	1.8	34404	5.0	22279	4.5	4500	0.1	4216	−0.1	4234	0.0	426	1.9
1960–1	18555	9.0	187548	91.0	187909	5.7	12846	5.4	40941	19.0	27981	##	4728	5.1	4429	5.1	4450	5.1	434	1.9
1961–2	20763	9.8	191736	90.2	191112	1.7	13757	7.1	38502	−6.0	24730	−11.6	4759	0.6	4449	0.4	4476	0.6	444	2.3
1962–3	24234	11.2	192760	88.8	193602	1.3	16693	21.3	43775	13.7	29070	17.6	4749	−0.2	4425	−0.5	4456	−0.4	454	2.3
1963–4	26607	11.7	201373	88.3	200804	3.7	20822	24.7	45962	5.0	30330	4.3	4883	2.8	4546	2.7	4576	2.7	464	2.2
1964–5	28969	11.8	216301	88.2	212800	6.0	21482	3.2	50839	10.6	34006	12.1	5137	5.2	4781	5.2	4819	5.3	474	2.2
1965–6	31717	13.4	204589	86.6	212988	0.1	23458	9.2	57911	13.9	39762	16.9	4833	−5.9	4459	−6.8	4498	−6.7	485	2.3
1966–7	33697	14.1	205013	85.9	215756	1.3	23725	1.1	60052	3.7	40632	2.2	4785	−1.0	4392	−1.5	4430	−1.5	495	2.1
1967–8	35916	13.9	222221	86.1	227962	5.7	24180	1.9	56137	−6.5	35712	−12.1	5056	5.7	4653	5.9	4698	6.0	506	2.2
1968–9	38928	14.7	225945	85.3	233950	2.6	25473	5.3	54839	−2.3	33386	−6.5	5071	0.3	4657	0.1	4699	0.0	518	2.4
1969–70	42032	14.9	240102	85.1	242640	3.7	27888	9.5	62355	13.7	39923	19.6	5289	4.3	4865	4.5	4909	4.5	529	2.1
1970–1	45805	15.5	250473	84.5	250880	3.4	30453	9.2	64638	3.7	41302	3.5	5433	2.7	5002	2.8	5045	2.8	541	2.3
1971–2	48516	16.2	250753	83.8	255761	1.9	33663	10.5	66704	3.2	42268	2.3	5355	−1.4	4914	−1.7	4961	−1.7	554	2.4
1972–3	51631	17.3	246685	82.7	257475	0.7	33761	0.3	65287	−2.1	39596	−6.3	5216	−2.6	4763	−3.1	4808	−3.1	567	2.3
1973–4	56891	18.2	255003	81.8	263793	2.5	33372	−1.2	77055	18.0	50167	26.7	5344	2.5	4880	2.5	4914	2.2	580	2.3
1974–5	58184	18.4	257330	81.6	263594	−0.1	31862	−4.5	68649	−10.9	40557	−19.2	5304	−0.8	4830	−1.0	4847	−1.4	593	2.2
1975–6	63313	18.4	280611	81.6	278563	5.7	35170	10.4	71655	4.4	42126	3.9	5654	6.6	5167	7.0	5179	6.9	607	2.4
1976–7	69958	20.1	278265	79.9	284118	2.0	37873	7.7	80238	12.0	49065	16.5	5605	−0.9	5103	−1.2	5114	−1.3	620	2.1
1977–8	73525	19.6	300710	80.4	307285	8.2	39011	3.0	90648	13.0	57934	18.1	5891	5.1	5375	5.3	5387	5.3	634	2.3

(contd.)

TABLE A1.1 (contd.)

(1)	(13)		(14)		(15)		(16)		(17)		(18)		(19)		(20)		(21)		(22)	
1978–9	78888	20.0	315940	80.0	326066	6.1	41862	7.3	105080	15.9	70477	21.6	6085	3.3	5551	3.3	5559	3.2	648	2.2
1979–80	82283	22.0	292008	78.0	318753	−2.2	44482	6.3	92895	−11.6	56379	−20.0	5642	−7.3	5092	−8.3	5087	−8.5	664	2.5
1980–1	88719	22.1	312409	77.9	347443	9.0	46581	4.7	99719	7.3	61166	8.5	5920	4.9	5352	5.1	5340	5.0	679	2.3
1981–2	93206	21.9	331867	78.1	362552	4.3	48675	4.5	100425	0.7	59649	−2.5	6144	3.8	5555	3.8	5553	4.0	692	1.9
1982–3	102535	23.4	335544	76.6	366178	1.0	53280	9.5	100271	−0.2	56968	−4.5	6166	0.4	5555	0.0	5576	0.4	708	2.3
1983–4	109445	23.2	362297	76.8	394599	7.8	55605	4.4	103784	3.5	57756	1.4	6491	5.3	5854	5.4	5888	5.6	723	2.1
1984–5	117738	23.9	374339	76.1	405973	2.9	59620	7.2	112567	8.5	63480	9.9	6620	2.0	5956	1.7	5994	1.8	739	2.2
1985–6	127845	24.9	386145	75.1	422916	4.2	66255	11.1	123113	9.4	71240	12.2	6769	2.3	6082	2.1	6121	2.1	755	2.2
1986–7	138862	25.9	397395	74.1	436262	3.2	72802	9.9	123552	0.4	68689	−3.6	6900	1.9	6189	1.8	6244	2.0	771	2.1
1987–8	147945	26.6	408833	73.4	451215	3.4	78698	8.1	142152	15.1	84055	22.4	6998	1.4	6260	1.2	6328	1.4	788	2.2
1988–9	158483	25.8	456615	74.2	479378	6.2	82775	5.2	160762	13.1	99127	17.9	7543	7.8	6777	8.3	6875	8.6	805	2.2
1989–90	171575	26.1	484756	73.9	503167	5.0	86659	4.7	172046	7.0	106455	7.4	7885	4.5	7087	4.6	7187	4.5	822	2.1
1990–1	176720	25.5	516151	74.5	525641	4.5	89601	3.4	195650	13.7	126185	18.5	8149	3.3	7321	3.3	7430	3.4	839	2.1
1991–2	187758	26.8	514105	73.2	536980	2.2	89008	−0.7	171553	−12.3	97782	−22.5	8074	−0.9	7212	−1.5	7338	−1.2	856	2.0
1992–3	192708	26.1	545084	73.9	550828	2.6	91795	3.1	187478	9.3	109285	11.8	8330	3.2	7433	3.1	7564	3.1	872	1.9
1993–4	202512	25.9	578833	74.1	574772	4.3	97725	6.5	198412	5.8	115059	5.3	8624	3.5	7690	3.4	7825	3.4	892	2.3
1994–5	216995	25.9	621036	74.1	601481	4.6	98935	1.2	243882	22.9	153424	33.3	9064	5.1	8070	4.9	8215	5.0	910	2.0
1995–6	230051	25.6	669512	74.4	638938	6.2	106881	8.0	271015	11.1	171863	12.0	9558	5.4	8489	5.2	8625	5.0	928	2.0
1996–7	240452	24.8	729630	75.2	689566	7.9	111640	4.5	268435	−1.0	161160	−6.2	10141	6.1	9007	6.1	9121	5.7	946	1.9
1997–8	269001	26.5	747594	73.5	707285	2.6	123978	11.1	289058	7.7	174198	8.1	10435	2.9	9244	2.6	9354	2.6	964	1.9
1998–9	288505	26.6	794242	73.4	752440	6.4	139963	12.9	290971	0.7	168778	−3.1	10893	4.4	9650	4.4	9772	4.5	983	2.0
1999–2000	304955	26.6	843412	73.4	797653	6.0	158432	13.2	351624	20.8	222553	31.9	11360	4.3	10071	4.4	10183	4.2	1001	1.8
2000–1	307177	25.6	891415	74.4	819637	2.8	159209	0.5	346682	−1.4	210582	−5.4	11643	2.5	10308	2.3	10427	2.4	1019	1.8
2001–2	328395	25.9	939550	74.1	866977	5.8	164146	3.1	336486	−2.9	194021	−7.9	12128	4.2	10754	4.3	10853	4.1	1037	1.8
2002–3	351018	26.6	967344	73.4	891419	2.8	160175	−2.4	395163	17.4	246594	27.1	12422	2.4	11013	2.4	11088	2.2	1055	1.7
2003–4$	357482	25.0	1073066	75.0	964865	8.2	166085	3.7	449539	13.8	293065	18.8	13257	6.7	11799	7.1	11874	7.1	1073	1.7
2004–5$$	—	—	—	—	—	—	—	—	—	—	—	—	13930	5.1	12416	5.2	12505	5.3	1091	1.7
1999–2000 Series																				
1999–2000	454283	25.3	1338009	74.7	1266294		252285		509289		322640		17751		15886		16040		1001	2.0
2000–1	—		—		1E+06	2.3	253001	0.3	486369	−4.5	291614	−9.6	18134	2.2	16223	2.1	16444	2.5	1019	1.8
2001–2	—		—		1371638	5.9	257334	1.7	477158	−1.9	275054	−5.7	18857	4.0	16910	4.2	17109	4.0	1038	1.9
2002–3	—		—		1393047	1.6	255847	−0.6	555762	16.5	345107	25.5	19278	2.2	17281	2.2	17459	2.0	1055	1.6
2003–4	—		—		1502502	7.9	262015	2.4	643480	15.8	422142	22.3	20580	6.8	18517	7.2	18683	7.0	1073	1.7
2004–5$	—		—		1596802	6.3	286196	9.2	744522	15.7	509569	20.7	21805	6.0	19649	6.1	19805	6.0	1090	1.6
2005–6$$	—		—		—		—		—		—		23228	6.5	21005	6.9	21222	7.2	1107	1.6

Notes: *** Based on mid-financial year (as on October 1 each year); $ Quick Estimates; $$ Revised Estimates; — Information not available; Figures in italics denote percentage changes over previous years.

Sources: NAS (2005), CSO and their various press notes, and NAS 1950–1 to 2002–3, EPWRF, December 2004.

TABLE A1.2
Gross and Net Domestic Savings by Type of Institutions (at Current Prices)

(Rupees, crore)

Year	GDP at current market prices	NDP at current market prices	Domestic savings GDS	Domestic savings CFC*	Domestic savings NDS		Household sector savings Gross		Household sector savings CFC*		Household sector savings Net		Private corporate sector savings Gross		Private corporate sector savings CFC*		Private corporate sector savings Net		Public sector savings Gross		Public sector savings CFC*		Public sector savings Net	
(1)	(2)	(3)	(4)	(5)	(6)		(7)		(8)		(9)		(10)		(11)		(12)		(13)		(14)		(15)	
1993–4 Series																								
1950–1	9934	9570	887 8.9	364 3.7	523 5.5		612 6.2		256 2.6		356 3.7		93 0.9		45 0.5		48 0.5		182 1.8		63 0.6		119 1.2
1951–2	10566	10155	985 9.3	411 3.9	574 5.7		583 5.5		285 2.7		298 2.9		136 1.3		52 0.5		84 0.8		266 2.5		74 0.7		192 1.9
1952–3	10366	9924	861 8.3	442 4.3	419 4.2		637 6.1		305 2.9		332 3.3		64 0.6		55 0.5		9 0.1		160 1.5		82 0.8		78 0.8
1953–4	11282	10818	888 7.9	465 4.1	423 3.9		655 5.8		321 2.8		334 3.1		90 0.8		56 0.5		34 0.3		143 1.3		88 0.8		55 0.5
1954–5	10678	10167	1005 9.4	511 4.8	494 4.9		719 6.7		354 3.3		365 3.6		118 1.1		64 0.6		54 0.5		168 1.6		93 0.9		75 0.7
1955–6	10873	10327	1370 12.6	546 5.0	824 8.0		1046 9.6		371 3.4		675 6.5		134 1.2		72 0.7		62 0.6		190 1.7		103 1.0		87 0.8
1956–7	12951	12340	1584 12.2	611 4.7	973 7.9		1178 9.1		408 3.2		770 6.2		155 1.2		80 0.6		75 0.6		251 1.9		123 1.0		128 1.0
1957–8	13349	12687	1384 10.4	661 5.0	723 5.7		997 7.5		430 3.2		567 4.5		121 0.9		88 0.7		33 0.3		266 2.0		142 1.1		124 1.0
1958–9	14874	14102	1407 9.5	772 5.2	635 4.5		1016 6.8		514 3.5		502 3.6		140 0.9		99 0.7		41 0.3		251 1.7		159 1.1		92 0.7
1959–60	15675	14832	1748 11.2	843 5.4	905 6.1		1301 8.3		544 3.5		757 5.1		185 1.2		113 0.7		72 0.5		262 1.7		186 1.2		76 0.5
1960–1	17167	16223	1989 11.6	944 5.5	1045 6.4		1254 7.3		592 3.4		662 4.1		281 1.6		136 0.8		145 0.9		454 2.6		217 1.3		237 1.5
1961–2	18196	17138	2127 11.7	1058 5.8	1069 6.2		1281 7.0		634 3.5		647 3.8		320 1.8		172 0.9		148 0.9		526 2.9		252 1.4		274 1.6
1962–3	19566	18401	2479 12.7	1164 5.9	1315 7.1		1533 7.8		673 3.4		860 4.7		344 1.8		198 1.0		146 0.8		602 3.1		293 1.5		309 1.7
1963–4	22482	21169	2763 12.3	1313 5.8	1450 6.8		1618 7.2		725 3.2		893 4.2		394 1.8		245 1.1		149 0.7		751 3.3		343 1.5		408 1.9
1964–5	26220	24743	3129 11.9	1477 5.6	1652 6.7		1875 7.2		776 3.0		1099 4.4		389 1.5		286 1.1		103 0.4		865 3.3		415 1.6		450 1.8
1965–6	27668	25998	3870 14.0	1671 6.0	2199 8.5		2602 9.4		872 3.2		1730 6.7		405 1.5		304 1.1		101 0.4		863 3.1		495 1.8		368 1.4
1966–7	31305	29330	4375 14.0	1975 6.3	2400 8.2		3223 10.3		1039 3.3		2184 7.4		424 1.4		348 1.1		76 0.3		728 2.3		587 1.9		141 0.5
1967–8	36649	34427	4355 11.9	2222 6.1	2133 6.2		3210 8.8		1174 3.2		2036 5.9		410 1.1		369 1.0		41 0.1		735 2.0		679 1.9		56 0.2
1968–9	38823	36407	4721 12.2	2416 6.2	2305 6.3		3349 8.6		1267 3.3		2082 5.7		439 1.1		394 1.0		45 0.1		933 2.4		755 1.9		178 0.5
1969–70	42750	40072	6104 14.3	2678 6.3	3426 8.5		4440 10.4		1428 3.3		3012 7.5		549 1.3		413 1.0		136 0.3		1115 2.6		837 2.0		278 0.7
1970–1	45677	42707	6649 14.6	2970 6.5	3679 8.6		4634 10.1		1521 3.3		3113 7.3		672 1.5		462 1.0		210 0.5		1343 2.9		988 2.2		355 0.8
1971–2	48932	45640	7367 15.1	3292 6.7	4075 8.9		5219 10.7		1658 3.4		3561 7.8		769 1.6		502 1.0		267 0.6		1379 2.8		1133 2.3		246 0.5
1972–3	53947	50226	7872 14.6	3721 6.9	4151 8.3		5624 10.4		1845 3.4		3779 7.5		806 1.5		564 1.0		242 0.5		1442 2.7		1312 2.4		130 0.3
1973–4	65613	61274	10999 16.8	4339 6.6	6660 10.9		7985 12.2		2096 3.2		5889 9.6		1083 1.7		656 1.0		427 0.7		1931 2.9		1588 2.4		343 0.6
1974–5	77479	71919	12380 16.0	5560 7.2	6820 9.5		8080 10.4		2634 3.4		5446 7.6		1465 1.9		876 1.1		589 0.8		2835 3.7		2049 2.6		786 1.1
1975–6	83269	76820	14346 17.2	6449 7.7	7897 10.3		9743 11.7		2980 3.6		6763 8.8		1083 1.3		1053 1.3		30 0.0		3520 4.2		2416 2.9		1104 1.4
1976–7	89739	82833	17408 19.4	6907 7.7	10501 12.7		11849 13.2		3180 3.5		8669 10.5		1181 1.3		1068 1.2		113 0.1		4378 4.9		2659 3.0		1719 2.1
1977–8	101597	94100	20142 19.8	7497 7.4	12645 13.4		14354 14.1		3405 3.4		10949 11.6		1413 1.4		1083 1.1		330 0.4		4375 4.3		3009 3.0		1366 1.5
1978–9	110133	101560	23676 21.5	8573 7.8	15103 14.9		17015 15.4		3903 3.5		13112 12.9		1652 1.5		1203 1.1		449 0.4		5009 4.5		3467 3.1		1542 1.5
1979–80	120841	110392	24314 20.1	10449 8.6	13865 12.6		16690 13.8		4748 3.9		11942 10.8		2398 2.0		1457 1.2		941 0.9		5226 4.3		4244 3.5		982 0.9

(contd.)

TABLE A1.2 (contd.)

(1)	(2)	(3)	(4)	(5)	(6)	(7)	(8)	(9)	(10)	(11)	(12)	(13)	(14)	(15)
1980–1	143764	131477	27136	*18.9*	12288	*8.5*	14848	*11.3*	19868	*13.8*	5579	*3.9*	14289	*10.9*	2339	*1.6*	1717	*1.2*	622	*0.5*	4929	*3.4*	4992	*3.5*	–63	*0.0*
1981–2	168600	153892	31355	*18.6*	14708	*8.7*	16647	*10.8*	21225	*12.6*	6709	*4.0*	14516	*9.4*	2560	*1.5*	2022	*1.2*	538	*0.3*	7570	*4.5*	5977	*3.5*	1593	*1.0*
1982–3	188262	171087	34368	*18.3*	17175	*9.1*	17193	*10.0*	23216	*12.3*	7690	*4.1*	15526	*9.1*	2980	*1.6*	2364	*1.3*	616	*0.4*	8172	*4.3*	7121	*3.8*	1051	*0.6*
1983–4	219496	199931	38587	*17.6*	19565	*8.9*	19022	*9.5*	28165	*12.8*	8531	*3.9*	19634	*9.8*	3254	*1.5*	2811	*1.3*	443	*0.2*	7168	*3.3*	8222	*3.7*	–1054	*–0.5*
1984–5	245515	223028	46063	*18.8*	22487	*9.2*	23576	*10.6*	35067	*14.3*	9650	*3.9*	25417	*11.4*	4040	*1.6*	3231	*1.3*	809	*0.4*	6956	*2.8*	9606	*3.9*	–2650	*–1.2*
1985–6	277991	251274	54167	*19.5*	26717	*9.6*	27450	*10.9*	39795	*14.3*	11109	*4.0*	28686	*11.4*	5426	*2.0*	3976	*1.4*	1450	*0.6*	8946	*3.2*	11632	*4.2*	–2686	*–1.1*
1986–7	311177	280788	58951	*18.9*	30389	*9.8*	28562	*10.2*	45072	*14.5*	12327	*4.0*	32745	*11.7*	5336	*1.7*	4675	*1.5*	661	*0.2*	8543	*2.7*	13388	*4.3*	–4845	*–1.7*
1987–8	354343	320369	72908	*20.6*	33974	*9.6*	38934	*12.2*	59157	*16.7*	13665	*3.9*	45492	*14.2*	5932	*1.7*	5052	*1.4*	880	*0.3*	7819	*2.2*	15257	*4.3*	–7438	*–2.3*
1988–9	421567	381874	87913	*20.9*	39693	*9.4*	48220	*12.6*	70657	*16.8*	15607	*3.7*	55050	*14.4*	8486	*2.0*	6130	*1.5*	2356	*0.6*	8770	*2.1*	17955	*4.3*	–9185	*–2.4*
1989–90	486179	439619	106979	*22.0*	46560	*9.6*	60419	*13.7*	86955	*17.9*	17813	*3.7*	69142	*15.7*	11845	*2.4*	7401	*1.5*	4444	*1.0*	8179	*1.7*	21346	*4.4*	–13167	*–3.0*
1990–1	568674	515410	131340	*23.1*	53264	*9.4*	78076	*15.1*	109897	*19.3*	20092	*3.5*	89805	*17.4*	15164	*2.7*	8861	*1.6*	6303	*1.2*	6279	*1.1*	24311	*4.3*	–18032	*–3.5*
1991–2	653117	588715	143908	*22.0*	64402	*9.9*	79506	*13.5*	110736	*17.0*	23356	*3.6*	87380	*14.8*	20304	*3.1*	11577	*1.8*	8727	*1.5*	12868	*2.0*	29470	*4.5*	–16602	*–2.8*
1992–3	748367	673855	162906	*21.8*	74512	*10.0*	88394	*13.1*	131073	*17.5*	26170	*3.5*	104903	*15.6*	19968	*2.7*	14451	*1.9*	5517	*0.8*	11865	*1.6*	33891	*4.5*	–22026	*–3.3*
1993–4	859220	775867	193621	*22.5*	83353	*9.7*	110268	*14.2*	158310	*18.4*	28941	*3.4*	129369	*16.7*	29866	*3.5*	17028	*2.0*	12838	*1.7*	5445	*0.6*	37384	*4.4*	–31939	*–4.1*
1994–5	1012770	914776	251463	*24.8*	97994	*9.7*	153469	*16.8*	199358	*19.7*	33933	*3.4*	165425	*18.1*	35260	*3.5*	20628	*2.0*	14632	*1.6*	16845	*1.7*	43433	*4.3*	–26588	*–2.9*
1995–6	1188012	1070086	298747	*25.1*	117926	*9.9*	180821	*16.9*	216140	*18.2*	41929	*3.5*	174211	*16.3*	58542	*4.9*	26059	*2.2*	32483	*3.0*	24065	*2.0*	49938	*4.2*	–25873	*–2.4*
1996–7	1368209	1231706	317261	*23.2*	136503	*10.0*	180758	*14.7*	233252	*17.0*	47552	*3.5*	185700	*15.1*	61092	*4.5*	32381	*2.4*	28711	*2.3*	22917	*1.7*	56570	*4.1*	–33653	*–2.7*
1997–8	1522547	1370550	352178	*23.1*	151997	*10.0*	200181	*14.6*	268437	*17.6*	52437	*3.4*	216000	*15.8*	63486	*4.2*	37826	*2.5*	25660	*1.9*	20255	*1.3*	61734	*4.1*	–41479	*–3.0*
1998–9	1740985	1572919	374659	*21.5*	168066	*9.7*	206593	*13.1*	326802	*18.8*	57251	*3.3*	269551	*17.1*	65026	*3.7*	43583	*2.5*	21443	*1.4*	–17169	*–1.0*	67232	*3.9*	–84401	*–5.4*
1999–2000	1936831	1754472	468681	*24.2*	182359	*9.4*	286322	*16.3*	404401	*20.9*	61814	*3.2*	342587	*19.5*	84329	*4.4*	48674	*2.5*	35655	*2.0*	–20049	*–1.0*	71871	*3.7*	–91920	*–5.2*
2000–1	2089500	1891605	490049	*23.5*	197895	*9.5*	292154	*14.0*	452268	*21.6*	66081	*3.2*	386187	*20.4*	86142	*4.1*	55563	*2.7*	30579	*1.6*	–48361	*–2.3*	76251	*3.6*	–124612	*–6.6*
2001–2	2271984	2054305	532274	*23.4*	217679	*9.6*	314595	*15.3*	513110	*22.6*	76822	*3.4*	436288	*21.2*	81076	*3.6*	58156	*2.6*	22920	*1.1*	–61912	*–2.7*	82701	*3.6*	–144613	*–7.0*
2002–3	2463324	2230372	642298	*26.1*	232952	*9.5*	409346	*18.4*	574681	*23.3*	82517	*3.3*	492164	*22.1*	94269	*4.4*	62780	*2.5*	31489	*1.4*	–26652	*–1.1*	87655	*3.6*	–114307	*–5.1*
2003–4	2760025	2506388	776420	*28.1*	253637	*9.2*	522783	*20.9*	671692	*24.3*	91775	*3.3*	579917	*23.1*	114157	*4.1*	67410	*2.4*	46747	*1.9*	–9429	*–0.3*	94452	*3.4*	–103881	*–4.1*
1999–2000 Series																											
1999–2000	1958814	1772165	487301	*24.9*	186649	*9.5*	300652	*17.0*	416726	*21.3*	71461	*3.6*	345265	*19.5*	87234	*4.5*	41827	*2.1*	45407	*2.6*	–16659	*–0.9*	73361	*3.7*	–90020	*–5.1*
2000–1	2107661	1904929	496272	*23.5*	202732	*9.6*	293540	*15.4*	446317	*21.2*	77438	*3.7*	368879	*19.4*	87017	*4.1*	47681	*2.3*	39336	*2.1*	–37062	*–1.8*	77613	*3.7*	–114675	*–6.0*
2001–2	2281305	2060144	537966	*23.6*	221161	*9.7*	316805	*15.4*	502674	*22.0*	83986	*3.7*	418688	*20.3*	81669	*3.6*	53434	*2.3*	28235	*1.4*	–46377	*–2.0*	83741	*3.7*	–130118	*–6.3*
2002–3	2449736	2214134	648994	*26.5*	235602	*9.6*	413392	*18.7*	565408	*23.1*	90058	*3.7*	475350	*21.5*	99767	*4.1*	57216	*2.3*	42551	*1.9*	–16181	*–0.7*	88328	*3.6*	–104509	*–4.7*
2003–4	2760224	2503654	797512	*28.9*	256570	*9.3*	540942	*21.6*	648634	*23.5*	99085	*3.6*	549549	*21.9*	120852	*4.4*	62578	*2.3*	58274	*2.3*	28026	*1.0*	94907	*3.4*	–66881	*–2.7*
2004–5$	3121414	2826656	907416	*29.1*	294758	*9.4*	612658	*21.7*	687079	*22.0*	115644	*3.7*	571435	*20.2*	150947	*4.8*	72439	*2.3*	78508	*2.8*	69390	*2.2*	106675	*3.4*	–37285	*–1.3*
2005–6$$	3531451	3207364	—	—	—	—	—	—	—	—	—	—	—	—	—	—	—	—	—	—	—	—	—	—	—	—

Notes: ** This has been worked out from the estimated value of capital stock and the expected age of various types of assets (see CSO 1989); $ Quick Estimates; $$ Revised Estimates; —Information not available; Figures in italics are as percentages to GDP at current prices except those for net savings in columns (6), (9), (12), and (15) which are as percentages to NDP at current market prices.

Source: Central Statistical Organisation (CSO), *National Accounts Statistics*, various issues.

TABLE A1.3
Gross Capital Formation by Type of Institutions at Current Prices

(Rupees, crore)

Year	Aggregate (3+4+5+6)		Gross capital formation (GCF)						Gross domestic savings	Net foreign capital inflow (−) outflow (+)	Finances for gross capital formation (7+8)	Errors and omissions (9−2)**	GCF adjusted (2+10)	
			Public sector		Private corporate sector		Household sector		Valuables*					
(1)	(2)		(3)		(4)		(5)		(6)	(7)	(8)	(9)	(10)	(11)
1993–4 Series														
1950–1	1044	10.5	276	2.8	218	2.2	550	5.5		887	−21	866	−178	866	8.7
1951–2	1146	10.8	321	3.0	256	2.4	569	5.4		985	183	1168	22	1168	11.1
1952–3	917	8.8	274	2.6	78	0.8	565	5.4		861	−34	827	−90	827	8.0
1953–4	833	7.4	311	2.8	9	0.1	513	4.5		888	−13	875	42	875	7.8
1954–5	1063	10.0	477	4.5	149	1.4	437	4.1		1005	16	1021	−42	1021	9.6
1955–6	1361	12.5	522	4.8	222	2.0	617	5.7		1370	39	1409	48	1409	13.0
1956–7	1881	14.5	691	5.3	345	2.7	845	6.5		1584	360	1944	63	1944	15.0
1957–8	1959	14.7	859	6.4	394	3.0	706	5.3		1384	473	1857	−102	1857	13.9
1958–9	1740	11.7	844	5.7	242	1.6	654	4.4		1407	376	1783	43	1783	12.0
1959–60	2103	13.4	932	5.9	303	1.9	868	5.5		1748	231	1979	−124	1979	12.6
1960–1	2516	14.7	1178	6.9	540	3.1	798	4.6		1989	481	2470	−46	2470	14.4
1961–2	2723	15.0	1187	6.5	744	4.1	792	4.4		2127	345	2472	−251	2472	13.6
1962–3	3063	15.7	1490	7.6	539	2.8	1034	5.3		2479	440	2919	−144	2919	14.9
1963–4	3477	15.5	1733	7.7	869	3.9	875	3.9		2763	440	3203	−274	3203	14.2
1964–5	4074	15.5	2007	7.7	906	3.5	1161	4.4		3129	600	3729	−345	3729	14.2
1965–6	4517	16.3	2282	8.2	705	2.5	1530	5.5		3870	599	4469	−48	4469	16.2
1966–7	5193	16.6	2209	7.1	625	2.0	2359	7.5		4375	923	5298	105	5298	16.9
1967–8	5580	15.2	2415	6.6	820	2.2	2345	6.4		4355	837	5192	−388	5192	14.2
1968–9	5582	14.4	2259	5.8	769	2.0	2554	6.6		4721	416	5137	−445	5137	13.2
1969–70	6557	15.3	2361	5.5	675	1.6	3521	8.2		6104	241	6345	−212	6345	14.8
1970–1	7227	15.8	2919	6.4	1045	2.3	3263	7.1		6649	394	7043	−184	7043	15.4
1971–2	8283	16.9	3415	7.0	1204	2.5	3664	7.5		7367	478	7845	−438	7845	16.0
1972–3	8721	16.2	3875	7.2	1350	2.5	3496	6.5		7872	297	8169	−552	8169	15.1
1973–4	10928	16.7	4904	7.5	1651	2.5	4373	6.7		10999	392	11391	463	11391	17.4
1974–5	14192	18.3	5753	7.4	2733	3.5	5706	7.4		12380	653	13033	−1159	13033	16.8
1975–6	15800	19.0	7806	9.4	2169	2.6	5825	7.0		14346	−117	14229	−1571	14229	17.1
1976–7	17144	19.1	8822	9.8	1325	1.5	6997	7.8		17408	−1309	16099	−1045	16099	17.9

(contd.)

TABLE A1.3 (contd.)

(1)	(2)		(3)		(4)		(5)		(6)		(7)	(8)	(9)	(10)	(11)
1977-8	18979	18.7	8101	8.0	2377	2.3	8501	8.4			20142	-1465	18677	-302	18677	18.4
1978-9	22810	20.7	10165	9.2	2288	2.1	10357	9.4			23676	128	23804	994	23804	21.6
1979-80	25824	21.4	12137	10.0	3078	2.5	10609	8.8			24314	580	24894	-930	24894	20.6
1980-1	26868	18.7	12105	8.4	3505	2.4	11258	7.8			27136	2094	29230	2362	29230	20.3
1981-2	37783	22.4	16986	10.1	9186	5.4	11611	6.9			31355	2611	33966	-3817	33966	20.1
1982-3	40786	21.7	20139	10.7	10170	5.4	10477	5.6			34368	2566	36934	-3852	36934	19.6
1983-4	43196	19.7	21265	9.7	7060	3.2	14871	6.8			38587	2517	41104	-2092	41104	18.7
1984-5	53026	21.6	25600	10.4	10238	4.2	17188	7.0			46063	3292	49355	-3671	49355	20.1
1985-6	65803	23.7	29990	10.8	14556	5.2	21257	7.6			54167	6234	60401	-5402	60401	21.7
1986-7	72203	23.2	34772	11.2	15695	5.0	21736	7.0			58951	6355	65306	-6897	65306	21.0
1987-8	78357	22.1	33757	9.5	12263	3.5	32337	9.1			72908	6825	79733	1376	79733	22.5
1988-9	99876	23.7	40136	9.5	16266	3.9	43474	10.3			87913	12304	100217	341	100217	23.8
1989-90	115035	23.7	46405	9.5	19673	4.0	48957	10.1			106979	12279	119258	4223	119258	24.5
1990-1	136854	24.1	53099	9.3	23498	4.1	60257	10.6			131340	18196	149536	12682	149536	26.3
1991-2	143260	21.9	57633	8.8	36992	5.7	48635	7.4			143908	3377	147285	4025	147285	22.6
1992-3	178019	23.8	63997	8.6	48316	6.5	65706	8.8			162906	13816	176722	-1297	176722	23.6
1993-4	182619	21.3	70834	8.2	48213	5.6	63572	7.4			193621	4791	198412	15793	198412	23.1
1994-5	236784	23.4	88206	8.7	69953	6.9	78625	7.8			251463	11893	263356	26572	263356	26.0
1995-6	315179	26.5	90977	7.7	113781	9.6	110421	9.3			298747	20780	319527	4348	319527	26.9
1996-7	297862	21.8	96187	7.0	110084	8.0	91591	6.7			317261	17738	334999	37137	334999	24.5
1997-8	343712	22.6	100653	6.6	121399	8.0	121660	8.0			352178	22302	374480	30768	374480	24.6
1998-9	372209	21.4	114545	6.6	111208	6.4	146456	8.4			374659	18362	393021	20812	393021	22.6
1999-2000	458262	23.7	134484	6.9	125120	6.5	198658	10.3			468681	21988	490669	32407	490669	25.3
2000-1	472708	22.6	131505	6.3	105709	5.1	235494	11.3			490049	8130	498179	25471	498179	23.8
2001-2	504012	22.2	140095	6.2	104771	4.6	259146	11.4			532274	-18731	513543	9531	513543	22.6
2002-3	557958	22.7	131966	5.4	105750	4.3	320242	13.0			642298	-32010	610288	52330	610288	24.8
2003-4	635694	23.0	154086	5.6	124177	4.5	357431	13.0			776420	-49552	726868	91174	726868	26.3
1999-2000 Series																
1999-2000	512214	26.1	146483	7.5	140088	7.2	210124	10.7	15519	0.8	487301	21988	509289	-2925	509289	26.0
2000-1	511590	24.3	145775	6.9	119993	5.7	231098	11.0	14724	0.7	496272	12754	509026	-2564	509026	24.2
2001-2	554468	24.3	157580	6.9	127503	5.6	255198	11.2	14187	0.6	537966	-14229	523737	-30731	523737	23.0
2002-3	619014	25.3	151246	6.2	141659	5.8	312152	12.7	13957	0.6	648994	-28486	620508	1494	620508	25.3
2003-4$	725630	26.3	180228	6.5	188728	6.8	332190	12.0	24484	0.9	797512	-45380	752132	26502	752132	27.2
2004-5$$	889245	28.5	225319	7.2	257478	8.2	366302	11.7	40146	1.3	907416	32139	939555	50310	939555	30.1

(contd.)

TABLE A1.3 (contd.)

Year	Con-sumption of Fixed Capital (CFC)	Net Capital Formation (NCF) (2−12)	NCF Adjusted (13+10)	GDCF (unadjusted)	Price Deflators (1993–4=100)					Aggregate GCF Con
					GDP at market prices	GDP C Mkt P CP	GDP C Mkt P CP	NDP C Mkt P CP	GDP C Mkt P Con	NDP C Mkt P Con	
(1)	(12)	(13)		(14)	(15)	(16)	(17)	(18)	(19)	(20)	(21)

1993–4 Series

Year	(12)	(13)		(14)	(15)	(16)	(17)	(18)	(19)	(20)	(21)
1950–1	364	680	7.1	502	4.1	6.7	9934	9570	148503	140958	25360
1951–2	411	735	7.2	757	4.4	6.9	10566	10155	152979	145131	26032
1952–3	442	475	4.8	385	4.2	6.6	10366	9924	156960	148796	21681
1953–4	465	368	3.4	410	4.2	6.8	11282	10818	166625	158194	20003
1954–5	511	552	5.4	510	4.5	6.1	10678	10167	174745	165803	23606
1955–6	546	815	7.9	863	4.6	6.0	10873	10327	180530	170996	29498
1956–7	611	1270	10.3	1333	4.9	6.8	12951	12340	190578	180365	38026
1957–8	662	1297	10.2	1195	4.9	7.0	13349	12687	189960	179106	39825
1958–9	772	968	6.9	1011	5.4	7.3	14874	14102	203958	192517	31971
1959–60	843	1260	8.5	1136	5.7	7.5	15675	14832	209408	197283	36641
1960–1	944	1572	9.7	1526	6.0	7.8	17167	16223	220560	207599	41729
1961–2	1058	1665	9.7	1414	6.4	7.9	18196	17138	228921	215148	42581
1962–3	1164	1899	10.3	1755	6.7	8.3	19566	18401	235834	221129	46030
1963–4	1313	2164	10.2	1890	7.0	9.0	21169	19566	250208	234577	50001
1964–5	1477	2597	10.5	2252	7.3	9.8	24743	21169	268821	251989	55697
1965–6	1671	2846	10.9	2798	7.7	10.6	25998	24743	262029	243879	58543
1966–7	1975	3218	11.0	3323	8.8	12.0	29330	25998	261586	242167	58824
1967–8	2222	3358	9.8	2970	9.2	13.0	34427	29330	281971	261546	60461
1968–9	2416	3166	8.7	2721	9.4	13.3	36407	34427	291759	270306	59613
1969–70	2678	3879	9.7	3667	10.2	13.8	38823	36407	310847	288415	64492
1970–1	2970	4257	10.0	4073	10.9	14.0	42750	40072	326925	303589	66382
1971–2	3292	4991	10.9	4553	11.7	14.7	45677	42707	332516	308080	70570
1972–3	3721	5000	10.0	4448	12.5	16.3	48932	45640	330594	304903	69738
1973–4	4339	6589	10.8	7052	14.8	19.2	53947	50226	341050	314161	73811
1974–5	5560	8632	12.0	7473	18.9	22.5	65613	61274	345101	317009	75127
1975–6	6449	9351	12.2	7780	19.8	22.1	77479	71919	376731	347202	79714
1976–7	6907	10237	12.4	9192	20.1	23.4	83269	76820	383163	351990	85485
1977–8	7497	11482	12.2	11180	20.6	24.7	89739	82833	410873	378160	92134
1978–9	8573	14237	14.0	15231	22.7	25.4	101597	94100	434437	399834	100639
1979–80	10449	15375	13.9	14445	26.8	29.4	110133	101560	411663	375147	96429

(contd.)

TABLE A1.3 (contd.)

(1)	(12)	(13)		(14)		(15)	(16)	(17)	(18)	(19)	(20)	(21)
1980–1	12288	14580	*11.1*	16942	*12.9*	29.3	32.7	143764	131477	439201	400648	91673
1981–2	14708	23075	*15.0*	19258	*12.5*	33.7	36.1	168600	153892	467139	426363	112085
1982–3	17175	23611	*13.8*	19759	*11.5*	36.8	38.9	188262	171087	484217	440915	110918
1983–4	19565	23631	*11.8*	21539	*10.8*	39.6	42.3	219496	199931	518491	472463	109094
1984–5	22487	30539	*13.7*	26868	*12.0*	43.8	45.5	245515	223028	539874	490787	121019
1985–6	26717	39086	*15.6*	33684	*13.4*	49.0	48.7	277991	251274	570267	518394	134197
1986–7	30389	41814	*14.9*	34917	*12.4*	52.9	52.0	311177	280788	597850	542986	136610
1987–8	33974	44383	*13.9*	45759	*14.3*	56.1	56.8	354343	320369	623371	565274	139701
1988–9	39693	60183	*15.8*	60524	*15.8*	62.3	61.6	421567	381874	684832	623197	160214
1989–90	46560	68475	*15.6*	72698	*16.5*	69.3	66.7	486179	439619	728952	663362	165963
1990–1	53264	83590	*16.2*	96272	*18.7*	76.4	73.7	568674	515410	771295	701831	179075
1991–2	64402	78858	*13.4*	82883	*14.1*	85.9	83.9	653117	588715	778289	704518	166866
1992–3	74512	103507	*15.4*	102210	*15.2*	94.3	91.3	748367	673855	819318	741125	188852
1993–4	83353	99266	*12.8*	115059	*14.8*	100.0	100.0	859220	775867	859220	775867	182619
1994–5	97994	138790	*15.2*	165362	*18.1*	108.0	109.7	1012770	914776	923349	832891	219245
1995–6	117926	197253	*18.4*	201601	*18.8*	117.9	119.5	1188012	1070086	993946	894794	267323
1996–7	136503	161359	*13.1*	198496	*16.1*	124.8	128.2	1368209	1231706	1067444	960169	238724
1997–8	151997	191715	*14.0*	222483	*16.2*	129.5	136.5	1522547	1370550	1115248	1000388	265331
1998–9	168066	204143	*13.0*	224955	*14.3*	135.1	147.3	1740985	1572919	1182020	1059827	275574
1999–2000	182359	275903	*15.7*	308310	*17.6*	139.6	153.0	1936831	1754472	1266283	1137212	328366
2000–1	197895	274813	*14.5*	300284	*15.9*	143.6	158.8	2089500	1891605	1316201	1180101	329198
2001–2	217679	286333	*13.9*	295864	*14.4*	152.6	164.2	2271984	2054305	1383705	1241240	330238
2002–3	232952	325006	*14.6*	377336	*16.9*	154.4	171.0	2463324	2230372	1440632	1292063	361347
2003–4	253637	382057	*15.2*	473231	*18.9*	161.5	176.4	2760025	2506388	1564620	1408146	393723
								3108561				
1999–2000 Series							(1999–2000=100)					
1999–2000	186649	325565	*18.4*	322640	*18.2*	100.0	100.0	1958814	1772165	1958814	1772165	512214
2000–1	202732	308858	*16.2*	306294	*16.1*	104.7	103.5	2107661	1904929	2036966	1842211	488818
2001–2	221161	333307	*16.2*	302576	*14.7*	109.8	106.4	2281305	2060144	2144483	1942379	505141
2002–3	235602	383412	*17.3*	384906	*17.4*	111.6	110.2	2449736	2214134	2222321	2011666	554425
2003–4$	256570	469060	*18.7*	495562	*19.8*	116.9	114.7	2760224	2503654	2406324	2184986	620655
2004–5$$	294758	594487	*21.0*	644797	*22.8*	126.2	119.5	3121414	2826656	2611511	2376558	704431
								3531451	3207364	2838222	2592194	

Notes: ** (Domestic Savings + Net Capital Inflow—Domestic Capital Formation); * Excluding works of art & antiques (valuables are a new item in the 1999–2000 series); $ Quick Estimates; $$ Revised Estimates; Figures in italics are as percentage to GDP at current prices, except for net capital formation in columns (13) and (14) which are as percentages to NDP at current market prices.

Source: Central Statistical Organisation (CSO), *National Accounts Statistics*, various issues.

TABLE A1.4
Net Capital Stock by Type of Institution and Capital–Output Ratio

Amount in rupees crore

Year (As on 31 March)	Net capital stock				Net fixed capital stock				Inventory				Fiscal year	Average capital-output ratio (ACOR)							Incremental capital-output (ICOR)	
			Private sector				Private sector							Net capital stock to Output*			Net Fixed Capital Stock to Output*			ND-CF to output	NFCF to output $
	Total (3+4)	Public sector	Total	Household sector	Total (7+8)	Public sector	Total	Household sector	Total (11+12)	Public sector	Total	Household sector		Total	Public sector	Private sector	Total	Public sector	Private sector		
(1)	(2)	(3)	(4)	(5)	(6)	(7)	(8)	(9)	(10)	(11)	(12)	(13)	(14)	(15)	(16)	(17)	(18)	(19)	(20)	(21)	(22)
							At 1993–4 prices							At 1993–4 prices							
1981	1231085	512169	718916	612928	1121610	471861	649749	577767	109475	40308	69167	35161	1980–1	–	–	–	–	–	–	2.47	2.10
1982	1312238	545386	766852	642779	1188209	500219	687990	606093	124029	45167	78862	36686	1981–2	3.31	6.95	2.41	3.01	6.39	2.17	2.75	2.61
1983	1379366	580645	798721	656008	1244576	532944	711632	617431	134790	47701	87089	38577	1982–3	3.41	6.71	2.52	3.08	6.16	2.25	5.44	5.43
1984	1433963	613846	820117	668652	1295600	565457	730143	627167	138363	48389	89974	41485	1983–4	3.30	6.69	2.41	2.98	6.15	2.14	1.87	1.91
1985	1496083	650509	845574	680021	1347822	598708	749114	635736	148261	51801	96460	44285	1984–5	3.31	6.59	2.40	2.98	6.07	2.13	3.67	3.57
1986	1568302	687969	880333	694032	1402628	632494	770134	645308	165674	55475	110199	48724	1985–6	3.32	6.41	2.41	2.98	5.89	2.12	3.72	3.44
1987	1640960	729394	911566	705716	1462759	672294	790465	652300	178201	57100	121101	53416	1986–7	3.33	6.23	2.44	2.98	5.74	2.12	3.56	3.59
1988	1699672	702288	937384	719174	1517223	707803	809420	662039	182449	54485	127964	57135	1987–8	3.35	5.91	2.45	2.99	5.70	2.12	4.86	4.47
1989	1771459	798155	973304	739929	1575554	744439	831115	674199	195905	53716	142189	65730	1988–9	3.14	5.78	2.26	2.79	5.59	1.94	1.81	1.55
1990	1839659	834418	1005241	754625	1634309	778117	856192	687930	205350	56301	149049	66695	1989–90	3.06	5.79	2.20	2.72	5.40	1.88	2.86	2.45
1991	1918761	872496	1046265	777430	1704760	813524	891236	707661	214001	58972	155029	69769	1990–1	3.01	5.90	2.14	2.68	5.50	1.83	3.86	3.09
1992	1995190	904901	1090289	792377	1781854	848542	933312	722573	213336	56359	156977	69804	1991–2	3.12	5.78	2.25	2.78	5.40	1.92	20.87	20.01
1993	2077675	936973	1140702	807065	1853469	877739	975730	735804	224206	59234	164972	71261	1992–3	3.09	5.86	2.22	2.76	5.49	1.90	3.47	3.17
1994	2144285	970452	1173833	808478	1921762	909237	1012525	737706	222523	61215	161308	70772	1993–4	3.02	5.78	2.17	2.70	5.41	1.87	3.00	2.63
1995	2283999	1011406	1272593	861463	2048289	950773	1097516	786379	235710	60633	175077	75084	1994–5	2.96	5.59	2.14	2.66	5.25	1.85	3.09	2.33
1996	2470063	1045338	1424725	938056	2212699	985081	1227618	854650	257364	60257	197107	83406	1995–6	2.97	5.46	2.20	2.66	5.14	1.90	3.24	2.77
1997	2611101	1075323	1535778	983904	2365943	1013446	1352497	907745	245158	61877	183281	76159	1996–7	2.94	5.37	2.22	2.65	5.06	1.94	2.58	2.28
1998	2754003	1103351	1650652	1029843	2498316	1038500	1459816	946589	255687	64851	190836	83254	1997–8	2.97	4.85	2.35	2.70	4.57	2.08	4.47	3.59
1999	2878178	1135160	1743018	1067948	2623861	1068576	1555285	985633	254317	66584	187733	82315	1998–9	2.93	4.61	2.36	2.67	4.34	2.10	2.87	2.63
2000	3017238	1175841	1841397	1108153	2737349	1099229	1638120	1021470	279889	76612	203277	86683	1999–2000	2.89	4.49	2.35	2.63	4.21	2.10	3.79	2.96
2001	3138233	1208598	1929635	1160453	2848732	1128608	1720124	1069887	289501	79990	209511	90566	2000–1	2.90	4.61	2.34	2.63	4.31	2.09	4.88	4.15
2002	3255205	1243954	2011251	1207622	2958839	1159888	1799151	1114480	296366	84266	212100	93142	2001–2	2.84	4.41	2.33	2.58	4.11	2.08	3.08	2.96
2003	3347520	1270531	2076989	1247140	3044377	1189686	1854691	1148379	303143	80845	222298	98761	2002–3	2.82	4.20	2.35	2.57	3.92	2.10	5.56	4.64
2004	3478797	1303113	2175684	1312270	3171098	1228473	1942625	1209341	307699	74640	233059	102929	2003–4	2.68	–	–	2.44	–	–	2.81	2.22

(contd.)

TABLE A1.4 (contd.)

(1)	(2)	(3)	(4)	(5)	(6)	(7)	(8)	(9)	(10)	(11)	(12)	(13)	(14)	(15)	(16)	(17)	(18)	(19)	(20)	(21)	(22)
					At current prices													At current prices			
1981	351395	146629	204766	167777	310669	131043	179626	155538	40726	15586	25140	12239	1980–1	—	—	—	—	—	—	0.87	0.74
1982	431181	176163	255018	206678	381653	157436	224217	192966	49528	18727	30801	13712	1981–2	2.85	6.38	2.05	2.52	5.70	1.80	0.99	0.89
1983	509014	208603	300411	240552	452612	188002	264610	225388	56402	20601	35801	15164	1982–3	3.09	6.27	2.28	2.74	5.63	2.01	1.32	1.27
1984	582900	240272	342628	274984	520828	218097	302731	257327	62072	22175	39897	17657	1983–4	3.05	6.29	2.24	2.72	5.69	1.98	0.81	0.82
1985	669406	279996	389410	309836	597918	254689	343229	289447	71488	25307	46181	20389	1984–5	3.13	6.29	2.30	2.79	5.71	2.03	1.27	1.21
1986	777279	333360	443919	347659	693136	304679	388457	323763	84143	28681	55462	23896	1985–6	3.25	6.29	2.39	2.90	5.74	2.10	1.49	1.35
1987	886426	381767	504659	391916	791770	350925	440845	364289	94656	30842	63814	27627	1986–7	3.36	6.21	2.49	3.00	5.69	2.18	1.39	1.40
1988	993908	431337	562571	435781	890329	399979	490350	404162	103579	31358	72221	31619	1987–8	3.33	6.12	2.48	2.98	5.65	2.16	1.34	1.23
1989	1127961	495583	632378	482372	1005150	461908	543242	441403	122811	33675	89136	40969	1988–9	3.13	5.87	2.30	2.80	5.46	1.99	1.07	0.91
1990	1286196	576172	710024	533239	1144039	537748	606291	486433	142157	38424	103733	46806	1989–90	3.08	5.89	2.23	2.75	5.50	1.91	1.38	1.18
1991	1457212	653192	804020	598616	1296299	609291	687008	545606	160913	43901	117012	53010	1990–1	3.00	5.91	2.14	2.67	5.51	1.83	1.45	1.16
1992	1711605	772374	939231	681228	1534234	725219	809015	624143	177371	47155	130216	57085	1991–2	3.02	5.74	2.18	2.70	5.37	1.87	1.24	1.19
1993	1944754	880457	1064297	747259	1737747	825616	912131	681975	207007	54841	152166	65284	1992–3	3.05	5.85	2.19	2.73	5.49	1.88	1.38	1.26
1994	2144285	970452	1173833	808478	1921762	909237	1012525	737706	222523	61215	161308	70772	1993–4	2.93	5.60	2.10	2.62	5.25	1.81	1.16	1.02
1995	2479822	1109118	1370704	926943	2222611	1041958	1180653	848783	257211	67160	190051	78160	1994–5	2.82	5.44	2.03	2.53	5.11	1.75	1.37	1.03
1996	2998698	1270492	1728206	1159654	2696837	1199172	1497665	1067742	301861	71320	230541	91912	1995–6	2.87	5.40	2.11	2.57	5.09	1.82	1.48	1.26
1997	3384845	1426154	1958691	1290942	3086238	1350268	1735970	1201887	298607	75886	222721	89055	1996–7	2.88	5.60	2.13	2.61	5.29	1.87	1.31	1.16
1998	3745028	1563424	2181604	1420215	3422806	1481724	1941082	1317796	322222	81700	240522	102419	1997–8	2.88	5.14	2.19	2.63	4.87	1.94	1.70	1.36
1999	4125124	1714274	2410850	1551295	3794555	1626912	2167643	1449121	330569	87362	243207	102174	1998–9	2.75	4.83	2.11	2.52	4.58	1.88	1.17	1.07
2000	4507095	1851659	2655436	1704478	4119239	1747838	2371401	1581303	387856	103821	284035	123175	1999–2000	2.73	4.73	2.11	2.51	4.48	1.89	2.06	1.60
2001	4834349	1960193	2874156	1824727	4412871	1844383	2568488	1689167	421478	115810	305668	135560	2000–1	2.74	4.90	2.10	2.50	4.61	1.88	2.39	2.08
2002	5265179	2113146	3152033	2054620	4823129	1987244	2835885	1912190	442050	125902	316148	142430	2001–2	2.71	4.82	2.09	2.48	4.53	1.88	1.86	1.79
2003	5566103	2228075	3338028	2167093	5103954	2105347	2998607	2013056	462149	122728	339421	154037	2002–3	2.68	4.62	2.09	2.45	4.36	1.88	2.39	1.99
2004	6071158	2417339	3653819	2397555	5579659	2298744	3280915	2231791	491499	118595	372904	165764	2003–4	2.57	—	—	2.36	—	1.94	1.53

Notes: Data as per 1999–2000 series are not available; —data are not available; * Average of beginning and year–end capital stock as ratio of the year's NDP at factor cost for respective sectors; $ Based on increase in NDP at factor cost.

Source: Central Statistical Organisation (CSO), *National Accounts Statistics*, various issues.

TABLE A1.5
Rank of States in Descending order of Per Capita State Domestic Product in Real Terms

(Three-yearly Annual Averages)

	Per Capita GSDP at 1980–1 prices					Per Capita GSDP at 1993–4 prices		
Rank	State	Annual Averages for 1980–1 to 1982–3	Rank	State	Annual Averages for 1990–1 to 1992–3	Relative Increase Between Two Periods (per cent)	Rank State	Annual Averages for 1993–4 to 1995–6	Rank State	Annual Averages for 2001–2 to 2003–4	Relative Increase Between Two Periods (per cent)

Part A: Per Capita Gross State Domestic Product (GSDP)

Rank	State	Annual Avg 1980–1 to 1982–3	Rank	State	Annual Avg 1990–1 to 1992–3	Rel. Incr. (%)	Rank	State	Annual Avg 1993–4 to 1995–6	Rank	State	Annual Avg 2001–2 to 2003–4	Rel. Incr. (%)
1	Delhi	4600	1	Delhi	6375	38.6	1	Chandigarh	22616	1	Goa	34029	64.2
2	Goa	3895	2	Goa	5987	53.7	2	Delhi	21041	2	Chandigarh	33140	46.5
3	Punjab	3174	3	Punjab	4286	35.0	3	Goa	20721	3	Delhi	30371	44.3
4	Pondicherry	3097	4	Maharashtra	3931	45.8	4	Andaman & Nicobar	16982	4	Pondicherry	26937	128.6
5	Andaman & Nicobar	2759	5	Haryana	3843	42.1	5	Punjab	14405	5	Maharashtra	17847	27.3
6	Haryana	2705	6	Sikkim	3729	112.3	6	Maharashtra	14019	6	Punjab	17775	23.4
7	Maharashtra	2695	7	Pondicherry	3213	3.7	7	Haryana	13000	7	Gujarat	17664	39.5
8	Gujarat	2280	8	Arunachal Pradesh	3150	70.3	8	Gujarat	12661	8	Andaman & Nicobar	17549	3.3
9	J & K	2019	9	Gujarat	3118	36.8	9	Pondicherry	11784	9	Haryana	17186	32.2
10	Himachal Pradesh	1888	10	A & N islands	3012	9.2	10	Tamil Nadu	10815	10	Tamil Nadu	14563	34.7
11	West Bengal	1871	11	Tamil Nadu	2579	48.0	11	Nagaland	10088	11	Karnataka	14133	56.1
12	Arunachal Pradesh	1850	12	Himachal Pradesh	2507	32.8	12	Arunachal Pradesh	9739	12	Himachal Pradesh	13657	44.5
13	Karnataka	1776	13	Karnataka	2462	41.6	13	Himachal Pradesh	9454	13	Kerala	13192	41.0
	Average for all states	1857	14	West Bengal	2448	30.8	14	Sikkim	9441	14	Nagaland	13127	30.1
	All-India GDP (CSO)	1757		Average for all states	2395	34.8	15	Kerala	9357	15	Sikkim	12611	33.6
13	Sikkim	1743		All-India GDP(CSO)	2538	36.7		All-India GDP(CSO)	9221		Average for all states	12592	38.9
14	Tamil Nadu	1742	15	Andhra Pradesh	2312	38.2		Average for all states	9065		All-India GDP(CSO)	12685	37.6
15	Nagaland	1739	16	Karnataka	2189	8.4	16	Karnataka	9054	16	Andhra Pradesh	12427	43.6
16	Karnataka	1683	16	J & K	2158	28.2	17	Andhra Pradesh	8653	17	West Bengal	12094	54.2
17	Kerala	1673	17	Kerala	2151	23.5	18	Meghalaya	8214	18	Mizoram	11923	—
18	Andhra Pradesh	1586	18	Nagaland	2129	50.4	19	Uttaranchal	7966	19	Meghalaya	11460	39.5
19	Manipur	1529	19	Rajasthan	2048	29.2	20	West Bengal	7844	20	Tripura	10965	79.5
20	Madhya Pradesh	1529	20	Manipur	2011	31.5	21	Rajasthan	7749	21	Arunachal Pradesh	10674	9.6
21	Meghalaya	1485	21	Meghalaya	1882	23.1	22	J & K	7664	22	Uttaranchal	10213	28.2
22	Assam	1449	22	Madhya Pradesh	1836	30.2	23	Chattisgarh	7626	23	Rajasthan	9935	28.2
23	Uttar Pradesh	1416	23	Tripura	1833	26.5	24	Madhya Pradesh	7490	24	Chattisgarh	9128	19.7
24	Rajasthan	1411	24	Uttar Pradesh	1719	15.8	25	Jharkhand	7277	25	Manipur	9118	39.7
25	Tripura	1371	25	Assam	1639	19.6	26	Manipur	6526	26	J & K	9069	18.3
26	Orissa	1080	26	Orissa	1291	19.6	27	Assam	6476	27	Jharkhand	8772	20.5
27	Bihar	—	27	Bihar	—	—	28	Tripura	6109	28	Madhya Pradesh	8761	17.0
28	Mizoram		28	Mizoram			29	Uttar Pradesh	5902	29	Assam	7258	12.1
							30	Orissa	5815	30	Orissa	7014	20.6
							31	Bihar	3326	31	Uttar Pradesh	6753	14.4
							32	Mizoram	—	32	Bihar	3990	20.0

(contd.)

TABLE A1.5 (contd.)

		Per Capita NSDP at 1980–1 prices						Per Capita GSDP at 1993–4 prices		
Rank	State	Annual Averages for 1980–1 to 1982–3	Rank	State	Annual Averages for 1990–1 to 1992–3	Relative Increase Between Two Periods (per cent)	Rank	State	Annual Averages for 1993–4 to 1995–6	Rank	State	Annual Averages for 2001–2 to 2003–4	Relative Increase Between Two Periods (per cent)

Rank	State	Annual Averages for 1980–1 to 1982–3	Rank	State	Annual Averages for 1990–1 to 1992–3	Relative Increase Between Two Periods (per cent)	Rank	State	Annual Averages for 1993–4 to 1995–6	Rank	State	Annual Averages for 2001–2 to 2003–4	Relative Increase Between Two Periods (per cent)
						Part B : Per Capita Net State Domestic Product (NSDP)							
1	Delhi	4229	1	Delhi	5845	38.2	1	Chandigarh	21102	1	Chandigarh	30973	46.8
2	Goa	3083	2	Goa	5017	62.7	2	Delhi	18968	2	Goa	29110	69.7
3	Punjab	2818	3	Punjab	3829	35.8	3	Goa	17155	3	Delhi	27688	46.0
4	Pondicherry	2817	4	Maharashtra	3573	45.7	4	Andaman & Nicobar	15579	4	Pondicherry	25558	161.4
5	Andaman & Nicobar	2544	5	Haryana	3476	43.7	5	Punjab	12834	5	Andaman & Nicobar	15881	1.9
6	Maharashtra	2452	6	Sikkim	3431	108.7	6	Maharashtra	12521	6	Punjab	15611	21.6
7	Haryana	2419	7	Arunachal Pradesh	2912	72.1	7	Haryana	11407	7	Maharashtra	15567	24.3
8	Gujarat	2011	8	Pondicherry	2833	0.6	8	Gujarat	10993	8	Haryana	14897	30.6
9	J & K	1777	9	Gujarat	2704	34.5	9	Pondicherry	9777	9	Gujarat	14850	35.1
10	West Bengal	1727	10	Andaman & Nicobar	2589	1.8	10	Tamil Nadu	9678	10	Tamil Nadu	12719	31.4
11	Himachal Pradesh	1718	11	Tamil Nadu	2290	47.3	11	Nagaland	9395	11	Karnataka	12563	55.1
12	Arunachal Pradesh	1692	12	Himachal Pradesh	2240	30.4	12	Arunachal Pradesh	8809	12	Nagaland	12303	30.9
13	Sikkim	1644	13	West Bengal	2236	29.5	13	Sikkim	8500	13	Himachal Pradesh	11970	42.7
14	Karnataka	1595	14	Karnataka	2193	40.3	14	Kerala	8483	14	Kerala	11565	36.3
	Average for all states	1672		Average for all states	2132	33.6	15	Himachal Pradesh	8387	15	Sikkim	11269	32.6
	All-India NDP(CSO)	1563		All-India NDP(CSO)	2264	35.4	16	Karnataka	8101		Average for all states	11189	38.4
15	Andhra Pradesh	1555	15	Tamil Nadu	2078	38.1		Average for all states	8083		All-India NDP(CSO)	11272	37.1
16	Nagaland	1553	16	Nagaland	2074	33.6		All-India NDP(CSO)	8222	16	Andhra Pradesh	11080	43.3
17	Rajasthan	1504	17	Andhra Pradesh	1891	49.9	17	Andhra Pradesh	7733	17	West Bengal	10981	54.4
18	Kerala	1487	18	Rajasthan	1858	24.9	18	Uttaranchal	7143	18	Mizoram	10836	–
19	Manipur	1443	19	Kerala	1822	26.3	19	Meghalaya	7123	19	Meghalaya	10321	44.9
20	Assam	1374	20	Manipur	1793	0.9	20	West Bengal	7114	20	Tripura	9972	80.2
21	Madhya Pradesh	1369	21	J & K	1705	24.7	21	Rajasthan	6844	21	Arunachal Pradesh	9388	6.6
22	Meghalaya	1367	22	Meghalaya	1650	27.1	22	Madhya Pradesh	6641	22	Rajasthan	8788	28.4
23	Uttar Pradesh	1299	23	Tripura	1631	25.6	23	J & K	6631	23	Uttaranchal	8787	23.0
24	Tripura	1298	24	Uttar Pradesh	1617	18.2	24	Chattisgarh	6486	24	Manipur	8081	42.6
25	Orissa	1265	25	Madhya Pradesh	1559	13.4	25	Jharkhand	6017	25	J & K	7702	16.1
26	Rajasthan	1261	26	Assam	1463	15.7	26	Assam	5737	26	Chattisgarh	7678	18.4
27	Bihar	933	27	Orissa	1106	18.6	27	Manipur	5668	27	Madhya Pradesh	7666	15.4
28	Mizoram	–	28	Bihar	–	–	28	Tripura	5535	28	Jharkhand	7273	20.9
							29	Uttar Pradesh	5177	29	Assam	6281	9.5
							30	Orissa	5051	30	Orissa	5985	18.5
							31	Bihar	3024	31	Uttar Pradesh	5803	12.1
							32	Mizoram	–	32	Bihar	3609	19.4

Note: – not available.

Source: EPWRF (2003) and CSO's Website (http://mospi.gov.in/mospi_nad_main.htm).

A2 PRODUCTION

TABLE A2.1
Production Trends in Major Agricultural Crops

(Million tonnes)

Year	Rice	Wheat	Coarse cereals	Cereals	Pulses	Food-grains	Oil-seeds#	Cotton (Lint)@	Jute and mesta*	Tobacco	Sugar-cane	Tea* (Jan.–Dec. Mn.kgs)	Coffee
(1)	(2)	(3)	(4)	(5)	(6)	(7)	(8)	(9)	(10)	(11)	(12)	(13)	(14)
1950–1	20.58	6.46	15.38	42.42	8.41	50.83	5.16	3.04	3.31	0.26	57.05	279.00	24.00
1951–2	21.30	6.18	16.09	43.57	8.42	51.99	5.03	3.28	4.72	0.21	61.63	291.00	24.00
1952–3	22.90	7.50	19.61	50.01	9.19	59.20	4.73	3.34	5.32	0.25	51.00	306.00	21.00
1953–4	28.21	8.02	22.97	59.20	10.62	69.82	5.37	4.13	3.77	0.27	44.41	267.00	25.00
1954–5	25.22	9.04	22.82	57.08	10.95	68.03	6.40	4.45	3.86	0.26	58.74	293.00	26.00
1955–6	27.56	8.76	19.49	55.81	11.05	66.85	5.73	4.18	5.39	0.30	60.54	308.00	35.00
1956–7	29.04	9.40	19.87	58.31	11.55	69.86	6.36	4.92	5.81	0.31	69.05	309.00	43.00
1957–8	25.53	7.99	21.23	54.75	9.56	64.31	6.35	4.96	5.33	0.24	71.16	311.00	44.00
1958–9	30.85	9.96	23.18	63.99	13.15	77.14	7.30	4.88	6.91	0.32	73.36	325.00	47.00
1959–60	31.68	10.32	22.87	64.87	11.80	76.67	6.56	3.68	5.69	0.29	77.82	326.00	50.00
1960–1	34.57	11.00	23.74	69.31	12.70	82.02	6.98	5.60	5.26	0.31	110.00	321.00	68.00
1961–2	35.66	12.07	23.22	70.95	11.76	82.71	7.28	4.85	8.24	0.34	103.97	354.00	46.00
1962–3	33.21	10.78	24.63	68.62	11.53	80.15	7.39	5.54	7.19	0.34	91.91	347.00	56.00
1963–4	37.00	9.85	23.72	70.57	10.07	80.64	7.13	5.75	7.98	0.36	104.23	346.00	69.00
1964–5	39.31	12.26	25.37	76.94	12.42	89.36	8.56	6.01	7.66	0.36	121.91	372.00	61.00
1965–6	30.59	10.40	21.42	62.41	9.94	72.35	6.40	4.85	5.78	0.29	123.99	366.00	64.00
1966–7	30.44	11.39	24.05	65.88	8.35	74.23	6.43	5.27	6.58	0.35	92.83	376.00	78.00
1967–8	37.61	16.54	28.80	82.95	12.10	95.05	8.30	5.78	7.59	0.37	95.50	385.00	71.00
1968–9	39.76	18.65	25.18	83.59	10.42	94.01	6.85	5.45	3.84	0.36	124.68	402.00	73.00
1969–70	40.43	20.09	27.29	87.81	11.69	99.50	7.73	5.56	6.79	0.34	135.02	396.00	63.00
1970–1	42.22	23.83	30.55	96.60	11.82	108.42	9.63	4.76	6.19	0.36	126.37	419.00	110.20
1971–2	43.07	26.41	24.60	94.08	11.09	105.17	9.08	6.95	6.84	0.42	113.57	435.00	68.90
1972–3	39.24	24.74	23.14	87.12	9.91	97.03	7.14	5.74	6.09	0.37	124.87	456.00	91.10
1973–4	44.05	21.78	28.83	94.66	10.01	104.67	9.39	6.31	7.68	0.46	140.81	472.00	86.40
1974–5	39.58	24.10	26.13	89.81	10.02	99.83	9.15	7.16	5.83	0.36	144.29	489.00	92.50
1975–6	48.74	28.84	30.41	107.99	13.04	121.03	10.61	5.95	5.91	0.35	140.60	487.00	84.00
1976–7	41.92	29.01	28.88	99.81	11.36	111.17	8.43	5.84	7.10	0.42	153.01	512.00	102.20
1977–8	52.67	31.75	30.02	114.44	11.97	126.41	9.66	7.24	7.15	0.49	176.97	556.00	125.10
1978–9	53.77	35.51	30.44	119.72	12.18	131.90	10.10	7.96	8.33	0.45	151.66	564.00	110.50
1979–80	42.33	31.83	26.97	101.13	8.57	109.70	8.74	7.65	7.96	0.44	128.83	544.00	149.80
1980–1	53.63	36.31	29.02	118.96	10.63	129.59	9.37	7.01	8.16	0.48	154.25	569.60	118.60
1981–2	53.25	37.45	31.09	121.79	11.51	133.30	12.08	7.88	8.37	0.52	186.36	560.40	150.00
1982–3	47.12	42.79	27.75	117.66	11.86	129.52	10.00	7.53	7.17	0.58	189.51	560.70	130.00
1983–4	60.10	45.48	33.90	139.48	12.89	152.37	12.69	6.39	7.72	0.49	174.08	581.50	105.00
1984–5	58.34	44.07	31.17	133.58	11.96	145.54	12.95	8.51	7.79	0.49	170.32	639.90	195.10
1985–6	63.83	47.05	26.20	137.08	13.36	150.44	10.83	8.73	12.65	0.44	170.65	656.20	122.30
1986–7	60.56	44.32	26.83	131.71	11.71	143.42	11.27	6.91	8.62	0.46	186.09	624.60	192.30
1987–8	56.86	46.17	26.36	129.39	10.96	140.35	12.65	6.38	6.78	0.37	196.74	674.30	123.00
1988–9	70.49	54.11	31.47	156.07	13.85	169.92	18.03	8.74	7.86	0.49	203.04	701.10	215.00
1989–90	73.57	49.85	34.76	158.18	12.86	171.04	16.92	11.42	8.29	0.55	225.57	684.10	180.00

(contd.)

TABLE A2.1: contd.

(1)	(2)	(3)	(4)	(5)	(6)	(7)	(8)	(9)	(10)	(11)	(12)	(13)	(14)
1990–1	74.29	55.14	32.70	162.13	14.26	176.39	18.61	9.84	9.23	0.56	241.05	720.34	170.00
1991–2	74.68	55.69	25.99	156.36	12.02	168.38	18.60	9.71	10.29	0.58	254.00	754.19	208.00
1992–3	72.86	57.21	36.59	166.66	12.82	179.48	20.11	11.40	8.59	0.60	228.03	703.93	169.40
1993–4	80.30	59.84	30.81	170.95	13.31	184.26	21.50	10.74	8.42	0.56	229.66	760.83	208.00
1994–5	81.81	65.77	29.88	177.46	14.04	191.50	21.34	11.89	9.08	0.57	275.54	752.90	180.00
1995–6	76.98	62.10	29.03	168.11	12.31	180.42	22.10	12.86	8.81	0.54	281.10	756.02	223.00
1996–7	81.73	69.35	34.11	185.19	14.25	199.44	24.38	14.23	11.13	0.62	277.56	780.14	205.00
1997–8	82.54	66.35	30.40	179.29	12.97	192.26	21.32	10.85	11.02	0.64	279.54	835.60	228.30
1998–9	86.08	71.29	31.33	188.70	14.91	203.61	24.75	12.29	9.81	0.74	288.72	855.20	265.00
1999–2000	89.68	76.37	30.34	196.39	13.41	209.80	20.71	11.53	10.56	0.52	299.32	836.80	292.00
2000–1	84.98	69.68	31.08	185.74	11.07	196.81	18.44	9.52	10.56	0.34	295.96	848.40	301.00
2001–2	93.34	72.77	33.37	199.48	13.37	212.85	20.66	10.00	11.68	0.55	297.21	847.40	301.00
2002–3	71.82	65.76	26.07	163.65	11.13	174.77	14.84	8.62	11.28	0.50	287.38	846.00	275.00
2003–4	88.53	72.15	37.60	198.28	14.91	213.19	25.19	13.73	11.17	0.54	233.86	850.50	270.00
2004–5	83.13	68.64	33.46	185.23	13.13	198.36	24.35	16.43	10.27		237.09	906.84	281.90
2005–6A	89.88	71.54	34.67	196.09	13.92	210.01	26.70	18.93	10.83		273.16	930.85	294.00
Decadal Growth Rates in per cent per annum													
1950–1 to 1959–60	4.34	4.93	2.51	3.75	3.51	3.72	4.11	3.98	4.82	2.81	6.98	1.73	11.96
1960–1 to 1969–70	1.92	9.46	1.92	3.35	–0.22	2.89	1.47	0.21	–2.60	0.91	2.29	2.21	4.16
1970–1 to 1979–80	2.58	5.02	1.56	2.98	0.12	2.72	1.53	2.85	2.90	2.43	2.59	2.99	5.98
1980–1 to 1989–90	4.03	3.29	0.43	2.97	1.27	2.83	6.10	3.50	0.91	–0.10	3.31	2.84	4.44
1990–1 to 2005–6	1.03	1.73	0.41	1.18	–0.02	1.09	0.43	0.98	1.88	–1.48	0.74	1.61	4.17

Notes: Decadal growth rate is worked out on three year moving averages. It indicates compound growth rate in the production data calculated for the specified period using the semi-log model lnY = a+bt, where t = time, Y = production, and the compound growth is obtained by taking antilog of 'b', deducting one from it and multiplying it with 100; A : Third advance estimate; * Production in million bales of 180 kgs each; @ Production in million bales of 170 kgs each; # Total of nine oilseeds out of eleven.

Source: GOI (2005), *Agricultural Statistics at a Glance*, Ministry of Agriculture and GOI (2006), *Economic Survey 2005–6*, Ministry of Finance and various earlier issues.

TABLE A2.2
Trends in Yields of Major Crops

(kg per hectare)

Year	Rice	Wheat	Coarse cereals	cereals	Pulses	food-grains	Total oil-seeds#	Sugar-cane	Tea	Coffee	Cotton (Lint)	Jute and mesta	Tobacco
(1)	(2)	(3)	(4)	(5)	(6)	(7)	(8)	(9)	(10)	(11)	(12)	(13)	(14)
1950–1	668	663	408	542	441	522	481	33422			88	1043	731
1952–3	714	653	414	557	448	536	430	31786			85	1074	723
1953–4	764	763	462	607	463	580	424	29495			89	1028	675
1954–5	902	750	506	678	489	640	488	31497			100	992	737
1955–6	820	803	520	664	500	631	511	36303			100	1021	737
1956–7	874	708	449	639	476	605	474	32779			88	1038	739
1957–8	900	695	473	664	495	629	509	33683			104	977	728
1958–9	790	682	495	630	424	587	502	34325			105	944	669
1959–60	930	789	519	707	541	672	561	37658			104	1130	836
1960–1	937	772	522	713	475	662	470	36414	971	448	86	1049	716
1961–2	1013	851	528	753	539	710	507	45549			125	1049	766
1962–3	1028	890	519	763	485	706	493	42349			103	1104	811
1963–4	931	793	556	733	475	680	482	40996			122	1041	842
1964–5	1033	730	540	757	416	687	481	46353			119	1130	817
1965–6	1078	913	514	817	520	757	561	46838			122	1136	876
1966–7	862	827	483	676	438	629	419	43717			104	936	778
1967–8	863	887	533	707	377	644	428	40336			114	1058	834
1968–9	1032	1103	608	840	534	783	530	40665			123	1137	871
1969–70	1076	1169	545	843	490	781	473	49236			122	855	821
1970–1	1073	1208	578	865	531	805	522	49121			122	1120	770
1971–2	1123	1307	665	949	524	872	579	48322	1182	816	106	1032	810
1972–3	1141	1380	564	936	501	858	526	47511	1221	499	151	1107	914
1973–4	1070	1271	548	886	474	813	452	50933	1271	620	127	1104	837
1974–5	1151	1172	623	918	427	827	555	51163	1311	554	142	1188	1001
1975–6	1045	1338	606	907	455	824	529	49855	1353	593	161	1068	954
1976–7	1235	1410	694	1041	533	944	627	50903	1341	488	138	1164	950
1977–8	1089	1387	689	985	494	894	512	53383	1407	544	144	1173	969
1978–9	1308	1480	710	1100	510	991	563	56160	1519	652	157	1108	979
1979–80	1328	1568	721	1136	515	1022	570	49114	1528	564	167	1186	1109
1980–1	1074	1436	652	982	385	876	516	49358	1455	749	160	1177	1031
1981–2	1336	1630	695	1142	473	1023	532	57844	1491	624	152	1130	1065
1982–3	1308	1691	733	1157	483	1032	639	58359	1461	691	166	1311	1172
1983–4	1231	1816	685	1150	519	1035	563	56441	1422	573	163	1265	1157
1984–5	1457	1843	813	1296	548	1162	679	55978	1468	453	141	1320	1120
1985–6	1417	1870	795	1285	526	1149	684	57673	1606	830	196	1242	1113
1986–7	1552	2046	664	1323	547	1175	570	59889	1641	507	197	1524	1111
1987–8	1471	1916	675	1266	506	1128	605	60444	1508	791	169	1454	1187
1988–9	1465	2002	721	1315	515	1173	629	60006	1628	508	168	1274	1155
1989–90	1689	2244	814	1493	598	1331	824	60992	1693	878	202	1540	1307
1990–1	1745	2121	922	1530	549	1349	742	65612	1652	478	252	1646	1335
1991–2	1740	2281	900	1571	578	1380	771	65395	1794	732	225	1634	1353
1992–3	1751	2394	778	1574	533	1382	719	66069	1800	746	216	1662	1369
1993–4	1744	2327	1063	1654	573	1457	797	63843	1664	582	257	1658	1425
1994–5	1888	2380	939	1701	598	1501	799	67120	1796	712	249	1713	1463
1995–6	1911	2559	929	1760	610	1546	843	71254	1767	614	257	1760	1486
1996–7	1797	2483	940	1703	552	1491	851	67787	1770	731	242	1712	1356
1997–8	1882	2679	1072	1831	635	1614	926	66496	1809	675	265	1818	1444
1998–9	1900	2485	986	1775	567	1552	816	71134	1865	746	208	1792	1394
1999–2000	1921	2590	1068	1856	634	1627	944	71203	1803	877	224	1722	1451
2000–1	1986	2778	1034	1926	635	1704	853	70935	1702	947	225	1836	1211
2001–2	1901	2708	1027	1844	544	1626	810	68577	1673	959	190	1867	1318
2002–3	2079	2762	1131	1980	607	1734	913	67370	1800	937	186	2007	1565
2003–4	1744	2610	966	1753	543	1535	691	63576	1800	839	191	1960	1529
2004–5	2077	2713	1238	1987	637	1731	1067	58986	na	824	309	2021	1474
2005–6	2026	2718	1166	1918	595	1703	967	63806	na	891	324	2107	na

Note: – Not Available.

Source: GOI (2005), *Agricultural Statistics at a Glance*, Ministry of Agriculture and GOI (2006), *Economic Survey 2005–6*, Ministry of Finance and various other issues.

TABLE A2.3
Horticulture and Livestock Production

(000 ' tonnes)

	1991–2	1992–3	1993–4	1994–5	1995–6	1996–7	1997–8	1998–9	1999–2000	2000–1	2001–2	2002–3	2003–4	2004–5	2005–6
Horticulture Production															
Total	96562	107388	114616	118394	125483	128482	128611	146020	149187	143806	146500	144400	152000	164100	178100
Fruits	28632	32955	37255	38603	41507	40458	43263	44042	45496	45370	43100	45200	49200	53100	57600
Apple	1148	1168	1298	1183	1215	1308	1321	1380	1047	1230	1420	na	na	na	na
Banana	7790	10460	11901	13168	13095	12440	13340	15073	16814	16170	16450	na	na	na	na
Citrus Fruit	2822	2979	3912	3701	3798	4456	4311	4575	4651	4400	4580	na	na	na	na
Lemon	na	na	924	970	920	1048	1101	1260	1492	na	na	na	na	na	na
Mosambi	na	na	825	887	880	844	882	773	1017	na	na	na	na	na	na
Orange	na	na	1058	709	1162	1720	1472	1674	na	na	na	na	na	na	na
Grapes	668	653	703	673	604	1135	969	1083	1138	1060	1100	na	na	na	na
Guava	1095	1204	1273	1388	1501	1601	1614	1801	1711	1630	1680	na	na	na	na
Litchi	244	261	313	333	365	378	455	429	433	400	420	na	na	na	na
Mango	8716	9223	10113	10993	10811	9981	10234	9782	10504	10240	10640	na	na	na	na
Papaya	805	804	1266	1373	1330	1299	1619	1582	1666	1770	1820	na	na	na	na
Pineapple	769	859	1007	1055	1071	925	937	1006	1025	1220	1260	na	na	na	na
Sapota	396	423	481	496	570	589	644	668	800	670	700	na	na	na	na
Vegetables	58532	63806	65787	67286	71594	75074	72683	87536	90831	93920	88600	84800	84800	91600	99400
Brinjal	na	na	4612	6232	6443	6586	7735	7882	8117	7700	7800	na	na	na	na
Cabbage	2771	3237	3593	3906	3862	3613	5324	5624	5909	5620	5700	na	na	na	na
Cauliflower	2998	3612	2873	3244	2474	3419	4471	4691	4718	4690	4700	na	na	na	na
Okra	1887	2738	3029	3989	4032	3040	3211	3380	3419	3340	3420	na	na	na	na
Onion	4706	5705	4006	4036	4080	4180	3140	5467	4900	4720	4850	na	na	na	na
Peas	852	1492	1528	2306	2341	2339	2422	2706	2712	3010	3110	na	na	na	na
Tomato	4243	4550	4934	5261	5442	5788	6184	8272	7427	7280	7420	na	na	na	na
Potato	18195	18479	17392	17401	18843	24216	17652	22495	25000	22240	24000	na	na	na	na
Sweet Potato	1131	1216	1221	1166	1138	1102	1048	1152	1007	na	na	na	na	na	na
Tapioca	5833	5413	6029	5857	5443	5663	6682	5830	6181	na	na	na	na	na	na
Coconuts*	10080	11241	11975	13300	12952	13061	12717	14925	12252	8700	8800	na	na	na	na
Flowers	na	na	233	261	334	367	366	419	509	560	570	na	na	na	na
Plantation Crops	7498	8347	8866	9767	9630	9730	9449	11063	9278	na	na	na	na	na	na
Spices	1900	2280	2470	2477	2410	2805	2801	2911	2911	3020	3200	2900	3800	4100	4400
Livestock Production															
Milk	56	58	61	64	66	69	72	75	78	81	84	86	88	91	na
Fish ('000 tonnes)	4157	4365	4644	4789	4949	5348	5388	5298	5675	5656	5956	6200	6399	6304	na
Eggs (Bn. Nos)	22	23	24	26	27	28	29	30	30	37	39	40	40	45	na

Notes: * Coconut production is in number of nuts in thousands (1453.24 nuts = 1 ton);   na—not available.

Source: National Horticulture Board, Ministry of Agriculture, Government of India, *Indian Horticulture Data Base, 2001* and *Economic Survey 2005–6*.

TABLE A2.4
Value of Output from Agriculture, Horticulture, and Livestock

(Rs crore)

Year	At Constant (1993–4) Prices											
	Agri-culture, Horti-culture, and Livestock	Agri-culture, (4 to 11)	Cereals	Pulses	Oilseeds	Sugars	Fibres	Drugs and Nar-cotics	Condi-ments and Spices	Others	Horti-culture# (Fruits and Vegetables)	Live-stock
(1)	(2)	(3)	(4)	(5)	(6)	(7)	(8)	(9)	(10)	(11)	(12)	(13)
1950–1	75462	55056	19186	7947	6437	4402	2817	1312	1790	11165	9529	20406
	(100.0)	(73.0)	(25.4)	(10.5)	(8.5)	(5.8)	(3.7)	(1.7)	(2.4)	(14.8)	(12.6)	(27.0)
1955–6	87963	66515	24446	10043	7318	5406	3766	1498	1957	12081	8914	21448
	(100.0)	(75.6)	(27.8)	(11.4)	(8.3)	(6.1)	(4.3)	(1.7)	(2.2)	(13.7)	(10.1)	(24.4)
1960–1	101953	78217	30355	11147	8655	7224	4780	1576	2254	12226	10164	23736
	(100.0)	(76.7)	(29.8)	(10.9)	(8.5)	(7.1)	(4.7)	(1.5)	(2.2)	(12.0)	(10.0)	(23.3)
1965–6	96816	72990	27067	8796	8175	8628	4041	1717	2190	12376	12552	23826
	(100.0)	(75.4)	(28.0)	(9.1)	(8.4)	(8.9)	(4.2)	(1.8)	(2.3)	(12.8)	(13.0)	(24.6)
1970–1	120802	95231	41162	10500	11733	8517	4432	2186	2972	13729	20010	25571
	(100.0)	(78.8)	(34.1)	(8.7)	(9.7)	(7.1)	(3.7)	(1.8)	(2.5)	(11.4)	(16.6)	(21.2)
1975–6	134664	104628	46357	11735	12264	9766	4783	2389	3068	14266	22706	30036
	(100.0)	(77.7)	(34.4)	(8.7)	(9.1)	(7.3)	(3.6)	(1.8)	(2.3)	(10.6)	(16.9)	(22.3)
1980–1	153023	116341	51263	9903	11301	10180	5865	2810	3722	21297	26214	36682
	(100.0)	(76.0)	(33.5)	(6.5)	(7.4)	(6.7)	(3.8)	(1.8)	(2.4)	(13.9)	(17.1)	(24.0)
1981–2	162189	123179	52109	10619	13465	12030	6703	3071	3737	21445	26466	39010
1982–3	160912	120243	49935	10800	11927	12319	6674	3139	4073	21376	27485	40669
1983–4	175923	132298	59703	11692	14556	11418	5524	2971	4260	22174	28929	43625
1984–5	176831	130298	57146	10878	14930	11040	7125	3514	4229	21436	31666	46533
1985–6	180379	131451	59379	11974	12798	10917	7754	3070	4703	20856	30116	48928
	(100.0)	(72.9)	(32.9)	(6.6)	(7.1)	(6.1)	(4.3)	(1.7)	(2.6)	(11.6)	(16.7)	(27.1)
1986–7	177763	126668	56816	10679	13162	11670	5867	3184	4548	20742	32576	51095
1987–8	177865	125574	55424	9860	14844	12320	5320	2966	4928	19912	29117	52291
1988–9	206650	152084	67783	12636	20487	12893	7219	3733	5583	21750	32702	54566
1989–90	209858	153218	68216	11642	19609	14273	9298	3445	5558	21177	31928	56640
1990–1	217745	158849	70273	13010	21253	15200	8248	3649	5561	21655	34141	58896
	(100.0)	(73.0)	(32.3)	(6.0)	(9.8)	(7.0)	(3.8)	(1.7)	(2.6)	(9.9)	(15.7)	(27.0)
1991–2	215328	154439	68437	10771	21366	15799	8247	3798	5388	20633	33720	60889
	(100.0)	(71.7)	(31.8)	(5.0)	(9.9)	(7.3)	(3.8)	(1.8)	(2.5)	(9.6)	(15.7)	(28.3)
1992–3	225154	161256	71474	11751	22881	14462	9372	3595	6267	21454	36746	63898
	(100.0)	(71.6)	(31.7)	(5.2)	(10.2)	(6.4)	(4.2)	(1.6)	(2.8)	(9.5)	(16.3)	(28.4)
1993–4	233419	166454	74523	12281	24096	14627	8961	4066	6740	21160	38420	66965
	(100.0)	(71.3)	(31.9)	(5.3)	(10.3)	(6.3)	(3.8)	(1.7)	(2.9)	(9.1)	(16.5)	(28.7)
1994–5	244678	175037	77698	12868	24843	17161	9972	3959	6803	21733	40298	69641
	(100.0)	(71.5)	(31.8)	(5.3)	(10.2)	(7.0)	(4.1)	(1.6)	(2.8)	(8.9)	(16.5)	(28.5)
1995–6	241680	169651	73212	11313	25151	17543	10749	4081	6492	21110	42593	72029
	(100.0)	(70.2)	(30.3)	(4.7)	(10.4)	(7.3)	(4.4)	(1.7)	(2.7)	(8.7)	(17.6)	(29.8)
1996–7	258938	184378	80252	13213	27780	17501	11944	4571	7276	21841	48455	74560
	(100.0)	(71.2)	(31.0)	(5.1)	(10.7)	(6.8)	(4.6)	(1.8)	(2.8)	(8.4)	(18.7)	(28.8)
1997–8	253442	176789	78630	12301	24774	17609	9377	4667	7278	22153	48958	76653
	(100.0)	(69.8)	(31.0)	(4.9)	(9.8)	(6.9)	(3.7)	(1.8)	(2.9)	(8.7)	(19.3)	(30.2)
1998–9	269471	189605	82645	14201	27935	18227	10589	4871	8696	22441	53545	79866
	(100.0)	(70.4)	(30.7)	(5.3)	(10.4)	(6.8)	(3.9)	(1.8)	(3.2)	(8.3)	(19.9)	(29.6)
1999–2000	270160	187832	85728	12422	23460	19056	9825	5314	8625	23402	54138	82328
	(100.0)	(69.5)	(31.7)	(4.6)	(8.7)	(7.1)	(3.6)	(2.0)	(3.2)	(8.7)	(20.0)	(30.5)
2000–1	261736	176285	80608	10351	21490	19920	8344	5130	8253	22189	59183	85451
	(100.0)	(67.4)	(30.8)	(4.0)	(8.2)	(7.6)	(3.2)	(2.0)	(3.2)	(8.5)	(22.6)	(32.6)
2001–2	280591	189901	86536	12621	24235	19535	8830	5579	9421	23144	58386	90690
	(100.0)	(67.7)	(30.8)	(4.5)	(8.6)	(7.0)	(3.1)	(2.0)	(3.4)	(8.2)	(20.8)	(32.3)
2002–3	255288	162411	70165	10523	18303	17891	7644	7123	8581	22181	60634	92877
	(100.0)	(63.6)	(27.5)	(4.1)	(7.2)	(7.0)	(3.0)	(2.8)	(3.4)	(8.7)	(23.8)	(36.4)
2003–4	285621	190312	84964	12636	28212	14778	11607	7163	8630	22322	60920	95309
	(100.0)	(66.6)	(29.7)	(4.4)	(9.9)	(5.2)	(4.1)	(2.5)	(3.0)	(7.8)	(21.3)	(33.4)

(contd.)

TABLE A2.4 (contd.)
Value of Output from Agriculture, Horticulture, and Livestock

(Rs crore)

Year	Agri-culture, Horti-culture, and Livestock	Agri-culture, (4 to 11)	Cereals	Pulses	Oilseeds	Sugars	Fibres	Drugs and Nar-cotics	Condi-ments and Spices	Others	Horti-culture[#] (Fruits and Vegetables)	Live-stock
(1)	(14)	(15)	(16)	(17)	(18)	(19)	(20)	(21)	(22)	(23)	(24)	(25)
1950–1	6385	5301	2082	335	464	248	214	138	173	1045	437	1084
	(100.0)	(83.0)	(32.6)	(5.2)	(7.3)	(3.9)	(3.4)	(2.2)	(2.7)	(16.4)	(6.8)	(17.0)
1955–6	5801	4737	1870	239	313	295	253	128	107	862	627	1064
	(100.0)	(81.7)	(32.2)	(4.1)	(5.4)	(5.1)	(4.4)	(2.2)	(1.8)	(14.9)	(10.8)	(18.3)
1960–1	8962	7493	3220	461	623	439	378	176	212	1005	829	1469
	(100.0)	(83.6)	(35.9)	(5.1)	(7.0)	(4.9)	(4.2)	(2.0)	(2.4)	(11.2)	(9.3)	(16.4)
1965–6	13301	11272	4951	706	1004	717	427	253	286	1312	1506	2029
	(100.0)	(84.7)	(37.2)	(5.3)	(7.5)	(5.4)	(3.2)	(1.9)	(2.2)	(9.9)	(11.3)	(15.3)
1970–1	22065	18786	8247	996	1865	1053	856	393	493	1916	2922	3279
	(100.0)	(85.1)	(37.4)	(4.5)	(8.5)	(4.8)	(3.9)	(1.8)	(2.2)	(8.7)	(13.2)	(14.9)
1975–6	35903	29623	13358	1589	2368	2007	1024	668	850	3037	4600	6280
	(100.0)	(82.5)	(37.2)	(4.4)	(6.6)	(5.6)	(2.9)	(1.9)	(2.4)	(8.5)	(12.8)	(17.5)
1980–1	60779	50236	19021	3186	4370	4025	1907	1000	1061	7177	8488	10543
	(100.0)	(82.7)	(31.3)	(5.2)	(7.2)	(6.6)	(3.1)	(1.6)	(1.7)	(11.8)	(14.0)	(17.3)
1981–2	68052	55295	21495	3150	5256	3783	2203	1107	1247	7685	9369	12757
1982–3	71800	57494	22403	3202	4999	3644	2129	1200	1422	7907	10589	14306
1983–4	85337	68740	27591	4332	7210	3796	2195	1379	1782	9025	11429	16597
1984–5	91464	71953	25723	4607	7266	4250	3401	1691	2160	9216	13639	19511
1985–6	98221	76389	28790	4975	5895	4722	2696	1652	2186	9887	15585	21832
	(100.0)	(77.8)	(29.3)	(5.1)	(6.0)	(4.8)	(2.7)	(1.7)	(2.2)	(10.1)	(15.9)	(22.2)
1986–7	105715	81268	28635	4619	8210	5007	2274	1844	2180	10308	18193	24447
1987–8	116794	88951	31378	5289	10309	5569	2908	1626	2828	11502	17541	27843
1988–9	142343	110327	40584	7770	12195	6408	3808	2219	3222	13430	20691	32016
1989–90	155447	117850	42707	7894	13416	8547	5010	2343	2980	13906	21047	37597
1990–1	181755	139822	48824	9353	18554	9411	5482	2947	3889	16135	25229	41933
	(100.0)	(76.9)	(26.9)	(5.1)	(10.2)	(5.2)	(3.0)	(1.6)	(2.1)	(8.9)	(13.9)	(23.1)
1991–2	213614	162811	60849	8276	20935	10159	6850	3226	5679	17804	29034	50803
	(100.0)	(76.2)	(28.5)	(3.9)	(9.8)	(4.8)	(3.2)	(1.5)	(2.7)	(8.3)	(13.6)	(23.8)
1992–3	236830	178658	66566	9656	20626	11686	6398	3249	6518	20201	33758	58172
	(100.0)	(75.4)	(28.1)	(4.1)	(8.7)	(4.9)	(2.7)	(1.4)	(2.8)	(8.5)	(14.3)	(24.6)
1993–4	271839	204874	74523	12281	24096	14627	8961	4066	6740	21160	38420	66965
	(100.0)	(75.4)	(27.4)	(4.5)	(8.9)	(5.4)	(3.3)	(1.5)	(2.5)	(7.8)	(14.1)	(24.6)
1994–5	312654	236608	84983	13614	26911	18123	13005	3884	8218	24390	43479	76046
	(100.0)	(75.7)	(27.2)	(4.4)	(8.6)	(5.8)	(4.2)	(1.2)	(2.6)	(7.8)	(13.9)	(24.3)
1995–6	342535	256698	86986	14018	28817	18276	13358	5312	8770	27959	53202	85837
	(100.0)	(74.9)	(25.4)	(4.1)	(8.4)	(5.3)	(3.9)	(1.6)	(2.6)	(8.2)	(15.5)	(25.1)
1996–7	399900	302743	107499	17204	34459	19474	14437	6227	10451	30718	62275	97157
	(100.0)	(75.7)	(26.9)	(4.3)	(8.6)	(4.9)	(3.6)	(1.6)	(2.6)	(7.7)	(15.6)	(24.3)
1997–8	426792	319586	106283	15171	30218	22330	12281	7787	11092	33276	81147	107206
	(100.0)	(74.9)	(24.9)	(3.6)	(7.1)	(5.2)	(2.9)	(1.8)	(2.6)	(7.8)	(19.0)	(25.1)
1998–9	488732	370365	128505	19591	36926	23076	13691	8152	14815	35584	90025	118367
	(100.0)	(75.8)	(26.3)	(4.0)	(7.6)	(4.7)	(2.8)	(1.7)	(3.0)	(7.3)	(18.4)	(24.2)
1999–2000	514718	384766	138767	18275	29996	24381	12636	9219	17468	40464	93560	129952
	(100.0)	(74.8)	(27.0)	(3.6)	(5.8)	(4.7)	(2.5)	(1.8)	(3.4)	(7.9)	(18.2)	(25.2)
2000–1	518693	378712	127704	16865	27264	27828	10920	9587	14147	41767	102630	139981
	(100.0)	(73.0)	(24.6)	(3.3)	(5.3)	(5.4)	(2.1)	(1.8)	(2.7)	(8.1)	(19.8)	(27.0)
2001–2	562023	412268	140293	22353	30626	27292	11570	10263	15106	40248	114516	149755
	(100.0)	(73.4)	(25.0)	(4.0)	(5.4)	(4.9)	(2.1)	(1.8)	(2.7)	(7.2)	(20.4)	(26.6)
2002–3	557036	397870	119200	18292	28649	25365	10851	15041	14145	41446	124881	159166
	(100.0)	(71.4)	(21.4)	(3.3)	(5.1)	(4.6)	(1.9)	(2.7)	(2.5)	(7.4)	(22.4)	(28.6)
2003–4	635104	470595	146948	21519	50890	22924	20147	14731	15128	46413	131896	164509
	(100.0)	(74.1)	(23.1)	(3.4)	(8.0)	(3.6)	(3.2)	(2.3)	(2.4)	(7.3)	(20.8)	(25.9)

Notes: 'Others' include other crops (rubber, gaurseed, and misc. crops), by product (straw and stalks, and others), kitchen garden products, and indigo, dyes and tannin material; [#] Horticulture includes floriculture; Figures in brackets are percentage shares in total value of output of agriculture, horticulture, and live stock.
Source: CSO (Various Issues), Ministry of Statistics and Programming implementation, Government of India.

TABLE A2.5
Structural Changes in Indian Industry and Decadal Growth

Sector group	Weight as per index numbers						Growth rates (per cent per annum)				
	1956=100	1960=100	1970=100	1980–1=100	1993–4=100		1970–1 to 1980–1	1980–1 to 1990–1	1990–1 to 1993–4	1993–4 to 2003–4	2004–5 to 2005–6	1993–4 to 2005–6
Mining and quarrying	7.47	9.72	9.69	11.5	10.47		4.6	7.6	1.4	3.1	0.70	3.2
Manufacturing	88.85	84.91	81.08	77.1	79.36		4.7	7.7	2.4	6.6	9.00	6.7
Electricity	3.68	5.37	9.23	11.4	10.17		4.2	9.1	6.8	5.5	5.10	5.3
General Index	100	100	100	100	100		7.6	7.9	2.9	6.1	8.00	6.2
Use-based category												
Basic goods	22.33	25.11	32.28	39.42	35.51		6.0	7.9	5.8	4.9	6.60	4.9
Capital goods	4.71	11.76	15.25	16.43	9.69		5.6	11.3	–3.9	6.7	15.50	7.5
Intermediate goods	24.59	25.88	20.95	20.51	26.44		3.5	6.3	4.9	7.1	2.30	6.5
Consumer goods	48.37	37.25	31.52	23.65	28.36		3.4	6.5	2.2	6.6	11.90	7.1
Consumer durables	2.21	5.68	3.41	2.55	5.12		4.6	14.8	0.7	9.9	14.60	9.9
Consumer non-durables	46.16	31.57	28.11	21.1	23.25		3.3	5.1	2.6	5.6	11.00	6.2

Note: Growth indicates compound growth rate in index numbers of industrial production for groups and general index calculated for the specified period using the semi-log model lnY = a+bt, where t = time, Y + index value, and the compound growth is obtained by taking antilog of 'b', deducting one from it and mutiplying it with 100.

Source: (i) EPWRF (2002): *Annual Survey of Industries 1993–4 to 1997–8, A Data Base on the Industrial Sector in India*, EPW Research Foundation, Mumbai; and as in Table A2.6.

TABLE A2.6
Index of Industrial Production with Major Groups and Sub-groups

Major groups	Weights	Annual average growth		Full fiscal year averages based on 1993–4=100												
		1993–4 to 2005–6	1980–1 to 1992–3	2005–6 (QE)	2004–5	2003–4	2002–3	2001–2	2000–1	1999–2000	1998–9	1997–8	1996–7	1995–6	1994–5	1993–4
(1)	(2)	(3)	(4)	(5)	(6)	(7)	(8)	(9)	(10)	(11)	(12)	(13)	(14)	(15)	(16)	(17)
General Index	100.00	6.9	6.8	221.2	204.8	189.0	176.6	167.0	162.6	154.9	145.2	139.5	130.8	123.3	109.1	100.0
				(8.0)	(8.4)	(7.0)	(5.7)	(2.7)	(5.0)	(6.7)	(4.1)	(6.7)	(6.1)	(13.0)	(9.1)	
Mining and Quarrying	10.47	3.8	7.0	154.5	153.4	146.9	139.6	131.9	130.3	126.7	125.4	126.4	118.2	120.5	109.8	100.0
				(0.7)	(4.4)	(5.2)	(5.8)	(1.2)	(2.8)	(1.0)	(–0.8)	(6.9)	(–1.9)	(9.7)	(9.8)	
Manufacturing	79.36	7.4	6.5	233.9	214.6	196.6	183.1	172.7	167.9	159.4	148.8	142.5	133.6	124.5	109.1	100.0
				(9.0)	(9.2)	(7.4)	(6.0)	(2.9)	(5.3)	(7.1)	(–4.4)	(6.7)	(7.3)	(14.1)	(9.1)	
Electricity	10.17	5.5	8.6	190.8	181.5	172.6	164.3	159.2	154.4	148.5	138.4	130.0	122.0	117.3	108.5	100.0
				(5.1)	(5.2)	(5.1)	(3.2)	(3.1)	(4.0)	(7.3)	(–6.5)	(6.6)	(4.0)	(8.1)	(8.5)	
Use-Based Classification																
Basic Goods	35.57	5.5	7.3	189.6	177.9	168.6	159.9	152.5	148.7	143.3	135.8	133.6	125.0	121.4	109.6	100.0
				(6.6)	(5.5)	(5.4)	(4.9)	(2.6)	(3.8)	(5.5)	(1.6)	(6.9)	(3.0)	(10.8)	(9.6)	
Capital Goods	9.26	8.6	8.8	265.1	229.6	201.5	177.4	160.6	165.6	163.3	152.7	135.6	128.2	115.0	109.2	100.0
				(15.5)	(13.9)	(13.6)	(10.5)	(–3.0)	(1.4)	(6.9)	(–12.6)	(5.8)	(11.5)	(5.3)	(9.2)	
Intermediate Goods	26.51	6.7	5.2	215.9	211.1	199.0	187.1	180.1	177.2	169.5	155.8	146.8	135.9	125.7	105.3	100.0
				(2.3)	(6.1)	(6.4)	(3.9)	(1.6)	(4.5)	(8.8)	(6.1)	(8.0)	(8.1)	(19.4)	(5.3)	
Consumer Goods	28.66	8.0	5.8	251.2	224.4	200.9	187.5	175.1	165.1	153.0	144.8	141.7	134.3	126.5	112.1	100.0
				(11.9)	(11.7)	(7.1)	(7.1)	(6.1)	(7.9)	(5.7)	(2.2)	(5.5)	(6.2)	(12.8)	(12.1)	
Consumer Durables	5.36	11.2	10.6	347.9	303.5	265.4	237.8	253.7	226.5	198.7	174.1	164.9	152.9	146.2	116.2	100.0
				(14.6)	(14.4)	(11.6)	(–6.3)	(–12.0)	(14.0)	(14.1)	(5.6)	(7.8)	(4.6)	(25.8)	(16.2)	
Consumer Non-durables	23.30	7.2	5.1	228.9	206.2	186.1	175.9	157.0	151.0	142.5	138.1	136.5	130.2	122.1	111.2	100.0
				(11.0)	(10.8)	(5.8)	(12.0)	(4.0)	(6.0)	(3.2)	(1.2)	(–4.8)	(6.6)	(9.8)	(11.2)	
Groupwise Index Number of Industrial Production																
Food Products	9.08	4.7	5.0	170.7	167.3	167.9	168.7	152.0	154.5	140.3	134.7	133.8	134.3	129.8	121.6	100.0
				(2.0)	(–0.4)	(–0.5)	(11.0)	(–1.6)	(10.1)	(–4.2)	(0.7)	(–0.4)	(3.5)	(6.7)	(21.6)	
Beverages, Tobacco, and Related Products	2.38	12.5	1.4	402.5	345.9	312.1	287.6	224.8	200.4	192.1	178.5	158.1	132.4	116.7	103.0	100.0
				(16.4)	(10.8)	(8.5)	(27.9)	(12.2)	(4.3)	(7.6)	(12.9)	(19.4)	(13.5)	(13.3)	(3.0)	
Cotton Textiles	5.52	2.8	3.7	137.0	126.3	117.4	121.2	124.5	127.3	123.7	115.9	125.6	122.7	109.5	99.1	100.0
				(8.5)	(7.6)	(–3.1)	(–2.7)	(–2.2)	(2.9)	(6.7)	(–7.7)	(2.4)	(12.1)	(10.5)	(–0.9)	
Wool, Silk, and Man-made Fibre Textiles	2.26	8.1	–0.6	249.4	249.0	240.5	225.1	218.5	209.3	197.8	176.8	172.0	145.1	131.3	114.5	100.0
				(0.2)	(3.5)	(6.8)	(3.0)	(4.4)	(5.8)	(11.9)	(2.8)	(–18.5)	(10.5)	(14.7)	(14.5)	

(contd.)

TABLE A2.6 (contd.)

(1)	(2)	(3)	(4)	(5)	(6)	(7)	(8)	(9)	(10)	(11)	(12)	(13)	(14)	(15)	(16)	(17)
Jute and Other Vegetable Fibre Textiles	0.59	0.8	−0.3	107.7	107.2	103.4	107.9	99.6	105.8	105.0	106.0	114.3	97.8	102.4	95.1	100.0
				(0.5)	(3.7)	(−4.2)	(8.3)	(−5.9)	(0.8)	(−0.9)	(−7.3)	(16.9)	(−4.5)	(7.7)	(−4.9)	
Textile Products (including wearing apparel)	2.54	8.7	7.4	255.6	219.6	184.3	190.3	166.3	162.4	156.1	153.1	158.7	146.3	133.7	98.5	100.0
				(16.4)	(19.2)	(−3.2)	(14.4)	(2.4)	(4.0)	(2.0)	(−3.5)	(8.5)	(9.4)	(35.7)	(−1.5)	
Wood and Wood Products, Furniture, and Fixtures	2.70	−2.4	6.6	69.7	74.8	81.7	76.5	92.8	104.3	101.4	121.0	128.5	131.9	123.2	99.3	100.0
				(−6.8)	(−8.4)	(−6.8)	(−17.6)	(−11.0)	(2.9)	(−16.2)	(−5.8)	(−2.6)	(7.1)	(−24.1)	(−0.7)	
Paper and Paper Products and Printing, Publishing and Allied Industries	2.65	7.4	6.2	228.2	230.7	208.7	180.5	169.0	164.0	180.5	169.8	146.4	136.9	125.5	108.6	100.0
				(−1.1)	(10.5)	(15.6)	(6.8)	(3.0)	(−9.1)	(6.3)	(16.0)	(6.9)	(9.1)	(15.6)	(8.6)	
Leather and Leather and Fur Products	1.14	3.7	4.9	148.4	156.9	147.0	152.9	158.0	150.0	135.5	119.1	110.2	107.8	98.5	86.6	100.0
				(−5.4)	(−6.7)	(−3.9)	(−3.2)	(5.3)	(10.7)	(13.8)	(8.1)	(2.2)	(9.4)	(13.7)	(−13.4)	
Basic Chemicals and Chemical Products (except products of petroleum and coal)	14.00	8.3	9.0	258.0	238.6	208.4	191.8	185.0	176.6	164.6	149.7	140.4	122.7	117.1	105.3	100.0
				(8.1)	(14.5)	(8.7)	(3.7)	(4.8)	(7.3)	(10.0)	(6.6)	(14.4)	(4.8)	(11.2)	(5.3)	
Rubber, Plastic, Petroleum, and Coal Products	5.73	6.0	6.6	200.4	192.2	187.7	179.7	170.4	153.4	137.2	138.7	124.6	118.4	116.1	107.7	100.0
				(−4.3)	(2.4)	(−4.5)	(−5.5)	(−11.1)	(−11.8)	(−1.1)	(−11.3)	(−5.2)	(−2.0)	(−7.8)	(7.7)	
Non-metallic Mineral Products	4.40	8.9	4.6	270.1	244.3	240.6	232.0	220.7	218.2	220.8	177.5	163.9	144.5	133.9	108.3	100.0
				(10.6)	(1.5)	(3.7)	(5.1)	(1.1)	(−1.2)	(−24.4)	(8.3)	(13.4)	(7.9)	(23.6)	(8.3)	
Basic Metal and Alloy Industries	7.45	7.2	2.1	226.9	196.1	186.0	170.4	156.0	149.6	146.9	139.9	143.5	139.8	131.0	113.1	100.0
				(15.7)	(5.4)	(9.2)	(9.2)	(4.3)	(1.8)	(5.0)	(−2.5)	(2.6)	(6.7)	(15.8)	(13.1)	
Metal Products and Parts except Machinery & Equipment	2.81	4.6	5.2	166.1	166.3	157.3	151.7	142.6	158.5	137.8	139.5	119.2	110.5	100.7	105.6	100.0
				(−0.1)	(5.7)	(3.7)	(6.4)	(−10.0)	(15.0)	(−1.2)	(−17.0)	(7.9)	(9.7)	(−4.6)	(5.6)	
Machinery and Equipment other than Transport Equipment	9.57	10.1	15.0	311.1	279.4	233.3	201.4	198.3	195.8	182.5	155.0	152.7	144.3	137.4	115.8	100.0
				(11.3)	(19.8)	(15.8)	(1.6)	(1.3)	(7.3)	(17.7)	(1.5)	(5.8)	(5.0)	(18.7)	(15.8)	
Transport Equipment and Parts	3.98	10.3	6.0	319.1	283.7	272.6	232.9	203.3	190.3	194.1	183.6	152.9	149.1	132.5	112.9	100.0
				(−12.5)	(4.1)	(17.0)	(14.6)	(6.8)	(−2.0)	(5.7)	(20.1)	(2.5)	(12.5)	(17.4)	(12.9)	
Other Manufacturing Industries	2.56	9.5	11.5	275.3	221.2	186.6	173.3	173.2	159.1	142.5	169.7	168.0	170.2	136.5	108.5	100.0
				(24.5)	(18.5)	(7.7)	(0.1)	(8.9)	(11.6)	(−16.0)	(1.0)	(−1.3)	(24.7)	(25.8)	(8.5)	

(contd.)

TABLE A2.6 (contd.)

Full fiscal year averages based on 1993–4=100

	Weight	1993–4	1992–3	1991–2	1990–1	1989–90	1988–9	1987–8	1986–7	1985–6	1984–5	1983–4	1982–3	1981–2	1980–1
		(14)	(15)	(16)	(17)	(18)	(19)	(20)	(21)	(22)	(23)	(24)	(25)	(26)	(27)
General Index	100.00	232.0	218.9	213.9	212.6	196.4	180.9	166.4	155.1	142.1	130.7	120.4	112.8	109.3	100.0
		(6.0)	(2.3)	(0.6)	(8.2)	(8.6)	(8.7)	(7.3)	(9.1)	(8.7)	(8.6)	(6.7)	(3.2)	(9.3)	
Mining and Quarrying	11.46	231.5	223.7	222.5	221.2	211.6	199.1	184.6	177.9	167.5	160.9	147.8	132.3	117.7	100.0
		(3.5)	(0.5)	(0.6)	(4.5)	(6.3)	(7.9)	(3.8)	(6.2)	(4.1)	(8.9)	(11.7)	(12.4)	(17.7)	
Manufacturing	77.11	223.5	210.7	206.2	207.8	190.7	175.6	161.5	149.7	136.9	124.8	115.6	109.4	107.9	100.0
		(6.1)	(2.2)	(−0.8)	(9.0)	(8.6)	(8.7)	(7.9)	(9.3)	(9.7)	(8.0)	(5.7)	(1.4)	(7.9)	
Electricity	11.43	290.0	269.9	257.0	236.8	219.7	198.2	181.0	168.1	152.4	140.4	125.4	116.5	110.2	100.0
		(7.4)	(5.0)	(8.5)	(7.8)	(10.8)	(9.5)	(7.7)	(10.3)	(8.5)	(12.0)	(7.6)	(5.7)	(10.2)	
Use-Based Classification															
Basic Goods	39.42	254.9	232.9	226.9	213.1	199.4	189.2	172.2	163.2	149.3	139.8	125.8	118.7	110.9	100.0
		(9.4)	(2.6)	(6.5)	(6.9)	(5.4)	(9.9)	(5.5)	(9.3)	(6.8)	(11.1)	(6.0)	(7.0)	(10.9)	
Capital Goods	16.43	255.4	266.4	266.8	291.8	251.5	206.4	192.8	166.3	140.7	127.2	123.5	110.6	106.7	100.0
		(−4.1)	(−0.1)	(−8.6)	(16.0)	(21.9)	(7.1)	(15.9)	(18.2)	(10.6)	(3.0)	(11.7)	(3.7)	(6.7)	
Intermediate Goods	20.51	203.9	182.6	173.2	176.9	168.9	161.9	145.0	141.2	135.7	126.2	115.0	104.7	103.7	100.0
		(11.7)	(5.4)	(−2.1)	(4.7)	(4.3)	(11.7)	(2.7)	(4.1)	(7.5)	(9.7)	(9.8)	(1.0)	(3.7)	
Consumer Goods	23.65	202.0	194.2	190.8	189.0	177.0	166.2	160.0	145.7	137.3	122.0	113.8	112.0	113.8	100.0
		(4.0)	(1.8)	(1.0)	(6.8)	(6.5)	(3.9)	(9.8)	(6.1)	(12.5)	(7.2)	(1.6)	(−1.6)	(13.8)	
Consumer Durables	2.55	369.4	318.1	320.5	359.7	325.0	317.5	259.6	241.3	212.2	178.8	140.5	121.0	110.9	100.0
		(16.1)	(−0.7)	(−10.9)	(10.7)	(2.4)	(22.3)	(7.6)	(13.7)	(18.7)	(27.3)	(16.1)	(9.1)	(10.9)	
Consumer Non-Durables	21.1	181.7	179.3	175.1	168.3	159.1	148.0	147.9	134.1	129.5	116.1	110.5	110.9	114.1	100.0
		(1.3)	(2.4)	(4.0)	(5.8)	(7.5)	(0.1)	(10.3)	(3.6)	(11.5)	(5.1)	(−0.4)	(−2.8)	(14.1)	
Groupwise Index Number of Industrial Production															
Food Products	5.33	160.0	175.3	178.0	169.7	150.9	148.5	139.0	133.2	125.6	120.0	121.1	129.5	113.5	100.0
		(−8.7)	(−1.5)	(4.9)	(12.5)	(1.6)	(6.8)	(4.4)	(6.1)	(4.7)	(−0.9)	(−6.5)	(14.1)	(13.5)	
Beverages, Tobacco, and Tobacco Products	1.57	137.8	113.7	107.3	104.3	103.0	92.1	84.9	98.5	112.1	111.7	104.5	107.8	104.3	100.0
		(21.2)	(6.0)	(2.9)	(1.3)	(11.8)	(8.5)	(−13.8)	(−12.1)	(0.4)	(6.9)	(−3.1)	(3.4)	(4.3)	
Cotton Textiles	12.31	160.5	150.1	139.0	128.7	112.3	107.8	111.3	112.5	110.4	102.2	100.2	89.4	99.7	100.0
		(6.9)	(8.0)	(8.0)	(14.6)	(4.2)	(−3.1)	(−1.1)	(1.9)	(8.0)	(2.0)	(12.1)	(−10.3)	(−0.3)	
Jute, Hemp, and Mesta Textiles	2.00	103.2	87.0	90.8	101.7	97.5	101.9	91.1	101.1	97.2	99.4	78.2	92.9	95.7	100.0
		(18.6)	(−4.2)	(−10.7)	(−4.3)	(−4.3)	(11.9)	(−9.9)	(4.0)	(−2.2)	(27.1)	(−15.8)	(−2.9)	(−4.3)	
Textile Products (including wearing apparel)	0.82	73.4	75.8	97.2	103.2	151.7	134.2	91.7	87.1	112.8	95.6	92.1	96.3	96.7	100.0
		(−3.2)	(−22.0)	(−5.8)	(−32.0)	(13.0)	(46.3)	(5.3)	(−22.8)	(18.0)	(3.8)	(−4.4)	(−0.4)	(−3.3)	
Wood and Wood Products, Furnitures, and Fixtures	0.45	199.3	190.5	185.0	198.4	176.0	171.7	161.7	246.1	223.2	216.5	167.5	153.0	153.2	100.0
		(4.6)	(3.0)	(−6.8)	(−12.7)	(2.5)	(6.2)	(−34.3)	(10.3)	(3.1)	(29.3)	(9.5)	(−0.1)	(53.2)	

(contd.)

TABLE A2.6 (contd.)

		(14)	(15)	(16)	(17)	(18)	(19)	(20)	(21)	(22)	(23)	(24)	(25)	(26)	(27)
Paper and Paper Products and Printing, Publishing, and Allied Industries	3.24	224.8 (6.6)	210.9 (3.9)	203.0 (2.6)	197.9 (9.0)	181.5 (6.0)	171.3 (3.0)	166.3 (1.9)	163.2 (10.0)	148.4 (12.5)	131.9 (20.7)	109.3 (3.6)	105.5 (−2.5)	108.2 (8.2)	100.0
Leather and Leather and Fur Products	0.49	204.3 (8.8)	187.7 (3.5)	181.3 (−6.6)	194.2 (3.1)	188.3 (6.1)	177.4 (−4.4)	185.5 (−3.8)	178.7 (5.6)	169.2 (21.1)	139.7 (20.1)	116.3 (−16.2)	100.1 (−21.9)	128.1 (−28.1)	100.0
Rubber, Plastic, Petroleum and Coal Products	4.00	176.4 (1.0)	174.6 (1.5)	172.0 (−0.9)	173.6 (0.1)	173.5 (3.1)	168.3 (8.3)	155.4 (3.9)	149.6 (−2.2)	153.0 (3.9)	147.2 (8.2)	136.1 (14.4)	119.0 (−0.1)	119.1 (19.1)	100.0
Chemicals and Chemical Products	12.51	297.9 (7.6)	276.9 (6.0)	261.2 (2.7)	254.3 (2.7)	247.6 (6.1)	233.4 (16.2)	200.9 (14.5)	175.5 (13.7)	154.3 (8.1)	142.8 (9.0)	131.0 (8.1)	121.2 (3.7)	116.9 (16.9)	100.0
Non-metallic Mineral Products	3.00	218.5 (4.5)	209.0 (1.9)	205.2 (6.2)	193.2 (1.7)	189.9 (2.9)	184.6 (16.8)	158.1 (−1.4)	160.3 (1.9)	157.3 (13.7)	138.4 (13.0)	122.5 (18.1)	103.7 (−2.8)	106.7 (6.7)	100.0
Basic Metal and Alloy Products	9.80	224.2 (33.1)	168.5 (0.4)	167.8 (5.5)	159.1 (10.7)	143.7 (−0.9)	145.0 (6.9)	135.6 (6.9)	126.8 (8.4)	117.0 (9.0)	107.3 (−12.8)	95.1 (−8.7)	104.2 (4.2)	100.0 (0.0)	100.0
Metal Products and Parts except Machinery & Equipment	2.29	126.5 (1.5)	124.6 (−6.4)	133.1 (−7.1)	143.2 (0.4)	142.6 (6.8)	133.5 (3.0)	129.6 (−4.2)	124.4 (8.5)	114.7 (9.2)	105.0 (19.2)	88.1 (−2.0)	89.9 (−5.0)	94.6 (−5.4)	100.0
Machinery, Machine Tools, and parts excluding Electrical Machinery	6.24	189.2 (4.5)	181.1 (−1.2)	183.3 (−2.0)	187.0 (8.8)	171.9 (6.7)	161.1 (15.7)	139.2 (−1.8)	141.8 (8.9)	130.2 (2.0)	127.6 (6.7)	119.6 (6.8)	112.0 (0.8)	111.1 (11.1)	100.0
Electrical Machinery, Apparatus Appliances	5.78	460.1 (−4.9)	483.6 (−2.0)	493.7 (−12.2)	562.0 (22.4)	459.2 (31.7)	348.7 (4.0)	335.2 (31.6)	254.7 (27.0)	200.6 (34.8)	148.8 (4.0)	143.1 (23.5)	115.9 (11.5)	103.9 (3.9)	100.0
Transport Equipment and Parts	6.39	211.2 (5.0)	200.6 (−0.7)	191.1 (6.3)	192.5 (5.0)	181.1 (13.7)	172.5 (4.7)	151.7 (6.7)	144.9 (3.2)	135.8 (6.6)	131.6 (10.9)	123.4 (3.0)	111.3 (8.1)	108.1	100.0
Other Manufacturing Industries	0.91 (−5.3)	267.0 (4.2)	281.3 (−16.6)	269.9 (−2.9)	323.7 (9.0)	333.2 (12.3)	305.6 (15.6)	272.1 (54.2)	235.4 (24.3)	152.7 (17.4)	122.8 (−32.5)	104.6 (3.9)	155.0 (49.2)	149.2	100.0

Note: Figures in brackets are percentage variations over the previous year; (QE = Quick Estimate).

Source: CSO, Ministry of Statistics and Programme Implementation, Periodic Press Releases.

A3 BUDGETARY TRANSACTIONS

Table A3.1
Budgetary Position of Government of India

(Rupees crore)

Budget Heads	2006–7 (Budget)	2005–6 (Revised)	2005–6 (Budget)	2004–5 (Actuals)	2003–4 (Actuals)	2002–3 (Actuals)	2001–2 (Actuals)	2000–1 (Actuals)	1999–2000 (Actuals)
(1)	(2)	(3)	(4)	(5)	(6)	(7)	(8)	(9)	(10)
(1) Revenue receipts 403465	348474	351200	306013	263878	231748	201449	192624	181513	128271
(a) Tax revenue (net to centre)	327205	274139	273466	224798	186982	159425	133662	136916	53242
(b) Non-tax revenue	76260	74335	77734	81215	76896	72323	67787	55708	11854
(2) Capital receipts 160526	160231	163144	191669	207490	182414	161004	132987	116571	10131
(a) Non-debt Capital Receipts of which:	11840	14056	12000	66467	84218	37342	20049	14171	1723
(a.1) Recovery of loans	8000	11700	12000	62043	67265	34191	16403	12046	1723
(a.2) Other Receipts of which:	3840	2356	0	4424	16953	3151	3646	2125	
(a.2.1) Disinvestment of equity of PSEs	3840	2356	0	4424	16953	3151	3646	2125	104717
(b) Borrowings and Other Liabilities	148686	146175	151144	125202	123272	145072	140955	118816	298084
(3) Total Receipts	563991	508705	514344	497682	471368	414162	362453	325611	221902
(4) Non-plan expenditure	391263	364914	370847	365406	349088	302708	261259	242942	202309
(a) On revenue account of which:	344430	326142	330530	296857	283502	268074	239954	226782	90249
(a.1) Interest payment	139823	130032	133945	126934	124088	117804	107460	99314	19593
(b) On capital account	46833	38772	40317	68549	65586	34634	21305	16160	
(5) Plan expenditure 172728	143791	143497	132276	122280	111455	101194	82669	76182	46800
(a) On revenue account	143762	114153	115982	87495	78638	71554	61657	51076	29382
(b) On capital account	28966	29638	27515**	44781	43642	39901	39537	31593	
(6) Total expenditure (4+5)	563991	508705	514344	497682	471368	414163	362453	325611	298084
	(10.9)	(2.2)	(3.3)	(5.6)	(13.8)	(14.3)	(11.3)	(9.2)	(6.7)
	[14.3]	[14.4]	[14.6]	[15.9]	[17.1]	[16.9]	[15.9]	[15.4]	[15.2]
(7) Revenue deficit (1–6.a)	84727	91821	95312	78338	98262	107880	100162	85234	67596
	[2.1]	[2.6]	[2.7]	[2.5]	[3.6]	[4.4]	[4.4]	[4.0]	[3.5]
(8) Fiscal deficit (2.c+8) or (1+2.a+2.b–6)	148686	146175	151144	125202	123272	145072	140955	118816	104717
	[3.8]	[4.1]	[4.3]	[4.0]	[4.5]	[5.9]	[6.2]	[5.6]	[5.3]
(9) Primary deficit (9–4.a1)	8863	16143	17199	–1732	–816	27268	33495	19502	14468
	[0.2]	[0.5]	[0.5]	[–0.1]	[–0.0]	[1.1]	[1.5]	[0.9]	[0.7]

(contd.)

TABLE A3.1 (contd.)

Budget Heads	1998–9 (Actuals)	1997–8 (Actuals)	1996–7 (Actuals)	1995–6 (Actuals)	1994–5 (Actuals)	1993–4 (Actuals)	1992–3 (Actuals)	1991–2 (Actuals)	1990–1 (Actuals)
(1)	(11)	(12)	(13)	(14)	(15)	(16)	(17)	(18)	(19)
(1) Revenue receipts	149510	133901	126279	110130	91083	75453	74128	66047	54954
(a) Tax revenue (net to centre)	104652	95672	93701	81939	67454	53449	54044	50070	42978
(b) Non-tax revenue	44858	38229	32578	28191	23629	22004	20084	15977	11976
(2) Capital receipts	129856	98167	74728	58338	68695	55440	36178	38528	39015
(a) Non-debt Capital Receipts of which:	16507	9230	7995	7902	11952	6143	8317	9058	5712
(a.1) Recovery of loans	10633	8318	7540	6505	6345	6191	6356	6020	5712
(a.2) Other Receipts of which:	5874	912	455	1397	5607	–48	1961	3038	0
(a.2.1) Disinvestment of equity of PSEs	5874	912	455	1397	5607	–48	1961	3038	0
(b) Borrowings and Other Liabilities	113349	88937	66733	50436	56743	49297	27861	29470	33303
(3) Total Receipts	279366	232068	201007	168468	159778	130893	110306	104575	93969
(4) Non-plan expenditure	212548	172991	147473	131901	113361	98998	85958	80469	76198
(a) On revenue account of which:	176900	145176	127298	110839	93847	83545	72925	67234	60850
(a.1) Interest payment	77882	65637	59478	50031	44049	36695	31035	26563	21471
(b) On capital account	35648	27815	20175	21062	19514	15453	13033	13235	15348
(5) Plan expenditure 66818	59077	53534	46374	47378	42855	36660	30961	29118	
(a) On revenue account	40519	35174	31635	29021	28265	24624	19777	15074	12666
(b) On capital account	26299	23903	21899	17353	19113	18231	16883	15887	16452
(6) Total expenditure (4+5)	279366	232068	201007	178275	160739	141853	122618	111430	105316
	(20.4)	(15.5)	(12.8)	(10.9)	(13.3)	(15.7)	(10.0)	(5.8)	(13.4)
	[6.0]	[15.2]	[14.7]	[15.0]	[15.9]	[16.5]	[16.4]	[17.1]	[18.5]
(7) Revenue deficit (1–6.a)	67909	46449	32654	29730	31029	32716	18574	16261	18562
	[3.9]	[3.1]	[2.4]	[2.5]	[3.1]	[3.8]	[2.5]	[2.5]	[3.3]
(8) Fiscal deficit (2.c + 8) or (1+2.a+2.b–6)	113349	88937	66733	60243	57703	60257	40173	36325	44650
	[6.5]	[5.8]	[4.9]	[5.1]	[5.7]	[7.0]	[5.4]	[5.6]	[7.9]
(9) Primary deficit (9–4.a1)	35467	23300	7255	10212	13655	23562	9138	9762	23134
	[2.0]	[1.5]	[0.5]	[0.9]	[1.3]	[2.7]	[1.2]	[1.5]	[4.1]

Notes: Figures in round brackets are variations over the previous year in percentages; Figures in square brackets are percentages to GDP at current market prices; GDP data is as per the revised series from 1999–2000 and it is at 1993–4 series before 1999–2000; GDP is estimated at 12 per cent growth from previous year for 2006–7.

Source: Budget at a Glance and Expenditure Budget, Vol. 1, Ministry of Finance, GOI (2006–7 and earlier budgets).

TABLE A3.2
Consolidated Budgetary Position of State Governments at a Glance

(Rs crore)

Year	Revenue account Receipts		Revenue account Expenditures		Revenue account Surplus(+)/deficit(−)	Capital account@ Receipts		Capital account@ Expenditures		Capital account@ Surplus(+)/deficit(−)	Aggregate Receipts		Aggregate Expenditures		Overall surplus(+)/deficit(−)	Gross fiscal deficit (GFD)		Revenue deficit (RD)		RD as per cent to aggregate disbursements	GFD as per cent to aggregate disbursements
(1)	(2)		(3)		(4)	(5)		(6)		(7)	(8)		(9)		(10)	(11)		(12)		(13)	(14)
1980–1	16294	(11.3)	14808	(10.3)	1486	5473	(3.8)	7856	(5.5)	−2383	21767	(15.1)	22664	(15.8)	−897	3713	(2.6)	−1486	(−1.0)	−6.6	16.4
1981–2	18455	(10.9)	17075	(10.1)	1380	5695	(3.4)	8095	(4.8)	−2400	24150	(14.3)	25170	(14.9)	−1020	4062	(2.4)	−1379	(−0.8)	−5.5	16.1
1982–3	21125	(11.2)	20238	(10.7)	887	6796	(3.6)	8504	(4.5)	−1708	27921	(14.8)	28742	(15.3)	−821	4986	(2.6)	−888	(−0.5)	−3.1	17.3
1983–4	24014	(10.9)	23803	(10.8)	211	8966	(4.1)	9737	(4.4)	−771	32980	(15.0)	33540	(15.3)	−560	6359	(2.9)	−210	(−0.1)	−0.6	19.0
1984–5	27425	(11.2)	28349	(11.5)	−924	10993	(4.5)	11508	(4.7)	−515	38418	(15.6)	39857	(16.2)	−1439	8199	(3.3)	923	(0.4)	2.3	20.6
1985–6	33424	(12.0)	32770	(11.8)	654	13131	(4.7)	12097	(4.4)	1034	46555	(16.7)	44867	(16.1)	1688	7521	(2.7)	−654	(−0.2)	−1.5	16.8
1986–7	38226	(12.3)	38057	(12.2)	169	12892	(4.1)	13729	(4.4)	−837	51118	(16.4)	51786	(16.6)	−668	9269	(3.0)	−170	(−0.1)	−0.3	17.9
1987–8	44000	(12.4)	45088	(12.7)	−1088	15806	(4.5)	14783	(4.2)	1023	59806	(16.9)	59871	(16.9)	−65	11219	(3.2)	1088	(0.3)	1.8	18.7
1988–9	50421	(12.0)	52228	(12.4)	−1807	17037	(4.0)	14850	(3.5)	2187	67458	(16.0)	67078	(15.9)	380	11672	(2.8)	1807	(0.4)	2.7	17.4
1989–90	56535	(11.6)	60217	(12.4)	−3682	20086	(4.1)	16565	(3.4)	3521	76621	(15.8)	76782	(15.8)	−161	15433	(3.2)	3682	(0.8)	4.8	20.1
1990–1	66467	(11.7)	71776	(12.6)	−5309	24693	(4.3)	19312	(3.4)	5381	91160	(16.0)	91088	(16.0)	72	18787	(3.3)	5309	(0.9)	5.8	20.6
1991–2	80535	(12.3)	86186	(13.2)	−5651	27238	(4.2)	21743	(3.3)	5495	107773	(16.5)	107929	(16.5)	−156	18900	(2.9)	5651	(0.9)	5.2	17.5
1992–3	91090	(12.2)	96205	(12.9)	−5115	30073	(4.0)	23129	(3.1)	6944	121163	(16.2)	119334	(16.2)	1829	20892	(2.8)	5114	(0.7)	4.3	17.5
1993–4	105564	(12.3)	109376	(12.7)	−3812	28623	(3.3)	25272	(2.9)	3351	134187	(15.6)	134648	(15.7)	−461	20596	(2.4)	3813	(0.4)	2.8	15.3
1994–5	122284	(12.1)	128440	(12.7)	−6156	43738	(4.3)	33114	(3.3)	10624	166022	(16.4)	161554	(16.0)	4468	27697	(2.7)	6156	(0.6)	3.8	17.1
1995–6	136803	(11.5)	145004	(12.2)	−8201	43630	(3.7)	32580	(2.7)	11050	180433	(15.2)	177584	(14.9)	2849	31426	(2.6)	8201	(0.7)	4.6	17.7
1996–7	152836	(11.2)	168950	(12.3)	−16114	42891	(3.1)	33819	(2.5)	9072	195727	(14.3)	202769	(14.8)	−7042	37251	(2.7)	16114	(1.2)	7.9	18.4
1997–8	170301	(11.2)	186634	(12.3)	−16333	59937	(3.9)	41501	(2.7)	18436	230238	(15.1)	228135	(15.0)	2103	44200	(2.9)	16333	(1.1)	7.2	19.4
1998–9	176448	(10.1)	220090	(12.6)	−43642	86394	(5.0)	46271	(2.7)	40123	262842	(15.1)	266361	(15.3)	−3519	74254	(4.3)	43642	(2.5)	16.4	27.9
1999–2000	207201	(10.6)	260998	(13.3)	−53797	103575	(5.3)	52891	(2.7)	50684	310776	(15.9)	313889	(16.0)	−3113	91480	(4.7)	53797	(2.7)	17.1	29.1
2000–1	237953	(11.3)	291522	(13.8)	−53569	111591	(5.3)	55677	(2.6)	55914	349544	(16.6)	347199	(16.5)	2345	89532	(4.2)	53569	(2.5)	15.4	25.8
2001–2	255675	(11.2)	314863	(13.8)	−59188	118211	(5.2)	62448	(2.7)	55763	373886	(16.4)	377311	(16.5)	−3425	95994	(4.2)	59188	(2.6)	15.7	25.4
2002–3	280340	(11.4)	335451	(13.7)	−55111	144734	(5.9)	85011	(3.5)	59723	425074	(17.4)	420462	(17.2)	4612	102123	(4.2)	55111	(2.2)	13.1	24.3
2003–4	309230	(11.2)	370468	(13.4)	−61238	208333	(7.5)	145883	(5.3)	62450	517563	(18.8)	516351	(18.7)	1212	121420	(4.4)	61238	(2.2)	11.9	23.5
2004–5 (RE)	377132	(12.1)	420322	(13.5)	−43190	200937	(6.4)	163751	(5.2)	37186	578069	(18.5)	584073	(18.7)	−6004	119288	(3.8)	43190	(1.4)	7.4	20.4
2005–6 (BE)	421324	(11.9)	445818	(12.6)	−24494	149155	(4.2)	122017	(3.5)	27138	570479	(16.2)	567835	(16.1)	2644	107041	(3.0)	24494	(0.7)	4.3	18.9

Notes: @ Excluding (i) ways and means advances (WMA) from the RBI and (ii) purchases and sales of securities from cash balance investment account; these serve as financing items for overall deficit (see cols. 11 and 12); Figures in brackets are percentages to GDP at current market prices; GDP data are as per revised series from 1999–2000 and as per 1993–4 series before 1999–2000, for 2006–7, GDP is estimated at 12 per cent growth from the previous year; In column 12 negative signs represent surpluses; Overall surplus or deficits shown in col. 10 represents conventional deficit, that is, difference between aggregate disbursements and aggregate receipts without any adjustments except for entries relating to temporary financing items mentioned above; The above aggregate disbursements and aggregate receipts are adjusted somewhat for deriving the figures of gross fiscal deficit (GFD). Thus, GFD is the difference between aggregate disbursements net of debt repayments and recovery of loans and total receipts consisting of revenue receipts and non-debt capital receipts (that is, in practice, only disinvestment proceeds); BE: Budget estimates; RE: Revised estimates.

Source: With a view to maintaining consistency in the series, this table has been prepared using RBI's *Handbook of Statistics on the Indian Economy 2004-5*.

A4 MONEY AND BANKING

TABLE A4.1

Money Stock Measures

(Rs. crore)

31 March	Currency with the Public					Deposit Money with the Public			M_1 (6+9)		Post Office Savings Bank Deposits	M_2 (10+11)	Time Deposits with the Banks	M_3 (10+13)		Total Post Office Deposits	M_4 (14+15)	
	Notes Circulation	Circulation of Rupee Coin	Small Coin	Cash in Hand with Banks	Total (2+3+4-5)	Demand Deposits with the Banks	Other Deposits with RBI	Total (7+8)										
(1)	(2)	(3)	(4)	(5)	(6)	(7)	(8)	(9)	(10)		(11)	(12)	(13)	(14)		(15)	(16)	(17)
2005-6	421922	6143	2553	17525	413093	405267	6914	412181	825273	(27.7)	5041	830314	1904700	2729972	(21.1)	25969	2755941	(20.9)
2004-5	361213	5984	1464	12893	355768	284017	6478	290495	646263	(11.7)	5041	651304	1607675	2253938	(12.4)	25969	2279907	(12.2)
2003-4	319732	5832	1464	12057	314971	258626	5119	263745	578716	(22.2)	5041	583757	1426960	2005676	(16.7)	25969	2031645	(16.5)
2002-3	275402	5613	1458	10892	271581	198757	3242	201999	473580	(12.0)	5041	478621	1244379	1717959	(14.7)	25969	1743928	(14.4)
2001-2	244608	4926	1440	10179	240795	179199	2850	182049	422844	(11.4)	5041	427885	1075512	1498356	(14.1)	25969	1524325	(13.8)
2000-1	212851	4053	1300	8654	209550	166270	3629	169899	379449	(11.0)	5041	384490	933771	1313220	(16.8)	25969	1339189	(16.4)
1999-2000	192483	3390	1188	7979	189082	149681	3033	152714	341796	(10.6)	5041	346837	782378	1124174	(14.6)	25969	1150143	(14.2)
1998-9	172000	2730	1116	6902	168944	136388	3736	140124	309068	(15.4)	5041	314109	671892	980960	(19.4)	25969	1006929	(18.8)
1997-8	147704	2297	1055	5477	145579	118724	3541	122265	267844	(11.3)	5041	272885	553488	821332	(18.0)	25969	847301	(17.4)
1996-7	134299	1927	991	5130	132087	105334	3194	108528	240615	(12.0)	5041	245656	455397	696012	(15.2)	25969	721981	(14.6)
1995-6	120066	1563	940	4311	118258	93233	3344	96577	214835	(11.7)	5041	219876	389172	604007	(13.7)	25969	629976	(13.0)
1994-5	102302	1498	881	4000	100681	88193	3383	91576	192257	(27.5)	5041	197298	339169	531426	(22.3)	25969	557395	(21.6)
1993-4	83405	1161	829	3094	82301	65952	2525	68477	150778	(21.5)	5041	155819	283629	434407	(18.4)	24029	458436	(18.0)
1992-3	69502	1044	780	3053	68273	54480	1313	55793	124066	(8.4)	4824	128890	242759	366825	(15.7)	21589	388414	(15.2)
1991-2	62034	975	729	2640	61098	52423	885	53308	114406	(23.2)	4620	119026	202643	317049	(19.3)	20141	337190	(20.2)
1990-1	53661	936	685	2234	53048	39170	674	39844	92892	(14.6)	4205	97097	172936	265828	(15.1)	14681	280509	(15.0)
1989-90	46730	916	639	1986	46299	34162	598	34760	81059	(21.7)	3994	85053	149890	230949	(20.2)	12980	243929	(19.6)
1988-9	38728	893	582	1788	38415	27730	462	28192	66607	(15.2)	3794	70401	125478	192085	(18.1)	11942	204027	(17.2)
1987-8	33812	839	541	1542	33650	23855	297	24152	57802	(12.9)	3639	61441	104858	162660	(15.7)	11490	174150	(14.5)
1986-7	28762	709	483	1369	28585	22240	352	22592	51177	(16.1)	3234	54411	89456	140633	(17.8)	11518	152151	(16.1)
1985-6	25584	531	409	1465	25059	18747	289	19036	44095	(11.2)	2971	47066	75299	119394	(17.1)	11687	131081	(16.8)
1984-5	23088	426	351	1202	22663	16382	603	16985	39648	(19.9)	2832	42480	62308	101956	(18.7)	10284	112240	(18.1)
1983-4	19888	386	333	1054	19553	13195	318	13513	33066	(15.9)	2648	35714	52833	85899	(17.9)	9112	95011	(17.1)
1982-3	16957	362	321	980	16660	11690	186	11876	28536	(15.4)	2496	31032	44333	72869	(16.7)	8296	81165	(16.1)
1981-2	14709	351	306	874	14492	10087	150	10237	24729	(5.6)	2351	27080	37697	62426	(11.9)	7470	69896	(12.0)
1980-1	13688	333	286	881	13426	9587	411	9998	23424	(17.4)	2334	25758	32350	55774	(19.2)	6632	62406	(19.0)
1979-80	11777	324	268	682	11687	7855	411	8266	19953	(15.8)	2036	21989	26848	46801	(17.4)	5658	52459	(17.5)
1978-9	10232	350	253	615	10220	6843	166	7009	17229	(-6.3)	1850	19079	22632	39861	(21.1)	4777	44638	(20.5)
1977-8	8559	353	240	521	8631	9683	70	9753	18384	(17.8)	1677	20061	14522	32906	(20.6)	4130	37036	(19.9)
1976-7	7700	335	233	395	7873	7636	100	7736	15609	(17.1)	1537	17146	11671	27280	(21.4)	3607	30887	(20.4)
1975-6	6498	331	224	348	6705	6543	77	6620	13325	(12.2)	1475	14800	9155	22480	(15.7)	3179	25659	(16.7)
1974-5	6147	322	210	332	6347	5483	44	5527	11874	(6.3)	1221	13095	7550	19424	(10.5)	2571	21995	(10.8)
1973-4	6083	314	188	277	6308	4819	45	4864	11172	(15.4)	1252	12424	6399	17571	(16.9)	2272	19843	(18.1)
1972-3	5210	290	167	247	5420	4213	51	4264	9684	(16.4)	1107	10791	5349	15033	(18.5)	1772	16805	(19.1)
1971-2	4594	263	148	205	4800	3441	79	3520	8320	(12.8)	1046	9366	4370	12690	(15.2)	1416	14106	(15.6)
1970-1	4173	247	137	186	4371	2943	60	3003	7374		990	8364	3646	11020		1184	12204	

Note: Figures in brackets are percentage variations over the previous year.
Source: RBI Bulletins.

TABLE A4.2
Selected Indicators of Scheduled Commercial Banks Operations (Year-End) (Outstandings)

(Rs crore)

Year	Aggregate Deposits (4+6)	Growth (per cent)	Demand Deposits	Growth (per cent)	Time Deposits	Growth (per cent)	Bank Credit (11+12)	Growth (per cent)	C-D Ratio	Food Credit	Non-food Credit	Growth (per cent)	Investment (16+17)	Investment Deposit Ratio	Govt. Securities	Other Securities	Cash in Hand	Balances with RBI	Borrowings from RBI
(1)	(2)	(3)	(4)	(5)	(6)	(7)	(8)	(9)	(10)	(11)	(12)	(13)	(14)	(15)	(16)	(17)	(18)	(19)	(20)
2005-6	2109049	24.0	364640	47.0	1744409	20.1	1507077	37.0	71.5	40691	1466386	38.4	717454	34.0	700742	16712	13046	127061	1488
2004-5	1700199	13.0	248028	10.2	1452171	13.5	1100428	30.9	64.7	41121	1059307	31.6	739154	43.5	718982	20172	8472	88105	50
2003-4	1504416	17.5	225022	32.1	1279394	15.2	840785	15.3	55.9	35961	804824	18.4	677588	45.0	654758	22830	7898	68997	0
2002-3	1280853	16.1	170289	11.3	1110564	16.9	729215	23.7	56.9	49479	679736	26.9	547546	42.7	523417	24129	7567	58335	79
2001-2	1103360	14.6	153048	7.4	950312	15.9	589723	15.3	53.4	53978	535745	13.6	438269	39.7	411176	27093	6245	62402	3616
2000-1	962618	18.4	142552	11.9	820066	19.5	511434	17.3	53.1	39991	471443	14.9	370160	38.5	340035	30125	5658	59544	3896
1999-2000	813344	13.9	127366	8.5	685978	15.0	435958	18.2	53.6	25691	410267	16.5	308944	38.0	278456	30488	5330	57419	6491
1998-9	714025	19.3	117423	14.5	596602	20.3	368837	13.8	51.7	16816	352021	13.0	254594	35.7	223217	31377	4362	63548	2894
1997-8	598485	18.4	102513	13.1	495972	19.5	324079	16.4	54.1	12485	311594	15.1	218705	36.5	186957	31748	3608	57698	395
1996-7	505599	16.5	90610	12.4	414989	17.5	278402	9.6	55.1	7597	270805	10.9	190514	37.7	158890	31624	3347	49848	560
1995-6	433819	12.1	80614	4.8	353205	14.0	254015	20.1	58.6	9791	244224	22.5	164782	38.0	132227	32555	3113	50667	4847
1994-5	386859	22.8	76903	35.9	309956	19.9	211561	28.7	54.7	12275	199286	29.8	149253	38.6	117685	31568	2972	60029	7415
1993-4	315132	17.3	56572	21.8	258560	16.4	164417	8.2	52.2	10907	153510	5.7	132523	42.1	101202	31321	2283	47760	1813
1992-3	268572	16.4	46461	3.0	222111	19.6	151982	21.0	56.6	6743	145239	20.1	105656	39.3	75945	29711	2293	28535	1619
1991-2	230758	19.8	45088	35.8	185670	16.5	125592	8.0	54.4	4670	120922	8.2	90196	39.1	62727	27469	2008	34179	577
1990-1	192541	15.3	33192	15.0	159349	15.4	116301	14.6	60.4	4506	111795	12.4	75065	39.0	49998	25067	1804	23861	3468
1989-90	166959	19.1	28856	23.6	138103	18.2	101452	19.8	60.8	2006	99446	18.5	64370	38.6	42292	22078	1649	23463	2399
1988-9	140150	18.7	23342	15.3	116808	19.4	84719	20.1	60.4	769	83950	22.8	54662	39.0	35815	18847	1444	21376	3527
1987-8	118045	14.9	20247	5.3	97798	17.1	70536	11.4	59.8	2190	68346	17.4	46504	39.4	30517	15987	1306	17656	1753
1986-7	102723	20.3	19227	23.2	83496	19.6	63308	12.9	61.6	5104	58204	15.2	38582	37.6	24847	13735	1174	14381	1293
1985-6	85404	18.2	15612	10.5	69792	20.1	56068	14.5	65.7	5535	50533	16.7	30554	35.8	19045	11509	1127	11053	954
1984-5	72245	19.2	14132	24.9	58113	17.9	48952	18.5	67.8	5665	43287	16.1	28138	38.9	18697	9441	1044	6884	1558
1983-4	60596	18.0	11312	13.3	49284	19.1	41294	16.3	68.1	4022	37272	14.6	21245	35.1	13473	7772	928	7783	1336
1982-3	51358	17.4	9984	19.1	41374	17.0	35493	19.6	69.1	2965	32528	18.0	18335	35.7	12078	6257	878	5208	815
1981-2	43733	15.1	8383	7.5	35350	17.1	29682	17.0	67.9	2127	27555	16.7	15141	34.6	10157	4984	788	4883	831
1980-1	37988	19.6	7798	17.4	30190	20.2	25371	17.8	66.8	1759	23612	21.5	13186	34.7	9219	3967	766	4092	589
1979-80	31759	17.6	6643	14.0	25116	18.5	21537	21.0	67.8	2100	19437	24.7	10625	33.5	7444	3181	616	3634	739
1978-9	27016	21.6	5826	19.6	21190	22.2	17795	19.1	65.9	2210	15585	20.3	9110	33.7	6622	2488	557	2634	546
1977-8	22212	26.4	4872	-29.8	17340	63.2	14939	13.4	67.3	1984	12955	18.0	7897	35.6	5907	1990	469	1674	331
1976-7	17566	24.1	6943	19.4	10623	27.4	13173	21.1	75.0	2191	10982	17.4	5536	31.5	3930	1606	354	1146	967
1975-6	14155	19.7	5817	17.2	8338	21.5	10877	24.1	76.8	1521	9356	14.8	4607	32.5	3283	1324	305	608	798
1974-5	11828	16.7	4963	14.5	6865	18.3	8762	18.4	74.1	613	8149	15.9	3915	33.1	2826	1089	296	612	473
1973-4	10139	17.3	4336	14.3	5803	19.7	7399	21.0	73.0	367	7032	21.8	3286	32.4	2362	924	246	610	409
1972-3	8643	21.6	3794	21.3	4849	21.9	6115	16.2	70.8	340	5775	17.4	2897	33.5	2161	736	221	279	139
1971-2	7106	20.3	3127	19.1	3979	21.3	5263	12.4	74.1	345	4918	10.0	2190	30.8	1650	540	181	267	208
1970-1	5906		2626		3280		4683		79.3	214	4469		1772	30.0	1362	410	167	197	368

Note: Data pertain to last Friday of march up to 1984-5 and last reporting Friday of March thereafter.
Source: RBI Bulletins.

TABLE A4.3
Trends in Statewise Bank Deposits and Credit and Credit–Deposit Ratios (For Scheduled Commercial Banks)

(Amount in rupees lakh; C–D ratio in per cent)

A. Credit as per Sanction

	Name of the State	All India								
		2005			1995			1985		
		Deposits	Credit	C–D Ratio	Deposits	Credit	C–D Ratio	Deposits	Credit	C–D Ratio
	(1)	(2)	(3)	(4)	(5)	(6)	(7)	(8)	(9)	(10)
	Northern Region	41040510	24420976	59.5	8496009	4128755	48.6	1859738	1010473	54.3
1	Haryana	3675305	1890786	51.4	747904	340650	45.5	155289	100950	65.0
2	Himachal Pradesh	1231437	447364	36.3	274413	71261	26.0	56274	21427	38.1
3	Jammu and Kashmir	1667324	778578	46.7	363038	103901	28.6	82175	29416	35.8
4	Punjab	6577064	3293518	50.1	1788454	740098	41.4	448194	202887	45.3
5	Rajasthan	4282322	2941210	68.7	1061994	506078	47.7	218088	145242	66.6
6	Chandigarh	1240825	1103352	88.9	321323	288820	89.9	63246	86332	136.5
7	Delhi	22366233	13966168	62.4	3938883	2077947	52.8	836472	424219	50.7
	North-eastern Region	2780098	973268	35.0	608496	216379	35.6	137655	64613	46.9
8	Arunachal Pradesh	119822	26336	22.0	32305	4017	12.4	4109	656	16.0
9	Assam	1778165	627076	35.3	395587	153024	38.7	96949	48627	50.2
10	Manipur	99666	42237	42.4	18277	10636	58.2	3179	2302	72.4
11	Meghalaya	306465	133712	43.6	65429	11142	17.0	12818	3197	24.9
12	Mizoram	78859	37720	47.8	18009	2969	16.5	3270	809	24.7
13	Nagaland	131276	30046	22.9	30002	11353	37.8	7769	2766	35.6
14	Tripura	265845	76141	28.6	48887	23238	47.5	9561	6256	65.4
	Eastern Region	20901201	9509073	45.5	4887888	2301647	47.1	1382531	674298	48.8
15	Bihar	4100740	1137856	27.7	1527408	496438	32.5	386206	140107	36.3
16	Jharkhand	2747344	812772	29.6						
17	Orissa	2661883	1644214	61.8	527523	287573	54.5	103370	84483	81.7
18	Sikkim	126428	37281	29.5	14703	3534	24.0	4550	713	15.7
19	West Bengal	11191940	5857456	52.3	2806177	1512051	53.9	886420	448304	50.6
20	Andaman and Nicobar Islands	72866	19494	26.8	12077	2051	17.0	1985	691	34.8
	Central Region	21950636	8954631	40.8	4944747	1929024	39.0	1160680	570567	49.2
21	Chhattisgarh	1654586	721110	43.6						
22	Madhya Pradesh	4795096	2620869	54.7	1338697	663359	49.6	302364	179243	59.3
23	Uttar Pradesh	13536012	5134490	37.9	3606050	1265665	35.1	858316	391324	45.6
24	Uttaranchal	1964942	478162	24.3						
	Western Region	49263353	41129124	83.5	10623635	6715172	63.2	2243637	1710312	76.2
25	Goa	1162373	291631	25.1	274998	67921	24.7	72255	22586	31.3
26	Gujarat	9768793	4539042	46.5	2344573	1092991	46.6	536799	273190	50.9
27	Maharashtra	38220925	36277139	94.9	7984183	5550971	69.5	1634037	1414155	86.5
28	Dadra and Nagar Haveli	36508	12709	34.8	6088	992	16.3	546	381	69.8
29	Daman and Diu	74754	8603	11.5	13793	2297	16.7			
	Southern Region	38745604	30259724	78.1	8356637	5802937	69.4	1807941	1385972	76.7
30	Andhra Pradesh	9822473	7346195	74.8	2017765	1472382	73.0	488164	361010	74.0
31	Karnataka	10768336	7946111	73.8	1969942	1295556	65.8	424701	357248	84.1
32	Kerala	6905845	3773650	54.6	1725008	772991	44.8	343002	208542	60.8
33	Tamil Nadu	10958511	11085222	101.2	2580659	2235367	86.6	539377	453872	84.1
34	Lakshadweep	9432	911	9.7	2081	160	7.7	348	79	22.7
35	Pondicherry	281007	107635	38.3	61182	26481	43.3	12349	5221	42.3
	All India Total	174681402	115246796	66.0	37917412	21093914	55.6	8592182	5416235	63.0

(contd.)

TABLE A4.3 (contd.)

B. Credit as per Utilization*

	Name of the State	All India								
		2005			1995			1985		
		Deposits	Credit	C–D Ratio	Deposits	Credit	C–D Ratio	Deposits	Credit	C–D Ratio
	(1)	(2)	(3)	(4)	(5)	(6)	(7)	(8)	(9)	(10)
	Northern Region	41040510	25527598	62.2	8496009	4032323	47.5	1859738	1007940	54.2
1	Haryana	3675305	2322831	63.2	747904	418588	56.0	155289	134721	86.8
2	Himachal Pradesh	1231437	626426	50.9	274413	81484	29.7	56274	22174	39.4
3	Jammu and Kashmir	1667324	847890	50.9	363038	103265	28.4	82175	29810	36.3
4	Punjab	6577064	3266345	49.7	1788454	774998	43.3	448194	252148	56.3
5	Rajasthan	4282322	3275858	76.5	1061994	541988	51.0	218088	149957	68.8
6	Chandigarh	1240825	1203864	97.0	321323	279223	86.9	63246	32703	51.7
7	Delhi	22366233	13984384	62.5	3938883	1832777	46.5	836472	386427	46.2
	North-eastern Region	2780098	1240785	44.6	608496	279077	45.9	137655	86186	62.6
8	Arunachal Pradesh	119822	36005	30.0	32305	6505	20.1	4109	1175	28.6
9	Assam	1778165	745575	41.9	395587	187459	47.4	96949	69084	71.3
10	Manipur	99666	42420	42.6	18277	10763	58.9	3179	2370	74.6
11	Meghalaya	306465	262668	85.7	65429	30868	47.2	12818	3014	23.5
12	Mizoram	78859	46623	59.1	18009	6322	35.1	3270	901	27.6
13	Nagaland	131276	30495	23.2	30002	13448	44.8	7769	3222	41.5
14	Tripura	265845	76999	29.0	48887	23712	48.5	9561	6420	67.1
	Eastern Region	20901201	10540768	50.4	4887888	2276998	46.6	1382531	659195	47.7
15	Bihar	4100740	1286846	31.4	1527408	516784	33.8	386206	150561	39.0
16	Jharkhand	2747344	840347	30.6						
17	Orissa	2661883	1988673	74.7	527523	294926	55.9	103370	87147	84.3
18	Sikkim	126428	36990	29.3	14703	3654	24.9	4550	1821	40.0
19	West Bengal	11191940	6356021	56.8	2806177	1459568	52.0	886420	418837	47.3
20	Andaman and Nicobar Island	72866	31891	43.8	12077	2066	17.1	1985	829	41.8
	Central Region	21950636	9951797	45.3	4944747	2036906	41.2	1160680	583748	50.3
21	Chhattisgarh	1654586	825481	49.9						
22	Madhya Pradesh	4795096	2835907	59.1	1338697	693212	51.8	302364	185257	61.3
23	Uttar Pradesh	13536012	5718136	42.2	3606050	1343694	37.3	858316	398491	46.4
24	Uttaranchal	1964942	572273	29.1						
	Western Region	49263353	35386292	71.8	10623635	6631240	62.4	2243637	1683336	75.0
25	Goa	1162373	352498	30.3	274998	70162	25.5	72255	23011	31.8
26	Gujarat	9768793	5947194	60.9	2344573	1163293	49.6	536799	295422	55.0
27	Maharashtra	38220925	29010025	75.9	7984183	5385046	67.4	1634037	1364294	83.5
28	Dadra and Nagar Haveli	36508	40446	110.8	6088	5771	94.8	546	609	111.5
29	Daman and Diu	74754	36129	48.3	13793	6968	50.5			
	Southern Region	38745604	22099554	57.0	8356637	5837367	69.9	1807941	1395830	77.2
30	Andhra Pradesh	9822473	8185712	83.3	2017765	1504608	74.6	488164	364469	74.7
31	Karnataka	10768336	8664858	80.5	1969942	1282572	65.1	424701	363477	85.6
32	Kerala	6905845	3971471	57.5	1725008	779774	45.2	343002	212242	61.9
33	Tamil Nadu	10958511	1151963	10.5	2580659	2239392	86.8	539377	449806	83.4
34	Lakshadweep	9432	2234	23.7	2081	201	9.7	348	71	20.4
35	Pondicherry	281007	123316	43.9	61182	30820	50.4	12349	5765	46.7
	All India Total	174681402	104746794	60.0	37917412	21093911	55.6	8592182	5416235	63.0

Notes: $ Data for the year 1985 includes Daman and Diu; * Use of bank credit in another place from the place of sanction captures utilization of bank credit and C–D ratio as per utilization; Data for 1995 and 2005 relate to end-March and those for 1985, to end-December.

Source: RBI: *Basic Statistical Returns of Scheduled Commercial Banks in India,* various issues.

TABLE A4.4
Trends in Districtwise Deposits and Credit (as per utilization) and Credit–Deposit Ratios

(Amount in rupees lakh; C–D ratio in per cent)

PUNJAB

Name of the District		2005			1995			1985		
		Deposits	Credit	C–D Ratio	Deposits	Credit	C–D Ratio	Deposits	Credit	C–D Ratio
	(1)	(2)	(3)	(4)	(5)	(6)	(7)	(8)	(9)	(10)
1	Amritsar	740092	338557	45.7	213348	82373	38.6	61267	25215	41.2
2	Bathinda	167713	105778	63.1	46956	33737	71.8	15217	17286	113.6
3	Faridkot	72275	44444	61.5	86210	36586	42.4	23817	16461	69.1
4	Fatehgarh Sahib	89683	66496	74.1	25734	7479	29.1			
5	Ferozpur	160985	120246	74.7	50981	29637	58.1	15700	13319	84.8
6	Gurdaspur	316256	137101	43.4	94123	24140	25.6	23674	9215	38.9
7	Hoshiarpur	464129	114573	24.7	129586	28969	22.4	32399	5839	18.0
8	Jalandhar	1434741	355664	24.8	435771	93983	21.6	103339	25260	24.4
9	Kapurthala	397833	78067	19.6	95726	18809	19.6	21285	6362	29.9
10	Ludhiana	1135894	1026559	90.4	318292	287260	90.3	77863	50075	64.3
11	Mansa	43650	33936	77.7	12418	4926	39.7			
12	Moga	156470	69591	44.5						
13	Muktsar	74356	50741	68.2						
14	Nawanshahar	244861	39954	16.3						
15	Patiala	493816	397196	80.4	138172	63187	45.7	38964	22075	56.7
16	Rupnagar	351828	120719	34.3	74700	23587	31.6	16328	7817	47.9
17	Sangrur	232485	166724	71.7	66437	40325	60.7	18342	13246	72.2
	Punjab Total	6577064	3266345	49.7	1788454	774998	43.3	448195	212170	47.3

Source and Notes: As in Table A4.3.

TABLE A4.5
Distribution of Outstanding Credit of Scheduled Commercial Banks According to Occupation

(Amount in rupees crore)

Occupation	No. of Accounts	Credit Limit Amount	Amount Outstanding		No. of Accounts	Credit Limit Amount	Amount Outstanding		No. of Accounts	Credit Limit Amount	Amount Outstanding	
	March 2005				March 2002				March 2000			
I. Agriculture (Direct, Indirect)	26656308	149143	124385	(10.8)	20351184	78759	64009	(9.8)	20532891	53554	45638	(9.9)
II. Industry	3716669	714005	446825	(38.8)	4232501	371630	271626	(41.4)	5354140	271867	213779	(46.5)
1. Mining and Quarrying	18141	31760	15817	(1.4)	9120	20819	11654	(1.8)	6611	6377	4852	(1.1)
2. Food Manufacturing and Processing	232424	66490	31050	(2.7)	217315	27548	20742	(3.2)	108750	22804	17624	(3.8)
3. Textiles	225788	91265	52407	(4.5)	236252	46881	34122	(5.2)	186917	38887	30586	(6.6)
4. Paper, Paper Products and Printing	47359	15948	10615	(0.9)	44921	9213	7445	(1.1)	45509	6033	4907	(1.1)
5. Leather and Leather Products	25988	6221	4148	(0.4)	29092	3867	2918	(0.4)	19693	3607	2731	(0.6)
6. Rubber and Rubber Products	45811	15272	8986	(0.8)	40795	9104	7435	(1.1)	14395	3687	2767	(0.6)
7. Chemicals and Chemical Products	97054	70565	39233	(3.4)	109160	43244	29895	(4.6)	94993	35783	26758	(5.8)
8. Basic Metals and Metal Products	133686	85590	53855	(4.7)	126761	41972	33262	(5.1)	93764	29842	24792	(5.4)
9. Engineering	229269	60410	40415	(3.5)	193984	49833	31852	(4.9)	112711	33734	25138	(5.5)
10. Vehicles, Vehicle Parts, and Transport equipments	40873	29420	18897	(1.6)	49430	14918	11090	(1.7)	41942	11713	8056	(1.8)
11. Other Industries	2313243	78474	52691	(4.6)	3042647	33747	26197	(4.0)	4546356	36708	30609	(6.7)
12. Electricity, Gas, and Water	5140	50744	36317	(3.2)	3376	26492	18824	(2.9)	2686	11296	8574	(1.9)
13. Construction	282672	76442	58376	(5.1)	110906	18614	15075	(2.3)	63972	6616	5599	(1.2)
III. Transport Operations	577543	17762	13721	(1.2)	657229	12451	9323	(1.4)	974401	10524	8075	(1.8)
IV. Professional and Other Services	1469713	80093	55266	(4.8)	1485331	36784	27702	(4.2)	1831185	18422	14653	(3.2)
V. Personal Loans	32835257	347598	255982	(22.2)	17594205	107950	82518	(12.6)	14420051	61077	51639	(11.2)
(i) Loans for Purchase of Consumer Durables	1510200	8057	6349	(0.6)	1213842	4168	3214	(0.5)	1187325	3426	2781	(0.6)
(ii) Loans for Housing	3666450	145034	126797	(11.0)	1816315	37566	32826	(5.0)	2253390	21001	18525	(4.0)
(iii) Rest of the Personal Loans	27658607	194507	122836	(10.7)	14564048	66217	46478	(7.1)	10979336	36650	30332	(6.6)
VI. Trade	6091108	173357	129646	(11.2)	6162035	118786	100872	(15.4)	7072533	85882	71618	(15.6)
1. Retail Trade	5591844	78494	56127	(4.9)	5791236	34075	27368	(4.2)	6595516	31197	25662	(5.6)
VII. Finance	107968	91440	73277	(6.4)	100761	49718	37614	(5.7)	70485	30166	21873	(4.8)
VIII. Miscellaneous	5696228	72867	53368	(4.6)	5805133	79351	62330	(9.5)	4114711	37604	32806	(7.1)
Total Bank Credit	77150794	1646266	1152468	(100)	56388379	855428	655993	(100)	54370397	569096	460081	(100)
Of which: 1. Artisans and Village Industries	1288321	7904	6149	(0.5)	1455000	6906	5600	(0.9)	2013171	3016	2677	(0.6)
2. Other Small Scale Industries	939186	62853	47076	(4.1)	1572798	39931	31970	(4.9)	2126150	43600	35070	(7.6)

(contd.)

TABLE A4.5 (contd.)

	Occupation	March 1990						December 1980						December 1975					
I.	Agriculture (Direct, Indirect)	24520595		19313		16626	(15.9)	10339615		4920		3722	(15.7)	3042170		1493		1071	(10.7)
II.	Industry	4125322		59762		50846	(48.7)	837313		17124		11555	(48.8)	304873		9009		5777	(57.7)
	1. Mining and Quarrying	8858		982		877	(0.8)	3987		267		191	(0.8)	1985		188		132	(1.3)
	2. Food Manufacturing and Processing	94534		5454		4288	(4.1)	37993		1737		955	(4.0)	18060		877		379	(3.8)
	3. Textiles	87634		8611		7495	(7.2)	54963		2943		1983	(8.4)	31457		1619		1056	(10.5)
	4. Paper Paper Products and Printing	36906		1860		1623	(1.6)	20952		550		417	(1.8)	10103		255		178	(1.8)
	5. Leather and Leather Products	11173		1093		1004	(1.0)	5117		234		169	(0.7)	2691		91		71	(0.7)
	6. Rubber and Rubber Products	11853		1002		887	(0.9)	6458		320		245	(1.0)	3330		145		104	(1.0)
	7. Chemicals and Chemical Products	64825		7493		6352	(6.1)	43149		2176		1410	(6.0)	20827		933		590	(5.9)
	8. Basic Metals and Metal Products	74936		6166		5398	(5.2)	45392		1962		1324	(5.6)	23462		1070		755	(7.5)
	9. Engineering	88135		10613		8926	(8.6)	54149		3454		2389	(10.1)	27082		1868		1231	(12.3)
	10. Vehicles, Vehicle Parts, and Transport equipments	25597		2667		2306	(2.2)	13991		855		550	(2.3)	8510		433		311	(3.1)
	11. Other Industries	357835		8740		7384	(7.1)	529390		1065		767	(3.2)	146478		829		547	(5.5)
	12. Electricity, Gas, and Water	2773		1121		843	(0.8)	702		291		125	(0.5)	1650		174		106	(1.1)
	13. Construction	23431		1566		1438	(1.4)	12638		230		180	(0.8)	5477		90		70	(0.7)
III.	Transport Operations	1240476		4146		3286	(3.2)	378273		1324		1078	(4.6)	103758		328		259	(2.6)
IV.	Personal Loans and Professional Other Services	8125421		11200		9791	(9.4)	1344474		637		527	(2.2)	262798		242		180	(1.8)
	1. Professional Services*	1592015		1129		967	(0.9)	187091		115		93	(0.4)	45752		38		30	(0.3)
	2. Other Services	1664209		2413		2126	(2.0)	1157383		522		433	(1.8)	217046		204		150	(1.5)
	3. Personal Loan	4869197		7,658		6698	(6.4)												
	(i) Loans for Purchase of Consumer Durables	420095		507		443	(0.4)												
	(ii) Loans for Housing	547114		2908		2536	(2.4)												
	(iii) Rest of the Personal Loans	3901988		4243		3719	(3.6)												
V.	Trade	8837621		17121		14486	(13.9)	1886767		7224		4653	(19.7)	444255		3252		1820	(18.2)
	1. Retail Trade	8438399		6319		5560	(5.3)	1735156		1050		801	(3.4)	360391		385		263	(2.6)
VI.	Financial Institutions	14122		2708		2234	(2.1)	2267767		937		810	(3.4)	12060		315		151	(1.5)
	1. Leasing/Hire Purchase and Finance Units	3801		920		771	(0.7)												
	2. Housing Finance Companies/Corporations	186		144		134	(0.1)												
VII.	Miscellaneous	6987129		7405		7042	(6.8)	3194086		1702		1328	(5.6)	3189168		1064		81	(0.8)
	Total Bank Credit	53850686		121654		104312	(100)	20248295		33867		23674	(100)	7359082		15703		10015	(100)
	Of which: 1. Artisans and Village Industries	2151263		1061		926	(0.9)												
	2. Other Small Scale Industries	1606146		14098		11986	(11.5)	668570		3709		2844	(12.0)	262301		1773		1178	(11.8)

Notes: – not available; Figures in brackets are percentages to total bank credit.

Source: RBI Banking Statistics: Basic Statistical Returns of Scheduled Commercial Banks in India, March 2005 (Vol. 34) and earlier issues.

TABLE A4.6
Resource Mobilization from the Primary Market

(Rupees crore)

Year	Total		Categorywise						Issue Type						Instrumentwise						
			Public		Right		Listed		IPOs		Equities				CCPS		Bonds		Others		
											At Par		At Premium								
	Number	Amount	Number	Amount	Number	Amount	Number	Amount	Number	Amount	Number	Amount	Number	Amount	Number	Amount	Number	Amount	Number	Amount	
(1)	(2)	(3)	(4)	(5)	(6)	(7)	(8)	(9)	(10)	(11)	(12)	(13)	(14)	(15)	(16)	(17)	(18)	(19)	(20)	(21)	
2006–7																						
Jun 2006	6	253	1	140	5	113	5	113	1	140	1	5	5	248	0	0	0	0	0	0	
May 2006	6	1300	6	1300	0	0	2	521	4	779	0	0	6	1300	0	0	0	0	0	0	
Apr 2006	9	8990	6	8923	3	67	4	199	5	8791	0	0	9	8990	0	0	0	0	0	0	
2005–6																						
Mar 2006	20	1351	14	947	6	403	9	522	11	829	2	164	18	1187	0	0	0	0	0	0	
Feb 2006	16	2780	15	2730	2	60	6	1035	11	1755	0	0	16	2780	0	0	0	0	0	0	
Jan 2006	13	3798	12	3796	1	3	4	2456	9	1342	0	0	13	3798	0	0	0	0	0	0	
Dec 2005	17	8984	10	6356	7	2629	10	7860	7	1124	0	0	17	8984	0	0	0	0	0	0	
Nov 2005	9	1007	9	1007	0	0	1	240	8	767	0	0	9	1007	0	0	0	0	0	0	
Oct 2005	7	706	7	706	0	0	1	275	6	431	0	0	7	706	0	0	0	0	0	0	
Sep 2005	12	1786	6	1650	6	135	8	198	4	1587	3	21	9	1765	0	0	0	0	0	0	
Aug 2005	9	950	4	560	5	390	5	390	4	560	3	53	6	897	0	0	0	0	0	0	
Jul 2005	9	2050	5	1826	4	224	5	474	4	1576	0	0	9	2050	0	0	0	0	0	0	
Jun 2005	9	932	9	932	0	0	3	372	6	560	1	16	8	916	0	0	0	0	0	0	
May 2005	8	325	4	54	4	271	4	271	4	54	1	118	7	207	0	0	0	0	0	0	
Apr 2005	8	2637	7	2625	1	12	3	2281	5	356	0	0	8	2637	0	0	0	0	0	0	
2004–5																						
Mar 2005	12	4782	10	4775	4	565	9	4423	5	917	1	174	11	4608	0	0	0	0	0	0	
Feb 2005	3	2142	3	2430	1	162	2	612	2	1980	0	0	3	2142	0	0	0	0	0	0	
Jan 2005	1	216	3	3074	0	0	3	3074	0	0	0	0	1	216	0	0	0	0	0	0	
Dec 2004	5	215	3	164	2	51	2	51	3	164	1	8	4	207	0	0	0	0	0	0	
Nov 2004	6	280	4	229	2	52	3	60	3	221	1	1	5	279	0	0	0	0	0	0	
Oct 2004	3	5451	1	5368	2	83	2	83	1	5368	0	0	3	5451	0	0	0	0	0	0	
Sep 2004	7	389	2	76	5	313	5	313	2	76	2	229	5	160	0	0	0	0	0	0	
Aug 2004	10	2408	2	46	8	2362	8	2362	2	46	1	9	9	2399	0	0	0	0	0	0	
Jul 2004	1	4713	1	4713	0	0	0	0	1	4713	0	0	1	4713	0	0	0	0	0	0	
Jun 2004	2	2858	0	0	0	0	0	0	0	0	0	0	0	0	0	0	2	2858	0	0	

(contd.)

TABLE A4.6 (contd.)

May 2004	3	478	0	0	2	27	2	27	0	0	0	2	27	0	0	451	0	0
Apr 2004	7	4324	5	3765	0	0	1	3500	4	265	0	5	3765	0	0	559	0	0
2005–6	138	27317	102	23190	36	4126	59	16375	79	10941	10	127	26934	0	0	0	0	0
2004–5	60	28255	34	24640	26	36616	37	14507	23	13749	6	49	23968	0	0	3867	0	0
2003–4	57	23273	35	22265	22	1007	36	19838	21	3434	14	37	18589	0	0	4324	0	0
2002–3	27	4070	14	3639	12	431	20	3032	6	1038	6	11	1314	0	0	2600	2	13
2001–2	35	7543	20	6502	15	1041	28	6341	7	1202	7	8	1121	0	0	5601	4	670
2000–1	151	6108	124	5379	27	729	37	3386	114	2722	84	54	2408	2	142	2704	1	36
1999–2000	94	7817	65	6257	28	1560	42	5098	51	2719	30	52	3780	0	0	3200	2	51
1998–9	59	5587	32	5019	26	568	40	5182	18	405	20	20	660	3	78	4450	6	202
1997–8	114	4569	62	2862	49	1708	59	3522	52	1048	64	33	1610	3	10	1550	10	1128
1996–7	889	14277	751	11557	131	2719	167	8326	717	5950	697	148	4412	5	75	5400	29	957
1995–6	1738	20804	1426	14240	299	6564	368	9880	1357	10924	1181	480	9727	8	145	2086	63	3888
1994–5	1735	27632	1342	21045	350	6588	453	11061	1239	16572	942	651	12441	7	124	0	135	9538
1993–4	1143	24372	773	15449	370	8923	451	16508	692	7864	608	383	9220	1	2	1991	142	9351

Note: Instrument-wise break up may not tally with the total number of issues because for one issue there could be more than one instruments.

Source: SEBI (2006), *Handbook of Statistics on the Indian Securities Market 2005* and SEBI Bulletins.

A5 CAPITAL MARKET

Table A5.1
Trends in Resource Mobilization by Mutual Fund

(Rs crore)

Year	Gross Mobilization				Redemption*				Net Inflow				Assets at the end of Period
	Private Sector	Public Sector	UTI	Total	Private Sector	Public Sector	UTI	Total	Private Sector	Public Sector	UTI	Total	
(1)	(2)	(3)	(4)	(5)	(6)	(7)	(8)	(9)	(10)	(11)	(12)	(13)	(14)
2006–7													
Jun–2005	113861	13048	9278	119737	119737	12144	8909	140790	-5876	904	369	-4603	265534
May–2005	130102	11718	10175	151995	99988	10034	6145	116168	30113	1684	4030	35827	276343
Apr–2005	110281	10712	4941	125934	91479	8476	5151	105106	18802	2236	-210	20828	257499
2005–6													
Mar–2006	113969	13300	9132	136400	103748	16549	8297	128594	10221	-3249	835	7807	231862
Feb–2006	80173	14012	6041	100226	75780	11031	3997	90808	4393	2981	2044	9418	207979
Jan–2006	78045	12913	3832	94790	70505	11949	4317	86771	7540	964	-485	8019	217707
Dec–2005	76794	10775	7179	94748	86603	10775	7839	105217	-9809	0	-660	-10469	199248
Nov–2005	-62453	9388	5861	77702	64578	9546	6591	80715	-2125	-158	-730	-3013	204519
Oct–2005	81429	8868	8068	98365	79696	7528	7024	94248	1733	1340	1044	4117	200209
Sep–2005	78791	11736	7156	97683	78625	9414	7828	95867	166	2322	-672	1816	201669
Aug–2005	91833	8608	7515	107956	80277	6679	6239	93195	11556	1929	1276	14761	195784
Jul–2005	70145	5855	5282	81282	64130	6087	5014	75231	6015	-232	268	6051	175916
Jun–2005	63887	6584	4106	74577	66128	6447	4532	77107	-2241	137	-426	-2530	164546
May–2005	54135	3264	5107	62506	48962	3836	4178	56976	5173	-572	929	5530	167978
Apr–2005	63049	5015	3849	71913	52693	4099	3847	60639	10356	916	2	11274	158422
2004–5													
Mar–2005	84535	6345	6650	97530	86127	9237	6473	101837	-1592	-2892	177	-4307	149600
Feb–2005	53512	5712	3993	63217	54767	4968	3821	63556	-1255	744	172	-339	153253
Jan–2005	51801	5308	3099	60208	50041	4398	3205	57644	1760	910	-106	2564	150378
Dec–2004	75048	4762	3450	83260	76320	5637	3759	85716	-1272	-875	-309	-2456	150537
Nov–2004	47229	3786	2376	53391	48473	4118	2882	55473	-1244	-332	-506	-2082	149581
Oct–2004	52074	3441	2769	58284	54949	4280	2772	62001	-2875	-839	-3	-3717	147995
Sep–2004	68359	-19949	2923	51333	72353	-25448	3526	50431	-3994	5499	-603	902	153108
Aug–2004	64060	30240	3090	97390	65527	36481	4629	106637	-1467	-6241	-1539	-9247	155686
Jul–2004	57961	5005	6669	69635	58783	4657	6458	69898	-822	348	211	-263	157747
Jun–2004	62776	3973	4090	70839	60327	3922	4792	69041	2449	51	-702	1798	155875

(contd.)

TABLE A5.1 (contd.)

															GDP
May–2004	55356	–3227	3341	55470		50793	–3178	2476	50091	4563	–49	865	5379	154018	
Apr–2004	63753	11193	4206	79152		50403	10194	4586	65183	13350	999	–380	13969	153214	
2005–6	914703	110319	73127	1098149	[31.1]	871727	103940	69704	1045370	42977	6379	3424	52779	231862	3531451
2004–5	736463	56589	46656	839708	[26.9]	728864	59266	49378	837508	7599	–2677	–2722	2200	149600	3121414
2003–4	534649	31548	23992	590189	[21.4]	492105	28951	22326	543382	42544	2597	1666	46807	139616	2760224
2002–3	284096	23515	7096	314707	[12.8]	272026	21954	16530	310510	12070	1561	–9434	4197	109299	2449736
2001–2	147798	12082	4643	164523	[7.2]	134748	10673	11927	157348	13050	1409	–7284	7175	100594	2281305
2000–1	75009	5535	12413	92957	[4.4]	65160	6580	12090	83830	9849	–1045	323	9127	90586	2107661
1999–2000	43726	3817	13698	61241	[3.1]	28559	4562	9150	42271	15167	–745	4548	18970	107946	1958814
1998–9	7847	1671	13193	22711	[1.3]	6394	1336	15930	23660	1453	335	–2737	–949	68193	1740985
1997–8	1974	332	9100	11406	[0.7]	na	na	na	na	na	na	na	na	na	1522547
1996–7	346	151	4280	4777	[0.3]	na	na	na	na	na	na	na	na	na	1368209
1995–6	312	296	5900	6508	[0.5]	na	na	na	na	na	na	na	na	na	1188012
1994–5	2084	2143	9500	13727	[1.4]	na	na	na	na	na	na	na	na	na	1012770
1993–4	1549	9527	51000	62076	[7.2]	na	na	na	na	na	na	na	na	na	859220

Notes: * Includes repurchases as well as redemption; na—not available; Figures in square brackets are percentages to GDP at current market prices (GDP data are as per revised series from 1999–2000 and as per 1993–4 series before 1999–2000; IDBI principal has now become principal MF, a private ector mutual fund; Erstwhile UTI has been divided into UTI mutual fund (registered with SEBI) and the specified undertaking of UTI (not registered with SEBI), above data contain information only of UTI mutual fund; Net assets pertaining to funds of funds schemes are not included in the above data.

Source: Securities and Exchange Board of India.

TABLE A5.2
Trends in Resource Mobilization by Mutual Funds

(Rs crore)

| Year | UTI | Bank-Sponsored MFs | | | Institution-Sponsored MFs | Total (8 to 11) | Private Sector MFs | | | Grand Total (2+3+6+7) |
		Total (4+5)	Joint Ventures (Predominantly Indian)	Others			Indian	Joint Ventures (Predominantly Indian)	Joint Ventures (Predominantly Foreign)	
(1)	(2)	(3)	(4)	(5)	(6)	(7)	(8)	(10)	(11)	(12)
Sales: All Schemes										
2006–7										
Jun–2006	na	15003	3888	11115	7322	113862	32607	45317	35938	136187
May–2006	na	16631	3934	12697	5262	130102	35079	50905	44118	151995
Apr–2006	na	10729	3090	7639	4924	110281	30582	46875	32824	125934
2005–6	na	137226	48167	89059	46220	914703	256752	346518	311433	1098149 [31.1]
2004–5	na	90446	30995	59451	12800	736462	242428	156925	337109	839708 [26.9]
2003–4	na	46661	na	na	21897	521632	143050	140545	238037	590190 [21.4]
2002–3	7062	11090	na	na	17535	278986	83351	71513	124122	314673 [12.8]
2001–2	4643	4242	na	na	9371	146267	33634	48396	64237	164523 [7.2]
2000–1	12413	2181	na	na	4011	74352	19901	20796	33655	92957 [4.4]
1999–2000	13536	1828	na	na	2211	42164	6688	15539	19937	59739 [3.0]
Redemptions: All Schemes										
2006–7										
Jun–2006	na	14880	3373	11507	6173	119737	34046	50234	35457	140790
May–2006	na	11595	3238	8357	4583	99989	28030	39360	32599	116167
Apr–2006	na	9528	2735	6793	4099	91479	26712	38441	26326	105106
2005–6	na	129535	43973	85562	44108	871727	238053	329429	304245	1045370 [29.6]
2004–5	na	92460	29970	62490	16183	728865	237060	156198	335607	837508 [26.8]
2003–4	na	43183	na	na	19796	480402	133131	127280	219991	543381 [19.7]
2002–3	7246	10536	na	na	16121	267322	79341	68333	119648	301225 [12.3]
2001–2	11927	3329	na	na	8550	133542	31181	43239	59122	157348 [6.9]
2000–1	12090	4125	na	na	3147	64467	17576	18353	28538	83829 [4.0]
1999–2000	9663	1744	na	na	1864	27933	5718	10641	11574	41204 [2.1]
Net Sales										
2006–7										
Jun–2006	na	123	515	–392	1149	–5875	–1439	–4917	481	–4603
May–2006	na	5036	696	4340	679	30113	7049	11545	11519	35828
Apr–2006	na	1201	355	846	825	18802	3870	8434	6498	20828
2005–6	na	7691	4194	3497	2112	42976	18699	17089	7188	52779 [1.5]
2004–5	na	–2014	1025	–3039	–3383	7597	5368	727	1502	2200 [0.1]
2003–4	na	3478	na	na	2101	41230	9919	13265	18046	46809 [1.7]
2002–3	–184	554	na	na	1414	11664	4010	3180	4474	13448 [0.5]
2001–2	–7284	913	na	na	821	12725	2453	5157	5115	7175 [0.3]
2000–1	323	–1944	na	na	864	9885	2325	2443	5117	9128 [0.4]
1999–2000	3873	84	na	na	347	14231	970	4898	8363	18535 [0.9]
Assets Under Management										
2006–7										
Jun–2006	na	46753	13634	33119	7557	211224	54943	85155	71126	265534
May–2006	na	48044	13670	34374	6722	221577	58071	91404	72102	276343
Apr–2006	na	48163	14506	33657	6134	203202	54482	84265	64455	257499
2005–6	na	45119	13186	31933	5229	181514	50602	74144	56768	231862
2004–5	na	29103	6595	22508	3010	117487	30750	30885	55852	149600
2003–4	na	28085	na	na	6539	108625	19885	33143	51964	143249
2002–3	13516	4491	na	na	5935	55522	10180	15459	29883	79464
2001–2	51434	3970	na	na	4234	40956	5177	15502	20277	100594
2000–1	58017	3333	na	na	3507	25730	3370	8620	13740	90587
1999–2000	76547	7842	na	na	3570	25046	2331	9724	12991	113005

Note: na—not available; figures in square brackets are percentages to GDP at current market prices (new series).

Source: Association of Mutual Funds in India (AMFI), (Website: *www.amfiindia.com*).

TABLE A5.3
Trends in FII Investments

Year	Gross Purchases			Gross Sales			Net Investment			Net Investment (US$ mn)	Cumulative Net Investment (US$ mn)
	Total (Rs crore)	Eqity	Debt	Total (Rs crore)	Eqity	Debt	Total (Rs crore)	Eqity	Debt		
(1)	(2)	(3)	(4)	(5)	(6)	(7)	(8)	(9)	(10)	(11)	(12)
2006–7											
Jun–2006	40408	39783	625	39532	97.8	39304	229	875	2.2	480	396	193	44153
May–2006	48738	47729	1009	55385	113.6	55083	302	–6647	–13.6	–7354	707	–1473	43960
Apr–2006	45235	44645	590	44464	98.3	44123	341	771	1.7	522	249	174	45433
2005–6											
Mar–2006	53162	52941	221	46732	87.9	46252	480	6430	12.1	6689	–258	1451	45260
Feb–2006	35671	35399	272	28235	79.2	27811	423	7436	20.8	7588	–152	1660	43809
Jan–2006	35415	35200	215	32658	92.2	31522	1136	2757	7.8	3678	–922	606	42149
Dec–2005	33548	33004	544	25187	75.1	23669	1518	8361	24.9	9335	–974	1831	41546
Nov–2005	23500	23086	414	21626	92.0	19047	2579	1874	8.0	4039	–2165	420	39715
Oct–2005	27166	26545	621	31794	117.0	30239	1555	–4628	–17.0	–3694	–933	–1054	39295
Sep–2005	26651	26348	304	22194	83.3	21701	492	4457	16.7	4646	–188	1023	40349
Aug–2005	28359	27837	522	23737	83.7	22786	951	4622	16.3	5051	–430	1062	39317
Jul–2005	25717	25532	185	17956	69.8	17597	359	7761	30.2	7934	–174	1784	38264
Jun–2005	25960	25915	45	20702	79.7	20586	115	5258	20.3	5329	–70	1210	36481
May–2005	15619	15364	256	17005	108.9	16504	502	–1386	–8.9	–1140	–246	–318	35271
Apr–2005	16210	16042	168	17686	109.1	16696	990	–1476	–9.1	–654	–821	–338	35588
2004–5											
Mar–2005	28444	27311	1133	20517	72.1	19808	709	7927	27.9	7502	425	1813	35926
Feb–2005	24360	22388	1972	15151	62.2	14012	1139	9209	37.8	8376	833	2101	34113
Jan–2005	17502	16651	851	17819	101.8	16194	1625	–317	–1.8	457	–774	–75	32012
Dec–2004	25841	20626	5215	15702	60.8	13943	1760	10139	39.2	6684	3456	2229	32087
Nov–2004	21302	18340	2962	13117	61.6	11600	1518	8185	38.4	6741	1445	1783	29858
Oct–2004	16063	15752	310	14035	87.4	12489	1546	2028	12.6	3263	–1236	439	28075
Sep–2004	13097	12385	712	10522	80.3	10000	522	2575	19.7	2385	190	556	27637
Aug–2004	12856	12595	261	10335	80.4	9702	633	2521	19.6	2893	–371	550	27080
Jul–2004	11247	11096	150	10534	93.7	10183	351	713	6.3	913	–201	157	26531
Jun–2004	10894	10634	261	11168	102.5	10117	1051	–274	–2.5	517	–790	–57	26374
May–2004	15655	15532	123	19201	122.7	18778	423	–3546	–22.7	–3247	–300	–806	26431
Apr–2004	19692	19692	0	12972	65.9	12053	919	6720	34.1	7638	–919	1483	27237
2005–6	532989	494654	38335	419867	78.8	389869	29998	113308	21.3	104799	8509	9332	45260
2004–5	216953	203001	13951	171072	78.9	158879	12193	45881	21.1	44122	1757	10172	35926
2003–4	144858	131762	13095	99094	68.4	91804	7144	45764	31.6	39958	5951	9949	25754
2002–3	47060	43999	3065	44371	94.3	41471	2902	2689	5.7	2528	162	562	15804
2001–2	49920	45465	4608	41165	82.5	37395	3922	8755	17.5	8067	685	1846	15242
2000–1	74051	70427	3616	64116	86.6	60320	3837	9935	13.4	10124	–46	2160	13396
1999–2000	56856	na	na	46734	82.2	na	na	10122	17.8	na	na	2339	11237
1998–9	16115	na	na	17699	109.8	na	na	–1584	–9.8	na	na	–386	8898
1997–8	18695	na	na	12737	68.1	na	na	5958	31.9	na	na	1649	9284
1996–7	15554	na	na	6979	44.9	na	na	8575	55.1	na	na	2432	7634
1995–6	9694	na	na	2752	28.4	na	na	6942	71.6	na	na	2036	5202
1994–5	7631	na	na	2835	37.2	na	na	4796	62.8	na	na	1528	3167
1993–4	5593	na	na	466	8.3	na	na	5127	91.7	na	na	1634	1638

Note: na—not available; Figures in italics indicate percentages to gross purchase; net investment in US$ million (mn) at monthly exchange rate.

Source: Securities and Exchange Board of India (SEBI), (Website: *www.sebi.gov.in*).

TABLE A5.4
Business Growth of Capital Market Segment of NSE

Year	No. of companies (listed)	No. of companies (permitted)	No. of companies (available for trading)	No. of trading days	No. of companies/ (scrips traded)	No. of trades (lakhs)	Traded quantity (lakhs)	Trading value (Rs crore)	Average daily trading value (Rs crore)	Average trade size (Rs)	Demat securities traded (lakhs)	Demat turnover (Rs crore)	Market capitalization (Rs crore)
(1)	(2)	(3)	(4)	(5)	(6)	(7)	(8)	(9)	(10)	(11)	(12)	(13)	(14)
2006–7													
Jun–2006	1099	0	962	23	1119	67	6675	151050	6567	22651	6675	151050	2524659
May–2006	1093	0	952	22	972	69	9537	201409	9155	29022	9537	201409	2612639
Apr–2006	1089	0	944	18	967	57	7289	177372	9854	31256	7289	177372	2990200
2005–6													
Mar–2006	1069	0	929	22	956	66	8579	209395	9518	31832	8579	209395	2813201
Feb–2006	1051	0	911	19	946	52	6163	135374	7125	25976	6163	135374	2512083
Jan–2006	1043	0	903	20	910	55	6672	149442	7472	26997	6672	149442	2434395
Dec–2005	1036	0	896	22	907	55	6370	149908	6814	27120	6370	149908	2322392
Nov–2005	1025	0	886	20	922	43	5387	109579	5479	25258	5387	109579	2166823
Oct–2005	1019	1	881	20	885	46	5767	120810	6041	26077	5767	120810	1927645
Sep–2005	1016	1	883	21	899	58	9200	145393	6924	25229	9200	145393	2098263
Aug–2005	1006	1	875	22	887	57	10072	145731	6624	25548	10072	145731	1957491
Jul–2005	999	1	868	20	995	50	8413	123008	6150	24449	8413	123008	1848740
Jun–2005	987	1	854	23	861	48	7048	111397	4843	23374	7048	111397	1727502
May–2005	977	1	842	22	875	41	5652	86802	3946	21020	5652	86802	1654995
Apr–2005	973	1	836	20	952	37	5127	82718	4136	22527	5127	82718	1517908
2004–5													
Mar–2005	970	1	839	22	870	46	8370	113055	5139	24626	8370	113055	1585585
Feb–2005	964	1	837	20	835	42	8967	99990	5000	23551	8967	99990	1614597
Jan–2005	958	5	833	19	823	41	8158	99732	5249	24343	8158	99732	1557444
Dec–2004	957	6	832	23	821	47	9933	115593	5026	24339	9933	115593	1579161
Nov–2004	954	6	831	20	816	33	6255	82035	4102	25013	6255	82035	1446292
Oct–2004	950	6	828	20	814	30	4727	75698	3785	25291	4727	75698	1253825
Sep–2004	945	7	824	22	809	37	6267	88508	4023	24124	6267	88508	1227550
Aug–2004	936	9	820	22	799	36	5754	86856	3948	24260	5754	86856	1143075
Jul–2004	929	12	815	22	793	38	6306	93836	4265	24918	6306	93836	1066087
Jun–2004	940	12	813	22	787	34	4199	84899	3859	25298	4199	84899	979700
May–2004	928	16	804	21	776	36	5465	98920	4711	27697	5465	98920	950494
Apr–2004	918	18	795	20	771	32	5369	100951	5048	31600	5369	100951	1171828
2005–6	1069	0	929	251	na	609	84449	1569558	6253	25777	84449	1569558	2813201 [79.7]
2004–5	970	1	839	253	na	451	79769	1140072	4506	25283	79769	1140072	1585585 [50.8]
2003–4	909	18	787	254	804	379	71330	1099534	4329	29090	71330	1099534	1120976 [40.6]
2002–3	818	107	788	251	899	240	36404	617989	2462	25776	36405	617985	537133 [21.9]
2001–2	793	197	890	247	1019	175	27841	513167	2078	29270	27772	512866	636861 [27.9]
2000–1	785	320	1029	251	1201	168	32954	1339510	5337	86980	30722	1264337	657847 [31.2]
1999–2000	720	479	1152	254	na	98	24270	839052	3303	85244	15377	711706	1020426 [52.1]
1998–9	648	609	1254	251	na	55	16533	414474	1651	75954	854	23818	491175 [28.2]
1997–8	612	745	1357	244	na	38	13569	370193	1520	97054			481503 [31.6]
1996–7	550	934	1484	250	na	26	13556	294503	1176	112086			419367 [30.7]
1995–6	422	847	1269	246	na	7	3991	67287	276	101505			401459 [33.8]
1994–5 (Nov–Mar)	135	543	678	102	na	0.3	139	1805	17	56310			363350 [35.9]

Notes: Figures in square brackets are percentages to GDP at current market prices (GDP data are as per revised series from 1999–2000 and as per 1993–4 series before 1999–2000); na—not available.

Source: NSE News, various issues.

APPENDIX TABLES 233

TABLE A5.5
Settlement Statistics of Capital Market Segment of NSE of India

Year	Number of Trades (million)	Traded Quantity (number)	Number of Shares (deliverable)	Percentage of Shares Delivered to Total Trade	Trading Value (Rs crore)	Value of Shares Deliverable (Rs crore)	Percentage of Delivered to Total Trading Value	Securities Pay-in (Rs crore)	Short Delivery (Auctioned quantity) (mn)	Percentage of Short Delivery to Total Delivery	Unrectified Bad Delivery (Auctioned quantity)	Percentage of Unrectified Bad Delivery to Total Delivery	Funds Pay-in (Rs crore)
(1)	(2)	(3)	(4)	(5)	(6)	(7)	(8)	(9)	(10)	(11)	(12)	(13)	(14)
2006–7													
Jun–2006	67	6633	1778	26.81	149842	36217	24.17	36126	5	0.30	0	0	13398
May–2006	72	9976	3058	30.65	216397	66750	30.85	66502	12	0.40	0	0	26471
Apr–2006	57	7287	2102	28.85	174555	48907	28.02	48761	9	0.44	0	0	13730
2005–6													
Mar–2006	62	7477	2229	29.81	174899	48029	27.46	47899	6	0.29	0	0	13256
Feb–2006	52	6032	1770	29.34	133753	37352	27.93	37246	6	0.31	0	0	10581
Jan–2006	55	6601	1861	28.19	148258	40098	27.05	39964	7	0.36	0	0	13633
Dec–2005	55	6211	1723	27.75	142814	36295	25.41	36194	5	0.29	0	0	11482
Nov–2005	42	5201	1416	27.24	104748	27653	26.40	27575	5	0.32	0	0	9155
Oct–2005	50	6473	1822	28.14	135376	33857	25.01	33741	7	0.40	0	0	13171
Sep–2005	54	8535	2300	26.94	132088	35618	26.97	35463	11	0.49	0	0	10373
Aug–2005	58	10013	2831	28.27	152561	42894	28.12	42745	12	0.43	0	0	13404
Jul–2005	47	7798	2101	26.95	114729	31308	27.29	31198	9	0.43	0	0	10174
Jun–2005	46	6679	1829	27.38	106133	30065	28.33	29964	8	0.42	0	0	10586
May–2005	41	5628	1527	27.14	88444	24561	27.77	24449	8	0.49	0	0	7921
Apr–2005	36	5195	1315	25.31	83038	21624	26.04	21539	6	0.48	0	0	7691
2004–5													
Mar–2005	47	8428	2002	23.76	114085	29903	26.21	29792	8	0.40	0.00	0.00	10417
Feb–2005	42	8815	2221	25.19	100267	28158	28.08	28062	9	0.40	0.00	0.00	9802
Jan–2005	41	8211	1950	23.74	97755	25031	25.61	24945	9	0.44	0.00	0.00	8083
Dec–2004	47	9524	2746	28.84	115867	33121	28.59	32994	14	0.49	0.00	0.00	11386
Nov–2004	32	5912	1897	32.08	79921	24359	30.48	24269	9	0.49	0.00	0.00	8401
Oct–2004	32	5140	1518	29.53	79879	21660	27.12	21588	7	0.46	0.00	0.00	7304
Sep–2004	35	5734	1559	27.19	81913	19656	24.00	19585	7	0.46	0.00	0.00	6171
Aug–2004	36	5830	1395	23.92	89597	18605	20.77	18554	6	0.40	0.00	0.00	6463
Jul–2004	39	6378	1403	22.00	97309	18164	18.67	18099	5	0.37	0.00	0.00	6523
Jun–2004	32	3928	858	21.84	81021	13999	17.28	13948	3	0.33	0.00	0.00	5862
May–2004	35	5478	1386	25.30	100203	22727	22.68	22668	5	0.35	0.00	0.00	8960
Apr–2004	33	5421	1293	23.86	103154	21719	21.05	21617	6	0.50	0.00	0.00	7870
2005–6	600	81844	22724	27.77	1516839	409353	26.99	407976	89	0.39	0.00	0.00	131426
2004–5	449	78799	20228	25.67	1140969	277101	24.29	276120	87	0.43	0.00	0.00	97241
2003–4	376	70453	17555	24.92	1090963	221364	20.29	220341	101	0.58	0.00	0.00	81588
2002–3	240	36541	8235	22.54	621569	87956	14.15	87447	47	0.57	0.00	0.00	34092
2001–2	172	27470	5930	21.59	508021	71766	14.13	64353	36	0.61	0.01	0.00	28048
2000–1	161	30420	5020	16.50	1263898	106277	8.41	94962	34	0.68	1.16	0.00	45937
1999–2000	96	23861	4871	20.42	803050	82607	10.29	79783	63	1.30	11.00	0.02	27992
1998–9	55	16531	2799	16.93	413573	66204	16.01	30755	31	1.09	6.97	0.25	12175
1997–8	38	13522	2205	16.31	370010	59775	16.15	21713	33	1.51	7.29	0.33	10827
1996–7	26	13432	1645	12.25	292314	32640	11.17	13790	38	2.32	6.63	0.40	7212
1995–6	6	3901	726	18.62	65742	11775	17.91	5805	18	2.46	3.22	0.44	3258
1994–5 (Nov–Mar)	0.3	133	69	51.74	1728	898	51.98	611	0.6	0.85	0.18	0.26	300

Source: NSE News, various issues.

TABLE A5.6
Business Growth Of The Futures and Options Market Segment, NSE

Year	Index Futures		Stock Futures		Interst Rate Futures		Index Options				Stock Options				Total		Average Daily Trading Value (Rs crore)	Open Interest at End Period	
							Call		Put		Call		Put						
	Number of Contracts Traded	Trading Value (Rs crore)	Number of Contracts Traded	Trading Value (Rs crore)	Number of Contracts Traded	Trading Value (Rs crore)	Number of Contracts Traded	Trading Value (Rs crore)	Number of Contracts Traded	Trading Value (Rs crore)	Number of Contracts Traded	Trading Value (Rs crore)	Number of Contracts Traded	Trading Value (Rs crore)	Number of Contracts Traded	Trading Value (Rs crore)		Number of Contracts Traded	Trading Value (Rs crore)
(1)	(2)	(3)	(4)	(5)	(6)	(7)	(8)	(9)	(10)	(11)	(12)	(13)	(14)	(15)	(16)	(17)	(18)	(19)	(20)
2006–7																			
Jun 2006	8437382	243571	6241247	243954	0	0	1118170	34158	793228	23814	206960	8767	57527	2541	16854514	556804	24209	580909	18807
May 2006	7666525	257328	9082184	409403	0	0	929908	33096	725769	25694	317774	14910	41904	1971	18764064	742401	33746	801589	26409
Apr 2006	5847035	204238	10021529	460555	0	0	773632	27524	715472	24897	393306	176270	67179	2998	17818153	737839	40991	1073728	43257
2005–6																			
Mar 2006	5952206	192035	10844400	473251	0	0	683979	22407	772372	24690	444604	18576	92657	3890	18790218	734849	33402	1028003	38470
Feb 2006	5186835	156359	7443178	288715	0	0	506714	15526	559682	16805	326233	12350	75740	2918	14098382	492673	25930	1023343	34400
Jan 2006	5760999	166127	7134199	265042	0	0	663684	19392	666782	19129	365493	14265	90562	3629	14681719	487584	24379	925680	30078
Dec 2005	6613032	183293	7571377	280283	0	0	775216	21862	764964	21125	361268	13630	95261	3614	16181118	523807	23809	808768	25323
Nov 2005	5238175	135478	6252736	216526	0	0	595900	15582	604657	15491	287136	10069	77052	2708	13055656	395854	19793	821223	24166
Oct 2005	6849732	170100	6526919	214398	0	0	695311	17632	715208	17954	309120	10753	80134	2822	15176424	433659	21683	803773	21083
Sep 2005	4701774	118905	6995169	236945	0	0	523948	13370	583081	14550	363872	12917	85897	3070	13253741	399757	19036	783718	23063
Aug 2005	4278829	100813	7124266	234817	0	0	444294	10620	485001	11372	350370	11935	81453	2750	12764213	372307	16923	892678	24788
Jul 2005	3451684	77399	6537794	199638	0	0	358867	8130	389154	8642	376129	11735	84989	2623	11198617	308167	15408	1024749	27198
Jun 2005	3626288	77218	5783428	163096	0	0	421480	9092	331753	7041	385640	11677	104478	3122	10653067	271246	11793	997984	24545
May 2005	3545971	70465	4466404	112882	0	0	382530	7726	353975	7056	288137	7642	100602	2609	9137619	208380	9472	670705	15863
Apr 2005	3332361	65598	4225623	106129	0	0	361544	7295	295020	5981	307994	8203	105955	2764	8628497	195970	9798	576056	12243
2004–5																			
Mar 2005	2076975	86398	4708687	175364	0	0	213632	9074	211385	8918	369895	14496	113590	4608	7694164	298858	13584	592646	21052
Feb 2005	1729103	71546	4167787	151743	0	0	168594	7128	144627	5998	367707	13890	83843	3247	6661661	253552	12678	404809	14901
Jan 2005	1931290	76151	4551564	159564	0	0	176682	7188	143416	5786	362345	13502	81618	3100	7246915	265291	13963	388354	13604
Dec 2004	1447464	58333	5238498	179387	0	0	130557	5355	108650	4356	481349	16952	108951	3845	7515469	268228	11662	426606	15221
Nov 2004	1023111	38277	3600135	113525	0	0	131218	4979	102223	3814	363158	11971	94810	3239	5314655	175805	8790	371842	12239
Oct 2004	1320173	47191	3660047	111695	0	0	138099	5030	97628	3500	357625	11684	93342	3124	5666914	182224	9111	321545	9845
Sep 2004	1463682	49500	3768178	107123	0	0	124547	4283	93808	3164	365187	10763	116304	3547	5931706	178380	8108	446299	13354
Aug 2004	1803263	57926	3577911	99591	0	0	127779	4192	98618	3193	284013	8499	86919	2604	5978503	176005	8000	261185	7332
Jul 2004	1971231	61125	3492774	94009	0	0	189179	6059	124352	3856	262755	7614	94222	2682	6134513	175345	7970	206709	5964
Jun 2004	2152644	64017	3125283	78392	0	0	158784	4914	117041	3559	193687	5340	75380	2084	5822819	158306	7196	201871	5367
May 2004	2551985	82149	3322799	92628	0	0	196198	6824	100430	3469	246630	7717	63156	1976	6481198	194763	9274	179487	4696
Apr 2004	2164528	79560	3829403	121048	0	0	115378	4347	80733	2968	292628	9640	85998	2736	6568868	220299	11015	249845	7668
2005–6	58537886	1513791	80905493	2791721	0	0	6413467	168632	6521649	169837	4165996	143752	1074780	36518	157619271	4824251	19220	1028003	38470
2004–5	21635449	772174	47043066	1484067	0	0	1870647	69373	1422911	52581	3946979	132066	1098133	36792	77017185	2547053	10067	592646	21052
2003–4	17191668	554463	32368842	1305949	10781	202	1043894	31801	688520	21022	4248149	168174	1334922	49038	56886776	2130649	8388	235792	7188
2002–3	2126763	43952	10676843	286532	0	0	269674	5670	172567	3577	2456501	69644	1066561	30489	16768909	439855	1752	97025	2194
2001–2	1025588	21482	1957856	51516	0	0	113974	2466	61926	1300	768159	18780	269370	6383	4196873	101925	413	93917	2150
2000–1 (Jun–Mar)	90580	2365	0	0	0	0	0	0	0	0	0	0	0	0	90580	2365	12	0	0

Source: NSE News, various issues.

Table A5.7
Settlement Statistics In Futures and Options Segment, NSE

(Rs crore)

Year	Index/Stock MTM Settlement	Futures Final Settlement	Index/Stock Premium Settlement	Options Exercise Settlement	Total
(1)	(2)	(3)	(4)	(5)	(6)
2006–7					
Jun 2006	6854	50	265	97	7267
May 2006	13594	135	326	124	14179
Apr 2006	7414	97	237	104	7852
2005–6					
Mar 2006	3611	70	232	159	4072
Feb 2006	1887	44	147	57	2135
Jan 2006	2035	107	140	52	2334
Dec 2005	2488	23	140	67	2718
Nov 2005	1831	32	123	76	2062
Oct 2005	3479	120	144	79	3822
Sep 2005	2367	17	136	96	2616
Aug 2005	2545	37	119	27	2728
Jul 2005	1568	38	93	59	1758
Jun 2005	1096	35	93	71	1295
May 2005	944	42	73	45	1104
Apr 2005	1737	31	83	30	1881
2004–5					
Mar 2005	1539	44	117	77	1777
Feb 2005	992	11	96	39	1138
Jan 2005	2318	32	96	42	2488
Dec 2004	1239	22	104	57	1422
Nov 2004	691	10	77	42	820
Oct 2004	838	23	69	31	961
Sep 2004	480	13	56	40	589
Aug 2004	548	9	51	15	623
Jul 2004	451	15	72	43	581
Jun 2004	535	20	47	10	612
May 2004	2556	13	91	36	2696
Apr 2004	837	16	65	25	943
2005–6	25586	598	1521	818	28523
2004–5	13024	228	941	456	14649
2003–4	10822	139	859	476	12296
2002–3	1738	46	331	196	2311
2001–2	505	22	165	94	786
2000–1	84	2	0	0	86

Source: NSE News, various issues.

Table A5.8
Business Growth On The WDM Segment, NSE

(Rs crore)

Year	Number of Trades	Trading Value (Rs crore)	Average Daily Trading Value (Rs crore)	Average Trade Size (Rs crore)
(1)	(2)	(3)	(4)	(5)
2006–7				
Jun 2006	950	11790	536	12.4
May 2006	1755	17986	818	10.3
Apr 2006	1962	23184	1364	11.8
2005–6				
Mar 2006	1732	17089	814	9.9
Feb 2006	2075	16485	868	7.9
Jan 2006	2572	21607	1080	8.4
Dec 2005	2505	20771	944	8.3
Nov 2005	2822	24360	1218	8.6
Oct 2005	2987	25387	1209	8.5
Sep 2005	4127	31960	1278	7.7
Aug 2005	5361	44717	1789	8.3
Jul 2005	8042	52309	2092	6.5
Jun 2005	14213	96108	3697	6.8
May 2005	9376	70114	2805	7.5
Apr 2005	6079	54617	2483	9.0
2004–5				
Mar 2005	6486	53812	2242	8.3
Feb 2005	10156	73588	3066	7.2
Jan 2005	8384	61205	2550	7.3
Dec 2004	10321	72593	2792	7.0
Nov 2004	5767	45541	1980	7.9
Oct 2004	8437	55770	2425	6.6
Sep 2004	12659	87695	3508	6.9
Aug 2004	9241	63806	2552	6.9
Jul 2004	9303	66013	2445	7.1
Jun 2004	11382	82453	3171	7.2
May 2004	13097	91340	3806	7.0
Apr 2004	19075	133478	6067	7.0
2005–6	61891	475524	1755	7.7
2004–5	124308	887294	3039	7.1
2003–4	189523	1316096	4477	6.9
2002–3	167778	1068701	3598	6.4
2001–2	144851	947191	3278	6.5
2000–1	64470	428582	1483	6.6
1999–2000	46987	304216	1035	6.5
1998–9	16092	105469	365	6.6
1997–8	16821	111263	385	6.6
1996–7	7804	42278	145	5.4
1995–6	2991	11868	41	4.0
1994–5 (Jun–Mar)	1021	6781	35	6.6

Source: NSE News, various issues.

TABLE A5.9
Business Growth and Settlement of Capital Market Segment, BSE

Year	Number of Companies Listed	Number of Trading Days	Number of Trades (lakhs)	Number of Shares Traded	Turnover (Rs crore)	Average Daily Turnover (Rs crore)	Market Capitalization (Rs crore)		Total Deliveries			
									Number of Shares	(Per cent to Total Shares Traded)	Value	(Per cent of Total Turnover)
(1)	(2)	(3)	(4)	(5)	(6)	(7)	(8)		(9)		(10)	
2006–7												
May 2006	4796	22	311	585	95819	4355	2842050		258	(44.1)	33188	(34.6)
Apr 2006	4796	18	257	479	87487	4860	3255565		205	(42.8)	28185	(32.2)
2005–6												
Mar 2006	4781	22	294	632	118765	5398	3022191		282	(44.6)	44978	(37.9)
Feb 2006	4782	19	222	421	70070	3688	2695543		178	(42.3)	22812	(32.6)
Jan 2006	4772	20	250	491	79316	3966	2616194		240	(48.9)	31742	(40.0)
Dec 2005	4763	22	234	452	77356	3516	2489385		228	(50.4)	29840	(38.6)
Nov 2005	4756	20	171	319	52694	2635	2323064		151	(47.3)	19269	(36.6)
Oct 2005	4748	20	183	365	59102	2955	2065611		176	(48.2)	22497	(38.1)
Sep 2005	4746	21	284	871	81291	3871	2254376		467	(53.6)	34006	(41.8)
Aug 2005	4752	22	272	1015	75933	3451	2123900		503	(49.6)	27059	(35.6)
Jul 2005	4743	20	219	677	61899	3095	1987170		297	(43.9)	20762	(33.5)
Jun 2005	4738	23	204	633	58479	2543	1850377		305	(48.2)	20446	(35.0)
May 2005	4734	22	170	434	43359	1971	1783221		199	(45.9)	14940	(34.5)
Apr 2005	4736	20	136	334	37809	1890	1635766		138	(41.3)	11398	(30.1)
2004–5												
Mar 2005	4731	22	222	610	59528	2706	1698428		256	(42.0)	19126	(32.1)
Feb 2005	4732	20	251	616	49686	2484	1730940		254	(41.2)	15786	(31.8)
Jan 2005	4730	19	220	535	43888	2310	1661532		224	(41.9)	13568	(30.9)
Dec 2004	4730	23	274	626	50226	2184	1685988		272	(43.5)	15994	(31.8)
Nov 2004	4725	20	201	423	35742	1787	1539595		203	(48.0)	12390	(34.7)
Oct 2004	4721	22	174	293	34608	1730	1337191		125	(42.7)	10318	(29.8)
Sep 2004	4733	22	205	370	39603	1800	1309317		146	(39.5)	10716	(27.1)
Aug 2004	4735	22	178	304	38195	1736	1216566		104	(34.2)	8260	(21.6)
Jul 2004	4730	22	175	286	39449	1793	1135588		82	(28.7)	7478	(19.0)
Jun 2004	5271	22	149	191	36990	1681	1047258		53	(27.7)	6500	(17.6)
May 2004	5296	21	170	259	45938	2188	1023128		79	(30.5)	10236	(22.3)
Apr 2004	5292	20	156	257	44864	2243	1255347		75	(29.2)	9685	(21.6)
2005–6	4781	251	2639	6644	816073	3251	3022191	[85.6]	3164	(47.6)	299749	(36.7)
2004–5	4731	253	2374	4772	518715	2050	1698428	[54.4]	1875	(39.3)	140056	(27.0)
2003–4	5528	254	2028	3904	503053	1981	1201206	[43.5]	1332	(34.1)	107153	(21.3)
2002–3	5650	251	1413	2214	314073	125	572197	[23.4]	699	(31.6)	48741	(15.5)
2001–2	5782	247	1277	1822	307292	1244	612224	[26.8]	577	(31.7)	59980	(19.5)
2000–1	5869	251	1428	2585	1000032	3984	571553	[27.1]	867	(33.5)	166941	(16.7)
1999–2000	5815	251	740	2086	686428	2735	912842	[46.6]	943	(45.2)	174740	(25.5)
1998–9	5849	243	354	1293	310750	1279	619532	[35.6]	506	(39.1)	85617	(27.6)
1997–8	5853	244	196	859	207113	849	630221	[41.4]	244	(28.4)	22512	(10.9)
1996–7	5832	240	155	809	124190	517	505137	[36.9]	212	(26.2)	10993	(8.9)
1995–6	5603	232	171	772	50064	216	563748	[47.5]	268	(34.7)	11527	(23.0)
1994–5	4702	231	196	1072	67749	293	468837	[46.3]	447	(41.7)	26641	(39.3)
1993–4	3585	218	123	758	84536	388	368071	[42.8]	na		15861	(18.8)

Note: Figures in square brackets are percentages to GDP at current market prices (GDP data are as per revised series from 1999–2000 and as per 1993–4 series before 1999–2000).

Source: BSE, *BSE Key Results* (www.bseindia.com).

TABLE A5.10
Secondary Market Turnover in Financial and Commodities Markets

(Rs crore)

Market Segments/Year	2005–6		2004–5		2003–4		2002–3	
	Amount	Percentage to GDP at current (market Prices)	Amount	Percentage to GDP at current (market prices)	Amount	Percentage to GDP at current (market prices)	Amount	Percentage to GDP at current (market prices)
(1)	(2)		(3)		(4)		(5)	
(1) Government Securities	2559260	72.5	2692129	86.2	2639244	95.6	1941673	79.3
(2) Forex Market	5239674	148.4	4042435	129.5	2318531	84.0	658035	26.9
(3) Total Stock Market Turnover	7209892	204.2	4221952	135.3	3744841	135.7	1374403	56.1
I Capital Market Derivatives (NSE)	4824251	136.6	2547053	81.6	2130612	77.2	439863	18.0
Cash	1569558	44.4	1140072	36.5	1099535	39.8	617989	25.2
Total	6393809	181.1	3687125	118.1	3230147	117.0	1057852	43.2
II Capital Market Derivatives (BSE)	9	0.0	16112	0.5	12074	0.4	2478	0.1
Cash	816074	23.1	518715	16.6	502620	18.2	314073	12.8
Total	816083	23.1	534827	17.1	514694	18.6	316551	12.9
(4) Commodities Market	2134000	60.4	571759	18.3	129400	4.7	66500	2.7
GDP at current market prices	3531451	100.0	3121414	100.0	2760224	100.0	2449736	100.0

Source: *Rakshitra*, Publications of CCIL, Sebi Bulletin, NSE News and FMC.

A6 INVESTMENT

TABLE A6.1
Trends in Total Investment and Investment Under Implementation by Industry

(Rs crore)

Industry	Total Investment by Industry April						Investment Under Implementation by Industry April					
	April 2006	April 2005	April 2004	April 2003	April 1999		April 2006	April 2005	April 2004	April 2003	April 1999	
Manufacturing	862777 (30.3)	493452 (24.7)	290871 (18.8)	242774 (17.2)	334512 (26.7)		188652 (21.0)	154308 (19.0)	118521 (16.6)	108802 (16.4)	143440 (29.2)	
Food and Beverages	21565 (0.8)	13224 (0.7)	10351 (0.7)	9200 (0.7)	5163 (0.4)		5310 (0.6)	4193 (0.5)	3421 (0.5)	3131 (0.5)	2454 (0.5)	
Food Products	19707 (0.7)	10591 (0.5)	8186 (0.5)	7458 (0.5)	4035 (0.3)		4513 (0.5)	3346 (0.4)	2668 (0.4)	2575 (0.4)	11830 (2.4)	
Beverages and Tobacco	1858 (0.1)	2633 (0.1)	2166 (0.1)	1743 (0.1)	1128 (0.1)		797 (0.1)	848 (0.1)	753 (0.1)	556 (0.1)	624 (0.1)	
Textiles	23528 (0.8)	12445 (0.6)	8418 (0.5)	6394 (0.5)	5369 (0.4)		9882 (1.1)	5786 (0.7)	3172 (0.4)	2776 (0.4)	3337 (0.7)	
Cotton Textiles	8849 (0.3)	4710 (0.2)	3136 (0.2)	3515 (0.2)	2636 (0.2)		4510 (0.5)	2000 (0.2)	1330 (0.2)	1612 (0.2)	1917 (0.4)	
Synthetic Textiles	3641 (0.1)	3247 (0.2)	2698 (0.2)	1069 (0.1)	2120 (0.2)		1976 (0.2)	2103 (0.3)	1201 (0.2)	820 (0.1)	973 (0.2)	
Chemicals	287416 (10.1)	197101 (9.9)	157185 (10.2)	132755 (9.4)	235632 (18.8)		95070 (10.6)	86621 (10.7)	62421 (8.7)	61785 (9.3)	86039 (17.5)	
Fertilizers	6271 (0.2)	5432 (0.3)	3862 (0.2)	2591 (0.2)	22784 (1.8)		830 (0.1)	770 (0.1)	669 (0.1)	687 (0.1)	5784 (1.2)	
Drugs and Pharmaceuticals	6890 (0.2)	5877 (0.3)	4897 (0.3)	3250 (0.2)	706 (0.1)		3272 (0.4)	3438 (0.4)	2262 (0.3)	1560 (0.2)	310 (0.1)	
Organic Chemicals	85744 (3.0)	54998 (2.8)	46151 (3.0)	37544 (2.7)	92195 (7.4)		11748 (1.3)	11192 (1.4)	12432 (1.7)	12734 (1.9)	24129 (4.9)	
Petroleum Products	171965 (6.0)	116049 (5.8)	91233 (5.9)	77570 (5.5)	108641 (8.7)		75624 (8.4)	66878 (8.2)	43749 (6.1)	43111 (6.5)	49710 (10.1)	
Tyres and Tubes	766 (0.0)	1189 (0.1)	1195 (0.1)	1815 (0.1)	3112 (0.2)		510 (0.1)	945 (0.1)	496 (0.1)	543 (0.1)	981 (0.2)	
Non-metallic Mineral Products	23782 (0.8)	16627 (0.8)	12753 (0.8)	12062 (0.9)	11028 (0.9)		5610 (0.6)	5497 (0.7)	4337 (0.6)	3354 (0.5)	4086 (0.8)	
Cement	16550 (0.6)	11223 (0.6)	9088 (0.6)	9773 (0.7)	9536 (0.8)		2628 (0.3)	3128 (0.4)	3603 (0.5)	2722 (0.4)	3015 (0.6)	
Other non-metallic Mineral Products	7232 (0.3)	5404 (0.3)	3665 (0.2)	2289 (0.2)	1492 (0.1)		2982 (0.3)	2369 (0.3)	734 (0.1)	632 (0.1)	1072 (0.2)	
Metals and Metal Products	438998 (15.4)	209746 (10.5)	67379 (4.4)	49904 (3.5)	51634 (4.1)		53688 (6.0)	39506 (4.9)	31687 (4.4)	23529 (3.6)	30820 (6.3)	
Ferrous Metals	389548 (13.7)	177497 (8.9)	51085 (3.3)	34346 (2.4)	35616 (2.8)		45628 (5.1)	32076 (3.9)	23830 (3.3)	18179 (2.7)	29394 (6.0)	
Non-ferrous Metals	49451 (1.7)	32249 (1.6)	16294 (1.1)	15559 (1.1)	16018 (1.3)		8060 (0.9)	7430 (0.9)	7856 (1.1)	5349 (0.8)	1426 (0.3)	
Aluminium & Aluminium Products	46537 (1.6)	30252 (1.5)	13206 (0.9)	12604 (0.9)	13919 (1.1)		6961 (0.8)	6260 (0.8)	6705 (0.9)	4498 (0.7)	479 (0.1)	
Machinery	22683 (0.8)	21033 (1.1)	14662 (0.9)	15066 (1.1)	9506 (0.8)		8106 (0.9)	6768 (0.8)	6809 (1.0)	6104 (0.9)	5727 (1.2)	
Non-electrical Machinery	6432 (0.2)	6783 (0.3)	4637 (0.3)	4203 (0.3)	3205 (0.3)		2422 (0.3)	2246 (0.3)	1561 (0.2)	1330 (0.2)	2092 (0.4)	
Electrical Machinery	4661 (0.2)	4253 (0.2)	3479 (0.2)	4656 (0.3)	2409 (0.2)		1932 (0.2)	2392 (0.3)	2217 (0.3)	2290 (0.3)	1550 (0.3)	
Electronics	11590 (0.4)	9997 (0.5)	6545 (0.4)	6207 (0.4)	3892 (0.3)		3753 (0.4)	2131 (0.3)	3031 (0.4)	2484 (0.4)	2085 (0.4)	
Transport Equipment	24756 (0.9)	15355 (0.8)	15568 (1.0)	14325 (1.0)	13095 (1.0)		7171 (0.8)	2802 (0.3)	4480 (0.6)	6800 (1.0)	9250 (1.9)	
Automobile	18267 (0.6)	10629 (0.5)	11296 (0.7)	10646 (0.8)	11051 (0.9)		5856 (0.7)	1855 (0.2)	3493 (0.5)	6212 (0.9)	8096 (1.7)	
Automobile Ancillaries	6489 (0.2)	4726 (0.2)	4272 (0.3)	3679 (0.3)	2044 (0.2)		1315 (0.1)	947 (0.1)	987 (0.1)	588 (0.1)	1154 (0.2)	
Miscellaneous Manufacturing	20049 (0.7)	7921 (0.4)	4555 (0.3)	3068 (0.2)	3085 (0.2)		3815 (0.4)	3135 (0.4)	2194 (0.3)	1323 (0.2)	1727 (0.4)	
Paper and Paper Products	18324 (0.6)	6992 (0.4)	3683 (0.2)	2058 (0.1)	2810 (0.2)		3425 (0.4)	2887 (0.4)	1865 (0.3)	993 (0.2)	1546 (0.3)	

(contd.)

TABLE A6.1 (contd.)

Industry	Total Investment by Industry April						Investment Under Implementation by Industry April					
	April 2006	April 2005	April 2004	April 2003	April 1999		April 2006	April 2005	April 2004	April 2003	April 1999	
Mining	109882	(3.9)	79881	(4.0)	71666	(4.6)	64266	(4.6)	56342	(4.5)	44484	(5.0)	42151	(5.2)	35410	(5.0)	24784	(3.7)	20910	(4.3)
Electricity	817725 (28.7)	570315 (28.6)	461611 (29.9)	430226 (30.5)	467435 (37.3)	238410 (26.6)	219862 (27.0)	183084 (25.7)	158609 (24.0)	120010 (24.5)
Generation	788781 (27.7)	546214 (27.4)	446107 (28.9)	416622 (29.6)	455710 (36.4)	224776 (25.1)	206837 (25.4)	175399 (24.6)	155379 (23.5)	115188 (23.5)
Distribution	28944 (1.0)	24101 (1.2)	15504 (1.0)	13604 (1.0)	11725 (0.9)	13634 (1.5)	13025 (1.6)	7684 (1.1)	3230 (0.5)	4822 (1.0)
Services	761332 (26.8)	623241 (31.2)	506143 (32.7)	464154 (33.0)	268420 (21.4)	283146 (31.6)	265619 (32.7)	245812 (34.4)	241192 (36.4)	103355 (21.1)
Hotels and Tourism	20862 (0.7)	15390 (0.8)	11436 (0.7)	11351 (0.8)	9744 (0.8)	5803 (0.6)	4597 (0.6)	4148 (0.6)	4061 (0.6)	4513 (0.9)
Recreational Services	10065 (0.4)	8189 (0.4)	5899 (0.4)	4093 (0.3)	640 (0.1)	2431 (0.3)	2490 (0.3)	2341 (0.3)	684 (0.1)	424 (0.1)
Health Services	12912 (0.5)	10945 (0.5)	7498 (0.5)	6208 (0.4)	1883 (0.2)	3569 (0.4)	3973 (0.5)	3306 (0.5)	2853 (0.4)	459 (0.1)
Transport Services	403888 (14.2)	331248 (16.6)	275227 (17.8)	255188 (18.1)	175340 (14.0)	154230 (17.2)	141819 (17.4)	125711 (17.6)	120731 (18.2)	65541 (13.4)
Road Transport	139549 (4.9)	125552 (6.3)	112510 (7.3)	105524 (7.5)	48015 (3.8)	54050 (6.0)	53698 (6.6)	51202 (7.2)	45900 (6.9)	9971 (2.0)
Railway Transport	162647 (5.7)	121063 (6.1)	85654 (5.5)	75612 (5.4)	48178 (3.8)	74767 (8.3)	69284 (8.5)	59036 (8.3)	56404 (8.5)	37186 (7.6)
Air Transport	34830 (1.2)	33773 (1.7)	32998 (2.1)	22297 (1.6)	9906 (0.8)	4367 (0.5)	4399 (0.5)	3052 (0.4)	2852 (0.4)	981 (0.2)
Shipping	61516 (2.2)	45492 (2.3)	38701 (2.5)	48506 (3.4)	45925 (3.7)	20924 (2.3)	13882 (1.7)	11866 (1.7)	15546 (2.3)	9279 (1.9)
Communication Services	105668 (3.7)	86421 (4.3)	84037 (5.4)	86589 (6.1)	42547 (3.4)	69227 (7.7)	67527 (8.3)	68096 (9.5)	72269 (10.9)	30311 (6.2)
Miscellaneous Services	177455 (6.2)	144766 (7.3)	103533 (6.7)	87745 (6.2)	38266 (3.1)	38976 (4.3)	36510 (4.5)	35518 (5.0)	34180 (5.2)	2108 (0.4)
Storage and Distribution	171106 (6.0)	139131 (7.0)	98833 (6.4)	83370 (5.9)	38267 (3.1)	37579 (4.2)	34958 (4.3)	34246 (4.8)	32515 (4.9)	2108 (0.4)
Information Technology	18774 (0.7)	16791 (0.8)	15304 (1.0)			(0.0)	4897 (0.5)	5624 (0.7)	6280 (0.9)	0 (0.0)	0 (0.0)
Irrigation	131125 (4.6)	127028 (6.4)	118692 (7.7)	115584 (8.2)	110926 (8.8)	110448 (12.3)	100199 (12.3)	99780 (14.0)	99052 (15.0)	96372 (19.7)
Construction	163225 (5.7)	101649 (5.1)	97173 (6.3)	91327 (6.5)	15819 (1.3)	32021 (3.6)	30981 (3.8)	31023 (4.3)	29443 (4.4)	6320 (1.3)
Commercial Complexes	151277 (5.3)	94450 (4.7)	97173 (6.3)	91327 (6.5)	15819 (1.3)	29899 (3.3)	29604 (3.6)	31023 (4.3)	29443 (4.4)	6320 (1.3)
All Industries	2846066 (100.0)	2E+06 (100.0)	1546156 (100.0)	1408331 (100.0)	1253454 (100.0)	897161 (100.0)	813120 (100.0)	713630 (100.0)	661882 (100.0)	490407 (100.0)

Notes: Total investment covers projects announced and proposed and those under implementation; Figures in brackets are percentages to total investment.

Source: Centre for Monitoring Indian Economy Pvt. Ltd., *Monthly Review of Investment Projects, CapEx*, various issues.

TABLE A6.2
Trends in Total Investment and Investments Under Implementation by States and Union Territories

(Rs crore)

State/UTs	Total Investment by States and Union Territories					Total Investment Under Implementation by States and Union Territories				
	April 2006	April 2005	April 2004	April 2003	April 1999	April 2006	April 2005	April 2004	April 2003	April 1999
Andhra Pradesh	239347 (8.41)	175157 (8.78)	126811 (8.20)	125947 (8.94)	102710 (8.19)	87342 (9.74)	61540 (7.57)	58062 (8.14)	56710 (8.57)	37721 (7.69)
Arunachal Pradesh	11192 (0.39)	11192 (0.56)	11339 (0.73)	2852 (0.20)	3738 (0.30)	2592 (0.29)	2592 (0.32)	95 (0.01)	95 (0.01)	1140 (0.23)
Assam	294133 (10.33)	17117 (0.86)	12838 (0.83)	14104 (1.00)	14028 (1.12)	11081 (1.24)	10234 (1.26)	10528 (1.48)	10413 (1.57)	11412 (2.33)
Bihar	39780 (1.40)	31039 (1.56)	29607 (1.91)	27401 (1.95)	23204 (1.85)	15008 (1.67)	14695 (1.81)	12978 (1.82)	10882 (1.64)	11559 (2.36)
Chhattisgarh	94817 (3.33)	52342 (2.62)	42116 (2.72)	35453 (2.52)		24050 (2.68)	24042 (2.96)	9305 (1.30)	3541 (0.53)	
Delhi	36096 (1.27)	36976 (1.85)	24537 (1.59)	18220 (1.29)	15510 (1.24)	13826 (1.54)	14721 (1.81)	8895 (1.25)	10180 (1.54)	6062 (1.24)
Goa	2389 (0.08)	3043 (0.15)	3168 (0.20)	2905 (0.21)	9050 (0.72)	960 (0.11)	1256 (0.15)	1512 (0.21)	1303 (0.20)	1255 (0.26)
Gujarat	239659 (8.42)	158465 (7.94)	141062 (9.12)	129897 (9.22)	144129 (11.50)	80041 (8.92)	73381 (9.02)	65981 (9.25)	64616 (9.76)	76214 (15.54)
Haryana	89332 (3.14)	39225 (1.97)	30531 (1.97)	24014 (1.71)	15592 (1.24)	19844 (2.21)	16674 (2.05)	14601 (2.05)	12395 (1.87)	2587 (0.53)
Himachal Pradesh	40271 (1.41)	36614 (1.83)	37531 (2.43)	35943 (2.55)	23745 (1.89)	25918 (2.89)	17314 (2.13)	19580 (2.74)	22958 (3.47)	10641 (2.17)
Jharkhand	236973 (8.33)	60719 (3.04)	34372 (2.22)	27005 (1.92)		18733 (2.09)	11012 (1.35)	10676 (1.50)	7425 (1.12)	
Jammu & Kashmir	28596 (1.00)	24593 (1.23)	21047 (1.36)	17481 (1.24)	11841 (0.94)	18286 (2.04)	14577 (1.79)	13315 (1.87)	10958 (1.66)	7515 (1.53)
Karnataka	225245 (7.91)	151656 (7.60)	115974 (7.50)	112900 (8.02)	100918 (8.05)	58663 (6.54)	56494 (6.95)	44690 (6.26)	42599 (6.44)	50119 (10.22)
Kerala	80120 (2.82)	70704 (3.54)	56051 (3.63)	67187 (4.77)	48959 (3.91)	21550 (2.40)	20623 (2.54)	18637 (2.61)	19821 (2.99)	7551 (1.54)
Madhya Pradesh	93006 (3.27)	47698 (2.39)	48273 (3.12)	47925 (3.40)	71025 (5.67)	40818 (4.55)	37158 (4.57)	41466 (5.81)	38605 (5.83)	36060 (7.35)
Maharashtra	249621 (8.77)	200114 (10.03)	170321 (11.02)	154540 (10.97)	149768 (11.95)	98647 (11.00)	99668 (12.26)	90449 (12.67)	85140 (12.86)	72155 (14.71)
Manipur	6149 (0.22)	6144 (0.31)	5610 (0.36)	5610 (0.40)	955 (0.08)	6136 (0.68)	6136 (0.75)	5602 (0.79)	438 (0.07)	388 (0.08)
Meghalaya	882 (0.03)	907 (0.05)	926 (0.06)	737 (0.05)	362 (0.03)	813 (0.09)	213 (0.03)	592 (0.08)	29 (0.00)	176 (0.04)
Mizoram	2537 (0.09)	2537 (0.13)	2650 (0.17)	1939 (0.14)	1594 (0.13)	609 (0.07)	609 (0.07)	722 (0.10)	705 (0.11)	0 (0.00)
Nagaland	888 (0.03)	385 (0.02)	338 (0.02)	387 (0.03)	94 (0.01)	187 (0.02)	187 (0.02)	228 (0.03)	228 (0.03)	41 (0.01)
Orissa	266652 (9.37)	196538 (9.85)	65769 (4.25)	44364 (3.15)	111503 (8.90)	60914 (6.79)	50357 (6.19)	27990 (3.92)	21923 (3.31)	21874 (4.46)
Punjab	39842 (1.40)	29207 (1.46)	23873 (1.54)	25143 (1.79)	25576 (2.04)	16956 (1.89)	13953 (1.72)	13002 (1.82)	12874 (1.95)	6636 (1.35)
Rajasthan	50705 (1.78)	38780 (1.94)	28417 (1.84)	34934 (2.48)	34032 (2.72)	12934 (1.44)	17044 (2.10)	15903 (2.23)	16295 (2.46)	15727 (3.21)
Sikkim	8119 (0.29)	7315 (0.37)	6531 (0.42)	6228 (0.44)	362 (0.03)	3904 (0.44)	3870 (0.48)	3089 (0.43)	3086 (0.47)	362 (0.07)
Tamil Nadu	163245 (5.74)	151902 (7.61)	132723 (8.58)	129350 (9.18)	138562 (11.05)	52087 (5.81)	42830 (5.27)	41120 (5.76)	49461 (7.47)	25716 (5.24)
Tripura	13122 (0.46)	11867 (0.59)	4876 (0.32)	5326 (0.38)	248 (0.02)	224 (0.02)	224 (0.03)	149 (0.02)	149 (0.02)	116 (0.02)
Uttar Pradesh	92191 (3.24)	82504 (4.13)	72746 (4.70)	69404 (4.93)	64959 (5.18)	26462 (2.95)	28559 (3.51)	26584 (3.73)	24275 (3.67)	24271 (4.95)
Uttranchal	39351 (1.38)	30887 (1.55)	24442 (1.58)	21768 (1.55)		20268 (2.26)	20280 (2.49)	18598 (2.61)	14973 (2.26)	0 (0.00)
West Bengal	118757 (4.17)	98790 (4.95)	73836 (4.78)	63386 (4.50)	63501 (5.07)	30063 (3.35)	26797 (3.30)	25684 (3.60)	20260 (3.06)	22667 (4.62)
Union Territories	5051 (0.18)	3795 (0.19)	3628 (0.23)	3771 (0.27)	932 (0.07)	2916 (0.33)	1817 (0.22)	1764 (0.25)	1508 (0.23)	584 (0.12)
Andaman and Nocobar	5 (0.00)	37 (0.00)	37 (0.00)	106 (0.01)	8 (0.00)	5 (0.00)	5 (0.00)	5 (0.00)	74 (0.01)	8 (0.00)
Chandigarh	1194 (0.04)	1189 (0.06)	1144 (0.07)	1629 (0.12)	179 (0.01)	600 (0.07)	695 (0.09)	550 (0.08)	565 (0.09)	79 (0.02)
Dadra & Nagar Haveli	1790 (0.06)	862 (0.04)	759 (0.05)	652 (0.05)	378 (0.03)	1749 (0.19)	696 (0.09)	656 (0.09)	480 (0.07)	306 (0.06)
Daman and Diu	266 (0.01)	195 (0.01)	71 (0.00)	88 (0.01)	168 (0.01)	58 (0.01)	15 (0.00)	30 (0.00)	10 (0.00)	68 (0.01)
Lakshadweep	6 (0.00)	27 (0.00)	24 (0.00)	21 (0.00)	4 (0.00)	0 (0.00)	21 (0.00)	21 (0.00)	18 (0.00)	0 (0.00)
Pondicherry	1790 (0.06)	1485 (0.07)	1593 (0.10)	1275 (0.09)	195 (0.02)	504 (0.06)	385 (0.05)	502 (0.07)	361 (0.05)	123 (0.03)
Multi States	284864 (10.01)	213902 (10.72)	179967 (11.64)	148340 (10.53)	0 (0.00)	125278 (13.96)	124264 (15.28)	111835 (15.67)	98041 (14.81)	0 (0.00)
Unallocated	17856 (0.63)	3452 (0.17)	14235 (0.92)	3871 (0.27)	0 (0.00)	0 (0.00)	1 (0.00)	0 (0.00)	0 (0.00)	0 (0.00)
All India	2846065 (100.00)	1995565 (100.00)	1546156 (100.00)	1408331 (100.00)	1253452 (100.00)	897160 (100.00)	813121 (100.00)	713629 (100.00)	661883 (100.00)	490406 (100.00)

Notes: Total investment covers projects announced and proposed and those under implementation; Figures in brackets are percentage to total investment.

Source: Centre for Monitoring Indian Economy Pvt. Ltd, Monthly Review of Investment Projects, CapEx, various issues (see Table A5.10).

A7 PRICES

TABLE A7.1
Wholesale Price Index: Point-to-Point and Average Annual Variation

Year	Point-to-Point				Average			
	All commodities	Annual change (per cent)	Food index	Annual change (per cent)	All commodities	Annual change (per cent)	Food index	Annual change (per cent)
(1)	(2)	(3)	(4)	(5)	(6)	(7)	(8)	(9)
				Base Year 1993–4=100				
2005–6	197.2	5.2	187.2	4.2	195.5	4.4	187.4	3.3
2004–5	187.5	4.2	179.6	1.7	187.2	6.4	181.4	3.5
2003–4	180.0	4.9	176.6	4.6	175.9	5.5	175.2	4.3
2002–3	171.6	6.1	168.8	3.4	166.8	3.4	167.9	2.9
2001–2	161.8	1.6	163.3	3.3	161.3	3.6	163.2	4.1
2000–1	159.2	5.5	158.1	−1.3	155.7	7.2	156.7	0.6
1999–2000	150.9	6.5	160.3	4.1	145.3	3.2	155.7	1.0
1998–9	141.7	5.3	154.0	9.2	140.8	6.0	154.2	11.9
1997–8	134.6	4.5	141.0	4.8	132.8	4.3	137.8	4.1
1996–7	128.8	5.4	134.6	10.8	127.3	4.7	132.4	7.8
1995–6	122.2	4.4	121.4	6.3	121.6	7.8	122.8	6.5
1994–5	117.1	17.1	114.2	14.2	112.8	12.8	115.3	15.3
				Base Year 1981–2=100				
1994–5	285.2	10.4	303.3	12.5	274.7	10.9	297.2	9.9
1993–4	258.3	10.8	269.7	3.8	247.8	8.4	270.5	6.6
1992–3	233.1	7.0	259.8	9.0	228.6	10.0	253.7	10.9
1991–2	217.8	13.6	238.4	17.1	207.8	13.7	228.8	18.2
1990–1	191.8	12.1	203.6	17.0	182.7	10.3	193.6	11.2
1989–90	171.1	9.1	174.1	5.6	165.7	7.4	174.1	4.7
1988–9	156.9	5.7	164.8	4.0	154.3	7.5	166.3	8.3
1987–8	148.5	10.7	158.4	14.1	143.6	8.2	153.5	8.9
1986–7	134.2	5.3	138.8	6.8	132.7	5.8	140.9	10.2
1985–6	127.4	5.1	130.0	5.4	125.4	4.4	127.9	2.2
1984–5	121.2	5.6	123.4	3.8	120.1	6.5	125.2	4.5
1983–4	114.8	7.1	118.8	8.4	112.8	7.5	119.8	12.2
1982–3	107.2	7.2	109.6	9.6	104.9	4.9	106.8	6.8
				Base Year 1970–1=100				
1982–3	295.3	6.6	258.1	8.0	288.7	2.6	252.3	−1.0
1981–2	277.1	2.4	239.0	−3.4	281.3	9.3	254.8	6.5
1980–1	270.7	16.7	247.3	19.5	257.3	18.2	239.2	22.3
1979–80	232.0	21.4	206.9	22.6	217.6	17.1	195.6	16.9
1978–9	191.1	4.5	168.8	0.3	185.8	0.0	167.4	−5.5
1977–8	182.8	0.4	168.3	−1.7	185.8	5.2	177.1	7.0
1976–7	182.1	12.0	171.2	17.5	176.6	2.1	165.5	−2.2
1975–6	162.6	−6.5	145.7	−15.4	173.0	−1.1	169.3	−4.2
1974–5	173.9	10.1	172.2	11.2	174.9	25.2	176.6	19.7

(contd.)

TABLE A7.1 (contd.)

Year	Point-to-Point				Average			
	All commodities	Annual change (per cent)	Food index	Annual change (per cent)	All commodities	Annual change (per cent)	Food index	Annual change (per cent)
(1)	(2)	(3)	(4)	(5)	(6)	(7)	(8)	(9)
1973–4	158.0	30.0	154.9	22.2	139.7	20.2	147.5	19.9
1972–3	121.5	12.3	126.8	15.5	116.2	10.0	123.0	15.8
1971–2	108.2	8.2	109.8	9.8	105.6	5.6	106.3	6.3
			Base Year 1961–2=100					
1971–2	192.3	6.4	216.0	8.0	188.4	4.0	210.0	2.9
1970–1	180.6	2.8	200.0	0.0	181.1	5.5	204.0	3.6
1969–70	175.7	6.4	200.0	7.5	171.6	3.7	197.0	0.0
1968–9	165.1	3.0	186.0	–4.1	165.4	–1.1	197.0	–5.3
1967–8	160.3	0.9	194.0	3.2	167.3	11.6	208.0	21.6
1966–7	158.9	15.6	188.0	25.3	149.9	13.9	171.0	17.9
1965–6	137.5	12.4	150.0	13.6	131.6	7.6	145.0	8.9
1964–5	122.3	7.9	132.0	10.0	122.3	11.0	133.1	16.9
1963–4	113.3	8.0	120.0	14.3	110.2	6.2	113.9	8.5
1962–3	104.9	4.9	105.0	5.0	103.8	3.8	105.0	5.0
			Base Year 1952–3=100					
1962–3	127.3	3.6	123.5	4.3	127.9	2.2	126.1	5.0
1961–2	122.9	–2.6	118.4	1.3	125.1	0.2	120.1	0.1
1960–1	126.2	6.4	116.9	0.3	124.9	6.7	120.0	0.6
1959–60	118.6	5.8	116.5	3.4	117.1	3.7	119.3	3.6
1958–9	112.1	5.7	112.7	9.0	112.9	4.2	115.2	8.3
1957–8	106.1	–2.9	103.4	–6.0	108.4	2.9	106.4	4.0
1956–7	109.3	7.8	110.0	11.1	105.3	13.8	102.3	18.5
1955–6	101.4	11.7	99.0	22.5	92.5	3.2	86.3	5.1
1954–5	90.8	–11.9	80.8	–22.5	89.6	–11.5	82.1	–18.0
1953–4	103.1	3.1	104.2	4.2	101.2	1.2	100.1	0.1
			Base Year August 1939=100					
1952–3	385.0	1.8	362.6	6.9	380.6	–12.4	351.3	–11.8
1951–2	378.2	–15.9	339.3	–18.1	434.6	6.1	398.3	–4.3
1950–1	449.6	–	414.1	–	409.7	–	416.4	–

Source: Office of the Economic Adviser, Ministry of Commerce and Industry, Government of India.

TABLE A7.2
Cost of Living Indices
(A) Consumer Price Index for Industrial Workers

Year	Annual Average				Point-to-Point			
	Total Index	Annual change (per cent)	Food Index	Annual change (per cent)	Total Index	Annual change (per cent)	Food Index	Annual change (per cent)
(1)	(2)	(3)	(4)	(5)	(6)	(7)	(8)	(9)
				Base Year 2001 = 100				
2005–6	117.1	4.3	na	na	119.0	5.3	na	na
2004–5	112.3	3.9	na	na	113.0	3.7	na	na
				Base Year 1982 = 100				
2004–5	520.0	3.9	506.0	2.2	525.0	4.2	502.0	1.6
2003–4	500.3	3.8	495.0	3.8	504.0	3.5	494.0	3.1
2002–3	482.0	4.1	477.0	7.0	487.0	4.1	479.0	3.7
2001–2	463.0	4.3	446.0	−1.5	468.0	5.2	462.0	3.6
2000–1	444.0	3.7	453.0	1.6	445.0	2.5	446.0	0.0
1999–2000	428.0	3.4	446.0	0.2	434.0	4.8	446.0	0.2
1998–99	414.0	13.1	445.0	14.7	414.0	8.9	445.0	11.0
1997–8	366.0	7.0	388.0	5.1	380.0	8.3	401.0	7.5
1996–7	342.0	9.3	369.0	9.5	351.0	10.0	373.0	10.0
1995–6	313.0	12.2	337.0	13.5	319.0	8.9	339.0	9.0
1994–5	279.0	8.1	297.0	9.2	293.0	9.7	311.0	10.7
1993–4	258.0	7.5	272.0	7.1	267.0	9.9	281.0	11.1
1992–3	240.0	9.6	254.0	10.4	243.0	6.1	253.0	5.0
1991–2	219.0	13.5	230.0	15.6	229.0	13.9	241.0	16.4
1990–1	193.0	11.6	199.0	12.4	201.0	13.6	207.0	16.3
1989–00	173.0	6.1	177.0	4.7	177.0	8.6	178.0	5.3
1988–9	163.0	9.4	169.0	11.2	163.0	6.5	169.0	8.3
1987–8	149.0	8.8	152.0	7.8	153.0	10.9	156.0	9.9
1986–7	137.0	8.7	141.0	10.2	138.0	6.2	142.0	7.6
1985–6	126.0	6.8	128.0	4.9	130.0	8.3	132.0	10.0
1984–5	118.0	6.3	122.0	4.3	120.0	5.3	120.0	2.6
1983–4	111.0	11.0	117.0	17.0	114.0	14.0	117.0	17.0
				Base Year 1960 =100				
1983–4	547.0	12.6	581.0	14.4	558.0	11.2	583.0	11.7
1982–3	486.0	7.8	508.0	6.7	502.0	9.8	522.0	9.9
1981–2	451.0	12.5	476.0	13.6	457.0	8.8	475.0	8.7
1980–1	401.0	11.4	419.0	12.3	420.0	12.6	437.0	13.5
1979–80	360.0	8.8	373.0	7.8	373.0	12.3	385.0	12.9
1978–9	331.0	2.2	346.0	0.3	332.0	3.4	341.0	1.5
1977–8	324.0	7.6	345.0	8.8	321.0	2.9	336.0	1.2
1976–7	301.0	−3.8	317.0	−7.3	312.0	9.1	332.0	12.2
1975–6	313.0	−1.3	342.0	−4.5	286.0	−10.9	296.0	−17.5
1974–5	317.0	26.8	358.0	28.3	321.0	16.7	359.0	17.7
1973–4	250.0	20.8	279.0	25.1	275.0	27.3	305.0	29.2

(contd.)

TABLE A7.2 (contd.)

Year	Annual Average				Point-to-Point			
	Total Index	Annual change (per cent)	Food Index	Annual change (per cent)	Total Index	Annual change (per cent)	Food Index	Annual change (per cent)
(1)	(2)	(3)	(4)	(5)	(6)	(7)	(8)	(9)
1972–3	207.0	7.8	223.0	8.8	216.0	11.3	236.0	15.1
1971–2	192.0	3.2	205.0	1.5	194.0	5.4	205.0	5.1
1970–1	186.0	5.1	202.0	4.7	184.0	2.8	195.0	0.5
1969–70	177.0	1.7	193.0	0.5	179.0	5.3	194.0	6.0
1968–9	174.0	–18.3	192.0	–15.8	170.0	na	183.0	na
				Base Year = 1949 = 100				
1968–9	212.0	–0.5	223.0	–2.2	207.0	–2.8	212.0	–6.2
1967–8	213.0	11.5	228.0	15.2	213.0	6.5	226.0	7.6
1966–7	191.0	13.0	198.0	13.8	200.0	14.9	210.0	18.6
1965–6	169.0	7.6	174.0	7.4	174.0	9.4	177.0	9.3
1964–5	157.0	14.6	162.0	17.4	159.0	11.2	162.0	13.3
1963–4	137.0	4.6	138.0	5.3	143.0	6.7	143.0	5.9
1962–3	131.0	3.1	131.0	4.0	134.0	2.3	135.0	3.8
1961–2	127.0	2.4	126.0	0.0	131.0	4.0	130.0	3.2
1960–1	124.0	0.8	126.0	0.8	126.0	1.6	126.0	0.0
1959–60	123.0	4.2	125.0	5.9	124.0	2.5	126.0	0.8
1958–9	118.0	5.4	118.0	5.4	121.0	4.3	125.0	5.9
1957–8	112.0	4.7	112.0	6.7	116.0	4.5	118.0	5.4
1956–7	107.0	11.5	105.0	14.1	111.0	5.7	112.0	6.7
1955–6	96.0	–3.0	92.0	–8.9	105.0	9.4	105.0	14.1
1954–5	99.0	–6.6	101.0	–7.3	96.0	–5.0	92.0	–8.9
1953–4	106.0	1.9	109.0	na	101.0	–2.9	101.0	–3.8
1952–3	104.0	–1.0	na	na	104.0	6.1	105.0	na
1951–2	105.0	4.0	na	na	98.0	–4.9	na	na
1950–1	101.0	na	na	na	103.0	na	na	na

(contd.)

TABLE A7.2 (contd.)

	(B) Consumer Price Index for Urban Non-manual Employees				(C) Consumer Price Index for Agricultural Laboureres							
	Annual Average		Point-to-Point		Annual Average*				Point-to-Point**			
	Total index	Annual change (per cent)	Food index	Annual change (per cent)	Total index	Annual change (per cent)	Food index	Annual change (per cent)	Total index	Annual change (per cent)	Food index	Annual change (per cent)
	(10)	(11)	(12)	(13)	(15)	(16)	(17)	(18)	(19)	(20)	(21)	(22)
					Base Year 1984–85 =100							
2005–6	456.3	4.8	463.0	4.8	358.1	4.7	351.1	4.9	370.0	7.2	364.0	8.3
2004–5	435.6	3.7	441.0	3.7	341.9	2.9	334.7	2.8	345.0	2.7	336.0	2.1
2003–4	420.3	3.7	424.0	3.7	332.3	3.0	325.6	3.0	336.0	1.8	329.0	1.5
2002–3	405.0	3.8	410.0	3.8	322.6	3.8	316.2	4.0	330.0	5.1	324.0	5.9
2001–2	390.0	5.1	395.0	4.8	310.8	2.2	304.0	1.6	314.0	2.6	306.0	2.3
2000–1	371.0	5.4	377.0	5.6	304.0	−1.7	299.1	−4.7	306.0	−1.3	299.0	−3.5
1999–2000	352.0	3.5	357.0	5.9	309.2	3.5	313.8	2.8	310.0	3.0	310.0	1.3
1998–99	340.0	12.6	337.0	8.0	298.7	11.1	305.2	13.3	301.0	6.7	306.0	7.0
1997–8	302.0	6.7	312.0	7.2	268.8	3.5	269.3	2.1	282.0	8.9	286.0	10.9
1996–7	283.0	9.3	291.0	10.2	259.8	8.6	263.7	9.3	259.0	4.9	258.0	3.2
1995–6	259.0	11.6	264.0	8.2	239.3	na	241.3	na	247.0	na	250.0	na
1994–5	232.0	7.4	244.0	9.9				Base Year 1960 =100				
1993–4	216.0	6.9	222.0	8.3	1381.0	7.6	na	na	1337.0	0.0	na	na
1992–3	202.0	10.4	205.0	6.8	1283.0	11.9	na	na	1337.0	12.4	na	na
1991–2	183.0	13.7	192.0	13.6	1147.0	6.9	na	na	1189.0	12.5	na	na
1990–1	161.0	11.0	169.0	13.4	1073.0	6.6	na	na	1057.0	−1.0	na	na
1989–00	145.0	6.6	149.0	8.0	1007.0	21.3	na	na	1068.0	21.9	na	na
1988–9	136.0	7.9	138.0	7.0	830.0	10.4	na	na	876.0	15.4	na	na
1987–8	126.0	9.6	129.0	10.3	752.0	3.9	na	na	759.0	3.1	na	na
1986–7	115.0	7.5	117.0	6.4	724.0	11.4	na	na	736.0	9.7	na	na
1985–6	107.0	7.0	110.0	10.0	650.0	12.5	na	na	671.0	14.1	na	na
	Base Year 1960 =100				578.0	4.1	na	na	588.0	4.8	na	na
1985–6	568.0	6.8	584.0	8.1	555.0	5.7	na	na	561.0	5.8	na	na
1984–5	532.0	8.1	540.0	6.9	525.0	0.4	na	na	530.0	3.7	na	na
1983–4	492.0	10.3	505.0	9.3	523.0	8.7	na	na	511.0	0.4	na	na
1982–3	446.0	8.0	462.0	9.2	481.0	7.4	na	na	509.0	14.9	na	na
1981–2	413.0	11.9	423.0	9.9	448.0	9.5	na	na	443.0	3.3	na	na
1980–1	369.0	11.8	385.0	12.2	409.0	13.6	na	na	429.0	14.1	na	na
1979–80	330.0	7.8	343.0	11.4	360.0	13.6	na	na	376.0	18.2	na	na
1978–9	306.0	3.4	308.0	3.7	317.0	−1.9	na	na	318.0	1.9	na	na
1977–8	296.0	6.9	297.0	4.2	323.0	7.0	na	na	312.0	−2.2	na	na
1976–7	277.0	0.0	285.0	7.5	302.0	−4.7	na	na	319.0	13.9	na	na
1975–6	277.0	2.6	265.0	−4.3	317.0	−13.9	na	na	280.0	−25.3	na	na
1974–5	270.0	22.2	277.0	16.4	368.0	30.0	na	na	375.0	16.8	na	na
1973–4	221.0	15.1	238.0	19.6	283.0	25.8	na	na	321.0	32.6	na	na
1972–3	192.0	6.7	199.0	8.2	225.0	12.5	na	na	242.0	18.6	na	na
1971–2	180.0	3.4	184.0	5.7	200.0	4.2	na	na	204.0	7.9	na	na
1970–1	174.0	4.2	174.0	2.4	192.0	−0.5	na	na	189.0	−3.6	na	na
1969–70	167.0	3.7	170.0	5.6	193.0	4.3	na	na	196.0	5.4	na	na
1968–9	161.0	1.3	161.0	1.3	185.0	−10.2	na	na	186.0	−2.6	na	na
1967–8	159.0	8.9	159.0	5.3	206.0	8.4	na	na	191.0	−7.7	na	na
1966–7	146.0	10.6	151.0	11.9	190.0	24.2	na	na	207.0	32.7	na	na
1965–6	132.0	6.5	135.0	na	153.0	7.0	na	na	156.0	na	na	na
1964–5	124.0	na	na	na	143.0	na	na	na	na	na	na	na

Note: Current series with base 1984–5 =100 was introduced w.r.f November 1987; na— not available; The conversion factor from the new to the old series is 5.32; * Averages based on agricultural year, that is, July–June of every year; ** June over June; The base is revised to 1986-87 w.e.f. November 1995; Though the base of the series is 1960–1, the indices are available from September 1964 only.
Sources: Various issues of *Economic Survey*, *RBI Bulletin*, and *Indian Labour Journal*.

EXTERNAL SECTOR
A8 BALANCE OF PAYMENTS

TABLE A8.1
Foreign Exchange Reserves (End Period)

End of	SDRs			Gold		Foreign Currency Assets		Reserve Tranche Position in IMF		Total	
	In million SDRs	Rupees crore	In million US Dollar	Rupees crore	In million US Dollar	Rupees crore	In million US Dollar	Rupees crore	In million US Dollar	Rupees crore	In million US Dollar
(1)	(2)	(3)	(4)	(5)	(6)	(7)	(8)	(9)	(10)	(11)	(12)
April 2006	4	25	6	28335	6301	690730	153598	3473	772	722563	160677
2005–06											
Mar 2006	2	12	3	25674	5755	647327	145108	3374	756	676387	151622
Feb 2006	2	12	3	25541	5747	603925	135897	3348	753	632826	142400
jan 2006	3	20	5	25030	5680	589526	133770	4051	919	618627	140374
Dec 2005	3	20	5	23770	5274	590497	131018	4096	909	618383	137206
Nov 2005	3	21	4	22626	4925	627455	136582	6017	1310	656119	142821
Oct 2005	3	20	4	21943	4864	619299	137286	6403	1419	647665	143573
Sep 2005	3	19	4	20727	4712	602309	136920	6260	1423	629315	143059
Aug 2005	3	19	4	19971	4535	608225	138107	6312	1433	634527	144079
Jul 2005	3	18	4	19116	4395	585319	134587	6766	1556	611219	140542
Jun 2005	3	18	4	19375	4453	575864	132352	6791	1561	602048	138370
May 2005	3	19	4	19119	4376	580749	132925	6780	1552	606667	138857
Apr 2005	3	20	5	19393	4443	593423	135950	6300	1443	619136	141841
2004–05											
Mar 2005	3	20	5	19686	4500	593121	135571	6289	1438	619116	141514
Feb 2005	3	20	5	19096	4376	567725	130093	6223	1426	593064	135900
Jan 2005	3	22	5	19181	4390	540246	123654	6177	1414	565626	129463
Dec 2004	3	22	5	19969	4582	545466	125164	6221	1427	571678	131178
Nov 2004	3	22	5	20316	4540	547377	122319	6097	1362	573812	128226
Oct 2004	4	24	5	19776	4351	525632	115651	6043	1330	551475	121337
Sep 2004	1	7	1	19349	4192	526605	114083	6015	1303	551976	119579
Aug 2004	1	7	1	19186	4140	522333	112717	6005	1296	547531	118154
Jul 2004	1	8	2	19150	4123	524732	112967	6007	1293	549897	118385
Jun 2004	2	8	2	18655	4057	524865	114151	5980	1301	549508	119511
May 2004	2	8	2	18104	3974	519847	114102	5927	1301	543886	119379
Apr 2004	2	10	2	18598	4191	501429	113011	5704	1286	525741	118490
2005–6	2	12	3	25674	5755	647327	145108	3374	756	676387	151622
2004–5	3	20	5	19686	4500	593121	135571	6289	1438	619116	141514
2003–4	2	10	2	18216	4198	466215	107448	5688	1311	490129	112959
2002–3	3	19	4	16785	3534	341476	71890	3190	672	361470	76100
2001–2	8	50	10	14868	3047	249118	51049			264036	54106
2000–1	2	11	2	12711	2725	184482	39554			197204	42281
1999–2000	3	16	4	12973	2974	152924	35058			165913	38036
1998–9	6	34	8	12559	2960	125412	29522			138005	32490
1997–8	1	4	1	13394	3391	102507	25975			115905	29367
1996–7	1	7	2	14557	4054	80368	22367			94932	26423
1995–6	56	280	82	15658	4561	58446	17044			74384	21687
1994–5	5	23	7	13752	4370	66006	20809			79781	25186
1993–4	76	339	108	12794	4078	47287	15068			60420	19254
1992–3	13	55	18	10549	3380	20140	6434			30744	9832
1991–2	66	233	90	9039	3499	14578	5631			23850	9220
1990–1	76	200	102	6828	3496	4388	2236			11416	5834

Notes: 1. Gold was valued at Rs 84.39 per 10 grams till 16 October 1990. It has been valued close to international market price with effect from 17 October 1990; Conversion of SDRs into US dollar is done at exchange rates released by the IMF; With effect from 1 April 1991, the conversion of foreign currency assets into US dollar is done at week end rates for week end-data and or month-end rate for month end-data based on New York closing exchange rates; Prior to that it was done by using representative exchange rate released by the IMF; Since March 1993, foreign exchange holdings are converted into rupees at rupee–US dollar market exchange rates; Reserve tranche position has been reported as part of reserves since 2002–3.

Source: RBI, *Monthly Bulletin*, Various Issues.

TABLE A8.2
Balance of Payments, 1990–1 to 2005–6

(US $ million)

Item	2005–6(P) Credit	2005–6(P) Debt	2005–6(P) Net	2004–5 PR Credit	2004–5 PR Debt	2004–5 PR Net	2003–4 R Credit	2003–4 R Debt	2003–4 R Net	2002–3 Credit	2002–3 Debt	2002–3 Net
(1)	(2)	(3)	(4)	(2)	(3)	(4)	(2)	(3)	(4)	(5)	(6)	(7)
A. Current Account	196261	206873	–10612	154004	159404	–5400	119793	105710	14083	95699	89354	6345
1. Merchandise Gold	104780	156334	–51554	82150	118779	–36629	66285	80003	–13718	53774	64464	–10690
2. Invisibles	91481	50539	40942	71854	40625	31229	53508	25707	27801	41925	24890	17035
B. Capital Account	139300	114607	24693	98827	67800	31027	75885	59149	16736	46368	35528	10840
1. Foreign Investment (a+b)	76635	58413	18222	46508	34361	12147	32682	18938	13744	14001	9840	4161
a. In India	75867	55687	20180	46190	31694	14496	32540	16862	15678	13928	7913	6015
b. Abroad	768	2726	–1958	318	2667	–2349	142	2076	–1934	73	1927	–1854
a1. Direct	8520	2787	5733	5972	2732	3240	4464	2076	2388	5168	1951	3217
i. In India	7752	61	7691	5654	65	5589	4322	0	4322	5095	59	5036
Equity	5820	61	5759	3779	65	3714	2229	0	2229	2825	59	2766
Reinvested Earnings	1676	0	1676	1508	0	1508	1460	0	1460	1832	0	1832
Other Capital	256	0	256	367	0	367	633	0	633	438	0	438
ii. Abroad	768	2726	–1958	318	2667	–2349	142	2076	–1934	73	1892	–1819
Equity	768	1746	–978	318	1579	–1261	142	1264	–1122	73	684	–611
Reinvested Earnings	0	364	–364	0	700	–700	0	552	–552	0	1104	–1104
Other Capital	0	616	–616	0	388	–388	0	260	–260	0	104	–104
a2. Portfolio	68115	55626	12489	40536	31629	8907	28218	16862	11356	8833	7889	944
i. In India	68115	55626	12489	40536	31629	8907	28218	16862	11356	8833	7854	979
ii. Abroad	0	0	0	0	0	0	0	0	0	0	35	–35
2. Loans (a+b+c)	36221	31484	4737	29749	18994	10755	19667	24031	–4364	11568	15418	–3850
a. External Assistance	3415	1977	1438	3809	1886	1923	3350	6208	–2858	2878	6006	–3128
a1. By India	20	104	–84	24	128	–104	24	128	–104	0	32	–32
a2. To India	3395	1873	1522	3785	1758	2027	3326	6080	–2754	2878	5974	–3096
b. Commercial Borrowings (MT & LT)	13451	11860	1591	8546	3506	5040	5228	8153	–2925	3514	5206	–1692
b1. By India	0	342	–342	0	23	–23	3	0	3	9	0	9
b2. To India	13451	11518	1933	8546	3483	5063	5225	8153	–2928	3505	5206	–1701
c. Short term (to India)	19355	17647	1708	17394	13602	3792	11089	9670	1419	5176	4206	970
3. Banking Capital (a+b)	21658	20285	1373	14507	10633	3874	19222	13189	6033	18958	8533	10425
a. Commercial Banks	20586	20144	442	14230	10251	3979	18887	12386	6501	18422	8287	10135
a1. Assets	772	3947	–3175	505	552	–47	950	161	789	6089	976	5113
a2. Liabilities	19814	16197	3617	13725	9699	4026	17937	12225	5712	12333	7311	5022
of which: Non-resident deposits	17835	15046	2789	8071	9035	–964	14281	10639	3642	10214	7236	2978
b. Others	1072	141	931	277	382	–105	335	803	–468	536	246	290
4. Rupee Debt Service	0	572	–572	0	417	–417	0	376	–376	0	474	–474
5. Other Capital	4786	3853	933	8063	3395	4668	4314	2615	1699	1841	1263	578
C. Errors and Omissions	971	0	971	532	0	532	602	0	602	0	200	–200
D. Overall Balance (A+B+C)	336532	321480	15052	253363	227204	26159	196280	164859	31421	1E+05	1E+05	16985
E. Monetary Movements (1+2)	0	15052	–15052	0	26159	–26159	0	31421	–31421	0	16985	–16985
1. I.M.F	0	0	0	0	0	0	0	0	0	0	0	0
2. Foreign Exchange Reserves Increase (–ve)/Decrease (+ve)	0	15052	–15052	0	26159	–26159	0	31421	–31421	0	16985	–16985

(contd.)

TABLE A8.2 (contd.)

Item	2001–2			2000–1			1999–2000			1998–9		
	Credit	Debt	Net	Credit	Debt	Net	Credit	Debt	Net	Credit	Debt	Net
(1)	(8)	(9)	(10)	(11)	(12)	(13)	(14)	(15)	(16)	(17)	(18)	(19)
A. Current Account	81440	78040	3400	77719	80385	-2666	67854	72552	-4698	60068	64106	-4038
1. Merchandise Gold	44703	56277	-11574	45452	57912	-12460	37542	55383	-17841	34298	47544	-13246
2. Invisibles	36737	21763	14974	32267	22473	9794	30312	17169	13143	25770	16562	9208
B. Capital Account	43257	34706	8551	54126	45286	8840	40531	30087	10444	34172	25735	8437
1. Foreign Investment (a+b)	15488	8802	6686	17720	11858	5862	12240	7123	5117	5892	3580	2312
a. In India	15389	7243	8146	17650	10859	6791	12121	6930	5191	5743	3331	2412
b. Abroad	99	1559	-1460	70	999	-929	119	193	-74	149	249	-100
a1. Direct	6229	1495	4734	4101	829	3272	2170	3	2167	2518	38	2480
i. In India	6130	5	6125	4031	0	4031	2170	3	2167	2518	38	2480
Equity	4096	5	4091	2399	0	2399	0	0	0	0	0	0
Reinvested Earnings	1644	0	1644	1352	0	1352	0	0	0	0	0	0
Other Capital	390	0	390	280	0	280	0	0	0	0	0	0
ii. Abroad	99	1490	-1391	70	829	-759	0	0	0	0	0	0
Equity	99	669	-570	70	414	-344	0	0	0	0	0	0
Reinvested Earnings	0	700	-700	0	340	-340	0	0	0	0	0	0
Other Capital	0	121	-121	0	75	-75	0	0	0	0	0	0
a2. Portfolio	9259	7307	1952	13619	11029	2590	9951	6927	3024	3225	3293	-68
i. In India	9259	7238	2021	13619	10859	2760	9951	6927	3024	3225	3293	-68
ii. Abroad	0	69	-69	0	170	-170	0	0	0	0	0	0
2. Loans (a+b+c)	11601	12862	-1261	23806	18542	5264	13060	11459	1601	14771	10353	4418
a. External Assistance	3352	2235	1117	2941	2531	410	3074	2183	891	2726	1927	799
a1. By India	0	87	-87	0	17	-17	0	10	-10	0	21	-21
a2. To India	3352	2148	1204	2941	2514	427	3074	2173	901	2726	1906	820
b. Commercial Borrowings (MT & LT)	2687	4272	-1585	9621	5318	4303	3207	2874	333	7231	2864	4367
b1. By India	3	0	3	0	5	-5	20	0	20	5	0	5
b2. To India	2684	4272	-1588	9621	5313	4308	3187	2874	313	7226	2864	4362
c. Short term (to India)	5562	6355	-793	11244	10693	551	6779	6402	377	4814	5562	-748
3. Banking Capital (a+b)	13870	11006	2864	9744	11705	-1961	10659	8532	2127	8898	8199	699
a. Commercial Banks	13385	10725	2660	9423	11305	-1882	10259	7955	2304	7469	7916	-447
a1. Assets	1267	1711	-444	206	4380	-4174	2653	1863	790	1344	2741	-1397
a2. Liabilities	12118	9014	3104	9217	6925	2292	7606	6092	1514	6125	5175	950
of which: Non-resident deposits	11435	8681	2754	8988	6672	2316	7405	5865	1540	6000	5040	960
b. Others	485	281	204	321	400	-79	400	577	-177	1429	283	1146
4. Rupee Debt Service	0	519	-519	0	617	-617	0	711	-711	0	802	-802
5. Other Capital	2298	1517	781	2856	2564	292	4572	2262	2310	4611	2801	1810
C. Errors and Omissions	0	194	-194	0	305	-305	656	0	656	0	177	-177
D. Overall Balance (A+B+C)	1E+05	1E+05	11757	1E+05	1E+05	5869	1E+05	1E+05	6402	94240	90018	4222
E. Monetary Movements (1+2)	0	11757	-11757	1448	7316	-5868	0	6402	-6402	0	4222	-4222
1. I.M.F	0	0	0	0	26	-26	0	260	-260	0	393	-393
2. Foreign Exchange Reserves Increase (–ve)/Decrease (+ve)	0	11757	-11757	1448	7290	-5842	0	6142	-6142	0	3829	-3829

(contd.)

TABLE A8.2 (contd.)

Item	1997–8			1996–7			1995–6			1994–5		
	Credit	Debt	Net	Credit	Debt	Net	Credit	Debt	Net	Credit	Debt	Net
(1)	(20)	(21)	(22)	(23)	(24)	(25)	(26)	(27)	(28)	(29)	(30)	(31)
A. Current Account	58924	64423	-5499	55538	60157	-4619	49974	55886	-5912	42409	45778	-3369
1. Merchandise Gold	35680	51187	-15507	34133	48948	-14815	32310	43670	-11360	26855	35904	-9049
2. Invisibles	23244	13236	10008	21405	11209	10196	17664	12216	5448	15554	9874	5680
B. Capital Account	39292	29448	9844	36192	24185	12007	24176	20087	4089	25915	17413	8502
1. Foreign Investment (a+b)	9266	3913	5353	7825	1861	5964	5644	1029	4615	5763	956	4807
a. In India	9169	3779	5390	7817	1663	6154	5629	826	4803	5753	831	4922
b. Abroad	97	134	-37	8	198	-190	15	203	-188	10	125	-115
a1. Direct	3596	34	3562	2864	22	2842	2174	30	2144	1351	8	1343
i. In India	3596	34	3562	2864	22	2842	2174	30	2144	1351	8	1343
Equity	0	0	0	0	0	0	0	0	0	0	0	0
Reinvested Earnings	0	0	0	0	0	0	0	0	0	0	0	0
Other Capital	0	0	0	0	0	0	0	0	0	0	0	0
ii. Abroad	0	0	0	0	0	0	0	0	0	0	0	0
Equity	0	0	0	0	0	0	0	0	0	0	0	0
Reinvested Earnings	0	0	0	0	0	0	0	0	0	0	0	0
Other Capital	0	0	0	0	0	0	0	0	0	0	0	0
a2. Portfolio	5573	3745	1828	4953	1641	3312	3456	795	2661	4402	823	3579
i. In India	5573	3745	1828	4953	1641	3312	3456	795	2661	4402	823	3579
ii. Abroad	0	0	0	0	0	0	0	0	0	0	0	0
2. Loans (a+b+c)	17301	12502	4799	17720	12925	4795	11331	9132	2199	10930	7895	3035
a. External Assistance	2885	2000	885	3056	1955	1101	2933	2066	867	3193	1675	1518
a1. By India	0	22	-22	0	8	-8	0	17	-17	2	10	-8
a2. To India	2885	1978	907	3056	1947	1109	2933	2049	884	3191	1665	1526
b. Commercial Borrowings (MT & LT)	7382	3372	4010	7579	4723	2856	4261	2977	1284	4249	3125	1124
b1. By India	11	0	11	8	0	8	9	0	9	97	3	94
b2. To India	7371	3372	3999	7571	4723	2848	4252	2977	1275	4152	3122	1030
c. Short term (to India)	7034	7130	-96	7085	6247	838	4137	4089	48	3488	3095	393
3. Banking Capital (a+b)	8910	9803	-893	8018	5789	2229	6453	5690	763	7020	7354	-334
a. Commercial Banks	8164	9424	-1260	7632	5407	2225	6172	5235	937	6449	7075	-626
a1. Assets	580	2775	-2195	755	1625	-870	867	1251	-384	241	1203	-962
a2. Liabilities	7584	6649	935	6877	3782	3095	5305	3984	1321	6208	5872	336
of which: Non-resident deposits	7532	6407	1125	6775	3425	3350	4929	3826	1103	5805	5633	172
b. Others	746	379	367	386	382	4	281	456	-175	571	279	292
4. Rupee Debt Service	0	767	-767	0	727	-727	0	952	-952	0	983	-983
5. Other Capital	3815	2463	1352	2629	2883	-254	748	3285	-2537	2202	225	1977
C. Errors and Omissions	166	0	166	0	595	-595	601	0	601	654	0	654
D. Overall Balance (A+B+C)	98382	93871	4511	91730	84937	6793	74752	75974	-1222	68978	63191	5787
E. Monetary Movements (1+2)	0	4511	-4511	0	6793	-6793	2936	1715	1222	0	5787	-5787
1. I.M.F	0	618	-618	0	975	-975	0	1715	-1715	0	1143	-1143
2. Foreign Exchange Reserves Increase (-ve)/Decrease (+ve)	0	3893	-3893	0	5818	-5818	2936	0	2937	0	4644	-4644

(contd.)

TABLE A8.2 (contd.)

Item	1993-4			1992-3			1991-2			1990-1		
	Credit	Debt	Net	Credit	Debt	Net	Credit	Debt	Net	Credit	Debt	Net
(1)	(32)	(33)	(34)	(35)	(36)	(37)	(38)	(39)	(40)	(38)	(39)	(40)
A. Current Account	34002	35160	-1158	28203	31729	-3526	27768	28946	-1178	25941	35621	-9680
1. Merchandise	22683	26739	-4056	18869	24316	-5447	18266	21064	-2798	18477	27915	-9438
2. Invisibles	11319	8421	2898	9334	7413	1921	9502	7882	1620	7464	7706	-242
B. Capital Account	28953	20060	8893	22617	18741	3876	23339	19424	3915	22764	15711	7053
1. Foreign Investment (a+b)	4609	376	4233	589	32	557	151	18	133	111	10	101
a. In India	4609	376	4233	589	32	557	151	18	133	111	10	101
b. Abroad	0	0	0	0	0	0	0	0	0	0	0	0
a1. Direct	651	65	586	345	30	315	147	18	129	106	10	96
i. In India	651	65	586	345	30	315	147	18	129	106	10	96
Equity	0	0	0	0	0	0	0	0	0	0	0	0
Reinvested Earnings	0	0	0	0	0	0	0	0	0	0	0	0
Other Capital	0	0	0	0	0	0	0	0	0	0	0	0
ii. Abroad	0	0	0	0	0	0	0	0	0	0	0	0
Equity	0	0	0	0	0	0	0	0	0	0	0	0
Reinvested Earnings	0	0	0	0	0	0	0	0	0	0	0	0
Other Capital	0	0	0	0	0	0	0	0	0	0	0	0
a2. Portfolio	3958	311	3647	244	2	242	4	0	4	5	0	5
i. In India	3958	311	3647	244	2	242	4	0	4	5	0	5
ii. Abroad	0	0	0	0	0	0	0	0	0	0	0	0
2. Loans (a+b+c)	9971	8159	1812	8671	8260	411	9419	5437	3982	9431	3899	5532
a. External Assistance	3476	1580	1896	3302	1446	1856	4367	1333	3034	3397	1193	2204
a1. By India	0	5	-5	0	3	-3	0	5	-5	0	6	-6
a2. To India	3476	1575	1901	3302	1443	1859	4367	1328	3039	3397	1187	2210
b. Commercial Borrowings (MT & LT)	3015	2330	685	1179	1545	-366	3152	1690	1462	4282	2028	2254
b1. By India	102	24	78	12	20	-8	19	13	6	30	25	5
b2. To India	2913	2306	607	1167	1525	-358	3133	1677	1456	4252	2003	2249
c. Short term (to India)	3480	4249	-769	4190	5269	-1079	1900	2414	-514	1752	678	1074
3. Banking Capital (a+b)	11500	9237	2263	11998	8172	3826	10961	10394	567	10105	9423	682
a. Commercial Banks	10614	8956	1658	10653	7723	2930	9068	8930	138	7959	7055	904
a1. Assets	276	1120	-844	1234	161	1073	1336	1107	229	426	789	-363
a2. Liabilities	10338	7836	2502	9419	7562	1857	7732	7823	-91	7533	6266	1267
of which: Non-resident deposits	8850	7645	1205	9188	7187	2001	7696	7406	290	7347	5811	1536
b. Others	886	281	605	1345	449	896	1893	1464	429	2146	2368	-222
4. Rupee Debt Service	0	1053	-1053	0	878	-878	0	1240	-1240	0	1193	-1193
5. Other Capital	2873	1235	1638	1359	1399	-40	2808	2335	473	3117	1186	1931
C. Errors and Omissions	800	0	800	0	940	-940	0	138	-138	134	0	134
D. Overall Balance (A+B+C)	63755	55220	8535	50820	51410	-590	51107	48508	2599	48839	51332	-2493
E. Monetary Movements (1+2)	321	8858	-8537	1623	1033	590	1245	3844	-2599	3137	644	2493
1. I.M.F	321	133	188	1623	335	1288	1245	460	785	1858	644	1214
2. Foreign Exchange Reserves Increase (-ve)/Decrease (+ve)	0	8723	-8723	0	698	-698	0	3384	-3384	1279	0	1279

Notes: PR: Partially Revised; P: Preliminary; R: Revised; * Relates to acquisition of shares of Indian companies by non-residents under Section 5 of FEMA 1999. Data on such acquisition have been included as part of FDI since January 1996; ** Represents fresh inflow of funds by FIIs; PR : Provisional; # Represents the amount raised by Indian corporates through Global Depository Receipts (GDRs) and American Depository Receipts (ADRs).

Source: RBI; *Monthly Bulletin*, Various Issues.

TABLE A8.3
Invisibles Account on Balance of Payments

(US$ million)

Item	2005–6(P)			2004–5(PR)			2003–4(R)			2002–3(R)		
	Credit	Debt	Net	Credit	Debt	Net	Credit	Debt	Net	Credit	Debt	Net
(1)	(2)	(3)	(4)	5	6	7	8	9	10	(11)	(12)	(13)
Invisibles	91481	50539	40942	71854	40625	31229	53508	25707	27801	41925	24890	17035
a. Services	60610	38345	22265	46031	31832	14199	26868	16724	10144	20763	17120	3643
a1. Travel	7789	6421	1368	6495	5510	985	5037	3602	1435	3312	3341	−29
a2. Transportation	6277	7394	−1117	4798	4539	259	3207	2328	879	2536	3272	−736
a3. Insurance	1042	985	57	909	722	187	419	363	56	369	350	19
a4. G.n.i.e.	305	480	−175	328	261	67	240	212	28	293	228	65
a5. Miscellaneous	45197	23065	22132	33501	20800	12701	17965	10219	7746	14253	9929	4324
of which : Software Services	23600	1338	22262	17200	674	16526	12800	476	12324	9600	737	8863
b. Transfers	25220	944	24276	21276	432	20844	22736	574	22162	17640	802	16838
b1. Official	667	486	181	623	32	591	554	0	554	451	0	451
b2. Private	24553	458	24095	20653	400	20253	22182	574	21608	17189	802	16387
c. Income	5651	11250	−5599	4547	8361	−3814	3904	8409	−4505	3522	6968	−3446
c1. Investment income	5477	10504	−5027	4431	7100	−2669	3774	7531	−3757	3405	6949	−3544
c2. Compensation to employees	174	746	−572	116	1261	−1145	130	878	−748	117	19	98

Item	2001–2(R)			2000–1(R)			1999–2000(R)			1998–9(PR)		
	Credit	Debt	Net	Credit	Debt	Net	Credit	Debt	Net	Credit	Debt	Net
(1)	(14)	(15)	(16)	(17)	(18)	(19)	(20)	(21)	(22)	(23)	(24)	(25)
Invisibles	36737	21763	14974	32267	22473	9794	30312	17169	13143	25770	16562	9208
a. Services	17140	13816	3324	16268	14576	1692	15709	11645	4064	13186	11021	2165
a1. Travel	3137	3014	123	3497	2804	693	3036	2139	897	2993	1743	1250
a2. Transportation	2161	3467	−1306	2046	3558	−1512	1707	2410	−703	1925	2680	−755
a3. Insurance	288	280	8	270	223	47	231	122	109	224	112	112
a4. G.n.i.e.	518	283	235	651	319	332	582	270	312	597	325	272
a5. Miscellaneous	11036	6772	4264	9804	7672	2132	10153	6704	3449	7447	6161	1286
of which : Software Services	7556	672	6884	6341	591	5750						
b. Transfers	16218	362	15856	13317	211	13106	12672	34	12638	10649	62	10587
b1. Official	458	0	458	252	0	252	382	0	382	308	1	307
b2. Private	15760	362	15398	13065	211	12854	12290	34	12256	10341	61	10280
c. Income	3379	7585	−4206	2682	7686	−5004	1931	5490	−3559	1935	5479	−3544
c1. Investment income	3254	7098	−3844	2554	7218	−4664	1783	5478	−3695	1893	5462	−3569
c2. Compensation to employees	125	487	−362	128	468	−340	148	12	136	42	17	25

(contd.)

TABLE A8.3 (contd.)

Item	1997–8(PR)			1996–7(PR)			1995–6(PR)			1994–5(PR)		
	Credit	Debt	Net	Credit	Debt	Net	Credit	Debt	Net	Credit	Debt	Net
(1)	(26)	(27)	(28)	(29)	(30)	(31)	(32)	(33)	(34)	(35)	(36)	(37)
Invisibles	23244	13237	10007	21405	11209	10196	17676	12216	5460	15554	9874	5680
a. Services	9429	8110	1319	7474	6748	726	7342	7542	−186	6135	5533	602
a1. Travel	2914	1437	1477	2878	858	2020	2711	1167	1544	2365	818	1547
a2. Transportation	1836	2522	−686	1953	2394	−441	2010	2169	−159	1696	1863	−167
a3. Insurance	240	183	57	217	153	64	178	142	36	152	181	−29
a4. G.n.i.e.	276	160	116	72	178	−106	13	218	−205	10	165	−155
a5. Miscellaneous	4163	3808	355	2354	3165	−811	2430	3846	−1416	1912	2506	−594
of which : Software Services												0
b. Transfers	12254	45	12209	12858	81	12777	8890	39	8851	8533	24	8509
b1. Official	379	0	379	423	13	410	351	6	345	421	5	416
b2. Private	11875	45	11830	12435	68	12367	8540	33	8507	8112	19	8093
c. Income	1561	5082	−3521	1073	4380	−3307	1429	4634	−3205	886	4317	−3431
c1. Investment income	1561	5020	−3459	1073	4380	−3307	1429	4633	−3204	886	4317	−3431
c2. Compensation to employees	0	62	−62									

Item	1992–3(PR)			1991–2(PR)			1990–1(PR)		
	Credit	Debt	Net	Credit	Debt	Net	Credit	Debt	Net
(1)	(41)	(42)	(43)	(44)	(45)	(46)	(47)	(48)	(49)
Invisibles	9334	7413	1921	9502	7882	1620	7464	7706	−242
a. Services	4730	3601	1129	5022	3815	1207	4551	3571	980
a1. Travel	2098	385	1713	1977	465	1512	1456	392	1064
a2. Transportation	982	1485	−503	939	1289	−350	983	1093	−110
a3. Insurance	158	146	12	108	126	−18	111	88	23
a4. G.n.i.e.	75	100	−25	17	119	−102	15	173	−158
a5. Miscellaneous	1417	1485	−68	1981	1816	165	1986	1825	161
of which : Software Services									
b. Transfers	4228	13	4215	4259	16	4243	2545	15	2530
b1. Official	364	1	363	461	1	460	462	1	461
b2. Private	3864	12	3852	3798	15	3783	2083	14	2069
c. Income	376	3799	−3423	221	4051	−3830	368	4120	−3752
c1. Investment income	376	3799	−3423	221	4051	−3830	368	4120	−3752
c2. Compensation to employees									

Source: RBI, *Handbook of Statistics on Indian Economy and RBI Bulletin.*

Table A9.1 A9 EXCHANGE RATE

Exchange Rate for the Indian Rupee vis-à-vis Some Select Currencies

(Indian Rupee per Currency; Per cent appreciation (+), depreciation (−))

Countries	Currency	2005–6	2004–5	2003–4	2002–3	2001–2	2000–1	1999–2000	1998–9	1997–8	1996–7	1995–6	1994–5	1993–4	1992–3	2001–2 to 2005–6	1992–3 to 2000–1
(1)	(2)	(3)	(4)	(5)	(6)	(7)	(8)	(9)	(10)	(11)	(12)	(13)	(14)	(15)	(16)	(17)	(18)
Developing Countries																	
Argentina	Pesos	15.0767	15.3410	16.1597	14.3886	38.8523	45.7084	43.3557	42.0833	37.1769	35.5186	33.4673	31.4292	31.4681	26.6057	203.2	−41.8
Bangladesh	Taka	0.6776	0.7430	0.7868	0.8360	0.8401	0.8638	0.8717	0.8850	0.8308	0.8408	0.8269	0.7803	0.7872	0.6772	27.5	−21.6
Brazil	Reais	19.0588	15.6705	15.6941	15.1325	19.7735	24.0767	23.8689	31.8292	33.8634	34.7196	35.3031	39.1494	na	na	26.3	62.6
China	Yuan	5.4380	5.4287	5.5518	5.8483	5.7623	5.5188	5.2347	5.0807	4.4845	4.2731	4.0212	3.6714	4.8262	4.7265	1.5	−14.4
Colombia	Pesos	0.0193	0.0177	0.0163	0.0181	0.0207	0.0211	0.0234	0.0284	0.0306	0.0340	0.0350	0.0376	0.0357	0.0336	9.6	59.2
Hongkong	Hongkong Dollar	5.6992	5.7654	5.9055	6.2067	6.1156	5.8603	5.5801	5.4298	4.7997	4.5883	4.3261	na	na	na	2.8	−26.2
Indonesia	Rupiah for Rs 100	0.4600	0.4900	0.5400	0.5380	0.4603	0.5065	0.5771	0.4271	0.7962	1.5020	1.4706	1.4396	1.4917	1.2915	10.1	155.0
Israel	New Sheqalim	9.7004	10.0834	10.2961	10.1067	11.0219	11.1494	10.4712	10.7340	10.5738	10.9408	11.0092	10.4087	10.9033	10.2729	14.9	−7.9
Iran	Rials	0.0049	0.0051	0.0055	0.0061	0.0210	0.0259	0.0247	0.0240	0.0212	0.0203	0.0191	0.0180	0.0189	0.0240	428.4	957.9
Kenya	Shillings	0.5948	0.5676	0.6059	0.6171	0.6069	0.5892	0.5950	0.6660	0.6176	0.6297	0.6108	0.6235	0.4816	0.7637	−0.9	29.6
Korea	Won	0.0437	0.0405	0.0388	0.0366	0.0366	0.0391	0.0370	0.0324	0.0327	0.0340	0.0434	0.0393	0.0389	0.0335	−10.5	−14.3
Kuwait	Dinar	151.591	152.818	154.811	160.355	155.448	148.829	142.074	138.258	122.215	118.223	112.003	105.496	104.756	88.890	−1.8	−40.3
Malaysia	Ringgit	11.7354	11.8240	12.0927	12.7384	12.5510	12.0225	11.4037	10.8537	11.6454	14.1980	13.3682	12.1725	12.0456	10.3802	2.4	−13.7
Mexico	Pesos	4.1236	3.9637	4.2427	4.8020	5.1857	4.7948	4.5998	4.4165	4.6122	4.6207	4.9147	7.7052	10.0183	8.5058	16.3	77.4
Myanmar	Kyats	7.5783	7.8673	7.7193	7.5343	7.0246	6.9312	6.8564	6.6762	5.9017	5.9233	5.8780	5.3482	5.1081	4.3172	−8.5	−37.7
Nigeria	Naira	0.3396	0.3394	0.3512	0.3915	0.4247	0.4379	0.4526	1.1099	1.6976	1.6222	1.5292	1.4286	1.4260	1.3372	28.9	205.4
Pakistan	Rupees	0.7414	0.7656	0.7980	0.8183	0.7683	0.8211	na	0.9248	0.8869	0.9462	1.0293	1.0230	1.0762	1.0377	10.7	26.4
Philippines	Pesos	0.8139	0.8052	0.8405	0.9254	0.9263	0.9858	1.0950	1.0413	1.1239	1.3523	1.2887	1.2171	1.1321	1.0440	21.1	5.9
Qatar	Riyals	12.1604	12.3438	12.6242	13.2984	13.1027	12.5510	11.9049	11.5556	10.2083	9.7530	9.1929	8.6258	8.6166	7.2559	3.2	−42.2
Russia	Rubles	1.5586	1.5705	1.5347	1.5333	1.6044	1.6229	1.6659	3.0225	6.3164	6.6361	na	na	na	na	4.1	308.9
Saudi Arabia	Riyals	11.8169	11.9817	12.2662	12.9255	12.7353	12.1991	11.5712	11.2316	9.9221	9.4795	8.9365	8.3839	8.3750	7.0525	3.2	−42.2
Singapore	Singapore Dollar	26.6126	26.8174	26.5658	27.3712	26.3138	26.2953	25.5899	25.0326	23.3932	25.1511	23.7289	21.0641	19.5843	16.2014	−1.2	−38.4
South Africa	Rand	6.9259	7.1835	6.4017	4.9676	5.0024	6.2406	7.0305	7.2370	7.8762	7.9170	9.0987	8.7600	9.3804	9.0462	−9.9	45.0
Sri Lanka	Rupees	0.4375	0.4423	0.4747	0.5021	0.5214	0.5705	0.6064	0.6349	0.6181	0.6331	0.6403	0.6332	0.6430	0.5868	30.4	2.9
Thailand	Baht	1.0944	1.1212	1.1322	1.1330	1.0702	1.1007	1.1406	1.0826	1.0132	1.3925	1.3392	1.2540	1.2397	1.0396	0.6	−5.6
UAE	Dirhams	12.0528	12.2345	12.5125	13.1807	12.9867	12.4399	11.7996	11.4533	10.1221	9.6706	9.1153	8.5529	8.5438	7.1946	3.2	−42.2

(contd.)

TABLE A9.1 (contd.)

(1)	(2)	(3)	(4)	(5)	(6)	(7)	(8)	(9)	(10)	(11)	(12)	(13)	(14)	(15)	(16)	(17)	(18)
Industrialized Countries																	
Australia	Australian Dollar	33.4597	33.2255	31.9391	27.2332	24.5242	25.4605	27.9504	26.1329	26.6049	27.9927	25.1736	23.2975	21.4904	18.9865	−23.9	−25.4
Canada	Canadian Dollar	37.1031	35.1410	33.9613	31.2670	30.4655	30.3841	29.4549	27.9707	26.4924	26.0882	24.5541	22.7636	23.9404	21.4763	−18.1	−29.3
Denmark	Kroner	7.2204	7.5888	7.2409	6.4496	5.6630	5.5580	6.0144	6.3500	5.4598	5.9560	6.0235	5.1095	4.7572	4.3740	−23.0	−21.3
Egypt@	Pounds	7.6980	7.5595	7.0436	8.3395	10.7979	12.1250	12.7805	12.4978	10.1804	10.5960	10.1179	9.2948	9.2811	9.3450	57.5	−22.9
Japan	Yen	0.3910	0.4177	0.4065	0.3968	0.3812	0.4134	0.3885	0.3285	0.3028	0.3152	0.3470	0.3160	0.2908	0.2116	5.7	−48.8
Sweden	Kroner	5.7616	6.2032	5.9038	5.2250	4.5397	4.8370	5.1488	5.2952	4.7664	5.1786	4.7913	4.1536	3.9656	4.2416	−16.0	−12.3
Switzerland	Swiss Francs	34.7475	36.7018	34.8506	32.7045	28.1828	26.9186	27.9034	29.2689	25.4335	27.3567	28.6217	23.8712	21.4164	18.6180	−22.5	−30.8
USA	Dollar	44.2640	44.9313	45.9523	48.4060	47.6938	45.6855	43.3340	42.0620	37.1580	35.5010	33.4670	31.3980	31.3640	26.4110	3.2	−42.2
UK	Pound	79.0826	82.9049	77.8144	74.8163	68.2784	67.5734	69.8414	69.5458	60.9916	56.3256	52.3998	48.8361	47.1939	44.6586	−14.6	−33.9
Euro*		53.8508	56.4764	53.8682	47.9158	42.1360	41.4221	44.7065								−23.1	
Belgium	Franc								1.1719	1.0151	1.1106	1.1382	0.9760	0.8235	0.8193		−30.1
France	Franc								7.2101	6.2329	6.7543	6.7500	5.8373	5.4622	4.9806		−30.9
Germany	Deutsche Mark								24.1751	20.9437	22.8698	23.4004	20.1036	18.7171	16.8710		−30.2
Italy	Lire								0.0245	0.0213	0.0228	0.0208	0.0196	0.0195	0.0201		−18.0
Netherlands	Guidars								21.4429	18.5996	20.3922	20.8949	17.9242	16.6752	14.9844		−30.1

Notes: * Consisting of currencies of Belgium, France, Germany, Netherlands, and Italy. The Euro came into existence with effect from 1 January 1998; in these cases percentage appreciation or depreciation worked out is for the period 1992–3 to 1998–9, and 2000–1 to 2005–6 for the purpose of comparability; @ Data for Egypt are as at the end of the period; The liberalized exchange rate management system (LERMS) was instituted in March 1992 in conjunction with other measures of liberalization in the areas of trade, industry, foreign investment, and the import of Gold. The ultimate convergence of the dual rates was made effective as of 1 March 1993.

Source: International Financial Statistics, IMF, various issues.

TABLE A9.2
Indices of Real Effective Exchange Rate (REER) and Nominal Effective Exchange Rate (NEER) of the Indian Rupee

	36-Currency Export and Trade Based Weights									6-Currency Trade Based Weights							
	Trade Based Weights Base: 1993–4 =100				Export Based Weights					Base: 1993–4 =100				Base: 2003–4 =100 (Moving one, Get updated every year)			
	REER		NEER		REER		NEER		NEER		REER		NEER		REER		
(1)	(2)	(3)	(4)	(5)	(6)	(7)	(8)	(9)	(10)	(11)	(12)	(13)	(14)	(15)	(16)	(17)
2005–6																
Mar 2006	101.66	(1.1)	89.47	(2.0)	100.04	(1.1)	90.85	(1.8)	71.61	(2.8)	108.09	(4.5)	103.40	(2.8)	106.64	(4.5)
Feb 2006	102.02	(0.9)	89.92	(2.0)	100.36	(0.9)	91.26	(1.8)	72.03	(2.8)	108.61	(4.5)	104.01	(2.8)	107.17	(4.5)
Jan 2006	101.8	(1.1)	89.51	(2.2)	100.18	(1.0)	90.90	(2.1)	71.46	(2.6)	107.57	(4.0)	103.18	(2.6)	106.13	(4.0)
Dec 2005	100.85	(0.8)	87.97	(1.2)	99.01	(0.3)	89.09	(0.6)	70.22	(2.2)	105.98	(4.4)	101.39	(2.2)	104.56	(4.4)
Nov 2005	101.73	(2.3)	88.36	(3.0)	99.80	(1.8)	89.40	(2.6)	70.27	(3.3)	106.18	(5.3)	101.46	(3.3)	104.76	(5.3)
Oct 2005	102.87	(3.5)	89.40	(3.8)	100.97	(3.6)	90.56	(3.9)	70.90	(3.8)	106.43	(5.9)	102.36	(3.8)	105.01	(5.9)
Sep 2005	104.27	(3.8)	90.45	(4.5)	102.43	(4.1)	91.80	(5.2)	71.57	(4.5)	107.27	(5.9)	103.34	(4.5)	105.84	(5.9)
Aug 2005	104.05	(4.5)	90.86	(5.6)	102.33	(4.9)	92.27	(6.3)	72.08	(5.8)	107.39	(7.2)	104.08	(5.8)	105.95	(7.2)
Jul 2005	105.09	(6.3)	92.02	(6.7)	103.12	(6.2)	93.20	(7.0)	73.04	(7.0)	108.38	(9.1)	105.46	(7.0)	106.94	(9.1)
Jun 2005	103.74	(3.9)	91.17	(4.1)	101.96	(4.2)	92.52	(4.7)	72.36	(4.3)	106.82	(6.7)	104.48	(4.3)	105.39	(6.7)
May 2005	102.24	(2.6)	90.10	(1.6)	100.73	(3.3)	91.68	(2.7)	71.18	(1.3)	104.62	(4.7)	102.77	(1.2)	103.23	(4.7)
Apr 2005	100.59	(–0.8)	88.92	(–1.7)	99.22	(–0.2)	90.60	(–0.7)	70.22	(–2.6)	102.63	(0.8)	101.38	(–2.6)	101.27	(0.8)
2004–5																
Mar 2005	100.56	(0.3)	87.72	(0.8)	99.00	(–1.1)	89.27	(1.2)	69.68	(0.5)	103.46	(3.1)	100.61	(0.5)	102.08	(3.1)
Feb 2005	101.16	(2.2)	88.20	(3.2)	99.51	(0.5)	89.66	(3.3)	70.09	(3.2)	103.92	(5.4)	101.20	(3.2)	102.54	(5.4)
Jan 2005	100.68	(2.4)	87.55	(2.7)	99.19	(0.8)	89.05	(2.9)	69.66	(2.6)	103.41	(5.6)	100.59	(2.6)	102.04	(5.6)
Dec 2004	100.05	(1.8)	86.92	(1.2)	98.74	(0.5)	88.55	(1.7)	68.68	(0.0)	101.48	(3.6)	99.17	(0.0)	100.13	(3.6)
Nov 2004	99.47	(–1.0)	85.75	(–2.1)	97.99	(–2.1)	87.14	(–1.5)	68.03	(–3.2)	100.87	(0.8)	98.23	(–3.2)	99.52	(0.8)
Oct 2004	99.37	(–1.5)	86.15	(–2.2)	97.47	(–2.9)	87.13	(–2.0)	68.33	(–3.1)	100.46	(0.5)	98.66	(–3.1)	99.12	(0.5)
Sep 2004	100.46	(–1.0)	86.52	(–2.6)	98.38	(–2.3)	87.29	(–2.2)	68.49	(–4.3)	101.28	(0.2)	98.89	(–4.3)	99.92	(0.2)
Aug 2004	99.54	(–1.8)	86.03	(–3.8)	97.54	(–2.8)	86.80	(–3.3)	68.13	(–5.1)	100.22	(–0.3)	98.37	(–5.1)	98.88	(–0.4)
Jul 2004	98.89	(–1.0)	86.21	(–2.1)	97.06	(–2.0)	87.12	(–1.5)	68.24	(–3.5)	99.30	(0.4)	98.53	(–3.4)	97.98	(0.4)
Jun 2004	99.86	(1.9)	87.62	(1.5)	97.89	(0.6)	88.40	(1.8)	69.35	(0.3)	100.10	(3.5)	100.13	(0.3)	98.76	(3.5)
May 2004	99.64	(2.2)	88.66	(3.1)	97.47	(0.6)	89.27	(3.2)	70.30	(2.0)	99.95	(3.8)	101.51	(2.0)	98.62	(3.8)
Apr 2004	101.42	(2.2)	90.43	(3.1)	99.37	(1.2)	91.21	(3.8)	72.12	(2.5)	101.79	(4.2)	104.13		100.43	
2005–6	102.58	(2.5)	89.84	(2.9)	100.85	(2.6)	91.18	(3.1)	71.41	(3.1)	106.66	(5.2)	103.11	(3.1)	105.24	(2.6)
2004–5	100.09	(0.5)	87.31	(0.2)	98.30	(–0.8)	88.41	(0.6)	69.26	(–0.7)	101.35	(2.5)	100.00	(–0.7)	102.53	(2.5)
2003–4	99.56	(1.4)	87.14	(–2.2)	99.07	(3.2)	87.89	(1.0)	69.75	(–1.9)	98.85	(1.5)	100.71	(–1.9)	100.00	(1.5)
2002–3	98.18	(–2.7)	89.12	(–2.7)	95.99	(–2.6)	87.01	(–2.3)	71.09	(–6.3)	97.43	(–4.9)	102.65	(–6.3)	98.56	(–4.9)
2001–2	100.86	(0.8)	91.58	(–0.6)	98.59	(–0.1)	89.08	(–1.2)	75.89	(–1.8)	102.49	(–0.1)	109.58	(–1.8)	103.68	(–0.2)
2000–1	100.09	(4.3)	92.12	(1.2)	98.67	(3.6)	90.12	(–0.3)	77.30	(0.3)	102.64	(5.3)	111.61	(0.3)	103.84	(5.3)
1999–2000	95.99	(3.2)	91.02	(2.2)	95.28	(1.0)	90.42	(0.1)	77.04	(–0.4)	97.52	(1.6)	111.23	(–0.4)	98.66	(1.6)
1998–9	93.04	(–7.7)	89.05	(–3.2)	94.34	(–8.5)	90.34	(–1.8)	77.37	(–11.9)	95.99	(–7.9)	111.71	(–11.9)	97.10	(–7.9)
1997–8	100.77	(4.1)	92.04	(3.1)	103.07	(4.2)	91.97	(3.3)	87.80	(1.2)	104.24	(3.2)	126.77	(1.2)	105.45	(3.2)
1996–7	96.83	(–1.4)	89.27	(–2.5)	98.95	(–1.1)	89.03	(–2.1)	86.73	(–1.9)	100.97	(–0.2)	125.22	(–1.9)	102.15	(–0.2)
1995–6	98.19	(–5.9)	91.54	(–7.5)	100.10	(–4.6)	90.94	(–7.4)	88.45	(–8.7)	101.14	(–4.3)	127.71	(–8.7)	102.31	(–4.3)
1994–5	104.32	(4.3)	98.91	(–1.1)	104.88	(4.9)	98.18	(–1.8)	96.86	(–3.1)	105.71	(5.7)	139.86	(–3.1)	106.94	(5.7)
1993–4	100.00		100.00		100.00		100.00		100.00		100.00		144.36		101.14	

Notes: Figures in brackets represent annual appreciation (+) or depreciation (–) of the rupee as per the respective NEER and REER Indices; For weights, see A9.1.
Source: RBI Bulletin, various issues.

TABLE A9.3
Weighing Diagrams for RBI's NEERs and REERs

A: Normalized Weights for 6-Currency REER/NEER Indices

(per cent)

Year	Euro	Japan	UK	USA	Hongkong	China
1993–4	42.06	14.01	12.04	26.33	4.55	1.01
1994–5	40.25	13.50	11.73	26.95	5.40	2.17
1995–6	39.22	13.44	11.33	26.95	6.07	2.98
1996–7	38.95	12.87	11.25	27.29	6.15	3.49
1997–8	39.28	11.76	11.55	27.46	6.03	4.20
1998–9	38.71	11.03	11.82	28.21	6.03	4.20
1999–2000	37.79	10.64	11.86	28.59	6.68	4.44
2000–1	36.67	9.92	12.15	29.12	7.48	4.65
2001–2	35.88	9.30	12.06	29.08	8.02	5.67
2002–3	35.55	8.31	11.67	29.51	7.67	7.29
2003–4	35.52	7.85	10.84	28.90	7.55	9.34
2004–5	35.12	7.15	10.13	28.19	7.45	11.96

Note: The new six currency indices will have two base years: 1993–4 as fixed base and 2003–4 as moving base which would change every year. These indices use a 3-year moving average trade weights to reflect the changing pattern of India's foreign trade with its major trading partners. To calculate weights, the geometric average of India's bilateral trade (exports + imports) with countries/regions represented by the six currencies during the preceding three years has been taken. This has then been normalized to arrive at the requisite weights (wi), which are provided in the table.

Source: *RBI Bulletin*, December 2006.

B: 36-Currency Normalized Weights for REER and NEER for 2005–6

(per cent)

Country	Trade Weight	Export Weight	Country	Trade Weight	Export Weight
Argentina	0.53	0.17	Myanmar	0.43	0.16
Australia	2.66	1.03	Nigeria	0.55	0.95
Bangladesh	1.40	2.61	Pakistan	0.34	0.55
Brazil	0.79	0.78	Philippines	0.48	0.69
Canada	1.30	1.33	Quatar	0.35	0.24
China	6.69	5.52	Russia	1.45	1.18
Hong Kong	4.08	5.52	Saudi Arabia	1.74	1.99
Denmark	0.40	0.41	Singapore	3.85	3.97
Egypt	0.47	0.63	South Africa	2.44	1.11
Euro	19.37	18.38	Sri Lanka	1.25	2.07
Indonesia	2.73	1.87	Sweden	0.81	0.36
Iran	1.09	1.58	Switzerland	3.63	0.79
Israel	1.36	1.35	Thailand	1.26	1.41
Japan	3.95	3.26	Turkey	0.55	0.92
Kenya	0.28	0.47	UAE	6.43	8.7
Korea	2.94	1.38	UK	5.56	5.23
Kuwait	0.47	0.56	USA	15.56	20.78
Malaysia	2.51	1.56	Total	100.00	100.00
Mexico	0.33	0.51			

Note: The choice of the base year 1993–4 is attributable to the significant changes in the macroeconomic environment due to structural reforms introduced in the wake of balance of payments crisis in 1990–1. Moreover, it is also the base year for WPI. The 36-currency indices use 3-year moving average normalized weights (both exports and trade weights) in the construction of new series, keeping in view the rapid change in the destinations of India's foreign trade in contrast to the fixed weights used hitherto for constructing REER and NEER series. The table gives the normalized weights for the 36-currencies for the year 2005–6 which is based on trade shares of the previous three years (2002–3 to 2004–5).

Source: *RBI Bulletin*, December 2005.

A10 FOREIGN TRADE

Table A10.1
Changing Scenerio in Foreign Trade

(US$ Million)

Export	2005–6	2004–5	2003–4	2002–3	2001–2	2000–1	1999–00	1998–9	1997–8	1996–7	1995–6	1994–5	1993–4	1992–3	1991–2	1990–1	1989–90	1988–9	1987–8
(1)	(2)	(3)	(4)	(5)	(6)	(7)	(8)	(9)	(10)	(11)	(12)	(13)	(14)	(15)	(16)	(17)	(18)	(19)	(20)
Gems and Jewellery	15547	13762	10573	9030	7306	7384	7502	5929	5346	4753	5275	4500	3996	3072	2738	2924	3181	3033	2015
	(15.1)	(16.5)	(16.6)	(17.1)	(16.7)	(16.6)	(20.4)	(17.8)	(15.3)	(14.2)	(16.6)	(17.1)	(18.0)	(16.6)	(15.3)	(16.1)	(19.1)	(21.7)	(16.8)
Chemicals and Products	15514	13164	9446	7455	6052	5886	4707	4009	4396	3913	3597	3067	2377	1786	1869	1728	1554	1091	792
	(15.1)	(15.8)	(14.8)	(14.1)	(13.8)	(13.2)	(12.8)	(12.1)	(12.6)	(11.7)	(11.3)	(11.6)	(10.7)	(9.6)	(10.5)	(9.5)	(9.4)	(7.8)	(6.6)
Textiles	15206	12918	12792	11617	10207	11285	9822	8866	9050	8636	8032	7118	5472	5007	4693	4343	3747	3038	3014
	(14.8)	(15.5)	(20.0)	(22.0)	(23.3)	(25.3)	(26.7)	(26.7)	(25.9)	(25.8)	(25.3)	(27.0)	(24.6)	(27.0)	(26.3)	(23.9)	(22.6)	(21.7)	(25.1)
Petroleum Products	11515	6989	3568	2577	2119	1870	39	89	353	482	454	417	398	476	415	523	418	349	500
	(11.2)	(8.4)	(5.6)	(4.9)	(4.8)	(4.2)	(0.1)	(0.3)	(1.0)	(1.4)	(1.4)	(1.6)	(1.8)	(2.6)	(2.3)	(2.9)	(2.5)	(2.5)	(4.2)
Machinery & Instruments	4796	3719	2776	2008	1734	1580	1183	1155	1196	1057	830	727	639	542	581	696	604	510	397
	(4.7)	(4.5)	(4.3)	(3.8)	(4.0)	(3.5)	(3.2)	(3.5)	(3.4)	(3.2)	(2.6)	(2.8)	(2.9)	(2.9)	(3.3)	(3.8)	(3.6)	(3.6)	(3.3)
Transport Equipment	4567	2830	1956	1334	1021	992	810	762	929	969	925	771	592	534	496	401	316	251	195
	(4.4)	(3.4)	(3.1)	(2.5)	(2.3)	(2.2)	(2.2)	(2.3)	(2.7)	(2.9)	(2.9)	(2.9)	(2.7)	(2.9)	(2.8)	(2.2)	(1.9)	(1.8)	(1.6)
Manufacture of Metals	4173	3401	2427	1848	1604	1578	1226	1040	1023	914	826	706	663	560	484	456	446	305	222
	(4.1)	(4.1)	(3.8)	(3.5)	(3.7)	(3.5)	(3.3)	(3.1)	(2.9)	(2.7)	(2.6)	(2.7)	(3.0)	(3.0)	(2.7)	(2.5)	(2.7)	(2.2)	(1.9)
Iron ore	3861	3277	1126	868	426	358	271	384	476	481	515	413	438	381	582	585	557	465	428
	(3.8)	(3.9)	(1.8)	(1.6)	(1.0)	(0.8)	(0.7)	(1.2)	(1.4)	(1.4)	(1.6)	(1.6)	(2.0)	(2.1)	(3.3)	(3.2)	(3.4)	(3.3)	(3.6)
Iron & Steel	3511	3921	2478	1856	898	1028	833	579	875	770	697	528	568	306	154	161	99	52	22
	(3.4)	(4.7)	(3.9)	(3.5)	(2.0)	(2.3)	(2.3)	(1.7)	(2.5)	(2.3)	(2.2)	(2.0)	(2.6)	(1.7)	(0.9)	(0.9)	(0.6)	(0.4)	(0.2)
Electronic goods	2244	1890	1728	1253	1171	1052	681	503	760	784	670	412	304	212	265	232	303	201	154
	(2.2)	(2.3)	(2.7)	(2.4)	(2.7)	(2.4)	(1.8)	(1.5)	(2.2)	(2.3)	(2.1)	(1.6)	(1.4)	(1.1)	(1.5)	(1.3)	(1.8)	(1.4)	(1.3)
Total Export	102725	83536	63843	52719	43827	44560	36822	33219	35006	33470	31795	26331	22238	18537	17865	18145	16613	13970	12009
	(100.0)	(100.0)	(100.0)	(100.0)	(100.0)	(100.0)	(100.0)	(100.0)	(100.0)	(100.0)	(100.0)	(100.0)	(100.0)	(100.0)	(100.0)	(100.0)	(100.0)	(100.0)	(100.0)
of which:																			
Top 10 commodities/groups	(78.8)	(78.9)	(76.5)	(75.6)	(74.2)	(74.1)	(73.5)	(70.2)	(69.7)	(68.0)	(68.6)	(70.9)	(69.5)	(69.5)	(68.7)	(66.4)	(67.6)	(66.5)	(64.4)
Import																			
Petroleum crude & Prodts	43963	29844	20570	17640	14000	15650	12611	6399	8164	10036	7526	5928	5754	6100	5325	6028	3768	3009	3118
	(30.9)	(26.8)	(26.3)	(28.7)	(27.2)	(31.0)	(25.4)	(15.1)	(19.7)	(25.6)	(20.5)	(20.7)	(24.7)	(27.9)	(27.4)	(25.0)	(17.8)	(15.4)	(18.2)
Electronic Goods	13192	9993	7506	5599	3782	3509	2797	2223	2088	1424	1752	1228	912	0	0	0	0	0	0
	(9.3)	(9.0)	(9.6)	(9.1)	(7.4)	(6.9)	(5.6)	(5.2)	(5.0)	(3.6)	(4.8)	(4.3)	(3.9)						

(contd.)

TABLE A10.1 (contd.)

Export	2005–6	2004–5	2003–4	2002–3	2001–2	2000–1	1999–00	1998–9	1997–8	1996–7	1995–6	1994–5	1993–4	1992–3	1991–2	1990–1	1989–90	1988–9	1987–8
(1)	(2)	(3)	(4)	(5)	(6)	(7)	(8)	(9)	(10)	(11)	(12)	(13)	(14)	(15)	(16)	(17)	(18)	(19)	(20)
Gold and Silver	11189	11150	6856	4288	4582	4638	4706	5072	3169	992	867	713	–	–	–	–	–	–	–
	(7.9)	(10.0)	(8.8)	(7.0)	(8.9)	(9.2)	(9.5)	(12.0)	(7.6)	(2.5)	(2.4)	(2.5)	(0.0)	(0.0)	(0.0)	(0.0)	(0.0)	(0.0)	(0.0)
Machinery	9894	6818	4744	3566	2971	2709	2745	3045	3622	3644	3924	2728	1882	1653	1458	2100	1930	1810	2017
	(6.9)	(6.1)	(6.1)	(5.8)	(5.8)	(5.4)	(5.5)	(7.2)	(8.7)	(9.3)	(10.7)	(9.5)	(8.1)	(7.6)	(7.5)	(8.7)	(9.1)	(9.3)	(11.8)
Pearls & Precious Stones	9141	9423	7129	6063	4623	4808	5436	3760	3342	2925	2106	1630	2635	2442	1957	2083	2555	2193	1557
	(6.4)	(8.4)	(9.1)	(9.9)	(9.0)	(9.5)	(10.9)	(8.9)	(8.1)	(7.5)	(5.7)	(5.7)	(11.3)	(11.2)	(10.1)	(8.7)	(12.0)	(11.2)	(9.1)
Organic & Inorganic Chemicals	6889	5700	4032	3025	2800	2444	2866	2684	2956	2661	2566	2137	1371	1428	1379	1276	1154	1308	834
	(4.8)	(5.1)	(5.2)	(4.9)	(5.4)	(4.8)	(5.8)	(6.3)	(7.1)	(6.8)	(7.0)	(7.5)	(5.9)	(6.5)	(7.1)	(5.3)	(5.4)	(6.7)	(4.9)
Iron and Steel	4432	2670	1506	944	834	778	952	1064	1421	1371	1446	1164	795	779	799	1178	1352	1335	1018
	(3.1)	(2.4)	(1.9)	(1.5)	(1.6)	(1.5)	(1.9)	(2.5)	(3.4)	(3.5)	(3.9)	(4.1)	(3.4)	(3.6)	(4.1)	(4.9)	(6.4)	(6.8)	(5.9)
Transport Equipment	3149	4327	3228	1897	1149	700	1137	798	1051	1484	1105	1114	1270	462	371	931	889	520	586
	(2.2)	(3.9)	(4.1)	(3.1)	(2.2)	(1.4)	(2.3)	(1.9)	(2.5)	(3.8)	(3.0)	(3.9)	(5.5)	(2.1)	(1.9)	(3.9)	(4.2)	(2.7)	(3.4)
Fertilizers	2069	1377	721	626	679	752	1399	1076	1117	911	1683	1052	826	978	954	984	1083	645	392
	(1.5)	(1.2)	(0.9)	(1.0)	(1.3)	(1.5)	(2.8)	(2.5)	(2.7)	(2.3)	(4.6)	(3.7)	(3.5)	(4.5)	(4.9)	(4.1)	(5.1)	(3.3)	(2.3)
Edible Oil	1969	2465	2543	1814	1356	1308	1857	1804	744	825	676	199	53	58	101	182	125	504	747
	(1.4)	(2.2)	(3.3)	(3.0)	(2.6)	(2.6)	(3.7)	(4.3)	(1.8)	(2.1)	(1.8)	(0.7)	(0.2)	(0.3)	(0.5)	(0.8)	(0.6)	(2.6)	(4.4)
Total Imports	142416	111517	78149	61412	51413	50537	49671	42389	41485	39132	36675	28654	23306	21882	19411	24073	21219	19497	17156
	(100.0)	(100.0)	(100.0)	(100.0)	(100.0)	(100.0)	(100.0)	(100.0)	(100.0)	(100.0)	(100.0)	(100.0)	(100.0)	(100.0)	(100.0)	(100.0)	(100.0)	(100.0)	(100.0)
of which:																			
Top 10 Commodities/groups	71.3	70.2	71.7	72.0	68.1	69.5	69.8	60.2	66.2	71.4	69.1	67.4	72.4	70.0	70.7	66.6	66.0	64.8	64.7

Note: – Official imports of gold and silver started in 1994–5; 0 : Separate data not reported; Figures in brackets are percentage shares to total.

Source: Directorate General of Commercial Intelligence and Statistics (DGCI & S).

TABLE A10.2
Foreign Trade with Major Trading Partners

(US $ million)

	China		Germany		Australia		USA		Switzerland		UK		Singapore		UAE		Japan		Italy		Hong Kong		Total	
	Export	Import	Export	Import	Export	Import	Export	Import	Export	Import	Export	Import	Export	Import	Export	Import	Export	Import	Export	Import	Export	Import	Export	Import
1	2		3		4		5		6		7		8		9		10		11		12		13	
2005–6	6721	10740	3517	5818	812	4851	17204	7778	474	6526	5146	3898	5570	2085	8593	4312	2459	3552	2490	1829	4457	2168	102725	142416
	(6.5)	(7.5)	(3.4)	(4.1)	(0.8)	(3.4)	(16.7)	(5.5)	(0.5)	(4.6)	(5.0)	(2.7)	(5.4)	(1.5)	(8.4)	(3.0)	(2.4)	(2.5)	(2.4)	(1.3)	(4.3)	(1.5)	(100.0)	(100.0)
2004–5	5616	7098	2826	4015	720	3825	13766	7001	541	5940	3681	3566	4001	2651	7348	4641	2128	3235	2286	1373	3692	1730	83536	111517
	(6.7)	(6.4)	(3.4)	(3.6)	(0.9)	(3.4)	(16.5)	(6.3)	(0.6)	(5.3)	(4.4)	(3.2)	(4.8)	(2.4)	(8.8)	(4.2)	(2.5)	(2.9)	(2.7)	(1.2)	(4.4)	(1.6)	(100.0)	(100.0)
2003–4	2955	4053	2545	2919	584	2649	11490	5035	450	3313	3023	3234	2125	2085	5126	2060	1709	2668	1729	1071	3262	1493	63843	78149
	(4.6)	(5.2)	(4.0)	(3.7)	(0.9)	(3.4)	(18.0)	(6.4)	(0.7)	(4.2)	(4.7)	(4.1)	(3.3)	(2.7)	(8.0)	(2.6)	(2.7)	(3.4)	(2.7)	(1.4)	(5.1)	(1.9)	(100.0)	(100.0)
2002–3	1976	2792	2107	2405	504	1337	10896	4444	383	2330	2496	2777	1422	1435	3328	957	1864	1836	1357	812	2613	973	52719	61412
	(3.7)	(4.5)	(4.0)	(3.9)	(1.0)	(2.2)	(20.7)	(7.2)	(0.7)	(3.8)	(4.7)	(4.5)	(2.7)	(2.3)	(6.3)	(1.6)	(3.5)	(3.0)	(2.6)	(1.3)	(5.0)	(1.6)	(100.0)	(100.0)
2001–2	952	2036	1788	2028	418	1306	8513	3150	409	2871	2161	2563	972	1304	2492	915	1510	2146	1207	705	2366	729	43827	51413
	(2.2)	(4.0)	(4.1)	(3.9)	(1.0)	(2.5)	(19.4)	(6.1)	(0.9)	(5.6)	(4.9)	(5.0)	(2.2)	(2.5)	(5.7)	(1.8)	(3.4)	(4.2)	(2.8)	(1.4)	(5.4)	(1.4)	(100.0)	(100.0)
2000–1	831	1502	1908	1760	406	1063	9305	3015	438	3160	2299	3168	877	1464	2598	659	1795	1842	1309	724	2641	852	44560	50537
	(1.9)	(3.0)	(4.3)	(3.5)	(0.9)	(2.1)	(20.9)	(6.0)	(1.0)	(6.3)	(5.2)	(6.3)	(2.0)	(2.9)	(5.8)	(1.3)	(4.0)	(3.6)	(2.9)	(1.4)	(5.9)	(1.7)	(100.0)	(100.0)
1999–2000	539	1287	1738	1842	403	1082	8396	3564	354	2598	2035	2707	673	1534	2083	2334	1685	2536	1120	735	2511	818	36822	49671
	(1.5)	(2.6)	(4.7)	(3.7)	(1.1)	(2.2)	(22.8)	(7.2)	(1.0)	(5.2)	(5.5)	(5.4)	(1.8)	(3.1)	(5.7)	(4.7)	(4.6)	(5.1)	(3.0)	(1.5)	(6.8)	(1.6)	(100.0)	(100.0)
1998–9	427	1097	1852	2141	387	1445	7200	3640	319	2942	1855	2621	518	1384	1868	1721	1652	2466	1055	1088	1881	449	33219	42389
	(1.3)	(2.6)	(5.6)	(5.1)	(1.2)	(3.4)	(21.7)	(8.6)	(1.0)	(6.9)	(5.6)	(6.2)	(1.6)	(3.3)	(5.6)	(4.1)	(5.0)	(5.8)	(3.2)	(2.6)	(5.7)	(1.1)	(100.0)	(100.0)
1997–8	718	1119	1924	2529	438	1486	6803	3717	368	2641	2141	2444	780	1198	1692	1780	1899	2145	1115	922	1932	316	35006	41485
	(2.1)	(2.7)	(5.5)	(6.1)	(1.3)	(3.6)	(19.4)	(8.6)	(1.0)	(6.4)	(6.1)	(5.9)	(2.2)	(2.9)	(4.8)	(4.3)	(5.4)	(5.2)	(3.2)	(2.2)	(5.5)	(0.8)	(100.0)	(100.0)
1996–7	615	757	1893	2831	385	1317	6555	3686	300	1127	2047	2135	978	1063	1476	1736	2006	2187	934	987	1863	319	33470	39132
	(1.8)	(1.9)	(5.7)	(7.2)	(1.2)	(3.4)	(19.6)	(9.4)	(0.9)	(2.9)	(6.1)	(5.5)	(2.9)	(2.7)	(4.4)	(4.4)	(6.0)	(5.6)	(2.8)	(2.5)	(5.6)	(0.8)	(100.0)	(100.0)
1995–6	333	812	1977	3145	376	1022	5520	3861	282	1021	2011	1918	902	1092	1428	1607	2216	2468	1014	1064	1821	388	31795	36675
	(1.0)	(2.2)	(6.2)	(8.6)	(1.2)	(2.8)	(17.4)	(10.5)	(0.9)	(2.8)	(6.3)	(5.2)	(2.8)	(3.0)	(4.5)	(4.4)	(7.0)	(6.7)	(3.2)	(2.9)	(5.7)	(1.1)	(100.0)	(100.0)
1994–5	254	761	1748	2187	346	915	5021	2906	247	824	1690	1559	770	900	1266	1533	2027	2040	858	741	1517	287	26331	28654
	(1.0)	(2.7)	(6.6)	(7.6)	(1.3)	(3.2)	(19.1)	(10.1)	(0.9)	(2.9)	(6.4)	(5.4)	(2.9)	(3.1)	(4.8)	(5.4)	(7.7)	(7.1)	(3.3)	(2.6)	(5.8)	(1.0)	(100.0)	(100.0)
1993–4	279	302	1539	1790	245	659	3999	2737	221	506	1379	1536	752	627	1158	1003	1741	1522	604	538	1250	189	22238	23306
	(1.3)	(1.3)	(6.9)	(7.7)	(1.1)	(2.8)	(18.0)	(11.7)	(1.0)	(2.2)	(6.2)	(6.6)	(3.4)	(2.7)	(5.2)	(4.3)	(7.8)	(6.5)	(2.7)	(2.3)	(5.6)	(0.8)	(100.0)	(100.0)
1992–1	141	126	1427	1657	223	838	3516	2147	199	378	1213	1417	589	632	814	1112	1437	1428	622	524	765	170	18537	21882
	(0.8)	(0.6)	(7.7)	(7.6)	(1.2)	(3.8)	(19.0)	(9.8)	(1.1)	(1.7)	(6.5)	(6.5)	(3.2)	(2.9)	(4.4)	(5.1)	(7.7)	(6.5)	(3.4)	(2.4)	(4.1)	(0.8)	(100.0)	(100.0)
1991–2	48	21	1270	1559	203	586	2921	1995	219	151	1138	1202	389	695	739	1248	1652	1369	580	448	614	106	17865	19411
	(0.3)	(0.1)	(7.1)	(8.0)	(1.1)	(3.0)	(16.4)	(10.3)	(1.2)	(0.8)	(6.4)	(6.2)	(2.2)	(3.6)	(4.1)	(6.4)	(9.2)	(7.1)	(3.2)	(2.3)	(3.4)	(0.5)	(100.0)	(100.0)
1990–1	18	31	1421	1936	179	816	2673	2923	224	268	1186	1613	379	796	439	1059	1694	1808	558	608	597	166	18145	24073
	(0.1)	(0.1)	(7.8)	(8.0)	(1.0)	(3.4)	(14.7)	(12.1)	(1.2)	(1.1)	(6.5)	(6.7)	(2.1)	(3.3)	(2.4)	(4.4)	(9.3)	(7.5)	(3.1)	(2.5)	(3.3)	(0.7)	(100.0)	(100.0)
1989–90	24	40	1064	1674	201	539	2686	2561	219	219	961	1783	280	540	427	857	1639	1692	457	464	537	149	16613	21219
	(0.1)	(0.2)	(6.4)	(7.9)	(1.2)	(2.5)	(16.2)	(12.1)	(1.3)	(1.0)	(5.8)	(8.4)	(1.7)	(2.5)	(2.6)	(4.0)	(9.9)	(8.0)	(2.7)	(2.2)	(3.2)	(0.7)	(100.0)	(100.0)
1988–9	91	98	854	1697	183	488	2574	2237	188	194	796	1656	223	429	293	602	1488	1817	373	347	565	121	13970	19497
	(0.7)	(0.5)	(6.1)	(8.7)	(1.3)	(2.5)	(18.4)	(11.5)	(1.3)	(1.0)	(5.7)	(8.5)	(1.6)	(2.2)	(2.1)	(3.1)	(10.6)	(9.3)	(2.7)	(1.8)	(4.0)	(0.6)	(100.0)	(100.0)
1987–8	15	119	817	1665	139	388	2252	1544	157	182	783	1410	211	323	239	588	1245	1640	384	395	344	93	12089	17156
	(0.1)	(0.7)	(6.8)	(9.7)	(1.1)	(2.3)	(18.6)	(9.0)	(1.3)	(1.1)	(6.5)	(8.2)	(1.7)	(1.9)	(2.0)	(3.4)	(10.3)	(9.6)	(3.2)	(2.3)	(2.8)	(0.5)	(100.0)	(100.0)

Notes: Figures in brackets are percentages to total export/import; The countries are selected as per the the following criteria; USA and China are top destinations of exports in 2005–6; Germany, Australia, and Switzerland are 5 top import destinations to India in 2005–6. Japan, Italy, and Hong Kong are three other partners in trade where both export and imports are more than $1000 million.

Source: DGCI & S.

A11 FOREIGN INVESTMENT AND NRI DEPOSITS

Table A11.1
Foreign Investment Inflows

(US$ Million)

Year/Month	Direct Investment (4 to10)	Equity (4 to 8)	Government (SIA+FIPB)	RBI	NRI Investments	Acquisition of shares*	Equity Capital of Unincorporated Bodies#	Reinvested Earnings$	Other Capital$$	Portfolio Investment (12 to 14)	GDRs/ADRs##	FIIs**	Offshore Funds and Others	Total
(1)	(2)	(3)	(4)	(5)	(6)	(7)	(8)	(9)	(10)	(11)	(12)	(13)	(14)	(15)
2005–6														
Mar 2006	1240	1240	96	674	0	470	0	0	0	966	282	684	0	2206
Feb 2006	127	127	16	92	0	19	0	0	0	1821	129	1692	0	1948
Jan 2006	482	482	78	144	0	260	0	0	0	1545	159	1386	0	2027
Dec 2005	342	342	46	117	0	179	0	0	0	2389	267	2122	0	2731
Nov 2005	746	746	39	102	0	605	0	0	0	271	288	–17	0	1017
Oct 2005	412	412	25	231	0	156	0	0	0	88	557	–469	0	500
Sep 2005	282	282	7	128	0	147	0	0	0	1342	302	1035	5	1624
Aug 2005	399	399	68	300	0	31	0	0	0	1289	85	1204	0	1688
Jul 2005	324	324	114	139	0	71	0	0	0	1809	63	1746	0	2133
Jun 2005	264	264	70	142	0	52	0	0	0	1382	60	1313	9	1646
May 2005	654	654	486	60	0	108	0	0	0	–123	347	–470	0	531
Apr 2005	268	268	80	104	0	83	0	0	0	–286	13	–299	0	–18
2004–5														
Mar 2005	274	274	71	68	0	135	0	0	0	1654	171	1475	8	1929
Feb 2005	238	238	101	99	0	38	0	0	0	2467	0	2467	–	2705
Jan 2005	152	152	30	67	0	55	0	0	0	–130	48	–178	–	22
Dec 2004	316	316	86	177	0	53	0	0	0	804	0	799	5	1120
Nov 2004	186	186	46	98	0	42	0	0	0	3051	224	2827	–	3237
Oct 2004	214	214	24	90	0	100	0	0	0	848	0	848	–	1062
Sep 2004	282	282	57	96	0	129	0	0	0	424	0	421	3	706
Aug 2004	601	601	329	137	0	135	0	0	0	450	0	450	–	1051
Jul 2004	173	173	30	112	0	31	0	0	0	–410	0	–410	–	–237
Jun 2004	380	380	103	162	0	115	0	0	0	–467	0	–467	–	–87
May 2004	217	217	56	83	0	78	0	0	0	–314	135	–449	–	–97
Apr 2004	217	217	129	69	0	19	0	0	0	938	35	903	–	1155
2005–6	7210	5750	1126	2233	0	2181	210	1257	203	12492	2552	9926	14	19702
2004–5	5652	3777	1062	1258	0	930	527	1508	367	9315	613	8686	16	14967
2003–4	4322	2229	928	534	0	735	32	1460	633	11377	459	10918	0	15699
2002–3	5035	2764	919	739	0	916	190	1833	438	979	600	377	2	6014
2001–2	6130	4095	2221	767	35	881	191	1645	390	2021	477	1505	39	8151
2000–1	4029	2400	1456	454	67	362	61	1350	279	2760	831	1847	82	6789
1999–2000	2155	2155	1410	171	84	490	0	0	0	3026	768	2135	123	5181
1998–9	2462	2462	1821	179	62	400	0	0	0	–61	270	–390	59	2401
1997–8	3557	3557	2754	202	241	360	0	0	0	1828	645	979	204	5385
1996–7	2462	2462	1821	179	62	400	0	0	0	3312	1366	1926	20	5774
1995–6	2144	2144	1249	169	715	11	0	0	0	2748	683	2009	56	4892
1994–5	1314	1314	701	171	442	0	0	0	0	3824	2082	1503	239	5138
1993–4	586	586	280	89	217	0	0	0	0	3567	1520	1665	382	4153
1992–3	315	315	222	42	51	0	0	0	0	244	240	1	3	559
1991–2	129	129	66	0	63	0	0	0	0	4	0	0	4	133
1990–1	97	0	0	0	0	0	0	0	0	6	0	0	6	103

Notes: * Relates to acquisition of shares of Indian companies by non-residents under Section 5 of FEMA 1999. Data on such acquisition have been included as part of FDI since January 1996; # Figures for equity capital of unincorporated bodies for 2005–6 are estimates; ## Represents the amount raised by Indian corporates through Global Depository Receipts (GDRs) and American Depository Receipts (ADRs); $ Data for 2004–5 and 2005–6 are estimated as average of previous two years; P: Provisional; $$ Data pertains to inter company debt transactions of FDI entities; ** Represents fresh net inflow of funds by FIIs.

Source: RBI Bulletin, various issues.

TABLE A11.2
NRI Deposits, Outstandings as at the End Period

(US$ million)

Year/Month	FCNR(A)	FCNR(B)	NR(E)RA	NR(NR)RD	Total
1	2	3	4	5	6
2005–6					
Mar 2006	0	13198	21954	0	35152
Feb 2006	0	12670	21823	0	34493
Jan 2006	0	12551	21661	0	34212
Dec 2005	0	11819	21420	0	33239
Nov 2005	0	11420	20850	0	32270
Oct 2005	0	11556	20848	0	32404
Sep 2005	0	11477	21384	0	32861
Aug 2005	0	11511	21170	0	32681
Jul 2005	0	11346	21404	0	32750
Jun 2005	0	11397	21333	0	32730
May 2005	0	11384	21358	0	32742
Apr 2005	0	11539	21378	0	32917
2004–5					
Mar 2005	0	11452	21291	232	32975
Feb 2005	0	11388	20456	503	32347
Jan 2005	0	11292	20094	701	32087
Dec 2004	0	11437	20475	801	32713
Nov 2004	0	11196	19940	895	32031
Oct 2004	0	11100	19616	965	31681
Sep 2004	0	11087	19472	1047	31606
Aug 2004	0	11067	19375	1155	31597
Jul 2004	0	11162	19459	1275	31896
Jun 2004	0	11054	19731	1379	32164
May 2004	0	11020	20272	1500	32792
Apr 2004	0	10889	21251	1630	33770
2005–6	0	13198	21954	0	35152
2004–5	0	11452	21291	232	32975
2003–4	0	10961	20559	1746	33266
2002–3	0	10199	14923	3407	28529
2001–2	0	9673	8449	7052	25174
2000–1	0	9076	7147	6849	23072
1999–00	0	8172	6758	6754	21684
1998–9	0	7835	6045	6618	20498
1997–8	1	8467	5637	6262	20367
1996–7	2306	7496	4983	5604	20389
1995–6	4255	5720	3916	3542	17433
1994–5	7051	3063	4556	2486	17156
1993–4	9300	1108	3523	1754	15685
1992–3	10617	0	2740	621	13978
1991–2	9792	0	3025	0	12817
1990–1	10103	0	3618	0	13721

Notes: All figures are inclusive of interest; FCNR(A)—foreign currency non-resident (accounts); NR(NR)RD—non-resident (non-repatriable) rupee deposits (introduced in June 2002); FCNR(A)—foreign currency non-resident (accounts) (introduced May 2003); NR(E)RA—non-resident (external) rupee accounts.

Source: RBI Bulletin, various issues.

TABLE A11.3
FDI Inflows : Year-wise, Route-wise, Sector-wise Break-up and Countrywise Break-up

	Year-wise and Route-Wise: Actual Inflows of FDI/NRI						
	(Equity capital components only)				(From August 1991 to March 2006)		
	(Amount Rupees in million)						
Year (Jan-Dec)	Govt's approval (FIPB, SIA route)	RBI's Automatic Approval	Amount of inflows on acquisition of shares	RBI's Various NRI Schemes	Total	Closing Balance of Advance	Grand Total
(1)	(2)	(3)	(4)	(5)	(6)	(8)	(9)
Total #	755194	315575	357531	84270	1512571	98690	1614109
2006$	8466	40452	33274	0	82191	0	82191
2005	49728	68685	74292	0	192706	0	192706
2004	48517	54221	45076	0	147814	24852	172665
2003	42957	23400	29284	0	95640	18808	114448
2002	69577	39030	52626	111	161344	19771	181116
2001	96386	32411	29622	2293	160711	7066	167777
2000	63425	16918	20581	3488	104411	19126	123537
1999	61894	7608	19608	3488	92599	9068	101667
1998	82397	6107	40594	3595	132692	0	132692
1997	101284	8672	9540	10396	129898	0	129898
1996	57589	6196	3038	20621	87522	0	87522
1995	38694	5302	0	19878	64854	0	64854
1994	15008	3626	0	11453	31122	0	31122
1993	9852	2411	0	5794	18620	0	18620
1992	4780	475	0	1530	6912	0	6912
1991*	1912	0	0	1623	3535	0	3535
	(Amount in US $ million)						
Total #	18822	7224	8109	2510	36664	2179	38904
2006$	191	912	750	0	1853	0	1853
2005	1137	1557	1660	0	4354	0	4354
2004	1055	1179	980	0	3213	540	3753
2003	934	509	637	0	2079	409	2488
2002	1450	813	1096	2	3361	412	3773
2001	2142	720	658	51	3571	157	3728
2000	1475	393	479	81	2428	445	2873
1999	1474	181	467	83	2205	216	2421
1998	2086	155	1028	91	3359	0	3359
1997	2824	242	266	290	3621	0	3621
1996	1675	180	88	600	2545	0	2545
1995	1232	169	0	633	2065	0	2065
1994	478	116	0	365	992	0	992
1993	321	79	0	189	608	0	608
1992	183	18	0	59	264	0	264
1991*	78	0	0	66	144	0	144

Notes: # Data as on 31 March 2006; $ Data pertain to January–March 2006; * Data pertains to August–December 1991; Inflows through ADRs/GDRs/FCCBs against the FDI approvals have been excluded; Advance amounts of FDI get adjusted under different routes of inflow; Figures in brackets are percentages to respective sub-total and grand total.

Source: www.Dipp.nic.in (*SIA Newsletter*).

(contd.)

TABLE A11.3 (contd.)
FDI Inflows : Year-wise, Route-wise, Sector-wise Break-up and Countrywise Break-up

Sector-wise Break-up For FDI Inflows From August 1991 to March 2006				Country-wise Break-up For FDI Inflows From August 1991 to March 2006			
	(Rs Mn)	(US$ Million)			(Rs Mn)	(US$ Million)	
Total (Industry & Services)	1355523	32306	(83.0)	Total Source Countries	1309412	31203	(80.2)
Electrical Equipment (incl.S/W & Elec)	237094	5496	(17.0)	*of which:*			
Telecommunications	143368	3372	(10.4)	Mauritius	504032	11785	(37.8)
Transportation Industry	133151	3178	(9.8)	USA	206751	5038	(16.1)
Service Sector	128042	3091	(9.6)	Japan	89309	2124	(6.8)
Fuels (Power & Oil Refinery)	109763	2581	(8.0)	Netherlands	84966	1994	(6.4)
Chemicals (Other than Fertilizers)	85798	2143	(6.6)	UK	82710	1979	(6.3)
Food Processing Industries	47023	1179	(3.6)	Germany	65204	1582	(5.1)
Drugs and Pharmaceuticals	43114	1007	(3.1)	Singapore	43880	1050	(3.4)
Cement and Gypsum Products	32313	747	(2.3)	France	32756	778	(2.5)
Metallurgical Industries	28163	655	(2.0)	South Korea	29123	752	(2.4)
Consultancy Services	20985	460	(1.4)	Switzerland	26219	636	(2.0)
Misc. Mechanical Engineering	19321	492	(1.5)	Italy	20546	496	(1.6)
Textiles (incl. Dyed and Printed)	17749	450	(1.4)	Sweden	19806	472	(1.5)
Trading	14968	379	(1.2)	Hongkong	13495	370	(1.2)
Paper and Pulp (incl. Paper Product)	14047	363	(1.1)	UAE	6991	156	(0.5)
Hotel and Tourism	13841	323	(1.0)	Australia	6689	159	(0.5)
Glass	10305	256	(0.8)	Denmark	6590	160	(0.5)
Rubber Goods	9849	234	(0.7)	Belgium	6265	152	(0.5)
Industrial Machinery	8684	215	(0.7)	Malaysia	5956	139	(0.4)
Comm., Office & Household Equipment	8465	233	(0.7)	Cyprus	5149	118	(0.4)
Agricultural Machinery	6898	167	(0.5)	Russia	4969	117	(0.4)
Machine Tools	6643	156	(0.5)	Cayman Islands	4753	103	(0.3)
Timber Products	4669	107	(0.3)	Canada	4440	105	(0.3)
Medical and Surgical Appliances	4482	102	(0.3)	British Virginia	3524	81	(0.3)
Soaps, Cosmetics, & Toilet Preparations	3950	90	(0.3)	Bermuda	2922	71	(0.2)
Ceramics	3495	90	(0.3)	Thailand	2832	75	(0.2)
Earth-moving Machinery	3352	74	(0.2)	Phillipines	1886	52	(0.2)
Fertilizers	3293	78	(0.2)	Finland	1743	44	(0.1)
Fermentation Industries	3158	77	(0.2)	Luxembourg	1722	41	(0.1)
Leather, Leather Goods, & Pickers	1968	52	(0.2)	Austria	1650	41	(0.1)
Vegetable Oils and Vanaspati	1498	37	(0.1)	Israel	1623	44	(0.1)
Glue and Gelatin	1476	36	(0.1)	Spain	1424	32	(0.1)
Prime Movers other than Electrical	1056	31	(0.1)	Baharain	1408	33	(0.1)
Industrial Instruments	842	22	(0.1)	South Africa	1403	31	(0.1)
Sugar	719	17	(0.1)	Indonesia	1391	30	(0.1)
Scientific Instruments	616	15	(0.0)	West Indies	1385	32	(0.1)
Photographic Raw Film and Paper	608	15	(0.0)	Oman	1076	24	(0.1)
Dye-Stuffs	592	16	(0.0)	Nevia	841	19	(0.1)
Boilers and Steam Generating Plants	183	5	(0.0)	Bahamas	813	21	(0.1)
Defence Industries	2	0	(0.0)	Iceland	812	19	(0.1)
Mathematical,Surveying and Drawing	0	0	(0.0)	*Memo Items:*	304698	7701	*(19.8)*
Miscellaneous Industries	179983	4267	(13.2)	NRI	33727	796	(2.0)
Memo Items:	*258588*	*6599*	*(17.0)*	Unindicated	12383	307	(0.8)
Acquisition of Shares	72780	1849	(4.8)	Acquisition of Shares	72780	1849	(4.8)
Advance Inflows	98690	2179	(5.6)	Advance Inflows	98690	2179	(5.6)
Stock Swapped	2849	61	(0.2)	Stock Swapped	2849	61	(0.2)
NRI–RBI Schemes	84269	2510	(6.5)	NRI–RBI Schemes	84269	2510	(6.5)
Grand Total	1614111	38905	(100.0)	Grand Total	1614110	38904	(100.0)

DEMOGRAPHY AND SOCIAL SECTOR
A12 POPULATION

TABLE 12.1
Statewise Population, 1951–2001

(million)

State/UTs	2001	Decadal growth (%) (1991–2001)	1991	Decadal growth (%) (1981–91)	1981	Decadal growth (%) (1971–81)	1971	Decadal growth (%) (1961–71)	1961	Decadal growth (%) (1951–61)	1951	Decadal growth (%) (1941–51)
(1)	(2)	(3)	(4)	(5)	(6)	(7)	(8)	(9)	(10)	(11)	(12)	(13)
India	1028.61	21.5	846.39	23.9	683.33	24.7	548.16	24.8	439.23	21.6	361.09	13.3
Andhra Pradesh	76.21	14.6	66.51	24.2	53.55	23.1	43.50	20.9	35.98	15.6	31.12	14.0
Arunachal Pradesh	1.10	27.2	0.87	36.9	0.63	35.0	0.47	38.9	0.34	–	–	–
Assam	26.66	18.9	22.41	24.2	18.04	23.4	14.63	35.0	10.84	35.0	8.03	19.9
Bihar	83.00	28.6	64.53	–7.7	69.92	24.1	56.35	21.3	46.45	19.8	38.78	10.3
Goa	1.35	15.4	1.17	16.2	1.01	26.7	0.80	34.7	0.59	7.9	0.55	1.1
Gujarat	50.67	22.7	41.31	21.2	34.09	27.7	26.70	29.4	20.63	26.9	16.26	18.7
Haryana	21.14	28.4	16.46	27.4	12.92	28.8	10.04	32.2	7.59	33.8	5.67	7.6
Himachal Pradesh	6.08	17.6	5.17	20.8	4.28	23.7	3.46	23.0	2.81	17.9	2.39	5.4
Jammu and Kashmir	10.14	29.9	7.80	30.3	5.99	29.7	4.62	29.7	3.56	9.4	3.25	10.4
Karnataka	52.85	17.5	44.98	21.1	37.14	26.7	29.30	24.2	23.59	21.6	19.40	19.4
Kerala	31.84	9.4	29.10	14.3	25.45	19.2	21.35	26.3	16.90	24.8	13.55	22.8
Madhya Pradesh	60.35	24.3	48.57	–8.0	52.79	26.7	41.65	28.7	32.37	24.2	26.07	8.7
Maharashtra	96.88	22.7	78.94	25.7	62.78	24.5	50.41	27.5	39.55	23.6	32.00	19.3
Manipur	2.17	18.1	1.84	29.3	1.42	32.4	1.07	37.6	0.78	34.9	0.58	12.9
Meghalaya	2.32	30.7	1.78	32.9	1.34	32.0	1.01	31.6	0.77	26.9	0.61	9.0
Mizoram	0.89	29.0	0.69	39.7	0.49	48.8	0.33	24.8	0.27	35.7	0.20	28.1
Nagaland	1.99	64.5	1.21	56.1	0.78	50.2	0.52	39.8	0.37	73.2	0.21	12.1
Orissa	36.80	16.2	31.66	20.1	26.37	20.2	21.95	25.0	17.55	19.8	14.65	6.4
Punjab	24.36	20.1	20.28	20.8	16.79	23.9	13.55	21.7	11.14	21.5	9.16	–4.6
Rajasthan	56.51	28.4	44.01	28.4	34.26	33.0	25.77	27.8	20.16	26.2	15.97	15.2
Sikkim	0.54	33.0	0.41	28.5	0.32	50.5	0.21	29.6	0.16	17.4	0.14	13.1
Tamil Nadu	62.41	11.7	55.86	15.4	48.41	17.5	41.20	22.3	33.69	11.8	30.12	14.7
Tripura	3.20	16.1	2.76	34.2	2.06	31.7	1.56	36.6	1.14	78.7	0.64	24.6
Uttar Pradesh	166.20	25.9	132.00	19.1	110.86	25.5	88.34	19.8	73.76	16.7	63.22	11.8
West Bengal	80.18	16.5	68.80	26.1	54.58	23.2	44.31	26.9	34.93	32.8	26.30	13.2
Uttaranchal	8.49	19.4	7.11	–	–	–	–	–	–	–	–	–
Jharkhand	26.95	23.4	21.84	–	–	–	–	–	–	–	–	–
Chhatisgarh	20.83	18.3	17.62	–	–	–	–	–	–	–	–	–
Union Territories												
Andaman & Nicobar	0.36	28.1	0.28	48.7	0.19	64.3	0.12	–82.0	0.64	106.5	0.31	–8.8
Chandigarh	0.90	40.2	0.64	42.0	0.45	75.9	0.26	114.2	0.12	–50.0	0.24	4.3
Dadra & Nagar Haveli	0.22	59.4	0.14	32.7	0.10	40.5	0.07	27.6	0.06	38.1	0.04	5.0
Daman and Diu	0.16	54.9	0.10	29.1	0.08	25.4	0.06	70.3	0.04	–24.5	0.05	14.0
Delhi	13.85	47.0	9.42	51.5	6.22	55.2	4.01	50.7	2.66	52.5	1.74	90.0
Lakshadweep	0.06	15.4	0.05	30.0	0.04	25.0	0.03	33.3	0.02	14.3	0.02	16.7
Pondicherry	0.97	20.5	0.81	33.8	0.60	28.0	0.47	27.9	0.37	16.4	0.32	11.2

Source: Census of India 2001, Primary Census Abstract and *Census of India 1991, Final Population totals,* Paper 1 of 1992, Vol. II.

TABLE A12.2
Statewise Rural and Urban Population of India, 1951–2001

(million)

State/Union Territory	2001 Rural	2001 Urban		1991 Rural	1991 Urban		1981 Rural	1981 Urban		1971 Rural	1971 Urban		1961 Rural	1961 Urban		1951 Rural	1951 Urban	
India	741.66	285.36	(27.7)	628.69	217.61	(25.7)	523.87	159.46	(23.3)	439.05	109.11	(19.9)	360.30	78.94	(18.0)	298.64	62.44	(17.3)
Andhra Pradesh	55.22	20.50	(26.9)	48.62	17.89	(26.9)	41.06	12.49	(23.3)	35.10	8.40	(19.3)	29.71	6.28	(17.4)	25.69	5.42	(17.4)
Arunachal Pradesh	0.48	0.06	(5.5)	0.75	0.11	(12.8)	0.59	0.04	(6.5)	0.45	0.02	(3.6)	0.34	—		—	—	
Assam	23.25	3.39	(12.7)	19.93	2.49	(11.1)	16.26	1.78	(9.9)	13.34	1.29	(8.8)	10.06	0.78	(7.2)	7.68	0.35	(4.3)
Bihar	74.20	8.68	(10.5)	75.02	11.35	(17.6)	61.20	8.72	(12.5)	50.72	5.63	(10.0)	42.53	3.91	(8.4)	36.16	2.63	(6.8)
Goa	0.68	0.67	(49.6)	0.69	0.48	(41.0)	0.59	0.32	(32.1)	0.50	0.20	(25.5)	0.50	0.09	(14.7)	0.48	0.07	(13.0)
Gujarat	31.70	18.90	(37.3)	27.06	14.25	(34.5)	23.48	10.60	(31.1)	19.20	7.50	(28.1)	15.32	5.32	(25.8)	11.84	4.43	(27.2)
Haryana	14.97	6.11	(28.9)	12.41	4.06	(24.6)	10.10	2.83	(21.9)	8.26	1.77	(17.7)	6.28	1.31	(17.2)	4.71	0.97	(17.1)
Himachal Pradesh	5.48	0.60	(9.8)	4.72	0.45	(8.7)	3.96	0.33	(7.6)	3.22	0.24	(7.0)	2.63	0.18	(6.3)	2.23	0.15	(6.5)
Jammu and Kashmir	7.57	2.51	(24.7)	5.88	1.84	(23.6)	4.73	1.26	(21.0)	3.76	0.86	(18.6)	2.97	0.59	(16.7)	2.80	0.46	(14.0)
Karnataka	34.81	17.92	(33.9)	31.07	13.91	(30.9)	26.41	10.73	(28.9)	22.18	7.12	(24.3)	18.32	5.27	(22.3)	14.95	4.45	(23.0)
Kerala	23.57	8.27	(26.0)	21.42	7.68	(26.4)	20.68	4.77	(18.7)	17.81	3.47	(16.2)	14.35	2.55	(15.1)	11.72	1.83	(13.5)
Madhya Pradesh	44.28	16.10	(26.7)	50.84	15.34	(31.6)	41.59	10.59	(20.1)	34.87	6.79	(16.3)	27.75	4.63	(14.3)	22.94	3.13	(12.0)
Maharashtra	55.73	41.02	(42.3)	48.40	30.54	(38.7)	40.79	21.99	(35.0)	34.70	15.71	(31.2)	28.39	11.16	(28.2)	22.80	9.20	(28.8)
Manipur	1.82	0.57	(26.3)	1.33	0.51	(27.5)	1.05	0.38	(26.4)	0.93	0.14	(13.1)	0.71	0.07	(8.7)	0.58	0.03	(4.8)
Meghalaya	1.85	0.45	(19.5)	1.45	0.33	(18.6)	1.09	0.24	(18.0)	0.87	0.15	(14.5)	0.65	0.12	(15.2)	0.55	0.06	(9.9)
Mizoram	0.45	0.44	(49.6)	0.37	0.32	(46.1)	0.37	0.12	(24.7)	0.30	0.04	(11.4)	0.25	0.01	(5.3)	0.19	0.01	(3.6)
Nagaland	1.64	0.35	(17.7)	1.00	0.21	(17.2)	0.66	0.12	(15.5)	0.47	0.05	(9.9)	0.35	0.02	(5.1)	0.21	0.00	(0.9)
Orissa	31.21	5.50	(14.9)	27.43	4.24	(13.4)	23.26	3.11	(11.8)	20.10	1.85	(8.4)	16.44	1.11	(6.3)	14.05	0.59	(4.1)
Punjab	16.04	8.25	(33.9)	14.29	5.99	(29.5)	12.14	4.65	(27.7)	10.34	3.22	(23.7)	8.57	2.57	(23.1)	7.17	1.99	(21.7)
Rajasthan	43.27	13.21	(23.4)	33.94	10.07	(22.9)	21.22	7.21	(21.0)	21.22	4.54	(17.6)	16.87	3.28	(16.3)	13.02	2.96	(18.5)
Sikkim	0.48	0.06	(11.1)	0.37	0.04	(9.1)	0.27	0.05	(16.1)	0.19	0.02	(9.5)	0.16	0.07	(43.2)	0.14	0.03	(21.7)
Tamil Nadu	34.87	27.24	(43.7)	36.78	19.08	(34.2)	32.46	15.95	(33.0)	28.73	12.47	(30.3)	24.70	8.99	(26.7)	22.79	7.33	(24.4)
Tripura	2.65	0.54	(17.0)	2.34	0.42	(15.3)	1.83	0.23	(11.0)	1.39	0.16	(10.4)	1.04	0.10	(9.0)	0.60	0.04	(6.8)
Uttar Pradesh	131.54	34.51	(20.8)	111.51	27.61	(20.9)	90.96	19.90	(17.9)	75.95	12.39	(14.0)	64.28	9.48	(12.9)	54.59	8.63	(13.6)
West Bengal	57.74	22.49	(28.0)	49.37	18.71	(27.2)	40.13	14.45	(26.5)	33.35	10.97	(24.7)	26.39	8.54	(24.5)	20.02	6.28	(23.9)
Uttaranchal	6.31	2.17	(25.6)	—	—		—	—		—	—		—	—		—	—	
Jharkhand	20.92	5.99	(22.2)	—	—		—	—		—	—		—	—		—	—	
Chhatisgarh	16.62	4.18	(20.0)	—	—		—	—		—	—		—	—		—	—	
Union Territories																		
Andaman & Nicobar	0.24	0.12	(32.2)	0.21	0.08	(26.7)	0.14	0.05	(23.8)	0.09	0.03	(22.6)	0.05	0.01	(2.2)	0.02	0.01	(2.6)
Chandigarh	0.09	0.81	(89.9)	0.07	0.58	(89.7)	0.03	0.42	(93.6)	0.02	0.23	(90.7)	0.02	0.10	(82.5)	0.02	0.00	(0.0)
Dadra & Nagar Haveli	0.17	0.05	(22.7)	0.13	0.01	(8.7)	0.10	0.01	(6.7)	0.07	0.00	(0.0)	0.06	0.00	(0.0)	0.04	0.00	(0.0)
Daman and Diu	0.10	0.06	(36.1)	0.05	0.05	(47.1)	0.05	0.03	(36.7)	0.04	0.02	(38.1)	0.02	0.01	(35.1)	0.03	0.02	(36.7)
Delhi	0.96	12.82	(92.6)	0.92	8.47	(89.9)	0.45	5.77	(92.7)	0.42	3.66	(91.5)	0.30	2.36	(88.7)	0.31	1.44	(82.4)
Lakshadweep	0.03	0.03	(45.0)	0.02	0.03	(55.8)	0.02	0.02	(47.5)	0.03	0.00	(0.0)	0.02	0.00	(0.0)	0.02	0.00	(0.0)
Pondicherry	0.33	0.65	(66.5)	0.30	0.52	(64.0)	0.29	0.32	(52.3)	0.27	0.20	(42.3)	0.28	0.09	(24.4)	0.32	0.00	(0.0)

Note: Figures within brackets represent urban share in total population (in percentage).

Source: Census of India 2001, *Provisional Population Totals*, Part 1 of 2001 and Census of India 1991, *Final Population Totals*, Paper-1 of 1992, Vol. II.

TABLE A12.3
Statewise Sex Ratio

(females per 1000 males)

State/Union Territory	2001	1991	1981	1971	1961	1951	1941	1931	1921	1911	1901
(1)	(2)	(3)	(4)	(5)	(6)	(7)	(8)	(9)	(10)	(11)	(12)
India	933	927	934	930	941	946	945	950	955	964	972
Andhra Pradesh	978	972	975	977	981	986	980	987	993	992	985
Arunachal Pradesh	893	859	862	861	894	na	na	na	na	na	na
Assam	935	923	910	896	869	868	875	874	896	915	919
Bihar	919	907	948	957	1005	1000	1002	995	1020	1051	1061
Goa	961	967	975	981	1066	1128	1084	1088	1120	1108	1091
Gujarat	920	934	942	934	940	952	941	945	944	946	954
Haryana	861	865	870	867	868	871	869	844	844	835	867
Himachal Pradesh	968	976	973	958	938	912	890	897	890	889	884
Jammu and Kashmir	892	896	892	878	878	873	869	865	870	876	882
Karnataka	965	960	963	957	959	966	960	965	969	981	983
Kerala	1058	1036	1032	1016	1022	1028	1027	1022	1011	1008	1004
Madhya Pradesh	919	912	921	920	932	945	946	947	949	967	972
Maharashtra	922	934	937	930	936	941	949	947	950	966	978
Manipur*	978	958	971	980	1015	1036	1055	1065	1041	1029	1037
Meghalaya	972	955	954	942	937	949	966	971	1000	1013	1036
Mizoram	935	921	919	946	1009	1041	1069	1102	1109	1120	1113
Nagaland	900	886	863	871	933	999	1021	997	992	993	973
Orissa	972	971	981	988	1001	1022	1053	1067	1086	1056	1037
Punjab	876	882	879	865	854	844	836	815	799	780	832
Rajasthan	921	910	919	911	908	921	906	907	896	908	905
Sikkim	875	878	835	863	904	907	920	967	970	951	916
Tamil Nadu	987	974	977	978	992	1007	1012	1027	1029	1042	1044
Tripura	948	945	946	943	932	904	886	885	885	885	874
Uttar Pradesh	898	876	882	876	907	908	907	903	908	916	938
West Bengal	934	917	911	891	878	865	852	890	905	925	945
Uttaranchal	962	936	936	940	947	940	907	913	916	907	918
Jharkhand	941	922	940	945	960	961	978	989	1002	1021	1032
Chhatisgarh	989	985	996	998	1008	1024	1032	1043	1041	1039	1046
Union Territories											
Andaman & Nicobar	846	818	760	644	617	625	574	495	303	352	318
Chandigarh	777	790	769	749	652	781	763	751	743	720	771
Dadra & Nagar Haveli	812	952	974	1007	963	946	925	911	940	967	960
Daman and Diu	710	969	1062	1099	1169	1125	1080	1088	1143	1040	995
Delhi	821	827	808	801	785	768	715	722	733	793	862
Lakshadweep	948	943	975	978	1020	1043	1018	994	1027	987	1063
Pondicherry	1001	979	985	989	1013	1030	na	na	1053	1058	na

Note: * Excludes Mao-Maram, Paomata, and Purul sub-divisions of Senapati district of Manipur.

Source: Census of India 2001, Provisional Population Totals, Part 1 of 2001.

TABLE A12.4
Statewise Literacy Rate, 1951 to 2001

(as percentage of population)

State/Union Territory	2001			1991			1981			1971			1961			1951		
	Persons	Male	Female	Persons	Male	Female	Persons	Male	Female	Persons	Male	Female	Persons	Male	Female	Persons	Male	Female
(1)	(2)	(3)	(4)	(5)	(6)	(7)	(8)	(9)	(10)	(11)	(12)	(13)	(14)	(15)	(16)	(17)	(18)	(19)
India	64.8	75.3	53.7	52.2	64.1	39.3	43.6	56.4	29.8	34.5	39.5	18.7	28.3	34.40	12.9	18.3	24.9	7.9
Male–female gap	(21.6)			(24.8)			(26.6)			(24.0)			(25.1)			(18.3)		
Andhra Pradesh	60.5	70.3	50.4	44.1	55.1	32.7	35.7	46.8	24.2	24.6	33.1	15.8	21.2	30.20	12.0	13.2	19.7	6.5
Arunachal Pradesh	54.3	63.8	43.5	41.6	51.5	29.7	25.5	35.1	14.0	11.3	17.8	3.7	47.9	na	na	na	na	na
Assam	63.3	71.3	54.6	52.9	61.9	43.0	na	na	na	28.7	na	na	33.0	37.30	16.0	18.3	27.4	7.9
Bihar	47.0	59.7	33.1	38.5	52.5	22.9	32.0	46.6	16.5	19.9	30.6	8.7	21.8	29.80	6.9	12.2	20.5	3.8
Goa	82.0	88.4	75.4	75.5	83.6	67.1	64.7	76.0	55.2	na	54.3	35.1	36.2	na	na	23.0	na	na
Gujarat	69.1	79.7	57.8	61.3	73.1	48.6	52.2	65.1	38.5	35.8	46.1	24.8	30.5	41.10	19.1	23.1	32.3	13.5
Haryana	67.9	78.5	55.7	55.9	69.1	40.5	43.9	58.5	26.9	26.9	37.2	14.9	24.1	na	na	na	na	na
Himachal Pradesh	76.5	85.3	67.4	63.9	75.4	52.1	51.2	64.3	37.7	32.0	43.1	20.2	24.9	27.20	6.2	7.7	12.6	2.4
Jammu and Kashmir	55.5	66.6	43.0	na	na	na	32.7	44.2	19.6	18.6	na	na	13.0	17.00	4.3	na	na	na
Karnataka	66.6	76.1	56.9	56.0	67.3	44.3	46.2	58.7	33.2	31.5	48.6	27.8	29.8	36.10	14.2	19.3	29.1	9.2
Kerala	90.9	94.2	87.7	89.8	93.6	86.2	81.6	87.7	75.7	60.4	74.0	64.5	55.1	55.00	38.9	40.7	50.2	31.5
Madhya Pradesh	63.7	76.1	50.3	44.2	58.4	28.9	34.2	48.4	19.0	22.1	32.7	10.9	20.5	27.00	6.7	9.8	16.2	3.2
Maharashtra	76.9	86.0	67.0	64.9	76.6	52.3	55.8	69.7	41.0	39.2	51.0	26.4	35.1	42.00	16.8	20.9	31.4	9.7
Manipur	70.5	80.3	60.5	59.9	71.6	47.6	49.6	64.1	34.6	32.9	46.0	19.5	36.0	45.10	15.9	11.4	20.8	2.4
Meghalaya	62.6	65.4	59.6	49.1	53.1	44.9	42.0	46.6	37.2	29.5	34.1	24.6	na	na	na	na	na	na
Mizoram	88.8	90.7	86.7	82.3	85.6	78.6	74.3	79.4	68.6	na	60.5	46.7	na	na	na	na	na	na
Nagaland	66.6	71.2	61.5	61.6	67.6	54.8	50.2	58.5	40.3	27.4	35.0	18.7	20.4	24.00	11.3	10.4	15.0	5.7
Orissa	63.1	75.3	50.5	49.1	63.1	34.7	41.0	56.5	25.1	26.2	38.3	13.9	25.2	34.70	8.6	15.8	27.3	4.5
Punjab	69.7	75.2	63.4	58.5	65.7	50.4	48.1	55.5	39.6	33.7	40.4	25.9	31.5	33.00	14.1	15.2	21.0	8.5
Rajasthan	60.4	75.7	43.9	38.6	55.0	20.4	30.1	44.8	14.0	19.1	28.7	8.5	18.1	23.70	5.8	8.9	14.4	3.0
Sikkim	68.8	76.0	60.4	56.9	65.7	46.7	41.6	53.0	27.4	17.7	na	na	14.2	19.60	4.3	7.3	12.8	1.3
Tamil Nadu	73.5	82.4	64.4	62.7	73.8	51.3	54.4	68.1	40.4	39.5	51.8	26.9	36.4	44.50	18.2	20.8	31.7	10.0
Tripura	73.2	81.0	64.9	60.4	70.6	49.7	50.1	61.5	38.0	31.0	40.2	21.2	24.3	29.60	10.2	15.5	22.3	8.0
Uttar Pradesh	56.3	68.8	42.2	41.6	55.7	25.3	33.3	47.4	17.2	21.7	31.5	10.6	20.7	27.30	7.0	10.8	17.4	3.6
West Bengal	68.6	77.0	59.6	57.7	67.8	46.6	48.6	59.9	36.1	33.2	42.8	22.4	34.5	40.10	17.0	24.0	34.2	12.2
Uttaranchal	71.6	83.3	59.6	na	na	na	na	na	na	na	na	na	na	na	na	na	na	na
Jharkhand	53.6	67.3	38.9	na	na	na	na	na	na	na	na	na	na	na	na	na	na	na
Chhatisgarh	64.7	77.4	51.9	na	na	na	na	na	na	na	na	na	na	na	na	na	na	na
Union Territories																		
Andaman & Nicobar	81.3	86.3	75.2	73.0	79.0	65.5	63.2	70.3	53.2	43.6	na	na	40.1	42.40	19.4	25.8	34.2	12.3
Chandigarh	81.9	86.1	76.5	77.8	82.0	72.3	74.8	78.9	69.3	61.6	na	na	55.1	na	na	na	na	na
Dadra & Nagar Haveli	57.6	71.2	40.2	40.7	53.6	27.0	32.7	44.7	20.4	15.0	na	na	11.6	14.70	4.1	4.0	na	na
Daman and Diu	78.2	86.8	65.6	71.2	82.7	59.4	59.9	74.5	46.5	44.8	na	na	34.9	na	na	22.9	na	na
Delhi	81.7	87.3	74.7	75.3	82.0	67.0	71.9	79.3	62.6	56.6	na	na	62.0	60.80	42.5	38.4	43.0	32.3
Lakshadweep	86.7	92.5	80.5	81.8	90.2	72.9	68.4	81.2	55.3	43.7	na	na	27.2	35.80	11.0	15.2	25.6	5.3
Pondicherry	81.2	88.6	73.9	74.7	83.7	65.6	65.1	77.1	53.0	46.0	na	na	43.7	50.40	24.6	na	na	na

Note: Excludes Mao-Maram, Paomata, and Purul sub-divisions of Senapati district of Manipur.

Source: Economic Survey 2002–3 and for the year 1981 *Economic Survey* 1991–2.

TABLE A12.5
Statewise Infant Mortality Rate; 1961, 1981, 1991, 2001, 2002, and 2003

(Number per thousand)

State/Union Territory	2003			2002			2001			1991			1981			1961		
	Persons	Male	Female	Persons	Male	Female	Persons	Male	Female	Persons	Male	Female	Persons	Male	Female	Persons	Male	Female
(1)	(2)	(3)	(4)	(5)	(6)	(7)	(8)	(9)	(10)	(11)	(12)	(13)	(14)	(15)	(16)	(17)	(18)	(19)
India	60	57	64	63	62	65	71	na	na	77	79	74	115	122	108	115	122	108
Andhra Pradesh	59	59	59	62	64	60	66	na	na	55	67	51	91	100	82	91	100	82
Arunachal Pradesh	59	59	59	62	64	60	44	na	na	91	111	103	126	141	111	126	141	111
Assam	67	69	65	70	70	71	78	na	na	92	96	87	-	-	-	-	-	-
Bihar	60	59	62	61	56	66	67	na	na	75	62	89	94	95	94	94	95	94
Goa	16	15	18	16	17	16	36	na	na	51	56	48	90	87	93	57	60	56
Gujarat	57	54	61	60	55	66	64	na	na	78	74	82	115	120	110	84	81	84
Haryana	59	54	65	62	54	73	69	na	na	52	57	54	126	132	119	94	87	119
Himachal Pradesh	49	54	44	61	66	55	64	na	na	82	84	81	143	160	126	92	101	89
Jammu and Kashmir	44	46	41	43	45	40	45	na	na	na	na	na	108	115	99	78	78	78
Karnataka	52	51	52	55	56	53	58	na	na	74	81	na	81	87	74	77	74	79
Kerala	11	11	12	10	9	12	16	na	na	42	45	41	54	61	48	52	55	48
Madhya Pradesh	82	77	86	85	81	88	97	na	na	133	131	136	150	158	140	150	158	140
Maharashtra	42	32	54	45	48	42	49	na	na	74	72	76	119	131	106	92	96	89
Manipur	16	18	13	10	13	7	25	na	na	28	29	27	32	31	33	32	31	33
Meghalaya	57	56	59	66	64	69	52	na	na	80	79	82	79	81	76	79	81	76
Mizoram	16	16	17	5	9	2	23	na	na	53	51	56	83	94	70	69	73	65
Nagaland	na	na	na	20	na	43	na	na	na	51	51	52	68	76	58	68	76	58
Orissa	83	82	83	87	95	79	98	na	na	125	129	111	163	172	153	115	119	111
Punjab	49	46	52	51	38	66	54	na	na	74	81	53	127	138	114	77	74	79
Rajasthan	75	70	81	78	75	80	83	na	na	87	94	79	141	146	135	114	114	114
Sikkim	33	34	31	25	23	27	52	na	na	60	58	62	127	135	118	96	105	87
Tamil Nadu	41	44	43	44	46	43	53	na	na	54	55	51	104	114	93	86	89	82
Tripura	35	36	27	33	35	31	49	na	na	82	81	84	130	143	116	111	106	116
Uttar Pradesh	76	69	84	80	76	84	85	na	na	99	98	104	130	131	128	130	131	128
West Bengal	46	45	46	49	53	45	53	na	na	62	75	51	95	103	57	95	103	57
Chhatisgarh	19	21	16	22	15	30	na	na	na	na	na	na	na	na	na	na	na	na
Jharkhand	51	50	52	41	44	37	na	na	na	na	na	na	na	na	na	na	na	na
Uttarakhand	41	31	53	34	16	55	na	na	na	na	na	na	na	na	na	na	na	na
Union Territories																		
Andaman & Nicobar	18	12	24	23	17	29	30	na	na	69	71	61	95	114	76	77	78	66
Chandigarh	19	21	16	22	15	30	32	na	na	48	50	47	118	141	96	53	53	53
Dadra & Nagar Haveli	54	69	39	51	51	52	61	na	na	81	84	73	117	149	82	98	102	93
Daman and Diu	39	43	34	30	46	12	na	na	na	56	61	50	90	87	93	57	60	56
Delhi	28	28	29	33	29	38	51	na	na	54	55	51	100	108	92	67	66	70
Lakshadweep	26	21	32	15	6	26	30	na	na	91	100	78	132	170	88	118	124	88
Pondicherry	24	29	18	25	24	25	21	na	na	34	32	35	84	100	68	73	77	68

Note: na—not applicable or not relevant.

Source: Economic Survey 2005–6 and 2002–3 and *National Human Development Report 2001,* Planning Commission.

A13 HUMAN DEVELOPMENT INDICES

Table A13.1
Human Development Index for India by State; 1981, 1991, and 2001

States/Union Territory	HDI 1981									HDI 1991								HDI 2001	
	Rural		Urban		Combined		Gender disparity index			Rural		Urban		Combined		Gender disparity index		Combined	
	Value	Rank	Value	Rank	Value	Rank	Value	Rank		Value	Rank	Value	Rank	Value	Rank	Value	Rank	Value	Rank
(1)	(2)	(3)	(4)	(5)	(6)	(7)	(8)	(9)		(10)	(11)	(12)	(13)	(14)	(15)	(16)	(17)	(18)	(19)
India	0.263		0.442		0.302		0.620			0.340		0.511		0.381		0.676		0.472	
Andhra Pradesh	0.262	25	0.425	23	0.298	23	0.744	10		0.344	23	0.473	29	0.377	23	0.801	23	0.416	10
Arunachal Pradesh	0.228	28	0.419	24	0.242	31	0.537	28		0.300	28	0.572	15	0.328	29	0.776	28	*	
Assam	0.261	26	0.380	28	0.272	26	0.462	32		0.326	26	0.555	19	0.348	26	0.575	30	0.386	14
Bihar	0.220	30	0.378	29	0.237	32	0.471	30		0.286	30	0.460	31	0.308	32	0.469	32	0.367	15
Goa	0.422	5	0.517	10	0.445	5	0.785	2		0.534	3	0.658	3	0.575	4	0.775	13	*	
Gujarat	0.315	14	0.458	18	0.360	14	0.723	6		0.380	18	0.532	23	0.431	17	0.714	22	0.479	6
Haryana	0.332	13	0.465	17	0.360	15	0.536	24		0.409	15	0.562	17	0.443	16	0.714	17	0.509	5
Himachal Pradesh	0.374	10	0.600	1	0.398	10	0.783	4		0.442	12	0.700	1	0.469	13	0.858	4	*	
Jammu and Kashmir	0.301	17	0.468	16	0.337	19	0.584	19		0.364	22	0.575	14	0.402	21	0.740	25	*	
Karnataka	0.295	18	0.489	14	0.346	16	0.707	20		0.367	21	0.523	24	0.412	19	0.753	11	0.478	7
Kerala	0.491	1	0.544	6	0.500	2	0.872	1		0.576	1	0.628	9	0.591	3	0.825	2	0.638	1
Madhya Pradesh	0.209	32	0.395	26	0.245	30	0.664	25		0.282	32	0.491	28	0.328	30	0.662	28	0.394	12
Maharashtra	0.306	15	0.489	15	0.363	13	0.740	15		0.403	16	0.548	21	0.452	15	0.793	15	0.523	4
Manipur	0.440	2	0.553	5	0.461	4	0.802	3		0.503	7	0.618	12	0.536	9	0.815	3	*	
Meghalaya	0.293	20	0.442	21	0.317	21	0.799	12		0.332	24	0.624	10	0.365	24	0.807	12	*	
Mizoram	0.381	9	0.558	4	0.411	8	0.502	18		0.464	10	0.648	5	0.548	7	0.770	6	*	
Nagaland	0.295	19	0.519	8	0.328	20	0.783	16		0.442	13	0.633	7	0.486	11	0.729	21	*	
Orissa	0.252	27	0.368	31	0.267	27	0.547	27		0.328	25	0.469	30	0.345	28	0.639	27	0.404	11
Punjab	0.386	8	0.494	13	0.411	9	0.688	14		0.447	11	0.566	16	0.475	12	0.710	19	0.537	2
Rajasthan	0.216	31	0.386	27	0.256	28	0.650	17		0.298	29	0.492	27	0.347	27	0.692	16	0.424	9
Sikkim	0.302	16	0.515	11	0.342	18	0.643	23		0.398	17	0.618	11	0.425	18	0.647	20	*	
Tamil Nadu	0.289	21	0.445	19	0.343	17	0.710	9		0.421	14	0.560	18	0.466	14	0.813	9	0.531	3
Tripura	0.264	23	0.498	12	0.287	24	0.422	31		0.368	20	0.551	20	0.389	22	0.531	29	*	
Uttar Pradesh	0.227	29	0.398	25	0.255	29	0.447	29		0.284	31	0.444	32	0.314	31	0.520	31	0.388	13
West Bengal	0.264	24	0.427	22	0.305	22	0.556	26		0.370	19	0.511	26	0.404	20	0.631	26	0.472	8
Andaman & Nicobar	0.335	12	0.575	2	0.394	11	0.645	21		0.528	5	0.653	4	0.574	5	0.857	1	*	
Chandigarh	0.437	4	0.565	3	0.550	1	0.719	7		0.501	8	0.694	2	0.674	1	0.764	7	*	
Dadra & Nagar Haveli	0.269	22	0.268	32	0.276	25	0.888	11		0.310	27	0.519	25	0.361	25	0.832	14	*	
Daman and Diu	0.409	6	0.518	9	0.438	6	0.760	5		0.492	9	0.629	8	0.544	8	0.714	8	*	
Delhi	0.439	3	0.531	7	0.495	3	0.595	22		0.530	4	0.635	6	0.624	2	0.690	10	*	
Lakshadweep	0.395	7	0.371	30	0.434	7	0.688	8		0.520	6	0.545	22	0.532	10	0.680	24	*	
Pondicherry	0.338	11	0.443	20	0.386	12	0.753	13		0.556	2	0.591	13	0.571	6	0.783	5	*	

Notes: * Not available for the year 2001; The HDI is a composite of variables capturing attainments in three dimensions of human development viz. economic, educational, and health. It has been worked out by a combination of measures: per capita monthly expenditures adjusted for inequality; a combination of literacy rate and intensity of formal education; and a combination of life expectancy at age 1 and infant mortality rate. For details see the technical note in the source for the estimation methodology and other details.

Source: Planning Commission (2002): *National Human Development Report, 2001*, March.

TABLE A13.2
Statewise Poverty Estimation HCR

State/Union Territory	1973–4			1977–8	1983	1987–8	1993–4	1999–00			Adjusted poverty Ratios (1999–2000) 55th Round	
	Rural	Urban	Combined					Rural	Urban	Combined	Rural	Urban
(1)	(2)	(3)	(4)	(5)	(6)	(7)	(8)	(9)	(10)	(11)	(12)	(13)
All India	56.44	49.01	54.88	51.32	44.48	38.86	35.97	27.09	23.62	26.10	30.2	24.7
Andhra Pradesh	48.41	50.61	48.86	39.31	28.91	25.86	22.19	11.05	26.63	15.77	14.9	27.7
Arunachal Pradesh	52.67	36.92	51.93	58.32	40.88	36.22	39.35	40.04	7.47	33.47		
Assam	52.67	36.92	51.21	57.15	40.47	36.21	40.86	40.04	7.47	36.09	44.1	8.3
Bihar	62.99	52.96	61.91	61.55	62.22	52.13	54.96	44.30	32.91	42.60	49.2	33.8
Goa	46.85	37.69	44.26	37.23	18.90	24.52	14.92	1.35	7.52	4.40		
Gujarat	46.35	52.57	48.15	41.23	32.79	31.54	24.21	13.17	15.59	14.07	15.4	16.0
Haryana	34.23	40.18	35.36	29.55	21.37	16.64	25.05	8.27	9.99	8.74	12.7	9.5
Himachal Pradesh	27.42	13.17	26.39	32.45	16.40	15.45	28.44	7.94	4.63	7.63	18.9	4.5
Jammu and Kashmir	45.51	21.32	40.83	38.97	24.24	23.82	25.17	3.97	1.98	3.48		
Karnataka	55.14	52.53	54.47	48.78	38.24	37.53	33.16	17.38	25.25	20.04	25.7	25.5
Kerala	59.19	62.74	59.79	52.22	40.42	31.79	25.43	9.38	20.27	12.72	12.6	18.7
Madhya Pradesh	62.66	57.65	61.78	61.78	49.78	43.07	42.52	37.06	38.44	37.43	36.4	37.9
Maharashtra	57.71	43.87	53.24	55.88	43.44	40.41	36.86	23.72	26.81	25.02	29.2	28.1
Manipur	52.67	36.92	49.96	53.72	37.02	31.35	33.78	40.04	7.47	28.54		
Meghalaya	52.67	36.92	50.20	55.19	38.81	33.92	37.92	40.04	7.47	33.87		
Mizoram	52.67	36.92	50.32	54.38	36.00	27.52	25.66	40.04	7.47	19.47		
Nagaland	52.67	36.92	50.81	56.04	39.25	34.43	37.92	40.04	7.47	32.67		
Orissa	67.28	55.62	66.18	70.07	65.29	55.58	48.56	48.01	42.83	47.15	47.3	41.4
Punjab	28.21	27.96	28.15	19.27	16.18	13.20	11.77	6.35	5.75	6.12	5.9	6.3
Rajasthan	44.76	52.13	46.14	37.42	34.46	35.15	27.41	13.74	19.85	15.28	19.6	22.8
Sikkim	52.67	36.92	50.86	55.89	39.71	36.06	41.43	40.04	7.47	36.55		
Tamil Nadu	57.43	49.40	54.94	54.79	51.66	43.39	35.03	20.55	22.11	21.12	19.9	24.4
Tripura	52.67	36.92	51.00	56.88	40.03	35.23	39.01	40.04	7.47	34.44		
Uttar Pradesh	56.53	60.09	57.07	49.05	47.07	41.46	40.85	31.22	30.89	31.15	33.7	30.4
West Bengal	73.16	34.67	63.43	60.52	54.85	44.72	35.66	31.85	14.86	27.02	37.1	19.5
Andaman & Nicobar	57.43	49.40	55.56	55.42	52.13	43.89	34.47	20.55	22.11	20.99		
Chandigarh	27.96	27.96	27.96	27.32	23.79	14.67	11.35	5.75	5.75	5.75		
Dadra & Nagar Haveli	46.85	37.69	46.55	37.20	15.67	67.11	50.84	17.57	13.52	17.14		
Delhi	24.44	52.23	49.61	33.23	26.22	12.41	14.69	0.40	9.42	8.23		0.7
Lakshadweep	59.19	62.74	59.68	52.79	42.36	34.95	25.04	9.38	20.27	15.60		
Pondicherry	57.43	49.40	53.82	53.25	50.06	41.46	37.40	20.55	22.11	21.67		

Source: Planning Commission (2002), *National Human Development Report, 2001*, March.

A14 EMPLOYMENT

TABLE A14.1
Total Population, Workers, and Non-workers as Per Population Censuses

(number in million)

Year	Total Population			Workers			Non-Workers		
	Persons	Males	Females	Persons	Males	Females	Persons	Males	Females
(1)	(2)	(3)	(4)	(5)	(6)	(7)	(8)	(9)	(10)
2001	1028.6	532.2	496.4	402.2	275.0	127.2	626.4	257.1	369.2
	(100.0)	(100.0)	(100.0)	(39.1)	(51.7)	(25.6)	(60.9)	(48.3)	(74.4)
1991	846.3	439.2	407.1	306.0	218.6	87.4	510.1	205.0	305.2
	(100.0)	(100.0)	(100.0)	(36.2)	(49.8)	(21.5)	(60.3)	(46.7)	(75.0)
1981	683.3	353.3	330.0	244.6	181.0	63.6	420.7	162.9	257.8
	(100.0)	(100.0)	(100.0)	(35.8)	(51.2)	(19.3)	(61.6)	(46.1)	(78.1)
1971	548.2	284.0	264.1	180.7	144.4	36.3	367.5	134.8	232.7
	(100.0)	(100.0)	(100.0)	(33.0)	(50.8)	(13.7)	(67.0)	(47.5)	(88.1)
1961	439.2	226.3	212.9	188.4	129.0	59.4	249.9	96.8	153.1
	(100.0)	(100.0)	(100.0)	(42.9)	(57.0)	(27.9)	(56.9)	(42.8)	(71.9)
1951	361.1	185.6	175.5	139.5	99.1	40.4	217.4	84.2	133.1
	(100.0)	(100.0)	(100.0)	(38.6)	(53.4)	(23.0)	(60.2)	(45.4)	(75.8)
1941	318.7	163.8	154.8	na	na	na	na	na	na
	(100.0)	(100.0)	(100.0)						
1931	279.0	143.1	135.9	120.6	83.0	37.6	157.9	59.5	98.5
	(100.0)	(100.0)	(100.0)	(43.2)	(58.0)	(27.7)	(56.6)	(41.6)	(72.5)
1921	251.3	128.6	122.8	117.9	77.8	40.1	133.4	50.7	82.7
	(100.0)	(100.0)	(100.0)	(46.9)	(60.5)	(32.7)	(53.1)	(39.4)	(67.3)
1911	252.1	128.4	123.7	121.4	79.6	41.8	131.1	49.0	82.1
	(100.0)	(100.0)	(100.0)	(48.1)	(62.0)	(33.8)	(52.0)	(38.2)	(66.4)
1901	238.4	120.9	117.5	111.4	74.1	37.3	127.6	47.1	80.5
	(100.0)	(100.0)	(100.0)	(46.7)	(61.3)	(31.7)	(53.5)	(39.0)	(68.5)

Notes: Figures in brackets are percentages to respective totals; The 1981 data include interpolated data for Assam and 1991 figures include projected data for Jammu & Kashmir; The 2001 data include estimated total for Kachch district, Morvi, Maliya–Miyana, and Wankaner talukas of Rajkot district, Jodiya taluka of Jamnagar district of Gujarat state, and entire Kinnaur district of HP where Census was not conducted due to natural calamities.

Source: Census documents 2001 and 1961 (in the 1961 census document, a note on the working force estimates for 1901–61 by BR Kalra is available).

TABLE A14.2
Number of Persons Employed per 1000 Persons according to Usual Status and Current Weekly Status Approaches
(Workers Population Ratios, WPRs also called Workforce Participation Rates, WFPRs)

Round	Survey Period		WPRs : Male								WPRs : Female							
	Month	Year	Usual Status				Current weekly Status		Current Daily Status		Usual Status				Current weekly Status		Current Daily Status	
			ps		All (ps+ss)						ps		All (ps+ss)					
			Rural	Urban	Rural	Urbn	Rural	Urban	Rural	Urban	Rural	Urban	Rural	Urabn	Rural	Urban	Rural	Urban
(1)	(2)	(3)	(4)	(5)	(6)	(7)	(8)	(9)	(10)	(11)	(12)	(13)	(14)	(15)	(16)	(17)	(18)	(19)
60	Jan–Jun	2004	527	531	542	540	511	525	471	504	228	121	315	150	245	136	190	118
59	Jan–Dec	2003	536	535	547	541	525	528			235	119	311	146	236	121		
58	Jul–Dec	2002	537	530	546	534	529	523			214	118	281	140	219	118		
57	Jul–Jun	2001–2	531	547	546	553	523	542			241	110	314	139	241	111		
56	Jul–Jun	2000–1	532	525	544	531	525	519			221	116	287	140	217	117		
55	Jul–Jun	1999–2000	**522**	**513**	**531**	**518**	**510**	**509**	**478**	**490**	**231**	**117**	**299**	**139**	**253**	**128**	**204**	**111**
54	Jan–Jun	1998	530	506	539	509	524	504			207	99	263	114	202	99		
53	Jan–Dec	1997	541	516	550	521	535	513			222	111	291	131	222	114		
52	Jul–Jun	1995–6	542	522	551	525	538	520			234	107	295	124	233	109		
51	Jul–Jun	1994–5	547	514	560	519	541	511			237	112	317	136	241	117		
50	**Jul–Jun**	**1993–4**	**538**	**513**	**553**	**521**	**531**	**511**	**504**	**496**	**234**	**121**	**328**	**155**	**267**	**139**	**219**	**120**
49	Jan–Jun	1993	532	506	545	509	527	504			243	113	311	130	232	109		
48	Jan–Dec	1992	541	502	556	507	536	501			250	125	313	146	244	122		
47	Jul–Dec	1991	538	511	546	516	534	509			244	120	294	132	238	117		
46	Jul–Jun	1990–1	542	508	553	513	535	506			242	123	292	143	230	124		
45	Jul–Jun	1989–90	537	501	548	512	528	503			252	124	319	146	230	121		
43	**Jul–Jun**	**1987–8**	**517**	**496**	**539**	**506**	**504**	**492**	**501**	**477**	**245**	**118**	**323**	**152**	**220**	**119**	**207**	**110**
38	**Jan–Dec**	**1983**	**528**	**500**	**547**	**512**	**511**	**492**	**482**	**473**	**248**	**120**	**340**	**151**	**227**	**118**	**198**	**106**
32	**Jul–Jun**	**1977–8**	**537**	**497**	**552**	**508**	**519**	**490**			**248**	**123**	**331**	**156**	**232**	**125**		
27	Oct–Sep	1972–3	na	na	565	533	549	521			na	na	330	143	287	131		

Notes: Figures in bold represent regular quinquennial surveys; others are thin sample surveys; Worker population ratios (WPRs) represent the ratio of worker population in total population in the respective categories; ps—principal status; SS—subsidiary status.

Source: NSS 60th round (January–July 2004) Report No.506(60/10/1) and earlier NSS Reports.

TABLE A14.3
Per 1000 distribution of the Usually Employed by Status of Employment for All (Principal Subsidiary Status Workers)

Round	Survey Month	Period Year	WPRs : Male						WPRs : Female					
			Self-employed	Rural Regular Wage/Salaried	Casual Labour	Self-employed	Urban Regular Wage/Salaried	Casual Labour	Self-employed	Rural Regular Wage/Salaried	Casual Labour	Self-employed	Urban Regular Wage/Salaried	Casual Labour
(1)	(2)	(3)	(4)	(5)	(6)	(7)	(8)	(9)	(10)	(11)	(12)	(13)	(14)	(15)
60	Jan–Jun	2004	572	93	335	441	406	153	616	38	347	446	362	192
59	Jan–Dec	2003	578	87	335	429	415	156	616	33	351	454	339	207
58	Jul–Dec	2002	569	88	344	443	407	150	558	36	406	459	308	233
57	Jul–Jun	2001–2	580	81	339	430	415	154	589	29	382	441	298	261
56	Jul–Jun	2000–1	589	95	316	414	411	175	593	32	375	444	315	241
55	Jul–Jun	1999–2000	550	88	362	415	407	168	573	31	396	453	333	214
54	Jan–Jun	1998	553	70	377	425	395	181	534	25	442	384	327	288
53	Jan–Dec	1997	594	73	333	400	415	185	570	21	409	397	313	290
52	Jul–Jun	1995–6	590	77	333	410	425	165	564	24	412	400	332	268
51	Jul–Jun	1994–5	604	68	328	404	431	165	570	22	408	426	301	273
50	Jul–Jun	1993–4	577	85	338	417	420	163	586	27	387	458	284	258
49	Jan–Jun	1993	591	79	330	389	395	216	585	23	392	407	262	331
48	Jan–Dec	1992	608	83	309	412	394	193	591	32	377	425	288	287
47	Jul–Dec	1991	595	92	313	489	399	172	568	31	401	470	280	250
46	Jul–Jun	1990–1	557	128	315	407	442	151	586	38	376	490	259	251
45	Jul–Jun	1989–90	597	98	305	423	413	164	609	28	363	486	292	222
43	Jul–Jun	1987–8	586	100	314	417	437	146	608	37	355	471	275	254
38	Jan–Dec	1983	605	103	292	409	437	154	619	28	353	458	258	284
32	Jul–Jun	1977–8	628	106	266	404	464	132	321	28	351	495	249	256
27	Oct–Sep	1972–3	659	121	220	392	507	101	645	41	314	484	279	237

Notes: Figures in bold represent regular quinquennial surveys; others are thin sample surveys; Worker population ratios (WPRs) represent the ratio of worker population in total population in the respective categories.

Source: NSS 60th round (January–July 2004) Report No.506(60/10/1) and earlier NSS Reports.

TABLE A14.4
Unemployed Rates

(Number of persons unemployed per 1000 persons in the labour force)

Round	Survey Month	Period Year	Male - Rural				Male - Urban				Female - Rural				Female - Urban			
			Usual Status	Usual Adjusted	Current Weekly Status	Current Daily Status	Usual Status	Usual Adjusted	Current Weekly Status	Current Daily Status	Usual Status	Usual Adjusted	Current Weekly Status	Current Daily Status	Usual Status	Usual Adjusted	Current Weekly Status	Current Daily Status
(1)	(2)	(3)	(4)	(5)	(6)	(7)	(8)	(9)	(10)	(11)	(12)	(13)	(14)	(15)	(16)	(17)	(18)	(19)
60	Jan–Jun	2004	24 (13)	18 (10)	47 (25)	90 (47)	46 (25)	40 (22)	57 (32)	81 (45)	22 (5)	13 (4)	45 (12)	93 (19)	89 (12)	67 (11)	90 (14)	117 (16)
59	Jan–Dec	2003	19 (10)	15 (9)	28 (15)	–	43 (24)	40 (23)	51 (28)	–	10 (2)	6 (2)	16 (4)	–	44 (5)	35 (5)	49 (6)	–
58	Jul–Dec	2002	18 (10)	15 (8)	28 (15)	–	47 (26)	45 (25)	55 (31)	–	10 (2)	6 (2)	16 (4)	–	61 (8)	47 (7)	57 (7)	–
57	Jul–Jun	2001–2	14 (7)	11 (6)	26 (14)	–	42 (24)	39 (22)	46 (26)	–	20 (5)	14 (5)	26 (7)	–	49 (6)	38 (5)	48 (6)	–
56	Jul–Jun	2000–1	16 (9)	14 (8)	23 (12)	–	42 (23)	39 (22)	48 (26)	–	6 (1)	4 (1)	18 (4)	–	38 (5)	29 (4)	39 (5)	–
55	Jul–Jun	1999–2000	21 (11)	17 (9)	39 (21)	72 (37)	48 (26)	45 (24)	56 (30)	73 (38)	15 (4)	10 (3)	37 (10)	70 (15)	71 (9)	57 (8)	73 (10)	94 (12)
54	Jan–Jun	1998	24 (13)	21 (11)	29 (15)	–	53 (28)	51 (27)	54 (29)	–	20 (4)	15 (4)	27 (6)	–	81 (9)	68 (8)	78 (8)	–
53	Jan–Dec	1997	16 (9)	12 (7)	20 (11)	–	37 (21)	39 (21)	43 (23)	–	9 (2)	7 (2)	18 (4)	–	51 (6)	44 (6)	58 (7)	–
52	Jul–Jun	1995–6	15 (8)	13 (7)	18 (10)	–	40 (22)	38 (21)	41 (22)	–	8 (2)	7 (2)	9 (2)	–	36 (4)	31 (4)	35 (4)	–
51	Jul–Jun	1994–5	12 (7)	10 (6)	18 (10)	–	37 (20)	34 (18)	39 (21)	–	5 (1)	4 (1)	12 (3)	–	41 (5)	34 (4)	40 (5)	–
50	Jul–Jun	1993–4	20 (11)	14 (8)	31 (17)	56 (30)	45 (24)	41 (22)	52 (28)	67 (36)	14 (3)	8 (3)	30 (8)	56 (13)	83 (11)	61 (10)	79 (12)	104 (14)
49	Jan–Jun	1993	16	–	–	–	38	–	–	–	10	–	–	–	43	–	–	–
48	Jan–Dec	1992	16	–	–	–	46	–	–	–	12	–	–	–	67	–	–	–
47	Jul–Dec	1991	20	16	22	–	43	39	45	–	18	7	12	–	56	51	50	–
46	Jul–Jun	1990–1	13	–	–	–	45	–	–	–	4	–	–	–	54	–	–	–
45	Jul–Jun	1989–90	16	13	26	–	44	39	45	–	8	6	21	–	39	27	40	–
43	Jul–Jun	1987–8	28	18	42	46	61	52	66	88	35	24	44	67	85	62	92	120
38	Jan–Dec	1983	21	14	37	75	59	51	67	92	14	7	43	90	69	49	75	110
32	Jul–Dec	1977–8	22	13	36	71	65	54	71	94	55	20	41	92	178	124	109	145
27	Oct–Sep	1972–3	–	12	30	38	–	48	60	80	–	5	55	112	–	60	90	137

Notes: Figures in bold represent regular quinquennial surveys; others are thin sample surveys; Worker population ratios (WPRs) represent the ratio of worker population in total population in the respective categories; Figures in brackets indicate the proportion of unemployed per 1000 (person–days).

Source: NSS 60th round (January–July 2004) Report No.506(60/10/1) and earlier NSS Reports.

TABLE A14.5
Statewise Labour Force and Work Force Participation Rates by Place of Residence and Sex, 1983 to 1999–2000

State	Year	Labour Force Participation Rate (LFPRs)						Work Force Participation Rate (WFPRs)					
		Rural			Urabn			Rural			Urabn		
		Male	Female	Persons	Male	Female	Persons	Male	Female	Persons	Male	Female	Persons
(1)	(2)	(3)	(4)	(5)	(6)	(7)	(8)	(9)	(10)	(11)	(12)	(13)	(14)
Andhra Pradesh	1999–2000	61.1	48.0	54.6	53.2	18.4	36.2	99.0	99.6	99.3	96.1	96.7	96.1
	1993–4	63.5	52.1	57.8	56.0	20.7	38.7	99.4	100.0	99.5	97.1	96.1	97.2
	1983	61.2	47.2	54.1	53.4	18.6	36.4	99.0	99.8	99.5	95.3	96.7	95.7
Assam	1999–2000	54.6	16.1	36.4	56.5	13.8	36.8	96.9	93.8	95.9	92.4	81.2	90.2
	1993–4	54.1	17.2	37.3	55.9	12.4	35.2	95.4	92.4	94.6	94.5	74.2	91.2
	1983	51.1	12.9	33.3	52.4	8.6	32.7	98.0	98.0	97.9	95.6	90.4	95.3
Bihar	1999–2000	50.3	17.4	34.4	46.6	8.2	28.7	97.8	99.4	98.3	92.7	91.5	92.7
	1993–4	52.1	17.3	35.6	47.1	7.6	29.1	98.1	99.4	98.6	93.2	90.8	93.1
	1983	51.5	24.9	38.3	49.5	21.0	45.5	98.7	99.7	98.9	95.1	99.2	95.6
Gujarat	1999–2000	58.7	41.3	50.1	54.7	13.8	35.2	99.5	100.0	99.6	98.0	97.8	98.0
	1993–4	58.1	39.7	49.2	55.1	14.8	35.9	98.8	99.7	99.2	97.1	95.9	96.7
	1983	55.4	41.2	48.5	54.5	13.6	35.3	99.2	99.8	99.5	95.4	96.8	
Haryana	1999–2000	48.1	20.2	34.9	52.0	10.1	32.3	98.8	100.0	99.1	97.3	97.0	95.3
	1993–4	47.0	27.2	37.7	53.2	15.7	36.1	98.5	99.6	98.7	97.6	96.8	97.5
	1983	48.0	23.3	36.4	55.8	11.6	35.2	96.8	99.6	97.9	95.7	93.9	
Himachal Pradesh	1999–2000	54.6	47.4	50.9	53.3	14.2	34.4	98.2	99.4	98.8	93.6	91.5	
	1993–4	59.5	52.0	55.6	50.5	20.2	37.2	99.2	100.0	99.6	96.6	99.5	97.6
	1983	53.6	47.8	50.7	57.6	18.5	40.2	98.7	99.5	99.0	92.5	92.8	93.6
Jammu and Kashmir	1999–2000	55.4	33.0	44.7	50.0	6.8	29.6	98.9	99.1	98.9	95.6	91.2	94.9
	1993–4	52.4	39.3	45.9	52.2	14.3	34.0	99.0	99.5	99.3	94.1	90.9	93.2
	1983	55.6	28.5	42.6	55.6	10.8	34.6	99.4	99.7	99.6	96.8	92.6	96.1
Karnataka	1999–2000	60.1	38.1	49.1	56.2	18.6	37.8	99.0	99.7	99.2	97.0	95.7	96.8
	1993–4	60.9	43.2	52.1	55.8	19.1	37.9	99.2	99.5	99.2	97.1	94.8	96.6
	1983	59.1	38.8	49.0	53.5	20.4	37.4	99.3	99.3	99.3	95.7	95.7	95.8
Kerala	1999–2000	58.7	27.3	42.2	59.1	25.4	41.5	94.2	87.2	91.7	94.4	79.9	89.9
	1993–4	56.8	26.4	40.9	59.9	25.0	42.0	94.5	90.2	93.2	93.3	81.2	89.8
	1983	52.2	33.8	42.8	55.1	25.9	39.8	93.1	92.8	92.9	90.6	84.7	88.5
Madhya Pradesh	1999–2000	54.0	38.3	46.4	50.9	13.6	33.4	99.3	99.7	99.6	95.9	98.5	96.4
	1993–4	57.6	41.1	49.7	49.8	14.8	33.2	99.3	99.8	99.4	94.6	95.9	94.9
	1983	56.4	43.3	49.9	49.3	14.7	33.2	99.7	100.0	99.8	96.9	98.8	97.1
Maharashtra	1999–2000	54.2	43.7	49.0	56.3	14.6	37.3	98.0	99.3	98.8	94.5	93.8	94.3
	1993–4	55.8	47.8	51.8	54.9	17.7	36.1	98.7	99.8	99.2	95.8	95.5	95.4
	1983	56.6	47.4	52.0	54.2	15.7	33.1	99.1	99.8	99.5	94.6	96.6	95.1
Orissa	1999–2000	56.4	30.2	43.2	51.1	15.3	33.9	97.7	99.0	97.9	93.0	94.8	93.5
	1993–4	57.7	31.9	44.9	54.6	16.1	33.1	98.1	99.4	98.4	93.4	93.8	93.4
	1983	58.3	29.6	43.9	52.6	11.8	36.7	98.5	99.4	99.0	95.4	94.1	95.0
Punjab	1999–2000	54.3	28.2	41.7	56.5	12.8	36.3	97.6	99.3	98.3	97.2	97.7	97.2
	1993–4	55.4	22.3	39.7	57.1	9.9	34.8	98.6	98.7	98.7	96.8	93.9	96.6
	1983	59.3	32.4	46.6	55.8	13.6	36.4	98.0	98.4	97.9	96.4	95.5	95.2
Rajasthan	1999–2000	50.3	38.9	44.8	49.9	14.1	33.2	99.4	99.7	99.6	97.4	97.9	97.3
	1993–4	54.2	45.8	50.2	49.8	16.3	34.0	99.6	99.8	99.6	98.4	100.0	98.5
	1983	55.3	46.5	51.1	49.6	19.7	35.3	99.5	100.0	99.7	96.2	99.1	97.1
Tamil Nadu	1999–2000	61.0	43.4	52.3	58.5	22.7	41.0	97.4	99.1	98.1	96.2	94.7	95.9
	1993–4	61.3	48.1	54.6	60.1	24.7	42.3	98.2	99.4	98.7	95.7	93.1	95.0
	1983	61.0	46.0	53.4	57.9	22.5	40.2	97.6	98.8	98.2	93.3	94.0	93.6
Uttar Pradesh	1999–2000	48.6	20.1	34.8	51.2	9.7	31.7	99.0	100.0	99.1	95.7	96.9	95.9
	1993–4	52.7	21.9	38.1	49.8	10.3	31.4	99.1	100.0	99.2	96.8	99.0	97.1
	1983	53.5	25.7	40.3	52.2	9.9	32.3	99.4	100.0	99.4	96.2	97.4	96.2
West Bengal	1999–2000	54.9	16.5	35.9	61.2	12.9	37.8	97.3	97.0	97.2	92.6	90.7	92.6
	1993–4	56.7	18.9	38.2	58.7	16.7	39.3	98.2	97.9	98.4	93.7	85.6	92.1
	1983	55.2	19.6	37.8	59.1	14.8	38.7	97.5	98.7	97.7	91.7	88.4	91.1
All India	1999–2000	54.0	30.2		54.2	14.7		53.1	29.9	41.7	51.8	13.9	33.7
	1993–4	56.1	33.0		54.3	16.5		55.3	32.8	44.4	52.1	15.5	34.7
	1983							54.7	34.0	44.5	51.2	15.1	34.0

Notes: Labour force participation rates (LFPRs) represent the ratio of worker population in total population in the respective categories; The work force participation rate (WFPR) represents the proportion of the labour force actually working (in percentage).

Sources: GOI (1990), *Sarvekshana*, Vol. XIV, Nos 1 & 2, July–September; GOI (1997), *Employment and Unemployment in India*, NSS Report No 409, March 1977, pp. 62–3, 78–9; GOI (2001), *Employment and Unemployment Situation in India*, 1999–2000: Part 1, NSS Report No. 458, May 2001, pp. 62–3, 80–1.

TABLE A14.6
Statewise Sectoral Distribution of Usual (Principal + Subsidiary) Status Workers, 1983 to 1999–2000

State	Year	Agriculture			Manufacturing			Non-agriculture		
		Rural	Urban	Total	Rural	Urban	Total	Rural	Urban	Total
(1)	(2)	(3)	(4)	(5)	(6)	(7)	(8)	(9)	(10)	(11)
Andhra Pradesh	1999–2000	78.8	9.6	65.5	6.2	22.0	9.2	21.2	90.4	34.5
	1993–4	79.2	16.5	67.1	7.6	22.0	10.1	20.8	83.5	32.9
	1983	80.1	15.7	69.3	7.9	25.0	10.7	19.9	84.3	30.7
Assam	1999–2000	67.6	5.9	60.2	5.4	12.9	6.3	32.4	94.1	39.8
	1993–4	78.9	3.0	70.5	5.5	13.8	6.4	21.1	97.0	29.5
	1983	79.3	7.4	72.3	4.4	16.2	5.6	20.7	92.6	27.7
Bihar	1999–2000	80.6	11.1	73.1	6.4	21.2	8.0	19.4	88.9	26.9
	1993–4	84.2	11.9	76.6	4.1	21.5	6.0	15.8	88.1	23.4
	1983	83.5	14.3	76.5	6.3	24.8	8.1	16.5	85.7	23.5
Gujarat	1999–2000	80.0	9.8	59.7	7.0	27.3	12.8	20.0	90.2	40.3
	1993–4	78.8	8.0	58.9	9.5	34.8	16.6	21.2	92.0	41.1
	1983	85.0	18.0	68.7	5.7	35.0	12.9	15.0	82.0	31.3
Haryana	1999–2000	68.4	10.6	53.0	8.3	23.9	12.5	31.6	89.4	47.0
	1993–4	71.7	11.6	56.9	4.8	28.3	10.6	28.3	88.4	43.1
	1983	77.1	16.0	64.1	6.4	26.1	10.6	22.9	84.0	35.9
Himachal Pradesh	1999–2000	73.8	10.4	69.6	4.7	9.5	5.0	26.2	89.6	30.4
	1993–4	79.6	17.8	75.9	3.6	4.6	3.7	20.4	82.2	24.1
	1983	87.0	12.4	82.8	3.4	12.0	3.9	13.0	87.6	17.2
Jammu and Kashmir	1999–2000	73.7	12.8	62.9	5.6	10.5	6.5	26.3	87.2	37.1
	1993–4	75.1	13.8	63.9	4.2	12.9	5.8	24.9	86.2	36.1
	1983	79.7	16.1	68.9	4.7	28.7	8.8	20.3	83.9	31.1
Karnataka	1983	84.4	19.9	69.6	6.0	28.9	11.3	15.6	80.1	30.4
	1993–4	81.9	16.6	65.7	6.7	26.9	11.7	18.1	83.4	34.3
	1999–2000	82.1	10.9	62.5	5.9	27.1	11.8	17.9	89.1	37.5
Kerala	1999–2000	48.5	9.6	38.7	14.3	23.5	16.6	51.5	90.4	61.3
	1993–4	56.0	25.4	48.1	13.5	21.4	15.5	44.0	74.6	51.9
	1983	92.8	27.7	56.3	14.7	22.5	16.1	37.2	72.3	43.7
Madhya Pradesh	1999–2000	87.2	15.5	73.9	4.2	21.7	7.4	12.8	84.5	26.1
	1993–4	89.9	16.4	77.7	3.5	20.5	6.3	10.1	83.6	22.3
	1983	90.3	15.4	79.5	3.9	25.9	7.1	9.7	84.6	20.5
Maharashtra	1999–2000	82.7	5.7	56.4	5.2	28.1	13.1	17.3	94.3	43.6
	1993–4	82.6	9.2	59.4	5.3	27.5	12.3	17.4	90.8	40.6
	1983	85.8	12.6	66.2	5.0	31.7	12.1	14.2	87.4	33.8
Orissa	1999–2000	78.5	13.3	71.0	8.5	21.7	10.0	21.5	86.7	29.0
	1993–4	81.0	15.8	73.8	6.8	19.9	8.2	19.0	84.2	26.2
	1983	79.2	16.2	73.3	8.7	24.0	10.1	20.8	83.8	26.7
Punjab	1999–2000	72.5	8.9	53.4	7.8	26.8	13.5	27.5	91.1	46.6
	1993–4	74.5	9.2	56.4	5.9	28.5	12.2	25.5	90.8	43.6
	1983	82.5	14.0	66.8	6.4	30.1	11.8	17.5	86.0	33.2
Rajasthan	1999–2000	77.6	13.1	65.9	4.9	24.3	8.4	22.4	86.9	34.1
	1993–4	79.8	16.3	69.2	4.6	21.7	7.4	20.2	83.7	30.8
	1983	86.7	27.3	77.6	4.3	23.0	7.2	13.3	72.7	22.4
Tamil Nadu	1999–2000	68.3	9.0	46.8	14.4	33.4	21.3	31.7	91.0	53.2
	1993–4	70.2	11.9	52.5	13.6	32.2	19.3	29.8	88.1	47.5
	1983	74.3	15.4	58.9	11.4	34.8	17.5	25.7	84.6	41.1
Uttar Pradesh	1999–2000	76.1	9.4	63.6	8.6	29.2	12.5	23.9	90.6	36.4
	1993–4	80.0	15.0	69.0	7.1	27.1	10.5	20.0	85.0	31.0
	1983	82.0	12.2	71.7	7.4	29.2	10.6	18.0	87.8	28.3
West Bengal	1999–2000	63.0	3.0	46.1	17.7	31.1	21.4	37.0	97.0	53.9
	1993–4	63.6	5.7	48.1	17.0	31.8	21.0	36.4	94.3	51.9
	1983	73.6	4.8	56.4	11.2	36.4	17.5	26.4	95.2	43.6

Source: Chadha, G.K. and P.P. Sahu (2002), 'Post-Reform Setbacks In Rural Employment—Issues That Need Further Scrutiny', *Economic and Political Weekly*, 25 May.

TABLE A14.7
Statewise Composition of Rural and Urban Usual (Principal + Subsidiary) Status Workers, 1983 to 1999–2000

State	Year	Rural Persons				Urban Persons				All Persons			
		SE	RE	CL	ICL	SE	RE	CL	ICL	SE	RE	CL	ICL
(1)	(2)	(3)	(4)	(5)	(6)	(7)	(8)	(9)	(10)	(11)	(12)	(13)	(14)
Andhra Pradesh	1999–2000	45.80	5.90	48.30	819	36.70	38.70	24.60	64	44.10	12.14	43.75	360
	1993–4	47.50	5.20	47.30	910	40.30	34.10	25.60	75	46.01	10.92	43.07	394
	1983	48.10	7.74	43.46	561	41.80	37.38	20.67	55	47.09	12.74	39.58	311
Assam	1999–2000	58.20	16.60	25.20	152	44.70	42.90	12.40	29	56.49	19.74	23.77	120
	1993–4	57.80	14.40	27.80	193	45.30	43.10	11.60	27	56.20	17.63	26.16	148
	1983	61.60	18.70	19.10	102	44.35	45.88	9.10	20	60.00	21.49	18.13	84
Bihar	1999–2000	52.30	3.50	44.20	1263	53.70	30.20	16.10	53	52.52	13.68	30.64	640
	1993–4	52.30	4.00	43.70	1093	47.80	35.60	16.60	47	51.72	7.19	41.09	572
	1983	56.62	4.88	37.89	776	48.45	33.57	17.64	53	55.67	8.06	35.68	443
Gujarat	1999–2000	54.20	6.30	39.50	627	41.00	34.10	24.90	73	50.36	14.45	35.19	244
	1993–4	50.20	6.80	43.00	632	38.30	40.90	20.80	51	46.91	16.22	36.87	227
	1983	59.75	5.15	34.64	672	41.66	39.94	18.32	46	55.30	13.68	30.64	224
Haryana	1999–2000	66.40	12.40	21.20	171	44.80	42.80	12.40	29	60.52	20.61	18.87	92
	1993–4	67.70	9.40	22.90	244	45.00	40.40	14.60	36	62.38	16.95	20.67	122
	1983	70.23	12.85	19.90	155	50.31	38.90	10.71	28	62.49	18.49	17.87	97
Himachal Pradesh	1999–2000	78.70	10.10	11.20	111	37.60	51.60	10.80	21	75.53	13.04	11.43	88
	1993–4	85.60	7.10	7.30	103	38.40	52.50	9.10	17	82.39	9.99	7.62	76
	1983	89.17	5.21	5.51	106	36.87	54.86	8.27	15	85.79	8.26	5.81	70
Jammu and Kashmir	1999–2000	81.80	8.60	9.60	112	48.10	40.40	11.50	28	75.90	14.25	9.84	69
	1993–4	82.40	10.00	7.60	76	45.00	50.30	4.70	9	75.20	17.68	7.12	40
	1983	82.57	6.38	10.79	169	56.06	36.89	6.57	18	77.79	11.85	9.52	80
Karnataka	1999–2000	50.20	5.30	44.50	840	38.80	39.60	21.60	55	47.03	14.83	38.14	257
	1993–4	55.90	4.80	39.30	819	41.30	36.90	21.80	59	52.40	12.78	34.82	272
	1983	55.93	4.65	38.82	835	35.36	36.80	27.65	75	51.16	12.20	36.18	297
Kerala	1999–2000	42.90	13.70	43.40	317	41.30	29.10	29.60	102	42.35	17.53	40.12	229
	1993–4	45.40	11.50	43.10	375	39.80	26.80	33.40	125	43.86	15.44	40.70	264
	1983	50.17	13.16	36.60	278	41.20	30.06	28.63	95	48.37	16.35	35.21	215
Madhya Pradesh	1999–2000	56.60	3.50	39.90	1140	46.30	33.00	20.70	63	54.63	9.01	36.36	404
	1993–4	61.90	4.00	34.10	853	41.30	38.50	20.20	52	58.56	9.67	31.77	329
	1983	66.20	6.13	27.28	445	40.58	42.42	16.87	40	62.49	11.33	25.76	227
Maharashtra	1999–2000	44.30	7.30	48.40	663	33.80	51.50	14.70	29	40.69	22.44	36.87	164
	1993–4	48.70	7.60	43.70	575	36.60	49.60	13.80	28	44.95	20.84	34.21	164
	1983	51.39	8.02	40.50	505	31.14	49.02	17.52	36	46.52	19.21	34.20	178
Orissa	1999–2000	48.70	4.20	47.10	1121	42.80	35.80	21.40	60	48.00	7.88	44.12	560
	1993–4	56.40	4.50	39.10	869	37.20	44.30	18.50	42	54.33	8.84	36.82	416
	1983	53.33	7.99	38.32	480	38.15	42.32	19.39	46	51.92	11.23	36.51	325
Punjab	1999–2000	65.50	13.00	21.50	165	47.70	40.90	11.40	28	59.88	21.47	18.65	87
	1993–4	62.70	10.50	26.80	255	48.90	40.00	11.10	28	58.84	18.75	22.41	120
	1983	73.82	9.44	16.67	177	48.95	42.89	7.48	17	68.03	16.93	14.94	88
Rajasthan	1999–2000	79.90	4.90	15.20	310	49.90	36.50	13.60	37	74.49	10.63	14.88	140
	1993–4	79.00	4.60	16.40	357	51.00	37.90	11.10	29	74.37	10.15	15.48	152
	1983	84.52	3.95	11.44	289	60.54	26.69	12.69	48	80.76	7.53	11.64	154
Tamil Nadu	1999–2000	36.70	11.80	51.50	436	34.70	44.10	21.20	48	36.00	23.51	40.49	172
	1993–4	41.60	9.30	49.10	528	36.10	37.30	26.60	71	39.89	17.86	42.24	236
	1983	44.24	8.23	47.18	574	35.63	35.20	29.07	83	41.94	15.44	42.17	273
Uttar Pradesh	1999–2000	72.70	5.60	21.70	388	55.00	32.30	12.70	39	69.32	10.61	20.07	189
	1993–4	74.30	4.50	21.10	469	58.70	29.50	11.80	40	71.68	8.65	19.66	227
	1983	77.78	4.77	17.30	363	55.06	32.42	12.27	38	74.40	8.91	16.53	185
West Bengal	1999–2000	52.20	7.00	40.80	583	43.20	40.00	16.82	42	49.60	16.25	34.15	210
	1993–4	55.70	9.50	34.80	366	37.30	47.00	15.70	33	50.76	19.60	29.63	151
	1983	52.34	9.85	37.57	381	35.64	49.79	14.57	29	48.02	20.20	31.61	156

Notes: SE—self-employed; RE—regular salaried; CL—casual; Labour; ICL—index of casualization; CIL shows the number of casual wage earners for every 100 regular salaried employees.

Source: As in Table A14.6.

TABLE A14.8
Trends in Number and Employment of Agricultural (excluding crop production and plantation)
and Non-Agricultural Enterprises, 1980–2005 and Growth

		Total Employment in Thousands										
		5th Economic Census 2005			4th Economic Census 1998			3rd Economic Census 1990			2nd Economic Census 1980		
		Rural	Urban	Combined	Rural	Urban	Combined	Rural	Urban	Combined	Rural	Urban	Combined
	All-India	50185	48782	98968	39901	43399	83299	33296	38780	72076	24474	29194	53668
1	Andhra Pradesh	5718	3152	8871	4635	2877	7512	4082	2652	6734	2658	2054	4712
2	Arunachal Pradesh	64	43	107	52	28	81	62	31	93	32	13	44
3	Assam	1792	943	2735	1551	644	2195	1120	570	1689	Census not conducted		
4	Bihar	1383	893	2276	1775	1654	3429	1743	1710	3454	1532	1245	2777
5	Chattisgarh	1014	597	1610	Included in Madhya Pradesh								
6	Goa	120	125	246	98	118	216	98	121	219	136	116	252
7	Gujarat	2569	3245	5814	2351	2929	5280	2022	2704	4726	1528	2124	3652
8	Haryana	1074	1138	2212	595	964	1559	524	829	1353	370	604	974
9	Himachal Pradesh	462	205	667	387	189	577	312	156	469	236	108	344
10	Jammu and Kashmir	364	387	752	217	256	474	Census not conducted			247	242	489
11	Jharkhand	580	589	1169	Included in Bihar								
12	Karnataka	3320	2659	5978	2757	2496	5253	2588	2495	5083	2003	1863	3866
13	Kerala	3684	1876	5559	2760	1089	3849	1889	1400	3289	1603	849	2452
14	Madhya Pradesh	1868	2352	4220	2441	2815	5256	2363	2522	4886	1601	1689	3290
15	Maharashtra	4625	7201	11827	3688	6756	10445	2847	6113	8960	2145	4605	6750
16	Manipur	121	114	235	97	104	201	77	80	157	46	59	105
17	Meghalaya	137	107	245	97	87	184	85	85	170	49	59	109
18	Mizoram	32	69	101	23	54	77	21	51	72	18	27	46
19	Nagaland	73	111	184	64	111	175	50	80	130	39	36	75
20	Orissa	2572	1004	3575	2158	937	3095	1716	896	2612	1250	699	1949
21	Punjab	1059	1628	2688	743	1357	2100	580	1190	1770	415	921	1336
22	Rajasthan	2271	1969	4240	1793	1749	3542	1318	1520	2838	1138	1179	2317
23	Sikkim	41	28	69	27	21	48	28	19	47	15	15	31
24	Tamil Nadu	5188	4678	9867	3583	3608	7191	2882	3354	6236	2305	2841	5146
25	Tripura	249	130	379	168	101	268	132	89	220	83	52	134
26	Uttar Pradesh	4196	4344	8540	3232	4248	7480	2949	3959	6909	2621	3122	5743
27	Uttranchal	396	353	749	Included in Uttar Pradesh								
28	West Bengal	4921	4397	9318	4374	4397	8771	3636	3811	7448	2242	3101	5343
	Chandigarh	13	239	252	6	212	218	8	195	203	4	117	121
	Delhi	73	4007	4080	86	3415	3501	73	2012	2085	96	1375	1471
	Pondicherry	64	129	193	49	132	182	30	90	120	26	55	81
	Andaman & Nicobar Islands	28	36	64	37	25	63	31	21	52	21	17	38
	Dadra and Nagar Haveli	47	18	65	28	5	33	12	3	14	5	2	7
	Daman and Diu	57	10	68	21	11	32	11	10	21	Included in Goa		
	Lakshadweep	7	5	12	5	11	16	6	10	16	8	6	14

(contd.)

TABLE A14.8 (contd.)

		Annual Growth Rate - Employment (per cent)										
		1990–2005			1998–2005			1990–8			1980–90		
		Rural	Urban	Combined	Rural	Urban	Combined	Rural	Urban	Combined	Rural	Urban	Combined
	All–India	(2.72)	(1.49)	(2.08)	(3.33)	(1.68)	(2.49)	(2.15)	(1.34)	(1.71)	(2.88)	(2.81)	(2.84)
1	Andhra Pradesh	(2.27)	(1.16)	(1.85)	(3.05)	(1.32)	(2.40)	(1.60)	(1.02)	(1.38)	(4.38)	(2.59)	(3.64)
2	Arunachal Pradesh	(0.26)	(2.09)	(0.93)	(3.07)	(6.02)	(4.17)	(–2.13)	(–1.23)	(–1.82)	(6.97)	(9.65)	(7.80)
3	Assam	(3.18)	(3.42)	(3.26)	(2.08)	(5.61)	(3.19)	(4.15)	(1.54)	(3.32)	na		
4	Bihar	(0.80)	(–0.95)	(–0.02)	(1.79)	(–1.77)	(0.27)	(–0.95)	(–0.42)	(–0.68)	(1.30)	(3.23)	(2.20)
5	Chattisgarh	na			(3.82)	(1.19)	(2.78)	na			na		
6	Goa	(1.41)	(0.23)	(0.78)	(2.99)	(0.88)	(1.87)	(0.04)	(–0.34)	(0.17)	na		
7	Gujarat	(1.61)	(1.22)	(1.39)	(1.27)	(1.48)	(1.39)	(1.90)	(1.01)	(1.40)	(2.84)	(2.44)	(2.61)
8	Haryana	(4.90)	(2.13)	(3.33)	(8.80)	(2.40)	(5.12)	(1.60)	(1.90)	(1.79)	(3.56)	(3.21)	(3.34)
9	Himachal Pradesh	(2.64)	(1.82)	(2.38)	(2.54)	(1.13)	(2.09)	(2.73)	(2.43)	(2.63)	(2.85)	(3.73)	(3.13)
10	Jammu and Kashmir	na			(7.65)	(6.08)	(6.82)	na			na		
11	Jharkhand	na			(0.66)	(–1.21)	(–0.32)	na			na		
12	Karnataka	(1.67)	(0.43)	(1.09)	(2.69)	(0.91)	(1.86)	(0.79)	(0.01)	(0.41)	(2.60)	(2.96)	(2.77)
13	Kerala	(4.55)	(1.97)	(3.56)	(4.21)	(8.08)	(5.39)	(4.85)	(–3.09)	(1.99)	(1.66)	(5.13)	(2.98)
14	Madhya Pradesh	(1.33)	(1.05)	(1.19)	(1.69)	(0.54)	(1.04)	(0.41)	(1.38)	(0.92)	(3.97)	(4.09)	(4.03)
15	Maharashtra	(3.29)	(1.10)	(1.87)	(3.29)	(0.91)	(1.79)	(3.29)	(1.26)	(1.93)	(2.87)	(2.87)	(2.87)
16	Manipur	(3.03)	(2.36)	(2.70)	(3.24)	(1.28)	(2.25)	(2.85)	(3.32)	(3.09)	(5.26)	(3.16)	(4.13)
17	Meghalaya	(3.28)	(1.54)	(2.46)	(5.05)	(3.02)	(4.12)	(1.76)	(0.26)	(1.03)	(5.55)	(3.71)	(4.58)
18	Mizoram	(2.91)	(1.99)	(2.27)	(4.96)	(3.45)	(3.91)	(1.15)	(0.74)	(0.86)	(1.27)	(6.51)	(4.67)
19	Nagaland	(2.65)	(2.17)	(2.35)	(1.95)	(0.02)	(0.75)	(3.27)	(4.08)	(3.78)	(2.44)	(8.46)	(5.70)
20	Orissa	(2.73)	(0.76)	(2.11)	(2.54)	(0.99)	(2.08)	(2.90)	(0.56)	(2.14)	(3.22)	(2.51)	(2.97)
21	Punjab	(4.10)	(2.11)	(2.82)	(5.19)	(2.64)	(3.59)	(3.15)	(1.65)	(2.16)	(3.40)	(2.60)	(2.85)
22	Rajasthan	(3.69)	(1.74)	(2.71)	(3.44)	(1.71)	(2.60)	(3.92)	(1.77)	(2.81)	(1.48)	(2.57)	(2.05)
23	Sikkim	(2.49)	(2.71)	(2.58)	(6.41)	(4.32)	(5.52)	(–0.81)	(1.33)	(0.08)	(6.36)	(2.22)	(4.48)
24	Tamil Nadu	(4.00)	(2.24)	(3.11)	(5.43)	(3.78)	(4.62)	(2.76)	(0.91)	(1.80)	(2.26)	(1.68)	(1.94)
25	Tripura	(4.34)	(2.58)	(3.68)	(5.84)	(3.71)	(5.07)	(3.05)	(1.60)	(2.48)	(4.80)	(5.50)	(5.07)
26	Uttar Pradesh	(2.99)	(1.15)	(1.99)	(4.98)	(1.40)	(3.03)	(1.76)	(0.88)	(1.27)	(1.19)	(2.40)	(1.87)
27	Uttranchal	na			(7.06)	(2.04)	(4.45)	na			na		
28	West Bengal	(2.04)	(0.96)	(1.51)	(1.70)	(–0.00)	(0.87)	(2.34)	(1.80)	(2.07)	(4.95)	(2.09)	(3.38)
	Chandigarh	(3.03)	(1.37)	(1.44)	(12.11)	(1.71)	(2.07)	(–4.30)	(1.07)	(0.89)	(6.94)	(5.25)	(5.31)
	Delhi	(0.05)	(4.70)	(4.58)	(–2.26)	(2.31)	(2.21)	(2.12)	(6.84)	(6.70)	(–2.81)	(3.88)	(3.55)
	Pondicherry	(5.09)	(2.46)	(3.22)	(3.83)	(–0.37)	(0.88)	(6.21)	(5.00)	(5.31)	(1.66)	(4.93)	(3.99)
	Andaman & Nicobar Islands	(–0.67)	(3.60)	(1.36)	(–3.90)	(5.15)	(0.35)	(2.25)	(2.26)	(2.25)	(4.02)	(2.39)	(3.33)
	Dadra and Nagar Haveli	(9.82)	(13.12)	(10.59)	(7.56)	(22.03)	(10.33)	(11.82)	(5.85)	(10.81)	(8.28)	(3.86)	(7.23)
	Daman and Diu	(11.91)	(0.29)	(8.25)	(15.32)	(–0.06)	(11.49)	(9.01)	(0.60)	(5.50)	Not available		
	Lakshadweep	(0.45)	(–4.13)	(–1.99)	(3.53)	(–9.60)	(–4.00)	(–2.17)	(0.91)	(–0.20)	(–2.99)	(5.89)	(1.40)

(contd.)

TABLE A14.8 (contd.)

		Number of Enterprises in Thousands											
		5th Economic Census 2005			4th Economic Census 1998			3rd Economic Census 1990			2nd Economic Census 1980		
		Rural	Urban	Combined	Rural	Urban	Combined	Rural	Urban	Combined	Rural	Urban	Combined
	All-India	25809	16314	42124	17707	12641	30349	14722	10280	25002	11141	7220	18362
1	Andhra Pradesh	2896	1128	4023	2007	895	2903	1737	749	2487	1152	462	1614
2	Arunachal Pradesh	19	10	29	15	6	21	16	5	21	9	2	11
3	Assam	633	293	926	404	189	593	353	143	495	census not conducted		
4	Bihar	872	418	1290	872	571	1443	783	445	1228	713	331	1045
5	Chattisgarh	454	202	656	Included in Madhya Pradesh							
6	Goa	43	38	81	38	34	72	34	27	61	32	21	53
7	Gujarat	1343	1075	2419	1084	830	1915	842	656	1498	699	490	1188
8	Haryana	453	375	828	237	295	533	209	248	457	159	161	320
9	Himachal Pradesh	219	52	272	182	44	225	148	35	183	115	24	139
10	Jammu and Kashmir	185	139	324	111	105	216	census not conducted			125	71	197
11	Jharkhand	294	197	491	Included in Bihar							
12	Karnataka	1598	902	2500	1152	760	1912	1033	661	1694	883	492	1375
13	Kerala	2117	731	2848	1241	324	1565	827	402	1229	659	213	872
14	Madhya Pradesh	953	826	1778	1207	917	2124	1154	720	1873	867	474	1341
15	Maharashtra	2262	2113	4375	1613	1621	3234	1308	1315	2624	965	874	1839
16	Manipur	58	46	104	43	37	80	34	27	61	19	16	35
17	Meghalaya	56	28	85	36	20	56	32	18	50	21	12	33
18	Mizoram	18	29	47	10	15	25	10	13	23	8	6	13
19	Nagaland	21	17	38	14	16	30	13	11	24	9	7	16
20	Orissa	1425	367	1791	1157	293	1450	853	240	1094	629	174	804
21	Punjab	497	576	1072	303	415	717	254	345	599	202	261	463
22	Rajasthan	1210	746	1957	911	620	1531	689	481	1169	606	357	964
23	Sikkim	14	6	19	8	5	13	7	3	11	5	3	8
24	Tamil Nadu	2737	1710	4447	1408	1106	2514	1167	944	2111	981	787	1767
25	Tripura	136	52	188	70	34	104	61	25	85	39	14	54
26	Uttar Pradesh	2194	1822	4016	1479	1564	3043	1291	1342	2633	1151	1015	2166
27	Uttranchal	200	128	329	Included in Uttar Pradesh							
28	West Bengal	2831	1455	4286	2044	1191	3234	1818	932	2750	1044	659	1704
	Chandigarh	8	58	66	3	37	40	5	29	33	1	15	16
	Delhi	28	726	754	30	656	686	23	432	455	28	262	290
	Pondicherry	17	33	50	13	29	43	10	21	31	10	13	23
	Andaman & Nicobar Islands	6	7	12	9	5	14	8	3	12	5	2	7
	Dadra and Nagar Haveli	5	4	9	3	1	4	2	1	3	1	0	2
	Daman and Diu	7	4	11	3	3	6	2	3	5	included in Goa	
	Lakshadweep	2	1	3	2	3	5	2	3	5	3	1	5

(contd.)

TABLE A14.8 (contd.)   (concluded)

		Annual Growth Rate - Number of Enterprises (per cent)										
		1990–2005			1998–2005			1990–8			1980–90		
		Rural	Urban	Combined	Rural	Urban	Combined	Rural	Urban	Combined	Rural	Urban	Combined
	All–India	(3.76)	(3.07)	(3.49)	(5.53)	(3.71)	(4.80)	(2.27)	(2.50)	(2.36)	(2.83)	(3.60)	(3.14)
1	Andhra Pradesh	(3.47)	(2.76)	(3.26)	(5.37)	(3.35)	(4.78)	(1.82)	(2.25)	(1.95)	(4.19)	(4.96)	(4.42)
2	Arunachal Pradesh	(1.07)	(4.86)	(2.15)	(3.65)	(7.08)	(4.74)	(−1.14)	(2.96)	(−0.07)	(5.72)	(10.25)	(6.61)
3	Assam	(3.98)	(4.91)	(4.26)	(6.62)	(6.46)	(6.57)	(1.72)	(3.58)	(2.28)	na		
4	Bihar	(2.69)	(2.18)	(2.51)	(4.50)	(0.50)	(3.07)	(1.35)	(3.15)	(2.03)	(0.94)	(3.00)	(1.63)
5	Chattisgarh	na			(3.24)	(2.64)	(3.06)	na			na		
6	Goa	(1.59)	(2.34)	(1.93)	(1.75)	(1.75)	(1.75)	(1.46)	(2.85)	(2.09)	na		
7	Gujarat	(3.17)	(3.35)	(3.25)	(3.11)	(3.77)	(3.40)	(3.22)	(2.99)	(3.12)	(1.88)	(2.96)	(2.34)
8	Haryana	(5.31)	(2.78)	(4.04)	(9.68)	(3.46)	(6.50)	(1.62)	(2.19)	(1.93)	(2.78)	(4.43)	(3.64)
9	Himachal Pradesh	(2.68)	(2.65)	(2.67)	(2.73)	(2.60)	(2.71)	(2.63)	(2.70)	(2.64)	(2.49)	(4.00)	(2.76)
10	Jammu and Kashmir	na			(7.64)	(4.06)	(5.99)	na			na		
11	Jharkhand	na			(3.44)	(2.41)	(3.02)	na			na		
12	Karnataka	(2.95)	(2.10)	(2.63)	(4.78)	(2.49)	(3.91)	(1.37)	(1.76)	(1.52)	(1.59)	(2.98)	(2.11)
13	Kerala	(6.47)	(4.07)	(5.77)	(7.93)	(12.33)	(8.93)	(5.21)	(−2.66)	(3.07)	(2.29)	(6.56)	(3.49)
14	Madhya Pradesh	(1.33)	(2.40)	(1.76)	(1.74)	(1.40)	(1.58)	(0.57)	(3.07)	(1.58)	(2.90)	(4.27)	(3.40)
15	Maharashtra	(3.72)	(3.21)	(3.47)	(4.95)	(3.86)	(4.41)	(2.65)	(2.65)	(2.65)	(3.09)	(4.17)	(3.61)
16	Manipur	(3.71)	(3.48)	(3.61)	(4.46)	(2.92)	(3.76)	(3.05)	(3.97)	(3.47)	(6.01)	(5.62)	(5.84)
17	Meghalaya	(3.81)	(3.18)	(3.59)	(6.48)	(5.05)	(5.98)	(1.54)	(1.56)	(1.55)	(4.44)	(4.43)	(4.24)
18	Mizoram	(4.34)	(5.33)	(4.94)	(8.40)	(10.39)	(9.60)	(0.91)	(0.98)	(0.95)	(2.23)	(8.77)	(5.53)
19	Nagaland	(3.34)	(2.96)	(3.17)	(6.05)	(1.22)	(3.64)	(1.02)	(4.51)	(2.75)	(3.91)	(4.64)	(4.24)
20	Orissa	(3.48)	(2.86)	(3.35)	(3.02)	(3.26)	(3.07)	(3.88)	(2.51)	(3.59)	(3.09)	(3.25)	(3.13)
21	Punjab	(4.56)	(3.47)	(3.95)	(7.34)	(4.80)	(5.91)	(2.19)	(2.33)	(2.27)	(2.35)	(2.81)	(2.61)
22	Rajasthan	(3.83)	(2.98)	(3.49)	(4.15)	(2.69)	(3.57)	(3.55)	(3.24)	(3.42)	(1.28)	(3.01)	(1.95)
23	Sikkim	(4.24)	(3.66)	(4.06)	(8.39)	(1.16)	(5.83)	(0.74)	(5.89)	(2.54)	(3.40)	(1.08)	(2.62)
24	Tamil Nadu	(5.85)	(4.04)	(5.09)	(9.96)	(6.43)	(8.49)	(2.38)	(2.00)	(2.21)	(1.75)	(1.84)	(1.79)
25	Tripura	(5.52)	(5.12)	(5.41)	(9.85)	(6.37)	(8.79)	(1.87)	(4.05)	(2.53)	(4.41)	(5.72)	(4.77)
26	Uttar Pradesh	(4.20)	(2.52)	(3.29)	(7.07)	(3.14)	(5.14)	(1.71)	(1.93)	(1.83)	(1.15)	(2.83)	(1.97)
27	Uttranchal	na			(7.72)	(4.16)	(6.21)	na			na		
28	West Bengal	(3.00)	(3.01)	(3.00)	(4.77)	(2.90)	(4.10)	(1.48)	(3.11)	(2.05)	(5.70)	(3.52)	(4.90)
	Chandigarh	(3.50)	(4.82)	(4.65)	(15.57)	(6.67)	(7.46)	(−6.01)	(3.22)	(2.25)	(15.16)	(6.92)	(7.72)
	Delhi	(1.19)	(3.53)	(3.43)	(−0.91)	(1.45)	(1.36)	(3.07)	(5.38)	(5.27)	(−1.84)	(5.12)	(4.60)
	Pondicherry	(3.70)	(3.16)	(3.33)	(3.37)	(1.67)	(2.22)	(3.99)	(4.47)	(4.32)	(−0.31)	(4.99)	(2.94)
	Andaman & Nicobar Islands	(−2.40)	(4.88)	(0.54)	(−6.16)	(4.92)	(−1.36)	(0.82)	(3.86)	(1.78)	(4.70)	(5.08)	(4.81)
	Dadra and Nagar Haveli	(6.49)	(12.78)	(8.32)	(8.65)	(20.98)	(12.31)	(3.69)	(4.82)	(3.94)	(4.14)	(2.29)	(3.71)
	Daman and Diu	(7.90)	(1.08)	(4.57)	(13.64)	(1.39)	(7.85)	(2.49)	(0.66)	(1.42)	na		
	Lakshadweep	(−0.04)	(−4.86)	(−2.36)	(1.80)	(−11.31)	(−5.02)	(−1.30)	(0.94)	(0.02)	(−4.73)	(5.77)	(−0.25)

Scope of Economic Censuses: Economic censuses cover all enterprises—public and private, big and small; they do not cover crop production and plantations. The emphasis in them is on non-farm enterprises but some of the allied agricultural enterprises in dairying, etc; are covered. The censuses cover only enterprises including 'household' enterprises but not "households" (which are consumption units and not producer units); thus they exclude house servants and home-based workers and possibly even part-time labour not reported as regular employers for any enterprises.

Notes: Annual growth rate for All-India between 1990 and 2005 is worked out after excluding Jammu and Kashmir as Economic Census for 1990 was not conducted; Annual growth rate for Bihar, Madhya Pradesh and Uttar Pradesh for 1990 to 2005 are worked out after including Jharkhand, Chattisgarh and Uttranchal, respectively; Similarly growth rate between 1980-90 and 1990-98 for all-India excludes Assam and Jammu and Kashmir as Economic Census of Assam was not conducted in 1980 and that for Jammu & Kashmir was not conducted in 1990.

Source: GOI (2006), Press note dated June 12 on Fifth Economic Census 2005 and earlier Economic Census Reports.

TABLE A14.9
Percentage Distribution of Gainfully Employed Persons (ie by usual status for all workers ie PS+SS), by Industry

Round Number	Survey Period Month	Survey Period Year	Agriculture and Allied Activities	Mining and Quarrying	Manufacturing	Construction	Electricity	Trade, Hotel, etc.	Transport, Storage, etc.	Other Services
			Rural—Persons							
59	Jan–Jul	2003	75.9	0.5	7.4	4.4	0.1	4.4	2.0	5.2
58	Jul–Dec	2002	74.0	0.5	7.4	4.0	0.2	5.2	2.6	6.4
57	Jul–Jun	2001–2	73.6	0.4	8.9	3.8	0.1	5.7	2.2	5.4
56	Jul–Jun	2000–1	73.2	0.4	9.0	3.9	0.2	5.1	2.6	5.5
55	Jul–Jun	1999–2000	76.3	0.5	7.4	3.3	0.2	5.1	2.1	5.2
54	Jan–Jun	1998	79.7	0.5	5.5	2.7	0.3	4.3	1.5	5.4
53	Jan–Dec	1997	80.0	0.5	6.3	2.4	0.2	3.7	1.4	5.5
52	Jul–Jun	1995–6	78.8	0.4	6.9	2.7	0.2	4.0	1.5	5.5
51	Jul–Jun	1994–5	79.6	0.4	6.7	2.2	0.2	4.1	1.4	5.2
50	Jul–Jun	1993–4	76.9	0.7	7.1	2.6	0.2	4.6	1.6	6.2
49	Jan–Jun	1993	79.2	0.5	6.8	3.1	0.3	4.2	1.3	5.6
48	Jan–Dec	1992	79.4	0.6	6.5	2.1	0.3	4.0	1.4	5.7
47	Jul–Dec	1991								
46	Jul–Jun	1990–1	75.5	0.6	7.7	2.2	0.4	3.9	1.5	8.2
45	Jul–Jun	1989–90	75.1	0.6	8.2	3.3	0.1	3.5	1.6	7.6
43	Jul–Jun	1987–8	78.3	0.6	7.2	3.3	0.2	4.0	1.3	5.1
38	Jan–Dec	1983	81.2	0.5	6.7	1.7	0.1	3.5	1.1	5.2
32	Jul–Jun	1977–8	83.4	0.4	6.2	1.3	0.1	3.3	0.8	4.5
27	Oct–Sep	1972–3	85.4	0.4	5.3	1.4	0.1	2.5	0.7	4.2
21	Jul–Jun	1966–7	80.3	0.7	7.4	2.6	0.1	2.6	0.9	5.5
19	Jul–Jun	1964–5	80.0	0.8	7.1	1.7	0.1	2.8	0.7	6.7
17	Sep–Jul	1961–2	79.6	0.4	8.0	2.0	0.2	2.8	0.9	6.2
16	Jul–Jun	1960–1	82.2	0.6	6.4	1.4	0.1	3.2	1.1	5.1
15	Jul–Jun	1959–60	79.6	1.0	7.7	1.9	0.2	3.2	0.9	5.7
14	Jul–Jun	1958–9	81.1	0.6	7.7	1.5	0.1	2.6	1.0	5.5
11–12	Aug–Aug	1956–7	78.2	0.7	8.8	1.5	0.1	3.5	1.3	6.0
10	Dec–May	1955–6	82.1	0.6	8.0	0.8	0.2	2.3	1.0	5.0
9	May–Nov	1955	84.0	0.5	7.7	0.9	0.2	1.9	0.8	4.1
7	Oct–Mar	1953–4	83.8	0.3	6.9	1.0	incl in con.	2.3	0.6	5.2

Note: Dark lines represent regular Quinquennial Surveys. Others are thin sample surveys. Quinquennial surveys are conducted at roughly 5-year intervals. In these surveys Sch 1.0 dealing with house hold consumer expenditure and Sch.10, with employment and unemployment were canvassed.

Source: NSS 59th Report.

(contd.)

TABLE A14.9 (contd.)

Round Number	Survey Period Month	Survey Period Year	Agriculture and Allied Activities	Mining and Quarrying	Manufac- turing	Construction	Electricity	Trade, Hotel, etc.	Transport, Storage, etc.	Other Services
					Rural—Males					
59	Jan–Jul	2003	70.8	0.6	7.5	5.7	0.2	6.0	3.1	6.0
58	Jul–Dec	2002	68.8	0.6	7.5	5.4	0.2	6.7	3.8	6.8
57	Jul–Jun	2001–2	67.8	0.5	8.4	5.4	0.2	8.1	3.3	6.2
56	Jul–Jun	2000–1	69.0	0.4	8.1	4.8	0.3	6.9	3.8	6.6
55	**Jul–Jun**	**1999–2000**	**71.4**	**0.6**	**7.3**	**4.5**	**0.2**	**6.8**	**3.2**	**6.1**
54	Jan–Jun	1998	75.7	0.6	5.7	3.5	0.4	5.5	2.1	6.4
53	Jan–Dec	1997	75.8	0.6	6.5	3.2	0.3	4.9	2.0	6.8
52	Jul–Jun	1995–6	74.8	0.5	7.2	3.4	0.3	4.9	2.2	6.6
51	Jul–Jun	1994–5	75.6	0.5	6.5	3.0	0.3	5.5	2.1	6.5
50	**Jul–Jun**	**1993–4**	**74.1**	**0.7**	**7.0**	**3.2**	**0.3**	**5.5**	**2.2**	**7.0**
49	Jan–Jun	1993	75.0	0.6	6.2	3.7	0.4	5.2	1.9	7.0
48	Jan–Dec	1992	75.7	0.9	6.4	2.7	0.4	4.9	2.1	6.9
47	Jul–Dec	1991								
46	Jul–Jun	1990–1	71.0	0.8	8.1	2.7	0.5	4.6	2.1	10.2
45	Jul–Jun	1989–90	71.6	0.7	7.0	4.2	0.2	4.4	2.4	9.5
43	**Jul–Jun**	**1987–8**	**74.5**	**0.7**	**7.4**	**3.7**	**0.3**	**5.1**	**2.0**	**6.2**
38	**Jan–Dec**	**1983**	**77.5**	**0.6**	**7.0**	**2.2**	**0.2**	**4.4**	**1.7**	**6.1**
32	**Jul–Jun**	**1977–8**	**80.6**	**0.5**	**6.4**	**1.7**	**0.2**	**4.0**	**1.2**	**5.3**
27	**Oct–Sep**	**1972–3**	**83.2**	**0.4**	**5.7**	**2.6**	**0.1**	**3.1**	**1.0**	**4.7**
21	Jul–Jun	1966–7	77.9	0.8	7.5	2.9	0.2	3.2	1.4	6.3
19	Jul–Jun	1964–5	78.6	0.9	7.2	2.0	0.1	3.4	1.0	6.9
17	Sep–Jul	1961–2	78.4	0.4	7.9	2.2	0.2	3.2	1.2	6.6
16	Jul–Jun	1960–1	80.3	0.7	6.5	1.7	0.1	3.9	1.4	5.5
15	Jul–Jun	1959–60	78.7	1.2	7.4	2.1	0.1	3.6	1.2	5.6
14	Jul–Jun	1958–9	80.3	0.7	7.4	1.8	0.1	3.0	1.4	5.4
10	Dec–May	1955–6	82.2	0.6	7.3	0.9	0.1	2.7	1.3	4.9
7	Oct–Mar	1953–4	82.9	0.4	6.3	1.1	incl in con.	2.8	0.9	5.6

Note: Dark lines represent regular Quinquennial Surveys. Others are thin sample surveys. Quinquennial surveys are conducted at roughly 5-year intervals. In these surveys Sch 1.0 dealing with house hold consumer expenditure and Sch.10, with employment and unemployment were canvassed.

Source: NSS 59th Report.

(contd.)

TABLE A14.9 (contd.)

Round Number	Survey Period Month	Survey Period Year	Agriculture and Allied Activities	Mining and Quarrying	Manufacturing	Construction	Electricity	Trade, Hotel, etc.	Transport, Storage, etc.	Other Services
			Rural—Females							
59	Jan–Jul	2003	85.2	0.4	7.3	1.9	0.0	1.6	0.1	3.7
58	Jul–Dec	2002	84.9	0.3	7.2	1.1	0.0	2.1	0.1	4.1
57	Jul–Jun	2001–2	84.0	0.3	9.9	0.8	0.0	1.4	0.1	3.6
56	Jul–Jun	2000–1	81.8	0.4	10.6	2.2	0.0	1.4	0.1	3.5
55	**Jul–Jun**	**1999–2000**	**85.4**	**0.3**	**7.6**	**1.1**	**0.0**	**2.0**	**0.1**	**3.7**
54	Jan–Jun	1998	88.5	0.2	5.3	1.0	0.2	1.7	0.1	3.1
53	Jan–Dec	1997	88.5	0.3	5.9	0.9	0.1	1.2	0.0	3.0
52	Jul–Jun	1995–6	86.8	0.3	6.3	1.3	0.1	2.0	0.0	3.2
51	Jul–Jun	1994–5	87.2	0.3	7.3	0.7	0.0	1.6	0.1	2.9
50	**Jul–Jun**	**1993–4**	**86.2**	**0.4**	**7.0**	**0.9**	**0.0**	**2.1**	**0.1**	**3.4**
49	Jan–Jun	1993	87.2	0.3	4.9	2.1	0.1	2.2	0.1	3.1
48	Jan–Dec	1992	86.2	0.2	6.6	0.9	0.1	2.3	0.1	3.6
47	Jul–Dec	1991								
46	Jul–Jun	1990–1	84.9	0.1	6.7	1.3	0.0	2.6	0.1	4.3
45	Jul–Jun	1989–90	81.5	0.4	10.3	1.7	0.0	1.9	0.2	4.0
43	**Jul–Jun**	**1987–8**	**84.7**	**0.4**	**6.9**	**2.7**	**0.0**	**2.1**	**0.1**	**3.0**
38	Jan–Dec	1983	87.5	0.3	6.4	0.7	0.0	2.1	0.1	2.8
32	Jul–Jun	1977–8	88.1	0.2	5.9	0.6	0.0	1.9	0.1	3.0
27	Oct–Sep	1972–3	89.7	0.2	4.7	1.1	0.0	1.5	0.0	2.8
21	Jul–Jun	1966–7	85.1	0.0	7.1	2.2	0.0	1.3	0.1	4.2
19	Jul–Jun	1964–5	83.3	0.5	7.0	1.1	0.1	1.5	0.1	6.3
17	Sep–Aug	1961–2	82.6	0.4	8.2	1.3	0.5	1.8	0.1	5.2
16	Jul–Jun	1960–1	86.3	0.4	6.2	0.8	0.2	1.7	0.5	4.2
15	Jul–Jun	1959–60	82.1	0.4	8.2	1.1	0.3	1.9	0.1	5.9
14	Jul–Jun	1958–9	82.8	0.2	8.5	0.9	0.1	1.7	0.2	5.6
10	Dec–May	1955–6	81.7	0.4	10.1	0.5	0.4	1.4	0.1	6.5
7	Nov–Mar	1953–4	85.4	0.2	8.0	0.7	incl in con.	1.3	0.1	4.4

Note: Dark lines represent regular Quinquennial Surveys. Others are thin sample surveys. Quinquennial surveys are conducted at roughly 5-year intervals. In these surveys Sch 1.0 dealing with house hold consumer expenditure and Sch.10, with employment and unemployment were canvassed.
Source: NSS 59th Report.

(contd.)

TABLE A14.9 (contd.)

Round Number	Survey Period Month	Survey Period Year	Agriculture and Allied Activities	Mining and Quarrying	Manufacturing	Construction	Electricity	Trade, Hotel, etc.	Transport, Storage, etc.	Other Services
			urban—Persons							
59	Jan–Dec	2003	8.8	0.6	23.8	8.1	0.7	23.8	8.5	25.8
58	Jul–Dec	2002	9.0	0.7	23.2	8.7	0.7	22.2	8.4	27.2
57	Jul–Jun	2001–2	10.3	1.1	23.8	7.0	0.5	24.2	8.4	24.7
56	Jul–Jun	2000–1	8.8	0.9	25.1	8.6	0.8	21.7	8.3	25.9
55	**Jul–Jun**	**1999–2000**	**8.8**	**0.8**	**22.7**	**8.0**	**0.7**	**26.9**	**8.7**	**23.6**
54	Jan–Jun	1998	11.3	1.2	20.0	8.7	1.7	21.5	7.8	27.9
53	Jan–Dec	1997	10.1	1.0	23.9	7.6	1.3	18.4	7.8	29.9
52	Jul–Jun	1995–6	10.4	0.8	24.5	6.6	1.2	20.2	8.0	28.3
51	Jul–Jun	1994–5	11.0	1.2	23.4	7.4	1.2	19.6	8.6	27.7
50	**Jul–Jun**	**1993–4**	**10.6**	**1.2**	**23.6**	**6.6**	**1.1**	**19.9**	**8.4**	**28.6**
49	Jan–Jun	1993	13.2	1.2	22.7	7.6	2.1	17.9	8.1	27.2
48	Jan–Dec	1992	13.1	1.0	25.7	5.7	1.3	17.3	7.7	28.2
47	Jul–Dec	1991								
46	Jul–Jun	1990–1	12.3	1.9	25.8	5.0	1.4	17.3	7.6	29.6
45	Jul–Jun	1989–90	12.8	0.9	23.8	5.7	1.2	18.1	9.3	28.2
44	Jul–Jun	1988–9								
43	**Jul–Jun**	**1987–8**	**7.5**	**1.5**	**23.3**	**5.1**	**1.3**	**17.2**	**9.6**	**26.3**
38	Jan–Dec	1983	16.5	1.4	23.8	4.7	0.9	18.4	8.1	25.6
32	Jul–Jun	1977–8			28.0	3.8	0.8	18.8	7.9	24.6
27	Oct–Sep	1972–3	14.8	0.9	26.5	4.1	0.7	18.1	7.5	27.4
21	Jul–Jun	1966–7	13.5	0.9	29.9	4.0	0.9	16.0	8.0	26.7
19	Jul–Jun	1964–5	12.9	1.0	30.4	4.1	0.6	16.1	7.8	27.3
18	Feb–Jun	1963–4	15.7	0.8	29.2	4.1	0.5	16.9	8.0	24.9
17	Sep–Jul	1961–2	16.6	0.4	29.4	3.5	0.7	15.6	8.3	25.5
16	Jul–Jun	1960–1	16.6	0.7	30.2	3.6	0.6	15.5	7.5	25.3
15	Jul–Jun	1959–60	15.5	0.5	31.1	3.6	0.6	15.0	7.5	26.6
14	Jul–Jun	1958–9	16.6	0.6	29.5	2.9	0.9	14.6	8.0	26.9
13	Sep–Mar	1957–8	16.7	0.3	30.5	3.5	0.8	15.5	8.2	24.3
11–12	Aug–Aug	1956–7	14.8	0.5	32.1	3.2	0.6	16.3	8.7	23.9
10	Dec–May	1955–6	19.9	0.3	28.7	3.3	1.1	14.2	8.0	26.5
9	May–Nov	1955	19.4	0.4	29.6	3.4	0.8	14.5	8.2	23.7
7	Oct–Mar	1953–4	23.9	0.5	23.9	3.6	incl in con.	14.0	6.6	25.4

Note: Dark lines represent regular Quinquennial Surveys. Others are thin sample surveys. Quinquennial surveys are conducted at roughly 5-year intervals. In these surveys Sch 1.0 dealing with house-hold consumer expenditure and Sch.10, with employment and unemployment were canvassed.

Source: NSS 59th Report.

(contd.)

TABLE A14.9 (contd.)

Round Number	Survey Period Month	Survey Period Year	Agriculture and Allied Activities	Mining and Quarrying	Manufac-turing	Construction	Electricity	Trade, Hotel, etc.	Transport, Storage, etc.	Other Services
					Urban—Males					
59	Jan–Jul	2003	6.3	0.7	23.0	9.1	0.8	26.7	10.3	23.2
58	Jul–Dec	2002	7.0	0.8	22.7	9.3	0.9	24.7	10.1	24.5
57	Jul–Jun	2001–2	7.8	1.0	22.9	7.7	0.5	27.5	9.9	22.6
56	Jul–Jun	2000–1	6.6	0.9	24.5	9.3	0.9	24.3	10.0	23.6
55	**Jul–Jun**	**1999–2000**	**6.6**	**0.9**	**22.4**	**8.7**	**0.8**	**29.4**	**10.4**	**21.0**
54	Jan–Jun	1998	9.2	1.2	20.2	8.8	2.0	23.3	9.0	26.3
53	Jan–Dec	1997	7.8	1.2	23.4	7.9	1.5	20.6	9.3	28.2
52	Jul–Jun	1995–6	8.2	0.9	24.2	7.0	1.4	22.1	9.4	26.8
51	Jul–Jun	1994–5	8.8	1.4	22.4	7.7	1.4	21.8	9.7	26.8
50	**Jul–Jun**	**1993–4**	**9.0**	**1.3**	**23.5**	**6.9**	**1.2**	**21.9**	**9.7**	**26.4**
49	Jan–Jun	1993	10.2	1.3	22.3	8.3	2.5	19.9	9.5	26.0
48	Jan–Dec	1992	10.7	1.1	25.5	6.2	1.5	19.4	9.3	26.3
47	Jul–Dec	1991								
46	Jul–Jun	1990–1	9.2	1.1	25.4	5.4	1.7	19.1	9.1	29.0
45	Jul–Jun	1989–90	10.0	1.0	23.2	6.3	1.4	20.1	11.1	26.9
43	**Jul–Jun**	**1987–8**	**9.1**	**1.3**	**25.7**	**5.8**	**1.2**	**21.5**	**9.7**	**25.2**
38	**Jan–Dec**	**1983**	10.3	1.2	26.8	5.1	1.1	20.3	9.9	24.8
32	Jul–Jun	1977–8	10.6	0.9	27.6	4.2	1.1	21.6	9.8	24.3
27	Oct–Sep	1972–3	10.7	1.0	26.9	4.3	0.8	20.1	9.0	27.0
21	Jul–Jun	1966–7	10.8	0.9	30.0	4.2	1.1	17.6	9.5	25.9
19	Jul–Jun	1964–5	9.9	1.1	29.9	4.6	0.6	18.1	9.2	26.7
15	Jul–Jun	1959–60	13.5	0.5	30.7	3.6	0.5	17.0	8.9	25.4
14	Jul–Jun	1958–9	14.4	0.4	29.0	3.0	0.8	16.5	9.4	26.5
13	Sep–Mar	1957–8	13.7	0.4	30.5	3.9	0.8	17.4	9.8	23.6
10	Dec–May	1955–6	17.3	0.3	29.3	3.4	0.9	15.7	9.2	24.0
9	May–Nov	1955	16.4	0.4	29.7	3.8	0.8	16.3	9.5	23.2
7	Oct–Mar	1953–4	22.2	0.6	24.7	4.0	incl in con.	16.6	8.2	23.8

Note: Dark lines represent regular Quinquennial Surveys. Others are thin sample surveys. Quinquennial surveys are conducted at roughly 5-year intervals. In these surveys Sch 1.0 dealing with house hold consumer expenditure and Sch.10, with employment and unemployment were canvassed.

Source: NSS 59th Report.

(contd.)

TABLE A14.9 (contd.)

Round Number	Survey Period Month	Survey Period Year	Agriculture and Allied Activities	Mining and Quarrying	Manufac-turing	Construction	Electricity	Trade, Hotel, etc.	Transport, Storage, etc.	Other Services
					Urban—Females					
59	jan–Jul	2003	19.0	0.2	27.0	4.0	0.1	12.3	1.0	36.6
58	Jul–Dec	2002	17.1	0.4	25.1	6.0	0.1	11.8	1.6	38.0
57	Jul–Jun	2001–2	21.1	1.5	27.4	4.2	0.4	10.2	1.7	33.8
56	Jul–Jun	2000–1	18.3	0.7	27.5	5.8	0.2	10.8	1.4	35.3
55	**Jul–Jun**	**1999–2000**	**17.7**	**0.4**	**24.0**	**4.8**	**0.2**	**16.9**	**1.8**	**34.2**
54	Jan–Jun	1998	22.1	0.7	19.2	7.8	0.3	12.6	1.6	35.6
53	Jan–Dec	1997	20.0	0.3	25.6	6.0	0.5	8.9	1.4	37.3
52	Jul–Jun	1995–6	20.9	0.4	25.5	4.7	0.3	11.4	1.3	35.5
51	Jul–Jun	1994–5	20.5	0.3	27.4	6.2	0.4	10.0	3.7	31.6
50	**Jul–Jun**	**1993–4**	**24.7**	**0.6**	**24.1**	**4.1**	**0.3**	**10.0**	**1.3**	**35.0**
49	Jan–Jun	1993	25.8	0.8	24.7	4.7	0.4	9.3	1.9	32.4
48	Jan–Dec	1992	22.4	0.5	26.0	3.6	0.7	9.0	1.6	36.2
47	Jul–Dec	1991								0
46	Jul–Jun	1990–1	24.9	0.4	27.2	3.6	0.4	10.2	1.7	31.6
45	Jul–Jun	1989–90								0.0
43	Jul–Jun	1987–8	29.4	0.8	27.0	3.7	0.2	9.8	0.9	27.8
38	Jan–Dec	1983	31.0	0.6	26.7	3.1	0.2	9.5	1.5	26.6
32	**Jul–Jun**	**1977–8**	**31.9**	**0.5**	**29.6**	**2.2**	**0.1**	**8.7**	**1.0**	**26.0**
27	Oct–Sep	1972–3	32.8	0.7	25.0	3.3	0.1	9.4	0.9	27.0
21	Jul–Jun	1966–7	27.2	0.9	29.3	2.8	0.3	7.5	0.9	31.8
19	Jul–Jun	1964–5	26.7	0.6	32.8	1.7	0.4	6.7	1.2	31.1
15	Jul–Jun	1959–60	25.0	0.6	32.8	2.3	0.8	5.3	0.8	37.9
14	Jul–Jun	1958–9	27.4	1.1	32.2	2.6	1.2	5.4	1.2	32.1
13	Sep–Mar	1957–8	30.7	0.2	30.6	2.0	0.7	7.0	1.2	30.4
10	Dec–May	1955–6	32.8	0.3	25.6	3.0	1.8	7.3	2.0	28.7
9	May–Nov	1955	34.5	0.7	28.9	1.7	1.2	6.1	1.6	27.2
7	Oct–Mar	1953–4	40.2	0.4	20.7	2.2	incl in con.	3.9	0.6	38.9

Note: Dark lines represent regular Quinquennial Surveys. Others are thin sample surveys. Quinquennial surveys are conducted at roughly 5-year intervals. In these surveys Sch 1.0 dealing with house hold consumer expenditure and Sch.10, with employment and unemployment were canvassed.

Source: NSS 59th Report.

A15 HOUSEHOLD INDEBTEDNESS

Table A15.1
Household Indebtedness in India: A Profile

1. Amount of Debt by Occupational categories of Households (Rs crore) | **2. Proportion of Households Reporting Debt**

Year	Rural Households			Urban Households			All House-holds (4+7)	Rural Households			Urban Households		
	Cultivator	Non-cultivator	All	Self-employed	Others	All		Cultivator	Non-cultivator	All	Self-employed	Others	All
(1)	(2)	(3)	(4)	(5)	(6)	(7)	(8)	(2)	(3)	(4)	(5)	(6)	(7)
2002	81709	29759	111468	24341	40977	65327	176795	29.7	21.8	26.5	17.9	17.8	17.8
1991	17668	4543	22211	6306	8805	15232	37443	34.6	26.8	32.0	28.5	25.9	26.9
1981	5737	456	6193	1406	1617	3023	9216	21.7	12.0	19.4	16.6	17.4	17.2
1971	3374	474	3848	na	na	na	na	44.4	33.3	41.3	na	na	na

3. Percentage Share of Outstanding Debt by Credit Agency, Rural and Urban

	Rural						Urban		
	2002	1991	1981	1971	1961	1951	2002	1991	1981
A. Institutional	57.1	56.6	61.2	29.2	17.3	7.2	75.1	64.3	59.9
Government	2.3	5.7	4.0	6.7	6.6	3.7	7.6	9.3	14.6
Co-op Society/Bank	27.3	18.6	28.6	20.1	10.4	3.5	20.5	14.2	17.5
Commercial Bank	24.5	29.0	28.0	2.2	0.3	0.0	29.7	17.7	22.5
Insurance	0.3	0.5	0.3	0.1	0.0	0.0	3.5	1.4	2.1
Provident Fund	0.3	0.9	0.3	0.1	0.0	0.0	2.0	3.3	3.2
Other Institutions	2.4	1.9	0.0	0.0	0.0	0.0	11.9	18.5	0.0
B. Non-institutional	42.9	39.6	38.8	70.8	82.7	92.8	24.9	32.0	40.1
Landlords	1.0	4.0	4.0	8.6	1.1	3.5	0.2	0.8	1.0
Agrl. Moneylenders	10.0	6.3	8.6	23.1	47.0	25.2	0.9	1.2	3.6
Prof. Moneylenders	19.6	9.4	8.3	13.8	13.8	46.4	13.2	7.9	8.9
Traders	2.6	6.7	3.4	8.7	7.5	5.1	1.0	5.8	4.8
Relatives/Friends	7.1	6.7	9.0	13.8	5.8	11.5	7.6	10.4	15.2
Others	2.6	9.9	5.5	2.8	7.5	1.1	1.9	5.9	6.6
C. Not Specified	0.0	3.8	0.0	0.0	0.0	0.0	0.0	3.6	0.0

4. Cash Debt of Households Classified By Purpose of Loan (per cent)

	Rural Households						All Households		
	Cultivators			Non-Cultivators					
	2002	1991	1981	2002	1991	1981	2002	1991	1981
1. Farm Business									
Capital Expenditure	34.3	14.4	45.3	6.3	2.4	8.4	26.8	12.0	42.4
Current Expenditure	18.2	3.2	18.5	3.0	0.7	5.9	14.2	2.7	17.6
2. Non-farm Business									
Capital Expenditure	7.4	4.7	6.3	14.2	9.8	18.8	9.2	5.8	7.2
Current Expenditure	2.0	1.5	1.5	4.8	3.8	4.5	2.8	2.0	1.7
3. Households									
Capital Expenditure in Residential Building	27.7	5.1	20.0	55.0	11.8	51.0	35.0	6.5	22.4
Current Expenditure	na	0.5	na	na	0.4	na	na	0.5	na
4. Productive Purposes (1+2+3)*	89.6 (61.9)	28.9 (23.8)	91.6 (71.6)	83.3 (28.3)	28.5 (16.7)	88.6 (37.6)	88.0 (53.0)	29.0 (22.5)	91.3 (68.9)
5. Other Purposes	10.4	45.4	8.1	16.4	57.6	11.4	12.0	48.0	8.5
Repayment of Debt	1.5	na	0.8	1.3	na	1.5	1.4	na	0.8
Expenditure on Litigation	0.3	na	0.1	0.2	na	0.0	0.3	na	0.2
Fin. Investment Exp.	0.6	na	1.0	1.0	na	0.5	0.7	na	0.9
Other purposes	8.0	na	6.2	13.9	na	9.4	9.6	na	6.6
6. Unspecified	0.0	25.2	0.3	0.3	13.5	0.0	0.1	22.8	0.2

(contd.)

TABLE A15.1: contd.

	Urban Households								
	Self-employed			Others			All Households		
	2002	1991	1981	2002	1991	1981	2002	1991	1981
1. Farm Business									
Capital Expenditure	7.3	5.7	7.2	0.9	0.3	4.3	3.3	2.5	5.6
Current Expenditure	4.4	0.2	8.1	0.4	0.1	1.1	1.9	0.1	4.4
2. Non-farm Business									
Capital Expenditure	36.1	21.1	41.6	4.8	3.3	7.3	16.5	10.8	23.2
Current Expenditure	7.5	8.1	15.0	0.7	1.0	2.5	3.2	4.0	8.3
3. Households									
Capital Expenditure in Residential Bldg	32.8	28.7	13.1	72.1	44.6	54.3	57.5	37.9	35.0
Current Expenditure	na	0.1	na	na	2.5	na	na	1.5	na
4. Productive Purposes	88.1	63.9	85.0	78.9	51.8	69.5	82.4	56.8	76.5
(1+2+3)*	(55.3)	(35.1)	(71.9)	(6.8)	(4.7)	(15.2)	(24.9)	(17.4)	(41.5)
5. Other Purposes	11.9	33.9	14.7	21.1	46.6	30.4	17.6	41.4	23.2
6. Unspecified	0.0	2.2	0.3	0.1	1.4	0.2	0.0	1.8	0.2

5. Amount of Cash Borrowing and Repayments by Occupational Category of Households

Year	Round	Amount of Borrowings (Rs crore)			Amount of Repayment (Rs crore)			Share of Cultivator hhs (%)		Per cent of Repayments to Borrowings	
		Cultivator	Non-cultivator	All Hhs	Cultivator	Non-cultivator	All Hhs	Total Borrowings	Total Repayment	All Hhs	Cultivator
Rural											
2002–3	59	39294	15825	55119	17729	7154	24883	71.3	71.3	45.1	45.1
1991–2	48	10636	2862	13498	4070	1133	5203	78.8	78.3	38.5	38.3
1981–2	37	3757	427	4185	1899	193	2091	89.8	90.9	50.0	50.5
1971–2	26	1155	190	1345	1009	146	1155	85.9	87.4	85.9	87.4
		Self-employed	Others	All Hhs (incl.n.r)	Self-employed	Others	All Hhs (incl.n.r)	Share of Self-employed (%)		Per cent of Repayments to Borrowings	
								Total Borrowings	Total Repayment	All Hhs	Self-employed
Urban											
2002–3	26	12215	21965	34181	6679	11768	18447	35.7	36.2	54.0	54.7
1991–2	37	2815	5098	7918	1513	3027	4540	35.7	33.3	57.3	53.7
1981–2	48	830	1156	1986	536	653	1189	41.8	45.1	59.9	64.6

Notes: * Figues in brackets relate to those given by NSSO for productive purposes (1+2); na—details are not available; nr—not reported.

Source: NSSO (2005), *Household Indebtedness in India as on 30 June 2002*, AIDIS Report No. 501(59/18.2/2), December; NSSO (2006), *Household Borrowing and Repayments in India during 1 July 2002 to 30 June 2003*, AIDIS Report No. 502(59/18.2/3), January.

A16 INTERNATIONAL COMPARISON

Table A16.1
Development Characteristics of Some Selected Countries

Country	Group*	Population (million) 2004	Density (people/ sq. km) 2004	GDP US$ billion 2003	GDP PPP US$ billion 2003	GDP Per capita US$ 2003	GDP Per capita PPP US$ 2003	PPP Gross National Income (GNI) $ billion 2004	PPP Gross National Income (GNI) $ per capita 2004	per capita GNI (US$) 2004	Life Expectancy at Birth Male Years 2003	Life Expectancy at Birth Female Years 2003
(1)	(2)	(3)	(4)	(5)	(6)	(7)	(8)	(9)	(10)	(11)	(12)	(13)
Norway	HI	4.6	15	220.1	171.9	48412	37670	177	38550	52030	77	82
Switzerland	HI	7.4	187	320.1	224.6	43553	30552	261	35370	48230	78	83
United States	HI	293.5	32	10948.5	10923.4	37648	37562	11655	39710	41400	75	80
Sweden	HI	9.0	22	301.6	239.6	33676	26750	267	29770	35770	78	82
United Kingdom	HI	59.4	247	1794.9	1610.6	30253	27147	1869	31460	33940	75	80
Netherlands	HI	16.3	480	511.5	476.5	31532	29371	507	31220	31700	76	81
France	HI	60.0	109	1757.6	1654.0	29410	27677	1759	29320	30990	76	83
Germany	HI	82.6	237	2403.2	2291.0	29115	27756	2310	27950	30120	76	81
Australia	HI	20.1	3	522.4	589.1	26275	29632	588	29200	26900	77	83
Singapore	HI	4.3	6470	91.3	104.0	21492	24481	115	26590	24220	76	80
Spain	HI	41.3	83	838.7	920.3	20404	22391	1035	25070	21210	76	84
New Zealand	HI	4.1	15	79.6	90.5	19847	22582	90	22130	20310	77	81
Korea, Rep.	HI	48.1	488	605.3	861.0	12634	17971	982	20400	13980	71	78
Saudi Arabia	HI	23.2	11	214.7	298.0	9532	13226	325	14010	10430	72	75
Hungary	UMC	10.1	109	82.7	147.7	8169	14584	157	15620	8270	69	77
Mexico	UMC	103.8	54	626.1	937.8	6121	9168	995	9590	6770	71	77
Poland	UMC	38.2	125	209.6	434.6	5487	11379	482	12640	6090	71	79
Chile	UMC	16.0	21	72.4	162.1	4591	10274	168	10500	4910	73	80
Malaysia	UMC	25.2	77	103.7	235.7	4187	9512	243	9630	4650	71	76
Uruguay	UMC	3.4	19	11.2	28.0	3308	8280	31	9070	3950	72	79
Turkey	UMC	71.7	93	240.4	478.9	3399	6772	551	7680	3750	66	71
South Africa	UMC	45.6	38	159.9	474.1	3489	10346	500	10960	3630	45	46
Russian Federation	UMC	142.8	8	432.9	1323.8	3018	9230	1374	9620	3410	60	72
Brazil	LMC	178.7	21	492.3	1375.7	2788	7790	1433	8020	3090	65	73
Jamaica	LMC	2.7	246	8.1	10.8	3083	4104	10	3630	2900	74	78
Thailand	LMC	62.4	122	143.0	471.0	2305	7595	500	8020	2540	67	72
Iran, Islamic Rep.	LMC	66.9	41	137.1	464.4	2066	6995	505	7550	2300	68	71
Algeria	LMC	32.4	14	66.5	194.4	2090	6107	203	6260	2280	70	72
Colombia	LMC	45.3	44	78.7	298.8	1764	6702	309	6820	2000	69	75
China	LMC	1296.5	139	1417.0	6445.9	1100	5003	7170	5530	1290	69	73
Philippines	LMC	83.0	278	80.6	352.2	989	4321	406	4890	1170	68	72
Indonesia	LMC	217.6	120	208.3	721.5	970	3361	753	3460	1140	65	69
Georgia	LMC	4.5	65	4.0	13.3	778	2588	13	2930	1040	69	78
Sri Lanka	LMC	19.4	301	18.2	72.7	948	3778	78	4000	1010	72	76
India	LIC	1079.7	363	600.6	3078.2	564	2892	3347	3100	620	63	64
Pakistan	LIC	152.1	197	82.3	311.3	555	2097	328	2160	600	63	65
Vietnam	LIC	82.2	252	39.2	202.5	482	2490	222	2700	550	68	72
Sudan	LIC	34.4	14	17.8	64.1	530	1910	64	1870	530	57	60
Kenya	LIC	32.4	57	14.4	33.1	450	1037	34	1050	460	45	46
Bangladesh	LIC	140.5	1079	51.9	244.4	376	1770	278	1980	440	62	63
Ghana	LIC	21.1	93	7.6	46.3	369	2238	48	2280	380	54	55
Cambodia	LIC	13.6	77	4.2	27.9	315	2078	30	2180	320	53	56
Uganda	LIC	25.9	132	6.3	36.8	249	1457	39	1520	270	43	44
Nepal	LIC	25.2	176	5.9	35.0	237	1420	37	1470	260	60	60
Zimbabwe	LIC	13.2	34	–	31.4	–	2443	28	2180	–	39	38

(contd.)

TABLE A16.1 (contd.)

Country	Group*	Infant Mortality Rate (per 1000 live births)		Adult Literacy Rate ages 15 and older (%) 1998–2004	International Poverty Line					Population below National Poverty Line			
		1980	2002		Survey Year	Population below $1 a day (%)	Poverty Gap $1 a day (%)	Population below $2 a day (%)	Poverty Gap $2 a day (%)	Survey Year	Rural (%)	Urban (%)	National (%)
(1)	(2)	(14)	(15)	(16)	(17)	(18)	(19)	(20)	(21)	(22)	(23)	(24)	(25)
Norway	HI	9	4	–	–	–	–	–	–	–	–	–	–
Switzerland	HI	9	5	–	–	–	–	–	–	–	–	–	–
United States	HI	13	7	–	–	–	–	–	–	–	–	–	–
Sweden	HI	7	3	–	–	–	–	–	–	–	–	–	–
United Kingdom	HI	12	5	–	–	–	–	–	–	–	–	–	–
Netherlands	HI	9	5	–	–	–	–	–	–	–	–	–	–
France	HI	10	4	–	–	–	–	–	–	–	–	–	–
Germany	HI	13	4	–	–	–	–	–	–	–	–	–	–
Australia	HI	11	6	–	–	–	–	–	–	–	–	–	–
Singapore	HI	11	3	93	–	–	–	–	–	–	–	–	–
Spain	HI	13	5	–	–	–	–	–	–	–	–	–	–
New Zealand	HI	13	6	–	–	–	–	–	–	–	–	–	–
Korea, Rep.	HI	16	5	–	1998#	<2.0	<0.5	<2.0	<0.5	–	–	–	–
Saudi Arabia	HI	65	23	79	–	–	–	–	–	–	–	–	–
Hungary	UMC	24	8	99	2002*	<2.0	<0.5	<2.0	<0.5	1997	–	–	17.3
Mexico	UMC	56	24	90	2000*	9.9	3.7	26.3	10.9	1988	–	–	10.1
Poland	UMC	21	8	–	2002*,@	<2.0	<0.5	<2.0	<0.5	1993	–	–	23.8
Chile	UMC	49	10	96	2000#	<2.0	<0.5	9.6	2.5	1998	–	–	17.0
Malaysia	UMC	31	8	89	1997#	<2.0	<0.5	9.3	2.0	1989	15.5		
Uruguay	UMC	37	14	–	2000#	<2.0	<0.5	3.9	0.8	–	–	–	–
Turkey	UMC	103	35	88	2002*,@	4.8	1.0	24.7	7.5	–	–	–	–
South Africa	UMC	64	52	–	2000*	10.7	1.7	34.1	12.6	–	–	–	–
Russian Federation	UMC	28	18	99	2002*	<2.0	<0.5	7.5	1.3	1994	–	–	30.9
Brazil	LMC	67	33	88	2001#	8.2	2.1	22.4	8.8	1998	51.4	14.7	22.0
Jamaica	LMC	28	17	88	2000*	<2.0	<0.5	13.3	2.7	2000	25.1	12.8	18.7
Thailand	LMC	45	24	93	2000*,@	<2.0	<0.5	32.5	9.0	1992	15.5	10.2	13.1
Iran, Islamic Rep.	LMC	92	34	77	1998*	<2.0	<0.5	7.3	1.5	–	–	–	–
Algeria	LMC	94	39	70	1995*	<2.0	<0.5	15.1	3.8	1998	16.6	7.3	12.2
Colombia	LMC	40	19	94	1999#	8.2	2.2	22.6	8.8	1999	79.0	55.0	64.0
China	LMC	49	30	91	2001*	16.6	3.9	46.7	18.4	1998	4.6	<2	4.6
Philippines	LMC	55	28	93	2000*	15.5	3.0	47.5	17.8	1997	50.7	21.5	36.8
Indonesia	LMC	79	32	88	2002*	7.5	0.9	52.4	15.7	1999	–	–	27.1
Georgia	LMC	34	24	–	2001*	2.7	0.9	15.7	4.6	1997	9.9	12.1	11.1
Sri Lanka	LMC	34	16	90	2002*,@	5.6	<0.5	41.6	11.9	1995–6	27.0	15.0	25.0
India	LIC	113	65	61	1999–2000*	35.3	7.2	80.6	34.9	1999–2000	30.2	24.7	28.6
Pakistan	LIC	105	76	49	2001*,@	17.0	3.1	73.6	26.1	1998–9	35.9	24.2	32.6
Vietnam	LIC	44	20	90	–	–	–	–	–	2002	35.6	6.6	28.9
Sudan	LIC	86	64	59	–	–	–	–	–	–	–	–	–
Kenya	LIC	73	78	74	1997*	22.8	5.9	58.3	23.9	1997	53.0	49.0	52.0
Bangladesh	LIC	129	48	41	2000*	36	8.1	82.8	36.3	2000	53.0	36.6	49.8
Ghana	LIC	96	60	54	1998–9*	44.8	17.3	78.5	40.8	1998–9	49.9	18.6	39.5
Cambodia	LIC	110	96	74	1997*	34.1	9.7	77.7	34.5	1999	40.1	13.9	35.9
Uganda	LIC	107	83	69	–	–	–	–	–	1997	–	–	44.0
Nepal	LIC	124	62	49	1995–6*	39.1	11.0	80.9	37.6	1995–6	44.0	23.0	42.0
Zimbabwe	LIC	69	76	90	1995–6*	56.1	24.2	83.0	48.2	1995–6	48.0	7.9	34.9

Notes: *—expenditure base; #—income base; @—primary data,–denotes no data; Col. 1 classifies all World Bank member economies and all other economies with population of more than 30,000. Economies are divided among income groups according to 2004 GNI per capita, calculated using the World Bank Atlas method ; Groups are: low-income economies (LIC) with $825 or less, lower middle income economies (LMC), $826–$3255, Upper-middle income economies (UMC), $3256–$10,065, and high-income economies, $10,066 or more.

Source: World Development Report 2004 and 2006 (http://devdata.worldbank.org/wdi2005/Section1.htm).